ENTITY-RELATIONSHIP APPROACH TO INFORMATION MODELING AND ANALYSIS

ENTITY-RELATIONSHIP APPROACH TO INFORMATION MODELING AND ANALYSIS

Proceedings of the Second International Conference on
Entity-Relationship Approach
Washington, D.C., October 12-14, 1981

edited by

Peter P. CHEN*

University of California
Los Angeles, U.S.A.

* Current Address:
Murphy J. Foster Distinguished Chair Professor
Department of Computer Science
Louisiana State University
Baton Rouge, Louisiana 70803-4020, U.S.A.

1983

NORTH-HOLLAND – AMSTERDAM • NEW YORK • OXFORD

© ER Institute, 1983

ISBN: 0 444 86747 3

Publishers:

ELSEVIER SCIENCE PUBLISHERS B.V.
P.O. BOX 1991
1000 BZ Amsterdam
The Netherlands

Sole Distributors for the U.S.A. and Canada:

ELSEVIER SCIENCE PUBLISHING COMPANY, INC.
52, Vanderbilt Avenue
New York, N.Y. 10017
U.S.A.

The original version of the book was published by the ER Institute, P.O. Box 617, Saugus, CA 91350, U.S.A. in 1981 (ISBN 0 941334 00 7).

Library of Congress Cataloging in Publication Data

International Conference on Entity-Relationship
    Approach (2nd : 1981 : Washington, D.C.)
    Entity-relationship approach to information modeling
and analysis.

    1. Data base management--Congresses. 2. Information
storage and retrieval systems--Congresses. I. Chen,
Peter P. S. II. Title.
QA76.9.D3I5583 1981   001.64   83-14121
ISBN 0-444-86747-3 (U.S.)

PRINTED IN THE NETHERLANDS

PREFACE

Information modeling and analysis is one of the most difficult tasks in information systems development and database design. A major reason is the lack of communication between users and systems analysts. One solution to this communication problem is to express user information requirements in a way that users can more readily understand. Each database in an organization is a representation of the users' view of the real world. Since we usually express our perceptions of the real world in terms of entities (objects) and relationships (relations, associations) between them, it seems natural to use the concepts of 'entities' and 'relationships' in information modeling and analysis. In the past few years, the so-called 'Entity-Relationship Approach' has attracted considerable attention in industry and the research community. Two international conferences based on this approach have been held to provide a forum for the inter-change of ideas between practitioners researchers, and the third conference is planned to be held in Anaheim, California in October of 1983. Elsevier Science Publishers B.V. (North-Holland) are the publishers of the proceedings of these conferences.

This book contains the papers presented at the second conference on Entity-Relationship Approach, which was held in October of 1981, in Washington, D.C. and attracted information systems specialists and managers from more than ten countries. Many high-quality papers (from 17 countries) were submitted for the second conference; however, due to the limitation of the available time slots, the program committee selected about one-third of the papers for presentation at the conference.

In total, twenty-eight full-length papers are included in this volume, and they are organized into twelve chapters. Chapter 1 presents a framework for classification of entity-relationship models and applications of the Entity-Relationship (ER) Approach to meta-schema definition. Chapter 2 describes two languages (EAS-E and GORDAS) which are based on the concepts of entities and relationships. Chapter 3 discussed the issues of integrity and completeness. Chapter 4 presents formal specifications of two versions of entity-relationship models (ERM's) and a decomposition approach to relational database design based on the ER Approach. Chapter 5 describes three practical applications of the ERM: the first one is related to a defense project, the second one is related to an accounting system, and the third one is related to item-tracking. Chapter 6 discusses the use of ERM's in the design of database management systems which can support multiple data models. Chapter 7 describes the use of the ERM in the design of IMS and ADABAS databases. Chapter 8 presents the use of the ERM as a basis for the conceptual schema in the ANSI/SPARC architecture. Chapter 9 describes three database design tools. Chapter 10 discusses several extensions to the ERM (to incorporate the concept of 'time dimension' and the idea of 'data abstraction'). Chapter 11 presents two database management systems which are based on the concepts of entities and relationships. The last chapter discusses the concept of 'relationships' (or 'association') and a self-defining ERM.

This second conference on the Entity-Relationship Approach was sponsored by the UCLA Graduate School of Management, the University of Maryland Computer Science Department, and the National Bureau of Standards (NBS) in cooperation with ACM Special Interest Group in Business Data Processing (SIGBDP) and Special Interest Group in Information Retrieval (SIGIR). This conference would not have been feasible without the support of many individuals. Dr. Edgar Sibley of the Alpha Omega Group, the conference chairman, contributed a lot of time to supervise the organization and operations of the conference. Dr. Dennis Fife of NBS and Professor Raymond Yeh of the University of Maryland also contributed significantly to the success of the conference. Professor Peter Ng of the University of Missouri at Columbia did an excellent job in the publicity for the conference. Ms. Pat Stevens of the Alpha Omega Group and Professor Nick Roussopoulos of the University of Maryland arranged excellent meeting facilities for the conference. Dr. Richards Adrion of the NSF, Mr. William Carlson of the Western Digital Corp., Professor Ephraim McLean of UCLA, and Dr. Eric Wolman of Bell Laboratories gave valuable advice on the organization of the conference. The program committee worked very hard in selecting papers for presentation at the conference and in providing comments to the authors of all papers submitted.

Two persons — Mr. Dennis Perry and Mr. Ilchoo Chung, both of UCLA — contributed enormous time to this effort. Mr. Perry took good care of every detail of the program and the conference, and Mr. Chung was involved heavily in the editing of the book. In addition, Mr. Bryan Hsiao of UCLA also spent considerable time in the organization of the conference.

The editor would like to thank all of them for their effort in making the second ER conference a success.

                                                      Peter Pin-Shan Chen
                                                      Editor

CONTENTS

CHAPTER 10: EXTENSIONS OF ERM

CHAPTER 11: ER-BASED DBMS

CHAPTER 12: MODELING APPROACHES

ORGANIZATION

CONFERENCE CHAIRMAN
Edgar H. Sibley
Alpha Omega Group Inc.
Room LL7 World Building
8121 Georgia Ave., Silver Spring
Maryland 20910, U.S.A.

PUBLICITY CHAIRMAN
Peter A. Ng
University of Missouri-Columbia, U.S.A.

ADVISORY COMMITTEE
Richards Adrion, NSF, U.S.A.
William Carlson, Western Digital Corp., U.S.A.
Ephraim McLean, UCLA, U.S.A.
Eric Wolman, Bell Laboratories, U.S.A.

PROGRAM COORDINATORS
Dennis Perry, UCLA, U.S.A.
Nick Roussopoulos, University of Maryland, U.S.A.

PROGRAM CHAIRMAN
Peter P. Chen
Graduate School of Management
UCLA
Los Angeles, California 90024
U.S.A.

INTERNATIONAL COORDINATORS
Raymond T. Yeh
University of Maryland, U.S.A.

Dennis Fife
National Bureau of Standards
U.S.A.

LOCAL ARRANGEMENTS
Pat Stevens
Alpha Omega Group, Inc. U.S.A.

PROGRAM COMMITTEE
T.C. Chiang, Bell Laboratories, U.S.A.
Wesley Chu, UCLA, U.S.A.
A.L. Furtado, Catholic University, Brasil
Steve Kimbleton, ITT-TTC, U.S.A.
Andre Flory, University of Lyon, France
Anne-Marie Glorieux, SIRIUS Project, France
Patrick Hall, SCICON, England
Rowland Johnson, Lawrence Livermore Laboratory, U.S.A.
Beverly Kahn, Boston University, U.S.A.
Ewing Lusk, Argonne National Laboratory, U.S.A.
William McCarthy, Michigan State University, U.S.A.
Michel Melkanoff, UCLA, U.S.A.
Fumio Nakamura, Hitachi Ltd., Japan
E.J. Neuhold, University of Stuttgart, Germany
Peter A. Ng, University of Missouri-Columbia, U.S.A.
Mario Schkolnick, IBM Research Laboratory, U.S.A.
Gary Sockut, National Bureau of Standards, U.S.A.
Hubert Tardieu, France
John Tsao, IBM, U.S.A.
Jeffrey Ullman, Stanford University, U.S.A.
Charles Vick, Systems Control Inc., Alabama, U.S.A.

REFEREES (Partial List)
All the program committee members, and
K.H. Kim, University of South Florida, U.S.A.
J. Robert Heath, University of Kentucky, U.S.A.
Robert Arnold, Honeywell, U.S.A.
W. Terry Hardgrave, National Bureau of Standards, U.S.A.
Benjamin Wah, Purdue University, U.S.A.
T.C. Ting, National Bureau of Standards, U.S.A.
Sandra B. Salazar, National Bureau of Standards, U.S.A.
Joseph C. Collica, National Bureau of Standards, U.S.A.

CHAIRPERSONS (Partial List)
Andre Flory, University of Lyon, France
Michel Melkanoff, UCLA, U.S.A.
Gary Sockut, National Bureau of Standards, U.S.A.
Steve Kimbleton, ITT-TTC, U.S.A.
Mario Schkolnick, IBM, U.S.A.
Dennis Fife, National Bureau of Standards, U.S.A.
Beverly Kahn, Boston University, U.S.A.
Peter Ng, University of Missouri-Columbia, U.S.A.
Al Dale, University of Texas-Austin, U.S.A.

PANEL CHAIRPERSONS (Partial List)
John Tsao, IBM, U.S.A.
T.C. Ting, National Bureau of Standards, U.S.A.
Hubert Tardieu, Ministere De L'environnement, France

PANELISTS (Partial List)
Mikhail Vaynshenker, Chemical Bank, U.S.A.
Martin Modell, Consultant, U.S.A.
Patrick Hall, SCICON Consultancy, England

DISCUSSANTS (Partial List)
Erich J. Neuhold, University of Stuttgart, Germany
Colette Rolland, University of Paris, France
John Ying, Bell Laboratories, U.S.A.
James Weeldreyer, Honeywell, U.S.A.
James Longstaff, Leeds Polytechnic, England

LUNCHEON SPEAKER
Robert Taylor, IBM Research, U.S.A.

Entity-Relationship Approach to
Information Modeling and Analysis, P.P. Chen (ed.)
Elsevier Science Publishers B.V. (North-Holland)
©ER Institute, 1983

Applications of The Entity-Relationship Approach

Daniel Teichroew
Industrial and Operations Engineering
University of Michigan
U.S.A.

Fernao Germano
Free Docent of Information Systems
University of S. Paulo
Brasil

Silva, Luca
Instituto de Pesquisas Energeticas e Nucelares
Brasil

ABSTRACT

This paper reports briefly on some results of
investigations using the ERA model as a basis for
documenting and analyzing information processing
systems. Previous work was summarized in a paper
presented at the first ERA conference, Teichroew
et al (1980).

1. INTRODUCTION

The Problem Statement Language (PSL) was originally designed in 1972
without the benefit of a formal model and the associated software, the
Problem Statement Analyzer (PSA), was essentially "hard coded" except for
the use of a network database management system. A language analyzer, XPL,
was used to verify that the language was syntatically consistant, but it did
not help to reduce the effort required to implement PSA. Beginning in 1975
it became clear that a formal definition of PSL should not only be useful
for analyzing the language, but also for reducing the amount of software
needed to provide a computer-aided tool. This lead to the development of the
Information System Language Definition System (ISLDS) and System Encyclopedia
Manager (SEM) described in Teichroew et al 1980.

Section 2 discusses some of the work concerned with verifying that the ERA model in ISLDS is sufficiently general to include many of the System Description Languages that have been proposed. Section 3 is concerned with the analogous validation for data models. Section 4 describes an application of the concept to the Metaschema approach proposed by Rochfeld and Tabourier (1974). In Section 5, some of the areas currently being investigated are outlined.

2. SYSTEM DESCRIPTION LANGUAGE

One of the first languages chosen to demonstrate that a computer aided development facility could be implemented with relatively little effort using ISLDS and SEM was the language specified as part of the Rational Design Methodology by Boyd, Pizzarello and Vestal (1978). All that is required is the definition of the underlying conceptual model and the syntax of the language using the ERA modeling facilities of ISLDS. A number of the other languages that were implemented are listed in Teichroew et al 1980, Figures 12 and 13.

Since that time many Software Development Facilities with associated system description languages have been proposed. See, for example, Hausen and Mullerberg (1981). Interest in this development has also been stimulated by the proposal for the Programming Support Environment (APSE) for ADA. (Buxton 1980, Stenning et al 1981, and Wolfe et al 1981).

The ISLDS has been used to implement a number of these proposed facilities including the Hierarchical Development Methodology, a software design system based on Nassi Schneiderman diagrams for representing control structures, the Performance Oriented Design methodology and the System Description Language developed by CCITT. Other implementations are described in Winters (1981), Spewak (1981), Winchester (1981), and Yamamoto (1981).

The Hierarchical Development Methodology (HDM) is a software life cycle system which divides the design process into several stages including the conceptual development stage, external interface definition stage, formal specification stage, formal representation stage, abstract implementation stage, and coding and verification stage. (Robinsen and Levitt, 1977). HDM provides three levels of software tools including the Hierarchical Specification Language (HSL), SPECIfication Assertion Language (SPECIAL), and an Intermediate Level Programming Language (ILPL). The language defined in ISLDS (HDML) is analogous to HSL and the specification aspects of SPECIAL. The analyst uses the language to specify one or more hierarchical systems; the specifications are maintained in a database. Each hierarchy is denoted by a user defined name which is the root of the hierarchy. The hierarchy has levels and the modules within each level should reference or map to modules within lower levels. Each module may have several subparts including assertions, definitions, parameters, declarations, designator types, scalar types and functions.

The Software Producing System (SPS) is an experimental, integrated system consisting of a Software Specification Language (SSL), an Algorithm

Translator, a Specification Database, and a Program Generator (Teichroew, Kang and Macasovic, 1980). It is designed to generate executable software automatically, by use of the FLECS Translator from a design expressed in SSL and stored in a SEM database. SSL was designed using the ISLDS, and has three types of statements: design description statements, algorithm description statements, and assertion statements. The Algorithm Translator is a subsystem of SPS that translates an algorithm in Nassi Shneiderman diagrams, (Nassi and Schneiderman, 1973) into SSL. The Specification Database is the SEM database that contains the software specification in SSL. The SEM processor is used to update or display the content of the Specification Database. The Program Generator generates a program in the FLECS source from the Specification Database, which is then translated by FLECS translator into FORTRAN.

The Performance Oriented Design Methodology (POD) was developed by Buzen, Goldberg et al (1979, 1980) and Levy (1980) to support the software development process. POD provides a tool for estimating system response to specific software and hardware configurations. POD approaches this problem by allowing for iterative refinement of system design specifications. POD provides software tools to facilitate performance analysis, including: (1) Specification Language - a language is provided to specify software and hardware aspects; (2) Interactive Modification - commands to interactively modify the system specification; (3) Reports - static and dynamic reports are provided. The ISLDS definition of POD is an implementation of the POD Specification Language. The definition of the POD language allows the user to enter system specifications into a database. Static reports, comparable to those provided by POD, are available.

The Functional Specification and Description Language (SDL) (Riesson, 1977) is a graphical language developed by CCITT for requirement specification of real time telephone switching systems. The primatives of the graphic language were defined by ISLDS to aid the methodology by storing the information in the database and providing the analysis tools of SEM.

For all of these methods a language reference manual is produced automatically as illustrated in Figure 2 in Teichroew et al 1980. A system can then be described or designed using the method and the language, and SEM can be used to store the design and retrieve and display the design on demand. Any algorithms or processing that are language specific can be implemented through a high level interface to the SEM database. (Kang, 1981).

3. DATA MODELS

The implementations described in the previous section may be considered as essentially "applications," to the area of computer aided system description, which are based on a database management system using an ERA schema. ISLDS and SEM are not limited to only this application area, instead they may be considered as a general Database Management System which can accommodate a number of data models. In this section the implementation of several recent data models is briefly described. The first generation data models, hierarchical, network and relational, have all been used as the basis for

database management systems (DBMS), though relational DBMS have only recently
become commercially available. A number of "2nd generation" data models have
been proposed in recent years (Chen, 1980). This development has been
prompted by the recognition that the 1st generation models are too "low
level" for adequate modeling of the real world, and for producing conceptual
schemas. A number of candidate models for conceptual schemas have recently
been studied by the ISO Working Group, Griethuysen 1981. The data models
that have been (or   are planned to be) implemented in ISLDS include the
models proposed by Chen (1976), Codd (1979), McLeod (1975), Brown and Ramey
(1979), Wiederhold and El-Masri (1979), and the Information System Definition
Language in ISLDS.

In the Entity-Relationship Model (ERM), Chen (1976, 1977) proposed to
model the real world in terms of entities, relationships, and attributes, and
described how to translate a conceptual schema expressed in this high-level
description into a database schema expressed in the "first generation" data
models. Scheuermann et al (1980) proposed an Extended Entity-Relationship
Model (EERM) to included the concepts of generalization and aggregation.
Dos Santos et al (1980) incorporated the data type concept developed in
programming languages into the Entity-Relationship Model. Recently, these
papers have stimulated a good deal of research activity in the Entity-
Relationship Approach.

In the Relational Model with extensions (RM/T), Codd (1979) added a
number of features to the usual relational concepts to express "more semantics." Semantics necessary in data model construction are expressed as
relation types. Structural and dynamic (time dependency of database) aspects
are included in the model as relation types. Entities are classified into
entity types according to the role (subordinate, superordinate or neither of
these) played in describing entities of some other type. Multivalued and
indirect properties of entities are supported. The graph nature of the
relations are included in the model. Operations and operators to support
these extended features are supplied. Rules for data integrity are specified.

The Semantic Data Model (SDM) was developed by McLeod (1975), and
Hammer and McLeod (1978). It provides a class of real world semantics which
are important in data modeling. The data organization principles of the
method may be summarized as follows. A database is a collection of entities
which may be objects (concrete or abstract), events (point event or duration
event) or names which are designators for object or event. Entities are
organized into classes, which are meaningful collections of relevant objects.
Each class is either a base class which may be defined independent of other
classes, or a nonbase class which is defined in terms of other classes using
interclass connections. The interclass connection may be subclass,
superclass, restrict, subset, merge member, extract missing member. Membership of subclass is determined by the attributes while the membership of
subsets is defined explicitly by the user. The classes are logically
connected via interclass connections.. The entities and classes have
attributes which describe their characteristics, and relate them to other
entities. Each attribute has a value and may be organized hierarchically.
An attribute has a semantic "kind", which identifies the type of relationship
the value of the attribute has with the entity. The value of the "kind" may

be one of property, component, participant, class determined property, class determined component and class determined participant.

The Entity-Link-Key-Attribute (ELKA) information model is a language developed as part of a general methodology for constructing models of integrated engineering and manufacturing systems (Brown and Ramey, 1979). The basic primitives of the ELKA modeling technique are entities, links, and attributes. Entity is an object which is described by properties whose values can be considered as remaining fixed over some intervals of space and time. Link is a directed connective between two entities. Attributes are properties of entities and should always be defined by concatenating entity name and attribute class (set) name. Some of the attributes of an entity may be key attributes of the entity.

The Structural Model (SM) is a relational model by Wiederhold and El-Masri (1979) which uses relations as "building blocks" and includes the following major extensions. Logical connections (direct reference, identity reference, ownership connection) are explicitly defined between the relations. Relations are classified into relation types (primary entity relation, reference entity relation, net relation, lexicon relation, or association) according to the connections with other relations. If a data model satisfies logical connection and relation type constraints, the model is considered as having structural integrity. A set of data model update algorithms are defined between the relation types to maintain structural integrity of the entire model.

The results indicate that, with some relatively minor accommodations, these models can be defined in ISLDL and be processed by the ISLDS. Once this is done, the resulting schemas can be used to make SEM appear to the user as a database management system for the particular data model selected.

4. META SCHEMA DEFINITION

One of the advantages of ERA models is that they can be represented diagrammatically and then a great deal of information can be conveyed in a small amount of space. In practice however, ERA models frequently can become so large and complex that it is worthwhile to use computer aided tools to analyze them and to check that they are complete and consistant. This section gives an example based on the Meta Schema definition reported by Rochfeld and Tabourier (1974). They present an effort to formalize databases, and apply their results to the process of software development for a Database Management System of the CODASYL type (CODASYL Database Task Group (1971)).

Rochfeld and Tabourier present the metaschema that would be useful for the development of the software for a CODASYL DBMS in terms of a terminology that is derived from CODASYL 1971 DBTG report. Adding the prefix meta indicates that the reference is to the Meta Database of the DBMS and not to the databases that it is to handle in its normal operations. Therefore they use the terms: metarecords, metasets, metadata items, etc.

They use a mathematical notation from set theory to describe the meta-base. In practice, the mathematical notation used by Rochfeld and Tabourier is not necessarily the most satisfactory way to supply information to a software development team that would develop a CODASYL DBMS because it is not compatible with their natural method of communication. Software people do use diagrams similar to that in Figure 1 to express database schema. All the information shown in Figure 1 was taken from Rochfeld and Tabourier's paper. Such diagrams consist of the records with their components and the relationships between them. In terms of formalization Figure 1 can be thought of as a representation of the diagram which is described by the expressions, so it does not loose information and it seems much easier to understand than the set of expressions in their paper.

Figure 2 shows the result of applying the ERA approach to the design of the Metabase. It is useful for the software development team because it identifies the entities involved in the metaschema, their attributes and the relationships between them that should be considered. The information in Figure 2 can be represented in PSL or an ISLDS language specifically designed for this application. Figure 3 shows the description in PSL of part of the schema shown in Figure 2. Through PSA, reports can be obtained showing different aspects of the database such as the names of its components arranged in different orders, the attributes of each entity, attributes common to different entities, the entities involved in each relationship, the relationships in which each entity is involved, a matrix representation of the database schema, the alternate paths that can be used to go from an entity to another using the relationships that connect them, etc.

Defining the Metaschema for the development of a DBMS can be increased by the use of a computer aided tool, in this case PSL/PSA. The real value is to guide and coordinate the efforts of the several members of the software development team. PSL/PSA can contribute effectively to the communication between the members of this team and thus speed the process of defining the metaschema and making this definition useful. Different reports that can be obtained using PSL/PSA to model the Real World Metaschema of Figure 2. The Dictionary Report shows that it is easy to discover if a name has been used in defining a component of the Metabase, which synonyms it has, etc. The Formatted Problem Statement is an example of the description of an entity, a relationship, an attribute (elementary or not) showing how they are related. The structure of the Metabase may be observed in terms of metarecords, metadata items, etc. in the Contents Report. The Similarity Matrix can be used to show that the matrix is empty outside the diagonal. This means that there are no attributes common to more than one entity or, in other words, that there is no data redundancy in the real world schema. (Paco (Paco 1978) studied this problem when the criterion is to avoid data redundancy to the maximum and proposed a computer-aided method using PSL/PSA; her method includes comparing the matrix representations of the Real World Schema and of the schema according to different DBMS's and choosing the DBMS for which the matrix is sparse outside the diagonal because off-diagonal elements are indications of data redundancy.) Communication of the metabase information to the software development team can be improved as one can observe all metabase components related to a certain word as shown in the KWIC Index report.

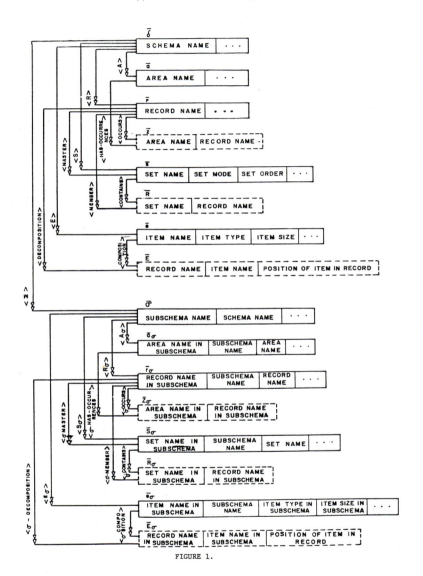

FIGURE 1.

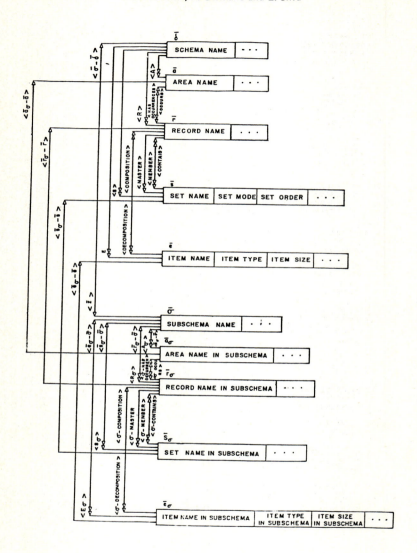

FIGURE - 2

```
DEFINE ENTITY                           INF-RECORD-SCH;
     SYNONYMS ARE:  R-BAR;
     CONSISTS OF:
          RECORD-NAME;


DEFINE ENTITY                           INF-ITEM-SCH;
     SYNONYMS ARE:  E-BAR;
     CONSISTS OF:
          ITEM-NAME,
          ITEM-SIZE,
          ITEM-TYPE;

DEFINE ELEMENT                          POSITION-OF-ITEM-IN-RECORD;
     ATTRIBUTES ARE:
          TYPE            NUMERIC;


DEFINE ELEMENT                          ITEM-NAME;
     ATTRIBUTES ARE:
          SIZE            30,
          TYPE            ALPHANUMERIC;


DEFINE RELATION                         REL-ITEM-RECORD-SCH;
     SYNONYMS ARE:  COMPOSITION;
     ASSOCIATED-DATA IS:
                    POSITION-OF-ITEM-IN-RECORD;
     CONNECTIVITY IS:
          MANY            MANY;
     LEFT IS:       INF-ITEM-SCH;
     RIGHT IS:      INF-RECORD-SCH;

DEFINE RELATION                         REL-RECORD-ITEM-SCH;
     SYNONYMS ARE:  DECOMPOSITION;
     ASSOCIATED-DATA IS:
                    POSITION-OF-ITEM-IN-RECORD;
     CONNECTIVITY IS:
          MANY            MANY;
     LEFT IS:       INF-RECORD-SCH;
     RIGHT IS:      INF-ITEM-SCH;


DEFINE RELATION                         REL-SCHEMA-ITEMS;
     SYNONYMS ARE:  E;
     CONNECTIVITY IS:
          ONE             MANY;
     LEFT IS:       INF-SCHEMA;
     RIGHT IS:      INF-ITEM-SCH;
                                   REL-ITEM-SUBSCH-ITEM-SCH;
DEFINE RELATION
     SYNONYMS ARE:  E-BAR-SUB-SIGMA-E-BAR;
     CONNECTIVITY IS:
          MANY            ONE;
     LEFT IS:       INF-ITEM-SUBSCH;
     RIGHT IS:      INF-ITEM-SCH;
```

FIGURE -3

These reports can be obtained on video terminals and the selection module
of PSA allows the efficient consulting of the aspects of PSL/PSA information Processing System Model, in particular of the ERA Database Model,
that are relevant to any member of the software development team. The
matrix diagram representation of the metaschema Figure 4 is easy to
understand even for those not familiar with mathematical notation. The
other matrices inspired by graph theoretical tools present very useful
information for the analyst on how many relationships relate to entities
and how many steps at a minimum would be required to go from one entity
to another using the relationships that exist in the database schema.

The proposal of Rochfeld and Tabourier for using the metaschema
concept in the development of the software for a DBMS is extremely valid
as is their idea of formalizing the database schema using mathematical
tools. Graph theoretical tools seem more proficient than their set
theoretic notation and PSL/PSA, with its built-in ERA Model that is
adequate for Meta Base formalization, can be used to computer-aid the
effort. The possibility of using the computer to aid the software
development effort is the result of adequately formalizing the DBMS
development process objective sought by Rochfeld and Tabourier.

5. CURRENT TOPICS

This paper has outlined some applications of the ERA approach to
documentation and analysis of information processing system. This
section briefly discusses two issues that have arisen in this work and
some investigation currently being pursued. The issues are concerned
with expressing procedural information in ERA based languages and the
relative advantages and disadvantages of the relational model versus
the ERA model.

5.1 EXPRESSING PROCEDURAL INFORMATION IN ERA BASED LANGUAGES

The ERA model in the System Description and Data Model applications
described above is used to describe static structure. Systems, however,
are not static - they also have dynamic aspects. In system description
it is necessary at some point to define the behavior of the system;
usually this is done by a procedural programming language.

In programming languages, much of the procedure is expressed by
position; a statement is executed immediately after the one that proceeds
it. The sequence may be altered by control statements. Sequence in
effect is implicit. When the ERA model is used, sequence must be
stated explicitly and consequently the number of statements that must be
stated explicitly made is much larger. One possibility currently being
investigated is to input a graphical representation of the ERA model via
a graphic terminal and have these representations translated automatically to acceptable transactions to update the database.

In the case of data models, it is necessary to describe the dynamics
of the database, i.e. the way it changes over time. Dynamic aspects of

Relation Structure Report

RELATION - ENTITY Matrix

Each RELATION (row) has entries indicating which ENTITIES
it connects. The type of entry denotes how the two ENTITIES
are RELATED. This matrix is based on the LEFT and RIGHT
statements in the RELATION section. For example:

    DEFINE RELATION XYZ;
        LEFT E1;
        RIGHT E2;

An L, left, means that the ENTITY is on the "left hand side"
of the RELATION. In the above example, E1 is the "left"
ENTITY. An R, right, indicates that the ENTITY is on the
"right hand side" of the RELATION. In the above example E2
is the "right" ENTITY. Thus an L in position (i,j) and an
R in position (i, k) indicates that ENTITY j is related to
ENTITY k via RELATION i. The mapping between ENTITIES j
and k is assumed to be directional, i.e., from j to k.

Row Names

```
 1 REL-AREA-RECORD-SCH                 RELATION
 2 REL-AREA-SUBSCH-AREA-SCH            RELATION                      1
 3 REL-SCHEMA-AREAS                    RELATION            1234567890
 4 REL-RECORD-AREA-SCH                 RELATION            +----+-----+
 5 REL-AREA-RECORD-SUBSCH              RELATION          1 |LR  |     |
 6 REL-AREAS-SUBSCHEMA                 RELATION          2 |R L |     |
 7 REL-RECORD-AREA-SUBSCH              RELATION          3 |R  L|     |
 8 REL-SUBSCHEMA-AREAS                 RELATION          4 |RL  |     |
 9 REL-ITEM-RECORD-SCH                 RELATION          5 +---L-R-----+
10 REL-SCHEMA-ITEMS                    RELATION          6 |  L |R    |
11 REL-ITEM-SUBSCH-ITEM-SCH            RELATION          7 |  R L     |
12 REL-RECORD-ITEM-SCH                 RELATION          8 |  R |L    |
13 REL-ITEM-RECORD-SUBSCH              RELATION          9 |R  |  L   |
14 REL-ITEMS-SUBSCHEMA                 RELATION         10 +---L+-R---+
15 REL-RECORD-ITEM-SUBSCH              RELATION         11 |    |  RL  |
16 REL-SUBSCHEMA-ITEMS                 RELATION         12 | L  |  R   |
17 REL-MEMBER-SCH                      RELATION         13 |    R  L  |
18 REL-MASTER-SCH                      RELATION         14 |    |R L  |
19 REL-SET-RECORD-SCH                  RELATION         15 +----L--R--+
20 REL-SCHEMA-RECORDS                  RELATION         16 |    |L R  |
21 REL-RECORD-SUBSCH-RECORD-SCH        RELATION         17 | L  |    R |
22 REL-MASTER-SUBSCH                   RELATION         18 | L  |    R |
23 REL-MEMBER-SUBSCH                   RELATION         19 | R  |    L |
24 REL-RECORDS-SUBSCHEMA               RELATION         20 +-R-L+-----+
25 REL-SET-RECORD-SUBSCH               RELATION         21 | R   L    |
26 REL-SUBSCHEMA-RECORDS               RELATION         22 |     L   R|
27 REL-SCHEMA-SETS                     RELATION         23 |     L   R|
28 REL-SCHEMA-SUBSCHEMAS               RELATION         24 |     LR   |
29 REL-SUBSCHEMAS-SCHEMA               RELATION         25 |     R   L|
30 REL-SET-SUBSCH-SET-SCH              RELATION            +----+-----+
31 REL-SETS-SUBSCHEMA                  RELATION         26 |     RL   |
32 REL-SUBSCHEMA-SETS                  RELATION         27 | L| R    |
   Column Names                                         28 | L|R    |
                                                        29 | R|L    |
 1 INF-AREA-SCH                        ENTITY           30 +----+---RL+
 2 INF-RECORD-SCH                      ENTITY           31 |  |R  L|
 3 INF-AREA-SUBSCH                     ENTITY           32 |  |L  R|
 4 INF-SCHEMA                          ENTITY              +----+-----+
 5 INF-RECORD-SUBSCH                   ENTITY
 6 INF-SUBSCHEMA                       ENTITY
 7 INF-ITEM-SCH                        ENTITY              FIGURE 4a
 8 INF-ITEM-SUBSCH                     ENTITY
 9 INF-SET-SCH                         ENTITY
10 INF-SET-SUBSCH                      ENTITY
```

D. Teichroew, F. Germano and L. Silva

Relation Structure Report

ENTITY Interaction Matrix

The row and column numbers refer to the column
names from above.

An entry n in position (i,j) indicates that ENTITY i is
related to ENTITY j via n RELATIONS.

```
                        1 2 3 4 5  6 7 8 9 0
                      +----------+----------+
                    1 |   1      |    1     |
                    2 | 1        |    1   2 |
                    3 | 1        | 1| 1     |
                    4 | 1 1      |   1 1   1|
                    5 |   1 1    |   1   1 2|
                      +----------+----------+
                    6 |   1 1 1| |     1   1|
                    7 |   1      |          |
                    8 |        1| 1 1      |
                    9 |   1      |          |
                   10 |        1| 1     1  |
                      +----------+----------+
```

FIGURE - 4b

Shortest Path Matrix

The row and column numbers refer to the column
names from above.

Path length is defined as the number of RELATIONS which
must be used to relate one ENTITY to another. An entry
n in location (i,j) is the length of the shortest "path"

from ENTITY i to ENTITY j. No entry in a position
indicates that there is no path. This path utilizes
directional RELATIONS, from "left" or "parent" ENTITY
to "right" or "child" ENTITY.

```
                        1 2 3 4 5  6 7 8 9 0
                      +----------+----------+
                    1 | 2 1      |   2   2  |
                    2 | 1 2      |   1   2  |
                    3 | 1 2 2 2 1| 1 3 2 3 2|
                    4 | 1 1 2 2 2| 1 1 2 1 2|
                    5 | 2 1 1 2 2| 1 2 1 2 2|
                      +----------+----------+
                    6 | 2 2 1 1 1| 2 2 1 2 1|
                    7 | 2 1      |   2   2  |
                    8 | 3 2 2 2 1| 1 1 2 3 2|
                    9 | 2 1      |   2   2  |
                   10 | 3 2 2 2 1| 1 3 2 1 2|
                      +----------+----------+
```

FIGURE - 4c

data model have been examined, for example, by Griethuysen (1981). The
ERA model used in ISDLS is being extended to incorporate dynamic concepts. (Kang, 1981).

5.2 RELATIONAL VERSUS ERA MODELS

It is clearly possible to implement a software development facility
using relational data model if a relational DBMS is available. This
has been demonstrated by Johnson (1981) using System R as the relational
DBMS.

Whether this will be a practical approach depends first and foremost
on the availability of a relational DBMS. Assuming that these will soon
be as common as hierarchical and network DBMS's are now, there are still
some issues to be resolved. Among the most important are performance,
application development time and system administrator functions.

The relative performance of relational and network DBMS has been
the subject of much research and debate (King, 1980), because it affects
the future of relational DBMS in general. While the database in software development facilities may be smaller than in many other applications, they tend to be more complex and the processing that must be
done is also complex. These factors will probably accentuate the relative disadvantage of the relational DBMS in the near future. Some
quantitative experiments are planned.

As in most other applications, using a DBMS does not eliminate the
need to write applications software. One of the advantages calimed for
relational DBMS is that with a single user interface, e.g. SEQUEL in the
case of System R, the time and effort required to write applications
software is reduced and it can even by done by the end user. It is
certainly true that the higher the level of procedural language, the
less the amount of programming required. However, it is also possible
to design very high level languages that understand the ERA model.
(Kang, 1981). Therefore, this factor, itself, does not necessarily
give relational DBMS an advantage.

Another advantage claimed for this relational DBMS is that there
need not be a distinction between the schema and the data structure
known by the application program. The set of relations may be modified
at any time. This may appear to be an advantage, but in practice, the
organization usually wants to have an organizational standard which the
end user is not allowed to modify. This can be done with a relational
DBMS with appropriate security controls, but requires substantial
overhead.

From the investigations and experience reported in this paper, it
appears that the ERA model is more general and provides a more natural
view of systems. The ERA model also bridges the gap between system
analysis, data modeling and functional analysis.

D. Teichroew, F. Germano and L. Silva

Acknowledgements

Section 4 is based on results obtained by Maria Clara Paco in a MSc program. This MSc program has been in part supported by CAPES and was developed in part at the Instituto de Ciencias Mathmaticas de Sao Carlos and in part at the Instituto de Pesquisas Energeticas de Sao Paulo.

REFERENCES

Boyd, D.L., Pizzarello, A. and Vestal, S.C., "Rational Design Methodology", Report HR-78-57: 17-38, Honeywell Inc., Rome Air Development Center, Information Science Division, Griffiss AFB, NY 13441, June 1978, 178 pp. (ADA06 2404).

Brown, R.R. and T.L. Ramey, "The Concept and Practice of ERA Information Modeling", Entity-Relationship Approach to Systems Analysis and Design, P.P. Chen (ed.), North-Holland, June 1980.

Buxton, J.N., "Requirements for Ada Programming Support Environments", DoD February 1980.

Buzen, J.P., Goldberg, R.P., et al., "POD - A Software Engineering Tool for Life Cycle Management of System Performance", BGS Systems, Inc. Lincoln, MA, 1980.

Buzen, J.P., Goldberg, R.P., et al., "Performance Oriented Design (POD) - Preliminary Reference Manual", BGS Systems, Inc., Lincoln, MA, March 1979.

Chen, P.P., "The Entity-Relationship Model: Toward a Unified View of Data," ACM Transactions of Database Systems, Vol. 1, No. 1, June 1976.

Chen, P.P., Entity-Relationship Approach to Logical Database Design, Q.E.D. Information Sciences, Inc., 141 Linden Street, Wellesley, Mass., 02181, 1977.

Chen, P.P. (ed.), Entity-Relationship Approach to Systems Analysis and Design, North-Holland Publishing Co., June 1980.

"CODASYL DBTG (Database Task Group)", CODASYL April 1971 Report., CODASYL (Conference on Data Systems Language), 1971.

Codd, E.F., "Extending the Database Relational Model to Capture More Meaning", ACM Transactions on Database Systems, Vol. 4, No. 4, Dec. 1979.

Hammer, H. and D. McLeod, "The Semantic Model: A Modeling Mechanism for Database Applications", ACM SIGMOD Proceedings, International Conference on Management of Data, May 1978, Austin, Texas.

Hausen, Hans-Ludwig and Monika Mullerburg, "Conspectus of Software Engineering Environments", 5th Intern. Conference of Software Engineering, San Diego, California, March 9-12, 1981, pp. 34-43.

Griethuysen, J.J. Van (ed.), Concepts and Terminology for the Conceptual
    Schema, ISO TC97/SC5/WG3 Preliminary Report, February 1981.

Johnson, David, "The Software Development Facility Approach to Improved
    Software Development," Ph.D. Dissertation, The University of
    Michigan, 1981.

Kang, K.C., "A Methodology for the Specification of Completeness and
    Consistency of System Descriptions," Ph.D. Dissertation, The
    University of Michigan, Expected 1981.

King, W.F., "Relational Database Systems: Where We Stand Today," Information
    Processing 80, S.H. Lanington (ed.), North Holland Publishing Co.,
    1980, pp. 369-381.

Levy, A.I., "An Integrated Approach to Capacity Planning Using Capture
    IMVS and BEST/II," Eighth Annual European Conference on Computer
    Measurement, London, England, October 1980.

McLeod, D., "A Semantic Database Model and Its Associated Structured User
    Interface," Ph.D. Dissertation, MIT, Cambridge, MA, 1975.

Nassi, I. and Shneiderman, B., "Flowchart Techniques for Structured
    Programming," SIGPLAN Notices of the ACM, Vol. 8, No. 8, pp. 12-26,
    August 1973.

Paco, M., Sobre aspectos logicos do projeto de Bases de Dados, MSc
    dissertation presented at Instituto de Ciencias Matematicas de Sao
    Carlos da Universidade de Sao Paulo, 1978.

Riesson, O.J., "The CCITT Functional Specification and Description Language
    SDL," ITU, Geneva, 1977.

Robinson, L. and K.N. Levitt, "Proof Techniques for Hierarchically
    Structured Programs, Comm. ACM 20 (4), pp. 271-283, April 1977.

Rochfeld, A. and Tabourier, Y., "Bases de donnees: un essai de formaliza-
    tion," Revue Metra v13 n04, 1974.

Santos, C.C. dos, Neuhold, E.J. and Furtado, A.L., "A Data Type Approach
    to the Entity-Relationship Model," in: Chen, P.P. (ed.), Entity-
    Relationship Approach to Systems Analysis and Design, North-Holland
    Amsterdam, June 1980.

Scheuermann, P., Schiffner, G., and Weber, H., "Abstraction Capabilities
    and Invariant Properties Modeling within the Entity-Relationship
    Approach" in Chen, P. (ed.), Entity-Relationship Approach to Systems
    Analysis and Design, North-Holland, Amsterdam, June 1980.

Spewak, Steven Howard, "Analysis of Dynamics of the Logical Design of Information Systems," Ph.D. Dissertation, The University of Michigan, 1981.

Stenning, V., Frogatt, T., Gilbert, R., Thomas., E., "The Ada Environment: A perspective," Computer, June 1981, pp. 26-45.

Teichroew Daniel, Petar Macasovic, Ernest A., Hershey III, and Yuzo Yamamoto, "Application of the Entity-Relationship Approach to Information Processing Systems Modeling," Entity-Relationship Approach to Systems Analysis and Design, P.P. Chen (ed.), North-Holland Publishing Company, 1980, pp. 15-38.

Teichroew, D., K.C. Kang and Petar Macasovic, "A Laboratory for Software Engineering Education and Research," Proceedings II International Symposium Computers at the University, University Computing Center, Zagrab, 1980, pp. 38-49.

Wiederhold, Gio and El-Masri, "A Structural Model for Database Systems," STAN-CS-79-722, Computer Science Department, Stanford University, February 1979.

Winchester, James, "Requirements Definition and Its Interface to the Sara Design Methodology for Computer-Based Systems," Ph.D. Dissertation, University of California at Los Angeles, 1981.

Winters, Edward William, "On the Analysis and Synthesis of Human and Computer Subsystems for Information Processing Systems," Ph.D. Dissertation, Union of Experimenting Colleges and Universities, 1981.

Wolfe, Martin I., Wayne Babich, Richard Simpson, Richard Thall, and Larry Weissman, "The Ada Language System," Computer, June 1981, pp. 37-45.

Yamamoto, Yuzo, "An Approach to the Generation of Software Life Cycle Support Systems," Ph.D. Dissertation, The University of Michigan, 1981.

Entity-Relationship Approach to
Information Modeling and Analysis, P.P. Chen (ed.)
Elsevier Science Publishers B.V. (North-Holland)
©ER Institute, 1983

A PRELIMINARY FRAMEWORK FOR ENTITY-RELATIONSHIP MODELS

PETER PIN-SHAN CHEN

Graduate School of Management
University of California, Los Angeles
Los Angeles, California 90024
U.S.A.

ABSTRACT

Many models have been proposed for use in information modeling
and analysis. Most of them use the concepts of entity, relationship, and attribute. The major difference of these models are
their definitions and use of the concepts of "relationship" and
and "attribute". This paper proposes a framework for classifying
entity-relationship models and discusses how these models might
be translated from one to the other.

I. <u>INTRODUCTION</u>

        In recent years, many entity-relationship models have been proposed for
use in information modeling and analysis. Most of them are based on the concepts of "entity", "relationship", and "attribute". The differences between
these entity-relationship models are their interpretations of (and limitations
on) the concepts of "relationship" and "attribute". The supporters of a particular model may claim that their model is more "powerful" than other models,
while others may claim their models are more "elegant" since fewer primitive
concepts are used. It is very difficult for a newcomer to this field to fully
understand these claims and to evaluate the merits of different models. Therefore, a framework for entity-relationship models is needed to put them in
perspective.

        In this paper, a preliminary framework for entity-relationship models
is proposed. The framework is based on the capabilities and limitations of
"relationship" and "attribute" in each model. In terms of "relationship",
models are diffrentiated by whether they allow n-ary relationships or allow
only binary relationships. In terms of "attribute", some models allow "attribute of relationship", while some others allow no attributes at all. By
diffrentiating on the treatment of "relationships " and "attributes", we
can present a framework for classifying entity-relationship models.

        The purpose of this paper is not only to classify entity-relationship
models into different categories but also to demonstrate the feasibility of
translating from one type of entity-relationship model to another.. If such
translations are feasible, there are several significant implications for

information modeling and analysis. First, the systems analyst may use their
favorite model to model the real world and then covert it into another model
for presentation to others. Second, it may be possible to implement a database management system which supports several types of entity-relationship
models. Third, it may be able to demonstrate that different types of entity-
relationship models are equivalent. The equivalence of "data models" has
been a subject of research for several researchers (for example, [SIBL74]).
We hope that our paper can stimulate more research in this direction.

II. CLASSIFICATION OF ENTITY-RELATIONSHIP MODELS

        Entity-relationship models can be divided into two major categories
based on the type of relationship allowed in the model. The first category
is called Generalized (N-ary) Entity-Relationship Models (GERM), which allows
relationships defined on more than two entities. The second category is called
Binary Entity-Relationship Models (BERM) which allows at most two entities to
be involved in a relationship.

        Each of these two major categories can be further divided into three
subcategories depending on their treatment of "attributes." The first subcategory of models allows attributes for both entity and relationship. The
second subcategory allows attributes for entities only. The third subcategory
does not allow attributes at all.

        Figure 1 illustrates a framework for entity-relationship models. An
example of a GERM which allows attributes for both entities and relationships
is the original version of the Entity-Relationship Model [CHEN76, DOSS80,
SCHE80]. A graphical representation of the ERM's in this category is given
in Figure 2. As shown, a project can participate in "m" (i.e., "many") "WORKS-
FOR" relationships, and an employee can participate in "N" (i.e., "many")
"WORKS-FOR" relationships. In other words, an employee can work for several
projects, and a project can have several employees as workers. Note the three-
way relationship between the SUPPLIER, PART, and PROJ entities. The SUPPLIED
relationship indicates that a particular supplier supplied a particular part
to a particular project. Note in this Entity-Relationship Diagram (ERD) that
both entities and relationships can have attributes. For example, a SUPPLY
entity has attribute S# and SNAME, and a SUPPLIED relationship has an attribute
DATE.

        The second subcategory of the GERM's does not allow attributes for re-
lationships. If a "relationship" has an attribute, the analyst will create a
"high-level entity" to replace it. Figure 3(a) indicates the graphical representation of this type of ERM. Note that the "SUPPLIED-BY" relationship has
been converted into a "high-level entity" called "SUPPLIES", and "DATE" is an
attribute of the newly-created SUPPLIES entities. Note that "relationships"
are represented by a "straight line" (or arc) between entity types. If the
SUPPLIED-BY relationship in Figure 2 does not have any attribute, Figure 3(b)
will be the new ERD. Note that the "SUPPLIED-BY" relationship is represented
by a "dot", which is the intersection of three lines originating from three
entity types: PROJ, PART, and SUPPLIER. The concept of a "high-level entity"
and the graphical symbol to represent it have been discussed in [SCHE80, DOSS80,
CHEN80]. However, in these papers, the conversion of a "relationship" into a

"high-level entity" is done at the analyst's option and is not enforced when
the relationship has an attribute.

The third subcategory is a GERM with no attributes at all. In this
case, Figure 3(b) will be converted into Figure 4. To the best of our knowledge, no one has proposed an ERM in this subcategory.

The binary ERM's can also be divided into three subcategories, which
are designated as (4), (5), and (6) in Figure 1. The (4) subcategory is a
binary ERM which allows attributes for both entities and relationships.
Figure 5 illustrates an ERD for this kind of ERM. An example of this kind
of ERM is the data model used in the IBM DB/DC data dictionary system.

Subcategory (5) in Figure 1 is the class of ERM which allows attributes
for entities only. This subcategory can be further divided into two groups
depending on whether or not "many-to-many" relationships are allowed. Subcategory (5.1) denotes a class of BERM's which allow many-to-many relationships. Figure 6, which correspond to Figure 2, illustrates an ERD based on
this kind of BERM. Note that "WORK-FOR" is a many-to-many relationship. Note
also that Figure 6 is the same as Figure 3(a). However, Figure 6 is the only
acceptable graphical representation corresponding to Figure 2 for this kind of
BERM. Figure 3(b) is not acceptable since it contains a 3-ary relationship
"SUPPLIED-BY". Any n-ary relationship has to be converted into an "entity" in
a binary model. Therefore, no matter whether the "SUPPLIED-BY" relationship
has an attribute or not, Figure 6 is the corresponding ERD for the BERM with
attributes for entities only. Examples of this type of BERM are the data models
used in many of the commercially available data dictionary systems. Another
example is the Simplified ERM used in [FURT81, LUSK81].

Subcategory (5.2) is the class of BERM, which does not allow "many-to-
many" relationships. In other words, only "one-to-one" or "one-to-many" relationships are allowed. This subcategory can be further divided into two
groups depending on whether the relationship is directional or non-directional.
Subcategory (5.2.1) denotes the class of BERM's in which the relationships are
non-directional. Figure 7, which corresponds to Figure 6, illustrates an ERD
based on this kind of BERM.

Subcategory (5.2.2) denotes the class of BERM's in which the relationships are directional. Each relationship has a direction: it starts with a
"parent" entity and ends with a "child" entity. Although it may be possible
to access the "parent" entities from a "child" entity, the treatment of these
two types of entities is usually quite different. This kind of BERM can be
found in many conventional database management systems. Let us divide this
subcategory into three groups depending on the number of "parent" entities
allowed for a "child" entity.

Subcategory (5.2.2.1) is the class of BERM's in which only one "parent"
entity is allowed for a "child" entity and no attributes are allowed for relationships. An example of this kind of BERM is a "pure" hierarchical database
management system. Figure 8 illustrates an ERD, which is acceptable in this
kind of BERM.

Subcategory (5.2.2.2) is the class of BERM's in which one "physical parent" entity and one "logical parent" entity are allowed for a "child" entity. An example of this kind of BERM is the data model used in the IBM's IMS system. Figure 9 illustrates an ERD which is acceptable in this kind of BERM.

Subcategory (5.2.2.3) is the class of BERM's in which many "parent" entities are allowed for a "child" entity. Figure 10, which is corresponding to Figure 7, illustrates an ERD for this kind of BERM. The CODASYL data model can be classified into this subcategory.

Subcategory (6) is the class of BERM's in which no attributes are allowed. This kind of BERM can be respresented by either Figure 11 or Figure 12. Note that in Figure 12 the entity identifying attribute is used to denote the entity itself. For example, PROJ# is used to denote "PROJ" entity itself. The binary data model [ABRI74] and the Entity set model [SEKO73] can be considered as close to the one represented by Figure 12, while the Functional model [SIBL77] can be considered as close to the one represented by Figure 11 after some modifications.

III. OBSERVATIONS

There are a few observations based on this framework of entity-relationship models:

(a) There is a spectrum of ERM's. On the one end, there is a GERM in which attributes for both entities and relationships are allowed. On the other end, there is a BERM in which no attributes are allowed. The conversion from the former to the latter involves the conversion of n-ary relationships into "entities" and the conversion of attributes into "entities". The reverse conversion is possible, but it needs human inputs to specify what attributes are and what entities are.

(b) Each kind of ERM has its own appeal in certain situations. It is difficult to judge which kind of ERM is always superior than other types.

(c) Although little work has been done for models in category (2), it is conceivable that a theory can be developed along the line of [DOSS80, SCHE80, CHEN80] as discussed earlier in the paper. However, research work on the ERM's in category (3) would be of theoretical value, but its practical value needs to be justified.

IV. SUMMARY

In this paper, we have presented a framework for entity-relationship models. We have also discussed previous research work or commercial systems, which fit into each of these categories. We have tried to use the same example to demonstrate the feasibility of translation from an ERD of one category to an ERD in another category. We hope that the results of this paper can increase the understanding of different types of ERM's and can stimulate more research in the Entity-Relationship approach.

REFERENCES

[ABRI74]   Abrial, J.R., Data Semantics, in: Klimbie, J.W. and Koffemann, K.L. (eds.), Data Base Management (North-Holland, Amsterdam, 1974).

[CHEN76]   Chen, P.P., The entity relationship model: toward a unified view of data, ACM Transactions on Database Systems, 1, 1 (March 1976),9-37.

[CHEN80]   Chen, P.P., Entity-Relationship diagrams and English sentence structures, (abstract only), in: Chen, P.P. (ed.), Entity-Relationship Approach to Systems Analysis and Design (North-Holland, Amsterdam, June 1980).

[DOSS80]   dos Santos, C.S., Neuhold, E.J. and Furtado, A.L., A data type approach to the entity-relationship model, in: Chen, P.P. (ed.), Entity- Relationship Apprcach to Systems Analysis and Design (North-Holland, Amsterdam, 1980).

[FURT83]   Furtado, A.L. Veloso, P.A.S., and de Castilho, J.M.V., Verification and testing of S-ER representations, in: Chen, P.P. (ed.), Entity-Relationship to Information Modeling and Analysis (Elsevier Science Publishers B.V., Amsterdam, 1983)

[LUSK83]   Lusk E., Petrie G., and Overbeek, R., Item tracking entity-relation-ship models, in: Chen, P.P. (ed.), Entity-Relationship Approach to Information Modeling and Analysis (Elsevier Science Publishers B.V., Amsterdam, 1983)

[SCHE80]   Scheuermann, P., Schiffner, G. and Weber, H., Abstraction Capabili-ties and invariant properties modeling within the entity-relationship approach, in: Chen, P.P. (ed.), Entity-Relationship Approach to Systems Analysis and Design (North-Holland, Amsterdam, June 1980).

[SENK73]   Senko, M.E., Altman, E.B., Astrahan, M.M. and Fehder, P.L., Data structures and accessing in data-base system, IBM Systems Journal, 12,1 (1973), 30-93.

[SIBL74]   Sibley, E.H., On the equivalence of data base systems, Proceedings of ACM SIGNOD 1974 Debate on Data Models, Ann Arbor, Michigan (May 1974), 43-76.

[SIBL77]   Sibley, E.H. and Kershberg, L. Data architecture and data model considerations, Proceedings of AFIPS National Computer Conference, Dallas, Texas (June 1977), 85-96.

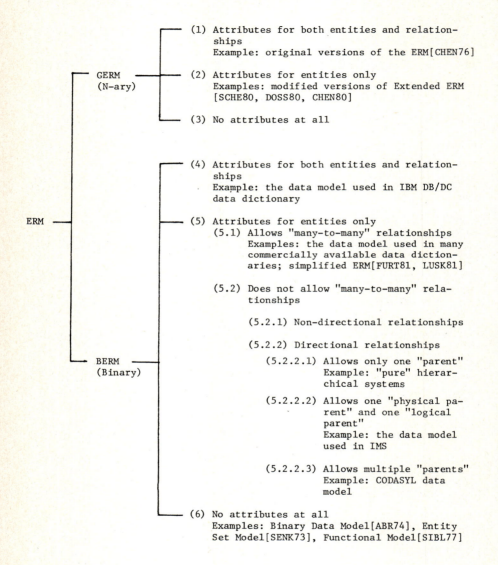

Figure 1: A Framework for Entity-Relationship Models

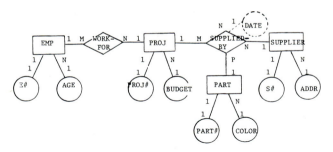

Figure 2: An ERD based on a **GERM** which allows
attributes on both entities and relationships

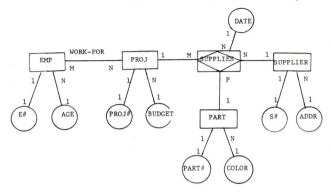

Figure 3(a): An ERD based on a **GERM** which allows
attributes on entities only (Note that
"DATE" is an attribute of a "high-level
entity" of type "SUPPLIES".)

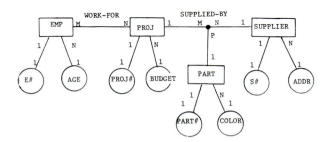

Figure 3(b): An ERD based on a **GERM** which allows
attributes on entities only (Note
that the "SUPPLIED" relationship
does not have an attribute.)

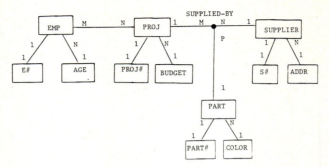

Figure 4: An ERD based a GERM with no attributes at all (This is a corresponding diagram of Figure 3(b).)

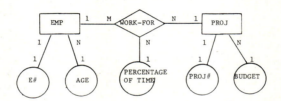

Figure 5: An ERD based on a BERM which allows attributes for both entities and relationships

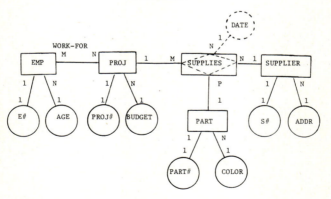

Figure 6: An ERD based on a BERM which allows attributes for entities only and allows "many-to-many" relationships

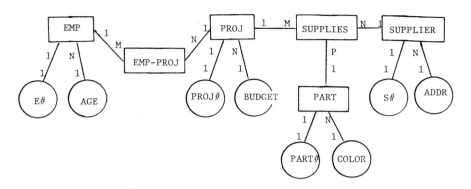

Figure 7: An ERD based on a BERM which allows only:
(i) attributes for entities, (ii) "one-
to-many" and "one-to-one" one-directional
relationships

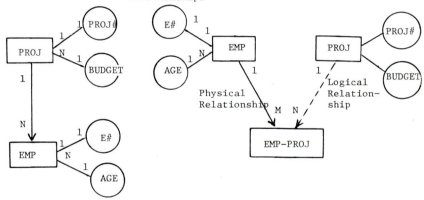

Figure 8: An ERD based on a BERM
which allows only: (i) attributes
for entities, (ii) "one-to-one"
and "one-to-many" directional
relationships, (iii) one "parent"
for each child.

Figure 9: Same as stated in Figure 6
except that one "logical parent" and
one "physical parent" are allowed

28   P.P. Chen

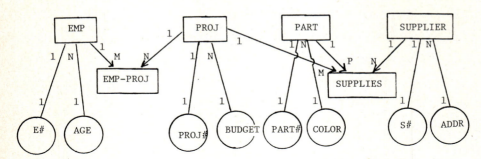

Figure 10: Same as stated in Figure 8 except that
multiple "parents" are allowed

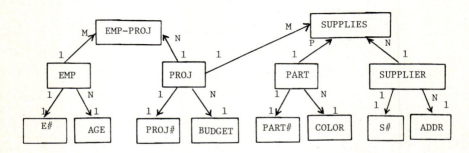

Figure 11: An ERD on a BERM in which no attribute
is allowed

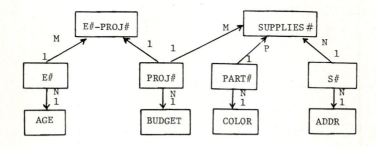

Figure 12: Another ERD on BERM in which no attribute
allowed and the entity identifying attributes
are used to identify entities themselves

Entity-Relationship Approach to
Information Modeling and Analysis, P.P. Chen (ed.)
Elsevier Science Publishers B.V. (North-Holland)
©ER Institute, 1983

The ER and EAS Formalisms for System Modeling,
and the EAS-E Language

H.M. Markowitz, A. Malhotra, and D.P. Pazel

IBM Thomas J. Watson Research Center,
P.O. Box 218, Yorktown Heights, N.Y. 10598

This paper reviews the relationships between the ER (Entity-Relationship) and the EAS (Entity-Attribute-and-Set) formalisms; describes the EAS-E implementation of the EAS view as far as we have developed it; considers where EAS-E could go from here, i.e., considers the natural long run goal of an EAS-based application development language; and draws implications of these observations for ER as well as EAS programming.

1. INTRODUCTION

EAS-E is an experimental application development system being developed at IBM's T. J. Watson Research Center. It is based on the Entity, Attribute and Set (EAS) formalism for system modeling. We were delighted to see in the call for papers that topics of interest for this conference include "relationships with...EAS-E." In this connection we would like to review the relationships between the ER and EAS views; describe the EAS-E implementation of the EAS view as far as we have developed it; consider where EAS-E could go from here, i.e., consider the natural long run goal of an EAS-based application development language; and draw implications of these observations for ER as well as EAS programming.

2. THE EAS WORLDVIEW

The Entity, Attribute and Set formalism for system description was introduced almost simultaneously by three simulation languages-- CSL(1), GASP(7), and SIMSCRIPT(10)--in the early 1960s. For each of these languages an entity is some concrete or abstract "thing" represented by the simulation; an attribute is some property or characteristic of the entity; and a set is an ordered collection of entities. In SIMSCRIPT, each instance of a set has one owner entity as well as zero, one or more member entities. For example, the simulation of a factory might include a type of set whose name is QUEUE; machine 1 owns one instance of a QUEUE, machine 2 owns a second instance, etc. Zero, one or more jobs belong to a particular queue.

The elemental acts for changing the status of such a system are to CREATE or DESTROY an entity, FILE an entity into or REMOVE an entity from a set, or assign a value to an attribute. A simulated activity or event may involve many such elemental acts.

The Entity, Attribute and Set view of the simulation languages is closely related to the network view of the database languages, with record corresponding to entity, field corresponding to attribute, and set corresponding to set. In a DBTG database, as in a SIMSCRIPT simulation, sets have owners as well as members; if only a single set with a given name is allowed, it is said to be owned by the system as a whole.

There are minor differences between the EAS concepts as incorporated, e.g., in SIMSCRIPT II(8) and the network concept as incorporated in DBTG(3). For example, SIMSCRIPT allows an entity of a given type to both own and belong to a set with a given name. This indeed is the easiest way to represent a tree structure: if an entity type, say ORGANIZATIONAL_UNIT owns a set called SUBORGANIZATIONs whose members are themselves ORGANIZATIONAL_UNITS (which own SUBORGANIZATIONS, etc.) an organization tree is represented. On the other hand SIMSCRIPT does not offer, but could and surely should offer, the options of mandatory and automatic sets as used by DBTG.

A more important difference, though some would discount this as mere quibbling over choice of words, is the use of entity-attribute as primitives in the one language as compared to record-field in the other. In part the difference is philosophical, the one terminology emphasizing that which is represented as distinguished from how this representation is achieved. The difference also has to do with such "practical" matters as how information is stored. To illustrate, let us briefly consider certain details concerning the SIMSCRIPT and EAS-E implementations.

The entity types in a SIMSCRIPT program, and the "main storage", as distinguished from database, entities of EAS-E, are divided into two classes: (a) those types whose individuals may be created and destroyed individually during the course of an execution; and (b) those types whose individuals are created en masse usually at the beginning of an execution and usually exist throughout the execution (e.g. throughout a simulation run). The former are called "temporary" entities, the latter "permanent" entities (at least they are "permanent" during the course of the run).

In part for reasons of efficiency, the attributes of temporary entities are stored in records whereas those of permanent entities are stored in arrays. Thus all the attributes of one temporary entity are stored in successive words of memory; whereas all the values on one attribute of all instances of some type of permanent entity are stored together in an array. Consequently, information concerning a particular permanent entity is dispersed in many arrays rather than grouped together into one record for the entity.

Both permanent and temporary entities can own sets, both can belong to sets, both have attributes which can be modified or referenced. The programmer FILEs, REMOVEs and assigns values to attributes with the same source program statements in either case. It is up to the software behind the scenes to remember what is stored where, and how to update it.

It is sometimes argued that, even in the case of a permanent entity, though its attributes are scattered they constitute a "logical record". While such terminology may be helpful in some contexts, we feel it normally more descriptive to say that EAS-E represents entities of various types, and it is up to the implementation to decide which are stored in records, which in arrays, and which in perhaps other ways.

3. EAS and ER

Chen(2) describes how entities and their relationships can be described by a network, therefore an EAS, model. In particular, an attribute of one entity may "point" to another entity; hence may be used to represent a one-one or many-one relationship. Sets obviously show a one-many relationship between the owner entities and the member entities respectively. An m-n relationship between, e.g., courses and students requires an intermediate entity like an "enrollment". Enrollment belongs to a set owned by course and another owned by student and thereby connects the two. (In EAS-E, entities belonging to database sets automatically point to their owner entities; hence each enrollment would know its student and course without further definition or programming.) Usually--in fact, in every case we have dealt with in either simulation or database applications--the intermediate entity carries other useful information, such as the date and grade of the enrollment.

In considering the representation of entity, attribute and set structures by the ER formalism, one must keep in mind that sets are ordered collections. A set of backorders for a given item, for example, not only remembers who is waiting for the item but also remembers that Mr. Jones is first, Ms. Smith is second, and so on. This sequence information is most easily represented in ER terms by use of an "ordinal path", in the sense of Griffith (5), from first member to last member as well as a 1-n relationship between owner and members.

The ER and the EAS views are similar in that they allow their users to model a (real or imagined) world rather than require him to spell out how the computer is to represent this world. They each provide their users with a simple but general set of modeling concepts. The strength of each view is at the same time its weakness. The fact that the entity, attribute and set view requires the user to declare in advance, in effect, which are 1-1 or many-1 relationships versus 1-many and m-n relationships, allows an EAS implementation to lay out a program to execute more efficiently. But more trouble is usually involved in an EAS than an ER system when database definitions are changed; e.g., the aforementioned efficient program must be recompiled when it is decided that an employee can belong to more than one department, therefore a set must now be used where previously an attribute sufficed.

The ER and EAS views seem to us sufficiently similar that experience with the implementation and use of an EAS-based application development system should be at least suggestive for, and perhaps formally generalizable to, the ER view. Accordingly, in the next section we briefly describe and illustrate the EAS-E implementation of the EAS view for database management; thereafter we consider possible extensions of EAS-E to other areas; and finally consider the corresponding possibilities for the ER view.

4. THE EAS-E LANGUAGE

EAS-E (which stands for "entities, attributes, sets and events") includes a procedural language which is now operational, and "direct" or nonprocedural facilities currently under development. We begin by describing the procedural language.

EAS-E is an integrated language, as distinguished from the usual database language embedded in a conceptually unrelated host language. Other salient features of the EAS-E procedural language are its entity, attribute and set view, and its English-like syntax. It also includes a simplified interface with DMS/CMS.

Below we illustrate these features in terms of the first application system developed using EAS-E: a rewrite and extension of the Workload Information System of Thomas. J. Watson's Central Scientific Services (CSS). CSS consists of about 90 craftsmen who do glass work, electronics, etc., for Thomas. J. Watson's scientists and engineers. The old Workload Information System, written in PL/I and assembler, was difficult to modify or extend. In the first instance an EAS-E version was built to operate in parallel with the old version, reading the same weekly inputs and generating the same weekly outputs. The EAS-E based system duplicated the functions of the prior system with about one-

fifth as much source code. The new system shows an even greater but
difficult to quantify advantage over the old in terms of ease of modification and extension.

Interface With DMS/CMS

EAS-E provides a simplified interface with the Display Management
System for CMS (DMS/CMS), an IBM program product that facilitates the
specification and manipulation of display screens (6). Panels designed
through DMS/CMS can be displayed by EAS-E programs via the DISPLAY
statement. This consists of the word DISPLAY, the name of the panel to be
displayed, perhaps followed by any or all of the following: a list of
variables "given" from the calling program to the panel, a list of variables "yielded" back from the panel to the calling program, instructions
as to cursor position, intensity of specified fields, special message
at the bottom of the screen, and audible signal.

The DISPLAY statement in exhibit 1 appears in the EAS-E version of the
CSS Workload Information System. The statement itself should be as
clear as any brief verbal explanation we could add here. The meaning of
the statement depends partly on a SUBSTITUTE statement, exhibit 2,
which appears in the program PREAMBLE and thus is global to the program's
various routines. Because of this SUBSTITUTE statement, whenever the
word REPORT_SPEC_DATA appears in the source program, as it does twice in
the DISPLAY statement of exhibit 1 and many times elsewhere in the program, a list of 17 variables is substituted in its place. In particular,
the DISPLAY statement gives current values of these 17 variables and
receives updated values as filled in by the user.

English-like Syntax

In general we have tried to design the EAS-E syntax to be English-like
and self-documenting, in part to facilitate review, communication and
maintenance. Examples of English-like EAS-E coding are given in the
preceding and the following sections illustrating certain aspects of
the language. Here we will discuss the PRINT and FIND statements as
further examples of EAS-E's English-like syntax.

Exhibit 3 is a routine from the CSS system whose function is, as it
says, to start a new page and print a heading on it. This routine is called
in the printing of several different reports. The START NEW PAGE statement is self-explanatory. The seven lines (including the blank seventh
line) following the PRINT 7 LINES... statement are printed during
run-time just as they appear in the source program, except that the first
variable, PAGE.V (automatically maintained by EAS-E) is printed in
place of the first grouping of ***s, the second variable TITLE is printed
in place of the second groupings of *s, etc. Though the routine is without comment, its action should be clear to anyone.

```
Exhibit 1:
DISPLAY FORM GIVEN REPORT_SPEC_DATA YIELDING REPORT_SPEC_DATA
  WITH DATA FIELDS 1, 2, 3 AND 4 BRIGHT, WITH SIGNAL,
  WITH CURSOR AT DATA FIELD 1, AND WITH COMMENT =
  |AT MOST ONE ON THIS LINE CAN BE SPECIFIED. REENTER OR PRESS PF12 TO QUIT.|
```

```
Exhibit 2:
SUBSTITUTE THESE 4 LINES FOR REPORT_SPEC_DATA
REP_DEPT_XX, REP_PROJ_XX, REP_JOB_XX, REP_WORKER_XX, REP_DETAIL_LINE_1,
REP_DETAIL_LINE_2, REP_DETAIL_LINE_3, REP_DETAIL_LINE_4, REP_ACTIVE_ONLY_XX
REP_COMPL_ONLY_XX, REP_BOTH_XX, REP_CUSTOMERS,
REP_HEADING, REP_ENTRY_FROM, REP_ENTRY_TO, REP_COMPL_FROM, REP_COMPL_TO
```

```
Exhibit 3:
ROUTINE TO START_NEW_PAGE_AND_PRINT_HEADING
START NEW PAGE
PRINT 7 LINES WITH PAGE.V, TITLE, SUBTITLE, DATE, AND WEEK THUS...
CSS Information System                                              Page ***
                        Central Scientific Services
      ****************************************************
********************************          ********** **
CSS CSS  DEPT  CHARGE ENTRY COMPL ESTIMT PRCDNG TOTAL TIME CUSTOMER NAME
AREA JOB NUM   TO  DAY DAY    WEEK TIME RMNING /AREA RESP.

RETURN    END
```

```
Exhibit 4:
PRINT 3 LINES WITH TASK_AREA_NUMBER, JOB_NUMBER, JOB_DEPT_NUMBER,
JOB_PROJ_NUMBER, TASK_ENTRY_DATE, TASK_COMPL_DATE, TASK_ESTIMATED_HOURS,
INHOUSE_HOURS_FOR_WEEK, TASK_INHOUSE_HOURS+TASK_VENDOR_HOURS,
TASK_ESTIMATED_HOURS - TASK_INHOUSE_HOURS - TASK_VENDOR_HOURS,
JOB_CUSTOMER, JOB_DESCRIPTION, TASK_EST_VENDOR_HOURS,
VENDOR_HOURS_FOR_WEEK, TASK_VENDOR_HOURS, TASK_ASSIGNEE_NAME, AND STAR THUS
** ***** **** **** *** *** ***** ***** ***** ***** *************
************************************ ****** ****** ******   ************ *
------------------------------------------------------------------------
```

```
Exhibit 5:
FIND THE JOB IN CSS_JOBS WITH JOB_NUMBER = PROPOSED_JOB_NUMBER
  IF ONE IS FOUND...
      CALL REJECT ( |JOB ALREADY EXISTS WITH SPECIFIED JOB NUMBER.| )
      RETURN
  ELSE...
```

```
Exhibit 6:
FOR EVERY GROUP IN CSS_GROUPS, FOR EVERY AREA IN GROUP_AREAS
          WITH AREA_TASKS NOT EMPTY AND AREA_TYPE ¬= VENDOR_TYPE, DO THIS...
  LET SUBTITLE = AREA_NAME
  CALL START_NEW_PAGE_AND_PRINT_HEADING
  FOR EACH TASK IN AREA_TASKS WITH TASK_COMPL_DATE=0, CALL PRINT_TASK_LINES
REPEAT
```

The PRINT statement in exhibit 4, slightly simplified from its CSS version, prints 3 lines containing the specified variables and expressions in the places indicated in the three form lines (last 3 lines of the exhibit). These lines will print data under the headings of exhibit 3. When controlled in a manner illustrated later, the print statements in exhibits 3 and 4 precisely duplicate reports from the old CSS system, but with a shorter and much more self-descriptive source program.

The example of a FIND statement reproduced in exhibit 5, including the IF ONE IS (NOT) FOUND statement that usually follows a FIND, finds the job in the set of CSS_JOBS with its job number as specified. The statement should be self-explanatory to anyone who understands the notion of a set as various database and simulation languages use the term.

Integrated Language

Exhibit 6 illustrates that a substantial amount of EAS-E's power could not be achieved by imbedding a database language in an unrelated host language. As background for this example we mention that tasks to be performed by CSS are divided into areas. These areas, in turn, are divided into groups. Thus the "Device and Mask Generation" group includes the "Electrochemistry" and "Mask Gen Lab" areas.

The first phrase of the exhibit (FOR EVERY GROUP IN CSS_GROUPS) instructs the compiled EAS-E program to have the reference variable GROUP point in turn to each member of the set called CSS_GROUPS. For each such GROUP, the next two phrases ("FOR... WITH...") instruct the executing program to look at each area in the group's areas that meet certain conditions. For each GROUP and AREA thus generated, the program sets the variable SUBTITLE used in the START_NEW_PAGE_PRINT_HEADING routine, and then calls the latter routine. Next, under the control of a FOR and a WITH phrase, it calls on a subroutine which includes the PRINT 3 LINES... statement of exhibit 4 for tasks in the AREA_TASKS set which have not yet been completed. These six lines thus select groups, areas and tasks for which heading lines and body lines are printed for one of the CSS weekly reports.

Now let us consider the coding required to perform the same functions if a database language (DBL) is imbedded in a host language (like PL/I-IMS or COBOL-DBTG) where the host language knows how to loop, call and print whereas the DBL knows how to access the database. Specifically, consider the coding required to perform the function expressed in the phrase "FOR EVERY GROUP IN CSS_GROUPS". In either of the aforementioned host-DBL systems (the coding details differ but the sequence of actions is the same) the following must be coded:

The DBL is called upon to "get first" GROUP in CSS_GROUPS; host
coding is used to test a flag or error-code to see if no member was
fetched because the set was empty; in the latter case host coding
transfers out of the loop. If the set was not empty, after processing the member the host coding transfers back to a point which calls
on the DBL to do a "get next" to obtain the next GROUP in CSS_GROUPS;
the result of this operation must also be tested to see if the last-
in-set has been processed.

Thus, several lines of host/DBL coding are required to perform the same
function, and the function performed is much less clear to the reader of
the coding than is the phrase "FOR EVERY GROUP IN CSS_GROUPS."

The FOR EVERY phrase is one example in which greater power (one short
phrase serving in place of several statements) and readability can only
be achieved by rejecting the customary division of labor between host
language and database language. The single statement at the beginning
of exhibit 6 (FOR EVERY GROUP IN CSS_GROUPS, ...) fetches database
entities, tests for conditions such as AREA_TYPE not equal to
VENDOR_TYPE, and controls looping--thus combining traditionally
separated host-vs.-DBL functions in a single statement.

In general, database and core (main storage) variables can appear
anywhere they make logical sense in any EAS-E statement-- READ, WRITE,
LET, IF, etc. To do otherwise is as restrictive and arbitrary as would be
a rule saying that such statements could contain only local variables,
not global variables, of a host (algorithmic) language.

Direct Query and Update Facilities

In addition to the procedural language, we have developed a direct
browsing facility ("Browser") and plan further direct (nonprocedural)
capabilities of a similar nature. Exhibits 7 through 11 illustrate how
the user interacts with the database using Browser.

Browser displays individual entities of the database on a screen as
in exhibit 7. The first line of the screen shows the type of the entity
plus certain internal identification information which we will ignore
here (see (9)). The region marked (2) in exhibit 7 shows attributes of
the entity. We see, for example, that the JOB in the exhibit has
JOB_NUMBER = 80150, JOB_DEPT_NUMBER = 461, etc. The line marked (3)
tells us that the JOB owns a set called JOB_TASKS, that the set for this
particular job has only one member, and that the set is ordered by job
number. The line marked (4) indicates that the job belongs to a set
called PROJ_JOBS.

You move through the database with the aid of the PF keys whose template is marked as shown in exhibit 8. To look at every task in the set
JOB_TASKS, for example, place an X as shown at (3), then press PF8 labeled
EVERY on the template. This brings the first (and in this case, only)
task of the set as shown in Exhibit 9. (Pressing the appropriate arrow on
the keyboard moves the cursor only to allowed input positions.)

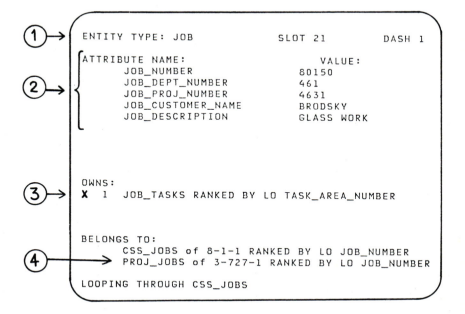

```
ENTITY TYPE: JOB                SLOT 21         DASH 1

ATTRIBUTE NAME:                      VALUE:
     JOB_NUMBER                  80150
     JOB_DEPT_NUMBER             461
     JOB_PROJ_NUMBER             4631
     JOB_CUSTOMER_NAME           BRODSKY
     JOB_DESCRIPTION             GLASS WORK




OWNS:
X    1   JOB_TASKS RANKED BY LO TASK_AREA_NUMBER



BELONGS TO:
     CSS_JOBS of 8-1-1 RANKED BY LO JOB_NUMBER
     PROJ_JOBS of 3-727-1 RANKED BY LO JOB_NUMBER

LOOPING THROUGH CSS_JOBS
```

Exhibit 7

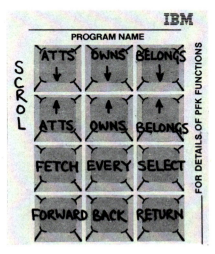

Exhibit 8

```
ENTITY TYPE: TASK              SLOT 141        DASH 1
ATTRIBUTE NAME:                      VALUE:
        TASK_AREA_NUMBER         113
        TASK_ASSIGNEEE_NAME      FISHER
        TASK_DEPT_NUMBER         461
        TASK_JOB_NUMBER          80150
        TASK_PROJ_NUMBER         4631
        TASK_ENTRY_DATE              41
        TASK_COMPL_DATE               0
        DATE_TASK_ENTRY_NOT          41
        TASK_TYPE                     1
        TASK_REAPPROVED_FLAG          1
                                             MORE.←
OWNS:
    0  SUBTASKS FIFO



BELONGS TO:
        SUBTASKS OF 9-129-1
        PR.AR_TASKS OF 11-70-1 RANKED BY LO TASK_JOB_NUMBER
        AREA_TASKS OF 6-18-1 RANKED BY LO TASK_DEPT_NUMBER

LOOPING THROUGH JOB_TASKS
```

⑤

Exhibit 9

The "more..." message at (5) in exhibit 9 indicates that there are more attributes of task than can be displayed in the space provided. PF1 scrolls attribute information down; PF4 scrolls attribute information up. PF2,3,5,6 similarly scroll ownership and membership information up and down. PF10 is used to advance to the next entity in a set (or to the next in a selected subset); PF11 is used to move back to the preceding member of the set. If the end of the set is reached, pressing the "forward" button pops the user up to the owner of the set. You can also pop up to the owner by pressing "return", PF12.

If you put an X in front of a set to which an entity belongs, e.g., on the line labelled (4) in exhibit 7, and press "fetch", PF7, Browser brings the owner of the set (in this case, the project shown in exhibit 10). To look at a subset of the 12 jobs in the set PROJ_JOBS of the project in exhibit 10, place an X on the screen as at the line marked (6); then press "select", PF9. A screen like that in exhibit 11 will be presented, but without entries under the headings "relation" or "value". In the exhibit a user is asking to see all jobs in the set with JOB_NUMBER not equal to 80150 and with JOB_CUSTOMER_NAME = BRODSKY.

The browsing session is initiated when the user types BROWSE at his terminal. Browser asks the user to specify the name of a database. After this is entered the authorized user is presented a screen, like those in the exhibits, showing the attributes of, and the sets owned by, the database as a whole. He then proceeds to browse as illustrated above, using PF functions as described on the template in exhibit 8. If he presses "enter" instead of a PF key, he is given the same 12 options again, plus an extended list of options. These allow him, for example, to review the still open paths by which he got to his current screen. In addition, we plan to add the ability to update the database by overwriting the value of an attribute on the screen, and to generate a tabulation and/or summary of specified entities.

5. THE REST OF THE ICEBERG

Preceding sections have described EAS-E's current procedural and direct facilities for examining and manipulating database and main-storage entities. But these capabilities are but a small part of what should be encompassed in an integrated EAS application development system. In the present section we cite 3 instances of desirable extensions; in the next section we generalize these instances into an "EAS principle"; and in the final section we consider the corresponding generalization for ER systems.

(I) As noted before, EAS-E's entity, attribute and set view has been used for simulation for two decades, and in database management prior to EAS-E under the name "network" model. The EAS view is also used, in effect, in computer graphics (see, for example, (4)). It is common in the

```
ENTITY TYPE: PROJECT              SLOT 727        DASH 1

ATTRIBUTE NAME:                         VALUE:
       PROJ_NUMBER                4631
       PROJ_NAME                  INTERFACE PHYSICS
       PROJ_MANGR_NAME            YOUNG
       PROJ_DEPT_NUMBER           461




OWNS:
     8   AREAS_USED_BY_PROJECT RANKED BY LO PR.AR_AREA
  ✗ 12   PROJ_JOBS RANKED BY LO JOB_NUMBER


BELONGS TO:
       LOC_PROJECTS of 10-1-1 RANKED BY LO NUMBER
       DEPT_PROJECTS of 2-35-1 RANKED BY LO PROJ_NUMBER
```

⑥ →

Exhibit 10

```
ENTITY TYPE: JOB

ATTRIBUTE NAME:              MODE:      RELATION:      VALUE:
    JOB_NUMBER               TEXT         NE           80150
    JOB_PROJ_NUMBER          ALPHA
    JOB_CUSTOMER_NAME        TEXT         =             BRODSKY
    JOB_DESCRIPTION          TEXT
    O.PROJ_JOBS              IDENTFR
    O.CSS_JOBS               IDENTFR
```

Exhibit 11

latter field to speak of geometric entities of types such as point, line, polygon, circle, plane and sphere. These entities have attributes such as the x and y coordinates of a point and the radius of a circle. Compound geometric entities are composed (e.g. by union or intersection, or variants thereof) from sets of primitive entities and/or other compound geometric entities. Sometimes these sets are called sets; sometimes they are called lists or some other synonym for set; sometimes an alternate structure, such as the binary tree, is used instead.

Clearly any general purpose programming system that aspires to build a wide variety of application systems should interface with some kind of graphics package. An application development system based on an EAS worldview would most naturally use an EAS view of the relationships among geometric objects. Furthermore, a programming system which aspires to be integrated in the sense already illustrated should allow the user to manipulate geometric entities in the same manner as he manipulates the database objects which he defines.

A graphics package for an EAS system, therefore, should include predefined entity types such as point, line, plane, sphere, etc. as well as compound objects made up of such primitive objects. The entity, attribute and set structure for such geometric objects should be made known to the user in the same manner as are other database objects. If the user knows that an entity of type circle has an attribute called radius he could, if required, create a circle, assign its radius attribute, and file it into the set of geometric objects of a picture using the same commands that he uses for database entities. Thus once the user knows the names of the geometric entity types, their attributes, the sets owned and the sets to which they belong, he has a substantial graphics capability and, for the most part, does not need to learn new commands beyond the already familiar CREATE, DESTROY, FILE, REMOVE, LET, FIND and FOR EACH.

A collection of the aforementioned capabilities—to create, destroy, file, etc.,—for graphic entities is not sufficient in itself to constitute a convenient graphics package. Two other things are needed. First, certain complex higher order operations must be provided even though they can be synthesized from the elemental operations. One example is the clipping of lines wi.   geometric world and its set of objects is associated with a window. The second requirement is for special input/output facilities to enter and display geometric objects. The latter capability is in part a matter of sensing the attributes of an I/O device such as the X- and Y- coordinates of a light-pen; and in part is a complex operation which may itself be described in terms of device sensing and other elemental EAS operations.

(II) A suitable graphics package for an integrated EAS language, then, should include predefined entity types with their attribute and set structures; the ability for the user to manipulate these geometric objects in the same way as he manipulates the objects which he has defined himself; commonly used complex operations which could be described in terms of elemental EAS operations, but would be a burden to do so for each particular application; and special input/output facilities. But such

capabilities (with the possible exception of special I/O facilities)
would be at least as valuable in another area.

The EAS-E programming system, like most programming systems is
dependent upon an operating system. In general, users of operating
systems frequently experience difficulties trying to get them to do
their bidding. Some operating systems can be instructed in only a
strange job control language. Large manuals are common for explaining
available facilities, and job control or EXEC languages. Users report
much frustration in trying to get the operating system to do things which
it should, but no one around knows how to instruct it to do.

Much of this difficulty is quite unnecessary. Job control systems
have quite ordinary EAS structures typically including jobs with one or
more tasks to be done, each task owning a set of resource requirements.
Resources include peripheral devices with queues of waiting work.
Users may also own sets such as virtual readers and virtual printers (or
whatever they are called in the particular system). The actions which
frustrated users seek from their recalcitrant operating systems are the
acts of any job shop: to schedule tasks, perhaps contingent on the outcomes of other tasks; to examine the contents of queues; to insert or
remove tasks from various queues, and the like.

This could be done easily if the user was told the names of the various
entities, attributes and sets of the particular operating system; was
allowed to use the same procedural commands or direct facilities to
create, destroy, file, remove, assign attribute values, and find entities as he can in an EAS-based database or simulation language, and the
same event scheduling commands as he can in an EAS-based simulation
language. The system itself is not particularly complex. The impres-
sion of great complexity comes from the fact that the user must use a
different, and usually not very powerful language, to direct it. Worse,
he often must use different "languages" with unrelated syntax rules to
direct different parts of the operating system. (Here "operating
system" is broadly defined as encompassing all the entities of the
computer system with which the user must interact.)

There are elemental actions which the user could specify which the
computer system cannot or should not fulfill. He may ask for information
for which he is not authorized. Justifiably or otherwise he may ask to
DESTROY THE (real) PRINTER. He may ask to take some elemental action when
certain prerequisite conditions (describable in EAS terms) have not
been met. In such cases the user should be instructed that he is not
authorized to take such an action, or that particular preconditions are
not met. At least the system should recognize the request, and responds
with the action or an appropriate message.

As at present, frequently used combinations of elemental actions
would be prepackaged and invocable by the user. Also, certain descriptive synonyms would be allowed. For example the user would probably
prefer to say PRINT and specify a file (n.) rather than say FILE (v.t.)
this file in the queue of the printer. It is not necessary to have a great

number of such higher order actions involving rarely used cases, since these can be composed from typically few elemental actions when and if necessary.

Thus, as in the case of the graphic entities, the user would be told the attribute and set structure of the entities of the operating system and, where authorized, could manipulate these as if these were his own defined simulation or database entities. In addition he could schedule events, either immediately or with delay, unconditionally or conditionally, as easily as he can do such now in EAS based simulation.

(III) Next consider the entities of text processing. We may think of an "ordinary" file (n.), the kind we build with an editor, as being an entity containing a set of lines, each line containing one text attribute. The file itself has attributes like name and date_last_modified. The lines could be thought of as containing a set of characters, or alternatively it may be thought of as containing a set of words. The word entities are not stored in records or arrays, as with other main storage and database entities, but are stored implicitly like words in a book, by putting at least one blank after each successive word in the set. We may alternately think of the file (document) as owning a set of paragraphs, each paragraph owning a set of words. We may speak of the one type of entity (the paragraph) on one occasion, and the other type (the line) on another.

Typically we do not think in terms of creating individual entities such as characters and words and filing them into their sets. Rather we think of higher order operations or special input/output operations such as the actions of an editor. On the other hand there are frequent occasions when it would be desirable to find and perhaps modify the entity, attribute and set structures of documents using the same commands applicable to other entities. This is illustrated in exhibit 12.

In the first instance assume the routine in exhibit 13 deals with user defined entities including the entity type PROGRAM that owns a set of ROUTINES, each ROUTINE pointing to an entity called its SOURCE program which owns a set of WORDS. The entity WORD has an attribute TEXT which is the actual contents of the word. The program in exhibit 13 searches the set of words of each routine in the set of routines of the program, changing the contents of certain words. It also schedules a recompilation of any routine for which at least one word is changed.

```
Exhibit 12
FIND THE PROGRAM IN MY.PROGRAMS WITH NAME = GIVEN.NAME
IF NONE ... ELSE...
FOR EACH ROUTINE IN ROUTINES ''OF PROGRAM'' DO...
    FOR EACH WORD IN WORDS (SOURCE (ROUTINE))
                        WITH TEXT (WORD) = OLD.WORD, DO...
        LET TEXT (WORD) = NEW.WORD
        LET FLAG = 1
    LOOP
    IF FLAG = 1
        SCHEDULE RECOMPILE (ROUTINE) AT NEXT_NONPRIME_TIME
    REGARDLESS...
LOOP  END
```

Except for the SCHEDULE statement, as long as we assume that PROGRAM, ROUTINE and WORD are user defined entities exhibit 13 only contains concepts and commands already discussed. What we add now is the notion that PROGRAM, ROUTINE and WORD should be automatically defined entities. A user would usually manipulate these implicitly with some editor. The proposal is that the user should also be allowed to manipulate these entities as he would entities which he defined himself. The exhibit illustrates a circumstance in which it would be convenient to do so; e.g., when we wish to loop through sets of such entities selecting those which meet certain conditions, taking one or more actions on those which do. The scheduling of the recompile in the exhibit is an operating system function rather than a text editing function. The exhibit thus also illustrates a circumstance in which it is convenient to mix the two.

6. THE EAS PRINCIPLE.

The ultimate goal of an integrated application development system should be to permit the user to process all entities, attributes and sets in a uniform manner whether these are entities which he defines, or entities which have been defined for him such as graphical entities, text entities or the entities of the computer system itself with which he is obliged to interact. The application development system may offer some alternatives for dealing with entities depending on the tastes and needs of the user. For example, it may offer the user a compact rather than an English-like syntax, allowing him to type ∀ rather than FOR EACH, and ∃ rather than CREATE. The purpose of this option would be to accommodate users who do not type very fast. But it would not force the user to change his style of programming, change his keywords, change his syntax rules simply because he has passed from a database entity to a graphic entity to an entity of the operating system.

Problems are encountered when you consider in detail how to implement this general principle. For example:

(1) There are alternate possible EAS structures for implementing a given function; e.g., alternate possible details for the EAS structure of an operating system.

(2) The same word may be desirable as the name of an entity, attribute or set in different contexts; e.g., as a name used in the graphics package and/or in the operating system and/or as a user defined entity.

(3) It is not a trivial matter to implement a proper response for each elemental action which the user may give for any entity relevant to him.

But, as far as we have seen, the problems are all solvable. For example

(1) The fact that there are alternate EAS structures for an operating system does not contradict the assertion that we should tell the user the EAS structure adopted, and respond reasonably (with action or message) to any request for any elemental act on this structure.

(2) The proper interpretation of words that can be used in different contexts can be solved by having a set of current contexts, each context owning a dictionary of words, the set of contexts being ordered by which should be considered first and which next in interpreting a word. (We know, of course, how to arrange and rearrange this set, since we know how to do this for ANY set with which we must interact.) Where the context order is to be overriden for a specific word usage, a qualifier can be added to the word (e.g., G.POINT referring to POINT as used in the Graphics context rather than any other).

(3) The above EAS principle was not proposed because it is easy to implement, but because we believe that it will make application development one or two orders of magnitude easier.

7. APPLICABILITY TO ER

We have argued that an integrated EAS language should allow the user to examine and manipulate entities in a uniform manner, whether these are entities of types which he defines himself, or those which are defined for him. In this way the user is spared having to learn new keywords and syntax to do the same old actions to new things.

It seems to us that this same desideratum applies if entities are characterized by their 1-1, 1-m, m-1 and m-n relationships rather than in terms of their attributes and sets. If it were necessary (not just convenient at the user's option, but actually necessary) for the user to switch in and out of the ER view as he moves from one type of entity to another, or express himself in a different manner as he moves from type to type, he would be hindered by the burden of learning two or more modes of expression, and further burdened by the requirement to know when to switch from one to the other. But such seems to us as unnecessary for ER as for EAS. We suggest that "integrated ER" should be as much a focal point for you as integrated EAS is for us.

7. REFERENCES

1. Buxton, J.N., & Laski, J.G., Control and Simulation Language., The Computer Journal 5, 1962, pp. 194-199.

2. Chen, P.P-S, The Entity-Relationship Model -- Towards a Unified View of Data., ACM Trans. Database Systems Vol 1, No. 1, March 1976, pp. 9-36.

3. CODASYL Data Base Task Group Report, Available from ACM, New York, NY, April 1971.

4. Giloi, W.K., Interactive Computer Graphics., Prentice-Hall, NJ, 1978.

5. Griffith, R.L., & Harlan, V.G., Theory of IDEA Structures., TR 02.559, IBM Systems Development Division, San Jose, CA, April 1973.

6. IBM Corporation, Virtual Machine/370 Display Management System for CMS: Guide and Reference. Program Number 5748-XXB File No. 5370-39 SC24-5198-0.

7. Kiviat, P.J., GASP -- A General Activity Simulation Program., Applied Research Laboratory, U.S.Steel Corp, Monroeville, PA, July 1963.

8. Kiviat, P.J., Villanueva, R., & Markowitz, H.M., The SIMSCRIPT II Programming Language., Prentice Hall, Englewood Cliffs, NJ, 1969.

9. Malhotra, A, Markowitz, H.M., & Pazel, D.P., EAS-E: An Integrated Approach to Application Development., RC 8457, IBM T. J. Watson Research Center, Yorktown Hts., NY 10598, August 29 1980.

10. Markowitz, H.M., Hausner, B., & Karr, H.W., A Simulation Programming Language., The RAND Corporation RM-3310-PR 1962. Prentice-Hall NJ, 1963.

Entity-Relationship Approach to
Information Modeling and Analysis, P.P. Chen (ed.)
Elsevier Science Publishers B.V. (North-Holland)
©ER Institute, 1983

GORDAS: A FORMAL HIGH-LEVEL QUERY LANGUAGE
FOR THE ENTITY-RELATIONSHIP MODEL

Ramez Elmasri
Honeywell Inc.
Corporate Computer Sciences Center
Bloomington, Minnesota 55420

Gio Wiederhold
Department of Computer Science
Stanford University
Stanford, California 94305

ABSTRACT

We present a formal high-level query language for the Entity-Relationship (ER) model. The language is called GORDAS (for Graph-Oriented Data Selection). GORDAS can be applied with slight modifications to the class of entity-attribute-relationship data models. We define the ER model as a graph, and augment an ER schema slightly by introducing connection names, which are used to specify relationship paths in a GORDAS query. We then define the language, give examples of its use, and briefly compare it to some other query languages.

1 INTRODUCTION

It is generally accepted that a database management system should have different types of interfaces to cater to the needs of different classes of users [Codd74]. One possible classification is the following:

Type(1) A procedural programming language interface, used by data processing professionals to define database application programs that are used routinely by the DBMS users.

Type(2) A stand-alone high-level, non-procedural query language for user interaction with the DBMS from a terminal, say. This interface is used by technical and semi-technical users for ad-hoc reference to the database.

Type(3) User-friendly interfaces. These include form or screen oriented interfaces which guide the user in specifying a request, and natural language-type interfaces. These interfaces may be used by non-technical users.

Early database management systems only had type(1) interfaces, with data selection statements embedded in a programming language, usually COBOL. An example is the CODASYL DML [CODA71]. Type(2) languages include SEQUEL [Cham76], implemented on SYSTEM-R [Astr76], QUEL, implemented on INGRES [SWKH76], and LINUS [Hone78], implemented on MRDS [Hone78a]. Some languages of this type are also used as embedded statements in a host programming

language (for example, SEQUEL statements in PL/I). An example of
a screen-oriented interface is QBE [Zloo75], and of a natural
language interface is LIFER [HSSS78]. The above list of
references is by no means comprehensive.

Many of the type(2) non-procedural interfaces are built on DBMS's
based on the relational model [Codd70]. This is because
relational query languages are well understood, and are based on
formal foundations such as the relational calculus [Codd71] and
the relational algebra [Codd72]. A weakness of query languages
based on the relational model is that users need to understand the
implicit semantics of their relational schema (or view) in order
to properly qualify attributes, and to correctly specify join
terms and restriction clauses [Ries77]. The formal specification
of relational languages however makes them excellent system
languages upon which one may build user-friendly interfaces, as
demonstrated by the QBE and IDA [Saga77] systems.

It is often easier for the user to specify a query in terms of a
hierarchical view of data. Query languages for non-computer
specialists have been especially successful here, for example the
SYSTEM-2000 query language [MRI79]. The IMS system, although it
supports a very complex internal structure and a complex Data
Manipulation Language (DL/1), can support simple hierarchical
interfaces to user submodels, and query languages have been
successful here (INQUIRY [INFO79], MCAUTO [McDonn], IQF [IBM]).

Query languages for network databases have been more difficult to
specify, since the network model they support may cause more than
one path to lead to the data elements to be retrieved. Hence,
procedural languages characterized by the concept of navigation
[Bach73] have been associated with the network model.

The objective of our work is to present a means to specify queries
in a formally complete but simple and natural form, using the
knowledge inherent in the entity-attribute-relationship models of
databases, such as the Entity-Relationship (ER) Model [Chen76] and
the Structural Model [Wied77]. The relationship connections in
these data models are at the logical (conceptual) level, and hence
are not limited to implemented connections, as are for instance
CODASYL sets.

We present a formal high-level query language, GORDAS, for the ER
model. The language is designed to support a type(2) user
interface. We present the language as a stand alone interface,
and do not discuss its embedding in a host programming language.
Our formalism is applicable to a class of graph-oriented data
models, which use three basic primitives to model the data:
entities (or objects), attributes (or properties) and
relationships (or associations): the entity-attribute-
relationship or entity-property-association data models [Chen76,
Pirr77, Wied77]. The language can also be used with extensions to

these models which include more recent modeling concepts of generalization [SmSm77], subclasses (IS-A hierarchies [Mins73]) and roles [BaDa77], such as the Entity-Category-Relationship Model [Weel80, Elma81] and the Structural Model [WiEl79, Elma80].

There is another class of graph-oriented data models, the functional, or binary relationship, data models (for example, see [Abri74, Senk75, BiNe78, Ship79]) which use two primitives to model data: entities and binary relationships (or binary functions). Several query languages have been proposed for this class of data models (DAPLEX [Ship79], FQL [BuFr79], TASL [HoWY79], FORAL [Senk80]).

The language we present here uses some of the concepts developed in the above query languages. However, the language is presented from a different point of view: that of an underlying ER graph database. The ER model [Chen76, Chen79] has proven quite popular because it provides a bridge between table-oriented and graph-oriented data models. We will consider the graph view of the ER model. Few formalisms for ER languages have been proposed (for example CABLE [Shos79], CLEAR [Poon79]). No complete specifications (as far as the authors know) of CABLE have been presented. CLEAR has some unnecessary restrictions which make formulation of some queries impossible [McCu79].

We note that the language presented here has some similarities to existing query languages and to path expressions [ShTh80]. We will give some brief comparisons and differences in Section 6.

2 THE ENTITY-RELATIONSHIP MODEL AS A GRAPH

In this section, we define the ER model as a graph. An ER schema is defined as a labeled, directed graph, the <u>schema graph</u>, and an ER database is also defined as a labeled, directed graph, the <u>database graph</u>. We assume the reader is familiar with the ER terminology in [Chen76].

The schema graph specifies the structure of the underlying database. The database graph is an abstract representation of the actual database. It can be considered an abstraction of a network database (or even of a relational database with all join connections between tuples specified by arcs).

Defining the schema graph as a <u>directed</u> graph is necessary for specification of queries on a relationship set among n entity sets when n>2. For n=2, direction is not necessary, since the relationship set provides sufficient information for query formulation. However, even in the latter case, the directed graph representation permits more natural query formulation because reference to the same relationship is through different names depending on the entity set from which one references the relationship (see Definition 2).

Definition 1 (Schema Graph):
    A schema graph is a labeled, directed graph. A node in the
    schema graph corresponds to either an entity-set (an ES node)
    or to a relationship-set (an RS node). An edge in the schema
    graph connects an ES node to an RS node, and is directed from
    the ES node to the RS node. Such an edge from an ES node X to
    an RS node Y specifies the participation of entity-set X in
    relationship Y.

Definition 2 (Labeling in a schema graph):
    Both nodes and edges of the schema graph are labeled. A node
    label is of the form (node-type, node-name: attr1=valset1,
    ..., attrn=valsetn). For an ES node, node-type is ES, and
    n>0.   For an RS node, node type is RS, and n>=0.   The
    node-name corresponds to the entity-set name or relationship-
    set name of the corresponding ER schema.   The attribute names,
    attri, 1<=i<=n, correspond to the names of the attributes of
    the entity-set or relationship-set in the ER schema.   The
    value set names, valseti (1<=i<=n), correspond to names of
    predefined value sets associated with a particular schema.

    An edge label is of the form (name1, name2:   i1, i2), where
    name1 refers to the direction of the edge (from an ES node to
    an RS node), and name2 refers to the reverse direction.   The
    two integers i1 and i2 are optional, and constrain the number
    of relationship nodes directly connected (by a single edge) to
    an entity node in the database graph (see Definitions 4-6) to
    between i1 and i2, i1>=0, i2>0, and i2>=i1. The name part of
    an edge label is (name1, name2), and the single name
    components of the name part (name1 or name 2) are called
    connection names.   The constraint part of the label is (i1,
    i2). If i1 or i2 or both are missing, the default values are
    i1=0 and i2=infinity.

The connection name (name1) is used by GORDAS to refer to the
relationship from the entity set, while (name2) is used to refer
to the entity set from the relationship. Hence, names that are
appropriate for such references should be chosen (see Figure 2).
The numbers i1 and i2 are a precise and general means of
specifying the relationship cardinality and dependency [ElWi80].
They were first introduced in [Abri74], although the definition
therein was restricted to binary relationships only.

Figure 1 shows an ER schema, and Figure 2 shows the corresponding
graph schema.   Note that there is a direct correspondence between
the two schemas except for the edges being directed and labeled in
the graph schema only.

Definition 3 (Naming constraints on the schema graph):
    The following naming constraints hold on the schema graph:
    (a) All node-names must be unique.
    (b) All attribute-names for a given node must be unique.

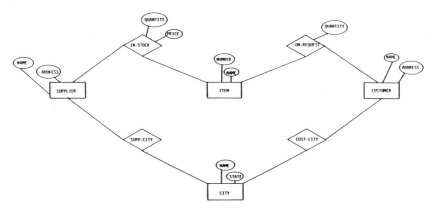

Figure 1: An Entity-Relationship Schema

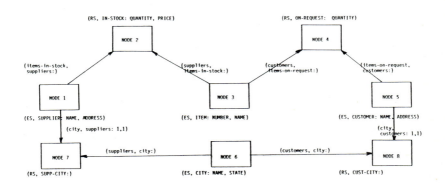

Figure 2: The Corresponding Schema Graph

(c) For an ES node X, if the name parts of the labels of any two edges directly connected to X are (A, B) and (C, D), then A≠C.

(d) For a binary relationship X (which is an RS node directly connected to exactly two edges), if the name part of the label of one of the edges connected to X is (A, B), then the name part of the label of the other edge must be (B, A). Also, the attribute names of X (if any) must be different from the attribute names of the two ES nodes directly connected to X.

(e) For an n-ary relationship X (which is an RS node directly
    connected to exactly n edges, n>2), if the name parts of
    the labels of any two edges connected to X are (A, B) and
    (C, D), then B≠D.

The above constraints are   required to make GORDAS queries
non-ambiguous, and can be easily checked for a given schema
[Elma80, Elma81].

<u>Definition 4</u> (Database graph):
    A <u>database</u> <u>graph</u> is a labeled, directed graph. A particular
    database graph, DBG, is <u>an</u> <u>instance</u> <u>of</u> a particular schema
    graph SG. Each node in DBG corresponds to an entity tuple
    (called an <u>E</u> <u>node</u>) or to a relationship tuple (called an <u>R</u>
    <u>node</u>) in the ER model.   Each edge in the database graph
    connects an E node to an R node, and is directed from the E
    node to the R node. For a given schema graph SG, a class of
    database graphs which <u>correspond</u> <u>to</u> SG is defined.   Each
    database graph DBG in this class must obey the constraints
    specified in SG.

<u>Definition 5</u> (Labeling in a database graph):
    The label of a node x in a database graph DBG, which
    corresponds to a schema graph SG, is of the form (set-name:
    attr1=val1, ..., attrn=valn). The set-name must be the same
    as some node-name of a node X in SG, and database node x is
    said to <u>belong</u> <u>to</u> the schema node X. The <u>type</u> of database
    node x is E if schema node X is of type ES, and R if schema
    node X is of type RS. The <u>attribute</u> <u>names</u> (attr1, ...,attrn)
    of database node x must be identical to the attribute names of
    schema node X to which x belongs. Each vali for node x is
    called the <u>value</u> of attribute attri, 1=<i<=n, for node x, and
    must be an element of the corresponding value set, valseti,
    specified in SG.

    The <u>label</u> of an edge d in DBG that connects an E-node x to an
    R-node y is of the form (name1, name2), and must be identical
    to the name part of a label of an edge D in the corresponding
    schema graph SG which connects the two schema nodes X and Y to
    which the database nodes x and y belong.   Edge d in DBG is
    said to <u>belong</u> <u>to</u> edge D in SG. As in the case of a schema
    graph labeling (Definition 2), single names of an edge label
    in the database graph are called <u>connection</u> <u>names</u>.

<u>Definition 6</u> (Constraints on a database graph):
    The following constraints must hold on a database graph DBG
    that corresponds to schema graph SG:
(a) (Basic relationship constraint) Given an R node x in DBG
    which belongs to RS node X in SG.   If X is directly
    connected to n ES nodes Y1, Y2, ..., Yn, (not necessarily
    distinct) by the edges D1, D2, ..., Dn, then x must be
    directly connected by exactly one edge di, which belongs

to Di, to a node yi which belongs to Yi, for 1<=i<=n.
(b) (Cardinality and dependency constraint) For some edge D in
SG which connects an ES node X to an RS node Y, if the
constraint part of the edge label of D is (i1, i2), then
each database node x that belongs to X must be directly
connected to n distinct edges d1, ..., dn, which belong to
D such that i1<=n<=i2. Each edge di will directly connect
x to some node yi, 1<=i<=n, which belongs to Y such that
yi≠yj if i≠j.

Figure 3 shows part of a database graph which corresponds to the
schema graph of Figure 2. Nodes NODE 11, ..., NODE 18 belong to
schema node NODE 1, nodes NODE 21, ..., N229, belong to schema
node NODE 2, and so on.

Now that we have defined our schema and database graphs, we can
start the definition of GORDAS. We first define path expressions
and predicates, which are the building blocks of GORDAS queries.

3 PATH EXPRESSIONS AND PREDICATES

Given a schema graph SG, and a corresponding database graph DBG.
A path expression generates a single schema path on SG, and
numerous database paths on DBG. (The reader may skip the formal
definitions, and come back to them after looking at the examples.)

In our definitions, we use c_1, c_2, ..., for connection names of
edges; X_1, X_2, ..., for node-names from the schema graph; and A_{i1},
A_{i2}, ..., A_{in} for attribute names from the label of node X_i in the
schema graph. We also use square brackets ([]) as meta-symbols to
delineate our expressions.

Definition 7 (Path expressions):
  First we define a prefix of a path expression. There are two
  types of prefixes, which are defined recursively as follows:
  (a) An attribute name A_{ij} of schema node X_i is a prefix of
      type 1. A connection name c_i is a prefix of type 2.
  (b) If P_i, 1<=i<=n, are prefixes; c_j, 1<=j<=m, are connection
      names; and p is a predicate (we will define predicate
      shortly), then:
      1.[<P_1, ..., P_n> of c_j] and [<P_1, ..., P_n> of c_j : p] are
        prefixes of type 2.
      2.[P_i of c_j] and [P_i of c_j : p] are prefixes whose type
        is the same as the type of P_i.
  (c) If P is a prefix of either type, then COUNT P is a prefix
      of type 1.

A path expression is either of the form [X] or [P of X], where
P is a prefix, and X is a node name from the schema graph.
The path expression is of type 1 if P is of type 1, and is of
type 2 if P is of type 2 or if P does not exist.

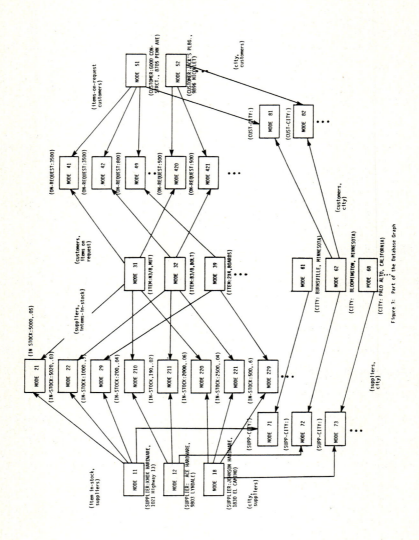

Figure 3: Part of the Database Graph

Type 1 prefixes and path expressions represent single values or sets of values from the database, while those of type 2 represent actual nodes, or tuples that are a mixture of nodes and values.

Definition 8 (Predicates):
  We first define constant expressions and set expressions. A <u>constant expression</u> is defined recursively as follows:
  (a) A constant value is a constant expression of type 1.
  (b) If c_1, ..., c_i are constant expressions, then {c_1, ..., c_i} (a set of constant expressions) is a constant expression of type 1, and <c_1, ..., c_n> (a tuple of constant expressions) is a constant expression of type 2.

  A <u>set expression</u> is defined as follows:
  (a) Any prefix, path expression, constant expression, or query (see Definition 10) is a set expression.
  (b) If P_i and P_j are set expressions of the same type, then P_i UNION P_j, P_i INTERSECT P_j, and P_i - P_j are set expressions of the same type as P_i and P_j.

  A <u>predicate</u> p is defined as follows. If each of P_i and P_j is a set expression such that both P_i and P_j are of the same type, then:
  (a) If P_i and P_j are both of type 1 or both of type 2, then $P_i=P_j$, $P_i{\neq}P_j$, P_i INCLUDES P_j, and P_j INCLUDES P_i, are predicates.
  (b) If P_i and P_j are both of type 1, and single-valued, then $P_i>P_j$, $P_i>=P_j$, $P_i<P_j$, and $P_i<=P_j$, are predicates.
  (c) If p_1 and p_2 are predicates, then so are p_1 AND p_2, p_1 OR p_2, NOT p_1, and NOT p_2.

For the definition of predicate, it is straightforward to check that a set expression is single-valued from the cardinality of the relationships in the ER schema (see [Elma80]).

Before proceeding further, we give some examples and discuss informally the meaning of path expressions. The examples refer to Figures 2 and 3. We use upper case for attribute and node names, and lower case for connection names. Some examples of <u>path expressions</u> on the schema graph of Figure 2 are:
     i. ITEM
    ii. NAME of CUSTOMER
   iii. <NAME, ADDRESS> of CUSTOMER
    iv. suppliers of ITEM
     v. suppliers:(<NAME, STATE> of city=<Bloomington, Minnesota>)
             of ITEM
    vi. NAME of suppliers:(QUANTITY>10) of ITEM
   vii. <NAME, <NAME, STATE> of city of customers,
             <NAME, STATE> of city of suppliers> of ITEM
  viii. <NAME, QUANTITY> of items-in-stock of SUPPLIER

Two predicates are shown in examples (v) and (vi) above. Some
other examples of <u>predicates</u> are:
    i. NAME of ITEM = "BOLT"
   ii. city of CUSTOMER = city of SUPPLIER
 iii. items-in-stock of SUPPLIER INCLUDES
                   items-on-request of CUSTOMER
  iv. COUNT(items-in-stock of SUPPLIER
          INTERSECT items-on-request of CUSTOMER) > 3
   v. COUNT(items-in-stock) > 0

The path expressions (i)-(iii) illustrate the use of attribute and
node names. Path expression (i), ITEM, specifies the single node
whose node-name is ITEM in the schema graph, which is NODE 3.
Implicitly, it also specifies the set of nodes in the database
graph which belong to NODE 3; {NODE 31, NODE 32,..., NODE 39,
...}.

Path expression (ii) specifies the attribute NAME of CUSTOMER in
the schema graph. In the database graph, it specifies for each
customer node {NODE 51, NODE 52, ...} the value of its NAME
attribute. Similarily, path expression (iii) specifies for each
customer node, the values of its NAME and ADDRESS attributes.

Next, we illustrate the use of connection names. Path expression
(iv) specifies the path from NODE 3 (node-name=ITEM) to NODE 1
through NODE 2 in the schema graph of Figure 2. This traversal
starts at the node specified by the node name at the end of the
path expression; ITEM in this case. Then, moving backward in the
path expression, the connection name [suppliers] is specified. A
search for an edge whose connection name in the direction <u>from</u>
NODE 3 is [suppliers] is conducted. (Recall that the first
connection name of the name part of an edge label refers to the
direction from the ES node, while the second name refers to the
direction from the RS node, see Definition 2). If no such edge is
found, the path expression is ill-specified. In our example, the
edge is found and traced to NODE 2 in Figure 2. Since NODE 2
represents a binary relationship (see Definition 3(d)), an edge
whose connection name from NODE 2 is [suppliers] exists. This
edge is now traced to NODE 1.

On the database graph of Figure 3, path expression (iv) specifies
a set of SUPPLIER nodes for each ITEM node.   For each ITEM node,
the set of edges connected to that node whose connection name in
the direction from the node is [suppliers] are located. Each such
database edge leads to a distinct R node that belongs to schema
node NODE 2.   Then a single database edge with the appropriate
connection name [suppliers] leads from each R node to an E node
that belongs to NODE 1. For example, database node NODE 31 traces
the appropriate edges as follows: NODE 31-->NODE 21-->NODE 11,
NODE 31-->NODE 210-->NODE 12, and NODE 31--> NODE 220-->NODE 18.
Hence, the set of SUPPLIER database nodes specified by path
expression (iv) for NODE 31 is {NODE 11, NODE 12, NODE 18}.

Similarily, for NODE 32 the set of SUPPLIER nodes specified is {NODE 11, NODE 12, NODE 18}, and for NODE 33 the set is {NODE 11, NODE 18}.

The next path expression (v) is similar to (iv). The only difference is that for each item, not all of its suppliers nodes are specified, but only those supplier nodes for suppliers located in Bloomington, Minnesota. This is specified by the <u>restricting predicate</u> following the [suppliers] connection name; [:<NAME, STATE> of city=<Bloomington, Minnesota>]. (The ':' should read 'such that'.) A path expression in the restricting predicate is traced in the schema graph starting from the node reached by the connection name that precedes it. Hence, in Figure 2, the path specified first is NODE 3-->NODE 2-->NODE 1 (by the connection name [suppliers]). Then, in the restricting predicate, a second path is specified by the connection name [city], which is traced starting from NODE 1-->NODE 7-->NODE 6. Again, the path expression would be ill-specified if no connection name [city] exists in the direction from NODE 1.

In the database graph, the subset of SUPPLIER nodes specified for each ITEM node are checked for satisfying the restricting predicate, and only those nodes that satisfy the predicate are the nodes specified by path expression (v). For example, the set of SUPPLIER nodes specified for ITEM node NODE 31 is {NODE 11, NODE 12, NODE 18}. Each of these nodes is connected to a CITY node via the connection name [city]. Only those connected to CITY node NODE 62, whose attributes <NAME, STATE> = <Bloomington, Minnesota> satisfy the restricting predicate. Hence, only NODE 12 satisfies the predicate. Similarily, for ITEM node NODE 32, the set of SUPPLIER nodes {NODE 11, NODE 12, NODE 18} is restricted to {NODE 12}, and for ITEM node NODE 39, the set of SUPPLIER nodes {NODE 11, NODE 18} is restricted to { } (the empty set). Note that each SUPPLIER node is connected to exactly one CITY node at all times because of the constraint (1, 1) on the edge from NODE 1 to NODE 7 in Figure 2.

Hence, we see that a path expression is well-specified only if the connection names along the path form a chain of connected edges. We now formalize this notion. To make it easier to understand the formalization, imagine that we refer to a path expression of the form: A of cn of ... of c2 of c1 of X.

<u>Definition 9</u> (Well-specified path expressions):
A path expression is <u>well-specified</u> with respect to a schema graph SG if every connection name along the path exists as a connection name of some edge in SG in the direction <u>from</u> the last reached node. The <u>last reached node</u> is defined as follows:
(a) The node X whose name is at the end of a path expression is the last reached node for the connection name c1 that precedes it in the path expression.

(b) The last reached node for a connection name c_i which is
followed by a connection name c_{i-1} in the path expression
is the node Y which is reached by tracing the connection
name c_{i-1} from the last reached node Z of c_{i-1} as follows:
  1. If Z is an ES node, and c_{i-1} is a connection name for a
     binary relationship, then two edges are traced: the
     first from Z to an RS node W, and the second from W to
     (the ES node) Y.
  2. If Z is an ES node, and c_{i-1} is a connection name for
     an n-ary relationship, $n>2$, then one edge is traced to
     (the RS node) Y.
  3. Finally, if Z is an RS node, then one edge is traced to
     (the ES node) Y.

An attribute name A in the path expression must be an
attribute of the last reached node Y by the connection name
cn, which precedes A in the path expression. If cn is a
connection name for a binary relationship, A may also be an
attribute name from the relationship node W which is on the
path to Y (see (b) above).

For example, path expression (vi) uses both the NAME and QUANTITY
attributes of [suppliers of ITEMS] because the IN-STOCK
relationship (NODE 2 in Figure 2) is binary. The attributes refer
to the NAME of a SUPPLIER and the QUANTITY IN-STOCK of the same
supplier for a given item. This is possible because of the basic
relationship constraint (Definition 6(a)) which says that a
database node that is a member of IN-STOCK is connected to exactly
one database node which is a member of SUPPLIER (and to exactly
one database node that is a member of ITEM). Similarily, path
expression (viii) above uses both the NAME and QUANTITY attributes
of [items-in-stock of SUPPLIER]. The attributes now refer to the
NAME of an ITEM and the QUANTITY IN-STOCK of the same item for a
given supplier.

4 QUERIES IN GORDAS

A GORDAS query is specified on a schema graph SG, and retrieves
information from a corresponding database graph DBG. The query is
formed from two clauses: the GET-clause and the WHERE-clause.

The GET-clause specifies n schema nodes, N1, N2,..., Nn, $n>=1$.
Some database nodes, which belong to these schema nodes, will be
selected (by the WHERE-clause). The GET-clause also specifies
what information about each of the selected database nodes is to
be retrieved. This information may be attribute values for the
selected nodes, or for nodes related to the selected nodes. The
GET-clause consists of n path expressions, $n>=1$, and the schema
nodes N1, ..., Nn are those whose names appear at the end of each
path expression. The information to be retrieved for the selected
database nodes is specified by the prefixes of the path
expressions.

If the same node name is to appear more than once in the GET-clause (or in the query), different versions of the node name occurrences are uniquely identified by appending an integer to the node name.

The WHERE-clause specifies a predicate on the schema nodes of the GET-clause, and is used to select the set of database nodes that belong to these schema nodes <u>and</u> satisfy the predicate.

Informally, the semantics of a query are as follows:
(a) Form the cross product of the sets of database nodes which belong to the schema nodes specified in the GET-clause.
(b) For each element in the cross-product, if that element satisfies the predicate of the WHERE-clause, then return the information specified in the prefixes of the GET-clause path expressions for each node in the element.

<u>Definition 10</u> (Queries):
A <u>query</u> specified on a schema graph SG is of the form:

    (GET-clause)   GET path-expr1, ..., path-exprn
    (WHERE-clause) WHERE predicate

The <u>semantics</u> of a query are as follows. Let $N1, ..., Nn$ be the schema nodes specified by path expressions path-expr1, ..., path-exprn, respectively, and let $S-N1, ..., S-Nn$ be the sets of database nodes such that $S-Ni = \{n \mid n$ belongs to $Ni\}$. Then do the following:
(a) (Form the cross product) Let $Q = S-N1 \times S-N2 ... \times S-Nn$.
(b) (Test each element in the cross product for selection) For each q in Q, test if q satisfies the predicate of the WHERE-clause. If yes, q is <u>selected</u>.
(c) For each selected q, assume $q = \langle n1, n2, .., nn \rangle$. Return the values specified by the prefix of path-expri in the GET-clause for database node ni for $1 <= i <= n$.

A query is of type 1 if the GET-clause is formed of a single path expression of type 1, and is of type 2 otherwise.

Note that we use no variable names in GORDAS. Multiple references to the same schema node (if ambiguous) are resolved by appending an integer to the node name (similar to the technique used in DAPLEX [Ship79]). We now give some examples of queries stated in GORDAS, based on the ER schema of Figure 1 (and the corresponding graph schema of Figure 2). The parts of queries between square brackets ([]) may be omitted without causing any ambiguity.

(1) Get the names and addresses of all suppliers located in Minnesota.

```
GET <NAME, ADDRESS, NAME of city> of SUPPLIER
WHERE STATE of city [of SUPPLIER]='Minnesota'
```

Note the uniform way in which path expressions are used in both the GET-clause and the WHERE-clause. The query refers to attributes of nodes related to SUPPLIER in both the predicate of the WHERE-clause and the prefix of the GET-clause. If a set of database nodes is referenced in the predicate (as in queries 3 to 5 below), appropriate set comparison operators may be used.

(2) For each city, get the name of the city, and the names of all suppliers and customers located in that city.

```
GET <NAME, <NAME of suppliers, NAME of customers>> of CITY
[WHERE TRUE]
```

Note the hierarchical style of the query. The entity set of primary interest to the user here is CITY. In formulating the query, the user may consider CITY as the root node of a hierarchy, with SUPPLIER and CUSTOMER as subordinate nodes (Figure 4). For other queries, the appropriate root node is the one that represents the entity set of primary interest, and can be any node in the schema graph. This ability to isolate the schema node of primary interest is a very natural feature of GORDAS, and allows the user to think of the data model as a hierarchy in the way that best suits the user in formulation of the query. It also implies a grouping of the query output (by NAME of CITY in this example) without the explicit need for a GROUP BY clause. The GROUP BY clause in SEQUEL was found to cause problems to users in query formulation [Ries77].

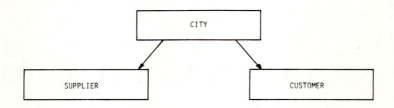

Figure 4: Conceptual Hierarchy for Formulating Query (2)

(3) Get the names of all suppliers who are located in the same city as customer 'Smith', and who have each item that Smith requires in stock.

```
GET NAME of SUPPLIER
WHERE (city [of SUPPLIER] = (GET city of CUSTOMER
                              WHERE NAME [of CUSTOMER]='Smith'))
   AND (items-in-stock [of SUPPLIER] INCLUDES
                              (GET items-on-request of CUSTOMER
                              WHERE NAME [of CUSTOMER]='Smith'))
```

Here, two inner queries are used. No ambiguity exists because references are bound to the innermost query. The first condition in the predicate uses equality comparison because it is known from the schema semantics that each supplier and each customer is related to exactly one city. In the second condition, it is known that a set of items is related to each supplier and each customer, so the set comparison operator INCLUDES is used.

(4) For each customer, get the name of the customer, and the names of all suppliers who are located in the same city as that customer, and who have each item that the customer requires in stock.

```
GET NAME of CUSTOMER, NAME of SUPPLIER
WHERE (city of SUPPLIER = city of CUSTOMER)
   AND (items-in-stock of SUPPLIER INCLUDES
                              items-on-request of CUSTOMER)
```

This query is a generalization of the previous query. Note the use of two path expressions in the GET-clause. Here, the user can consider the query formulation in terms of two hierarchies: one with CUSTOMER as the root node and the other with SUPPLIER as the root node.

(5) For each customer, get the name of the customer, and the name of each supplier who has in stock all the items the customer requires in quantities more than the customer requests (this query was suggested by Hank Korth).

```
GET NAME of CUSTOMER, NAME of SUPPLIER
WHERE
    (GET ITEM
     WHERE QUANTITY of suppliers [of ITEM]:NAME=NAME of SUPPLIER
        > QUANTITY of customers [of ITEM]:NAME=NAME of CUSTOMER)
    INCLUDES
    (items-on-request of CUSTOMER)
```

This last query illustrates many of the finer points of GORDAS. A complete inner query is used in the predicate of the outer query, and restricting logical expressions within the inner query reference the nodes of the outer query.

The semantics of the query are as follows:
(a) Form the cross-product {<c, s>} of <CUSTOMER, SUPPLIER> nodes
    in the database.
(b) For each <c,s> in <CUSTOMER, SUPPLIER>, the inner query
    selects the set of ITEM nodes {i} such that: (1) there exists
    a node k which belongs to IN-STOCK that connects i and s, (2)
    there exists a node q which belongs to ON-REQUEST that
    connects i and c, and (3) the value of the QUANTITY attribute
    for k is larger than the value of the QUANTITY attribute for
    q. (Note that at most one k and one q will exist.) If {i}
    includes the set of ITEM nodes connected to CUSTOMER node c by
    the [items-on-request] connection, then <c, s> satisfies the
    WHERE clause, and is selected.

5 ADDITIONAL FEATURES

GORDAS has many other features which we now briefly mention. We
only presented the formal specifications for queries in the
previous sections. As in other query languages, we use several
standard functions and arithmetic operators to enhance GORDAS
capabilities. The functions we use are SUM, AVG, SD, MAX[i], and
MIN[i]. The SUM, AVG, and SD functions return the sum, average,
and standard deviation of the values of a numeric-valued attribute
over a set of nodes, while MAX[i] and MIN[i] return the ith
highest or ith lowest value, respectively, of a numeric or
alphabetic attribute over a set of nodes.

For example, to get the number of items each supplier has in
stock, and the average price of these items, we write:

GET <NAME, <COUNT, AVG PRICE> of items-in-stock> of SUPPLIER

GORDAS also has powerful facilities for defining derived
attributes and relationships. For example, if we want to define
an attribute CITY of SUPPLIER for direct reference, we write:

DEFINE CITY of SUPPLIER TO BE NAME of city of SUPPLIER

or, if we want to define a multi-valued attribute CITIES for each
ITEM which gives the cities where the item is currently in stock,
we write:

DEFINE CITIES of ITEM TO BE NAME of city of suppliers of ITEM

The user does not see a difference between actual and derived
attributes when formulating a query. The derivation definition is
kept with the schema.

For a complete discussion of functions, arithmetic, derivation
facilities, and also update statements in GORDAS, refer to the
versions of GORDAS for the Structural Model (called SMQL), given
in [Elma80], or the Entity-Category-Relationship model [Elma81].

Conditions for non-ambiguous schema names, and algorithms to test
for well-formedness of expressions are given in these references,
which we do not include here due to space limitations.

6 DISCUSSION

We think of GORDAS as a graph 'calculus' language rather than a
graph 'algebra' if we compare it with relational languages. The
relational algebra is formed of relational operators (PROJECT,
SELECT, JOIN) and set operators (UNION, INTERSECTION, CROSS
PRODUCT) which manipulate relations forming new relations. The
relational calculus does not manipulate relations, but a calculus
expression selects the desired information from existing relations
forming a single result relation. It is in this sense that GORDAS
is a calculus rather than an algebra, since it selects the desired
information without manipulating the underlying graph database.

GORDAS does not include the universal and existential quantifiers,
as in the relational calculus, but achieves similar selection
capabilities using COUNT, and the set formation (UNION, INTERSECT,
DIFFERENCE) and set comparison (INCLUDES) operators. It has been
shown [Pirr78] that the latter operators are equivalent to the
universal and existential quantifiers in a relational framework.

To compare GORDAS with a relational-calculus based language, such
as QUEL, the main differences are:
(1) QUEL uses tuple variables, while GORDAS does not.
(2) QUEL does not have a set comparison operator.
(3) QUEL does not have universal and existential quantifiers.
    Hence, queries that require the power of quantifiers must be
    phrased as a sequence of requests in QUEL, while in GORDAS a
    single query suffices.

On the surface, GORDAS may appear similar to a functional
language, such as DAPLEX [Ship79]. However, there are several
significant differences:
(1) In GORDAS, a query is clearly separated into two clauses:
    the GET clause which specifies the entity-sets of interest,
    and the information to be retrieved for selected entities
    from those sets, and the WHERE clause, which specifies the
    conditions that entities in these sets must satisfy to be
    selected. This is a clean and natural separation of
    different parts of a query.
(2) DAPLEX does not have set comparison operators as defined in
    GORDAS, which correspond naturally to some selection
    conditions.
(3) DAPLEX is meant to be part of a programming language (type
    1) interface while GORDAS is intended to have sufficient
    power to also act as a stand-alone (type 2) interface.

(4) GORDAS is formally defined using a technique similar to that used to define the predicate and relational calculus [Codd72]. Although the syntax of GORDAS may appear cumbersome, it is quite concise, and the concepts of prefix, path expression, and predicate are the only building blocks of a query. The semantics of GORDAS are simple and straightforward.

(5) DAPLEX uses some variant of the universal and existential quantifiers (FOR ALL, FOR SOME statements). GORDAS acheives similar selection power by using the COUNT operator, and the set formation and set comparison operators, which make query formulation simpler and more natural.

GORDAS has more similarities to FORAL [Senk80], although it was developed independently. However, GORDAS is defined for a different class of data models than the binary fact model upon which FORAL is based.

Two other query languages have been specified for the ER model: CLEAR [Poon79] and CABLE [Shos79]. A brief comparison of CLEAR, CABLE, and GORDAS follows:

(a) All three languages use the explicit relationship information in an E-R schema. CABLE uses the relationship name as a "bead" along a "chain". CLEAR uses either the relationship name or connection names that have been added to an E-R schema. GORDAS uses only connection names.

(b) CABLE and CLEAR do not have set comparison and set formation operators, which are fundamental operators in GORDAS.

(c) GORDAS query formulation is hierarchical, while CABLE and CLEAR queries are formulated in a linear fashion.

(d) The semantics of GORDAS are simple and well-defined, which may make query formulation easier.

From the above observations, it seems that a fundamental difference between relational query languages and query languages based on the ER model is the use of relationship information in the latter to specify "join" operations. This seems to make query formulation closer to the natural language equivalent.

7 CONCLUSION

We presented a formal high-level query language, GORDAS, for the ER model. Path expressions, predicates, and queries were formally defined, and examples to demonstrate the use of the language were given.

GORDAS demonstrates an approach to the definition of a formal query language for the ER model. The only addition that is needed to the ER model to support GORDAS is the definition of connection names on the ER schema.

A version of GORDAS for the Entity-Category-Relationship (ECR) model [Weel80] is being implemented as a type(2) user interface to DDTS (Distributed Database Test Sestem [DeWe80]), being developed at Honeywell Corporate Computer Sciences Center. The ECR model is an extension of the ER model which allows direct representation of generalization, subclasses, and the grouping of entities according to the roles they play in a relationship. Queries are automatically translated to a relational algebra internal form.

ACKNOWLEDGEMENTS

The authors wish to acknowledge the comments of Cory Devor, Jonathan King, Susan Owicki, Daniel Sagalowicz, Jeff Ullman, Jim Weeldreyer, and Eugene Wong on different versions of the language. This research was partially supported by NSF grant ECS-8007683 A01. The work for the version of GORDAS for the Structural Model presented in [Elma80] was partially supported by ARPA grant MDA903-77-C-0322.

REFERENCES

[Abri74] Abrial,J.R., "Data Semantics"; in Klimbie,J.W., and Koffeman,K.L. (editors); Data Base Management (Proceedings of the IFIP Conference on Data Base Management), North-Holland, 1974, pp.1-60.

[Astr76] Astrahan,M.M., et.al., "System R: Relational Approach to Data Base Management", ACM Transactions on Database Systems, Volume 1, Number 2, June 1976, pp.97-137.

[Bach73] Bachman,C., "The Programmer as a Navigator", Communications of the ACM, Volume 16, Number 11, November 1973, pp.653-658.

[BaDa77] Bachman,C., and Daya,M., "The Role Concept in Database Models", VLDB77 Proceedings, IEEE, Tokyo, Japan, September 1977, pp.464-476.

[BiNe78] Biller,H., and Neuhold,E., "Semantics of Data Bases: The Semantics of Data Models", Information Systems, Volume 3, Number 1, September 1978, pp.11-30.

[BuFr79] Buneman,P., and Frankel,R.E., "FQL: A Functional Query Language", Proceedings of the ACM SIGMOD Conference, Boston, Massachusetts, May 1979, pp.52-57.

[Cham76] Chamberlin,D.D., et.al,,"SEQUEL 2: A Unified Approach to Data Definition, Manipulation, and Control", IBM Journal of Research and Development, Volume 20, Number 6, November 1976, pp.560-575.

[Chen76] Chen,P.P-S., "The Entity-Relationship Model: Towards a Unified View of Data", ACM Transactions on Database Systems, Volume 1, Number 1, March 1976, pp.9-36.

[Chen79] Chen,P.P-S., ed., Proceedings of the International Conference on Entity-Relationship Approach to Systems Analysis and Design, Los Angeles, California, December 1979 (North-Holland).

[CODA71] Committee on Data Systems Languages, CODASYL Data Base Task Group Report, ACM, 1971.

[Codd70] Codd,E.F., "A Relational Model for Large Shared Data Banks", Communications of the ACM, Volume 13, Number 6, June 1970, pp.377-387.

[Codd71] Codd,E.F., "A Data Base Sublanguage Based on the Relational Calculus", Proceedings of the ACM SIGFIDET Workshop on Data Description, Access, and Control, November 1071, pp.35-68.

[Codd72] Codd,E.F., "Relational Completeness of Data Base Sublanguages", Courant Computer Science Symposium, Volume 6, Prentice-Hall, 1972, pp.33-64.

[Codd74] Codd,E.F., "Seven Steps to Rendezvous with the Casual User", in Klimbie,J., and Koffeman,K., eds., Data Base Management Systems, (Proceedings of the IFIP TC-2 Working Conference on Data Base Management Systems), North-Holland, 1974.

[DeWe80] Devor,C., and Weeldreyer,J., "DDTS: A Testbed for Distributed Database Research", Proceedings of the ACM Pacific 80 Conference, San Fransisco, California, November 1980, pp.86-94.

[Elma80] El-Masri,R., "On the Design, Use, and Integration of Data Models", Ph.D. Thesis, Computer Science Department, Stanford University, Report STAN-CS-80-801, May 1980.

[Elma81] Elmasri,R., "GORDAS: A Data Definition, Query and Update Language for the Entity-Category-Relationship Model of Data", Report HR-81-250:17-38, Honeywell CCSC, Bloomington, Minnesota, January 1981.

[ElWi80] El-Masri,R., and Wiederhold,G., "Properties of Relationships and Their Representations", Proceedings of the National Computer Conference, Volume 49, AFIPS, May 1980, pp.319-326.

[Hone78] Multics Logical Inquiry and Update System (LINUS) Reference Manual, Order Number AZ49, Honeywell Information Systems, Waltham, Massachussetts, March 1978.

[Hone78a] Multics Relational Data Store (MRDS) Reference Manual, Order Number AW53, Honeywell Information Systems, Waltham, Massachussetts, March 1978.

[HoWY79] Housel,B., Waddle,V., and Yao,S., "Functional Dependency Model for Logical Data Base Design", Proceedings of the 5th International Conference on VLDB, Rio de Janeiro, Brazil, October 1979, pp.194-208.

[HSSS78] Hendrix,G., Sacerdoti,E., Sagalowicz,D., and Slocum,J., "Developing a Natural Language Interface to a Complex System", ACM Transactions on Database Systems, Volume 3, Number 2, June 1978, pp.105-147.

[IBM] IMS Interactive Query Facility (IQF), IBM, White Plains, New York.

[Info79] Technical System Description, INQUIRY IV/IMS, Informatics Inc., Canoga Park, California, July 1979.

[McCu79] McCue, D., "Evaluation of an E-R Query Language", presented at the Entity-Relationship Conference, Los Angeles, California, December 1979.

[McDonn] MCAUTO INQUIRY Language for IMS, McDonnel Douglas.

[Mins73] Minsky,M. "Computer Science and Representation of Knowledge", Proceedings of the National Computer Conference, AFIPS, Volume 42, 1973.

[MRI79] MRI Systems Corporation, SYSTEM 2000 Syntax Guide for IBM OS/VS, Austin, Texas, 1979.

[Pirr77] Pirrotte,A., "The Entity-Property-Association Model: An Information-Oriented Database Model", Report R343, MBLE, Brussels, Belgium, March 1977.

[Pirr78] Pirrotte,A., "High Level Data Base Query Languages", in Gaillaire,H., and Minker,J., eds., Logic and Database Design, Plenum Press, New York, 1978.

[Poon79] Poonen,G., "CLEAR: A Conceptual Language for Entities and Relationships", reprinted in Chu,W., and Chen,P., eds., Tutorial: Centralized and Distributed Data Base Systems, IEEE, 1979, pp.194-215.

[Ries77] Riesner,P., "The Use of Psychological Experimentation as an Aid to Development of a Query Language", IEEE Transactions on Software Engineering, Volume SE-3, Number 3, May 1977.

[Saga77]   Sagalowicz,D.,   "IDA: An Intelligent   Data   Access
Program", Proceedings of the Third VLDB Conference, Tokyo, Japan,
IEEE, September 1977, pp.293-302.

[Senk75] Senko,M., "Specification of Stored Data Structures and
Desired Output Results in DIAM II with FORAL", Proceedings of the
International Conference on Very Large Data Bases, IEEE, September
1975.

[Senk80] Senko,M., "A Query-Maintenance Language for the Data
Independent Accessing Model II", Information Systems, Volume 5,
Number 4, Pergamon Press, 1980, pp.257-272.

[Ship79] Shipman,D., "The Functional Data Model and the Data
Language DAPLEX", Supplement to the Proceedings of the ACM SIGMOD
Conference, Boston, Massachusetts, May 1979, pp.1-19.

[Shos79]   Shoshani,A.,   "CABLE: A Chain-Based Language for the
Entity-Relationship Model", Abstract and presentation in [Chen79].

[ShTh80] Shneiderman,B., and Thomas,G., "Path Expressions for
Complex Queries and   Automatic Database Program Conversion",
Proceedings of the 6th Intenational Conference on VLDB, ACM and
IEEE, Montreal, Canada, October 1980, pp.33-44.

[SmSm77] Smith,J., and Smith,D., "Database Abstractions:
Aggregation and Generalization", ACM Transactions on Database
Systems, Volume 2, Number 2, June 1977, pp.105-133.

[SWKH76] Stonebraker,M., Wong,E., Kreps,P., and Held,G., "The
Design and Implementation of INGRES", ACM Transactions on Database
Systems, Volume 1, Number 3, September 1976, pp.189-222.

[Weel80]   Weeldreyer,J.A.,   "Structural   Aspects   of   the
Entity-Category- Relationship Model of Data", Honeywell CCSC,
Technical Report, HR-80-251, Bloomington, Minnesota, March 1980.

[Wied77]   Wiederhold,G.,   Database Design,   McGraw-Hill, 1977,
Chapter 7.

[WiEl79] Wiederhold,G., and El-Masri,R., "A Structural Model for
Database Systems", Computer Science Department, Stanford
University, Report STAN-CS-79-722, February 1979.

[Zloo75] Zloof,M., "Query by Example", Proceedings of the National
Computer Conference, AFIPS Volume 44, 1975.

Appendix

Syntax of GORDAS in BNF

We now give the BNF for the GORDAS syntax. This BNF covers only the concepts presented in this paper. For a complete BNF of GORDAS which also covers data definition, arithmetic operations, and updates, refer to the Appendix in [Elma81].

In the BNF specifications, we use the following metasymbols:

```
[x]           x appears 0 or 1 times
{x}           x appears 0 or more times
x|y           x or y
xy            x followed by y
(...)         used to group alternatives
'm'           literal metasymbol (m is [, ], {, }, (, or ))
```

```
<GORDAS query> ::= <type1_query> | <type2_query>

<type1_query> ::= GET <type1_pathexpr> WHERE <predicate>

<type2_query> ::= GET (<type1_pathexpr> <path_expr> {,<pathexpr>}
  | <type2_pathexpr> {,<pathexpr>}) WHERE <predicate>

<pathexpr> ::= <type1_pathexpr> | <type2_pathexpr>

<type1_pathexpr> ::= <type1_prefix> OF <class_name>

<type2_pathexpr> ::= <type2_prefix> OF <class_name>

<class_name> ::= <entityset_name> | <relationshipset_name>

<type1_prefix> ::= [COUNT] <attribute_name> [OF <type2_prefix>]
  | COUNT <type2_prefix>

<type2_prefix> ::= <connection_name> [: <predicate>]
  {OF <connection_name> [: <predicate>]}

<predicate> ::= <condition> {(AND | OR) <condition>} |
  [NOT] '(' <predicate> ')'

<condition> ::= (<type1_setexpr> (< | <= | > | >=) <type1_setexpr>
  | <setexpr> (= | ≠ | INCLUDES) <setexpr>)
```

NOTE: In this last rule, <type1_setexpr> must be single-valued as determined by the schema semantics (cannot be a set of values). Also, both <setexpr>s in a condition must be compatible (of the same type).

```
<setexpr> ::= <type1_setexpr> | <type2_setexpr>
```

```
<type1_setexpr> ::= <type1_expr> (UNION | INTERSECT| MINUS)
  <type1_expr>

<type2_setexpr> ::= <type2_expr> (UNION | INTERSECT | MINUS)
  <type2_expr>

<type1_expr> ::= <type1_prefix> | <type1_pathexpr> | <type1_query>
  | <type1_constant_expr>

<type2_expr> ::= <type2_prefix> | <type2_pathexpr> | <type2_query>
  | <type2_constant_expr>

<type1_constant_expr> ::= <constant> | '{'<constant_term_list>'}'

<type2_constant_expr> ::= '<' <constant_term_list> '>'

<constant_term_list> ::= <constant> {, <constant>}
```

Entity-Relationship Approach to
Information Modeling and Analysis, P.P. Chen (ed.)
Elsevier Science Publishers B.V. (North-Holland)
©ER Institute, 1983

THE OCCURRENCES STRUCTURE CONCEPT

AN APPROACH TO STRUCTURAL INTEGRITY CONSTRAINTS IN THE ENTITY
RELATIONSHIP (ER) MODEL, WITH APPLICATION TO RELATIONSHIP DE-
COMPOSITION AND METAMODEL ACHIEVEMENT

Yves TABOURIER
GAMMA INTERNATIONAL

Paris - FRANCE

Dominique NANCI
CECIMA

Aix en Provence - FRANCE

SUMMARY

Some kinds of integrity constraints cannot be represented in the
present ER formalism, for instance, constraints which involve two
or more relationship-types, or constraints which would invoke two
or more occurrences of the same entity-type and/or relationship-type.
We propose the introduction of the OCCURRENCES STRUCTURE concept,
which gives a solution to such problems. In addition, the new integrity
constraints, based on this concept, provide improved accuracy in
relationship decomposition, metamodel achievement and (in the future)
in external model validation and programming.

TOPIC

Theory and Graphical Representation : Modification and Extension to
Entity Relationship Models and Diagrams.

INTRODUCTION

Integrity constraints are all those constraints which must hold at
any time for a database to be valid. They may be classified in 3
categories :

- VALUE constraints, which are related to ATTRIBUTE values within
  a unique occurrence of entity or relationship (for definition,
  see §1.11)

- STRUCTURAL constraints, which do not invoke any attribute value,
  but only the presence of entity-occurrences within relationship-
  occurrences

- MIXED constraints, which invoke both attribute values and several
  occurrences of entities and relationships, bound in a given way

As an example, let us consider the conceptual schema below:

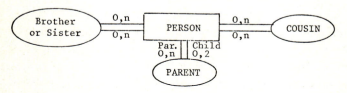

We assume that the "cousin" relationship-type is necessary because we may
know that two persons are cousin, without knowing their parents. Nevertheless, if a person (x) is child of a person (y) who is brother or sister
of a person (z), who is parent of a person (t), we expect that (x) and (t)
be cousin: this is a <u>structural</u> constraint.

If an AGE attribute is defined on PERSON, $0 \leqslant AGE (x) \leqslant 120 \ \forall \ x$ is a <u>value</u>
constraint. If we specify that $AGE (x) \leqslant AGE (y) - 12$, provided that (x)
is the child of (y), this specification is a <u>mixed</u> constraint.

In this introductory paper we shall focus on <u>structural</u> constraints (mixed constraints, and also external schema validation [TARD 80], need an additional concept corresponding to attribute values, which will not be needed here).

There are two main types of approaches [ISO 81] to specify integrity constraints: <u>static</u> approaches, which try to define them directly on the conceptual schema, and <u>dynamic</u> approaches, which consider the consequences of actions on the information base (creating, deleting, updating, retrieving).

An interesting example of the static approach is the clausal form of logic [KOWA 79]. The structural constraint about cousinhood, presented in the example above, would be written as follows:

[Cousin (x,t) ⟵ Parent (y,x), Brother or Sister (y,z), Parent (z,t)]

In the dynamic approach it would be necessary to consider separately the effects of various creations or deletions of relationship occurrences in various external updating schemas. A typical example of such an approach is presented in [SCHE 80] (propagation path concept).

We prefer the <u>static</u> approach, because:

i) external updating schemas [ANSI 75] [ANSI 77] change quicker than the conceptual schema; thus, if we define integrity constraints in a static way (on the conceptual schema), we shall have a stable reference for developing new control programs even if they are to be written by hand

ii) we believe that it is a better job for human beings to develop artificial intelligence procedures for generating control programs from static integrity specifications, than to specify (or to write by hand) each of them.

The reason why we created the Occurrences Structure Concept, is our belief in the power of ER diagrams for human understanding and communication concerning the way objects are bound together [CHEN 76 & 77].

For specifing the cousinhood constraint with the Occurrences Structure
Formalism, we shall write as follows:

i) S =

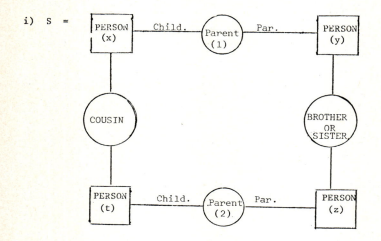

(S is an "occurences structure" diagram, not an ER diagram)

ii) AFFIRMATION (S/Cousin)

We are aware this may seem heavy, but the only difference between this
and the logical clause [Cousin (x,t) ◀— Parent (y,x), Brother or Sister
(y,z), Parent (z,t)] is that we show the four separate occurrences of
PERSON and the way they are bound together, instead of Kowalski's
simply invoking them. We deeply think that the structure S actually
exists in the logical clause, hidden behind its elegant formulation.
Moreover, it is clear that the constraint we have chosen is of a type
which fits particularly well with the clausal form of logic. For other
types of constraints which will be described later, the formulation
as logical clauses would be less easy. Nevertheless, we are working
to define new primitives, easier to handle, and new ways of showing
the structures directly on the ER diagram when it is feasible.

But our feeling is that this kind of job is at the surface of the
problem, and that the occurrences structure concept will go on working
fairly well as we will introduce new types of constraints (structural
and/or mixed), or use the concept for external schemas validation
purpose, instead of conceptual subschemas which are not precise enough.

We believe that the concept will work later as the basis for an open
language for defining and handling sets of occurrences. The problem of
primitives will then disappear.

The paper is structured as follows:

1. Structural integrity constraints in the present ER formalism :
   problems already solved, problems not yet solved

2. The concept of OCCURRENCES STRUCTURE within an ER model, with
   application to unsolved problems : new integrity primitives

3. Application to relationship decomposition

4. Application to metamodel achievement

5. Conclusion

1. - STRUCTURAL INTEGRITY CONSTRAINTS IN THE PRESENT ER FORMALISM

1.1. PROBLEMS ALREADY SOLVED

1.11 RECALL ON THE ER FORMALISM: VOCABULARY AND "LEG EQUIVALENCE"

The objects under consideration are defined as OCCURRENCES of
ENTITY-TYPES, which are sets of objects.

We now define n-ary RELATIONSHIP-TYPES as mathematical n-ary
relationships, defined on n-tuples of ENTITY-TYPES (seen as

sets of objects). An OCCURRENCE of the RELATIONSHIP-TYPE R
is defined by an n-tuple of entity-occurrences for which R
holds. We call COLLECTION of R, the n-tuple of entity-types
on which R is defined. Each of its n positions is called a
LEG of R, and we shall write as E(L) the entity-type corresponding to the leg L of a given relationship-type.

Any piece of information must be defined as an ATTRIBUTE VALUE
related to an OCCURRENCE of ENTITY or RELATIONSHIP : any
ENTITY-TYPE or RELATIONSHIP-TYPE is characterized by a given
list of ATTRIBUTES availabe for it.

If E(L) = E(L') for two different legs L and L' of a given
relationship-type R, we assume that E(L) plays two different
ROLES in R, according to L and L'. If it is not true, L and
L' are said to be EQUIVALENT. From a theoretic   point of view,
that means only that all occurrences of R, obtained by exchanging
entity-occurrences on equivalent legs, must be simultaneously
present or absent (and, if attributes defined on the relationship-
type, values must be equal).

This constraint, which may be written as EQUIV(R:L$\equiv$L') is the
first structural constraint in the ER formalism, in addition
to self-evident built-in constraints.

1.12 *"ENTITY-RELATIONSHIP" CARDINALITIES*

Let R be a n-ary relationship-type, C its Collection, L one of
its legs and E(L) the related entity-type. Let us call e(L) $\in$ E(L)
an occurrence of E(L). We shall write as Card (R:e(L)) the
number of occurrences of R which have got e(L) on the leg L.
The present formalism accepts constraints such as :

$$m \leqslant \text{Card } (R: e(L)) \leqslant M, \quad \forall \quad e(L) \in E(L)$$

This constraint will be written as CARD (R:E(L)) = (m,M)

In the ER DIAGRAM, in which RECTANGLES stand for entity-types,
OVALS for relationship-types and oval-to-rectangle LINES for
legs, it is shown by writing (m,M) near the representative line
of L.

1.13 FUNCTIONAL DEPENDENCY (FD) CONSTRAINTS

Let now C' be a sublist of C, which does not include the leg L.
Its number of legs n' is such that n' $<$ n. If r is an occurrence
of R, we shall call <u>projection</u> of r on C', written as $r[C']$,
the n'-tuple of entity-occurrences obtained from r by dropping
those which correspond to legs out of C'. In the same way, the
occurrence e(L) $\in$ E(L) invoked in r is viewed as the projection
of r on L: $e(L)=r[L]$.

We shall say that the relationship-type R holds a <u>Functional
Depedency Constraint from its Subcollection C' towards L</u> if,
given two occurrences r1 an r2 of R, the equality of their
projections on C' implies the equality of their projections
on L:

$$r1[C'] = r2[C'] \implies r1[L] = r2[L]$$

The pictorial representations for both cases n' = n-1 and
n' $<$ n-1 are the following:

i) <u>n' = n-1</u>   ii) <u>n' $<$ n-1</u>

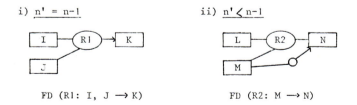

FD (R1: I, J $\rightarrow$ K)   FD (R2: M $\rightarrow$ N)

1.2. PROBLEMS NOT YET SOLVED

We do not claim to do an exhaustive inventory of those problems:

indeed, such an inventory would not be the correct way of finding
a good formalism. Nevertheless, it seems useful to point out some
of those problems, in order to test that the formalism we propose
is a good framework to solve them.

We think that the CAR REGISTRATION AUTHORITY PROBLEM, presented in
[ISO 81] is promised to a famous future, so we will take it as a
basis for our (unexhaustive) inventory (see Appendix 1 for description of the case).

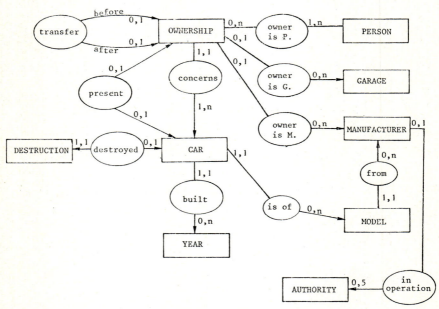

Plenty of constraints of the problem are not recorded in the
schema above. We will present a number of them, all of the .
STRUCTURAL TYPE (no attribute involved).

1.21 INCOMPATIBILITY CONSTRAINTS

   Cst 1.1. Any ownership is related to no more than one kind of
            owner (person, garage or manufacturer)

Cst 1.2. A manufacturer may not be a transferee

Cst 1.3. Ownership may not be transferred from a garage to another one

Cst 1.4. Ownership may not be transferred from manufacturer to person(s)

Cst 1.5. A present ownership may not be known as "before" another ("after") ownership through a transfer

1.22 OBLIGATION CONSTRAINTS

Cst 2.1. An ownership which is the present ownership of a car, must concern this specific car

Cst 2.2. Both ownerships invoked in a transfer must concern the same car

Cst 2.3. If a manufacturer is owning cars it must be in operation

1.23 GENERALIZED CARDINALITY CONSTRAINTS

Cst 3.   A garage may not presently own cars built by more than 3 manufacturers

1.24 ADDITIVE CARDINALITY CONSTRAINTS

Cst 4.1. Any ownership must invoke some person, garage or manufacturer

Cst 4.2. Any car must be presently owned or have been destroyed, not both

Cst 4.3. Any ownership of a car must be either related to a manufacturer, or due to a transfer, not both

1.25 IMPLICATION CONSTRAINTS

Cst 5.   If a car is owned, or has been owned, by a manufacturer, it must be one of his own models

Cst 5'. If a car is a model from a given manufacturer, it must
         be owned, or have been owned, by this manufacturer

1.26 CONNECTIVITY CONSTRAINTS

Cst 6.   If two ownerships concern the same car, they must be
         chained by a transfer or a sequence of transfers

2. - THE OCCURRENCES STRUCTURE CONCEPT

2.1. OCCURRENCES STRUCTURE DEFINED OVER A CONCEPTUAL SCHEMA

An OCCURRENCES STRUCTURE is a bipartite multigraph. Its two classes
of nodes are called SQUARES and CIRCLES and its edges are called
BINDINGS. An ENTITY-TYPE is assigned to each SQUARE, a RELATIONSHIP-
TYPE to each CIRCLE. The rules are the following:

- Any entity-type of the conceptual schema may be assigned to 0, 1,
  or several SQUARE(S). In that case, the squares are distinguished
  by an index

- The same rule holds for relationship-types and circles

- Each binding between a square and a circle must correspond
  unambiguously to a specific leg of the relationship-type assigned
  to the circle, on the entity-type assigned to the square (Recall:
  2 legs of a given relationship-type on the same entity-type
  correspond a priori to different ROLES. The case of "equivalent
  legs" means only that occurrences of the relationship obtained
  by exchanging occurrences of entities on equivalent legs, must be
  present or absent simultaneously)

- Two bindings from a unique circle must correspond to different legs
  of the related relationship-type

- Any square and any circle must bear at least one binding, but
  it is not presently expected that the structure be "connected"

Example Occurrences Structure

S.22 =

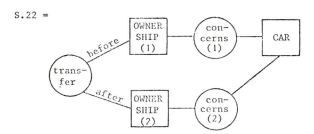

(invoked in §2.4.2)

In S22, 2 of the 3 <u>squares</u> refer the same entity-type OWNERSHIP: they will correspond to <u>a priori</u> different occurrences of OWNERSHIP, bound together through an occurrence of TRANSFER relationship. They have to be distinguished through different indices (1 and 2). The 2 <u>circles</u> which refer the same relationship-type "CONCERNS" are distinguished the same way.

There is a unique square for CAR, because we expect a car will not be changed "by magic" into another one through a transfer.

We have written the <u>roles</u> near the two <u>bindings</u> of the <u>circle</u> "TRANSFER", corresponding to the <u>legs</u> of the <u>relationship</u> TRANSFER.

2.2. *FIRST LEVEL RELATED NOTIONS*

- We call <u>E-tuple</u> a <u>set of squares</u>, <u>R-tuple</u> a <u>set of circles</u> of a given occurrences structure

- The E-tuple made from all squares of a structure, the R-tuple made from all its circles, are called <u>principal</u>

- An <u>occurrence of E-tuple</u> is defined by assigning to each square of the E-tuple an occurrence of its assigned entity-type. An occurrence of R-tuple is obtained by assigning to each circle of that R-tuple an occurrence of its assigned relationship-type

- An occurrence of E-tuple and an occurrence of R-tuple are said to be compatible if, for any binding between a square of the E-tuple and a circle of the R-tuple, the occurrence of entity assigned to that square is the very one specified on the corresponding leg, within the occurrence of relationship assigned to the circle

- An occurrence of E-tuple is said to be compatible with a given R-tuple if there exists an occurrence of that R-tuple, compatible with the occurrence of E-tuple (or if the R-tuple is the "empty" R-tuple)

- An occurrence of E-tuple is said to be compatible with the structure (or simply "compatible") if it is compatible with the principal R-tuple of the structure

- An occurrence of a given structure is an occurrence of its principal E-tuple, compatible with the structure

- Let E, F be E-tuples such that $E \supset F$, and e an occurrence of E: we call projection of e on F, written as $e[F]$, the occurrence f of F which has got the same entity-occurrences as E for the squares of F

Example   1st Level notions

E = {OWNERSHIP (1), OWNERSHIP (2)}   is an E-tuple of S 22
R = {TRANSFER, CONCERNS (1)}   is a R-tuple of S 22
Ep = {OWNERSHIP (1), OWNERSHIP (2), CAR}   is the principal E-tuple
Rp = {TRANSFER, CONCERNS (1), CONCERNS (2)} is the principal R-tuple

Let $\emptyset 1$, $\emptyset 2$, $\emptyset 3$ be values of OWNERSHIP identifier, and C1, C2 be values of CAR identifier. We will write as CAR (C1) the occurrence of car identified with C1, TRANSFER ($\emptyset 3$, $\emptyset 1$) the transfer from OWNERSHIP ($\emptyset 3$) to OWNERSHIP ($\emptyset 1$);

Then:

- e = (OWNERSHIP (∅3), OWNERSHIP (∅1)) may be an occurrence of E, provided that occurrences identified with ∅3 and ∅1 are in the database; we use ( ) instead of { } to mean that the ordering is significant

- r = (TRANSFER (∅3, ∅1), CONCERNS (∅3, C2)) may be an occurrence of R. r is compatible with e if we consider the collection of TRANSFER in the ordering: before, after

- r' = (TRANSFER (∅3, ∅1), CONCERNS (∅1, C1)) would not be compatible with e since the OWNERSHIP occurrence invoked in CONCERNS (∅1, C1), namely OWNERSHIP (∅1), does not fit with the good one in e

- let ep = (OWNERSHIP (∅3), OWNERSHIP (∅1), CAR (C2)): it may be an occurrence of Ep. ep is compatible with r, and we can write: e = ep [E]; ep is an occurrence of S if CONCERNS (∅1, C2) is in the database

2.3. SECOND LEVEL CONCEPTS ABOUT OCCURRENCES STRUCTURES

2.31 CORRESPONDENCE

- **E-tuple correspondence between two structures**

  Let S, T be structures from a conceptual schema (may be S=T) and let C be a one-to-one correspondence (bijection) between an E-tuple I from S and an E-tuple J from T. For a simplified notation, we shall write I= {I1, I2...Ip} and J= {J1, J2...Jp} in such ordering that squares Ik and Jk are homolog within C. We shall say that C is an E-tuple correspondence between S and T, if Ik and Jk are assigned to the same entity type, for k=1,...,p. We shall write this as COR (S, T/C), or explicitly as COR (S, T/I1=J1, I2=J2,... Ip=Jp), or COR (S, T/I=J).

- **Compatibility between occurrences of corresponding structures**

Given the occurrences s of S and t of T, bound in a correspondence COR (S, T/I=J), we say that s and t are <u>compatible</u>
if s $[I]$ =t $[J]$.

● <u>Compatibility between an occurrence of a structure and a</u>
<u>corresponding structure</u>

Let S, T be structures in correspondence COR (S, T/C), and
let t be an occurrence of T: t is said to be <u>compatible with</u>
S, if there exists an occurrence s of S such that <u>s and t are</u>
compatible

<u>Example correspondences</u>:

Let us split S22 into 2 parts, giving S6 and T6 (invoked in
§2.4.6)

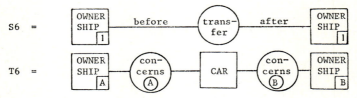

We may define between S6 and T6 various correspondences, among
which:

    C'   = COR (S6, T6/OWNERSHIP (1) = OWNERSHIP (A),
                        OWNERSHIP (2) = OWNERSHIP (B))

    C''   = COR (S6, T6/OWNERSHIP (1) = OWNERSHIP (B),
                        OWNERSHIP (2) = OWNERSHIP (A))

Let s6 = (OWNERSHIP (∅3), OWNERSHIP (∅1)) an occurrence of S6,

t6 = (OWNERSHIP (∅3), CAR (C2), OWNERSHIP (∅1)) an occurrence of
T6: s6 and t6 are compatible through C' but not through C''

It is also possible to define a correspondence between a
structure and itself. As an example:

C''' = COR (S6, S6/OWNERSHIP (2) = OWNERSHIP (1))

Let s'6 = (OWNERSHIP (Ø1), OWNERSHIP (Ø2)) an occurrence of S6:
(s6, s'6) are compatible through C''' but it is not true for
(s'6, s6)

2.32 GRAPHS

- ### Arc of structures

    Let S and T be structures such that COR (S, T/I=J). This
    correspondence may be viewed as a way to jump from S to T
    or the reverse. If we select such a possibility, for instance
    a jump from S to T, we shall say we define an Arc from S to T,
    written as A=(S→T/I=J). We note that different arcs may be
    defined from a structure to another, if there exist several
    correspondences between them.

- ### Occurrence of arc

    With the notations above, (s,t) is said to be an occurrence
    of A if s and t are compatible occurrences of S and T, that
    is if s$[I]$=t$[J]$. Note that (t, s) is not an occurrence of A:
    it is an occurrence of A' if we have defined A'=(T→S/J=I).

- ### Graph of structures, path, occurrence of path

    Let X={... Si... Sj...} be a set of structures, U={... Ak...}
    a set of arcs over X. The couple G=(X, U) is called a graph
    of structures.
    A path in G is a sequence P=(S1, S2,..., Sp) such that there
    exists some Ak=(Si→Si+1/Ii=Ji+1), for i=1... (p-1).
    Remark: May be p=1.

    An occurrence p of P is a sequence p=(s1, s2,... sp) such
    that (si, si+1) is an occurrence of Ak =(Si→Si+1/Ii=Ji+1)
    for i=1... (p-1)

• External structure bound to a graph

Let G=(X, U) be a graph, with X={S1... Sn}, and let T be a
structure out of G: T is said to be bound to G if there exists
some "input" arcs from T to some Si's and "output" arcs from
some Sj's to T.

2.4. APPLICATION OF STRUCTURE CONCEPTS

As we said at the beginning of §1.2., we do not claim for the
exhaustivity of the set of primitives presented here: we consider
it as open. We matched it with various problems encountered in
writing conceptual schemas for various companies and we think it
already solves a broad class of problems, but our belief is that it
will be easily extended for solving new ones as it will be needed.

2.41 "INCOMPATIBILITY" PROBLEMS: NEGATION PRIMITIVE

Let S be a structure: NEGATION (S) means that no occurrence of
S may exist at any time.

Application to Cst !.1. thru 1.5.:

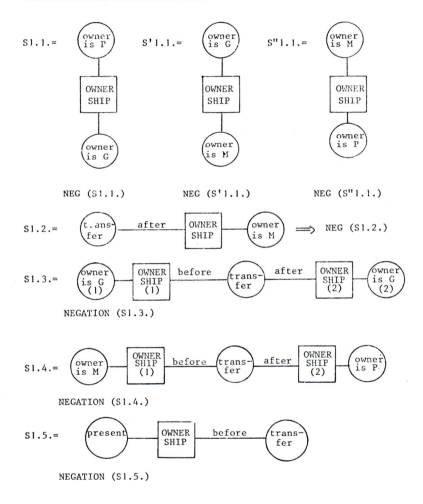

2.42 *"OBLIGATION" PROBLEMS:* AFFIRMATION *PRIMITIVE*

Let S be a structure, E its principal E-tuple, R its principal
R-tuple, Rj a circle: AFFIRMATION (S/Rj) means that any occurrence
of E, compatible with R - {Rj}, must be also compatible with Rj
(thus with R, that is with S). We say that "circle Rj is forced"
by the other ones in S.

Application to Cst 2.1. thru 2.3.:

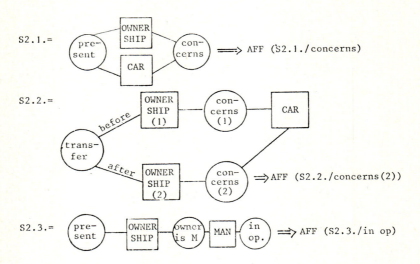

2.43 "GENERALIZED CARDINALITY" PROBLEMS

2431 SCARDS PRIMITIVE

Let S be a structure and E, F two non-empty, disjoint
E-tuples from S. Let e be an occurrence of E. We call
strict cardinality of e with respect to F in S, written
as $SCard_S$ (e/F), the number of occurrences f of F, such
that there exists an occurrence s of S with $s[E]$=e and
$s[F]$=f.

The constraint

$m \leqslant S\ Card_S\ (e/F) \leqslant M\ \forall$ e: occurrence of E

will be written as : SCARDS(S:E/F)=(m, M)

Application to Cst 3:

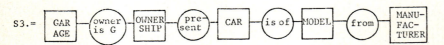

SCARDS (S3:GARAGE/MANUFACTURER)=(0,3)

2432 CARDINALITY IN A SUBSTRUCTURE: CARDS PRIMITIVE

Let G be an E-tuple from S, such that $G \supseteq (EUF)$ and R an R-tuple from S. We call substructure of S restricted to G and R, the structure $S[G](R)$ made from the squares in G, the circles in R and the bindings in S which bind squares of G and circles of R.

Let I=G-(EUF): we define

$$Card_S (e/F[I](R))=S \ Card_{S[G](R)}(e/F)$$

The constraint $m \leqslant Card_S (e/F[I](R)) \leqslant M$

is written as   CARDS $(S:E/F[I](R))=(m, M)$

Implicit clauses

- If I is empty, $[I]$ is omitted

- If R is the R-tuple made from the circles which are bound to squares of FUI (=G-E), (R) is omitted

2.44 *"ADDITIVE CARDINALITIES" PROBLEMS: V CARDS PRIMITIVE*

Let E be a non-empty E-tuple of a structure S, and p triples (Fk, Ik, Rk) where Fk is a non-empty E-tuple disjoint from E, Ik an E-tuple disjoint from E and Fk, Rk an R-tuple, for k=1...p.

We define the additive cardinality

$$V \ Card_S (e/F1[I1](R1) +...+ Fp[Ip](Rp))=\sum_{k=1}^{p} Card_S(e/Fk[Ik](Rk))$$

The constraint

$m \leqslant V \ Card_S (e/F_1[I_1](R_1)+...+Fp[Ip](Rp)) \leqslant M \ \forall e: occ. of E$

is written as

$V \ CARDS (S:E/F1[I1](R1) +...+ Fp[Ip](Rp))=(m, M)$

with the same implicit clauses as above.

Application to Cst 4.1. thru 4.3.:

S4.1.=

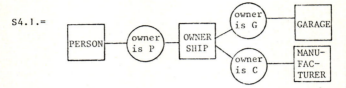

V CARDS (S4.1.: OWNERSHIP/PERSON + GARAGE + MANUFACTURER)=(1,n)

S4.2.=

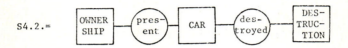

V CARDS(S4.2.: CAR/OWNERSHIP + DESTRUCTION)=(1,1)

S4.3.=

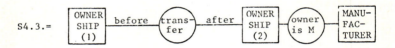

V CARDS (S4.3.: OWNERSHIP(2)/OWNERSHIP(1) + MANUFACTURER)=(1,1)

2.45 *IMPLICATION PROBLEMS: IMPL PRIMITIVE*

Let S, T be structures and COR (S, T/I=J). We shall say that S implies T, according to COR (S, T/I=J), if any occurrence s of S is compatible with T. This constraint is written as
IMPL (S ➡ T/I=J)

Application to Cst 5 and 5':

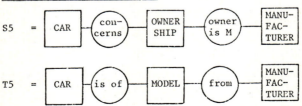

Cst 5: IMPL (S5 ⇒T5/CAR(S5)=CAR(T5), MANUFACTURER (S5)=
MANUFACTURER (T5))

Cst 5: IMPL (T5 ⇒S5/CAR(T5)=CAR(S5), MANUFACTURER (T5)=
MANUFACTURER (S5))

<u>NOTA</u>: There is complete equivalence between AFFIRMATION, and
an IMPL in which T has got only one circle. For instance,

Cst 2.3. is equivalent to :

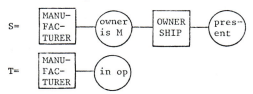

IMPL (S ⇒T/MANUFACTURER(S)=MANUFACTURER(T))

2.46 CONNECTIVITY CONSTRAINTS: CONNECT PRIMITIVES

Let G=(X, U) be a graph of structures and T a structure bound
to G with an "input" arc A'=(T → Si/J'=Ii) and an "output" arc
A"=(Sj → T/Ij=J"). May be there is in addition a "self-
correspondence" C=COR (T, T/J'=J"). In that case, there exists
implicitly an "alternate input" arc $\overline{A'}$ = (T→Si/J"=Ii) and an
"alternate output" arc $\overline{A''}$ = (Sj→T/Ij=J').

We say that G supports a <u>direct connection</u> on T, thru A' and A",
and written as D-CONNECT (G, T(A', A")), C) (C may be omitted),
if for any occurrence t of T:

. <u>either</u>, C being defined, $t\left[J'\right]$ = $t\left[J''\right]$ holds,

. <u>or</u>, there exists an occurrence of path p = (s1,...sn) in G
such that (t, s1) is an occurrence of A' and (sn, t) an
occurrence of A".

When C is defined, the connection is said to be <u>alternate</u> if the
conditions (t, sl) occ. of A' and (sn, t) occ. of A" may be
replaced by (t, sl) occ. of $\overline{A'}$ and (sn, t) occ. of $\overline{A''}$. Alternate
connection is written as A-CONNECT.

Other concepts such as strong and semi-strong connection may be
useful but are not needed here.

Application to Cst 6.:

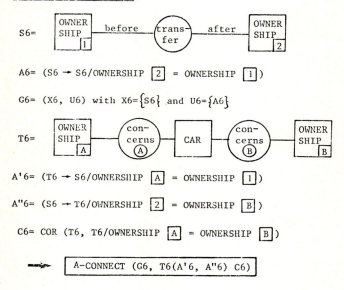

A6= (S6 → S6/OWNERSHIP $\boxed{2}$ = OWNERSHIP $\boxed{1}$)

G6= (X6, U6) with X6=$\{$S6$\}$ and U6=$\{$A6$\}$

A'6= (T6 → S6/OWNERSHIP $\boxed{A}$ = OWNERSHIP $\boxed{1}$)

A"6= (S6 → T6/OWNERSHIP $\boxed{2}$ = OWNERSHIP $\boxed{B}$)

C6= COR (T6, T6/OWNERSHIP $\boxed{A}$ = OWNERSHIP $\boxed{B}$)

→ | A-CONNECT (G6, T6(A'6, A"6) C6) |

3. - RELATIONSHIP DECOMPOSITION

3.1. CARDINALITY DECOMPOSITION

It is well known that a n-ary relationship (n > 2) which has got a
(1,1) min-max cardinality on a leg may be decomposed into (n-1)
binary relationships, as follows:

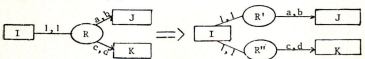

When it has got a (0,1) cardinality, the decomposition is no longer
possible, due to a lack of synchronization between R' and R"

It is now possible, thanks to the statements:

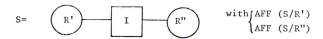

$$S = \quad \text{with} \begin{cases} \text{AFF } (S/R') \\ \text{AFF } (S/R'') \end{cases}$$

3.2. DECOMPOSITION BY REIFICATION

Reification is the following process:

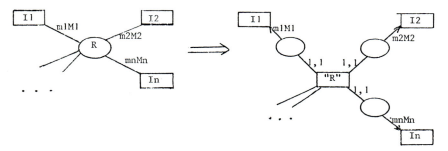

The new model is equivalent to the first one if we guarantee unicity
of "R" occurrence for a given occurrence (il...in) of the n-tuple
(Il...In)

Solution:

$$\Sigma (R) =$$

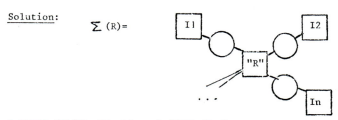

S CARDS (Σ(R): Il, l2,..,In/"R")=(0,1)

3.3. TRANSFORMATION OF CONSTRAINTS IN A DECOMPOSITION PROCESS

- Any constraint of the type AFF($\sum$/Rj) in which Rj is to be decomposed or reified is to be previously transformed into an IMPL thru the following process:

AFF ($\sum$/Rj)   IMPL (S$\Longrightarrow$T/I=J)

- Transformation of a structure follows that of the conceptual model: a circle referring a decomposed relationship is to be decomposed and so are its bindings, a circle referring a reified relationship gives a square, its bindings give each a circle and two bindings.

- Cardinality decomposition saves all integrity statements, except for AFF when Rj is decomposed (it must be replaced by an IMPL as above).

- Concerning reification, in addition to some AFF transformation into IMPL, CARDS and VCARDS must be modified as follows:

  - add into I (or Ik) the squares produced by reification of circles from R (or Rk)

  - add into R (or Rk) the circles produced by transformation of bindings of circles from R (or Rk) which are reified

Consequence: Any ER model may be transformed into an equivalent
one, with only binary "one to n" relationships,
without lack of information.

4. - METAMODEL INSTALLATION

By metamodel, we mean the conceptual schema of an ER model, written
in the ER formalism. Thus, we shall find in the metamodel a meta-entity-
type called "ENTITY", another one called "RELATIONSHIP" and so on.

We present, in appendix 2, the part of the metamodel useful for our
purpose, which is to instal the new concepts and the integrity primitives.

As for any model, there are a number of integrity constraints which must
hold for a model implementation to be valid: all of them are formulated
in terms of the new concepts and primitives, so that the new formalism is
self consistent.

5. - CONCLUSION

The concept of OCCURRENCES STRUCTURE makes it possible to define a set
of primitives for solving a broad class of structural integrity constraints.
The new formalism is self-consistent, since its rules may be expressed in
terms of its own concepts and primitives.

It provides a way to produce an equivalent model with only "1 to n" binary
relationships, without lack of integrity information.

What we now expect is that the new concepts will also provide better
accuracy on external schemas validation and on the generation of related
programs.

APPENDIX 1 (copied from ISO text)   EXAMPLE UNIVERSE OF DISCOURSE.
==

4.1. INTRODUCTION.

The example which follows has been created expressly for the purpose of having a single universe of discourse of at least moderate plausibility which can be described by each of the various approaches. It is sufficiently small so that a large description is not required, but sufficiently complex to exhibit the essential differences among the various approaches. In addition, there is enough dynamic specification to permit the same universe of discourse to be used to exemplify the dynamic approaches.

In this chapter we present a prose description of the classifications and rules in our example universe of discourse, i.e. we state our abstraction system in natural English language. This could be considered as an informal conceptual schema.

We also give some example entities and happenings in our universe of discourse. This could be regarded as an informal (and incomplete) information base.

4.2. ABSTRACTION SYSTEM.

The universe of discourse to be described has to do with the registration of cars and is limited to the scope of interest of the registration authority. The registration authority exists for the purpose of:

1. Knowing who is or was the registered owner of a car at any time from construction to destruction of the car.

2. To monitor certain laws, for example regarding fuel consumption of cars and their transfer of ownership.

Manufacturers of cars:

There are a number of manufacturers, each with one unique name. Manufacturers may start operation, with the permission of the registration authority (which permission cannot be withdrawn). No more than five manufacturers may be in operation at any time. A manufacturer may cease to operate provided he owns no cars, in which case permission to operate lapses.

Cars:

A car is of a particular model and is given a serial number by its manufacturer that is unique among the cars made by that manufacturer. The manufacturer is registered as the owner of the car as soon as practicable. At this time it is given one registration number, unique for all cars and for all time. The year of production is also recorded. During the month of January only, a car may be declared to have been produced in the previous year. Eventually a car is destroyed and the date of destruction is registered. The history of a car must be kept until the end of the second calendar year following its destruction.

Car models:

A model of car has one universally unique name. Cars of each model are made by
only one manufacturer. New models may be introduced without limit. All cars of
one model are recorded as having the same fuel consumption.

Fuel consumption:

Fuel consumption is a number of litres of hydrocarbon fuel per 100 kilometres,
which will be between 4 and 25 litres. The fuel consumption averaged over all
registered cars produced by a particular manufacturer in a particular year is
required not to exceed a maximum value, which is the same for each manufacturer
and may change from year to year. At the end of each January an appropriate
message is sent by the registration authority to each manufacturer which has
failed to meet this requirement.

Garages:

There are a number of garages, each with one unique name. New garages may start
trading. Garages may own cars, but at any time the cars they own must have originated from no more than three manufacturers (which three is unimportant, and
may vary with time). A garage cannot cease to trade as long as it owns cars.

Persons:

There are a number of persons who can own one or more cars. Each person has one
unique name. Only those persons are of interest who own, or have at some time
owned, a car still known to the registration authority.

Car ownership:

At any time a car may be owned by either its manufacturer, or a trading garage,
or a person or group of persons. If a car is owned by a group of persons, each
is regarded as an owner.

Transfer of ownership:

Ownership of a car is transferred by registration of the actual transfer, including the date. A manufacturer can transfer only to garages, and cannot be a
transferee. A garage can transfer only to people. After destruction of the car
it cannot be transfered anymore. Earlier transfer though still can be recorded.

There are no specifications except as above.

In the example, it is inevitable that a number of simplifying assumptions have
been made, e.g. reasons, prices and circumstances of transfer of ownership are
not considered.

4.3. SOME THINGS AND HAPPENINGS IN THE OBJECT SYSTEM.

The following describes some of the things and happenings of the assumed object system:

Some of the car manufacturers with permission to operate are Ford, General Motors, Renault, Jowett, and Volkswagen. A couple of Ford's models are the Mustang and the Granada. General Motors constructs, among others, the Impala model.

The history of a Ford Mustang, serial number PCXX999 is as follows. It was constructed in 1975 and presented for registration on 21 January 1975. It got the registration number GMF 117. On 29 January 1975 it was distributed to Smith's garage, which sold it on 15 March 1975 to Mr. Johnson. Mr. Baker bought the car from Mr. Johnson on 24 May 1978. The car was destroyed on 13 January 1980.

A General Motors Impala car, serial number QGTM783F, was registered under number ABC 653 on 9 April 1978 and distributed to Jones Brothers Ltd. This car was bought by Mr. Johnson on 26 May 1978. The car was destroyed on 14 August 1979.

General Motors made an Impala car with serial number QAVP864B in 1977. It was registered on 21 January 1978 and given registation number PQR 456. On 14 February 1978 it was sold to RN Cars who already owned other cars made by General Motors, Renault and Volkswagen. Mr. and Mrs. J. Soap bought this car on 31 March 1978, but were unable to trade in their Datsun as part of the deal.

In 1978, a new manufacturer PSC (Pretty Small Cars) requested permission to manufacture, and was refused. Following the failure of Jowett in 1979, the request was resubmitted, and this time PSC (Pretty Small Cars) got permission to operate on the market on 1 January 1980.

The first model produced was the Gasmiser. The first series of this model with serial numbers GAM1001, GAM1002, and GAM1003 were all registered on 4 January 1980. They got the registration numbers XYZ 101, XYZ 102, and XYZ 103 respectively.

The car XYZ 101 was distributed to the garage named South Station on 25 January 1980, but was destroyed by an accident on the same day. The latter two cars were distributed to the North Station Garage on 20 January 1980. Both cars were sold to Messrs. Gödel, Escher, and Bach on 26 January 1980. Mr. Bach died in an accident with car XYZ 103 on 2 March 1980. The car was registered as destroyed on 5 March 1980. On 5 March 1980 the Messrs. Gödel and Escher were registered as sole owners of the remaining car XYZ 102. They sold this car to Smith's garage on 15 march 1980 and bought from it a Mustang, serial number PCXX010, which was registered first on 5 January 1980, built in 1979. The registration number of this latter car was XYZ 109. XYZ 102 was destroyed by dismantling, because Smith's garage had a shortage of spare parts. Therefore at the end of 1982 the registration authority can forget all about the cars XYZ 101 - XYZ 103.

On 1 December 1980 PSC gave notice of withdrawal from the car business.

For 1979 the average fuel consumption was established as a maximum of 12 litres per 100 kilometres, for 1980 it was established as a maximum of 10 litres per 100 kilomitres, which will be the rate for 1981.

APPENDIX 2

METAMODEL INSTALLATION

1. - BASIC CONCEPTS

1.1. METAMODEL

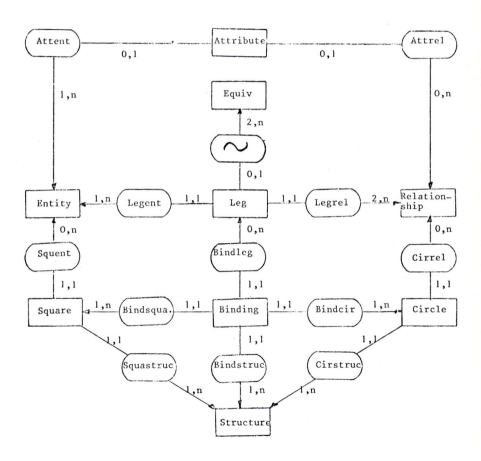

1.2. *CONSTRAINTS ON THE BASIC CONCEPTS*

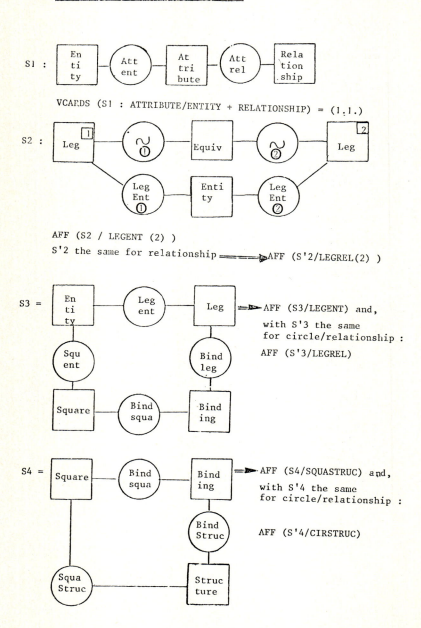

S1 :

VCARDS (S1 : ATTRIBUTE/ENTITY + RELATIONSHIP) = (1,1.)

S2 :

AFF (S2 / LEGENT (2))
S'2 the same for relationship ══════▶ AFF (S'2/LEGREL(2))

S3 =

══▶ AFF (S3/LEGENT) and,

with S'3 the same
for circle/relationship :

AFF (S'3/LEGREL)

S4 =

══▶ AFF (S4/SQUASTRUC) and,

with S'4 the same
for circle/relationship :

AFF (S'4/CIRSTRUC)

2. - AFFIRMATION AND NEGATION

2.1. METAMODEL IMPLEMENTATION

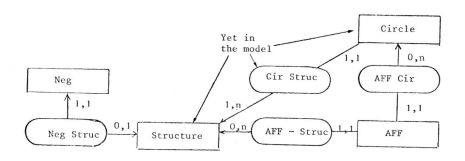

2.2. CONSTRAINTS

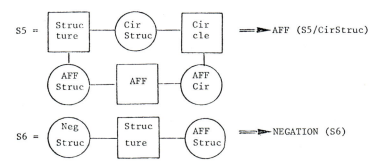

NOTA : This is a semantic constraint.

3. - SCARDS, CARDS and VCARDS

3.1. METAMODEL IMPLEMENTATION

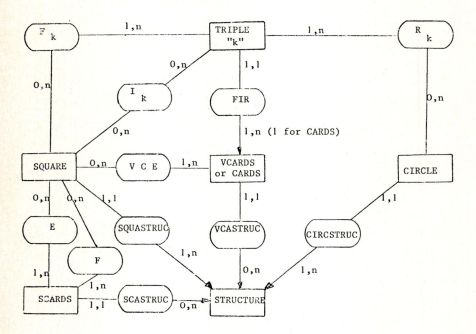

3.2. CONSTRAINTS

SCARDS

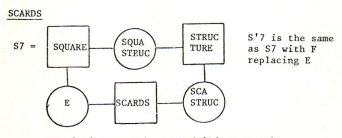

S7 =

S'7 is the same
as S7 with F
replacing E

AFF (S7/SQUASTRUC) ; AFF (S'7/SQUASTRUC)

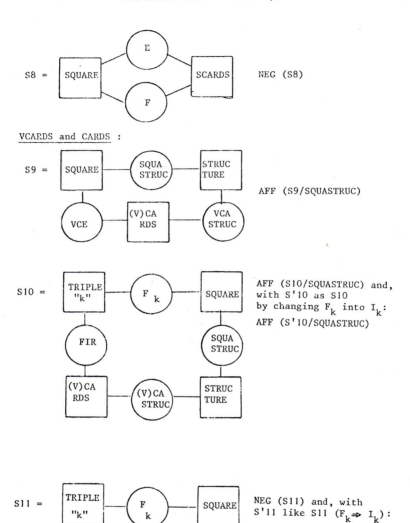

$S12 =$ 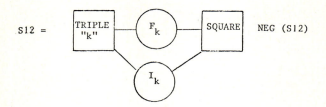 NEG (S12)

$S13 =$ 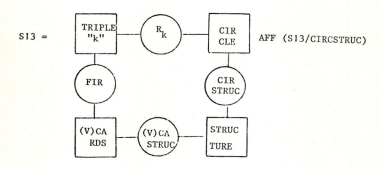 AFF (S13/CIRCSTRUC)

4. - CORRESPONDENCE AND IMPLICATION

4.1. METAMODEL INSTALLATION

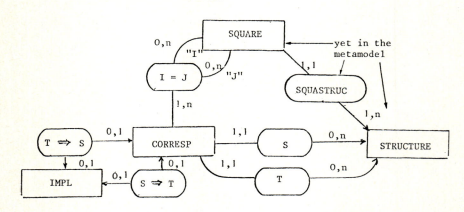

4.2. *CONSTRAINTS*

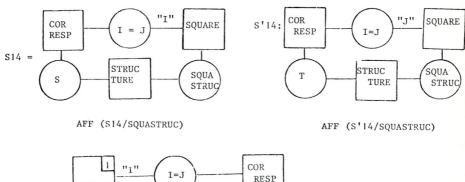

AFF (S14/SQUASTRUC)   AFF (S'14/SQUASTRUC)

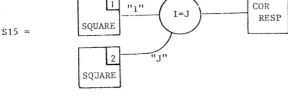

$$
\begin{cases}
\text{SCARDS (S15: SQUARE } \boxed{1} \text{, CORRESP/SQUARE } \boxed{2} \text{) } = (0,1) \\
\text{SCARDS (S15: SQUARE } \boxed{2} \text{, CORRESP/SQUARE } \boxed{1} \text{) } = (0,1)
\end{cases}
$$

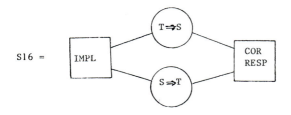

VCARDS (S16 : IMPL/CORRESP (T⇒S) + CORRESP (S⇒T))= (1,1)

5. - <u>GRAPH AND CONNECT</u>

Graph and connect are based on correspondence; their implementation is easy but rather long, we think there is no interest in developping it in this paper.

R E F E R E N C E S

ANSI 75   ANSI/X3/SPARC, "Study Group on Data Base Management Systems: Interim
            Report 75-02-08". FDT-Bulletin of the ACM SIGMOD, Vol 7, No. 2, 1975.

ANSI 77   ANSI/X3/SPARC, Report of Study Group on Data Base Management Systems,
            1977.

CHEN 76   Chen, P.P., The entity-relationship model: Toward a unified view of
            data, ACM Tran. on Data Base Systems. Vol 1, No. 1, 1976.

CHEN 77   Chen, P.P., The entity-relationship model: A basis for the entreprise
            view of data, Proceedings of 1977 National Computer Conference, Dallas,
            Texas, AFIPS Conference Proceedings, Vol 46, pp. 77-84.

CHEN 80   Chen, P.P., Entity-relationship diagrams and English sentence struc-
            tures, in: Chen P. (ed.), Entity-relationship Approach to Systems
            Analysis and Design (North-Holland, Amsterdam, 1980).

KOWA 79   Kowalski R., Logic for Problem Solving (North-Holland, 1979).

ISO 81   ISO/TC97/SC5/WG3, Van Griethuysen, J.J., Editor, "Concepts and
            Terminology for the Conceptual Schema", Feb. 1981.

MOUL 76   Moulin P., Randon J., Scappapietra S., Tardieu H., Teboul M.,
            Conceptual Model as a Data Base Design Tool, Proc. IFIP TC-2 Working
            Conference. Black Forest, Germany (Jan. 1976) 459-479.

NIJS 77   Nijssen, G.M., Current issues in conceptual schema concepts, in:
            Nijssen, G.M. (ed.), Architecture and Models in Data Base Management
            Systems (North-Holland, Amsterdam, 1977).

SCHE 80   Scheuermann P., Schiffner G., and Weber H., Abstraction capabilities
            and invarient properties modeling within the entity-relationship
            approach, in: Chen P. (ed.), Entity-relationship Approach to Systems
            Analysis and Design (North-Holland, Amsterdam, 1980).

TARD 80   Tardieu H., Pascot D., Nanci D., and Heckenroth H., Method, Models
            and Tools for Data Base Design: Three years of experiment in: Chen P.
            (ed.), Entity-relationship Approach to Systems Analysis and Design
            (North-Holland, Amsterdam, 1980).

Entity-Relationship Approach to
Information Modeling and Analysis, P.P. Chen (ed.)
Elsevier Science Publishers B.V. (North-Holland)
©ER Institute, 1983

COMPLETENESS OF QUERY LANGUAGES FOR
THE ENTITY-RELATIONSHIP MODEL*

Paolo Atzeni   and   Peter P. Chen

Instituto di Automatica   Graduate School of Management
Universita´ di Roma   UCLA
Via Eudossiana 18   Los Angeles, California 90024
00184 Roma Italy

ABSTRACT

The notion of completeness for query languages based on the
Entity-Relationship model is proposed. It is based on predicate
calculus, like relational completeness but also takes into account
the ability of the Entity-Relationship model to capture the semantics
of the real world. Two formal definitions of completeness are given:
E-R completeness and simplified E-R completeness, the latter being a
weak version of the former. Finally, a modified version of a recently proposed language, the Executable Language, is briefly described and it is shown to satisfy the property of simplified E-R
completeness.

1. INTRODUCTION

Since its definition [4], relational completeness has usually been considered a fundamental requirement for the relational languages. According to
Date [5], "what relational completeness means to the user is that, very loosely
speaking, if the information wanted is in the database, then it can be retrieved by means of a single self-contained request." In [4], a particular
language, the relational calculus based on the first order predicate calculus,
is formally defined. Then a language L is said to be relationally complete if
it has at least the same expressive power as the relational calculus. That is,
for any relational calculus expression E there is an L expression equivalent to
E. In truth, there are some features that a good language should possess and
that are not taken into account by the definition of completeness, namely aggregate functions and arithmetic capability (see, for instance, [9]). Thus,
some popular relational languages are "more than complete."

The notion of completeness has seldom been extended to other models than
the relational one. (To the best of our knowledge, the only case is [8], where
a definition for the network model is sketched.) Here we want to define completeness in the framework provided by the Entity-Relationship model (E-R model
in the following) [3].

*This work was partially performed while P. Atzeni, sponsored by an Italsiel
S.P.A. grant, was visiting the Graduate School of Management of UCLA.

The E-R model has been widely accepted in the recent years both by researchers and by practitioners, mainly for its ability to capture most of the important semantics of the real world and to express them in an easily understandable way. Moreover, languages based on the E-R model [1], [2], [6], [7] are more natural to non-technical users than conventional data manipulation languages.

An important property of the E-R model is that in a well-designed E-R schema, most of the semantic links of interest for the application are explicitly described. The queries usually have to follow connected paths in the schema (called "chains" in [7] or "navigations" in [2]). As a consequence, we will define the concept of completeness in such a way that a "complete language" need not be able to express queries involving comparisons between unrelated objects.

Similarly to what has been done for relational completeness, we will first define an E-R language based on first order predicate calculus and then say that an E-R language is complete if it is at least as powerful as the E-R calculus.

We will actually give two different definitions of completeness, the first requiring the ability to extract data from any number of different entity-sets and/or relationship-sets and the other one requiring just the ability to select instances in a single entity-set or relationship-set, with conditions that may involve any object in the schema. We will call the former E-R completeness and the latter simplified E-R completeness. We want to stress the fact that simplified completeness is very important (perhaps more than completeness itself) for at least two reasons:

1. The objects of interest for the application are not usually split in an E-R schema, but appear as entity-sets or relationship-sets. This does not always happen in the case of models that do not attempt to capture the semantics of the real world but just its "syntax".

2. Some of the update operations (insertion of relationships, deletion or modification of entities or relationships) require the previous retrieval of the involved entities or relationsips by means of operations that are exactly those required by simplified E-R completeness.

All the high-level languages presented until now for the E-R model (CLEAR [6], CABLE [7], Executable Language [1], [2]) satisfy neither of the definitions of completeness.

The paper is organized as follows: In section 2, the two definitions of completeness are given, preceded by the definition of the E-R calculus. In section 3, the modified version of the Executable Lanaguage is presented and its simplified completeness is shown. In Section 4, our conclusions are presented.

2. THE E-R CALCULUS AND ITS SIMPLIFIED VERSION

The E-R calculus we define in this section is similar to the relational calculus, defined in [4] (see also [9]) as a query language for the relational model. The only great difference is that the atoms containing references to two or more different objects-sets* are allowed by our definition only if the object-sets are explicitly related in the schema of interest. This reflects the fact that in an E-R schema all the semantic links of the piece of the real world to be modelled are explicitly represented. In this way, since the E-R calculus is used to define the notion of E-R completeness, an E-R complete language need not be able to express queries involving comparisons among unrelated object-sets.

<u>Definition 1</u>. An expression of the E-R calculus has the form:

<range list>(<target list>):< predicate>

where:

1. <range list> has the form $x_1:X_{i1}, x_2:X_{i2}, \ldots, x_H:X_{iH}$, where, for each h, x_h indicates a variable that appears in <predicate>, and X_{ih} is the object-set that constitutes its range (that is, the set of values it may assume);

2. <target list> has the form $x_{i1}, x_{i2}, \ldots, x_{jK}$, where the x_{jk} are different variables appearing in the range list;

3. <predicate> is a formula, built from atoms and operators, and satisfying certain conditions as follows.

   There are three types of atoms:

   1. $x_h.X_{ik} = x_k$, where x_h is a variable whose range X_{ih} is a relation-ship-set which involves, among others, the entity-set X_{ik}, that is the range of the variable x_k. This atom assumes the boolean value true for a couple of values (x_h, x_k) of x_h, x_k if and only if x_k is the component of the relationship x_h relevant to the entity-set X_{ik};

   2. $x_h.A_p \; \theta \; x_k.A_q$, where x_h and x_k are variables having the same range X_{ik}, θ belongs to the set of the comparison operators $\{=, \neq, >, \geq, <, \leq\}$ and A_p, A_q are attributes of X_{ik} with θ-comparable domains †. This atom assumes the boolean value true for a couple of values (x_h, x_k) if and only if the value that x_h assumes for the attribute A_p is in relation θ with the value that x_k assumes for A_q;

---

* An object-set is either an entity-set or a relationship-set.

† Two domains D_1, D_2 are said θ-comparable [4] if the comparison $a_1 \; \theta \; a_2$ is meaningful (i.e., is either true or false, but defined) for any $a_1 \varepsilon D$, $a_2 \varepsilon D$.

3. $x_h.A_p \ \theta \ c$, where x_h is a variable with range X_{ih}, A_p is an attribute of X_{ih}^p, θ is as above and c is a constant value θ-comparable with the domain of A_p. The atom assumes the boolean value true for a certain value $\bar{x}_h$ of x_h if and only if the value that $\bar{x}_h$ assumes for the attributes A_p is in relation θ with the constant c.

Formulas defined as follows (assuming reader's familiarity with the elementary logic we do not explain the meaning of symbols $\vee$, $\wedge$, $\neg$, $\exists$, $\forall$, and of the concepts of free and bounded variables):

1.   Each atom is a formula;

2.   If Ψ and Ω are formulas, then $\Omega \wedge \Psi$, $\Omega \vee \Psi$, $\neg \Psi$ (with parentheses if needed) are formulas;

3.   If Ψ is a formula containing at least a free variable x' different from x, $\exists x(\Psi)$ and $\forall x(\Psi)$ are formulas.

4.   Nothing else is a formula.

<predicate>, in an expression of the E-R calculus, is a formula whose free variables are exactly those appearing in the target list of the expression. □

Definition 2. An expression of the simplified E-R calculus is an expression of the E-R calculus that has only one variable in its target list. □

Example 1. Given the E-R diagram below,

the query: "Select the parts whose price is greater than $100" may be expressed as follows:

x_1:PART (x_1) :x_1.PRICE > 100.

The query: "Find the parts needed by the project 'ABC'" may be expressed as follows:

x_1:PART, x_2:PP, x_3: PROJECT (x_1): $\exists x_3(x_3.\text{NAME}='\text{ABC}' \wedge \exists x_2 \ (x_2.\text{PART}=x_1 \wedge$

$$x_2.\text{PROJECT}=x_3)),$$

The query: "Find the suppliers that supply all the parts needed by the project 'ABC' ', may be expressed as follows:

x_1:PROJECT, x_2:PP, x_3:PART, x_4:SP, x_5:SUPPLIER (x_5):
$\exists x_1(x_1.\text{NAME}='\text{ABC}' \wedge \forall x_3 \ (\neg \exists x_2(x_2.\text{PROJECT} = x_1 \wedge x_2.\text{PART}=x_3) \vee$
$$\exists x_4(x_4.\text{PART} = x_3 \wedge x_4.\text{SUPPLIER} = x_5)))$$

Finally, the query: "Find the couples <supplier, project> such that the supplier supplies at least a part to the project," may be expressed as follows:

x_1:PROJECT, x_2:PP, x_3:PART, x_4:SP, x_5:SUPPLIER(x_1,x_5):
$\exists x_3(\exists x_2(x_2.\text{PART}=x_3 \wedge x_2.\text{PROJECT}=x_1) \wedge \exists x_4(x_4.\text{PART}=x_3 \wedge x_4.\text{SUPPLIER}=x_1))$

We now give the two definitions of completeness, which resemble the usual definition of relational completeness.

Definition 3. A language L satisfies the property of E-R completeness if for any expression E of the E-R calculus there is an expression of L equivalent to E.

Definition 4. A language L satisfies the property of simplified E-R completeness if for any expression E of the simplified E-R calculus, there is an expression of L equivalent to E.

3. AN E-R COMPLETE LANGUAGE

As we said in the introduction, various high-level languages have been proposed for the E-R model, but none of them satisfies the property of simplified E-R completeness (and as a consequence, none of them satisfies the criteria for E-R completeness). In this section, we describe a modified version of the Executable Language (originally presented in [1], [2]), and show that it satisfies the property of simplified completeness.

The fundamental operation of the language is the selection of entities or relationships from an entity-set or a relationship-set, respectively. The selection of entities may be specified in the following ways:

1. Indicating a condition on the attributes of an entity-set:

    FIND <entity-set name> WITH (<condition>)

    where <condition> is a boolean expression whose operators are AND, OR, NOT, (,), and whose terms have the form:

    <attribute-name>θ<attribute-name> or <attribute-name>θ<constant>
    (with $\theta \ \varepsilon \ \{=, \neq, >, \geq, <, \leq \}$).

2. Requiring that they take part in relationships of a given relationship-set, selected with a condition on attributes analogous to the one described above:

```
FIND <entity-set-name>
     THROUGH HAVING <relationship-set name> WITH (<condition>)
```

3. Requiring that they take part in relationships of a given relationship-set selected, indicating that they involve entities of another entity-set that satisfy a "WITH" condition:

```
FIND <entity-set name1>
     THROUGH <relationship-set name>
     HAVING <entity-set name2> WITH (<condition>)
```

The selection of relationships may be specified in similar ways:

1. Indicating a condition on attributes

```
FIND <relationship-set name> WITH <condition>
```

2. Indicating that they involve entities of a given entity-set selected with a "WITH" clause:

```
FIND <relationship-set name>
     HAVING <entity-set name> WITH <condition>
```

The constructs described above may be combined to form more complex queries with the following three rules:

1. Branching: Several different conditions on a single object-set may be combined with the operators AND, OR, NOT and parentheses to form a boolean expression, as in the following example.

<u>Example 2</u>. Given the following schema:

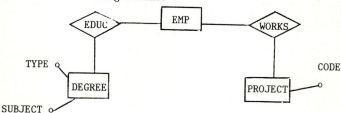

The query: "Find the employees that have a Ph.D. degree in Electrical Engineering (EE) and that do not work for the project Integrated Circuits (IC)" may be expressed as follows:

```
FIND emp
     (THROUGH educ
     HAVING degree WITH (type= 'PhD' AND subject = 'EE'))
     AND
     NOT (THROUGH work
     HAVING project WITH (code = 'IC'))
```

2. Chaining: Two queries such that the first one ends on the same object-set as that on which the second begins,

        ...HAVING <object-name> WITH <condition>

and

        FIND <object-name>...

may be combined as follows:

        ...HAVING FOUND <object-name> WITH <condition>...

3. Among the terms of a selection predicate ("WITH" clause) there may appear terms referring to the results of other subqueries. The following example shows such a situation.

Example 3. Given the E-R diagram:

AGE   CODE

| EMPLOYEE | — | MANAGES | — | PROJECT |

the query "Find the employees that are older than the manager of the project 'IC'" may be expressed as follows:

```
FIND employee WITH (age > age OF FOUND employee
                    THROUGH manages
                    HAVING project
                           WITH (code = 'IC'))
```

Another example of nesting will be shown after the introduction of the concept of variable.

In order to perform queries involving correlation between various references to the same object-set, the language allows the definition of variables. A variable may appear several times in an expression (either always in the place of an entity-set name or always in the place of a relationship-set name) and once and only once it must appear together with the name of the object-set that constitutes its domain.

Example 4.   Given the schema below:

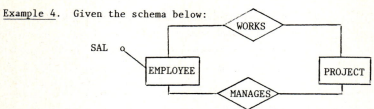

the query "Find the employees whose salary is greater than the salary of the
manager of the project they work for" may be expressed as follows:

```
FIND e: employee WITH (sal > sal OF FOUND employee
      THROUGH manages
      HAVING FOUND project
            THROUGH works
            HAVING e)
```

Note that a variable could have been used for any other object-set referred to
in the query, without changing its meaning.   So the following statement is
equivalent to the preceding:

```
FIND e: employee WITH (sal > sal OF FOUND f:employee
      THROUGH m:manages
      HAVING FOUND project
            THROUGH works
            HAVING e)
```

The introduction of variables allows us to specify another kind of nesting
which has the following structure: among the terms of a "WITH" clause referring to an object-set X, there may appear a term that compares two sets of
entities (or relationships) of a given entity-set (or relationship-set) selected by means of operations that, in general, involve X:

$$\text{FIND } x:X \text{ WITH } (\ldots(\text{FIND } Y_1 \ldots x \ldots) \; \eta \; (\text{FIND } Y_1 \ldots x \ldots)\ldots)$$

where η indicates the one of the set-comparison operators (=, $\neq$, $\subset$, $\supset$, $\subseteq$, $\supseteq$).

Example 5.   Given the E-R schema below:

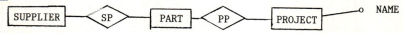

the query "Find the suppliers that supply all the parts needed by the project
'ABC'" may be expressed as follows:

```
FIND s:supplier WITH ((FIND part
                       THROUGH sp
                       HAVING s ) ⊇ (FIND part
                                      THROUGH pp
                                      HAVING project WITH (name = ABC))
```

The language also allows the specification of aggregation functions, but for the sake of brevity we do not describe them here.

With the following theorem, we prove the simplified completeness of this language, showing how an equivalent expression of it may be built for any expression of the simplified E-R calculus.

Theorem 1. The Executable Language satisfies the property of simplified E-R completeness.

Proof: Let

$$x_1:X_{i1}, \; x_2:X_{i2}, \; \ldots, \; x_H:X_{iH} \; (x_j): \; \Psi$$

be an expression of the E-R simplified calculus, where, without loss of generality, Ψ is a formula containing only the operators $\wedge, \neg$, $\forall$ and such that the scope of any occurrence of the quantifier $\forall$ in it is an expression built with the operators $\wedge, \neg$, and whose terms are either atoms involving the variable which is bounded by that occurrence of the quantifier or quantified formulas(*). So, for any subformula Φ in Ψ we can define one of the variables that appear in as the "local target," in this way:

-   if there is no quantifier whose scope contains Φ, then the variable in the target list is the local target;

-   if there is at least a quantifier whose scope bounds Φ, then the local target is the variable that is quantified by the quantifier whose scope is the smallest among the scopes of quantifiers that contain Φ.

We prove the theorem by induction on the number of operators in any subformula Φ of Ψ: First we prove that an equivalent expression exists for any formula with no operators, and then that if for each subformula of a formula Φ with one or more operators an equivalent expression exists, then an equivalent expression exists also for Φ.

Basis.   No operators in Φ: Φ is an atom. Let x be the local target of Φ and X its range. The atom may have one of the three forms defined in def. 1; for each of them we give the corresponding expression of the Executable Language.

(*)   It may easily be proved that for each formula there exists an equivalent formula of this kind.

1. $x_h.X_{ik} = x_k$. We have to distinguish two cases:

    (1) $x=x_h$ (the range of the local target is the relationship-set involved in the atom); in this case the expression of the Executable Language is the following:

$$\text{FIND } x:X$$
$$\text{HAVING } x_k$$

    (2) $x=x_k$ (the range of the local target is the entity-set involved in the atom); the corresponding expression is:

$$\text{FIND } x:X$$
$$\text{THROUGH HAVING } x_h$$

2. $x_h.A_p \; \theta \; x_k.A_q$. Again we have two cases:

    (1) $x=x_h=x_k$; the corresponding expression is:

$$\text{FIND } x:X \text{ WITH } (A_p \; \theta \; A_q)$$

    (2) $x=x_h \neq x_k$ (or $x=x_k \neq x_h$); the corresponding expression is:

$$\text{FIND } x:X \text{ WITH } (A_p \; \theta \; A_q \text{ OF } x_k)$$
$$\text{or FIND } x:X \text{ WITH } (A_q \; \theta \; A_p \text{ OF } x_h))$$

3. $x_h.A_p \; \theta \; c$. In this case $x_h=x$, (obviously), and the corresponding expression is:

$$\text{FIND } x:X \text{ WITH } (A_p \; \theta \; c)$$

Induction. Let Φ have at least one operator and assume that each subformula of Φ has a corresponding expression in the Executable Language. We have three cases:

1. $\Phi = \neg \Phi_1$. Let FIND x:X <string> be the expression corresponding to Φ_1. The expression for Φ is the following:

    FIND x:X NOT (<string>)

2. $\Phi = \Phi_1 \wedge \Phi_2$. For the assumptions made at the beginning of the proof, Φ_1 and Φ_2 have the same target. Let FIND x:X <string$_1$> and FIND x:X <string$_2$> be the expressions corresponding to Φ_1 and Φ_2, respectively. The expression corresponding to Φ is the following:

    FIND x:X (<string$_1$> AND <string$_2$>)

3. $\Phi = \forall_y (\Phi_1)$ Let FIND y:Y <string> be the expression corresponding to Φ_1. The expression corresponding to Φ is the following:

    FIND x:X WITH ((FIND y:Y <string>) = FIND Y)

This expression describes the quantification because it requires that the elements of the object-set Y selected by the condition <string> coincide with the elements found with no restrictions, that is, with all the elements of Y.

Thus, we have completed the induction and proved the theorem. □

4. CONCLUSIONS

The definitions of completeness presented here may serve as an effective means for evaluating Entity-Relationship-based query languages, both existent and to be developed in the future. Moreover, they can be extended to other semantic data models.

At this point, we want to remind the reader that there are at least two features that a good E-R query language should possess that are not taken into account by the definition of completeness. They are:

- capability of expressing arithmetic and aggregate functions (see introduction);

- simplicity and readability.

Both of them are, at least partially, possessed by the original versions of CLEAR, CABLE and Executable Language, although they are not complete. Actually we think that an E-R complete language is likely to be very complex, but, since most queries require only local selection of instances and linear navigation in the schema, it is very important that at least these queries be expressed in an easy and expressive way (this concept is analogous to that expressed in [9] with regard to relational queries and projection-selection-join expressions).

ACKNOWLEDGMENT

The authors wish to express their thanks to Ilchoo Chung and Dennis Perry for their valuable comments.

REFERENCES

1.   P. Atzeni, C. Batini, M. Lenzerini, F. Villanelli. INCOD: A system for
     Conceptual Design of Data and Transactions in the Entity Relationship
     Model. Submitted for publication.

2.   P. Atzeni, F. Villanelli. A Query and Manipulation Language for the
     Entity Relationship Model (in Italian). Submitted to the AICA Conference,
     Italy, 1981.

3.   P.P. Chen. The Entity-Relationship Model: Toward a Unified View of Data.
     ACM Trans. on Database Syst. 1, 1, March 1976.

4.   E.F. Codd. Relational Completeness of Data Base Sublanguages. Data Base
     Systems (R. Rustin ed.) Prentice Hall, 1972.

5.   C.J. Date. An Introduction to Data Base Systems 2nd ed., Addison Wesley,
     1977.

6.   G. Poonen. CLEAR; a Conceptual Language for Entities and Relationships.
     Proc. LCMOD, Milan, Italy, 1978.

7.   A. Schoshani. CABLE: a Language Based on the Entity Relationship Model
     Rep UCID-8005, Lawrence Berkeley Laboratory, University of California,
     Berkeley, 1977.

8.   D. Trischritzis, F. Lochovsky. Data Base Management Systems, Academic
     Press, 1978.

9.   J.D. Ullman, Principle of Data Base Systems. Computer Science Press,
     1980.

APPENDIX

Syntax of the Executable Language

<retrieve>::=<outent> |<outrel>

<outent>::= {$^{FIND}_{FOUND}$} <entity>[<ent-expr>]

<outrel>::= {$^{FIND}_{FOUND}$} <relationship>[<rel-expr>]

<ent-expr>::=<ent-term> |NOT (<ent-expr>) | (<ent-expr> <op> <ent-expr>)

<ent-term>::=<with-clause> |THROUGH HAVING <relationship>

                 THROUGH <relationship> <rel-expr>

<rel-expr>::=<rel-term> |NOT (<rel-expr>) | (<ent-expr> <op-diad> <ent-expr>)

<rel-term>::= HAVING <outent> |HAVING <entity> |< with-clause>

<with-clause>::=WITH (<predicate>)

<predicate>::=<term> |NOT (<predicate>) (<predicate> <op> <predicate>)

<term>::=<attribute> <θ> <attribute> |<attribute ><θ>< constant>

     <attribute> <Θ> <attribute> OF {$^{<retrieve>}_{<varible>}$} |

    (<outent> <η> <outent>) | (<outrel> <η> <outrel>)

<entity>::=<variable>[:<entity-name>][<with-clause>][<comment>] | <entity-name>
         [with-clause>] [<comment>]

<relationship>::=<relationship-name> [<with-clause>] [<comment>] |[<variable>]

               [:<relationship-name>] [<with-clause>] [<comment>]

```
<entity-name>::=<id>

<attribute>::=<id>

<relationship-name>::=<id>

<variable>::=<id>

<θ>::= =|≠|<|>|≥|≤

<η>::= =|≠| ⊂ | ⊃ |⊆| ⊇

<op>::=AND|OR

<id>::=<alph> [<char-string>]

<char-string>::=<char>[<char-string>]

<char>::=<alpha>|1|2|3|...|0|-

<alph>::= A|B|C|...| Z

<comment>::=/*<char-string>*/
```

Entity-Relationship Approach to
Information Modeling and Analysis, P.P. Chen (ed.)
Elsevier Science Publishers B.V. (North-Holland)
©ER Institute, 1983

VERIFICATION AND TESTING OF S-ER REPRESENTATIONS

A.L.Furtado, P.A.S.Veloso, J.M.V. de Castilho
Pontifícia Universidade Católica do Rio de Janeiro
Brasil

A methodology is proposed for representing data base applications, formally specified as abstract data types, by the abstract
data type corresponding to the S-ER data model. The methodology
includes the verification and testing of the representation. An
example data base application is used to illustrate   the dis -
cussion.

1. Introduction

Capturing the intended behavior of a data base application from   informal
descriptions supplied by its prospective users is a critical task.   Misunder-
standings are often perceived only too late, when an executable implementation
becomes available after lengthy and costly efforts.

Our approach to this problem involves the following steps:

a) Express the informal description of the data base application   formally
   as an abstract data type [GTW,GUT], keeping however the very same   terminology of the data base application.

b) Represent the application data type by an abstract data type corresponding
   to the data model.

c) Verify formally the correctness of the representation.

d) Test the representation against the original specification.

Notice that we stress testing as an opportunity for the users to   confirm
the faithfulness of the specification to their perhaps vague mental   image.
Since it is impossible to prove the equivalence between the initial   informal
specification and the formal ones, the availability of experimental usage   is
paramount to confirming that the original intentions were captured [SHA,VCF].

In line with the above remarks we shall use the formalism of procedural
specifications [FVE]. It presents the advantage of allowing early usage   and
testing by means of symbolic programs.

As data model we shall employ the entity-relationship data model [CHE]. It is important to note that the entity-relationship view has been praised for its closeness to real world situations but has been regarded as informal [ULL], whereas we shall present it here in the same precise data type formalism. For the sake of simplicity, we shall confine ourselves to a simplified version of the entity-relationship model, presented in section 2.

In section 3 we introduce a simple data base application, which will be used as a running example in order to illustrate the main ideas involved in representing a data base application by the data model as well as verifying and testing the representation.

2. SPECIFICATION OF THE S-ER DATA MODEL

In order to simplify the presentation, we shall confine ourselves to a restricted version of the entity-relationship data model to be denominated the S-ER data model. The S-ER data model supports only binary relationships and allows attributes for entities but not for relationships. The remaining features of the full ER model appear to be easily incorporated.

Its update operations permit to initialize (phi) the data base to an empty state, create and delete (cr,del) entities within entity-sets, modify (mod) values of attributes ('*' stands for the undefined value) and link or unlink (lk,ulk) entities via a relationship. The query operations are predicates referring to the existence (exs) of entities within entity-sets, values (hv) of attributes and relatedness (isr) of entities. These operations were first introduced in [SAN].

An obvious integrity constraint is that only entities that exist in the data base may have defined values for attributes and may be related to other entities. Dynamically this constraint is enforced by causing the operations that assign values to attributes or establish links to have no effect if the entities involved do not exist. On the other hand, an entity that exists in only one entity-set cannot be deleted until all its attribute-values are set to undefined and all incident links are removed.

Any ser-object can be created through — and can therefore be denoted by — expressions, involving applications of the update operations. It is possible to identify sets of expressions that denote the same ser-object, but one may choose representatives for each one of those sets, defining a convenient canonical form containing only some of the update operations. The operations are phi, cr, mod and lk. The canonical terms will therefore contain only these operations, arranged in the sequence

lk(...lk(mod(...mod(...cr(...cr(...phi( )...)...)...)...)...)...)

Occurrences of the same operation are ordered lexicographically with respect to their arguments (apart from the canonical term argument), in increasing sequence, from left to right; the implied order of execution is inside out:

the first is phi and the last is the most external operation.

However, not all expressions conforming to the above syntax correspond   to
canonical terms. The procedural specification [FVE] given in Figure 1 can   be
shown to generate only expressions that are valid with respect to the integrity
constraints.

Each procedure has commands corresponding to the rewriting rules   which
transform a data base expressed by a canonical term into another canonical term,
when an additional operation (corresponding to the procedure) is applied. Whenever update operations depend on integrity constraints for their applicability,
these are checked at the outset and the canonical term given as argument   is
returned unchanged in case of failure. The remaining part of the   procedure
bodies is a case-like statement, inside which occurs the recursive   scanning
of the canonical term argument.

The language features are self-explanatory except perhaps for "?",   which
stands for any valid value of an argument, and "?<variable>"which, in addition,
assigns the value found to a variable, as in PLANNER [HEW]. In order to improve
readability, the canonical terms are written using square brackets instead   of
parentheses and "|" instead of comma.

If the operations in the expression below

    mod(A,ATTR,10,lk(A,B,REL,del(B,ES2,cr(A,ES1,cr(B,ES2,phi( ))))))

are executed, the resulting canonical term is

    MOD[A|ATTR|10|CR[A|ES1|PHI]],

which would also be the result of executing

    mod(A,ATTR,10,CR[A|ES1|PHI]).

This "backtracking" property of canonical term specifications [GTW] will   be
found useful in the sequel.

Both in this section and in the next, all our query operations are   predi -
cates. Thanks to the use of the already introduced PLANNER-like   notation
"?<variable>", predicates also play the role of selectors. For example   exs
(a,?t,s) will be true if there is in s an entity a in some entity-set   and ,
in addition, the name of one such entity-set will be assigned to the   variable
t. More formally the notation corresponds to "computing" the Skolem   function
associated with $\exists t$ exs(a,t,s). Without this convenient feature we   would
need in the order of 2^n selectors to cope will all possible combinations   of
constants (given) and variables (for selection) per predicate with n parameters
(not counting the special parameter of type ser).

```
type ser
sorts ser,ent,eset,attr,val,rel,logical

  op phi( ):ser
     ⇒ PHI

  endop

  op cr(x:ent,t:eset,s:ser):ser
     var y:ent,z:ent,u:eset,a:attr,i:val,r:rel,sl:ser
     exs(x,t,s) ⇒ s;
     match s
       LK[y|z|r|sl] ⇒ LK[y|z|r|cr(x,t,sl)]
       MOD[y|a|i|sl] ⇒ MOD[y|a|i|cr(x,t,sl)]
       CR[y|u|sl] ⇒ if x.t > y.u then CR[y|u|cr(x,t,sl)]
                         else CR[x|t|s]
       otherwise ⇒ CR[x|t|s]
     endmatch
  endop

  op mod(x:ent,a:attr,i:(val,{*}),s:ser):ser
     var y:ent,z:ent,b:attr,j:val,r:rel,sl:ser
     ~ (exs(x,?,s) ∧~ hv(x,a,i,s)) ⇒ s;
     match s
       LK[y|z|r|sl] ⇒ LK[y|z|r|mod(x,a,i,sl)]
       MOD[y|b|j|sl] ⇒ if x.a = y.b then
                            if i = * then sl
                            else MOD[x|a|i|sl]
                         else if x.a > y.b then
                                 MOD[y|b|j|mod(x,a,i,sl)]
                              else MOD[x|a|i|s]
       otherwise ⇒ MOD[x|a|i|s]
     endmatch
  endop

  op lk(x:ent,y:ent,r:rel,s:ser):ser
     var z:ent,w:ent,q:rel,sl:ser
     ~(exs(x,?,s) ∧ exs(y,?,s) ∧~ isr(x,y,r,s)) ⇒ s;
     match s
       LK[z|w|q|sl] ⇒ if x.y.r > z.w.q then
                         LK[z|w|q|lk(x,y,r,sl)]
                      else LK[x|y|r|s]
       otherwise ⇒ LK[x|y|r|s]
     endmatch
  endop

  op del(x:ent,t:eset,s:ser):ser
     var y:ent,z:ent,u:eset,a:attr,i:val,r:rel,sl:ser
     ~(exs(x,t,s) ∧ (inothereset(x,?,t,s) ∨
                 (~ isr(x,?,?,s) ∧~ isr(?,x,?,s) ∧~ hv(x,?,?,s)))) ⇒ s;
     match s
       LK[y|z|r|sl] ⇒ LK[y|z|r|del(x,t,sl)]
       MOD[y|a|i|sl] ⇒ MOD[y|a|i|del(x,t,sl)]
```

```
          CR[y|u|s1] ⇒ if x.t = y.u then s1
                         else CR[y|u|del(x,t,s1)]
      endmatch
  endop

  op ulk(x:ent,y:ent,r:rel,s:ser):ser
     var z:ent,w:ent,q:rel,s1:ser
     ∿ isr(x,y,r,s) ⇒ s;
     match s
       LK[z|w|q|s1] ⇒ if x.y.r = z.w.q then s1
                        else LK[z|w|q|ulk(x,y,r,s1)]
     endmatch
  endop

  op exs(x:ent,t:eset,s:ser):logical
     var y:ent,z:ent,v:eset,a:attr,i:val,r:rel,s1:ser
     match s
       LK[y|z|r|s1] ⇒ exs(x,t,s1)
       MOD[y|a|i|s1] ⇒ exs(x,t,s1)
       CR[y|v|s1] ⇒ if x.t = y.v then true
                      else if x.t > y.v then exs(x,t,s1)
                             else false
       otherwise ⇒ false
     endmatch
  endop

  op hv(x:ent,a:attr,i:val,s:ser):logical
     var y:ent,z:ent,b:attr,j:val,r:rel,s1:ser
     match s
       LK[y|z|r|s1] ⇒ hv(x,a,i,s1)
       MOD[y|b|j|s1] ⇒ if x.a.i = y.b.j then true
                         else if x.a > y.b then hv(x,a,i,s1)
                                else false
       otherwise ⇒ false
     endmatch
  endop

  op isr(x:ent,y:ent,r:rel,s:ser):logical
     var z:ent,w:ent,q:rel,s1:ser
     match s
       LK[z|w|q|s1] ⇒ if x.y.r = z.w.q then true
                        else if x.y.r > z.w.q then isr(x,y,r,s1)
                               else false
       otherwise ⇒ false
     endmatch
  endop

  hidden op inothereset(x:ent,v:eset,t:eset,s:ser):logical
    ⇒ exs(x,v,s) ∧ v ≠ t
  endop
endtype
```

FIGURE 1: The ser data type

3. SPECIFYING A DATA BASE APPLICATION

As an example of a (simplified) data base application, we shall use   the
data base of an employment agency, where persons apply for positions, companies
subscribe by offering positions, and persons are hired by or fired from   com -
panies. A person applies only once, thus becoming a candidate to some position;
after being hired, the person is no longer a candidate but regains this   status
if fired. The same company can subscribe several times, the (positive)   number
of positions being added up. Only persons that are currently candidates can be
hired and only by companies that have at least one vacant position. One   consequence of these integrity constraints is that a person can work for at   most
one company.

Apply, subscribe, hire and fire, together with initag (which creates an initially empty agency data base) are our update operations. As query operations we
shall use the predicates iscandidate, worksfor and haspositions, the latter referring to the number of unfilled positions in a company.

An agency data base (agdb) object will be created through - and can there -
fore be denoted by - expressions involving applications of the update   opera -
tions initag, apply, subscribe and hire.   The canonical terms will therefore
contain only these operations, arranged in the sequence:

        hire(...subscribe (...apply (...initag( )...)...)...)

Occurrences of the same operation are ordered   lexicographically
with respect to their first argument (person for hire and apply, company   for
subscribe), in increasing sequence, from left to right; the order of execution
is from the inside out: the first is initag and the last is the most   external
operation.

Figure 2 shows the procedural specification of the agdb data type. If   the
operations in the expression below

fire(E3,C2,hire(E2,C2,hire(E1,C2,subscribe(C2,1,hire(E1,C1,
hire(E4,C1,apply(E1,hire(E3,C2,apply(E2,apply(E4,subscribe(C2,3,
apply(E3,subscribe(C1,2,initag( )))))))))))))))

are executed, the resulting canonical term is

HIRE[E1|C1|HIRE[E2|C2|HIRE[E4|C1|SUBSCRIBE[C1|2|
SUBSCRIBE[C2|4|APPLY[E1|APPLY[E2|APPLY[E3|APPLY[E4|INITAG]]]]]]]]]

Notice that the same result would be obtained, in view of the   "backtracking"
property, with the execution of, e.g.

hire(E1,C1,hire(E2,C2,hire(E4,C1,subscribe(C1,2,
SUBSCRIBE[C2|4|APPLY[E1|APPLY[E2|APPLY[E3|APPLY[E4|INITAG]]]]]))))

where the subscribe (C1,2,...) and the three hire(...) operations are executed sequentially, provided the initial agdb state is the one described by the canonical term beginning with SUBSCRIBE[C2| .... above.

```
type agdb

sorts agdb,person,company,natural,logical

op initag():agdb
   ⇒ INITAG
endop

op apply(x:person,s:agdb):agdb
   var z:person,w:company, m:natural, t:agdb
   ∿(∿iscandidate(x,s) ∧∧ worksfor(x,?,s)) ⇒ s;
   match s
      HIRE[ z|w|t ] ⇒ HIRE[ z|w|apply(x,t)]
      SUBSCRIBE[w|m|t] ⇒ SUBSCRIBE[w|m|apply(x,t)]
      APPLY[z|t] ⇒
         if x>z
         then APPLY[z|apply(x,t)]
         else APPLY[x|s]
      otherwise ⇒ APPLY[x|s]
   endmatch
endop

op subscribe(y:company,m:natural,s:agdb):agdb
   var x:person, t:agdb, w:company, n:natural
   ∿(m>0) ⇒ s;
   match s
      HIRE[x|w|t ] ⇒ HIRE[x|w|subscribe(y,m,t)]
      SUBSCRIBE[w|n|t] ⇒
         if y=w
         then SUBSCRIBE[y|n+m|t]
         else if y>w
                 then SUBSCRIBE[w|n|subscribe(y,m,t)]
                 else SUBSCRIBE[y|m|s]
      otherwise ⇒ SUBSCRIBE[y|m|s]
   endmatch
endop

op hire(x:person,y:company,s:agdb):agdb
   var m:natural,z:person, w:company, t:agdb, n:natural
   ∿(iscandidate(x,s) ∧ (haspositions(y,?m,s) ∧ m>0)) ⇒ s;
   match s
      HIRE[ z|w|t] ⇒
         if x > z
         then HIRE[ z|w|hire(x,y,t) ]
         else HIRE[x|y|s]
      otherwise ⇒ HIRE[x|y|s]
   endmatch
endop
```

```
op fire (x:person,y:company,s:agdb):agdb
   var t:agdb, w:company, z:person
   ¬worksfor(x,y,s) ⇒ s
   match s
       HIRE[z|w|t] ⇒
           if x>z
           then HIRE[z|w|fire(x,y,t)]
           else t
   endmatch
endop
op iscandidate(x:person,s:agdb):logical
   var z:person, w:company, t:agdb, m:natural
   match s
       HIRE[z|w|t] ⇒
           if x=z
           then false
           else iscandidate(x,t)
       SUBSCRIBE[w|m|t] ⇒ iscandidate(x,t)
       APPLY[z|t] ⇒
           if x=z
           then true
           else iscandidate(x,t)
       otherwise ⇒ false
   endmatch
endop
op haspositions(y:company,m:natural,s:agdb):logical
   var z:person, w:company, t:agdb, n:natural
   match s
       HIRE[z|w|t] ⇒
           if w=y
           then haspositions(y,m+1,t)
           else haspositions(y,m,t)
       SUBSCRIBE[w|n|t] ⇒
           if w≠y
           then haspositions(y,m,t)
           else if m=n
                   then true
                   else false
       otherwise ⇒ false
   endmatch
endop
op worksfor(x:person,y:company,s:agdb):logical
   var z:person, w:company, t:agdb, m:natural
   match s
       HIRE[z|w|t] ⇒
           if x.y = z.w
           then true
           else worksfor(x,y,t)
       otherwise ⇒ false
   endmatch
endop
endtype
```

FIGURE 2 : the agdb data type

4. REPRESENTING THE DATA BASE APPLICATION BY THE DATA MODEL

We are viewing both the data application and the data model as   abstract
data types. Thus, representing the former by the latter consists of implementing
one data type by another [GTW,GUT,HOA].

In our example of the employment agency data base, it seems natural to   represent persons (candidates and employees) and companies as entities and agdb -
objects as ser-objects. This establishes a correspondence from the non-primiti-
ve sorts of type agdb into the sorts of type ser (mirrored in the sort   defi -
nitions of Figure 3). We now have to refine this correspondence to a   function
rep assigning to each agdb-object an ser-object representing it. This can   be
done as follows.

For each basic operation op-agdb, an operation op-ser is defined by means of
a procedure using the basic operations of the ser data type, so that the   following diagram commutes.

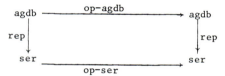

Figure 3 shows a procedural specification of such a representation.Some   points
are worth mentioning. Firstly, the representation is independent of any parti -
cular implementation of the data model. Secondly, the representation   function
rep is defined only implicitly by viewing a sequence of agdb operations as calls
to the corresponding procedures in the representation. Thirdly, the data   model
needs only the entity-sets CAND, EMP and COMP, only one attribute NPOS associ -
ated with entities from the COMP set), and only one relationship set,   WORKS,
linking entities from EMP to entities from COMP. Lastly, the integrity   cons -
traints of agdb are to be respected in the representation, the data   model
having of course its own integrity constraints.

    repr of agdb by ser
    sort definitions
        agdb :: = ser
        person ::= ent
        company ::= ent
    {sorts natural and logical are primitive}

    op initag( ):agdb
        ⇒ phi( )
    endop

    op apply(x:person,s:agdb):agdb
        ∿(∿ exs(x,CAND,s) ∧∿ isr(x,?,WORKS,s))⇒ s;
        ⇒ cr(x,CAND,s)
    endop

```
op subscribe(y:company,m:natural,s:agdb):agdb
   var n:natural
   ∿(m>0) ⇒ s;
   hv(y,NPOS,?n,s) ⇒ mod(y,NPOS,n+m,s);
                  ⇒ mod(y,NPOS,m,cr(y,COMP,s))
endop

op hire(x:person,y:company,s:agdb):agdb
   var n:natural
   ∿(exs(x,CAND,s) ∧ hv(y,NPOS,?n,s) ∧ n>0) ⇒ s;
              ⇒ lk(x,y,WORKS,mod(y,NPOS,n-1,cr(x,EMP,del(x,CAND,s))))
{the value of n in the last command is obtained by the ?n construction, as
 in PLANNER}
endop

op fire(x:person,y:company,s:agdb):agdb
   var n:natural
   ∿isr(x,y,WORKS,s) ⇒ s;
   hv(y,NPOS,?n,s) ⇒ ulk(x,y,WORKS,mod(y,NPOS,n+1,cr(x,CAND,del(x,EMP,s))))
{the effect of the condition hv(y,NPOS,?n,s) is simply retrieving the  value
 of n}
endop

op iscandidate(x:person,s:agdb):logical
          ⇒ exs(x,CAND,s)
endop

op haspositions(y:company,m:natural,s:agdb):logical
          ⇒ hv(y,NPOS,m,s)
endop

op worksfor(x:person,y:company,s:agdb):logical
          ⇒ isr(x,y,WORKS,s)
endop
endrepr agdb/ser
```

FIGURE 3: the representation module

5. VERIFYING THE REPRESENTATION

As stated in section 4 a representation of agdb by ser implicitly defines   a
map rep:agdb → ser and verifying the correctness of the representation amounts
to verifying the commutativity of a diagram for each basic agdb-operation.   An
expanded version of such a diagram appears in Figure 4, where the upper   and
the lower paths have been decomposed into three steps each. We have to   start
with a generic agdb-object C, which will be mapped to a ser-object e, via   the
upper path, and to a ser-object g, via the lower path. In order to check   the
equality of e and g (which are given by sequences of ser operations), we   use
the procedural specification of ser and check whether the corresponding   cano -
nical terms, A and B are syntactically identical.

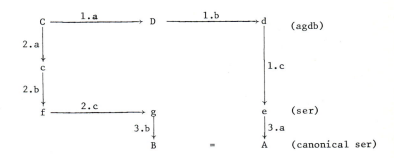

FIGURE 4: Steps to verify the correctness of the representation

As an illustration consider the simple case of the operation of firing   E2
from C2, on the agdb state given by the canonical term

C = HIRE[E1|C1|HIRE[E2|C2|SUBSCRIBE[C1|2|SUBSCRIBE[C2|3
    APPLY[E1|APPLY[E2|APPLY[E3|INITAG]]]]]]]

By applying to this term the agdb operation fire (E2,C2,..), we obtain

D = HIRE[E1|C1|SUBSCRIBE[C1|2|SUBSCRIBE[C2|3|APPLY[E1|APPLY[E2|
    APPLY[E3|INITAG]]]]]]

which, by the backtracking property, is

d = hire(E1,C1,subscribe(C1,2,subscribe(C2,3,apply(E1,apply(E2,
    apply(E3,initag( )))))))

The above terms pertain to the agdb level. Now, the representation of Figure 3
applied to d, gives an ser term representing d, namely

e = lk(E1,C1,WORKS,mod(C1,NPOS,2-1,cr(E1,EMP,del(E1,CAND,
    mod(C1,NPOS,2,mod(C2,NPOS,3,cr(E1,CAND,cr(E2,CAND,cr(E3,
    CAND,phi( )))))))))

which, according to the data model procedural specification, corresponds   to
the canonical term

A = LK[E1|C1|WORKS|MOD[C1|NPOS|1|MOD[C2|NPOS|3|CR[E1|EMP|
    CR[E2|CAND|CR[E3|CAND|PHI]]]]]]

On the other hand, along the lower path, the canonical term C is, by the backtracking property

c = hire(E1,C1,hire(E2,C2,subscribe(C1,2,subscribe(C2,3,apply(E1,apply(E2,
    apply(E3,initag( ))))))))

which is represented, according to Figure 3, by the ser term

f = lk(E1,C1,WORKS,mod(C1,NPOS,2-1,cr(E1,EMP,del(E1,CAND,lk(E2,C2,WORKS,
    mod(C2,NPOS,3-1,cr(E2,EMP,del(E2,CAND,mod(C1,NPOS,2,
    mod(C2,NPOS,3,cr(E1,CAND,cr(E2,CAND,cr(E3,CAND,phi( )))))))))))))))))

By applying to f the procedure fire(E2,C2,.) of Figure 3, we obtain

g = ulk(E2,C2,WORKS,mod(C2,NPOS,3-1+1,cr(E2,CAND,del(E2,EMP,f))))

whose corresponding canonical term is

B = LK[E1|C1|WORKS|MOD[C1|NPOS|1|MOD[C2|NPOS|3|CR[E1|EMP|CR[E2|CAND|
    CR[E3|CAND|PHI]]]]]]

which is identical to the above A.

    The steps involved are as follows (see Fig. 4):

- upper path

1a: operation op-agdb given by the procedural specification (Figure 2), giving
    D;

1b: application of the backtracking property for agdb canonical terms,yielding
    d;

1c: execution of the procedures according to the representation (Figure 3)   ,
    giving e;

- lower path

2a: application of the backtracking property for agdb canonical terms,yielding
    c;

2b: execution of the procedures according to the representation   (Figure 3)
    giving f;

2c: execution of the procedure op-ser on f according to the representation (Fi-
    gure 3), yielding g.

    Notice that both e and g are sequences of basic ser operations. By applying
to them the procedural specification for the data model (Figure 1) we obtain the
canonical terms A and B which are to be identical if the representation   is
correct.

    In general, the representation will be verified to be correct by proving,for
each agdb operation (initag, apply, ..., worksfor) and for every agdb canonical
term, the syntactical identity of the corresponding A and B, as above.   This

can be a laborious task, but the very form of the procedure texts suggests how to break it into cases. In fact, this amounts to proving the equivalence of two programs mapping agdb to ser. One program has procedure calls according to the upper path: first apply the procedure op-agdb of Fig. 2, then interpret the capital letters in the result as calls to the corresponding procedures in Fig. 3. For the other program the calling sequence follows the lower path : first the capital letters are interpreted as calls to the corresponding procedures in Figure 3, then the procedure op-ser of the representation is applied to the result.

By means of a formal specification of the data type ser (say, the procedural specification in Figure 1), we can verify the equivalence of these programs. We have indicated above how to do this by means of symbolic execution [KNG].

6. TESTING THE REPRESENTATION

Testing a representation means, of course, running a systematically chosen series of programs against the original specification and then against the representation, and checking if the results are the same. This step would seem redundant after the verification phase; however, it may be a useful redundancy, since verification is not immune to error.

Also, as said in the introduction, an additional benefit of testing lies in the opportunity given to users to actually experiment with the specification to see whether it corresponds to their, perhaps somewhat vague, intentions.For this purpose either the original specification or the representation, both executable in our methodology, can be used.

In order to provide experimental usage and testing of a specified data type, we developed a SNOBOL-based processor, which is a single program with three identifiable parts:

1. initializations and utilities
2. operations
3. interactive handler for test programs

Part 2 varies according to the data type to be tested. In our present case, two sets of operations where separately included:

- for running the original specification: operations of the agdb data type (Figure 5);
- for running the representation: operations of the ser data type (Figure 6) and operations of the representation of agdb by ser (Figure 7).

Parts 1 and 3 are given in Appendix A. Part 3 is essentially a loop which keeps prompting the user to submit SNOBOL programs, compiles and runs them. During a session, a user sitting at a terminal may submit one or more programs utilizing the operations for initializing, updating and querying the data base in its canonical term representation.

Appendix B contains a short sample session, involving various test programs which, except in two cases for reasons that will be obvious, yield the   same results with both sets of operations.

We began by performing a series of updates (grouped in a long "nested" ex - pression, noting that it can also be broken into as many lines each with   a single operation and an assignment). Then the resulting canonical term   is printed, providing a "dump" for a complete examination of the result.   What is displayed in the Appendix is the canonical term as in the representation.

Next, there are tests for query operations, noting that "arg . <variable>" corresponds to the "?<variable>" notation. The third query test includes   a search for the employees working for each company and uses a CURSOR   [DAT] feature, analogous to the iterators in [LIS].

Finally, there are tests involving the definition of an additional   oper- ation and the redefinition of an existing one. The new operation, c2-hire,   is designed to be used by a company c2, authorized to hire a person who has   not applied to the employment agency, provided that at least 10 vacant   positions (in the same company) are reserved for applicants. The operation however   does not violate the integrity constraint that only registered candidates can   be hired: what happens is that c2 is permitted to apply on the person's   behalf or, in other words, that an apply operation is "triggered" if c2 attempts   to hire an unregistered person.

The ability to redefine an operation for the duration of a session   (con- veniently supported by SNOBOL) is fundamental for experimenting with possible changes to the specification and investigating its consequences. Here,   we redefined the query iscandidate (using the representation) so that a   person who has applied retains his status of candidate even if hired; a   consequence of this redefinition is then observed: now the same person can be hired by and therefore work for more than one company.

We regard our processor as a short-sized and relatively unsophisticated software tool. Since it is entirely contained in this paper and given the wide availability of SNOBOL, it becomes easy for others to reproduce and extend the experiment.

```
        DEFINE('INITAG()')                          :(INEND)
INITAG      INITAG = 'INITAG'                        :(RETURN)
INEND
*
*
        DEFINE('APPLY(X,S)Z,W,N,S1')                 :(APEND)
APPLY      APPLY = ¬(¬ISCANDIDATE(X,S)  ¬(WORKSFOR(X,ARG,S))
+               S                                    :(RETURN)
        S  'HIRE(' ARG . Z ',' ARG . W ',' ARG . S1 ')' :F(AP1)
            APPLY = 'HIRE(' Z ',' W ',' APPLY(X,S1) ')' :(RETURN)
AP1     S  'SUBSCRIBE(' ARG . W ',' ARG . N ',' ARG . S1 ')' :F(AP2)
```

```
                APPLY = 'SUBSCRIBE(' W ',' N ',' APPLY(X,S1) ')' :(RETURN)
AP2        S  'APPLY(' ARG . Z ',' ARG . S1 ')'    :F(AP3)
                APPLY = LGT(X,Z) 'APPLY(' Z ',' APPLY(X,S1) ')' :S(RETURN)
                APPLY = 'APPLY(' X ',' S ')'              :(RETURN)
AP3        APPLY = 'APPLY(' X ',' S ')'              :(RETURN)
APEND
*
*
     DEFINE('SUBSCRIBE(Y,M,S)Z,W,N.S1')               :(SUEND)
SUBSCRIBE   SUBSCRIBE = EQ(M,O)  S                     :S(RETURN)
           S  'HIRE(' ARG . Z ',' ARG . W ',' ARG . S1 ')' :F(SU1)
                SUBSCRIBE = 'HIRE(' Z ',' W ','
+                               SUBSCRIBE(Y,M,S1) ')'    :(RETURN)
SU1        S  'SUBSCRIBE(' ARG . W ',' ARG . N ',' ARG . S1 ')' :F(SU2)
                SUBSCRIBE = IDENT(Y,W) 'SUBSCRIBE(' Y ','
+                               N + M ',' S1 ')'         :S(RETURN)
                SUBSCRIBE = LGT(Y,W) 'SUBSCRIBE(' W ',' N ','
+                               SUBSCRIBE(Y,M,S1) ')'    :S(RETURN)
                SUBSCRIBE = 'SUBSCRIBE(' Y ',' M ',' S ')' :(RETURN)
SU2        SUBSCRIBE = 'SUBSCRIBE(' Y ',' M ',' S ')'      :(RETURN)
SUEND
*
*
     DEFINE('HIRE(X,Y,S)Z,W,S1')                       :(HIEND)
HIRE       HIRE = ¬(ISCANDIDATE(X,S) HASPOSITIONS(Y,ARG . NUM,S)
+                GT(NUM,0))  S                          :S(RETURN)
           S  'HIRE(' ARG . Z ',' ARG . W ',' ARG . S1 ')' :F(HI1)
                HIRE = LGT(X,Z) 'HIRE(' Z ',' W ','
+                               HIRE(X,Y,S1) ')'         :S(RETURN)
                HIRE = 'HIRE(' X ',' Y ',' S ')'        :(RETURN)
HI1        HIRE = 'HIRE(' X ',' Y ',' S ')'             :(RETURN)
HIEND
*
*
     DEFINE('FIRE(X,Y,S)Z,W,S1')                       :(FIEND)
FIRE       FIRE = ¬WORKSFOR(X,Y,S)   S                  :S(RETURN)
           S  'HIRE(' ARG . Z ',' ARG . W ',' ARG . S1 ')'
                FIRE = IDENT(X,Z)  S1                   :S(RETURN)
                FIRE = 'HIRE(' Z ',' W ',' FIRE(X,Y,S1) ')' :(RETURN)
FIEND
*
*
     DEFINE('ISCANDIDATE(X,S)Z')                       :(ISEND)
ISCANDIDATE  S  ARB 'APPLY(' X $ Z
+                   *(¬WORKSFOR(Z,ARG,S))              :S(RETURN)F(FRETURN)
ISEND
*
*
     DEFINE('HASPOSITIONS(Y,M,S)W,N')                  :(HAEND)
HASPOSITIONS   S  ARB 'SUBSCRIBE(' Y $ W ',' ARG $ N
+                   *COMPARE(((N - NHIRED(W,S)) ',' ),M) :S(RETURN)F(FRETURN)
HAEND
*
*
```

```
        DEFINE('NHIRED(Y,S)S1')                              :(NHEND)
NHIRED       S   ARB 'HIRE(' ARG ',' Y ',' ARG . S1 ')'  :F(NH1)
                 NHIRED = NHIRED(Y,S1) + 1                :(RETURN)
NH1          NHIRED = 0                                   :(RETURN)
NHEND
*
*
        DEFINE('COMPARE(S,P)')                               :(CMEND)
COMPARE      S   P                                       :S(RETURN)F(FRETURN)
CMEND
*
*
        DEFINE('WORKSFOR(X,Y,S)')                            :(WOEND)
WORKSFOR     S   ARB 'HIRE(' X ',' Y                     :S(RETURN)F(FRETURN)
WOEND
```

FIGURE 5: Executable specification of agdb

```
        DEFINE('PHI()')                                      :(PEND)
PHI          PHI = '$'                                    :(RETURN)
PEND
*
*
        DEFINE('CR(X,T,S)Y,Z,U,A,I,R,S1')                    :(CREND)
CR           CR = EXS(X,T,S)  S                           :S(RETURN)
             S   'LK(' ARG . Y ',' ARG . Z ',' ARG . R ','
+                     ARG . S1 ')'                        :F(C1)
             CR = 'LK(' Y ',' Z ',' R ',' CR(X,T,S1) ')' :(RETURN)
C1           S   'MOD(' ARG . Y ',' ARG . A ',' ARG . I ','
+                     ARG . S1 ')'                        :F(C2)
             CR = 'MOD(' Y ',' A ',' I ',' CR(X,T,S1) ')' :(RETURN)
C2           S   'CR(' ARG . Y ',' ARG . U ',' ARG . S1 ')' :F(C3)
             CR = LGT(X T,Y U) 'CR(' Y ',' U ','
+                                   CR(X,T,S1) ')' :S(RETURN)
             CR = 'CR(' X ',' T ',' S ')'                 :(RETURN)
C3           CR = 'CR(' X ',' T ',' S ')'                 :(RETURN)
CREND
*
*
        DEFINE('MOD(X,A,I,S)Y,Z,B,J,R,S1')                   :(MEND)
MOD          MOD = ¬(EXS(X,ARG,S) ¬HV(X,A,I,S))  S      :S(RETURN)
             S 'LK(' ARG . Y ',' ARG . Z ',' ARG . R ','
+                     ARG . S1 ')'                        :F(M1)
             MOD = 'LK(' Y ',' Z ',' R ',' MOD(X,A,I,S1) ')' :(RETURN)
M1           S   'MOD(' ARG . Y ',' ARG . B ',' ARG . J ','
+                     ARG . S1 ')'                        :F(M3)
             IDENT(X A,Y B)                               :F(M2)
               MOD = IDENT(I,'*')  S1                     :S(RETURN)
               MOD = 'MOD(' X ',' A ',' I ',' S1 ')'   :(RETURN)
M2           MOD = LGT(X A,Y B) 'MOD(' Y ',' B ',' J ','
```

```
+                                           MOD(X,A,I,S1) ')' :S(RETURN)
                 MOD = 'MOD(' X ',' A ',' I ',' S ')'        :(RETURN)
M3           MOD = 'MOD(' X ',' A ',' I ',' S ')'            :(RETURN)
MEND
*
*

     DEFINE('LK(X,Y,R,S)Z,W,Q,S1')                          :(LEND)
LK        LK = ¬(EXS(X,ARG,S) EXS(Y,ARG,S) ¬ISR(X,Y,R,S)) S :S(RETURN)
          S  'LK(' ARG . Z ',' ARG . W ',' ARG . Q ','
+                        ARG . S1 ')'                        :F(L1)
            LK = LGT(X Y R,Z W Q) 'LK(' Z ',' W ',' Q ','
+                                          LK(X,Y,R,S1) ')'   :S(RETURN)
             LK = 'LK(' X ',' Y ',' R ',' S ')'         :(RETURN)
L1        LK = 'LK(' X ',' Y ',' R ',' S ')'             :(RETURN)
LEND
     DEFINE('DEL(X,T,S)Y,Z,U,A,I,R,S1')                     :(DEND)
DEL       DEL = ¬EXS(X,T,S)  S                             :S(RETURN)
          V1 = T
          EXS(X,ARG $ V2 *DIFFER(V2,V1),S)                 :S(D1)
          DEL = ¬(¬ISR(X,ARG,ARG,S) ¬ISR(ARG,X,ARG,S)
+                   ¬ HV(X,ARG,ARG,S))  S                  :S(RETURN)
D1        S  'LK(' ARG . Y ',' ARG . Z ',' ARG . R ','
+                    ARG . S1 ')'                          :F(D2)
            DEL = 'LK(' Y ',' Z ',' R ',' DEL(X,T,S1) ')' :(RETURN)
D2        S  'MOD(' ARG . Y ',' ARG . A ',' ARG . I ','
+                    ARG . S1 ')'                          :F(D3)
            DEL = 'MOD(' Y ',' A ',' I ',' DEL(X,T,S1) ')' :(RETURN)
D3        S  'CR(' ARG . Y ',' ARG . U ',' ARG . S1 ')'
            DEL = IDENT(X T,Y U)  S1                       :S(RETURN)
            DEL = 'CR(' Y ',' U ',' DEL(X,T,S1) ')'       :(RETURN)
DEND
*
*

     DEFINE('ULK(X,Y,R,S)Z,W,Q,S1')                        :(UEND)
ULK       ULK = ¬ISR(X,Y,R,S)   S                          :S(RETURN)
          S  'LK(' ARG . Z ',' ARG . W ',' ARG . Q ','
+                    ARG . S1 ')'
            ULK = IDENT(X Y R,Z W Q)  S1                   :S(RETURN)
            ULK = 'LK(' Z ',' W ',' Q ',' ULK(X,Y,R,S1) ')' :(RETURN)
UEND
*
*

     DEFINE('EXS(X,T,S)')                                  :(EEND)
EXS       S  ARB 'CR(' X ',' T                   :S(RETURN)F(FRETURN)
EEND
*
*
```

```
      DEFINE('HV(X,A,I,S)')                                :(HEND)
HV          S   ARB 'MOD(' X ',' A ',' I                   :S(RETURN)F(FRETURN)
HEND
*
*

      DEFINE('ISR(X,Y,R,S)')                               :(IEND)
ISR         S   ARB 'LK(' X ',' Y ',' R                    :S(RETURN)F(FRETURN)
IEND
```

FIGURE 6: Executable specification of ser.

```
      DEFINE('INITAG()')                                   :(INEND)
INITAG     INITAG = PHI()                                  :(RETURN)
INEND
*
*
      DEFINE('APPLY(X,S)')                                 :(APEND)
APPLY      APPLY = ¬(¬ISCANDIDATE(X,S) ¬WORKSFOR(X,ARG,S))
+                    S                                     :S(RETURN)
           APPLY = CR(X,'CAND',S)                          :(RETURN)
APEND
*
*
      DEFINE('SUBSCRIBE(Y,M,S)')                           :(SUEND)
SUBSCRIBE   SUBSCRIBE = EQ(M,O)  S                         :S(RETURN)
            SUBSCRIBE = HV(Y,'NPOS',ARG . N,S)
+            MOD(Y,'NPOS',N + M,S)                         :S(RETURN)
            SUBSCRIBE = MOD(Y,'NPOS',M,CR(Y,'COMP',S))     :(RETURN)
SUEND
*
*
      DEFINE('HIRE(X,Y,S)')                                :(HIEND)
HIRE       HIRE = ¬ (ISCANDIDATE(X,S) HASPOSITIONS(Y,
+                  (ARG $ N *GT(N,O)),S))   S              :S(RETURN)
           HIRE = LK(X,Y,'WORKS',DEL(X,'CAND',CR(X,'EMP',
+                  MOD(Y,'NPOS',N - 1,S))))               :(RETURN)
HIEND
*
*
      DEFINE('FIRE(X,Y,S)')                                :(FIEND)
FIRE       FIRE = ¬WORKSFOR(X,Y,S)   S                     :S(RETURN)
           HV(Y,'NPOS',ARG . N,S)
           FIRE = ULK(X,Y,'WORKS',DEL(X,'EMP',CR(X,'CAND',
+                  MOD(Y,'NPOS',N + 1,S))))                :(RETURN)
FIEND
*
*
```

```
      DEFINE('ISCANDIDATE(X,S)')                    :(ISCEND)
ISCANDIDATE  EXS(X,'CAND',S)                        :S(RETURN)F(FRETURN)
ISCEND
*
*

      DEFINE('HASPOSITIONS(Y,M,S)')                 :(HAEND)
HASPOSITIONS HV(Y,'NPOS',M,S)                       :S(RETURN)F(FRETURN)
HAEND
*
*

      DEFINE('WORKSFOR(X,Y,S)')                     :(WOEND)
WORKSFOR    ISR(X,Y,'WORKS',S)                      :S(RETURN)F(FRETURN)
WOEND
```

FIGURE 7: Executable ser representation of agdb

7. CONCLUSIONS

We have presented a methodology for the crucial task of producing, verifying
and testing a precise specification of a data base application. After   this
becomes available, the way is paved for an orderly succession of design steps,
finally leading to some file structure representation that can be implemented
efficiently. In fact, we do not have to go through all such steps for each data
base application, which would require a considerable effort that we would   not
be willing to expend except for critical or extraordinary applications. If   a
data model, regarded as an abstract data type, has alread been effectively implemented, all we have to do is to build upon it the representation of our data
base application, as we did in this paper using a restricted version of   the
entity-relationship data model (see [POO;BEN] for implementations of the   ER
model; also its translation into the more data-structure oriented models   has
been for a long time under investigation [CHE]).

Figure 8 illustrates this strategy.

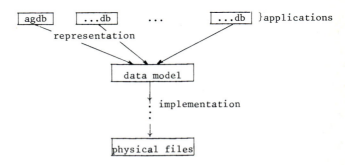

FIGURE 8: Steps along the representation axis

This discussion stresses one important role of data models: a data model can be regarded as the most general (least restricted) member of a family of   data base applications.

We shall now give a more general perspective of what we did putting together two data types (agdb and ser). In agdb the <u>behavior</u> of the application   is fully specified as intended, whereas certain other aspects are covered in   a rudimentary way. Three such aspects are representation, accessibility and usage interfaces. By providing a representation module (repr, in figure 3),   whereby we substituted ser operations for the agdb operations, we initiated the   design of an architecture of data types [EHR;CAF] centered around agdb, which   is obtained by decoupling and refining aspects of the specification of agdb. Large applications indeed require complex architectures, combining several data types.

The accessibility aspect corresponds in practice to "auxiliary"   structures superimposed on the data base. These can be formally introduced by way of what we shall call transference modules, whose operations combine queries from   agdb and updates (or constructors) from some other data type (say sets, other   pos- sibilities being lists, mappings, etc. [Jones]), appropriate for collecting and possibly ordering selected components of agdb. If the need to determine   the employees working for each company arises frequently, this may be a case   where one such structure should be built (which can be done as in   the   search   in section 6 and Appendix B, using set constructors instead of printing operations).

Since data base applications are handled by different classes of users with different needs and degrees of authorization, they must be given usage   inter- faces (external schemata [ANS]) tailored to their distinct characteristics. The usage interfaces give origin in the architecture to interface   modules,   one for each class of users, the operations of which use certain   agdb   operations, possibly restricted by incorporating further applicability conditions; also   , besides the operations whose effects are the ones that the user had in mind   , other agdb operations may be triggered (again an example is supplied in section 6 and Appendix B: the c2.hire operation of user c2). Since the interface   (or external schema) operations are defined on the agdb (conceptual schema)   oper- ations, the agdb data type is not disturbed; this constitutes a simple   case of enrichment [GTW].

Figure 9 sketches the proposed architecture.

As we proceed along the representation axis towards the data   files   level, other modules can also "slide down" to lower levels of representation.   Thus the auxiliary access structures will eventually become, say,   inverted   files and, at that level, transference may correspond to setting records   of   an inverted file to point to data file records.

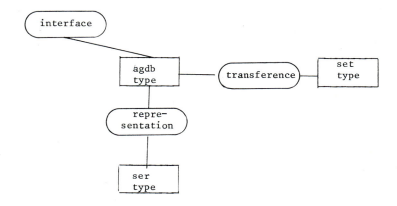

FIGURE 9: An abstract data type architecture

REFERENCES

[ANS]   ANSI/X3/SPARC - Interim Report of the Study Group on Data Management Systems. FDT Bulletin, ACM, 1975.

[BEN]   Benneworth, R., Bishop, C., Turnbull, C., Holman, W., Monette, E. - The implementation of GERM, an entity relationship data base management system. Proc. 7th VLDB, 1981.

[CAF]   Castilho, J.M.V.de, and Furtado, A.L. - Algebraic specification of data base applications. PUC - Rio de Janeiro, T.R. DB108004, 1980.

[CHE]   Chen, P. - The entity-relationship model - toward a unified view of data. ACM-TODS v.1, n.1, 1976.

[DAT]   Date, C.J. - An introduction to data base systems. Addison-Wesley , 1977.

[EHR]   Ehrig, H., Kreowski, H.J., Weber, H.J. - Algebraic Specification Schemes for data base systems - Proc. 4 th VLDB, 1979.

[FVE]   Furtado, A.L. and Veloso, P.A.S. - Procedural specifications and im-
        plementations for abstract data types. SIGPLAN Notices, vol. 16,no 3,
        1981, pp. 53-62.

[GTW]   Goguen, J.A., Thatcher, J.W. and Wagner, E.G. - An initial   algebra
        approach to the specification, correctness and implementation   of
        abstract data types, in R.T. Yeh (ed.) Current trends in programming
        methodology, vol. IV, Prentice-Hall, 1978, p. 81-149.

[GUT] Guttag, J. - Abstract data types and the development of data structu-
        res. CACM, vol. 20, n. 6, 1977.

[HEW]   Hewitt, C. - PLANNER: a language for proving theorems in robots.Proc.
        IJCAI, 1971.

[HOA]   Hoare, C.A.R. - Proof of correctness of data representations.   Acta
        Informatica, vol. 1, 1972, p. 271-281.

[JON]   Jones, C.B. - Software development: a rigorous approach,   Prentice-
        Hall, 1980.

[KNG]   King, J.C. - Symbolic execution and program testing. Communications
        of the ACM, Vol. 19 no. 7, 1976, pp. 385-394.

[LIS]   Liskov, B.H., Snyder, A., Atkinson, R. and Schaffert, C. - Abstrac -
        tion mechanisms in CLU. CACM, vol. 20, n. 8, 1977.

[POO]   Poonen, G. - CLEAR: a conceptual language for entities and   relation-
        ships, Proc. of International Conference on Management of Data, 1978.

[SAN]   Santos, C.S., Neuhold, E.J. and Furtado, A.L. - A data type approach
        to the entity-relationship model, in P. Chen (ed), Entity-relation -
        ship approach to systems analysis and design, North-Holland,1980.

[SHA]   Shaw, M. - Presentation in the workshop on data abstraction,   data-
        bases and conceptual modelling, SIGMOD Record, vol. 11, n.2, 1981 ,
        p.43-46.

[ULL]   Ullman, J.D. - Principles of database systems. Computer Science Press,
        1980.

[VCF]   Veloso, P.A.S., Castilho, J.M.V. and Furtado, A.L. - Systematic de-
        rivation of complementary specifications. Proc. 7th VLDB, 1981.

ACKNOWLEDGEMENTS:

   Financial support was granted by Conselho Nacional de Desenvolvimento Cien
tifico e Tecnológico (CNPq) and IBM do Brasil.

```
*                 APPENDIX A:  THE SNOBOL-BASED PROCESSOR
*
*
*                     INITIALIZATIONS AND UTILITIES
*
*
      εFULLSCAN = 1
      εANCHOR = 1
      INPUT(.INTERM,'INTERM',80)
      OUTPUT(.OUTERM,'OUTERM','(1X,72A1)')
      ARG = BREAK(',(') '(' BAL ')' | BREAK(',)')
*
      DEFINE('CURSOR(C)')                             :(CEND)
CURSOR    $(C 1) = 0
          $C = ARG  @CUR *GT(CUR,CUR1) @($(C 1))  :(RETURN)
CEND
*
      DEFINE('NEXT(C)')                               :(NXEND)
NEXT      CUR1 = $(C 1)
          NEXT = $C                                   :(RETURN)
NXEND
*
      DEFINE('DISPLAY(VAR)T,V')                       :(DIEND)
DISPLAY   T = ''
DI1       VAR BREAK(',') . V ',' = ''                 :F(DI2)
          T = T V ' = ' $V ' '                        :(DI1)
DI2       OUTERM = T  VAR ' = ' $VAR                  :(RETURN)
DIEND
      OPSYN('!','DISPLAY',1)


*
*              INTERACTIVE HANDLER FOR TEST PROGRAMS
*
      NPRG = 0
CONTSESS   NPRG = NPRG + 1
STRT OUTERM = '???'
      TEST = ''
CONTRQ    TEST = TEST TRIM(INTERM)
          TEST ARB 'CANCEL'                           :S(STRT)
          TEST ARB 'FINIS'                            :S(ENDSESS)
          TEST ARB 'OLD('   ARG . P ')'               :F(TSV)
          NPRG = NPRG - 1                             :<$('PRG' $P)>
TSV       TEST ARB . LD 'SAVE(' ARG . SV ')' = LD :F(NWRQ)
          $SV = NPRG
NWRQ      TEST ARB . TS '.' RPOS(0) = TS '; :(CONTSESS)' :F(CONTRQ)
          P = CODE(TEST)                              :F(CFAIL)
          $('PRG' NPRG) = P                           :<P>
CFAIL OUTERM = 'COMPILATION FAILED'                   :(STRT)
ENDSESS
*
*
END
```

APPENDIX B: SAMPLE SESSION

```
 ???
"processes a series of updates
recording the corresponding canonical term";

    z = fire('e3','c2',hire('e2','c2',hire('e1','c2',
        subscribe('c2',1,hire('e1','c1',hire('e4','c1',
        apply('e1',hire('e3','c2',apply('e2',apply('e4',
        subscribe('c2',3,apply('e3',subscribe('c1',2,
        initag())))))))))))) ;
    !'z'.

Z = LK(E1,C1,WORKS,LK(E2,C2,WORKS,LK(E4,C1,WORKS,
    MOD(C1,NPOS,0,MOD(C2,NPOS,3,CR(C1,COMP,CR(C2,
    COMP,CR(E1,EMP,CR(E2,EMP,CR(E3,CAND,CR(E4,EMP,
    $)))))))))))

 ???

"queries
1. finds a candidate";

    iscandidate(arg . candidate,z) ; !'candidate'.

 CANDIDATE = E3

???

"2. finds a company with no vacant positions";

    haspositions(arg . company,0,z) ; !'company'.

COMPANY = C1

???

"3. lists for each company its vacant positions and employees";
    cursor('comp');
contcomp haspositions(next('comp') . company,arg . vacant,z)
        !'company,vacant'              :f(emp.comp.end);
        cursor('emp');
contemp       worksfor(next('emp') . employee,company,z)
              !'employee'             :s(contemp)f(contcomp);
emp.comp.end.

   COMPANY = C1 VACANT = 0
   EMPLOYEE = E1
   EMPLOYEE = E4
   COMPANY = C2 VACANT = 3
   EMPLOYEE = E2
```

```
        ???
```

"defines and uses an external schema operation allowing company c2 to hire
people who have not applied yet, applying on their behalf, provided that at
least 10 openings remain";

```
            define('c2.hire(x,s)')                   :(c2hend);
c2.hire        c2.hire = haspositions('c2',(arg $ np *gt(np,10)),s)
                    hire(x,'c2',apply(x,s)) :s(return);
                c2.hire = hire(x,'c2',s)          :(return);
c2hend;
        z = subscribe('c2',17,z);
        z = c2.hire('e5',z);
        worksfor('e5',arg . company,z);
        outerm = 'e5 works for ' company.

  E5 WORKS FOR C2


    ???
```

"tries to hire a person already working for a company and fails";

```
            save(try);
            z = hire('e4','c2',z);
            status = worksfor('e4','c2',z) 'hired';
            status = ¬worksfor('e4','c2',z) 'not hired';
            outerm = status.

NOT HIRED

???
```

"redefines a conceptual schema operation :
now a person who has applied always remains a candidate";

```
            define('iscandidate(x,s)')           :(iscend);
iscandidate exs(x,('cand' | 'emp'),s)            :s(return)f(freturn);
iscend.

    ???
```
"tries again to hire the already employed person";
```
        old(try)

  HIRED

  ???
```

"terminates the session";

```
        finis
```

Entity-Relationship Approach to
Information Modeling and Analysis, P.P. Chen (ed.)
Elsevier Science Publishers B.V. (North-Holland)
©ER Institute, 1983

A DECOMPOSITION OF RELATIONS USING
THE ENTITY-RELATIONSHIP APPROACH[+]

Ilchoo Chung*, Fumio Nakamura[†], and Peter P. Chen*

*Graduate School of Management
University of California, Los Angeles
Los Angeles, California 90024
U.S.A.

[†]Systems Development Laboratory
Hitachi, Ltd., 5030 Totsuka-Machi
Totsuka-Ku, Yokohama 244
JAPAN

ABSTRACT

Recently many researchers have begun to investigate the translation process from the E-R model to conventional data models. This
paper studies some issues involved in translating from an E-R schema
to a relational schema. The notion of entity-relationship relations
is defined from a bottom-up viewpoint. Data dependencies in E-R
relations are investigated. As a vehicle for the translation process, the E-R normal forms (ER-NF) are introduced. In conjunction
with E-R normal forms, we propose a way of decomposing an E-R diagram
to arrive at a normalized E-R diagram, which has a one-to-one correspondence to a relation scheme. The E-R relations which are in ER-NF
seem to be more natural and more closely represent the real world
semantics than those obtained by conventional methods.

1.   INTRODUCTION

The Entity-Relationship (E-R) model (abbreviated into E-R model) and its
extensions have been advocated by many researchers [e.g., BROW80, CHEN76,
CHEN77b, LIEN78, SANT80, SCHE80, SCHI79, SHOS78, TING80]. There are several
reasons for increasing interest in the E-R model and its variants. First, the
E-R model allows us to capture and preserve some of the important semantics of
the real world [MCCA79, TEIC80]. Second, computer languages based on entities
and relationships are more natural to non-technical users than conventional
data manipulation languages [POON78, SHOS78]. Third, the ease of translation
from the E-R model to the conventional data models (such as hierarchical,
network, and relational models) makes the E-R model an attractive candidate for
modeling the conceptual schema in the ANSI/SPARC DBMS architectures [CHIA80,
DOGA80, SAKA80] and for handling data translation in a heterogeneous database
environment [CARD80, CHU80, GARD77, LIEN78].

[+]This research is supported in part by the National Science Foundation, Grant
No. MCS 78-20005 and MCS 77-20829.

[†]This author was a visiting scholar at UCLA from August 1, 1979 to July 30,
1980.

Perhaps the most practical use of the E-R model today is as a database design tool [CHAN80, CHEN78, DAVE80, LUSK80, ULLM80]. Information about the real world of interest is organized into an E-R schema, and then the E-R schema is translated into a hierarchical schema, a network schema, or a relational schema. In order to automate the database design process, the translation rules from the E-R Model to conventional data models have to be well-defined. Many researchers have recently begun to investigate this subject. Within this context, this paper studies some issues involved in translating from an E-R schema to a relational schema.

Several ways to translate an E-R diagram to a relational schema have been proposed [CHEN76, CHEN77, SAKA78, NG80]. Chen [CHEN76, CHEN77] suggests one-to-one mapping between each entity (or relationship) type and a relation, and gives a set of rules for translation from an E-R diagram to relations in Third Normal Form (3NF), which are meaningful and close to the real world. Sakai [SAKA78] applies the notion of first-order hierarchical decomposition [DELO78] and transitive relationships among relationship types in addition to 3NF conditions in order to implement more integrity constraints and to eliminate redundant relationship types. Ng and Paul [NG80] demonstrate another method of deriving 3NF relations from an E-R model, particularly the relationship between regular and weak entity types and between single-valued and multivalued attributes.

In addition, several researchers have worked on the equivalence of the E-R model and the relational model [LIEN80, MELK80]. Lien [LIEN80] shows a formal correspondence between the semantics of the E-R model and the semantics of the relational model to provide a theoretical foundation for supporting the coexistence of data views that are based on graphs and those that are based on relations. Melkanoff and Zaniolo [MELK80] propose a method of designing an E-R diagram by deriving a "CAZ-graph" which graphically represents FDs and MVDs among attributes. The concepts of atomic subrelation and elementary dependencies are suggested to meet the requirements of complete relatability, and these concepts are combined into a graphical representation called CAZ-graph.

This paper studies some of the issues involved in translating from an E-R schema to a relational schema. We begin by studying the mapping between E-R data values and relational data values by means of the E-R relation. Data dependencies (such as functional dependency, multivalued dependency, join dependency, etc.) are studied within the context of E-R relations. We then introduce the "entity-relationship normal form" as a basis for the translation process, and propose algorithms to arrive at the normal form.

2. RELATIONAL CONCEPTS

Attributes are symbols taken from a finite set $\{A_1, A_2,\ldots,A_n\}$. Each attribute A is associated with it a domain denoted by $DOM(A)$, which is the set of possible values for that attribute. For a set of attributes X, an X-value is an assignment of values to the attributes from their domains. A relation on the set of attributes $\{A_1,\ldots,A_n\}$ is a subset of the cross product $DOM(A_1)\times\ldots\times$

Dom(A_n). The elements of the relations are called <u>tuples</u> or <u>rows</u>. A <u>relation</u> R on $\{A_1,\ldots,A_n\}$ will be denoted by $R(A_1,\ldots,A_n)$, or $\overline{R(T)}$ where T is the set of attributes. The word <u>relation scheme</u> denotes the structure (description) of the relation. A <u>relational schema</u> is a set of relation schemes. In this paper, we will use "relation" instead of "relation scheme" when there is no confusion.

Let u be a tuple in R(T). If Y is a subset of T, the u[Y] is the tuple which contains the components of u corresponding to the elements of Y. The <u>projection</u> of R on Y, denoted by R[Y], or R(T)[Y] is defined by: R[Y]= $\{u[Y]$ uεR$\}$. Similarly, the conditional projection of R on Y by a value x for the attribute X, where $X \subseteq T$ is defined as follows: $R[x,Y]= \{u[Y] \mid u \; \varepsilon \; R$ and $u[X]=x\}$. The <u>restriction</u> R[x] of R(T) on an X-value, x, is defined to be the relation: $\{u|u\varepsilon R$ and u is a mapping on the set of attributes T such that $u[X]=x\}$.

The <u>natural join</u> is an operator that combines several relations into one. For $1\leq i\leq m$, let $R_i(T_i)$ be a relation on the set of attributes, T_i. Then $*_{i=1}^{m}R_i$ (T_i) the join of $R_1(T_1),R_2(T_2),\ldots,R_m(T_m)$ is defined to be relation:

$\{$ u$|$ u is a mapping on the set of attributes $U_{i=1}^{m}Ti$ such that all $1\leq i\leq m$, there is mapping v in $R_i(T_i)$ such that $u[T_i]=v[T_i]\}$.

If all T_i's are disjoint, then the join is the Cartesian product of the $R_i(T_i)$'s. Also if $R_i(T_i)=R_j(T_j)$, then $R_i(T_i)*R_j(T_j)=R_i(T_i) \cap R_j(T_j)$. We use the symbol, $|R(T)|$, to denote the Cardinality of the relation R(T), i.e., the number of tuples of R(T). Similarly $|R[x,Y]|$ is the number of tuples in a relation R[x,Y].

A <u>functional dependency</u> (FD), X→Y, holds in R(X,Y,Z) if each value of X in R is associated with exactly one value of Y. The equality of the X values implies the equality of the Y values. A <u>multivalued dependency</u> (MVD), denoted by X↠Y, holds for R(X,Y,Z), if and only if for every XZ-value xz in R, R[x,z,Y]=R[x,Y]. An MVD: X↠Y in R(X,Y,Z) is called trivial if $Y \subseteq X$ or Z=φ. If a nontrivial MVD: X↠Y exists, we call it a <u>strong</u> MVD if there is no FD X→Y. From a given set of FDs and MVDs we can infer new FDs and MVDs using the inference rules [AMST74, BEERI77]. We say that X is a superkey of R(T) if X → T holds for R, where X$\subseteq$T. X is a key if X is a superkey and no X'$\subset$X is.

3. <u>PROPERTIES OF THE E-R MODEL</u>

In order to translate an E-R schema into a relational schema, we have to map the E-R values into a set of relations (or just a single relation) in a specific manner. The problem involves two issues: (1) to find the correspondence between the two models; and (2) to synthesize some properties of the two models in a meaningful way. In this section we first give formal definitions of the E-R model. By combining these formal properties of the E-R model with some relational database concepts, we define E-R relations from a bottom-up viewpoint, i.e., to construct E-R relations. The following E-R diagram is used to illustrate some of these concepts.

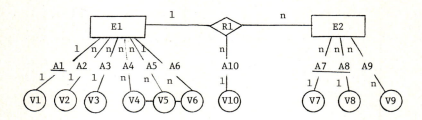

Figure 1:   An E-R Diagram

3.1   Entity-sets and Entity-relations

Let e denote an <u>entity</u> taken from the set of entities that exists in the real world and in our mind. Entities are classified into different <u>entity-sets</u>, $E_1, E_2, \ldots, E_n$. An entity-set E_i has a name associated with it and has a finite number of entities. For simplicity, we use E instead of E_i to represent an entity-set.

A <u>value-set</u> V is a set of values. An entity in E is described by one or more values taken from each of the value-sets associated with E. We use the same symbol to represent a value-set or the name of a value-set interchangeably, if there is no confusion.

An entity-set E is associated with a set of attributes, $A = \{A_1, A_2, \ldots, A_m\}$. An <u>attribute</u> A in AE is a mapping from E into a value-set V. In this paper, we assume that an attribute is associated with only <u>one</u> value-set. Four types of mappings from E into V exist in the E-R model: one-to-one, many-to-one, one-to-many, and many-to-many.

In the E-R diagram, an attribute A is represented by a string of symbols located at the end of an edge from a rectangular box, i.e., E. From A, one edge comes out which connects A to a value-set V. The type of mapping of A between E and V is specified by two symbols: N1 and N2 located on an edge between E and A, and between A and V, respectively.

> (1) N1=1 and N2=1: A is a one-to-one function E into V.
> (2) N1=n and N2=1: A is a many-to-one function from E into V.
> (3) N1=1 and N2=n: A is a one-to-many mapping from E into V.
> (4) N1=n and N2=n: A is a many-to-many mapping from E into V.

An attribute is called <u>singled-valued</u> if N2 is "1", and called <u>multivalued</u> if N2 is "n". We also express an attribute A as a relation R(E,A) where E and A represent the name of an entity-set E and a value-set V, respectively. In figure 1, we can find the following attributes for entity type E1: (1) Single-valued attributes: A1, A2, A3; (2) Multivalued attributes: A4, A5, A6. Also in Figure 1, we can easily verify that the four types of mapping exist.

When an entity-set E is associated with more than one multivalued attribute, it is not clear how to represent data values in a relation. For example, let an entity e of E be associated with m1,m2 of a value-set M, and n1,n2 of N. Let R(E,M,N) be a relation.

E	M	N
e	m1	n1
e	m2	n2

E	M	N
e	m1	n1
e	m1	n2
e	m2	n1
e	m2	n2

E	M	N
e	m1	n1
e	m2	n1
e	m2	n2

The choice among the above three and other possibilities should depend upon the relationships among value-sets. The relationships among value-sets are expressed by "relation-mapping."

Definition 1: Let C be a set of attributes, $\{A1,A2,...,Ak\}$. Let R(E,C) be a mapping from E into the Cartesian product of value-sets, $\{V1,V2,..., Vk\}$. We call C a relation-mapping iff (1) there exist some $e\varepsilon E$ such that for any two disjoint and proper subsets, X and Y of C, $R[e,X,Y] \subset R[e,X] \times R[e,Y]$, and (2) if there exist two relation-mappings C_1 and C_2, then $C_1 = C_2$ or $C_1 \cap C_2 = \phi$. In the E-R diagram, a relation-mapping is represented by a set of value-sets connected by edges. $\square$

Example: In Figure 1, $\{A4,A5,A6\}$ is a relation-mapping. The relation-mapping is also represented by a relation, R(E1,A4,A5,A6).

Definition 2: The entity-identifier K is a set of attributes, $\{K_1,K_2,..., K_m\}$, if there exist a one-to-one (total) function from E into a subset of the Cartesian product of all the value-sets $V_1,V_2,...,V_m$ associated with K_1, $K_2,...,K_m$, respectively. We can also represent an entity-identifier as a relation R(E,K). Let R(K) be R(E,K)[K]. We call R(K) an entity-identifier-set. In the E-R diagram, we explicitly show the entity-identifier K by putting an underline for all K_i's in K. When there are multiple identifiers, only one is selected. $\square$

From the definition of an entity-identifier, it immediately follows that there exists a function from an entity-identifier-set R(K) into a value-set V if a function exists from an entity-set E into V. The existence of FDs is also a consequence of the entity-identifier.

Lemma 1: Let R(E,K) and R(E,A) be relations defined on an entity-identifier K, and a single-valued attribute A of an entity-set E. An FD $K \rightarrow A$ holds in R(E,K) $*R(E,A)[K,A]$.

Proof: Omitted.

Up to this point, we have defined several notions, namely, an entity-set, entity-identifier, attribute, and value-set. We have not shown, however, how these notions are combined together to form a relation, which is our major concern. We temporarily call such a relation the "entity-relation" without giving a precise definition of it. We first intuitively characterize entity-relations as the following, and then give a formal definition of it.

(1) We should be able to select all the tuples that describe an entity "e" by some operation, e.g., R[e].

(2) We should be able to select all the relationships between any non-identifier value-sets for an entity "e" by some operations, e.g., R[e,X,Y].

(3) We should be able to select all the relationships between any value-sets, e.g., R[X,Y].

(4) We should be able to select mappings between an entity and a value-set or a subset of the Cartesian product of value-sets by some operations, e.g., R[e,X], R[e,Y,Z].

Definition 3: Let K be an entity-identifier of an entity-set E. Let $R(K,A_i)$ be a relation on a mapping A_i (i.e., an attribute) from R(K) into V_i, $1 \le i \le m$. Let $R(K,C_j)$ be a relation on a relation-mapping C_j (i.e., a set of attributes) from $R(K)$ into a subset of the Cartesian product of all the value-sets in C_j, $1 \le j \le n$. For all i and j, $A_i \cap C_j = \phi$, and $R(K,Ai)[K]=...=R(K,Cj)[K]$. Let T be $\{\overline{K},\overline{A}_1,...,A_m,C_1,...,C_n\}$. The entity-relation E(T) is a relation defined to be:

$$E(T)=R(K,A_1)*...*R(K,A_m)*R(K,C_1)*...*R(K,C_n) \qquad \square$$

Remarks: Note that K is not necessarily the key of an entity-relation. For example, the following instances have two entities and three tuples.

EMPLOYEE	NAME	SALARY	ADDRESS
entity 1 100	Smith	20k	312 Oak Street
100	Smith	20k	331 Pine Street
entity 2 200	John	30k	112 Maple Street

3.2 Relationship-sets and Relationship-relations

A <u>relationship-set</u> R is a subset of the Cartesian product of entity-sets which are related. We represent a relationship-set R as a relation, $R(E_1,E_2,...,E_m)$ or R(ER) where ER = $\{E_1,E_2,...,E_m\}$. An element r in R(ER) is called a <u>relationship</u>. In the E-R diagram a relationship-set R(ER) or R is represented by a diamond symbol. Edges from a diamond symbol connect entity-sets which are related. We use a symbol R to represent a relationship-set or the name of a relationship-set, interchangeably, if there is no confusion. Two types of mapping exist between R(ER) and an entity-set E_i in ER.

(1) One-to-one function from R(ER) into E_i.
(2) Many-to-one function from R(ER) into E_i.

For one-to-one case, $|R[e]|=1$ for any $e \varepsilon E_i$. For many-to-one case, $|R[e]|$ can be greater than 1. In the E-R diagram we use "1" and "n" to represent one-to-one and many-to-one mapping, respectively. Note that there is no one-to-many and many-to-many mapping from a relationship-set into an entity-set. In Figure 1, a one-to-one function exists from R1 into E1. The mapping between R1 and E2 is many-to-one.

A relationship-set R(ER) is associated with a set of value-sets, VR={V_1, V_2,...,V_m}, consisting of all the entity-identifier-sets of entity-sets in R and non-identifier value-sets. Only non-identifier attribute-value-set pairs are connected to a diamond symbol.

Definition 4: Let R(ER) be a relationship-set where ER is {E_1,...,E_n}. Let $R(E_1,K_1)$,...,$R(E_n,K_n)$ be relations on one-to-one mappings (i.e., entity-identifiers) K_1,...,K_n from E_1,...,E_n into V_1,...,V_n, respectively. We call a set G={K_1,...,K_n}, the general relationship-identifier of a relationship-set R(ER). The general relationship-identifier-set R(K_1,...,K_n) or R(G) is a relation defined to be:

$$R(G)=R(ER)*R(E_1,K_1)*...*R(E_n,K_n)[K_1,...,K_n].$$

A subset K of G is called the relationship-identifier if for any kεR(G)[K], |R(G)[k]| =1, and for K' K, |R(G)[k]| can be greater than one. The relationship-identifier-set R(K) is R(G)[K]. □

Example: In Figure 1, G={A1,A7,A8}. The general relationship-identifier-set R(G) for R1 is:

R(E1,E2)*R(E1,A1)*R(E2,A7,A8)[A1,A7,A8].

The relationship-identifier K is A1. The relationship-identifier-set R(K)= R(G)[A1].

Lemma 2: Let R(G) be a relation defined in Definition 4. Let K be a relationship-identifier of a relationship-set R(ER). An FD K→Y always holds in R(G), where Y=G-K.

Proof: In order to see the existence of an FD K→G-K, it suffices to show that for any two <k_1,y_1> and <k_2,y_2> in R(G), where k_1,k_2 ε R(G)[K] and y_1,$y_2$$\varepsilon$R(G) [Y], if k_1=k_2 then y_1=y_2. Assume that k_1=k_2. By definition of a relationship-identifier, any k is unique, i.e., for any kεR(G)[K], |R(G)[k]| = 1. Therefore <k_1,y_1> and <k_2,y_2> must be the same tuple, otherwise we have duplicate tuples, which is impossible. □

Example: In Figure 1, we have an FD, A1→A7A8 in R(A1,A7,A8).

A non-identifier attribute of a relationship-set is a mapping from a relationship-identifier-set into a value-set. We also represent all the attributes of a relationship-set as a set AR={A_1,...,A_n}. Then G⊆AR and also K⊆AR. Since R(ER), R(K), and R(G) are isomorphic, an A_i in AR is a mapping from R(G) or R(K) into a corresponding value-set. The relation-mapping is allowed only on those value-sets that are not entity-identifier-sets. Similarly, we define a relationship-relation as below.

Definition 5: Let G be a general relationship-identifier, and R(G) be a general relationship-identifier-relation (or -set). Let R(G,A_i) be a relation defined on a mapping A_i (i.e., an attribute), from R(G) into V_i, 1≤i≤m. Let R(G,C_j) be a relation defined on a relation-mapping C_j (i.e., a set of attributes) from R(G) into the Cartesian product of all the value-sets in C_j, 1≤j≤n.

For all i and j, $A_i \cap C_j = \phi$, and $R(K,Ai)[K] = \ldots = R(K,Cj)[K]$. Let T be $\{G, A_1, \ldots, A_m, C_1, \ldots, C_n\}$. The relationship-relation, $R(T)$ is a relation defined to be:

$$R(T) = R(G,A_1) * \ldots * R(G,A_m) * R(G,C_1) * \ldots * R(G,C_n).$$ □

4.   DATA DEPENDENCIES IN E-R RELATIONS

So far our interest has been focused on describing each entity (or relationship) by means of mappings between an entity-identifier-set and non-identifier value-sets. However, data dependencies in E-R relations have not been studied. In this section, we investigate several types of data dependencies that exist in entity or relationship-relations: FDs, MVDs, join dependency, and first order hierarchical decomposition (FOHD).

We say that a relation $R(K,A)$ on a mapping A (i.e., an attribute) is _preserved_ in an E-R relation $R(T)$ iff $R(K,A) = R(T)[K,A]$. Before we study data dependencies in the E-R relation, we first show that all the mappings between an entity-identifier-set and value-sets (or between a relationship-identifier-set and value-sets) are preserved in entity-relations (or relationship-relations).

Lemma 3:   Let $R(K,A_i)$ and $R(K,C_j)$ be relations defined on a mapping A_i and a relation-mapping C_j, respectively, for $1 \leq i \leq m$ and $1 \leq j \leq n$. $R(K,A_i)$ and $R(K,C_j)$ are preserved in E-R relations.

Proof: In order to prove the lemma, it suffices to show that the set of relations (i.e., all the $R(K,A_i)$'s and $R(K,C_j)$'s) has a lossless join. Let $k \varepsilon R(K)$. By definition of an entity-relation,

$$R[k,A_1,\ldots,A_m,C_1,\ldots,C_n] = R[k,A_1] * \ldots * R[k,A_m] * R[k,C_1] * \ldots * R[k,C_n].$$

Hence we have a full FOHD (due to [DELO78]), $K:A_1|\ldots|A_m|C_1|\ldots|C_n|$, and as a result, a set of MVDs, $K \twoheadrightarrow A_1, \ldots, K \twoheadrightarrow A_m, K \twoheadrightarrow C_1, \ldots, K \twoheadrightarrow C_n$. Let $R_1, R_2, \ldots, R_p$ be $R(K,A_1), R(K,A_2), \ldots, R(K,C_n)$, respectively. A set R_1 and R_2 has a lossless join since $R_1 \cap R_2 = K$, $K \twoheadrightarrow KA_1$, $K \twoheadrightarrow KA_2$, and $KA_1 \cup (R_1 \cap R_2) = R_1$ and $KA_2 \cup (R_1 \cap R_2) = R_2$ (By corollary 6 in [AHO79]). Assume a set $\{R_1, \ldots, R_k\}$ has a lossless join. By union and augmentation rule of MVD, we have an MVD, $K \twoheadrightarrow KA_1 A_2 \ldots$. Similarly, a set $\{R_1, \ldots, R_k, R_{k+1}\}$ has a lossless join. Therefore for all $1 \leq i \leq m$ and $1 \leq j \leq n$, $R(K,A_i)$ and $R(K,C_j)$ are preserved in $R(K,A_1,\ldots,A_m,C_1,\ldots,C_n)$.   □

In the following sections, attributes in E-R relations are grouped into four different types. We represent an entity (or relationship) relation as $R(K,S,M,P)$ where K is an entity (or relationship) identifier, S is a set of single-valued attributes, P is a set of one-to-many multivalued attributes, M is a set of many-to-many multivalued attributes. We assume that K,S,M,P are disjoint.

4.1 Functional Dependencies in E-R Relations

Some FDs are implied in E-R relations, e.g., K→S. But FDs cannot exist among certain attributes due to conflicts. Certain FDs are not implied in E-R relations, but may exist. The following table summarizes FDs among some combinations of attributes. Let S',S'',M',M'',P',P'' are disjoint, and S',S'' ⊂ S, M',M'' ⊂ M, P',P'' ⊂ P.

Table 1: FDs in E-R relations

LHS \ RHS	K	S''	M''	P''
K		I	X	X
S'	X	V	X	X
M'	X	V	V	X
P'	I	I	V	V

I: Implied, V: Not implied, but may exist,
X: Cannot exist

Lemma 4, below, shows one of the cases in Table 1.

Lemma 4: Let S'⊆S. An FD K→S' always holds in R(K,S,M,P,).

Proof: By Lemma 1 and 3, any $R_i(K,S_i)$ is preserved in R, where $S_i \varepsilon S$. By union rule of FD, K→S' holds. □

We can make similar proofs using Lemma 3 and the definition of E-R relations, and omit the rest of cases. The FDs among multivalued attributes indicate that one or more relation-mappings exist.

Lemma 5: Let X,Y⊂M and X∩Y=φ. If an FD X→Y holds in R(K,S,M,P), then XY is a relation-mapping.

Proof: Assume XY is not a relation-mapping. Then R[k,XY]=R[k,X]×R[k,Y]. Since X and Y are multivalued attributes, |R[x,Y]| ≥1. Hence, we obtain X≠Y, a contradiction. □

4.2 Multivalued Dependencies in E-R Relations

Lemma 6 through 11 show the existence of MVDs in E-R relations. The result is that most MVDs are implied in E-R relations, i.e., we can identify them from the E-R diagram.

Lemma 6: A strong MVD K→→MP always holds in R(K,S,M,P).

Proof: Omitted □

Lemma 7: Let X,Y⊂S. A strong MVD X→→Y does not hold in E(K,S,M,P).

Proof: By Lemma 1, $K \to X$ and $K \to Y$. Let Z be SMP-XY. Assume $X \twoheadrightarrow Y$. Then $\overline{R[x,Y]} = R[x,k,z,Y]$ and $R[x,k,z,Y]$ can have $y_1, y_2, \ldots, y_m$, m>1. Hence we obtain $K \not\to Y$, which is a contradiction. □

Lemma 8: Let $X, Y \subset P$ and $X \cap Y = \phi$. A strong MVD $X \twoheadrightarrow Y$ always holds in E(K,S,M,P).

Proof: Since $X, Y \subset P$, $X \to K$ and $Y \to K$. By Lemma 1, $K \twoheadrightarrow X$ and $K \twoheadrightarrow Y$. By transitivity and FD-MVD rule 1, $X \twoheadrightarrow Y$. □

Lemma 9: Let $X \subseteq S$ and $Y \subseteq P$. An MVD $X \twoheadrightarrow Y$ does not hold in E(K,S,M,P).

Proof: By definition of an entity-relation, $K \to S$, $P \to K$, $S' \not\to K$, and $S' \not\to P$, where $S' \subseteq S$. Assume $X \twoheadrightarrow Y$. Since $S' \not\to P$, $X \twoheadrightarrow Y$ must be a strong MVD. Let W be SMP-XY. Consider $E[x,Y,K,W]$. Since $X \twoheadrightarrow Y$, $E[x,Y,K,W] = E[x,Y] \times E[x,K,W]$. Since $X \twoheadrightarrow Y$ is a strong MVD, $E[x,Y] = \{y_1, y_2, \ldots, y_m\}$ and m>1. Also $E[x,y_1, K,W] = E[x,y_2,K,W] = \ldots = E[x,y_m,K,W]$. Hence $E[x,y_1,K] = \ldots = E[x,y_m,K]$. Let $E[x,y,K]$ be $k_1, k_2, \ldots, k_n$. If n=1, then it implies $X \to K$, obtaining a contradiction. If n>1, then $Y \not\to K$, which is also a contradiction. Therefore, $X \not\twoheadrightarrow Y$ in E(K,S,M,P). □

Lemma 10: MVDs $X \twoheadrightarrow Y$ and $Y \twoheadrightarrow X$ do not hold in E(K,S,M,P), where $X \subseteq P$ and $Y \subseteq M$.

Proof: Omitted. □

Lemma 11: If a strong MVD $X \twoheadrightarrow Y$ holds in E(K,S,M,P), where $X, Y \subseteq M$ and $X \cap Y = \phi$, then $\overline{E[K,X,Y]} = E[K] \times E[X] \times E[Y]$.

Proof: By definition 3, and Lemma 1, $K \twoheadrightarrow X$ and $K \twoheadrightarrow Y$. By the projectivity of $\overline{MVD}$, $X \twoheadrightarrow Y$, $K \twoheadrightarrow X$, and $K \twoheadrightarrow Y$ also hold in R(K,X,Y), where R(K,X,Y)=E[K,X,Y]. By definition of MVD, $R[k,Y] = R[k,x,Y]$. Also $X \twoheadrightarrow Y$ implies that $R[x,Y] = R[k,x,Y]$. Hence we obtain $R[k,Y] = R[x,Y]$. Since k and x are an arbitrary K-value and X-value, respectively, the only case where $R[k,Y] = R[x,Y]$ holds is R(K,X,Y)=$R[K] \times R[X] \times R[Y]$. □

4.3 E-R Relation, Join Dependency, and FOHD

We say that a relation R satisfies the join dependency $*R(R_1, \ldots, R_n)$ if $R = R[R_1] * \ldots * R[R_n]$, that is, when we project R onto the sets of attributes $\{R_i\}$, then join the results, we get back no more than we started with. As shown in Definition 3 and 5, we have constructed R (i.e., E(T) or R(T)) by joins of smaller relations whose common attribute is the identifier. Hence the join dependency is a way of characterizing entity-relationship relations. The mappings between an entity-identifier-set and value-sets are also MVD statements since the join dependency j, $*(R_1, \ldots, R_n)$ is implied by MVD(j), the set of multivalued dependencies that j logically implies, that is, which hold in any relation in which j holds [FAGI80].

As shown in Lemma 3, entity-relationship relations can also be viewed from the first order hierarchical decomposition (FOHD) [DELO78]. A relation where $X, Y_1, Y_2, \ldots, Y_k, W$ are disjoint sets of attributes, obeys the FOHD if for every X-value we have:

$$R[x, Y_1, Y_2, \ldots, Y_p] = R[x, Y_1] \times \ldots \times R[x, Y_p]$$

This condition is equivalent to the condition:

$$R[X,Y_1,Y_2,\ldots,Y_p]=R[X,Y_1]*\ldots*R[X,Y_p]$$

by Proposition 1 of [DELO78]. In entity-relationship-relations, a FOHD k: $A_1|A_2|\ldots|C_n$ holds since the latter condition is equivalent to the definition of an entity-relationship relation when X=K and $Y_1,\ldots,Y_p$ are $A_1,\ldots,C_n$. In entity-relationship relations, we have a full FOHD since W is empty. A full FOHD implies a set of MVDs. To summarize, entity-relationship relations can also be characterized in terms of sets of FDs, MVDs, join dependencies, and FOHDs.

5.   ENTITY-RELATIONSHIP NORMAL FORMS

Our goal in this section is to describe our approach to combining certain notions together, namely, key, FD, entity-identifier, relationship-identifier, and entity-relationship relation. We first outline some basic ideas and then define the entity-relationship normal form (ER-NF). In the next section an algorithm to arrive at the ER-NF is suggested as an extension of this effort.

First, we make the notion of entity-relationship-identifier compatible with the key of relations. Intuitively, if these two notions are equivalent, it would allow us to implement a relational database based on the E-R constructs, e.g., we may formulate a query using the E-R diagram to the relational database. Second, we consider a form where all the functional dependencies are implied by the entity or relationship-identifier. The complexity of data dependencies in E-R relations would be redued by decomposing them into simple and basic structures. The relational normalization theory has aimed at this goal by means of various normal forms [CODD70, 72, FAGI77, ZANI76, etc.]. Third, we adopt the universal relation assumption for each entity or relationship-relation which is not yet normalized, i.e., entity-relationship relation that have been defined in Section 3. However, we do not consider that the universal relation exists a priori but rather view that the universal relation as constructed by some rules. Our view of the universal relation assumption is from the bottom-up rather than starting from a giant relation, which has many implications but is hard to grasp intuitively. We believe that by assuming a large relation for each E-R relation (or local relation) we can express some important semantics more freely, e.g., multiple relationship types among a given set of entity types. Based on these considerations, we introduce the entity-relationship normal form.

5.1   Entity-Relationship Normal Form

Definition 6: An entity relation, E(T), is said to be in Entity Normal Form (E-NF) if and only if the following two conditions are satisfied in E(T).

   (1)   All the attributes are single-valued.
   (2)   The left hand side (LHS) of every non-trivial FD in E(T) includes at least one entity-identifier.   □

Example: In the E-R diagram in Appendix I, entity-relation EMPLOYEE is not in
E-NF since ADDRESS is a multivalued attribute, and therefore it violates condition (1). PROJECT, however, is in E-NF since the only FDs in the entity-relation are: PROJ-NO→P-NAME and PROJ-NO→TYPE. It meets both conditions.

Definition 7: A relationship relation, R(T), is said to be in Relationship
Normal Form (R-NF) if and only if the following two conditions are satisfied in
R(T):

   (1) All the attributes in R are single-valued attributes.
   (2) The LHS of every non-trivial FD in R includes at least one rela-
        tionship-identifier. □

Example: In the diagram of Appendix I, EMP-PROJ is in R-NF since EMP-NO is a
relationship identifier and PROGRESS is a single-valued attribute.

5.2 Relationship Between ER-NF and Other Normal Forms

   We consider two normal forms, Boyce-Codd Normal Form (BCNF) and Fourth
Normal Form (4NF). A relation is in BCNF if for any non-trivial FD $X{\to}Y$, X is a
superkey of the relation. Let $X{\twoheadrightarrow}Y$ be any nontrivial MVD in R. R is in 4NF if
for all such MVD, X is a superkey of R. We can easily see that E-NF relations
are always in BCNF. The following lemma shows that.

Lemma 12: E-NF relations are in BCNF.

Proof: Let K be an entity identifier and T be the set of all the attributes
in E. Let X and Y be the LHS and RHS of any FD in E, respectively. By condi-
tion 2, $X \supseteq K$. By Lemma 1 and condition 1, $K{\to}\{T{-}K\}$. Since $X{\supseteq}K$, $X{\to}K$. Since
$X{\to}K$ and $K{\to}\{T{-}K\}$, we have $X{\to}T$. Therefore, for any FD $X{\to}Y$, X is a superkey of E.
This implies that E is in BCNF. □

   Syntactically, E-NF is close to BCNF, but it is not true that every BCNF
relation is also in E-NF. The distinction depends upon whether the key of a
relation is an entity-identifier or not. For instance, suppose that we have an
entity-relation EMPLOYEE(EMPLOYEE-NUMBER,ADDRESS), and further assume that
ADDRESS→EMPLOYEE-NUMBER holds. Clearly, the relation EMPLOYEE is in BCNF. But
since EMPLOYEE-NUMBER is an entity-identifier and ADDRESS is a multivalued
attribute, the EMPLOYEE relation is not in E-NF.

   Based on several practical examples that we examined, they seem to be also
in 4NF. However, from a formal point of view, there is a possibility that they
are not in 4NF. To make our discussion formally complete, we shall identify
such a condition that prevents an E-NF relation to be in 4NF.

Lemma 13: Let R(X,Y,Z) be a BCNF relation, where X, Y and Z are disjoint sets
of attributes. Let K be a key of R. If a strong MVD $X{\twoheadrightarrow}Y$ holds for R, then K
$\supseteq$ YZ.

Proof: Assume $K \not\supseteq Y$. Let $Y{=}Y_1Y_2$ such that $K \supseteq Y_1$ and $K \cap Y_2{=}\phi$ ($Y_2{\neq}\phi$). Let
$R[x,Y]{=}Y_0$ and $R[x,Z]{=}Z_0$. If $y_1y_2, y_1y_2' \in Y_0$ and $z^1 \in Z_0$, then both (x,y_1y_2,z)
and (x,y_1y_2',z) are tuples of R since $X{\twoheadrightarrow}Y$. This violates the FD; $XY_1Z{\to}Y_2$ since

there are two Y_2-values, y_2 and y_2', for the same XY_1Z-value xy_1z. ($XY_1Z{\to}Y_2$ is derived by $K{\to}Y_2$ and $K \subseteq XY_1Z$.) Therefore, if $y_1y_2 \varepsilon Y_o$, then $y_1y_2' \varepsilon Y_o$. This implies $XY_1{\to}Y_2$. $XY_1{\not\to}\bar{Z}$ is obvious by $X{\to\to}Y$. This contradicts the assumption that R is in BCNF. Hence, we obtain $K \supseteq Y$. Similarly, $K \supseteq Z$. Therefore, $K \supseteq YZ$ is obtained. $\square$

Lemma 13 states that if a strong MVD: $X{\to\to}Y$ holds for a BCNF relation $R(X,Y,Z)$, every key of R includes Y and Z. Since an entity-identifier is a key in an E-NF relation, every identifier of R includes Y and Z if R is an E-NF relation.

6. ER-NF DESIGN ALGORITHM

In this section, we introduce an algorithm by which we can arrive at ER-NF entity-relation types (including attributes and value-sets) and also ER-NF relations. Once all the entity and relationship types are normalized, each entity or relationship type is directly translated into a relation scheme.

6.1 Input to the Algorithm

The design algorithm uses three types of input for each entity or rela-tionship type to be normalized. From the E-R diagram, we first group attri-butes into three different classes: identifier, single-valued, and multi-valued. And then, FDs which are not implied in the E-R diagram are identified. Particularly the algorithm requires that FDs satisfy three conditions: (1) an FD, f in F (the set of FDs that includes implied FDs) cannot be derived by F-f using FD, MVD, and FD-MVD inference rules; (2) the RHS of f is a single attri-bute; and (3) f does not have entity-identifier attributes. The input to the algorithm is summarized as the followings:

(1) Attributes: K (Entity-identifier attributes); K'(Candidate entity-identifiers); S(Single-valued non-identifiers attributes); M(Multi-valued many-to-many attributes); P(Multivalued one-to-many attributes and $P \cap C_i = \phi$); P'(Multivalued one-to-many attributes including those attributes in relation-mappings).

(2) Relation-mappings: $C=\{C_i\}$, where C_i is a relation-mapping.

(3) FDs: $F=\{<a,b>\}$, where "a" and "b" are LHS and RHS attributes, respec-tively, and $<a,b>$ satisfies the above three conditions.

6.2 Output of the Algorithm

As the output of the algorithm, we obtain a set of entity types and rela-tionship types which are decomposed from the original entity and relationship type. Also a set of relation schemes are derived by the algorithm.

(1) Entity types: $ES=\{<a,b>\}$, where "a" is the set of entity-identifiers and "b" is the set of non-identifier attributes.

(2) Relationship types: RS={<a,b,c>}, where "a" is the set of relation-
     ship-identifiers, "a" and "b" constitute the general relationship-
     identifier, and "c" is the set of non-identifier attributes. If "b"
     and "c" are empty, the relationship type is one-to-one, i.e., every
     attribute is a relationship-identifier.

(3) Relation schemes: R($\underline{A}$,B), where R is a relation name, A is the key,
     and B is the set of non-key attributes.

6.3 Design Algorithm

    The algorithm consists of three steps. In the first step, certain attri-
butes are identified, which will be shifted to entity types. Also, non-identifier attributes are identified. The second step is to generate relationship
types with identifiers and non-identifier attributes. At this point, we can
draw an E-R diagram for the entity and relationship types obtained. The final
step is simply to translate each entity or relationship type into a relation
scheme.

Step 1:   Construct entity types

    1.   ES={ϕ}; F'=UUF;   C'=UC; /* U is the union operator */
    2.   ES=ESU{<K',S-F'>}; S'=S∩F';
          /* Find non-identifier attributes and their entity-identifiers */
    3.   For all wεF'
             if $\exists$ x={<w,b_1>,...,<w,b_n>} F and $b_i \notin$ UU(F-x), $1 \leq i \leq n$,
                then do;
                      ES=ESU{<w,{b_1U...Ub_n}>};
                      F=F-x; C'=C'-Ux; S'$\stackrel{n}{=}$S'-Ux;
                      For all cεC if X$\subseteq$c then c=c-{b_1,...,b_n};
                      end;
          /* Remaining attributes become an entity identifier of entity types
              created, and the new entity types have no non-identifier attri-
              butes */
    4.   For all wε(S'UC'UMUP), ES=ESU{<w,ϕ>};
end Step 1;

Step 2:   Construct relationship types

    1.   RS={ϕ}; For all mεM, RS=RSU{<{K,m},ϕ,ϕ>};
    2.   For all pεP, RS=RSU{<p,K,ϕ>};
          /* Find non-identifier attributes and their relationship identifiers
          */
    3.   W={w | <w,b>εF and w is not a singleton};
    4.   For all wεW, if $\exists$ x={<w,b_1>,...,<w,b_n>} F and $b_i \notin$ UU(F-x), $1 \leq i \leq n$
                then do; RS=RSU{<w,ϕ,{b_1U...Ub_n}>}; F=F-x;
                      For all cε C, if Ux$\subseteq$c then c=c-{b_i,...,b_n};
                      ES=ES-{b_1,...,b_n};   end;
          /*Decompose relation-mappings: Attributes which are functionally
          determined by other attributes are grouped together as an all-
          identifier relationship type (many-to-many) */

5. For all cεC, do; w=c;
      for all <a,b>εF if b$\subset$c then c=c-b;
      if c=ϕ then c={w_1};   /* w={$w_1,\ldots,w_n$} */
      /* If c has one-to-many multivalued attributes, then a rela-
      tionship type is created for each attribute */
      X=c$\cap$P';
      if X$\neq\phi$ then do; for all xεX , ES=ESU{<x,ϕ>};
                     for all xεX, RS=RSU{<x,K,ϕ>}; end;
           else RS=RSU{<cUK,ϕ,ϕ>};
      end;
      /* Eliminate loops (e.g., A→B→C→A), and instead, create one-to-
      one relationship types (each attribute becomes a relationship-
      identifier) */
6. For all w={<x_1,x_2>,<x_2,x_3>,...,<x_{p-2},x_{p-1}>,<x_{p-1},x_p>}$\subseteq$F
      such that x_1 = x_p, and for any other loop w'$\subset$F, Uw $\cap$ Uw'=ϕ,
      do; F=F-{w}; RS=RSU{<Uw,ϕ,ϕ>};
      for all yεUw, if $\nexists$ <a,b> ε F such that yεb, then RS=RS
      U{<K,y,ϕ>}; end;
  /* Create many-to-one relationship types using FDs. For those
      attributes which do not appear in any RHS of FDs, create re-
      lationship types which connect to the original entity type */
7. For all sεS', if there is no <a,b>εF such that s$\subset$b, then RS=RS
   U{<K,s,ϕ>};
8. For all <a,b>εF, if $\exists$<a',b,ϕ>εRS such that a=a',
      then do; RS=RSU{<a',b'Ub,ϕ>}; RS=RS-{<a',b',ϕ>}; end;
end Step 2;

Step 3: Define relation schemes

1. For all <a,b>εES,
      if a=K then E becomes the relation name;
          else aUb becomes the relation name;
      "a" is the key of the relation;
      "b" is a set of non-key attributes;
2. For all <a,b,c>εRS,
      "a" is the key of the relation;
      aUb becomes the relation name;
      "b" and "c" are non-key attributes;
end Step 3;

6.4 An Example

The following E-R diagram is used to illustrate the algorithm.

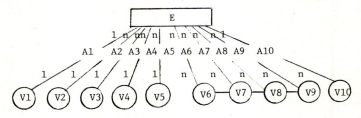

Figure 2: An Example

We assume that there exist four FDs which satisfy the three conditions (see 6.1): A3→A4, A4→A3, A4→A5, A6A7→A8. From the E-R diagram, we can see a relation-mapping. Single-valued and multivalued attributes can be located by "1" or "n" on the edge between an attribute and a value-set.

Input: F ={<A3,A4>,<A4,A3>,<A4,A5>,<A6A7,A8>}

K'=K={A1}^{*1} S={A2,A3,A4,A5}   M={φ}^{*2}

P'=P={A10}   C={A6,A7,A8,A9}

*1   There is only one entity-identifier.
*2   No one-to-many (multivalued) attributes are in relation-mappings.

Step 1:   We obtain the following entity types.

ES = {<A1,A2>,<A4,A5>,<A3,φ>,<A6,φ>,<A7,φ>,<A8,φ>,<A9,φ><A10,φ>}

Note that φ indicates there are no non-identifier attributes.

Step 2:   We obtain the following relatinship types in sequence.

1.   <A10,A1,φ>: A10 is the relationship identifier. The general relationship-identifier is A10,A1.

2.   <A6A7,φ,A8>: Since <A8,φ> was an entity type which was created in Step 1, <A8,φ> is removed from ES.

3.   <A1A6A7A9,φ,φ>: This relationship type is created by attributes in the relation-mapping. Attributes which are the RHS of FDs are not included in this relationship type.

4.   <{A3,A4},φ,φ>: This relationship type has two relationship-identifiers, namely, A3 and A4. The two FDs A3→A4 and A4→A3 form a loop.

5.   <A1,A3,φ>: Since A3 and A4 form a loop, any one attribute is connected to the original entity type.

Step 3:   As a final output of the algorithm, we arrive at the following seven relation schemes.

E($\underline{A1}$,A2),   A1A3($\underline{A1}$,A3),   A4A5($\underline{A4}$,A5),   A10A1($\underline{A10}$,A1),   A6A7A8($\underline{A6A7}$,A8)

A1A6A7A9($\underline{A1A6A7A9}$),   A3A4($\underline{A3}$,$\underline{A4}$)[*1]

*1 Each attribute is a key of the relation.

We can easily verify that each entity or relationship type in ES and RS is in E-NF and R-NF, respectively.

6.5   Diagrammatic Procedure

The algorithm in 6.3 can be followed diagrammatically by creating and deleting appropriate entity or relationship types. Each element in ES and RS corresponds to an entity or relationship type. Instead of describing the whole procedure, which is basically the same as the algorithm, we present a diagrammatic version of the example in section 6.4.

Step 1:   At the end of step 1, we have entity types which are not yet connected via relationship types. For simplicity, if an entity type has just entity-identifier attribute, we omit the attribute in the diagram.

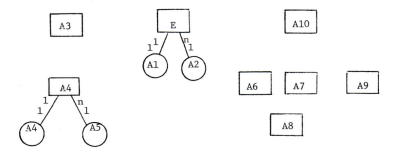

Step 2:   At the end of step 2, a complete E-R diagram can be drawn from ES and RS.

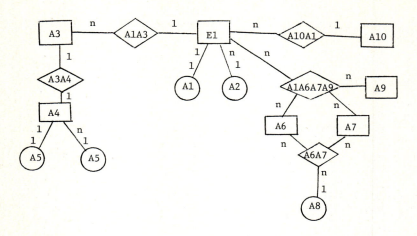

7.   CONCLUSIONS

In this paper, we have studied several issues involved in translating an
E-R schema into a relational schema.   The entity-relationship-relation was
defined from a bottom-up viewpoint.   The data dependencies in E-R relations
were investigated.   As a vehicle for the translation process, we introduced E-R
normal forms.   In conjunction with ER-NFs, we proposed a way of decomposing an
E-R diagram to arrive at a normalized E-R diagram.   The ER-NF relations seem to
possess one major advantage: Relations derived from the E-R diagram seem to be
more natural than those obtained by the conventional methods.

ACKNOWLEDGEMENT

The authors would like to thank D.S. Parker, Jr. for his valuable comments.

APPENDIX I

Entity-Relationship Relation

E-R Diagram

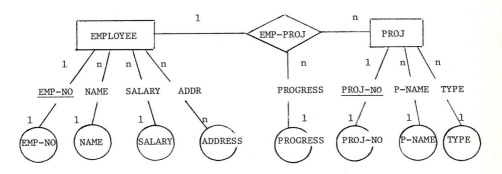

Entity-relations (schemes)

    EMPLOYEE (EMP-NO, NAME, SALARY, ADDRESS)
    PROJECT (PROJ-NO, P-NAME, TYPE)

Relationship-relation (scheme)

    EMP-PROJ (EMP-NO, PROJ-NO, PROGRESS)

Entity-identifiers

    In entity type EMPLOYEE: EMP-NO
    In entity type PROJECT: PROJ-NO

Multivalued attribute: ADDRESS

Single-valued attributes: All the attributes except ADDRESS

BIBLIOGRAPHY

[AHO79]   Aho, A. V., Berri, C., and Ullmann, J. D., The Theory of Joins in Relational Databases, ACM Transactions on Database Systems, Vol. 4, No. 3, September 1979, pp. 297-314

[AMST74] Amstrong, W. W., Dependency Structures of Data-Base Relationships, Proc. of IFIP74. North Holland, 1974, pp. 580-583.

[BEERI77] Beeri, C., Fagin, R., and Howard, H., A Complete Axiomatization for Functional and Multivalued Dependencies, Proc. ACM-SIGMOD Conference, Toronto, August 1977, pp. 7-61.

[BEERI78] Beeri, C., Bernstein, P., and Goodman, N., A Sophisticates Introduction to Database Normalization Theory, Proc. of 4th VLDB Conference, September 13-15, Berlin, 1978, pp. 113-124.

[BROW80] Brown, R. R., and Ramey, T. L., The Concept and Practice of ERA Information Modeling, in Chen, P. (ed.), Entity-Relationship Approach to Systems Analysis and Design, North-Holland, Amsterdam, 1980.

[CARD80] Cardenas, A. F. and Pirahesh, The E-R Model in a Heterogeneous Data Base Management System Network Architecture, in Chen, P. (ed.), North-Holland, Amsterdam, 1980.

[CHAN80] Chan, E. P. F. and Lochovsky, A Graphical Database Design Aid Using the Entity-Relationship Model, in Chen, P. (ed.), Entity-Relationship Approach to Systems Analysis and Design, North-Holland, Amsterdam, 1980.

[CHEN76] Chen, P. P., The Entity-Relationship Model: Towards a Unified View of Data, ACM TODS, Vol. 1, No. 1, March 1976, pp. 9-36.

[CHEN77] Chen, P. P., Entity-Relationship Approach to Logical Data Base Design, Monograph Series, Q.E.D. Information Sciences,

[CHEN77b] Chen, P. P., The Entity-Relationship Model: A Basis for Enterprise View of Data, Proc. of National Computer Conference, Vol. 46, AFIPS Press, 1977, pp. 77-84.

[CHEN78] Chen, P. P., Applications of the Entity-Relationship Model, NYU Symposium on Database Design, May 1978.

[CHIA80] Chiang, T. C., A Data Base Management System with an E-R Conceptual Model, in Chen, P. (ed.), Entity-Relationship Approach to Systems Analysis and Design, North-Holland, Amsterdam, 1980.

[CHU80]   Chu, W. W. and To, V. T., A Hierarchical Conceptual Data Model for Data Translation in a Heterogeneous Database System, in Chen, P. (ed.), Entity-Relationship Approach to Systems Analysis and Design, North-Holland, Amsterdam, 1980.

[CODD70] Codd, E. F., A Relational Model of Data for Large Shared Data Banks, Comm. of ACM, Vol. 13, No. 6, June 1970, pp. 377-387.

[CODD72] Codd, E. F., Further Normalization of the Data Base Relational Model, in Data Base Systems (R. Rustin, ed.), Prentice-Hall, Englewood Cliffs, N.J., 1972, pp. 33-64.

[DAVE80] Davenport, R. A., The Application of Data Analysis - Experience with the Entity-Relationship Approach, in Chen, P. (ed.), Entity-Relationship Approach to Systems Analysis and Design, North-Holland, Amsterdam, 1980.

[DELO78] Delobel, C., Normalization and Hierarchical Dependencies in the Relational Data Model, ACM Transactions on Database Systems, Vol. 3, No. 3, September 1978, pp. 201-222.

[DOGA80] Dogac A. and Ozkarahan, E. A., A Generalized DBMS Implementation on a Database Machine, Proc. of 1980 ACM-SIGMOD Conference, Santa Monica, California, May 1980, pp. 133-143.

[FAGI77] Fagin, R., Multivalued Dependencies and a New normal Form for Relational Databases, ACM TODS, Vol. 2, No. 3, September 1977, pp. 262-278.

[FAGI80] Fagin, R., Mendelson, A. O., and Ullmann, J. D., A Simplified Universal Relation Assumption and Its Properties, IBM Technical Report. RJ2900 (36596), November 14, 1980.

[GARD77] Gardarin, G. and Bihan, J. Le, An Approach Toward a Virtual Database Protocol for Computer Network, Proc. of AICA '77, Pisa, Italy, 1977.

[LIEN78] Lien, Y. E. and Ying, J. H., Design of a Distributed Entity-Relationship Database System, Proc. of IEEE 2nd International Computer Software and Applications Conference, Chicago, November 1978.

[LIEN80] Lien, Y., On the Semantics of the Entity-Relationship Data Model, in: Chen, P. (ed.), Entity-Relationship Approach to Systems Analysis and Design, North Holland, Amsterdam, 1980.

[LUSK80] Lusk, E. L., Overbeek, R. A. and Parrello, A Practical Design Methodology for the Implementation of IMS Databases, using the Entity-Relationship Model, Proc. of 1980 ACM-SIGMOD Conference, Santa Monica, California, May 1980, pp. 9-21.

170   *I. Chung, F. Nakamura and P.P. Chen*

[MELK80] Melkanoff, M. A. and Zaniolo, Decomposition of Relations and Synthesis of Entity-Relationship Diagrams, in: Chen, P. (ed.), Entity-Relationship Approach to Systems Analysis and Design, North-Holland, Amsterdam, 1980.

[MCCA79] McCarthy, W. E., An Entity-Relationship View of Accounting Models, The Accounting Review 54, October 1979, pp. 667-687.

[NG80] Ng, P. and Paul, J., A Formal Definition of Entity-Relationship Models, in Chen P. (ed.), Entity-Relationship Approach to Systems Analysis and Design, North-Holland, Amsterdam, 1980.

[POON78] Poonen, G., CLEAR: A Conceptual Language for Entities and Relationships, Proc. of International Conference of Management of Data, Italy, August 1978; Technical Report, R&D Group, Digital Equipment Corporation.

[SAKA78] Sakai, H., On the Optimization of an Entity-Relationship Model, Proc. of 3rd U.S.A. - Japan Computer Conference, October 1978, pp. 145-149.

[SAKA80] Sakai, H., Entity-Relationship Approach to the Conceptual Schema Design, Proc. of 1980 ACM-SIGMOD Conference, Santa Monica, California, May 1980, pp. 1-8.

[SANT80] Dos Santos, C. S., Neuhold, E. J. and Futardo, A. L., A Data Type Approach to the Entity-Relationship Model, in: Chen, P. (ed.), Entity-Relationship Approach to Systems Analysis and Design, North-Holland, Amsterdam, 1980.

[SCHE80] Scheuermann, P., Schiffner, G. and Weber H., Abstraction Capabilities and Invariant Properties Modeling within the Entity-Relationship Approach, in Chen, P. (ed.), Entity-Relationship Approach to Systems Analysis and Design, North-Holland, Amsterdam, 1980.

[SCHI79] Schiffner, G. and Schuermann, P., Multiple View and Abstractions with an Extended Entity-Relationship Model, Journal of Computer Languages, Vol. 4, pp. 139-154.

[SHOS78] Shoshani, A., CABLE: A Language Based on the Entity-Relationship Model, Presented on the Conference of Database Management (oral presentation only), Israel, August 1978; Working Paper, Computer Science and Applied Mathematics Department, Lawrence Berkeley Laboratory.

[TEIC80] Teichroew, D. et. al., Application of the Entity-Relationship Approach to Information Systems Modeling, in Chen, P. (ed.), Entity-Relationship Approach to Systems Analysis and Design, North-Holland, Amsterdam, 1980.

[TING80]   Ting, T. C., Some Other Potential Uses of the E-R Model, in Chen, P. (ed.), <u>Entity-Relationship Approach to Systems Analysis and Design</u>, North Holland, Amsterdam, 1980.

[ULLM80]   Ullmann, J. D., <u>Principles of Database Systems</u>, Computer Science Press, January 1980.

[ZANI76]   Zaniolo, C., Analysis and Design of Relational Schemata for Database Systems, <u>Computer Methodology Group Report</u>, Computer Science Department, UCLA-ENG-7669, June 1976.

Entity-Relationship Approach to
Information Modeling and Analysis, P.P. Chen (ed.)
Elsevier Science Publishers B.V. (North-Holland)
©ER Institute, 1983

AN EXTENDED ENTITY-RELATIONSHIP MODEL AND ITS USE ON A DEFENSE PROJECT

NEIL W. WEBRE

COMPUTER SCIENCES CORPORATION   *DEPARTMENT OF COMPUTER SCIENCE & STATISTICS
APPLIED TECHNOLOGY DIVISION   CALIFORNIA POLYTECHNIC STATE UNIVERSITY
P. O. BOX 7   AND SAN LUIS OBISPO, CALIFORNIA 93407
PRINCE GEORGE, VIRGINIA 23875   U. S. A.

ABSTRACT: The basic E-R approach is extended by a) a redefinition of existence dependencies, and b) development of
classification schemes for relationships which classify them
in each of three independent categories - mapping class,
restriction class, and completeness class. The result is a
rich composite classification scheme for relationships. The
Department of The Army's Standard Ports System - Enhanced is
described, as is the application of the extended E-R approach
to it. Significant points of the design effort are identified and discussed.

1 INTRODUCTION

Chen (2) has proposed the Entity-Relationship (E-R) approach to the problem
of modeling of database semantics. Biller (1) has discussed the need for a
canonical form for semantic modelling, and a number of researchers have proposed a variety of schemes (1, 9, 12, 16, 17, 18) for solving the problem.
However, the E-R model as described by Chen and extended by Scheuermann et
al (15) was chosen for use on the U. S. Department of Defense project described in section 3 because of the following: a) the E-R model was judged
to be an important step in the solution of the semantic modeling problem,
b) it appeared to be practical, relatively simple to apply, and applicable
without the need for developing software tools to support its use, c) the
simple but effective graphics provide both global and detail information,
and facilitate communication between technical and non-technical personnel,
and d) the extension (15) provides both several classes of relationships,
which in turn allowed for more accurate semantic modeling, and a method for
retaining the model's integrity under update operations on the database.

Application of the E-R technique to model the Department of the Army Standard Port System - Enhanced (DASPS-E) database, while for the most part successful, brought to light two problems. The first concerned existence
dependencies between two entity types. There appeared to be need for
mutual existence dependencies between two entity types - each, in Chen's
terminology, being both weak and strong with respect to the other. In addition, it was felt that the roles of relationship types between two entity

*Current Address

types between which there was an existence dependency(s) were not clearly
defined.

A second problem arose due to the relationship classifications defined for
both the E-R model and its extension. A number of situations were encountered which did not appear to fit well into any of the classifications
defined. In addition, there appeared to be obvious semantic information
which was not being modeled.

A review of these two facets of the extended E-R model led to a redefinition
of existence dependency which both allows mutual existence dependency and
which is independent of relationships between the two entities. Review of
the relationship classification scheme led to the identification of three
independent relationship characteristics. These characteristics are used
to form a five-dimensional space containing 108 discrete points - each being
in effect a composite relationship type (though not all are distinct).
These extensions are developed in section 2.

The Department of The Army's Standard Ports System - Enhanced is briefly
described in section 3, and the application of the extended E-R analysis
developed in section 2 to the modeling of that system is described in section 4. Section 5 discusses some significant points of our experience with
the design process.

2   EXTENSION OF THE E-R MODEL

The E-R model is independent of any host database management system, but has
well defined transformations (3) to each of the three most common data
models- hierarchical, network, and relational (7). The E-R approach is
relatively simple in application and has precise but simple graphics which
provide a strong visual component. The E-R Diagram, which is produced as a
natural result of the analysis, provides both means of obtaining a global
picture of a database and of precisely specifying database semantics at a
relatively detailed level.

2.1   REVIEW OF E-R CONCEPTS

A number of basic concepts assumed in this paper are defined and discussed
in the literature. In particular, the reader is referred to Smith, et al
(17, 18) for the general notions of abstraction and aggregation, to Codd (5)
for a discussion of keys, and to Chen (2, 3) for a discussion of basic E-R
concepts-in particular, the notions of entity, entity type, entity set,
domain of an entity type, attributes, relationship, relationship type, relationship set, mapping class, and E-R diagrams. The discussion in this paper
will assume that the occurance of an entity in an entity set of entity type
A is synonomous which the occurance of the key value of that entity. The
values of the non-key attributes are not important to the discussion, and
each key value (=entity) in an entity set is unique. The domain of entity

type X, DOM (X), can then be considered to be the set of all possible key
values which may occur in any entity set of X.

2.2   REDEFINITION OF EXISTENCE DEPENDENCY

Chen (3) defined <u>weak entities</u> which depend for their existence in an entity
set on the existence in another (or possibly the same) entity set of other
entities. For example, the inclusion of a child in an entity set of the
entity type CHILD might be dependent on the existence of the child's
parent(s) in an entity type ADULT. The ADULT entity type would be considered the <u>strong entity type</u>, CHILD the <u>weak entity type</u>. A graphic was
defined to indicate existence dependency (Figure 2.1).

This notion of existence dependency suffers from some limitations. The
graphics used becomes ambiguous if a third entity type which is also related
to the weak entity type is involved. For example, in Figure 2.1 it is not
possible to determine whether ADULT or SCHOOL is the strong entity type.

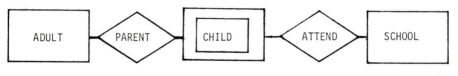

AMBIGUOUS EXISTENCE DEPENDENCY
FIGURE 2.1

Another limitation of the notion as defined by Chen is that of the asymmetric weak side - strong side concept. The implication, although perhaps
not intended, is that the reverse should not simultaneously be the case. If
A is weak with respect to B, then B cannot be also weak with respect to A.

A third problem is that the notion of existence dependency affects relationship types between the weak and strong entity types. Such may or may not be
the case. Consider the following example (Figure 2.2): a driver is allowed
into the database if one or more automobiles which he owns is in the database. However, once in the database, he can be assigned to any automobile,
regardless of ownership. DRIVER is existence dependent with respect to

AUTO, and OWNS is somehow involved in this dependency. However, ASSIGN,
even though it relates existence dependent entity types, is not concerned
with that dependency.

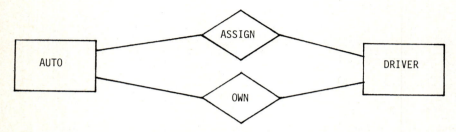

RELATIONSHIPS AND EXISTENCE DEPENDENCY
FIGURE 2.2

Application of the notion of existence dependency as defined by Chen to the
DASPS-E brought these problems to light. For example, it became obvious
that mutual existence dependencies were not uncommon. If in Figure 2.2, a
driver were allowed in DRIVER only if an automobile which he owned were present in AUTO, while simultaneously an auto were allowed in AUTO only if a
driver who owned it were present in DRIVER, then there would exist a mutual
existence dependency. In the following paragraphs, existence dependency is
defined to allow for such two-way dependencies and to be independent of
relationships in the database which relate the two entity types.
Relationships which involve the existence dependency are discussed in section 2.3.2. In addition, a new graphic is defined which is unambiguous.

An entity type A is defined to be existence dependent on an entity type B if
the existence of each entity a of DOM(A) in the current entity set of A,
A_c, is dependent on the existence in the current entity set of B, B_c of one
or more members b which are also members of S_a, the existence subset of a
with respect to DOM(B). S_a is a subset of DOM(B) and are those entities of
DOM(B), one or more of which must be B_c for a to exist. For example, given
two entity types ADULT and CHILD, and an existence dependency of CHILD on
ADULT such that a child may only be in the database if that child's
parent(s) are in the current ADULT entity set, then the existence subset
(S_a) of child a chosen from DOM(CHILD) is composed of those of the child's
parents who are in DOM(ADULT). An alternative statement of the existence
dependency is that a can exist in A if and only if

$$S_a \cap B_c \neq null.$$

Gathering all a of DOM(A) and their corresponding existence subsets S_a, the existence <u>dependency set</u> of DOM(A) on DOM(B) can be defined as

$$E_{A,B} = \left\{ \langle a, S_a \rangle \right\} \quad \text{for all } a \in \text{DOM(A)}, \text{ where } S_a \subseteq \text{DOM(B)}$$

If the point of view were inverted, and to each b of DOM(B) were associated all of the entities of DOM(A) which depend for their existence on b, denoted by T_b, then the <u>existence determination set</u> of B on A can be defined as

$$D_{A,B} = \left\{ \langle b, T_b \rangle \right\} \text{ for all } b \in \text{DOM(B)}, \text{ where } T_b \subseteq \text{DOM(A)}$$

If there were a mutual existence dependency of A on B and B on A, then

$$E_{B,A} = D_{A,B}$$

Note that existence dependency as defined above is a property of two entity types and not of any particular relationship types relating them. Certain relationships types between them can be restricted by the established existence dependency. These restrictions are discussed in section 2.3.

Note too that an entity type can have existence dependencies on more than one entity type of the database.

The graphic chosen to specify the existence dependency is simple and unambiguous - a directed line from the dependent to the determining entity type (Figure A-1). A directed graph (10) is formed representing a network of existence dependencies. Figure 4.2 is the <u>existence digraph</u> of the entities of DASPS-E is Export subsystem. <u>Existence dependency paths</u> can be formed which show hiearchical or cyclical dependencies. For example, there is a directed cycle between CARGO CLEARANCE ORDERS and VOYAGE showing a mutual existence dependency. There is a path from VESSEL through VOYAGE to CARGO CLEARANCE ORDER. In order for a cargo clearance order to exist, the associated voyage must exist. But for a voyage to exist, the vessel which is making that voyage must exist.

Existence dependency sets are not normally stored in the database, although it is possible to do in some cases. Often the database has only incomplete knowledge of DOM(A) and DOM(B), and even if they were completely known, $E_{A,B}$ is likely to be so large as to rule out inclusion on the grounds of practicality. Quite often, information about $E_{A,B}$ resides with the database user, be he/it human or a program. However, the database often has some a posteriori knowledge of $E_{A,B}$ residing in certain kinds of relationship types between A and B - the "current existence relationship" discussed in section 2.4.

2.3   RELATIONSHIP TYPE CLASSIFICATIONS

Chen (2) has specified the categorization of relationship types according to their mapping class. Several authors (4, 14, 15, 18, 25) have attempted to

extend the basic E-R model to include typologies of relationships which
involved other characteristics in addition to mapping classification. One
of these by Scheuermann, Schiffner, and Weber (15) was applied to the
DASPS-E database. Several cases were encountered which could not be fit
comfortably into any of the defined classifications. This situation
prompted the review of the classification scheme itself, with the realiza-
tion that independent characteristics of relationships (and existence
dependencies) were not completely separated. The review lead to the identification of three independent relationship characteristics: mapping
class, restriction class, and completeness class.

2.3.1 MAPPING CLASS

The review of the characteristic of mapping class lead to the retention of
the same classifications as defined in (3) - 1:1, 1:m, m:1, and n:m. It
should be noted that the mapping class is a statement of the maximum number
of times an entity of one entity type is allowed to appear in a relationship
type relating two entity types. The number of times that it must appear is
a completely separate characteristic addressed in section 2.3.3. The
graphic used for denoting mapping class is the same as that used by Chen and
is shown in Figure 4.1.

2.3.2 RELATIONSHIP RESTRICTION CLASS

The ability of the entities of one entity type, A, to be related to the
entities of a second entity type, B, through the relationship type AB may be
restricted in some way other than by mapping class. Suppose, for example,
that in the E-R Diagram of Figure 2.3 drivers holding regular operating
licenses are restricted to operating only those vehicles of gross weight two
tons or less, while drivers holding commercial licenses can operate any
vehicle in the database. Each driver may be restricted to possible relationship with only a certain subset of all vehicles. The question of
whether each driver must be related to one or more vehicles is a separate
question, a question of the completeness class of the relationship (section
2.3.3). The question of how many vehicles a driver is allowed to be
assigned at any time is a question of the mapping class of the relationship.

If a relationship type AB is __restricted__ in relating entity types A and B,
then each entity a of DOM(A) can be related through AB to an entity b of
DOM(B) if b is a member of C_a, the __restriction subset__ of a, where C_a
DOM(B). C_a is the set of those entities of DOM(B) with which a can be associated through AB. The set of ordered pairs

$$R_{A,B} = \left\{ \langle a, C_a \rangle \right\} \text{ where } C_a \subseteq DOM(B)$$

is called the __restriction set__ of AB.

Note that either $R_{A,B}$ or $R_{B,A}$ can be specified since the establishment of one determined the other.

An <u>unrestricted</u> relationship type is one for which there is no restriction. In that case, C_a = DOM(B) for all a in DOM(A). Note that unrestricted is a special case of restricted, and $R_{A,B}$ becomes simply another form of the cartesian product DOM(A) X DOM(B).

The graphic symbol for an unrestricted relationship type is a simple diamond. That for a restricted relationship type is a diamond with a bottom chevron (Figure 2.3).

Note that the graphics imply a symmetry which is indeed the case. Although the definition of restriction was stated in an asymmetric way, the restriction is in reality on AB with respect to both A and B, and the definition can alternatively be stated in that way.

Often the database does not know R_{AB} in the form defined. Instead the restriction takes another form such as the rule restricting ordinary drivers to vehicles of two tons or less. However, R_{AB} can always in theory be constructed.

It is often the case when relating two entity types, say A and B, between which there is an existence dependency, say of A on B, that entities of A are restricted to being related to those entities of B for which they depend on their existence. More formally, if there is an existence dependency of A on B, and there is a restriction on a relationship AB relating A and B such that C_a = S_a (the restriction subset of a equals its existence subset of a for all a $\in$ DOM(A)), then AB is said to be <u>existence</u> <u>restricted</u> with respect to A and B. For example, if the ASSIGN relationship type of figure 2.3 is redefined so that a driver is allowed into the database only if one or more of the automobiles which he owns is in the AUTO entity set, and in addition a driver may be assigned only to one or more of the automobiles which he owns, then the relationship type ASSIGN can be said to be existence restricted with respect to AUTO and DRIVER. Figure 2.4 shows the E-R Diagram and the double diamond graphic which is used to indicate existence restriction. Note that while existence dependency is directional, an existence restriction is not and the symmetry of the graphic is accurate.

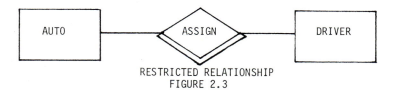

RESTRICTED RELATIONSHIP
FIGURE 2.3

EXISTENCE RESTRICTED RELATIONSHIP
FIGURE 2.4

2.3.3 RELATIONSHIP COMPLETENESS CLASS

Recall that the mapping class of a relationship specified the number of
allowable appearances of an entity in a relationship set. In constrast, the
completeness class of a relationship type with respect to an entity type
refers to the number of necessary appearances which each entity of the
entity set must make in the relationship set.

Each entity of entity set A is either not required to be related to any members of its restriction subset C_a which are in B_c, is required to be related
to at least one member of its restriction subset C_a which is in B_c, or is
required to be related to all of the members of its restriction subset
C_a which are in B_c, where B_c is the current entity set of entity type B.
These are the three categories of completeness class - a lower limit on the
appearance in AB of each entity a in the current entity set A_c of entity
type A of none, some, or all. Basing the completeness requirement on the
restriction subsets C_a in effect makes the definition of the completeness
class independent of the restriction class since both unrestricted and
existence restricted are special cases of restricted.

If the entities A_c are not required to be represented in relationship type
AB which relates A and another entity type B, then AB is said to be <u>partial</u>
with respect to A.

If the entities of A_c are required to be represented one or more times in
AB, then AB is said to be <u>total</u> with respect to A, indicated by a small
solid circle added to the line on the A side of AB.

If each entity of A_c is required to be related to all of entities of B_c to
which it can be related (ie to all members of its restriction subset)
through relationship type AB, then AB is said to be <u>complete</u> with respect to
A, indicated by a solid pointer tip added to the line on the A side of AB.

The graphics which indicate the completeness class of AB with respect to A
are shown in Figure A-1.

Figure 2.5 shows a small sample E-R diagram where the existence digraph (not shown) states that PERSON is existence dependent on AUTO. Each person must be related through OWN to all autos which he owns which are in entity set AUTO, and each driver must be assigned to at least one auto through ASSIGN. In addition, each AUTO must also be assigned to a person.

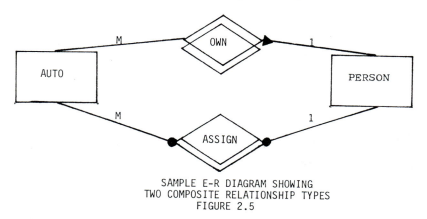

SAMPLE E-R DIAGRAM SHOWING
TWO COMPOSITE RELATIONSHIP TYPES
FIGURE 2.5

2.3.4 SUMMARY OF RELATIONSHIP CHARACTERISTICS

Figure A-1 summarizes the graphics chosen to indicate the classification of a relationship type with respect to each of the three characteristics - mapping class, restriction class, and completeness class. The three characteristics are completely independent of each other and, with one exception, of any existence dependency between the two entity types being related. The sole exception is that a relationship type may only be existence restricted if there is an existence dependency. The overall relationship classification is a composite formed by overlaying the individual characteristic classifications. The number of possible composite classifications resulting from five individual classifications (the mapping class of each side, the restriction class, and the completeness class of each side) is 108. Adding the existence dependency characteristics of the two entities being related, a total of four possible conditions, results in a pair of entity types and a relationship between them being categorized into one of 396 possible states of combined existence dependency and composite relationship classification, a very rich set of possibilities (though not all are distinct) resulting from the total of seven categorizations. (Existence dependency of (1) A on B, (2) B on A; mapping class of AB on (3) side A, (4) side B; (5) restriction class of AB; completeness class of AB on (6) side A, (7) side B).

2.4   CURRENT EXISTENCE AND RESTRICTION RELATIONSHIPS

If A is existence dependent on B, then any relationship type between them which is existence restricted and complete with respect to A supplies partial knowledge of the existence dependency set $E_{A,B}$. If AB is such a relationship, then not only is $AB \subseteq E_{A,B}$, but it is also the largest possible subset of $E_{A,B}$ which can be formed from the current entity sets of A and B. If $E_{A,B}$ does not exist in the database, then AB supplies the most complete information which the database has about $E_{A,B}$. For example, in Figure 2.5, if an auto is deleted from AUTO, OWNS provides the information about which members of PERSON must be also deleted to preserve existence dependency constraints. In determining if a PERSON can be entered, it is of no help and $E_{A,B}$ must be referenced. AB contains only a posteriori knowledge - knowledge of only those entities already in the database.

In a similar fashion, if there is a restriction set $R_{A,B}$ governing the possible associations of members of A to members of B through relationship AB, and AB is complete with respect to either A or B, then $AB \subseteq R_{A,B}$ and is the maximum subset of $R_{A,B}$ which can be formed from the current entity sets A and B.

2.5   PROPOGATION OF DATABASE UPDATES

Sheuermann et al (15) addressed the problem of retaining the invariant properties of the semantic model during update processes which modified entity sets or relationship sets. Adds, deletes, and updates may require supporting update operations in adjacent relationship types and related entity types, and such supporting updates may propogate in paths through the E-R diagram.
        A full discussion of the construction of update propogation paths is beyond the scope of the paper and is the subject of further research. Designers and programmers of the DASPS-E project were instructed to provide the necessary checks in designing and in the programs to insure that after each update operation the database retained its integrity with respect to existence dependencies and composite relationship classifications. If a supporting update were required, then it must in turn be checked for integrity retention, and so on until the update propogation terminated.

3.0   DASPS-E SYSTEM

The Department of The Army currently has in operation at overseas water terminals a computer based system for scheduling, routing, tracking, and controlling waterborne cargo - the Department of the Army Standard Ports System (DASPS). This system is nearing the end of its useful life. It is a punched card based batch procesing system with many ancillary manual activities. A new system, DASPS-Enhanced (DASPS-E), is currently under development and is due for extension into the field in 1983. The system is under

development at Fort Lee, Virginia by the U. S. Army Logistics Command with
the U. S. Army Computer Systems Command as the assigned development agency.
Computer Sciences Corporation is the Contractor providing the technical
design. DASPS-E will automate many of the existing manual operations,
change the processing base from batch to an interactive/batch combination,
and make use of telecommunications to link the system into existing military
telecommunications networks. The system will conform to the Military
Standard Transportation Movement Procedures (MILSTAMP) (13). Development
and testing is controlled by DOD and USA Standards (7, 19, 22).

DASPS-E is a completely new design starting with the production of a functional description document (FD) (20) and a data requirements document (RD)
(21). These documents were produced by a functional design team of the U.
S. Army Logistics Command. Members of the team had experience in water terminal operation, but little if any in data processing. The FD is a combination of data flow diagrams and structured English, with supporting
report formats, screen layouts, and table definitions. The RD contains a
data element dictionary and files as defined by the functional design team.
Files were defined as needed and no attempt was made to reduce data redundancy, to simplify the files' internal (sometimes quite complex) structures,
or to define any sort of data model or access method. Flat files were
assumed and all questions of access efficiency were ignored. The designers
simply assumed that they had available a hypothetical set level database
query facility and proceeded accordingly.

The system is composed of three major subsystems - Import, Export, and MIS.
Import, the largest of the three in volume of data handled, provides for
the receipt of advance manifest data concerning cargo and vessels on route.
This data is used to plan and record the discharge of cargo from vessels,
record subsequent movement and possible unpacking of consolidated cargo at
the port, and to schedule and route the onward movement of cargo out of the
port with automatic customs documentation.

Export provides for the receipt of cargo transportation movement and control
documentation, for subsequent offering of the cargo to Military Sealift
Command for booking on vessels, for consolidating cargo into containers, for
vessel loading, and for automatic manifest generation and transmission.

A variety of reports and statistics necessary for port operation, planning,
and scheduling is produced by both subsystems.

MIS, using mainly Import and Export data, produces a variety of reports concerning port operation, generates data on which to base the payment of
contractors and shippers, and bills governmental agencies for shipping
cargo.

The technical design effort (23), following DOD and USA guidelines and standards, uses structured design (26) to produce structure charts and IPO
charts (11) which are enhanced by appropriate structured English (24) statements for clarification and complete specification. The technical database
design employs the extended Entity-Relationship analysis described in section 2 to produce the conceptual database model.

4.0 DATABASE DESIGN

The sequencing of the design processes is shown in Figure 4.3.

The database design task was divided into two major phases:

1. Conceptual design - description of the database semantics
    independent of any dbms data model.

2. Detail design - translation of the conceptual design into
    the data model of the host dbms, and the specification of
    the underlying file structures and data elements.

The Entity-Relationship approach extended by the existance and relationship
classification schemes defined in section 2 was used for the conceptual
design.

Design of the semantic or conceptual database proceeded using the following
design steps: For each view,

1. Identify the entities

2. Identify the existence dependencies among entities and con-
    struct an existence dependency graph.

3. Identify the relationships and construct an E-R Diagram.

4. Classify each relationship with respect to its
    A. mapping class
    B. restriction class
    C. completeness class
    and extend the E-R diagram using the graphics defined in
    Figure A-1.

5. Identify the attributes and key attributes of each entity

6. Identify the attributes and key attributes of each rela-
    tionship

7. After completing all views, merge the view E-R diagrams to
    produce the database schema.

Figure 4.1 shows the extended E-R subdiagram for the Export subsystem view
of the DASPS-E database. The characteristics of the database are suggested
by the statistics given in Figure 4.4   Figure 4.2 shows the corresponding
existance dependency digraph. The Export subsystem view encompasses roughly
one third of the database.

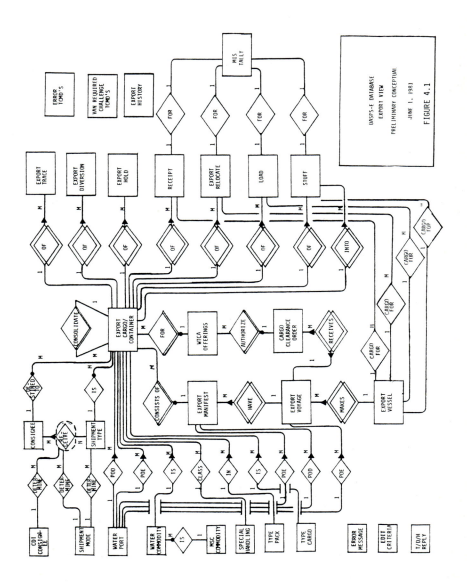

DASFS-E DATABASE
EXPORT VIEW
PRELIMINARY CONCEPTUAL

JUNE 1, 1981

FIGURE 4.1

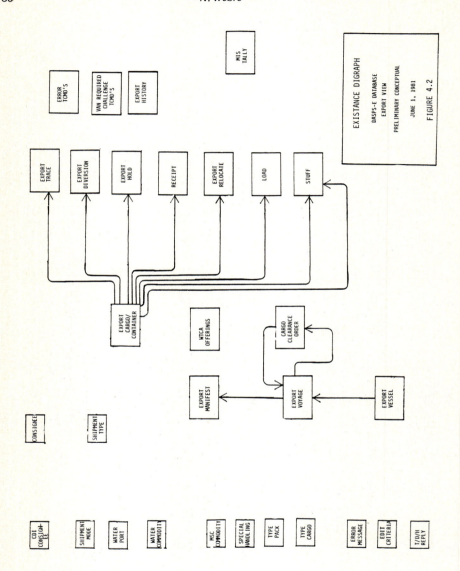

EXISTANCE DIGRAPH

DASPS-E DATABASE
EXPORT VIEW
PRELIMINARY CONCEPTUAL

JUNE 1, 1981

FIGURE 4.2

SYSTEM DESIGN TASK:

SUBTASK SEQUENCE

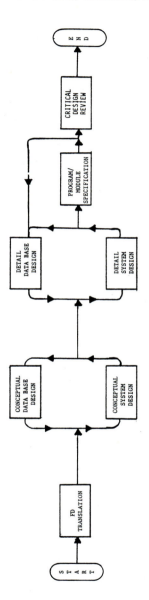

FIGURE 4.3

| | | VIEW | | | |
		IMPORT	EXPORT	MIS	TOTAL
ENTITY TYPES		29	30	50	91
RELATIONSHIP TYPES		33	38	68	129
EXISTANCE DEPENDENCIES		15	11	2	28
MAPPING CLASS	1:1	5	4	1	9
	1:M	27	33	38	89
	N:M	1	1	29	31
RESTRICTION CLASS	UNRES.	16	23	64	95
	RESTR.	2	4	2	6
EX.	RESTR.	15	11	2	28
COMPLETENESS CLASS	PARITAL	46	50	107	187
	TOTAL	3	5	2	9
	COMPLETE	17	21	25	62

DASPS-E DATABASE STATISTICS
FIGURE 4.4

5 SIGNIFICANT FEATURES OF THE DESIGN PROCESS

The process of extended E-R design using the approach outlined in section 4 raised a number of significant design issues.

5.1 LEVELS OF ABSTRACTION

Smith and Smith (16, 17) discuss the notion of abstraction and the concept of variation of abstraction level. The need for more than one level of abstraction for an entity or cluster of entities and relationships became apparent as the design progressed. For example, in Figure 4.1 the entity "EXPORT CARGO/CONTAINERS" is shown with a relationship "CONSOLIDATED" between members of itself. This entity type abstracts the notion of any type of cargo being exported, including basic shipment units of real cargo, consolidation containers which are used for consolidating shipment units, and vans, which can consolidate both shipment units and consolidation containers. For most purposes, the highest level of abstraction, that presented in Figure 4.1, is sufficient and in fact desirable to avoid unnecessary complexity since most of the entities related to EXPORT CARGO/CONTAINERS can relate to all three types of cargo or containers. However, the details of consolidation are not apparent. In order to clarify them, a second level of abstraction is necessary to accurately model the database semantics. Figure 5.1 shows the high and low levels of abstraction. At the high level, the relationship CONSOLIDATED is restricted since shipment units can be consolidated only into consolidation containers or vans, and not into other shipment units; consolidation containers can only be consolidated into vans; vans have no higher level of consolidation. Note the change in the relationship classes of the new CONSOLIDATE relationship, since the former restriction is now accurately modeled by the lower level of abstraction. Such cases appeared at several places in the database. Both levels were provided to the designers. In the case above, the higher level is shown in the Export E-R diagram, with the lower provided as a localized blow-up as shown in Figure 5.1. In other cases, the lower level was included, with a localized higher level appended.

5.2 RELATING RELATIONSHIPS

Chen (2) did not directly address the issue of relating to a relationship. However, several authors (15, 16, 14) have considered the problem and there appears to be no particular difficulty. Figure 4.1 shows a dotted oval around a diamond in the upper left region to indicate that the relationship type RECEIVES is to be reconsidered as an entity type for the purpose of constructing a relationship to it. The semantics of the situation is as follows: each piece of cargo is a certain type of goods -shipment type - and is destined to a specified consignee. However, the combination of shipment type and consignee determine to which shipping address - the CDI consignee - the cargo is to be routed. In addition, the same combination might determine the kind of conveyance used to move the cargo from the port to the CDI Consignee - the SHIPMENT MODE of the E-R diagram. If it does not, then the shipment type alone is used to determine the shipment mode. If that in turn fails, then the shipment mode is entered from outside the database.

a) High-Level Abstraction

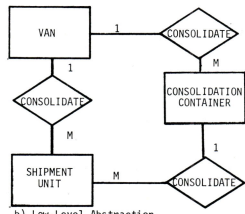

b) Low-Level Abstraction

FIGURE 5.1

5.3   COMMUNICATION WITH USERS

The Entity-Relationship diagram even in its extended form as described in
this paper, appears to have the admirable property that it is effective in
communicating both with technical personnel (designers, programmers) and
with non-technical personnel (functional designers, management). On the
one hand, it seems to convey an overall sense of the database to those not
needing too much detail. (However, we were quite surprised at the speed
with which non-technical personnel grasped the nuances of the extensions.)
On the other hand, the overall view provided by the basic E-R diagram and
the precise and sometime subtle constraints specified by the extensions both
prove extremely valuable to technical designers and programmers. By no
means the least important aspect of the E-R approach, the simple and stepwise constructed graphics convey a great deal of information with a minimum
of symbols.

In practice, Chen's (3) method of depicting attributes by a bubble graphic
is too cumbersome for the large number of atributes per entity type in this
database. Separate lists of entity types and relationship types, and their
attributes and keys were constructed and were much more convenient.

The existance digraph could have been incorporated directly onto the
extended E-R Diagram with, for example, broken directed lines. However, as
the reader will note, space is already at a premium on the E-R Diagram of
Figure 4.1 and the inclusion of more graphics would have further cluttered
an already crowded picture.

5.4   DBMS INDEPENDENCE

The need for a dbms independent design tool was especially important since
the Department of the Army's date for specification of the host system coin-
cided with the completion date for conceptual database design. In effect,
the conceptual database designers did not know what dbms they were designing
for until the conceptual design was complete. The E-R approach proved to be
completely dbms independent, and none of the design effort was wasted. (At
the time of final revision of this paper, a final decision on the development and target host systems has not been made by the Department of the
Army. It appears that in order to maintain the portability of DASPS-E among
Army Computer Systems, no generalized database management system is to be
used, and design is progressing using a system of files with key propogation
and inversions providing essentially a network model.)

6   CONCLUSIONS

The basic E-R model as defined by Chen would have alone provided a substantial and powerful design tool. The extensions defined in section 2 provided
                                    the inclusion of important and sometimes

subtle semantic constraints. The graphics for the extensions were defined
to be compatible with those defined by Chen and greatly increase the information content of the E-R diagram.

The E-R approach is compatible with U. S. D.O.D. and U.S.A. standards for
database design, mainly because there is little in the way of standards in
this aspect of system design. The E-R approach appears to be a good candidate for adoption as part of any future standards of these agencies.

ACKNOWLEDGEMENT: The author would like to thank Mr. Will Burke for his many
helpful discussions and Messrs. Napoleon Booker, Vaughn Sones, and Ron
Wilson for their support.

REFERENCES:

1.   Biller, Horst, "On the Equivalence of Database Schemas- A Semantic
     Approach To Data Translation" Info. Syst. 4, #1, 1979, pp 35-48.
2.   Chen, P.P.S., "The Entity-Relationship Model: Toward a Unified View of
     Data" ACM Transactions on Database Systems, Vol. 1, #1, March 1976,
     pp 3-36.
3.   Chen, P.P.S., "The Entity-Relationship Approach to Logical Database
     Design", Q.E.D. Monograph Series, No. 6, Q.E.D. Information Sciences,
     Inc., Wellesley, MA. 1977.
4.   Chiang, T.C. and Bergeron, R.F., "A Database Management System With An
     E-R Conceptual Model" Entity-Relationship Approach to Systems Analysis
     and Design, Chen, P. (Ed.), North Holland, Amsterdam, 1980.
5.   Codd, E.F., "Further Normalization of the Database Relational Model"
     Courant Computer Sciences Symposia, Vol. 6, Data Base Systems, R.
     Rustim (Ed.), Prentice Hall, New York 1971.
6.   Date, C.J., An Introduction to Database Systems, (2nd Ed.) Addison-
     Wesley, Reading, MA, 1977.
7.   Department of the Army, Army Automation: Software Design and Develop-
     ment, TB 18-103.
8.   Fong, E. & Kimbleton, S. "Database Semantic Integrity for A Network
     Data Manager", Proc. AFIPS N.C.C. Vol. 49, May 1980.
9.   Hammer, M. & McLeod, Dennis, "The Semantic Data Model: A Modelling
     Mechanism for Database Applications", Proc. Sigmod Int. Conf. on Mgt.
     of Data May 31-June 2, 1978 Lowenthar, E. & Dale, N.B. (Eds.), ACM, NY.
     1978, pp 26-36.
10. H rary, F., Graph Theory, Addison-Wesley, Reading MA. 1969.
11. IBM Corporation, "HIPO: A Design Aid and Documentation Technique",
     Form GC 20-1851-0, IBM, 1974.
12. Langefors, B. & Sundgren, B., Information Systems Architecture,
     Petrocelli/Charter, N.Y. 1975.
13. Department of Defense, "Military Standard Transportation and Movement
     Procedures-(MILSTAMP)" DOD 4500.32-R, Vol. 1, 1 August 1979.
14. dos Santos, C.S., Neuhold, E.J., and Furtado, A.L., "A Data Type Ap-
     proach to The Entity-Relationship Model" Entity-Relationship Approach
     to Systems Analysis and Design, Chen, P. (Ed.) North Holland, Amster-
     dam, 1980.

15. Scheuermann, P., Scheffner, G., and Weber, H., "Abstraction Capabili-
     ties and Invariant Properties Modelling Within the Entity-Relationship
     Approach", Entity Relationship Approach to Systems Analysis and Design,
     Chen, P. (Ed.), North Holland, Amsterdam, 1980.
16. Smith, J.M. and Smith, D.C.P., "Database Abstractions: Aggregation",
     Communications of ACM, Vol. 20, #6, June, 1977, pp 405-413.
17. Smith, J.M. and Smith, D.C.P., "Database Abstractions: Aggregation and
     Generalization", ACM Transactions on Database Systems, Vol. 2, #2,
     June, 1977, pp 105-133.
18. Su, S.Y.W. and Lo, D.H., "A Semantic Association Model for Conceptual
     Database Design", Entity-Relationship Approach to Systems Analysis and
     Design, Chen, P., (Ed), North Holland, Amsterdam, 1980.
19. United States Army Computer Systems Command, <u>Automatic Data Processing
     Systems Development, Maintenance, and Documentation Standards and
     Procedures Manual</u>, USACSC Manual 18-1, Vol. 1 (General).
20. U. S. Army Logistics Center, "Functional Description for Department of
     The Army Standard Port System - Enhanced", TM 38-L72-1, Headquarters,
     Department of the Army, January, 1981.
21. U. S. Army Logistics Center, "Data Requirements for the Department of
     the Army Standard Port System - Enhanced", TM 38-L72-1, Headquarters,
     Department of the Army, January, 1981.
22. United States Department of Defense, <u>DOD Automated Data Systems
     Documentation Standards</u>, Standard 7935.1-S.
23. Webre, N. and Wilson, R., "Techniques and Procedures, DASPS-E Project -
     System Design Task", DASPS-E Group, Computer Sciences Corporation, Fort
     Lee, Virginia.
24. Weinberg, Victor, <u>Structured Analysis</u>, Prentice-Hall, 1980.
25. Wilson, M. L., "The Measurement of Usability", Entity-Relationship
     Approach to Systems Analysis and Design, Chen, P. (Ed) North Holland,
     Amsterdam, 1980.
26. Yourdon, E., and Constantine, L.L., <u>Structured Design: Fundamentals of
     a Discipline of Computer Program and Systems Design</u>, 2nd Ed., Yourdon
     Press, New York, 1978.

FIGURE A-1

SUMMARY OF GRAPHICS

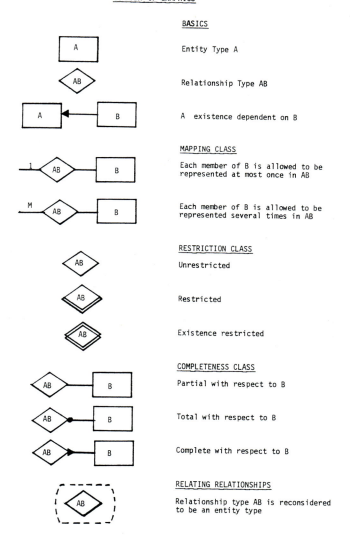

BASICS

Entity Type A

Relationship Type AB

A existence dependent on B

MAPPING CLASS

Each member of B is allowed to be
represented at most once in AB

Each member of B is allowed to be
represented several times in AB

RESTRICTION CLASS

Unrestricted

Restricted

Existence restricted

COMPLETENESS CLASS

Partial with respect to B

Total with respect to B

Complete with respect to B

RELATING RELATIONSHIPS

Relationship type AB is reconsidered
to be an entity type

Entity-Relationship Approach to
Information Modeling and Analysis, P.P. Chen (ed.)
Elsevier Science Publishers B.V. (North-Holland)
©ER Institute, 1983

DECLARATIVE AND PROCEDURAL FEATURES OF A
CODASYL ACCOUNTING SYSTEM

William E. McCarthy and Graham Gal
Department of Accounting
Graduate School of Business Administration
Michigan State University
East Lansing, Michigan 48824
U.S.A.

This paper presents selected aspects of an information system whose
data files have been specified in accordance with "events" accounting
principles and maintained with a CODASYL database management system
(DBMS). The accounting constructs employed in this implementation are
based on entity-relationship modeling, and the particular DBMS used is the
GPLAN system developed at Purdue University. The paper reviews derivation and use of both declarative and procedural features of the events
model.

1.   INTRODUCTION

During the last two decades, accounting researchers have been repeatedly faced
with the challenge of adapting conventional accounting models to fit well with
the capabilities provided by modern computer systems [1] [2]. A prominent
stream of research concerned with these adaptations has come to be known as
"events accounting," a term that is now used to describe any accounting system
whose primary distinguishing feature is the storage and maintenance of transaction data in disaggregate form. Sorter [24] first proposed the events
philosophy in 1969 as an alternative approach to public reporting of financial
data, but later work in this area [9] [16] [14] [12] [18] has concentrated
almost exclusively on the development of multidimensional accounting systems
and the integration of such systems with the shared use and modeling concepts
of database management. Readers interested in a review of the events accounting literature may consult [22].

In this present paper, we describe an actual events accounting implementation
that was built using the network or CODASYL [8] approach to database management. The particular system implemented in this case is an events model
based on an entity-relationship (E-R) view of accounting [18]. Such a view
discards traditional conventions such as debits, credits, and accounts in
favor of data models describing economic resources, events, and agents. Data

This project was funded by a grant from the Peat, Marwick, Mitchell Foundation
through its Research Opportunities in Auditing program. The views expressed
herein are those of the authors and do not necessarily reflect the views of the
Peat, Marwick, Mitchell Foundation. We also would like to acknowledge the
assistance provided by Dennis Miller, Brenda Spiewak, and Debbie North.

definitions are specified by mapping E-R constructs (such as entity-relationship tables [7]) into CODASYL constructs (such as record types and owner-
coupled sets). Following exhibition of these definitions, procedural aspects
of the implemented system are illustrated using process description tools
recommended by DeMarco [11]. These procedural aspects include transaction
processing and information retrieval for both accounting and non-accounting
decision makers.

The events implementation described herein has been programmed using the
GPLAN database management system (DBMS), a CODASYL system developed at Purdue
University in FORTRAN [15]. In the examples presented in the paper however,
we have chosen to use more English-like descriptions of both data elements and
processes in an effort to make our illustrations more readable. Readers
interested in seeing the actual data definitions and program code may consult
[23].

2.   DECLARATIVE FEATURES OF THE EVENTS SYSTEM

2.1 Introduction

The declarative features of a commercial database system can be developed by
(1) analyzing the entity-relationship structure of the corporate enterprise's
data environment, (2) translating that E-R structure into the logical model
employed by a particular DBMS, and (3) mapping that logical model into physical storage definitions. An overview of this process is illustrated in Figure
1 and explained below.

2.2 Object System —→ E-R Data Model

The object system [25] is a term used to describe those aspects of a certain
reality that are of interest to potential database users. For accountants,
the object system consists primarily of phenomena that directly concern a
given corporate enterprise's financial status, phenomena such as economic resources ("cash" and "inventory"), economic events ("sales" and "services"),
and economic agents ("customers" and "vendors"). The object system also will
include both relationships among the economic phenomena (vendors "participating in" purchases or cash receipts "paying for" sales) and detailed characteristics of the phenomena (the "name," "address," and "current balance" of
customers).

The steps involved in mapping elements of an accounting object system to an
E-R data model are explained in detail by McCarthy [18]. This abstraction
process is represented by the two top blocks of Figure 1, and its final output is a data model consisting of entity and relationship tables (also referred to as entity and relationship relations [7]) plus an E-R diagram
showing how the various tables correspond to each other. In the model shown
in Figure 1, there are three entity sets (rectangles) and two relationship
sets (diamonds).

2.3   E-R Data Model → CODASYL DBMS Processable Schema

The translation of an E-R data model to a CODASYL schema is illustrated by
the conversion of an E-R diagram to a data structure diagram [4] in Figure 1.
Chen [7, pp. 29-32] has established rules for this conversion which can be
summarized as follows:

(1)   All entity sets (such as A, B, and C) become CODASYL record types.

(2)   All m-to-n relationship sets (such as Y) also become record types;
      this kind of record type is usually called a link record.

(3)   All 1-to-n relationships (such as X) are represented by declara-
      tions of owner-coupled sets with the "1" entity as owner and the
      "n" entity as member. This is shown in the data structure diagram
      by the arrow pointing from the owner (A) to the member (B) with the
      set name (Set 1) written beside it.

(4)   All m-to-n relationships are represented by declaring two sets
      (Set 2 and Set 3) with the related entities (B & C) as owners and
      the link record (Y) as members.

Illustrated in Figure 2 is the same type of conversion just discussed. The
top part of the figure contains a subset of an E-R accounting model taken from
[20]. The bottom part of the figure was derived using the four rules summarized above plus declarations of three "system-owned" sets (S1, S8, and
S10). These system-owned sets are entry points to the database and allow access to customers, inventory, and vendors in a manner analogous to sequential
reading of tape files.

Fields of selected record types for the CODASYL structure are illustrated in
Figure 3. These fields represent selected characteristics of the modeled entities and relationships, and similar fields would have to be specified for
all record types used in a particular implementation.

2.4   CODASYL DBMS Processable Schema → Storage Structure Definition

The mapping from record types and owner-coupled sets to storage structures is
an implementation feature peculiar to the specific database management system
being used. The physical storage features of the GPLAN DBMS (on which the
events accounting system described herein is implemented) are explained by
Haseman and Whinston [15, Chap. 11].

2.5   Declarative Features Summary

The derivation of the declarative features of our events system, as illustrated in Figure 1, has now been explained completely. In the rest of the paper,
we will concentrate on explaining procedural aspects of the CODASYL structure
outlined in Figures 2 and 3. These procedural aspects are concerned primarily
with the maintenance and use of data defined in the sections above.

3.   PROCEDURAL FEATURES OF THE EVENTS SYSTEM

3.1 Introduction

This section illustrates transaction processing and information retrieval for
the events system. For example cases, we answer the questions: "how do we
get the data into the system?" and "how do we get it out for a particular
use?" Transaction processing logic is displayed first, using sale events as
an example.

3.2 Transaction Processing

In Figure 2(b), the 1-to-n relationship between customers and sales was effected in the database by declaring a set (S7) with the "customer" record
type as owner and the "sale" record type as member. Two occurrences of this
set are illustrated in Figure 4: customer White was the party to whom sales
1, 4, & 5 were made and customer Nelson was the party to whom sales 2 & 9 were
made. The dotted lines connecting members of S1 (system-owned) simply signify
that not all members of that set instance are shown in the diagram.

The processing logic that inserts information concerning a particular sale into
the database is illustrated in Figure 5(a) along with a dictionary enumeration
of the data elements contained on a sale invoice. Both the process description
and the dictionary entry are outlined using methods recommended by De Marco
[11]. In Figure 5(b), an example sale invoice is shown; the paragraphs below
explain how data contained on that document is fitted into the system.

    (1) First of all, a sale record occurrence is created containing field
         values for sale characteristics (the particular characteristics were
         shown in Figure 3).

    (2) Next, an owning customer is found for the sale (in this case, custo-
         mer White) by searching through the customer records via set S1 and
         then the customer and sale occurrences are linked. This linking is
         illustrated in Figure 4 by an arrow. Because the set ordering in
         this instance is specified as FIFO (first-in, first-out), "SALE 1"
         is inserted first in line next to the owning customer. Sales 4 & 5
         are events that occur later and consequently will be added further
         down the chain extending from the owner record.

    (3) Finally in the processing, each line item on the sale document is
         added to the database and linked in turn to both its sale owner (set
         S6) and its inventory owner (set S5). Illustrations of line item
         occurrences and linkages for "SALE 1" are shown at the bottom of
         Figure 6.

In the actual DBMS implementation [23], the algorithm illustrated in Figure
5(a) is coded using a programming language (FORTRAN) and a data manipulation
language (GPLAN DML). Additionally, readers should realize at this point that
similar processing of all economic events (including the "cash receipts" and
"purchases" shown in Figure 2) would be needed in the full implementation.

3.3   Information Retrieval

An important feature of the entity-relationship view of accounting, on which the described CODASYL system is based, is its deliberate exclusion of many double-entry conventions. Conventions such as debits, credits, and accounts are not used at all, but in spite of their absence, traditional accounting numbers can be retrieved without difficulty. Two examples of such retrieval are outlined in Figure 7 and explained briefly below. These explanations are followed by a discussion of non-accounting decision use.

Accounts-receivable (A/R) retrieval for the data structure outlined in Figure 2(b) can be computed using the following summary steps.

(1)   Those events that generate claims to future receipts of monetary resources are determined. For the modeled enterprise, this simply means identifying sales transactions.

(2)   Requited sales are determined. This means identifying cash receipts and then using that information further to determine the sales for which the receipts paid.

(3)   Unrequited sales are determined. This is done by subtracting the set of paid-for sales from the set of all sales. Following determination of this difference, the dollar amounts of the remainder are summed to get total receivables.

Execution of the first two steps explained above requires a sequential scan of all customers (to determine their sales and their cash receipts); therefore, the steps have been grouped together in one repetition block of Figure 7(a). The set difference operation is then accomplished by sorting and matching the two outputs to identify the set of transactions to be summarized.

The record-by-record orientation of the accounts-receivable retrieval is a feature characteristic of CODASYL database languages; readers interested in seeing a set-theoretic specification for the same retrieval may consult [19, p. 633]. It is also interesting to note at this point that, despite the absence of debits and credits, the controls inherent in a conventional subsidiary-control account structure are still present. The subsidiary receivables in this case are characteristics of the customers and are updated by transactions while the controlling figure is simply a redundant check of the data calculated at a certain time for verification purposes.

Cost-of-goods-sold (COGS) retrieval involves three record types--"inventory," "purchases," and "P-line-item"--and three owner-coupled sets--S8, S9, and S12. Some occurrences of these components are illustrated at the top of Figure 6. The additional instances of purchase line items shown in the "cloud" will allow us to be more specific about part of the COGS calculation.

Before studying the COGS retrieval procedure in Figure 7(b), the reader should understand the following aspects of the CODASYL system.

(1) The cost of goods sold for this company is calculated on a LIFO
     (last in, first out) basis. To facilitate the calculation, we have
     designated the ordering of set S9 also as LIFO. If this ordering
     were not present, an additional sort[1] would be necessary for the
     process.

(2) In Figure 3, the field "line-item-remnant" of "P-line-item" repre-
     sents that quantity of the particular line item that has not yet been
     charged off to cost of goods sold.

(3) The variable "sold-quantity" represents the total quantity sold for
     each inventory item during the reporting period in question. Again
     to facilitate the calculation, we have assumed that correct values
     for this variable have been previously materialized from the member
     instances of set S5.

The COGS derivation is another procedure involving sequential processing of a
system-owned set, in this case set S8. For this procedure, each inventory
type is retrieved in turn, and its cost is calculated by looking at its purchase history. For inventory type "A" with 12,000 units sold this period, the
COGS calculation would involve these components (objects used in the calculation are illustrated in Figure 6):

Total sold = 12,000 at a cost of $22,600 consisting of:

            6,000 units @ 2.00 = $12,000 (Purchase 10)
            4,000 units @ 1.90 =   7,600 (Purchase 9)
            2,000 units @ 1.50 =   3,000 (Purchase 8)

When the procedure is finished, "Purchase 8" would have 3,000 items of "A"
(that is, "line-item-remnant" = 3,000) left to be charged off to future COGS.

Non-accounting data retrieval can be accomplished either by the same technique
used above with accounting data--record-by-record processing with a programming
language--or by another technique that emphasizes non-programmer use--pro-
cessing with a query language. GPLAN implementation of both methods are explained by Haseman and Whinston [15, Chaps. 7-9].

Some potential data needs for non-accounting decisions that would use the accounting framework of Figure 2(b) include those shown below.

(1) To analyze the effects of discount policy on cash flows, a manager
     might request, "For certain groups of customers, plot the lag time
     between sales and cash receipts against the dollar amount of the

---

[1]This sort would require a time stamp on the "P-line-item" record type;
this stamp could be effected either by having a "time" field whose virtual
source was its owning record or by retrieving the "purchase" record itself.
Since GPLAN does not support the former, we have used the latter in [23].

receipts." This query would involve navigation[2] along the paths of
S1, S33 and S28.

(2)   To assess vendor performance, a manager might request, "For each
      vendor, construct a histogram of the quality ratings of our purchases
      with that firm during a certain period." This query would involve a
      navigation along the paths of S10 and S11.

(3)   To obtain a preliminary indication of the desirability of using
      distributed warehousing, a manager might ask, "List the names and
      dollar sales of customers who could have been supplied with their
      purchased products directly from our vendors located in the same city
      (or state or area)." This query would involve first a navigation
      through S1, S7, S6, & S5, then a navigation through S10, S11, S12, &
      S9, and finally a matching of the data obtained.

3.4   Summary of the Procedural Features of the Events System

We are now finished reviewing various types of transaction processing and information retrieval for the events database. Before moving on to a summary, we
discuss briefly an important procedural aspect of this type of accounting system: its maintenance of transaction histories.

The CODASYL system described in this paper, with a few exceptions, incorporates
completely the concept of events accounting; that is, it maintains all transaction or flow data indefinitely in disaggregate form. Such an implementation
is compatible with Sorter's [24] original principles which asked that accounting systems be designed so as to maximize the reconstructability of detailed event histories and thus make the outputs of the system available to a
wider range of unspecified decision makers. Sorter's thinking in this regard
is echoed in the following quote that deals with information systems development in a different functional area--marketing.

      Care must be taken not to accumulate data in ways that appear reasonable
      at one time, but preclude analysis at a subsequent time. A disaggregated
      data file is an important feature of any MIS that hopes to respond to
      needs or problems that are identified only after the MIS is operational.
      Disaggregation refers to the maintenance of individual data in a detailed
      time sequence as they are generated, so that new data are not combined
      with existing data. [13, p. 3]

Despite these opinions however, there will certainly be times when a cost-
benefit assessment of both accounting and non-accounting data usage will identify situations where the desirability of using events principles ought to be

---

[2]The analogy of a CODASYL database user to a navigator in n-dimensional
data space is due to Charles Bachman, the originator of most network data model
concepts. See [5].

analyzed further.[3]   Two such situations were used in our data retrieval
examples; they were (1) the "current-balance" field of "customer" and (2) the
"sold-quantity" variable which we materialized procedurally but which alternatively could have been maintained as a field in the "inventory" record type.
In the former case we decided (for control purposes) to temporally aggregate
data, while in the latter case we decided (somewhat arbitrarily) not to.   The
important point about transaction recording to remember during decision requirements analysis is that the data usage needs of one functional area, such
as accounting, should not be allowed to dictate the aggregation levels presented to the other functional areas.   This is precisely why an accounting system built with data modeling is better suited to a shared use environment than
one built with a debit-credit orientation.   Certain accounting actions, such as
the preparation of adjusting and closing journal entries, should be performed
independent of normal transaction maintenance if they result in aggregations
that lose or obscure information for other users.

As a final point in our discussion of procedural features, we should note that
our emphasis on events principles, coupled with the very simple nature of the
example enterprise which we chose to use, led us to build a system that needed
no chart of accounts or general ledger processing.   In [23], we illustrate
financial statements produced without these conventions.   However, with
relatively minor alterations, the accounting system described herein could produce (as a byproduct of transaction processing) the information needed to maintain a traditional general ledger [10, Chaps. 15-19].   If such a situation were
necessary, we recommend that the general ledger elements (the accounts) be
either specified as a view (subschema) or maintained as a separate file outside
the scope of the centrally-defined data model.

4.   CONCLUSION

This paper has described part of an events accounting system, one which was
implemented using the GPLAN database management system [15].   CODASYL data definitions and data manipulation programs were developed from an entity-relationship view which considers that accounting object systems are modeled best
as sets of economic resources, events, and agents plus relationships among
those economic phenomena.   The accounting theories underlying this view are explained in [21].

This implementation has demonstrated, at least in a partial sense, the feasibility of constructing data-modeled accounting systems, accounting systems designed from the start to encourage the shared use and maintenance of economic
data.   For at least two reasons however, the generalizability of our results is
hard to assess.   First of all, the DBMS used was decidedly limited and less
complex than most commercial systems.   GPLAN is a research/education system,
and it does not support features such as CALC (direct) access, virtual data
fields, and subschema specifications.   Certainly, an accounting system built on

---

[3]Quite apart from technical considerations, there are other behavioral
factors that might also necessitate this further analysis.   See [6].

a better equipped DBMS might differ in many ways. Second, the enterprise we
modeled was very simple [20]. It consisted of a retail company with a limited
capital structure, a limited set of products and services, and no departmental
structure. Future implementation efforts will have to concentrate on the
modeling of more complex object systems (such as a manufacturing firm with
multiple departments) and on the use of more detailed and wide-ranging design
methodologies (such as those outlined in [3] and [17]).

5.   REFERENCES

[1]   American Accounting Association. "Report of the Committee on Managerial
      Decision Models." The Accounting Review, Vol. 44 (Supplement 1969), pp.
      43-76.

[2]   American Accounting Association. "Report of the Committee on Non-
      Financial Measures of Effectiveness." The Accounting Review, Vol. 46
      (Supplement 1971), pp. 164-211.

[3]   Armitage, H., and W. E. McCarthy. "An Entity-Relationship Methodology
      for the Analysis and Design of Integrated Accounting Systems."
      Department of Accounting, Michigan State University, 1981. (Working
      Paper).

[4]   Bachman, C. W. "Data Structure Diagrams." Data Base, Vol. 1 (Summer
      1969), pp. 4-10.

[5]   Bachman, C. W. "The Programmer as Navigator." Communications of the ACM,
      Vol. 16 (November 1973), pp. 653-658.

[6]   Benbasat, I., and A. S. Dexter. "Value and Events Approaches to
      Accounting: An Experimental Evaluation." The Accounting Review, Vol. 54
      (October 1979), pp. 735-49.

[7]   Chen, P. P. "The Entity-Relationship Model--Toward a Unified View of
      Data." ACM Transactions on Database Systems, Vol. 1 (March 1976), pp.
      9-36.

[8]   CODASYL Programming Language Committee, Data Base Task Group Report.
      New York: Association for Computing Machinery, 1971.

[9]   Colantoni, C. S.; R. P. Manes; and A. B. Whinston. "A Unified Approach
      to the Theory of Accounting and Information Systems." The Accounting
      Review, Vol. 46 (January 1971), pp. 90-102.

[10] Cushing, B. E. Accounting Information Systems and Business Organizations.
      Reading, Mass.: Addison-Wesley, 1978.

[11] De Marco, T. Structured Analysis and System Specification. Englewood
      Cliffs, N. J.: Prentice-Hall, 1979.

[12] Everest, G. C., and R. Weber. "A Relational Approach to Accounting
      Models." The Accounting Review, Vol. 52 (April 1977), pp. 340-359.

[13]   Gibson, L. D.; C. E. Nugent, E. Christopher; and T. E. Vollman. "An
       Evolutionary Approach to Marketing Information Systems." Journal of
       Marketing, Vol. 37 (April 1973), pp. 2-6.

[14]   Haseman, W. D., and A. B. Whinston. "Design of a Multidimensional
       Accounting System." The Accounting Review, Vol. 51 (January 1976), pp.
       65-79.

[15]   Haseman, W. D., and A. B. Whinston. Introduction to Data Management.
       Homewood, Ill.: Richard D. Irwin, 1977.

[16]   Lieberman, A. Z., and A. B. Whinston. "A Structuring of an Events-
       Accounting Information System." The Accounting Review, Vol. 50 (April
       1975), pp. 246-258.

[17]   Lum, V. S.; G. M. Schkolnick; D. Jefferson; S. Su; J. Fry; T. Teorey;
       and B. Yao. "1978 New Orleans Data Base Design Workshop Report."
       Research Report RJ2554, San Jose, California: IBM Research Laboratories,
       1979.

[18]   McCarthy W. E. "An Entity-Relationship View of Accounting Models."
       The Accounting Review, Vol. 54 (October 1979), pp. 667-686.

[19]   McCarthy, W. E. "Construction and Use of Integrated Accounting Systems
       with Entity-Relationship Modeling." In Entity-Relationship Approach to
       Systems Analysis and Design. edited by P. Chen. Amsterdam: North-
       Holland, 1980. pp. 625-637.

[20]   McCarthy, W. E. "A Case Study Demonstrating the Applicability of Data
       Modeling to Accounting Object Systems." Proceedings of the 1980 Southeast
       Regional Meeting of the American Accounting Association, (April 1980),
       pp. 319-324.

[21]   McCarthy, W. E. "The REA Accounting Model: A Generalized Framework for
       Accounting Systems in a Shared Data Environment." Department of
       Accounting, Michigan State University, 1980. (Working Paper).

[22]   McCarthy, W. E. "Multidimensional and Disaggregate Accounting Systems:
       A Review of the 'Events' Accounting Literature." MAS Communication,
       Vol. 5 (July 1981), pp. 7-13.

[23]   McCarthy, W. E. and G. Gal. "Declarative and Procedural Features of a
       CODASYL Accounting System." Department of Accounting, Michigan State
       University, 1981. (Working Paper).

[24]   Sorter, G. H. "An 'Events' Approach to Basic Accounting Theory." The
       Accounting Review, Vol. 44 (January 1969), pp. 12-19.

[25]   Sundgren, B. "Conceptual Foundation of the Infological Approach to Data
       Bases." In Data Base Management. edited by J. W. Klimbie and K. L.
       Koffeman. Amsterdam: North-Holland Publishing Company, 1974. pp. 61-
       96.

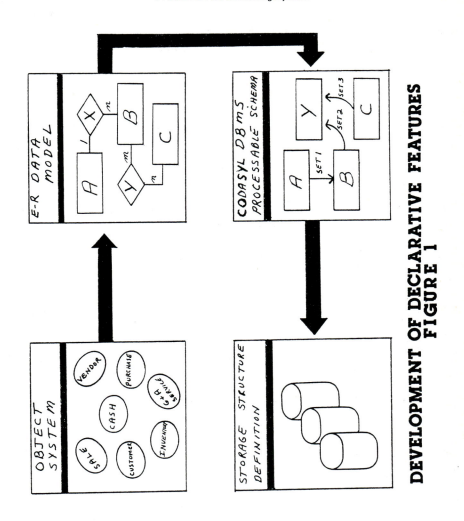

DEVELOPMENT OF DECLARATIVE FEATURES
FIGURE 1

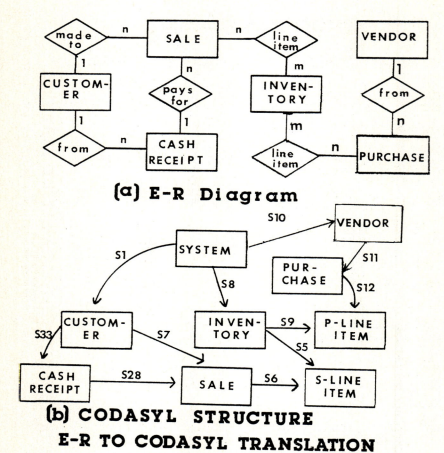

(a) E-R Diagram

(b) CODASYL STRUCTURE

E-R TO CODASYL TRANSLATION

FIGURE 2

CUSTOMER

NAME	NUMBER	ADDRESS	BALANCE

INVENTORY

STOCK NUMBER	QOH	DESCRIPTION	COST

SALE

INVOICE NUMBER	DATE	AMOUNT	ORDER NUMBER

S-LINE-ITEM

NUMBER	COST

P-LINE-ITEM

NUMBER	COST	LINE ITEM REMNANT

CODASYL RECORD FIELDS
FIGURE 3

W.E. McCarty and G. Gal

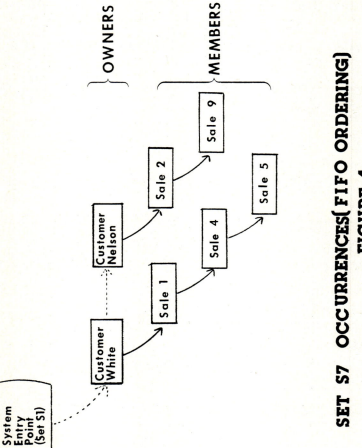

SET S7 OCCURRENCES (FIFO ORDERING)

FIGURE 4

```
Perform the following steps for each new sale invoice

        Create a SALE record type occurrence
        Find the appropriate CUSTOMER member of S1
        Update customer's account
        Add this SALE to S7
        Perform the following steps for each line-item on this sale invoice

                Create an S-LINE-ITEM record type occurrence
                Add this S-LINE-ITEM to S6
                Find the appropriate INVENTORY member of S8
                Update inventory status information
                Add this S-LINE-ITEM to S5
```

```
Sale-Invoice  =   Sale-Invoice-Number + Customer-Name +
                  Customer-Number + Customer-Information +
                  1{Inventory-Number + Quantity + Unit Price}7 +
                  Sale-Amount
```

(a) Sale Processing

WILSON CORP.
Sales Invoice

invoice no. _1_

Customer name _White_
Customer no. _100_
Customer info. _____

line-item	inv#	quantity	price	extension
1	A	2,000	3.00	6,000
2	B	1,000	5.00	5,000
3	C	700	12.00	8,400
4				
5				
6				
7				
			TOTAL	19,400

(b) Source Document for Sale

FIGURE 5

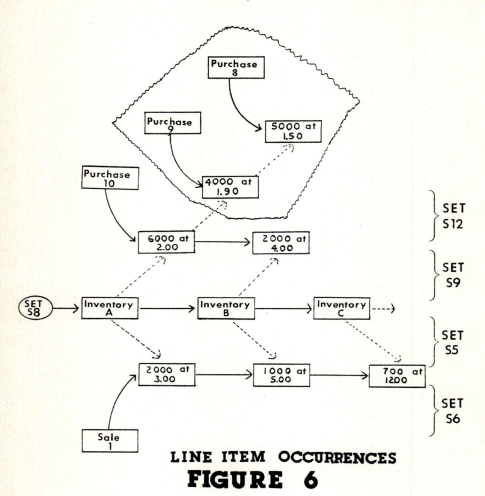

LINE ITEM OCCURRENCES

FIGURE 6

```
Perform the following steps for each CUSTOMER member of S1

     Get a CUSTOMER occurrence
     Accumulate detail A/R balance
     Perform the following steps for each CASH-RECEIPT member of S33
         with this CUSTOMER owner

             Get a CASH-RECEIPT occurrence
             Perform the following steps for each SALE member of S28 with
                 this CASH-RECEIPT owner

                     Get a SALE occurrence
                     Output sale invoice number and sale amount to paid-list

     Perform the following steps for each SALE member of S7 with this CUSTOMER
         owner

             Get a SALE occurrence
             Output sale invoice number and sale amount to total-list

Sort paid and total lists
Match lists sequentially to identify unpaid sales
Total unpaid sales and compare with accumulated detail balance
```

(a) A/R Retrieval

```
Perform the following steps for each INVENTORY member of S8

     Get an INVENTORY occurrence
     For each P-LINE-ITEM member of S9 with this INVENTORY as owner,
         perform the following steps until sold-quantity is gone

             Get a P-LINE-ITEM occurrence
             If line-item-remnant < sold-quantity
                 Then, contributed-quantity equals line-item-remnant
                 Otherwise, contributed-quantity equals sold-quantity
             Subtract contributed-quantity from line-item-remnant
             Subtract contributed-quantity from sold-quantity
             Multiply contributed quantity by unit-price and add product
                 to COGS for this inventory element

     Output Inventory-number and COGS amount

Add COGS for each inventory item and output final figure.
```

(b) COGS Retrieval

FIGURE 7

Entity-Relationship Approach to
Information Modeling and Analysis, P.P. Chen (ed.)
Elsevier Science Publishers B.V. (North-Holland)
©ER Institute, 1983

ITEM TRACKING ENTITY-RELATIONSHIP MODELS

Ewing L. Lusk
Northern Illinois University
DeKalb, Illinois

Gene Petrie
Software Architects
Chicago, Illinois

Ross A. Overbeek
Northern Illinois University
DeKalb, Illinois

This paper is a discussion of the design of a class of databases
which we call "item tracking" systems. We consider in detail an import tracking system, an airline reservation system, and a general
distribution system. These systems turn out to be similar enough to
support the claim that there are fundamental elements of design applicable to a very large number of specific systems.

1. INTRODUCTION

This paper is an outgrowth of meetings of the Chicago Area Database Design
Group. Several participants of that group advanced the thesis that there are
a few basically distinct types of databases. Most production databases will
be variations of these basic types. Therefore it was decided to compile prototype designs for these basic systems as a useful design tool. The prototype
designs will be criticized by those who have worked on production implementations of the corresponding systems. Hopefully, the result will be a portfolio
of designs which emphasize the results of past experience.

The basic category of systems discussed in this paper grew out of a detailed evaluation of an import tracking system. This system was generalized
from tracking only import products to tracking and scheduling movement of any
items. We shall first consider the import tracking system. Then we will present a design of an airline reservation system (which is similar to other
transportation reservation systems) and a distribution system. Our goal will
be to emphasize the similarities in the systems.

The airline reservation system and the distribution system have two distinct components: the entities that are used to track movement of items and
those that are used to select paths and schedule movements. Normally, the

tracking component, while complex, is easier to implement than the scheduling
component. These comments should become clearer after a detailed examination
of the three designs. For now it is only important to grasp that

a) the import tracking system is a good example of a tracking system -- it
   will be similar to the item tracking components of the airline reservation and distribution systems

b) the scheduling components of the airline reservation system and the distribution system again represent instances of a common problem.

The next section discusses the principles that were used to determine when
entities should be generalized (and amalgamated). As such it provides a background for the three sections that follow. These sections cover the designs
of the three application systems - the import tracking system, the airline
reservation system, and the distribution system. In each case an attempt is
made to designate the characteristics that generalize.

2.   GENERALIZATION OF ENTITIES

The problem of whether or not to generalize a given entity repeatedly con-
fronts anyone trying to use ER-models as an analysis tool. Several papers
have appeared offering guidance [1,2,3,6]. In this section, we shall describe
in relatively pragmatic terms the principles that were used in creating our
generic models.

First we will consider the advantages of generalizing the description of a
given entity. Several cases will be considered - including both cases in
which overlapping sets are generalized to a single entity-set and cases in
which disjoint sets are amalgamated. It is critically important that analysts
understand the motivations for generalization.

Then we consider the reasons for not generalizing. In particular we investigate the question of why all databases should not be represented as a single
entity, THING, with a variety of relationships between THINGs. In analyzing
this case we develop some practical guidelines that we have used repeatedly in
constructing our generic models.

2.1   GENERALIZING OVERLAPPING ENTITY-SETS

One of the most common classes of overlapping entity-sets results from the
different roles people may play. As an example, consider a data base for a
typical university. One is certainly tempted to introduce three distinct entity-sets: STUDENT, FACULTY, and STAFF. However, it is clear that a single
person could belong to two (or perhaps, all three) of these sets. It is worth
taking time to understand the disadvantages of keeping the sets distinct:

a) Redundant data will be maintained on people that occur in more than one set.

b) Common processing functions will normally be duplicated. For example, separate "name change" transactions would probably be implemented (perhaps, as submodules of a global logic that coordinated changes in all three of the data bases).   This reason is in our opinion the least understood, but probably the most significant.

c) It is more difficult (although certainly possible) to form a "composite" picture of the person - including data from several roles. For example, answering a query such as

   Give the names and addresses of faculty members who have enrolled in courses

   becomes difficult.

These reasons have caused us to advocate forming a more encompassing entity (such as PERSON).

   Before moving on to examine generalizing disjoint sets, let us consider two more examples:

a) In many business models the CUSTOMER, SUPPLIER, and EMPLOYEE sets are all distinct.   Note, however, that a single person may be in all three sets. This situation is complicated by the fact that some members in at least the CUSTOMER and SUPPLIER sets need not be people.   This has led us to advocate the use of the CONTRACTING-ENTITY set as a generalization of the three sets.   This almost always strikes people as quite unnatural. However, we urge the reader to at least consider the question seriously before rejecting it. It does seem to allow the definition of some generalized functions that are both natural and useful (for example, accounting functions for CONTRACTING-ENTITYs absorb what are often implemented as quite distinct systems).

b) In the Item Tracking generic model a specific import tracking system is discussed.   A number of documents such as BILL-OF-LADING, ORDER, and COMMERCIAL-INVOICE, are grouped into a single entity DOCUMENT. This allows generalized extraction and updating functions to be defined and results in a reasonably powerful and flexible implementation.

2.2   GENERALIZING DISJOINT SETS

Frequently disjoint entity-sets can profitably be merged, if similar processing functions apply to the sets. For example, in a work management generic model a discussion of a bus maintenance system was considered. It was found that merging the BUS and TRAIN sets in a single set, VEHICLE, was appropriate. Clearly the two original sets were disjoint, but because the processing requirements and attributes were so similar, the generalization led to an improved design.

2.3   DISADVANTAGES OF AMALGAMATING ENTITY-SETS

Having argued for combining commonly separated entity-sets, we shall now discuss the disadvantages of attempting to use increasingly general entity-sets. To focus on the problem we suggest considering the case in which all entity-sets are combined in a single set, THING, with many relationships between THINGs. A somewhat less drastic approach is to use VEGETABLE, ANIMAL, and MINERAL - but the difficulties (and advantages) are similar:

a) Since all possible attributes are grouped onto a single record, most fields in a record are null. This may or may not be serious depending on which DBMS is used to implement the system.

b) The visual and descriptive utility of ER-models is lost.

c) The size of the data base is large - which can lead to a host of implementation problems (recovery, degraded access time, etc.)

d) A set with a primary access structure of hashed, when merged with one that has an indexed structure, may experience degradation.

Some careful analysis will show, we believe, that in many cases such forms of extreme generalization would in fact function reasonably well (although we certainly do not advocate their use).

2.4 SUMMARY

We have tried to point out some of the advantages and difficulties that have arisen in our discussions concerning generalization of entity-sets. In our opinion designers err far more often by not generalizing than by over-generalizing. This is due to failure to visualize the more general class and failure to consider the common functions that can be defined. We strongly advocate the use of abstractions such as CONTRACTING-ENTITY, and suggest that entity-sets should not be created to reflect mere roles of real entities.

3. THE IMPORT TRACKING SYSTEM

The system that we are going to consider was implemented to maintain the status of imported items for a major retail outlet chain. Some types of processing performed by the system are:

1. It is possible to rapidly access the status of any outstanding order.

2. The system maintains records of actual and estimated costs for the various stages of bringing goods from a foreign manufacturer to a U. S. port.

3. It provides the company with timely cost control information.

We will present the system by considering several of the events that take place during the life of each order. As we cover each event we will present the entities involved in processing the event. As a summary the complete ER diagram will be given.

3.1 THE STRUCTURE OF THE RETAIL CORPORATION

The corporation for which the system was designed had a hierarchical structure of COST-CENTERs. This is normal and does not reflect any peculiarity of this system or company. The import department, wholesale distributors, and retail outlets are all specific COST-CENTERs within the company.

3.2 CREATION OF AN ORDER

An order is an agreement made between a buyer representing the corporation and a foreign manufacturer. The order will be for designated quantities of one or more products. It will also include:

a) scheduled shipping dates and destinations (ports and perhaps distribution centers) for partial amounts of the order,

b) how missed schedules will be handled (penalty clauses, etc.),

c) payment agreements, which frequently involve agreeing on a nontrivial sequence of events involving letters of credit at one or more banks and verification procedures,

d) an estimate of each component of "landed cost" for the order. The term "landed cost" refers to the cost of delivering the actual products in the order to a port in the United States. The components of landed cost are as follows:

1.   F. O. B. price - This is the cost of the merchandise delivered onto a ship in the originating country.

2.   Agent's fee - This is a commission paid to the individual or firm that protects the corporation's interests in the foreign country.

3.   Ocean Freight Charges - These represent the cost of transporting the goods from the foreign port to the destination port in the United States.

4.   Duty - This is a collection of taxes paid to the U. S. government.

5.   Port Handling Charges - These charges represent the cost of processing items in the port.

6.   Import Charges - These are the overhead costs in the import department to administer the importation process.

This brief description does not really do justice to the complexity of an actual order, but it does introduce a set of important entities:

a) Orders and letters of credit are instances of the DOCUMENT entity. We will find many types of documents in such a system. After evaluating alternatives according to the criteria discussed in Section 2, we decided to amalgamate them into a single entity set. In the discussion below, these are partially separated in order to better illustrate their interrelationships, but in the implementation they were combined.

b) The buyer, manufacturer, and banks represent instances of the CONTRACTING-ENTITY entity. Similarly, all employees of the corporation, as well as all customers, fall within this entity. Superficially, one would certainly think of keeping the sets distinct (such as EMPLOYEE, CUSTOMER, BANK, MANUFACTURER, etc.). However, since an employee might be a customer (and even a manufacturer), it is important to form the more general set. In general, if a single real entity might occur in several different entity-sets (in different roles) then we consider the design suspect.

c) Related to orders (which are DOCUMENTs), we have two more entities, SCHEDULE and SCHEDULED-EVENT. A SCHEDULE is normally a set of SCHEDULED-EVENTs. It might clarify this to illustrate the sort of schedule that actually occurs in an order.

Order Schedule

Order 1234   Product 567

New York   San Francisco   New Orleans

	New York	San Francisco	New Orleans
May 1, 1980	1000 units	2500 units	800 units
June 15, 1980	4000	10000	3200
Sept 1, 1980	4000	10000	3200
Jan 10, 1981	1000	7500	800
Totals	10000	30000	8000

For this system each column represents a schedule. Each entry represents a scheduled event. It is possible for a distribution center, as
well as the port, to be specified; this could result in multiple columns
for a single port. It is reasonably common for schedules to change
(normally an entire schedule is altered, not just a scheduled event).
Further, as goods are actually shipped and received it would seem natural to relate quantities to the scheduled events. Such a mechanism
proved prohibitively complex and was not implemented.

d) It will become necessary to record the exact status of financial agreements with contracting entities. This leads to two more entities, AC-
COUNTs and FINANCIAL-TRANSACTIONs. An account will be related to both
the contracting entity and the cost center which manages the account. A
record of each transfer of funds will be kept in the
FINANCIAL-TRANSACTION entity-set. A more complex accounting model will
be presented in a later paper.

e) PRODUCTs are the items manufactured, shipped, and sold.

So far we have arrived at the following ER diagram:

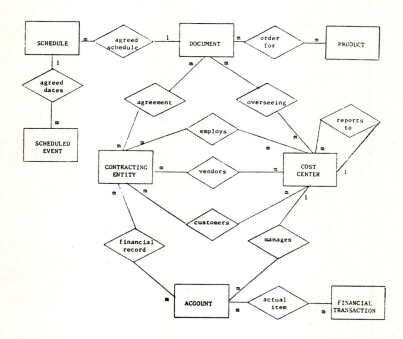

3.3   VERIFICATION OF PAYMENT AGREEMENT

As soon as an order has been approved, applications for letters of credit
are directed to one or more banks. Approved letters of credit are returned by
the bank to the corporation. Copies are forwarded to the foreign manufacturer
to indicate that payment is guaranteed.

We will summarize the fact that different documents relate to one another as follows:

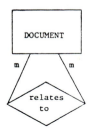

This drawing is not particularly edifying. Hence, to illustrate the details
of how the documents relate we will use a drawing like this one:

In our data structure all documents are actually grouped into a single entity
set.   However, as we continue introducing more types of documents, illustrating the more complex interrelationships will be necessary to convey the essential details of the data structure.

3.4   SHIPPING GOODS FROM THE MANUFACTURER TO THE PORT

   When the manufacturer has goods from one or more orders ready for shipment,
he prepares one or more Commercial Invoices listing the goods, quantities,
and original order numbers, and transports the items to the shipping docks.
At this point, an agent representing the corporation verifies the quality and
quantities of the products.   Once verified, the goods are placed on one or
more ships.   The goods become the responsibility of the shipping company at
this point.   The shipping company produces one or more Bills of Lading (BOL's)
for the goods.   A BOL designates batches of items loaded onto a given ship.
Each of these batches contain the order number and quantities of products in
the batch.   Such a batch is called a TRACKABLE-QUANTITY (TQ).

   The TQ's for a given commercial invoice may go on several ships.   However,
all of the commercial invoices and BOL'S for the goods are grouped together
into a "staple." The staple should be reconcilable; that is, the commercial
invoice line items should balance against the line items in the BOL's.   This
staple is sent to the Import Department (a Cost Center), which can then au-
thorize payment for the goods.

Certain complexities can arise. For example, if a ship becomes inoperable, the cargo may have to be loaded onto one or more new ships. In some cases TQ's may be split in this process. Thus TQ's have a time span of existence. It would be nice to relate TQ's to the corresponding previous TQ's in the case of splits, but in practice this proved infeasible. Also, a given ship may be used by several shipping companies, but only one per voyage.

The two new entities that result from this short discussion are the TRACKA-BLE-QUANTITYs and the VESSEL/VOYAGEs (i. e. ships on voyages). In addition new types of documents (Commercial Invoices and Bills of Lading) and contracting entities (shipping lines) were introduced.

These new entities are depicted in the following ER-diagram:

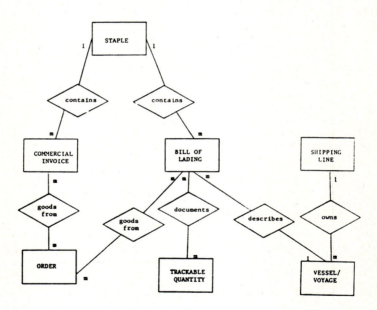

3.5   COMMERCIAL INVOICE PAYMENT

We need to digress from following the flow of goods to discuss several financial transactions.   When the import department receives a stapled group of
CI's and BOL's, they are validated and payment is sent to the manufacturer.
At the same time, one or more Import Invoices (IIs) is sent to the port for
which goods are destined.   This document removes the cost of the goods from
the import department and places it on the port. The import invoice is introduced into the ER-diagram as follows:

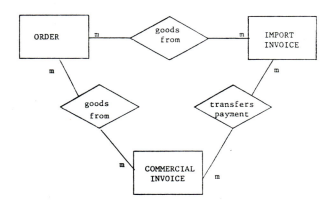

3.6   ARRIVAL IN THE PORT

In order to discuss the arrival of a ship in the port, we must introduce
two new contracting entities. First, a broker representing the corporation
oversees the process of handling goods at the port; and second, the United
States government (a particularly significant contracting entity) enters the
picture to collect import duties.   After inspection by customs agents, the
goods are unloaded and the shipping company's responsibilities are fulfilled.
At this point a customs charge is imposed for bringing the goods into the
country.   A new document, a Consumption Entry (CE), is created by the government, reflecting customs charges.   It should be noted that the amount on a CE
is only an estimate and may be adjusted at a later time at the government's
discretion.

Next, the broker pays the ocean freight charges to the shipping company and
the custom charges to the government.   He sends to the import department one
or more Broker Invoices (BIs) and an Ocean Freight and Duty Sheet (OFDS).
These documents bill the corporation for expenses and also provide supporting
documentation to reconcile the expenses against BOL's and original orders.
Finally, the goods are moved to the port warehouse, where they are beyond the
scope of the import tracking system and fall in the domain of a domestic distribution system.   The ER-diagram, including port contracting entities and do-

cuments is as follows:

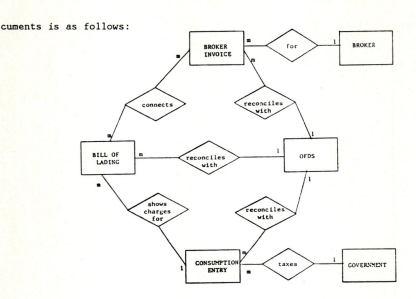

4. THE AIRLINE RESERVATION SYSTEM

In this section we will describe an airline reservation system, with an eye toward those features which it has in common with the import tracking system described above.   Both systems involve both scheduled and actual movement of entities along a series of connecting paths.   Our airline reservation system will place more emphasis on the scheduling of such movement, which will make it more complex than the import tracking system.   In fact the basic elements of the import tracking system will be readily apparent as a subset of the system now under consideration.

4.1   CORPORATE STRUCTURE

We begin with that part of the model which is entirely analogous to part of the import system.   Airlines, like other complex organizations, have a hier- archical structure of COST-CENTERs.   EMPLOYEEs are assigned responsibilities within one or more of these, and each of the COST-CENTERs transacts business and maintains financial records through a number of ACCOUNTs.   The airline has a very large number of CUSTOMERs, which often include its own EMPLOYEEs.   As above, we combine EMPLOYEEs, CUSTOMERs, and other persons and companies with whom the airline does business into an entity called CONTRACTING-ENTITY.   At this point we have developed the following part of our system:

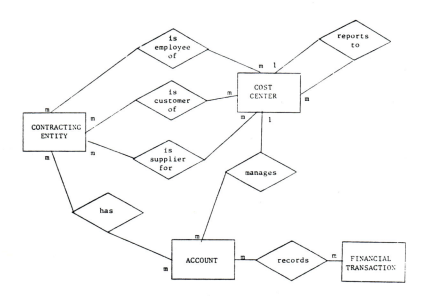

Now in the case we are considering we have the added feature that customers frequently book reservations through a travel agency. Both CONTRACTING-ENTI-TYs (the customer and the agent) will relate to different portions of the re-sulting model. Thus, a "represents" relationship will have to be added relat-ing a travel agency and its customers.

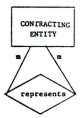

Further, a customer of a travel agency or airline creates one or more RES-ERVATIONs which record a major transaction, sometimes involving several TICK-

ETs.   The actual flights that a customer takes will have to relate back to
this RESERVATION. The RESERVATION may relate to both the customer and a travel agency.

4.2   FLIGHTS AND HOPS

A plane trip is made up of a series of segments from one airport to another. Such a segment we will call a HOP.   Certain sequences of HOPs are always
made together, with the same individual PLANE and with short intervals on the
ground between HOPs. Such a sequence is called a FLIGHT.   HOPs are instances
of SCHEDULED-HOPs, and FLIGHTs are instances of SCHEDULED-FLIGHTs.   The SCHE-
DULED-HOPs and SCHEDULED-FLIGHTs are what appear in the airlines' schedules.

Customers or travel agents (CONTRACTING-ENTITYs) buy tickets, which are for
particular series of HOPs.   These bear no particular relation to FLIGHTs in
the sense that a ticket may involve only one HOP of a FLIGHT,   all the HOPs
from several FLIGHTs, or a sequence of connecting HOPs from different FLIGHTs.

Finally, a crew member (another CONTRACTING-ENTITY),   though he has no
TICKET, is associated with the sequence of HOPs on which he is assigned.
These often, but not always, comprise a FLIGHT.   Our model has now been ex-

tended in the following way:

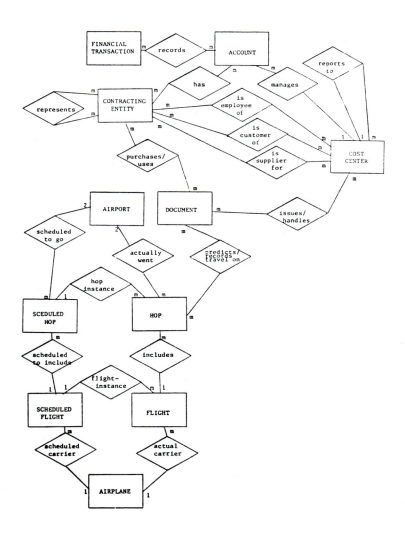

Although differences exist, there are strong similarities to the import tracking system. Here the DOCUMENTs include reservations, tickets, and coupons (which represent a single HOP). The trackable quantities are the customers themselves. The carrier corresponds to the plane. There are here, as before, scheduled events and actual events.

Perhaps some extra comments on the DOCUMENTs involved is in order. A customer makes a RESERVATION which represents scheduled space on a sequence of HOPs. The RESERVATION may be for more than one person, as in the case of a family traveling together. Either before or after making a RESERVATION, the customer buys a TICKET, which consists of one or more COUPONs. A COUPON (surrendered when a passenger boards an airplane) represents a sequence of HOPs which are part of the same FLIGHT. A RESERVATION is related to the CONTRACTING-ENTITY who made it and to the HOPs it reserves space on. A TICKET is related to the COUPONs of which it is composed - which are in turn related to the HOPs they represent. The TICKET also relates to the actual passenger. Finally, once both a RESERVATION and corresponding TICKET exist, they must be related. A single RESERVATION may be related to more than one TICKET in the case of complicated itineraries or group reservations.

4.3   MAKING A RESERVATION

In order to assist a customer (or travel agent) in determining which HOPs should appear on his ticket and whether space is available we will add to the model the entities and relationships necessary to make a reservation. The customer is interested in finding a convenient PATH between two CITYs. Each PATH is made up of a number of SCHEDULED-HOPs. The CITYs are served by a number of AIRPORTs, which are connected by the SCHEDULED-HOPs. In order to facilitate the calculation of a path when a precalculated PATH does not already exist, certain CITYs are designated as regional centers, between which PATHs are precalculated and stored. Each CITY which is not a regional center is related to one or more regional centers which serve it. It is thus possible to calculate a path between two relatively small CITYs by considering PATHs between the regional centers which serve them. If it becomes clear that a particular path is very frequently being calculated in this way, then it can be stored in the database as one of the precalculated PATHs.

We now have the following extended model:

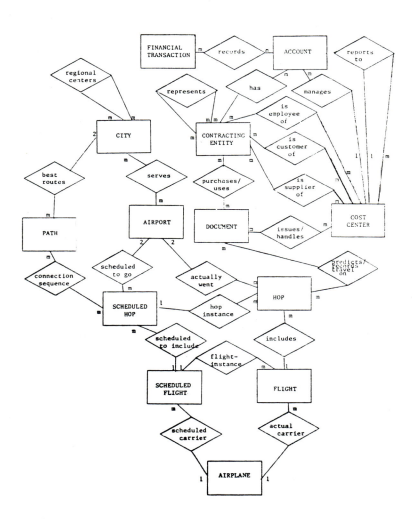

5.   DISTRIBUTION SYSTEMS

Distribution systems form a fundamental class of system.   They range from
the trivial to the very extreme of complexity, and are found everywhere, from
the internal distribution of reports within an office to the worldwide distribution of manufactured products by multinational corporations.

5.1   GENERALIZING THE CONCEPT OF DESTINATION

Let us begin with a simple example which came out of an investigation into
how addresses were to be treated in a banking database model.   Reports of financial transactions were . to be sent to individual customers, corporations,
trustees, and many others.   Individuals often received mail at corporate addresses.   In order to reduce postage and handling costs, it was desired to
combine the reports destined for various individuals at the same corporate address into the same envelope, which would be handled as a unit until it
reached the destination corporation, at which time it became the responsibility of that corporation's internal distribution system.   This led to the following model:

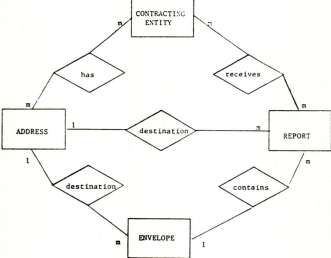

In this model,

1.   REPORT represents an individual copy of a report which is to be sent to
     a specific destination.

2.   CONTRACTING-ENTITY refers to the entities which get the reports.   They
     may be individuals, departments, corporations, etc.

3. ADDRESS is an address (as read by the post office) where REPORTs are to be delivered. CONTRACTING-ENTITYs receive various reports at various addresses.

4. An ENVELOPE is a physical package containing several reports (perhaps destined for various individuals) to be sent to the same ADDRESS.

This report distribution system is an instance of a more general distribution system model. In the above case all envelopes originated at the same place (the bank), the delivery mechanism was not an important part of the system (it was always either the postal system or a bank-operated hand-carrying system), and delivery of reports was automatic rather than being driven by requests from the contracting entities. In the next example, we remove these restrictions, and get a model of the delivery system of a medium-sized manufacturing firm. The company accepts orders from its customers for its products, packages the products into shippable units, combines packages into shipments to individual customers, and then sends out a delivery truck containing shipments for several customers on trip which delivers each shipment to its destination before returning to the warehouse.

We retain from the report distribution system the separation of address as a separate entity. This is necessary because not only may several customers take delivery at the same address, but a given customer may take delivery of various packages at different addresses. This leads us to the following diagram:

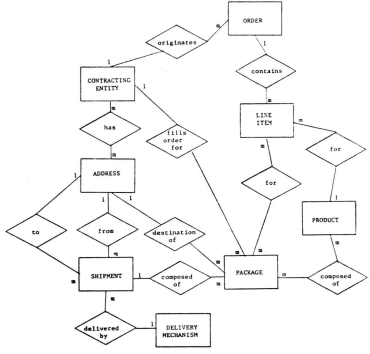

Some discussion should be made of the DELIVERY MECHANISM entity. In the case of our manufacturing firm which delivers its own products, the delivery mechanism consists of TRIPs made by TRUCKs of given capacity, which limits the number of SHIPMENTs which can be carried on a given TRIP. Scheduling a delivery via this mechanism depends on whether the company's trucks have regular routes, make different trips each day, or utilize some other scheduling mechanism. In some cases all the complexity of the airline reservation system may be present. In other cases, for example when the delivery mechanism is the Post Office, the delivery mechanism may be so straightforward from the company's point of view that it may be omitted from the model altogether.

In the most complicated cases, the complexity of the airline reservation system may be compounded with that of the import tracking system to make up the delivery mechanism. This occurs, for example, when shipments are to be made through various countries, changing carriers several times in the process. In this case a SHIPMENT may relate to several DELIVERY MECHANISMs.

In fact, the DELIVERY MECHANISM shown in the above model is really just the root of a hierarchy of distribution systems, each one implementing HOPs of the system at the next higher level. That is, from one point of view the delivery mechanism may be simply the Post Office, but the Post Office has trucks which make trips, and contracts with airlines whose schedules it must know, etc. Different companies need to maintain information on this hierarchy to different depths. Input for the scheduling process at one level of the hierarchy consists of output from the scheduling process of the next level down.

6. CONCLUSION

This paper grew out of a project initiated to develop prototype entity-relationship models. It reflects the outlook developed by a number of practicing consultants that in fact most industrial data base design problems represent variations on a small number of basic designs. In this paper we have briefly sketched the basic components of systems that schedule and track the movement of items.

The actual systems that were presented are abstractions of those discussed in detail by the Chicago Area Data Base Design Group. They resulted from interchanges between people that had implemented similar systems. Since the purpose of this paper was to emphasize the similarities of the abstractions, we have completely ignored the details involved in actual implementations. However, we believe that ER models represent far more than just an analysis tool that is relatively disconnected from the decisions required in completing a physical design. Rather, an extended ER model can more or less automatically be translated into a physical model that offers an excellent initial point for detailed physical design. In previous work we have discussed the process of translating ER models into IMS designs [4,5]. Similar translations into competing data base systems are equally straightforward.

REFERENCES

1. Bachman, C. and Daya, M., The role concepts in data models, in: Proceedings of 3rd Very Large Data Base Conference, (1977).

2. Chen, P. P., The entity-relationship model: Toward a unified view of data, ACM Transactions on Database Systems 1. 1 (March 1976) 9-37.

3. Chen, P. P., The entity-relationship model: A basis for the enterprise view of data, Proceedings of 1977 National Computer Conference, Dallas, Texas, AFIPS Conference Proceedings, Vol. 46, 77-84.

4. Lusk, Ewing L., Overbeek, Ross A., and Parrello, Bruce, A practical design methodology for the implementation of IMS databases, using the entity-relationship model, Proceedings of the ACM SIGMOD International Conference on Management of Data, Los Angeles, 1980.

5. Lusk, Ewing L., Overbeek, Ross A., and Parrello, Bruce, The design of IMS databases from entity-relationship models, unpublished manuscipt.

6. Schiffner, G. and Scheuermann, P., Multiple views and abstractions with an extended entity-relationship model, Technical Report, Dept. of Electrical Engineering and Computer Science, Northwestern University, Evanston, Illinois (1979).

Entity-Relationship Approach to
Information Modeling and Analysis, P.P. Chen (ed.)
Elsevier Science Publishers B.V. (North-Holland)
©ER Institute, 1983

Using The Entity-Relationship Model
For Implementing Multi-Model Database Systems

Hai-Yann Hwang
The University of Texas at Austin
Department of Computer Sciences

Umeshwar Dayal
Computer Corporation of America
Cambridge, Massachusetts

ABSTRACT

This paper shows how to use the Entity-Relationship Model as an intermediate mapping model in the design of relational interfaces to network and hierarchical database systems. Algorithms for defining an equivalent relational view of an Entity-Relationship schema and for translating operations at the relational interface down into equivalent operations on the database are developed.

1. INTRODUCTION

Multi-model database systems have been envisaged [ANSI 77]. In such a system, the users' views (external schemas) might be expressed in data models different from that of the conceptual database schema. Central to the implementation of a multi-model system is the problem of mapping schemas and operations from one data model to another. Mapping directly between two arbitrary data models (especially models with very different data manipulation languages, e.g., CODASYL and Relational) is not an easy matter. The task may be made simpler if we perform the mapping via a common intermediate model. It has been suggested that the Entity-Relationship (abbreviated E-R) Model can fulfill this function of an intermediate mapping model [Chen 76, Chen 77, LY 78, CP 80, CT 80, WK 80]. This paper demonstrates the feasibility of that proposal.

We consider the following scenario. The conceptual schema is defined in a network or hierarchical model, e.g., CODASYL, IMS. (Henceforth, we shall use CODASYL as our example network model, although our methodology can be applied to any network or hierarchical model.) To support relational users of the system, we want to provide a relational interface. This requires that a relational view equivalent to the conceptual schema be defined for these users, and that the users' programs written in a relational language be translated into equivalent CODASYL DML programs. In [Zaniolo 79a, Zaniolo 79b] an algorithm for transforming a CODASYL schema into an equivalent relational view is presented; however, the problem of mapping operations from the relational view down to the CODASYL database is not addressed. In this paper, we propose a two-step procedure. The CODASYL conceptual schema is first transformed into an equivalent Entity-Relationship schema, and then an equivalent relational view is defined over the latter. Correspondingly, relational operations from the user level are first translated into equivalent operations at the Entity-Relationship level, and these equivalent operations are then implemented by CODASYL DML programs.

We examine these issues in turn. In Section 2 we show that Entity-Relationship schemas can be described as graphs. Thus, the data structure diagram of a CODASYL schema can be directly interpreted as an Entity-Relationship schema, with the record types interpreted as entity types and the set types interpreted as relationship types. The primary keys of the entity types can be determined from the constraints on the CODASYL schema, using, for example, the algorithm described in [Zaniolo 79a, Zaniolo 79b]. Furthermore, to use the Entity-Relationship Model as an intermediate mapping model, we require a high-level non-procedural data manipulation language for it. A language, ERL, is defined in Section 2 for this purpose.

Section 3 addresses the problem of deriving a relational view equivalent to an Entity-Relationship schema. In [Dayal 79, DB 80], the notion of schema equivalence is defined precisely, and a functor that transforms general network schemas into provably equivalent relational schemas is presented. In Section 3, this transformation is adapted to obtain a procedure for mapping an Entity-Relationship schema into an equivalent relational one.

Section 4 describes procedures for translating relational queries and updates (we use the relational language QUEL [HSW 75] as an example) into equivalent ERL queries and updates. Translating the non-procedural ERL statements into CODASYL DML programs is then a compilation problem, and is not addressed in this paper.

Thus, this paper makes two contributions. First, it contributes to the theory of schema equivalence by developing procedures for mapping operations from a relational view into equivalent operations against an Entity-Relationship schema (and, hence, against a general network schema). Second, it contributes to the practical problem of constructing a relational interface to a network or hierarchical database system by showing how to use the Entity-Relationship Model as an intermediary.*

---

*In [Dayal 79, DB 80], we give algorithms for translating operations for the network model into equivalent operations in the relational model. These algorithms can be trivially adapted to translating from ERL into QUEL. Thus, the E-R model could be used as an interface to a relational system. This architecture might appeal to users since an E-R Schema conveys more semantic information than flat relational tables.

2. ERL — A QUERY LANGUAGE FOR THE ENTITY-RELATIONSHIP MODEL

In this section, we first show how to describe schemas in the E-R model as graphs. We then introduce ERL, a graph-based query language for this model. ERL is a variant of NQUEL, a non-procedural query language for a general network model, introduced in [Dayal 79, DB 80]. NQUEL is itself an extension of the relational language QUEL [HSW 75]. (We base our work on QUEL only because of its popularity. Any relational language could be similarly extended to obtain a language for the E-R model. Other approaches to defining query languages for the E-R model are described in [Poonen 78, Shoshani 78].)

2.1 Entity-Relationship Schemas

A <u>database</u> <u>schema</u> in the E-R model can be thought of as a graph $\mathscr{G} = (\mathscr{E}, \mathscr{R})$, where $\mathscr{E}$ is a set of nodes and $\mathscr{R}$ is a set of edges. Each node in the graph represents an <u>entity</u> <u>type</u>, and each edge a <u>relationship</u> <u>type</u>.

Each entity type has a set of <u>attributes</u>. Each attribute has a <u>domain</u> of values associated with it. Each entity type has a primary key that serves to uniquely identify entities of that type. An entity type is <u>regular</u> if its primary key is a subset of its own attributes. An entity type E is <u>weak</u> if its primary key is the union of some of its own attributes together with the primary keys of other entity types to which E is related. Thus, an entity of weak type is not uniquely identified by its own attribute values, but via relationships that it participates in with other entities [Chen 76]. (Weak entities correspond to AUTOMATIC MANDATORY members in CODASYL.) A relationship type is <u>regular</u> if it is between two regular entity types, and is <u>weak</u> otherwise. (We assume that relationship types do not have attributes. This is not a restrictive assumption, for such relationship types can always be modelled as entity types. Furthermore, we describe only binary relationships here. The model can be extended in a straightforward manner to include general k-ary relationships either by treating schemas as hypergraphs [Dayal 79] or by treating a k-ary relationship as a collection of k binary relationships as in CODASYL.)

A <u>database</u> <u>state</u> is an occurrence of the database schema, and can also be thought of as a graph. Each node in the graph represents an entity and is labelled with the type of the entity. Each edge represents a relationship and is labelled with the type of the relationship. There is the obvious typing constraint, viz., if edge [e1,e2] is of type R, and entities e1, e2 are of type E1, E2 respectively, then R must have been defined in the schema as a relationship type between entity types E1 and E2. For each entity type E, we shall refer to the set of all entities of that type in the current database state as the <u>entity</u> <u>set</u> E. Figure 1 shows a schema graph for a manufacturing company (adapted from [Chen 76]).

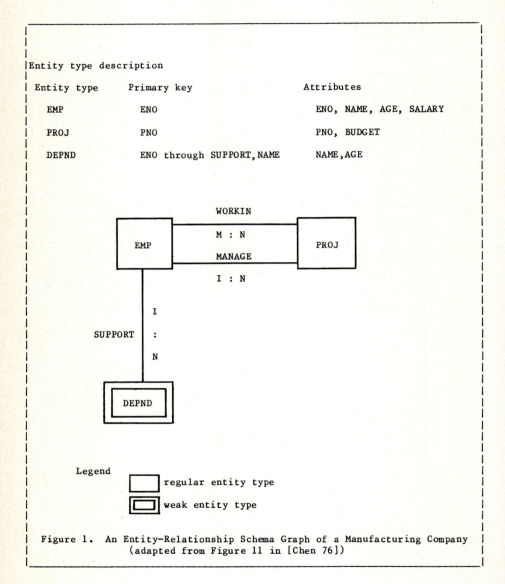

Entity type description

Entity type	Primary key	Attributes
EMP	ENO	ENO, NAME, AGE, SALARY
PROJ	PNO	PNO, BUDGET
DEPND	ENO through SUPPORT, NAME	NAME, AGE

Legend

☐ regular entity type

▣ weak entity type

Figure 1. An Entity-Relationship Schema Graph of a Manufacturing Company
(adapted from Figure 11 in [Chen 76])

2.2 Retrieval Queries In ERL

Queries in ERL are formulated using <u>entity variables,</u> which are declared by range statements: Range of e is E. At any instant e denotes some entity in entity set E. The value of an attribute A of e is denoted A(e). The syntax of a retrieval query in ERL is:

> Retrieve into <result-name> (<target-list>)
>   where <qualification>.

Here, <<u>target-list</u>> is a list of <u>terms,</u> which are either constants or attributes of entity variables; <<u>qualification</u>> is a Boolean combination of <u>join clauses</u> (<term> op <term>) and/or <u>relationship clauses</u> ([e1,e2] in R), where op is a comparison operator, e.g., "=", ">", and R is a relationship type in the schema. The clause ([e1,e2] in R) is satisfied by the entities e1, e2 iff there is a relationship (i.e., an edge) of type R between e1 and e2 in the current database state.

The semantics of the above query are as follows: for each entity variable e in the query, get its range, viz., entity set E; form the product of these entity sets; restrict the product by the qualification; project on the target list; then treat the result as a new set of entities of type <result-name>.

Some ERL queries with their English translations are given in Figure 2a.

2.3 Updates In ERL

There are seven update statements in ERL. Their syntax and semantics are explained below.

1. <u>Insert</u> into E(A1:=f1,..,Ak:=fk) where qual.

    This statement evaluates terms f1,..,fk for the entities satisfying qual. For each k-tuple of values, an entity is created with value(fi) assigned to attribute Ai, and is inserted into entity set E provided an entity with the same primary key value does not already exist in E. E should be a regular entity type. (For weak entity types, see statement 3.)

2. <u>Connect</u> R(e1,e2) where qual.

    This statement inserts a relationship of type R for each pair of entities

---

a. Queries

  1. Find the name of the manager of Project 254.
          Range of e is EMP
          Range of p is PROJ
          Retrieve into Result(NAME(e)) where [e,p] in MANAGE
                                        AND PNO(p)=254.

  2. Find the names of the dependents of all employees who work for pro-
     jects with budget exceeding 100K.
          Range of e is EMP
          Range of p is PROJ
          Range of d is DEPND
          Retrieve into Result(NAME(d)) where [e,d] in SUPPORT
                      AND [e,p] in WORKIN AND BUDGET(p)>100K.

b. Updates

  1. Assign the employee with ENO 100 to manage Project 254.
          Range of e is EMP
          Range of p is PROJ
          Connect MANAGE(e,p) where ENO(e)=100 AND PNO(p)=254.

  2. Fire all employees who support dependents older than 30.
          Range of e is EMP
          Range of d is DEPND
          Delete e where [e,d] in SUPPORT AND AGE(d)>30.

  3. Give all employees working with Manager Charlie Brown a 10% raise.
          Range of e,m is EMP
          Range of p is PROJ
          Replace e(SALARY:=1.1*SALARY(e)) where [e,p] in WORKIN
              AND [m,p] in MANAGE AND NAME(m)="Charlie Brown".

        Figure 2. Some ERL Queries and Updates and Their Meanings

in the ranges of e1, e2 that satisfy qual.

3. **Insert** into E(A1:=f1,..,Ak:=fk)
      and **connect** via R1 to e1,...,via Rp to ep where qual.

      This statement creates an entity of type E for each tuple
value(f1),..,value(fk)>, and connects the new entity through relationship
Rt to each entity et, t=1,..,p that satisfies qual. This combined statement is used for creating weak entities along with the weak relationships

necessary to identify them.

4. <u>Delete</u> e where qual.

This statement deletes all the entities in the range of e that satisfy qual. (Deleting an entity causes the deletion of all its relationships and its dependent weak entities.)

5. <u>Disconnect</u> R(e1,e2) where qual.

This statement deletes the relationships of type R between each pair of entities in the ranges of e1, e2 that satisfy qual.

6. <u>Replace</u> e(A1:=f1,...,Ak:=fk) where qual.

This statement replaces each entity in the range of e that satisfies qual by a new entity with value(fi) for attribute Ai.

7. <u>Reconnect</u> R([e1,e2]:=[e1´,e2´]) where qual.

This statement is equivalent to the (indivisible) sequence of connecting e1´, e2´ then disconnecting e1, e2. It is useful for changing the association of weak entities (and corresponds to moving MANDATORY members from one occurrence of a CODASYL set type to another).

Some examples of ERL updates and their English translations are given in Figure 2b.

3. TRANSFORMATION OF AN ENTITY-RELATIONSHIP SCHEMA INTO A RELATIONAL VIEW

To construct a relational interface to an E-R database, the E-R schema has to be transformed into its relational equivalent. Some work has been done on the transformation of schemas from the network model to the relational model. Zaniolo presented an algorithm to translate a CODASYL schema into a relational one [Zaniolo 79a, Zaniolo 79b], which incorporates each set association into the corresponding member record relation. (This is possible because in the CODASYL model, the "sets" represent 1 : N associations.) A general transformation H from the general network model to the relational model was proposed in [Dayal 79, DB 80]. This transformation models each relationship type and each record type with separate relations.

In this section, we propose an algorithm analogous to H for translating an E-R schema $\mathscr{S}$ into an equivalent relational schema.

Algorithm $\mathscr{S}$TRANS

1. For each regular entity type E in $\mathscr{S}$, create a relation scheme containing all of E´s attributes. Designate E´s primary key (denoted ID_E) to be the key of this relation scheme. Such relations are called <u>regular</u> <u>entity</u> <u>relations</u>.

2. For each weak entity type E in $\mathscr{S}$, create a relation scheme containing the union of E´s attributes and E´s primary key. Designate E´s primary key to be the key of this relation scheme. Such relations are called <u>weak</u> <u>entity</u> <u>relations</u>. (Recall that the primary key may contain some attributes not belonging to E, called <u>foreign attributes</u>. Thus, the relation scheme, in fact, incorporates the weak relationships used in identifying entities of type E.)

3. For each regular relationship type or weak relationship type not used in step 2, create a relation scheme R containing the primary keys of the participating entity relations. Such relations are called <u>relationship</u> <u>relations</u>. The key of relation scheme R depends on whether R is 1 : N or M : N.

   For the relationship or weak entity relation schemes, which contain attributes coming from other relation schemes, the corresponding subset constraints have to be imposed. The algorithm is illustrated in Figure 3.

```
                Relation schemes


                   EMP ( ENO, NAME, AGE, SALARY )

                   PROJ ( PNO, BUDGET )

                   DEPND ( ENO, NAME, AGE )

                   WORKIN ( ENO, PNO )

                   MANAGE ( ENO, PNO )


             Subset constraints


                   EMP[ENO]   ⊇ WORKIN[ENO]

                   PROJ[PNO]  ⊇ WORKIN[PNO]

                   EMP[ENO]   ⊇ MANAGE[ENO]

                   PROJ[PNO]  ⊇ MANAGE[PNO]

                   EMP[ENO]   ⊇ DEPND[ENO]
```

Figure 3.   The Relational Equivalent of the E-R Schema
in Figure 1 Derived by Algorithm $\mathscr{S}$ TRANS

4. MAPPING QUEL QUERIES AND UPDATES AGAINST THE VIEW
INTO EQUIVALENT ERL OPERATIONS

Once a relational view is set up over the E-R database, the users access
and manipulate the database by posing relational queries and updates against
this view. These relational commands have to be translated into the
corresponding ERL queries or updates against the underlying E-R schema for
processing. This section describes translation procedures for this purpose.
QUEL0, the aggregation-free subset of QUEL [HSW 75] is assumed to be the relational language used at the interface, although the translation procedures can

be adapted to other relational languages. The translation procedures have the important property that the ERL queries/updates produced by them are <u>equivalent</u> to the given QUELO queries/updates. (The notion of equivalence is defined precisely in the Appendix.)

4.1 Transformation Of QUELO Queries

To convert a QUELO query against the relational view

q: Retrieve Result(Al:=fl,...,Ak:=fk) where qual

into its ERL equivalent against the E-R schema, there are two issues to be dealt with:

1. q might contain tuple variables ranging over relationship relation schemes. Those variables have to be eliminated, with corresponding relationship clauses added to the qualification, instead.

2. q might contain indexed tuples e.X where X is a foreign attribute in the entity relation scheme over which e ranges. These attributes have to be shifted back to the correct ancestor entity type, with the addition of appropriate relationship clauses to the qualification.

In the following algorithm, step 1 handles the first problem, and step 2 the second. Step 3 changes the indexed tuple notation used in QUELO (e.g., e.X) to the functional notation in ERL (viz., X(e)).

<u>Algorithm QTRANS</u>

1. For each tuple variable r in q ranging over a relationship relation scheme R that associates entity relation schemes El and E2, do the following:

   i. Delete the range declaration for r.

   ii. If there is a tuple variable el, ranging over El and qual contains the join clause r.ID_El=el.ID_El,* then delete the join clause and take el to be the entity in El that r associates. Otherwise introduce a new variable, say el, with the range declaration: Range of el is El,

---

*If ID_El contains more than one attribute, then there should be a join clause for each attribute.

to refer to the entity in El that r associates.

   iii. Replace each occurrence of r.A by el.A where A is an attribute in ID_El.

   iv. Do (ii) and (iii) for E2.

   v. Conjoin the relationship clause ([el,e2] in R) to qual.

2. For each indexed tuple e2.X, where e2 ranges over entity relation scheme E2, and X is a foreign attribute introduced into E2 through weak relationship R between El and E2, do the following:

   i. If there is a tuple variable el ranging over El and qual contains the join clause e2.ID_El=el.ID_El, then delete the join clause and take el to be the ancestor from which e2 inherits X´s value. Otherwise create a new variable, say el, with the range declaration: Range of el is El, to refer to that ancestor.

   ii. Replace each occurrence of e2.A by el.A where A is in ID_El (e.g., X).

     For schemas containing a hierarchy of weak relationships through which primary keys are inherited, step 2 must be applied bottom-up.

3. Replace each indexed tuple e.A by the functional notation A(e).

The algorithm is illustrated in Figure 4.

Assume the E-R schema in Figure 1,
        the relational view in Figure 3,

  for Query 2 in Figure 2: Find the names of the
        dependents of all employees who work for projects
        with budget exceeding 100K,

  the QUELO query is:

        Range of d is DEPND
        Range of w is WORKIN
        Range of p is PROJ
        Retrieve into Result(d.NAME) where d.ENO=w.ENO
                    AND w.PNO=p.PNO AND p.BUDGET>100K.

Apply Algorithm QTRANS step by step:

  1. Eliminate w by creating variable e ranging over EMP,
     with [e,p] referring to the relationship w:
        Range of d is DEPND
        Range of e is EMP
        Range of p is PROJ
        Retrieve into Result(d.NAME) where d.ENO=e.ENO
                    AND [e,p] in WORKIN AND p.BUDGET>100K.

  2. For foreign attribute ENO of variable d, find d's
     ancestor e, modify the query to:
        Retrieve into Result(d.name) where [e,d] in SUPPORT
                    AND [e,p] in WORKIN AND p.BUDGET>100K.

  3. Replace d.NAME and p.BUDGET with NAME(d) and BUDGET(p)
     respectively.

The resulting query is identical to Query 2 in Figure 2.

  Figure 4.   Translating QUELO Queries into ERL Equivalents

4.2 Transformation Of QUELO Updates

To translate a query, only the target list and the qualification need to be considered. For an update, we also have to convert the command itself into the corresponding ERL command. This section discusses the translation procedures, called <u>Algorithm</u> <u>UTRANS</u> collectively, for the three update statements in QUELO, viz., Append, Delete, and Replace.

4.2.1 Insertion

Consider the following QUELO insertion statement:

Append to Z(A1:=f1,...,Ak:=fk) where qual.

In case Z is an entity relation scheme, the insertion corresponds to the insertion of entities, or to an insertion and connection if Z contains foreign attributes. (The subset constraints ensure that the ancestor entities already exist.) Treating insertion as a special case of insertion and connection, the translation procedure is as follows:

1. For the foreign attributes Ai in the target list that Z inherits from ancestor type E through relationship R, do the following:

   i. Create a new variable e ranging over E.

   ii. Delete assignment Ai:=fi from the target list, then conjoin a new join clause e.Ai=fi to qual.

   iii. Change the command to "Insert and connect", attach "via R to e" to specify the connecting relationship.

2. Apply Algorithm QTRANS to transform the target list and qualification.

In case Z is a relationship relation scheme associating entity types E1 and E2, then the insertion corresponds to a connection. The transformation procedure, then, is:

1.

i. Create new variables el, e2 ranging over El, E2 respectively.

ii. Delete the whole target list; for each i from 1 to k, if Ai is in
     ID_El, conjoin (el.Ai=fi) to qual; otherwise, conjoin (e2.Ai=fi) to
     qual.

iii. Change the statement to "Connect Z(el,e2) where qual".

2. Apply Algorithm QTRANS to transform the qualification.

4.2.2 Deletion

Consider the following QUELO deletion statement:

        Range of z is Z
        Delete z where qual.

In case Z is an entity relation scheme, the deletion corresponds to the
deletion of entities. In ERL semantics the effect of deleting an entity might
propagate, whereas in QUEL semantics the effect of deleting a tuple does not
propagate. However, the subset constraints imposed over the relational view
will force the user to remove all the relationships that an entity participates in and all its dependent weak entities before deleting the entity
itself, thus making the two deletions equivalent. Hence, we need only apply
Algorithm QTRANS to transform the qualification.

In case Z is a relationship relation scheme associating El and E2, the
deletion corresponds to a disconnection:

1.

i. Create new variables el, e2 ranging over El, E2 respectively.

ii. Conjoin to qual (el.Ai=z.Ai) for Ai in ID_El; (e2.Ai=z.Ai) for Ai in
     ID_E2.

iii. Change the statement to "Disconnect Z(el,e2) where qual".

2. Apply Algorithm QTRANS to transform the qualification.

4.2.3 Replacement

Consider the following QUEL0 replace statement:

```
Range of z is Z
Replace z(Al:=fl,...,Ak:=fk) where qual.
```

In case Z is an entity relation scheme, the replacement corresponds to the replacement of entities, or to a replacement and reconnection if Z contains foreign attributes. For the first case, we need only apply Algorithm QTRANS to transform the target list and the qualification. For the second case, since ERL has no single statement for replacement and reconnection, we decompose the QUEL replacement into a sequence of QUEL retrieval, deletion and insertion statements; then use the transformation procedures of Sections 4.1, 4.2.1 and 4.2.2 to complete the transformation. (Of course, we could directly translate the QUEL0 replace statement , but that translation procedure would be messier.)

The replace statement partitions Z's attributes into several groups. Let A denote the key attributes occurring in the target list, B denote the key attributes not occurring in the target list, C denote the non-key attributes not occurring in the target list. The transformation procedure is:

1. Decompose the replacement statement into the following sequence:

```
Retrieve into Temp(Al:=fl,...,Ak:=fk, OLDA:=z.A,
      z.B, z.C) where qual.
Range of t is Temp
Delete z where z.A=t.OLDA AND z.B=t.B.
Append to Z(t.Al,...,t.Ak, t.B, t,C)
```

2. Call Algorithms QTRANS, UTRANS to translate the above sequence.

In case Z is a relationship relation scheme associating El and E2, the replacement corresponds to a reconnection:

1.

i. Create new variables el, el' ranging over El; and variables e2, e2' over E2.

ii. Conjoin to qual (el.Ai=z.Ai) and (el'.Ai=fi) for Ai in ID_El; conjoin to qual (e2.Ai=z.Ai) and (e2´.Ai=fi) for Ai in ID_E2.

   iii. Change the statement to "Reconnect Z([e1,e2]:=[e1´,e2´]) where qual".

2. Call Algorithm QTRANS to transform the qualification.

An example of update transformation is given in Figure 5.

We argue in the Appendix that the translation procedures of this section preserve query- and update-equivalence, i.e., the translated ERL query/update will result in the same effect on the database as the original QUELO query/update would have on the user´s view.

```
Assume the E-R schema in Figure 1,
      the relational view in Figure 3,

   for the update: Rename dependent "Snoopy" of
      Employee 100 to "Woodstock",

   the QUELO update is:

      Range of d is DEPND
      Replace d(NAME:="Woodstock") where d.ENO=100
                                    AND d.NAME="Snoopy".

   Apply Algorithm UTRANS step by step:

      1. Decompose the replacement into the following QUELO
         statements:
         Range of d is DEPND
         Retrieve into Temp(NAME:="Woodstock", OLDA:=d.NAME,
           d.ENO, d.AGE) where d.ENO=100 AND d.NAME="Snoopy".
         Range of t is Temp
         Delete d where d.NAME=t.OLDA AND d.ENO=t.ENO.
         Append to DEPND(t.NAME, t.ENO, t.AGE)

      2. Translate the above statements into ERL equivalents:

         Range of d is DEPND
         Range of e is EMP
         Retrieve into Temp(NAME:="Woodstock", OLDA:=NAME(d),
            ENO(e), AGE(d)) where [e,d] in SUPPORT AND
            ENO(e)=100 AND NAME(d)="Snoopy".
         Range of t is Temp
         Delete d where NAME(d)=OLDA(t) AND [e,d] in SUPPORT
                    AND ENO(e)=ENO(t).
         Insert into DEPND(NAME(t), AGE(t))
            and connect via SUPPORT to e where ENO(e)=ENO(t).

         Figure 5.  Translating QUELO Updates into ERL Equivalents
```

5. CONCLUSION

This paper presents a practical approach to the implementation of multi-model database systems. Specifically, it considers the design of a relational interface to a network or hierarchical system and proposes the use of the Entity-Relationship Model as an intermediate mapping model. In this approach, the underlying network or hierarchical schema is first transformed into an equivalent E-R schema, and then an equivalent relational view is defined over the latter. User queries and updates are first translated into equivalent queries and updates at the E-R level, and then these are compiled into programs that execute on the underlying network or hierarchical database. Algorithms for defining an equivalent relational view of an E-R schema and for translating operations on the relational view into equivalent operations on the E-R database are developed.

6. REFERENCES

[ANSI 77]
    Tsichritzis, D., and A.C. Klug. "ANSI/X3/SPARC DBMS Framework. Report of the Study Group on Data Base Management Systems." AFIPS Press, Montvale, NJ, 1977.

[CP 80]
    Cardenas, A., and M.H. Pirahesh. The E-R Model in Heterogeneous Database Management Systems Network Architecture. in: Chen, P. (ed.), Entity-Relationship Approach to Systems Analysis and Design (North-Holland, Amsterdam, 1980).

[Chen 76]
    Chen, P.P.-S. "The entity-relationship model : Toward a unified view of data". ACM Trans. on Database Systems, 1:1, March 1976.

[CHEN 77]
    Chen, P.P. The Entity-Relationship Approach to Logical Database Design. Q.E.D. Monograph Series, No. 6, Q.E.D. Information Sciences, Inc., Wellesley (1977).

[CT 80]
    Chu, W., and V. To. A Hierarchical Conceptual Model for Data Translation in Heterogeneous Database Environment. in: Chen, P. (ed.), Entity-Relationship Approach to Systems Analysis and Design (North-Holland, Amsterdam, 1980).

[Dayal 79]
    Dayal, U. "Schema-Mapping Problems in Database Systems". Ph.D. Diss., Tech. Rep. TR-11-79, Center for Research in Computing Technology, Harvard University, Cambridge, Mass., August 1979.

[DB 80]
Dayal, U., and P.A. Berstein. "On the Updatability of Network Views — Extending Relational Views Theory to the Network Model". September 1980, submitted for publication.

[HD 81]
Hwang, H.Y., and U. Dayal. "Transformations from the Relational Model into the Network Model". Tech. Rep., University of Texas at Austin, Austin, TX., 1981 (in preparation).

[HSW 75]
Held, G.D., M.R. Stonebraker, and E. Wong. "INGRES — a Relational Database System". Proc. AFIPS National Computer Conf., 1975, pp.409-416.

[Iossiphidis 80]
Iossiphidis, J. A Translator to Convert the DDL of ERM to the DDL of System 2000. in: Chen, P. (ed.), Entity-Relationship Approach to Systems Analysis and Design (North-Holland, Amsterdam, 1980).

[LY 78]
Lien, Y.E., and J.H. Ying. Design of a Distributed Entity-Relationship Database System. Proc. of IEEE 2nd International Computer Software and Applications Conference (Compsac '78), Chicago, November 1978.

[LOP 80]
Lusk, E.L., R.A. Overbeek, and B. Parrello. A Practical Design Methodology for the Implementation of IMS Databases, Using the E-R Model. SIGMOD 1980, pp. 9-21.

[MZ 80]
Melkanoff, M.A. and C. Zaniolo. Decomposition of Relations and Synthesis of Entity Relationship Diagrams. in: Chen, P. (ed.), Entity-Relationship Approach to Systems Analysis and Design (North-Holland, Amsterdam, 1980).

[Poonen 78]
Poonen, G. CLEAR: A Conceptual Language for Entities and Relationships. Proc. of International Conference of Management of Data, Italy, August 1978; Technical Report, R&D Group, Digital Equipment Corporation.

[Sakai 80]
Sakai, H. A Unified Approach to the Logical Design of a Hierarchical Data Model, in: Chen, P. (ed.), Entity-Relationship Approach to Systems Analysis and Design (North-Holland, Amsterdam, 1980).

[Shoshani 78]
Shoshani, A. CABLE: A Language Based on the Entity-Relationship Model. presented at the Conference of Database Management, Israel, August 1978 (oral presentation only); Working Paper, Computer Science and Applied Mathematics Department, Lawrence Berkeley Laboratory.

[Tsao 80]
    Tsao, J.H. Enterprise Schema -- An Approach to IMS Logical Database
    Design. in: Chen, P. (ed.), <u>Entity-Relationship</u> <u>Approach</u> <u>to</u> <u>Systems</u>
    <u>Analysis</u> <u>and</u> <u>Design</u> (North-Holland, Amsterdam, 1980).

[WK 80]
    Wong, E., and R.H. Katz. Logical Design and Schema Conversion for Rela-
    tional and DBTG Databases. in: Chen, P. (ed.), <u>Entity-Relationship</u>
    <u>Approach</u> <u>to</u> <u>Systems</u> <u>Analysis</u> <u>and</u> <u>Design</u> (North-Holland, Amsterdam, 1980).

[Zaniolo 79a]
    Zaniolo, C. "Design of Relational Views Over Network Schemas". Proc.
    ACM-SIGMOD Intl. Conf. on Management of Data, Boston, May-June 1979,
    pp.179-190.

[Zaniolo 79b]
    Zaniolo, C. "Multimodel External Schemas for CODASYL Database Management
    Systems". IFIP TC2, Venice, June 1979.

A.   OPERATIONAL EQUIVALENCE

The query- and update-equivalences mentioned in the paper are formally
defined as follows (for details, see [Dayal 79, DB 80, HD 81]).

Assume M1, M2 are two data models; $\mathscr{S}1$, $\mathscr{S}2$ are two schemas in M1, M2
respectively; S1, S2 are two database states of $\mathscr{S}1$, $\mathscr{S}2$ respectively.

Definition of <u>State</u> <u>Query-Equivalence</u>

A database state S1 is <u>query-equivalent</u> to a database state S2 iff for
all queries q1 on S1, there exists a query q2 on S2 such that the retrieval

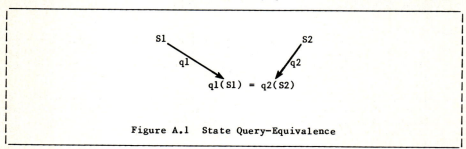

Figure A.1   State Query-Equivalence

results are the same, i.e., q1(S1)=q2(S2). (see Figure A.1)

Definition of <u>State</u> <u>Update-Equivalence</u>

A database state S1 is <u>update-equivalent</u> to a database state S2 iff for every update ul on Sl, there exists an update sequence u2 such that the two updates result in query-equivalent database states, i.e., ul(Sl) is query-equivalent to u2(S2). (see Figure A.2)

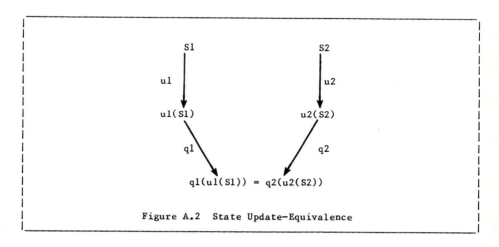

Figure A.2   State Update-Equivalence

The view mapping described in the paper, denoted V, includes the transformation 𝒮TRANS from E-R schemas into relational schemas, and the transformation QTRANS and UTRANS from QUELO queries/updates to ERL statements. Via the schema transformation   TRANS, an E-R database state S2 is mapped into a relational view state Sl as follows:

Algorithm STRANS

1. For each entity e of entity type E in S2, create a tuple V(e) in the corresponding entity relation V(E) in Sl, such that e and V(e) have the same values for corresponding attributes and keys.

2. For each pair of entities el, e2 associated with relationship type R in S2, if R is modelled in Sl as a relationship relation V(R), create a tuple V(r) in V(R) with the primary key values of el, e2 assigned to the corresponding attributes of V(r).

The state mapping is one-to-one.

It has been proved in [HD 81] that V induces operational equivalence, i.e., the relational state Sl derived through V is query- and update-equivalent to the original E-R database state S2 (see Figures A.3 and A.4).

The proof is based on the observation that for each entity in the E-R database there is a unique tuple in the corresponding entity relation in the view; and, similarly, for each relationship in the E-R database there is a unique tuple in the corresponding relationship relation in the view. Furthermore, the translation procedures have the property that the retrieval, insertion or deletion of each tuple in the view is translated into the retrieval, insertion or deletion, respectively, of the corresponding (unique) entity or relationship in the database.

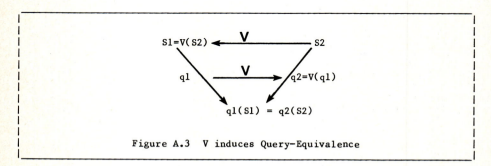

Figure A.3   V induces Query-Equivalence

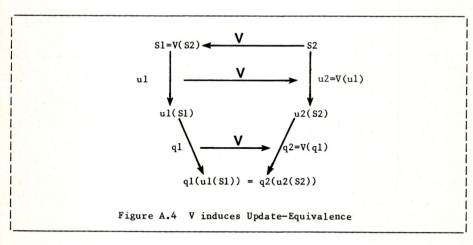

Figure A.4   V induces Update-Equivalence

Entity-Relationship Approach to
Information Modeling and Analysis, P.P. Chen (ed.)
Elsevier Science Publishers B.V. (North-Holland)
©ER Institute, 1983

View Processing in MULTIBASE,
A Heterogeneous Database System

R. H. Katz and N. Goodman
Computer Corporation of America
575 Technology Square
Cambridge, MA 02139

ABSTRACT: Views are used in MULTIBASE to provide an integrated global schema over distributed local databases. The user interface
language is DAPLEX and the system supports a functional model of
data. We propose a language for defining views for this data model
and give an algorithm for mapping queries over a virtual schema into
queries over the original schema. The approach is based on that proposed for relational query languages, with differences due to the
functional data model's support for two primitive modelling constructs: entity sets and functional interrelationships.

1. Introduction

MULTIBASE [SMIT81] is a system that provides a uniform query interface to
heterogeneous, distributed databases. The user is provided with an integrated
view of these databases that is independent of location and data model. This
paper is concerned with the translation of queries expressed over this
integrated view into queries over the original databases. This translation is
called view processing. The problem is well understood for relational databases (e.g., [STON75]); our approach is to adapt this relational technology to
the MULTIBASE environment.

The MULTIBASE query language is DAPLEX [SHIP81] which supports a functional data model [BUNE79, HOUS79, SIBL77]. The functional data model is
essentially a rephrasing and simplification of the entity-relationship model
(e.g., [CHEN76]). The primitive schema objects are entity sets, value sets,
and binary relationships over entities or values. DAPLEX schemas have a convenient graph representation, e.g.,

Research supported by Defense Advanced Project Research Agency and Naval Elec-
tronic Systems Command under Contract No. N00039-80-C-0402.

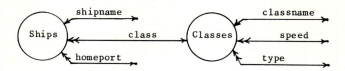

<u>Ships</u> and <u>Classes</u> are entity sets; the various <u>dots</u> represent value sets; and <u>shipname</u>, <u>class</u>, etc., are relations. A single headed arrow indicates that the relation is functional (many-to-one) in that direction, while a double headed arrow indicates nonfunctionality. Thus, <u>class</u> is a function from Ships to Classes (because each ship belongs to a single class), but the inverse relation from Classes to Ships is not a function (because a class will typi-cally contain many ships).

DAPLEX also supports <u>generalization hierarchies</u>. A <u>generalization entity set</u> is formed from the disjoint union of other entity sets. Thus if <u>USShips</u> is an entity set of American ships, and <u>URShips</u> is an entity set of Russian ships, then we can define <u>Ships</u> to be the generalization of these two sets. A convenient graph representation for this is:

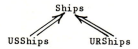

Compatible relationships across the specific objects can be inherited by the generalized object.

Other high-level languages proposed for entity-based data models include [LUSK80, MCCU80, POON78, SHOS78]. These previous works have concentrated on language design issues, but have not addressed the problem of view support for schema integration.

The schema architecture of MULTIBASE is given in Figure 1. At the bottom are <u>local host schemas</u>, the schemas of the databases being integrated. These are expressed in the data models of the local systems. Each local host schema is also represented by a DAPLEX <u>local schema</u>; the local schema is essentially a transliteration of the local host schema into the DAPLEX data model. Finally, the collection of local schemas is composed into a <u>global schema</u> that provides the desired integrated view. In addition, there is an <u>integration schema</u> to resolve certain types of incompatibilities among the local data-bases.

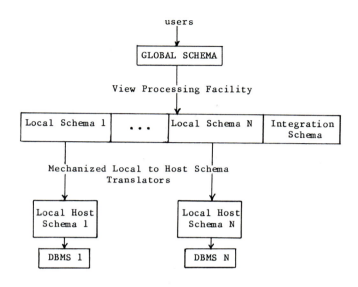

Figure 1.   Schema Integration Architecture

For example, suppose we wish to integrate a database of American ships with one of Russian ships. And suppose the American database is relational, while the Russian database uses the CODASYL model. The <u>local host schemas</u> for these databases might be:

<u>American</u>

USShips(shipname, shipclass, homeport)
USClasses(classname, type, speed)

<u>Russian</u>

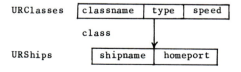

The <u>local schemas</u> are simply the transliteration of these into DAPLEX:

American

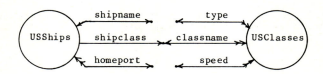

Russian

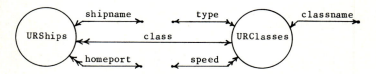

A <u>global schema</u> is then formed over these local schemas (and the <u>integration schema</u>) to permit global queries to be expressed. Scalar-valued functions are not shown.

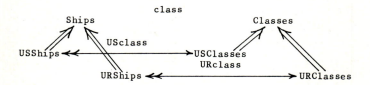

     The <u>integration schema</u> is used while defining the global schema to rectify the differences in "terminology" between the databases. For example, the Russian database might have "Pago Pago" as a valid homeport, but the global users know the port by the island name: "Tahiti". Or the Russian database might measure speed in kilometers per hour, but the global users prefer knots. The integration schema contains data (tables of synonyms, conversion formulas, etc.) to unify differences of this sort.

     <u>Structural incompatibilities</u> arise when the local schemas do not provide identical information about objects to be integrated. For example, the local schemas may record the captains of USShips, but not of URShips. The generalized Ships object could not be described by the captain relation in this case (note: captain could be generalized if a virtual relation is first defined which maps every Russian ship to the null string).

     Users submit queries expressed in terms of the global schema. Consider the query:

"Print the names of battleships based in Tahiti"

To execute this query, we translate it into a query over the collection of local schemas and the integration schema, e.g.,

"Print the following set of names:

    (1) U.S. Battleships based in Tahiti

union

    (2) U.R. Battleships based in P where P is
        the Russian synonym for Tahiti"

This translation is called <u>view processing</u> and is the subject of this paper.

The final step is to translate subqueries (1) and (2) into queries expressed in the local DML over the local systems. This step is highly dependent on details of the local system and is not considered here.

Our approach is based on the relational approach to view processing. This is discussed in Section 2. In Section 3, we present the salient features of the DAPLEX datalanguage. This forms the basis of the view definition language presented in Section 4. Algorithms to translate queries over objects into queries over base objects, and to simplify the resulting queries, are given in Section 5. In the final section, Section 6, we summarize our conclusions and make some observations on applying relational techniques to functional data models.

2. <u>View</u> <u>Processing</u> <u>for</u> <u>Relational</u> <u>Systems</u>

A <u>view</u> is a derived schema object. In the relational model, a view is always a <u>relation</u> and is defined by a <u>query</u> which could materialize the view. For example, a view of American battleships, constructed from USShips and USClasses, is defined in the query language QUEL [HELD75] as:

```
Range of s is USShips
Range of c is USClasses
Define View
BBShips (shipname = s.shipname, homeport = s.homeport)
where s.shipclass = c.classname and c.type = "BB"
```

To process a query that references a view one could, in principle, materialize the view by executing its definition. However, this step is not necessary. It is possible to translate the query over the view into a query over the actual database by syntactically replacing the view with its definition. This mapping is called <u>query modification</u> [STON75].

For example, consider a query to retrieve the names of U.S. battleships based in Tahiti:

```
Range of b is BBShips
Retrieve (b.shipname) where b.homeport = "Tahiti"
```

Query modification proceeds in three steps:

1. The range statement over the view is replaced by range statements over base relations (i.e., relations in the actual database),

```
Range of s is USShips
Range of c is USClasses
Retrieve (b.shipname) where b.homeport = "Tahiti"
```

2. The qualification from the view definition is appended to the user's query,

```
Range of s is USShips
Range of c is USClasses
Retrieve (b.shipname) where b.homeport = "Tahiti"
                         and   s.shipclass = c.classname
                         and   c.type = "BB"
```

3. References to view attributes are replaced by references to attributes in the base relations, as denoted by the target list of the view definition.

```
Range of s is USShips
Range of c is USClasses
Retrieve (s.shipname) where s.homeport = "Tahiti"
                         and   s.shipclass = c.classname
                         and   c.type = "BB"
```

It is easy to verify that the modified query is a <u>correct</u> <u>translation</u> of the original query. That is, the data retrieved by the modified query is identical to the data that would have been retrieved had we materialized the view (thereby obtaining the relation BBShips), and then run the original query against BBShips.

3. The <u>DAPLEX</u> <u>Language</u>

In this section, we review the DAPLEX language [SHIP81] and point out the difficulties it poses for view processing. To keep the discussion short, we present only a subset of the complete language.

A DAPLEX query consists of nested <u>iteration</u> <u>statements,</u> which associate <u>entity</u> <u>variables</u> with entity sets. Each execution of the iteration assigns a new entity to the entity variable. For example, the following is an iteration statement that associates entity variable b with battleship entities:

FOR EACH b IN BBShips
.
.
.

The language provides a function-like syntax for referencing relation names. Consider the DAPLEX schema:

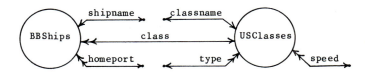

The functional syntax for relations requires that we identify the position of arguments to each relation, e.g., <u>shipname</u> would typically be defined as "a function <u>from</u> BBShips <u>to</u> a value set of ship names"; similarly <u>homeport</u> might be "a function <u>from</u> BBShips <u>to</u> port names"; etc. To print out the names of battleships based in Tahiti, we would write:

FOR EACH b IN BBShips WHERE homeport(b) = "Tahiti"
    PRINT shipname(b)

Similarly, if <u>class</u> were defined as "a function <u>from</u> BBShips <u>to</u> USClasses", then the following query would find the names of North Carolina-class battleships based in Tahiti:

```
FOR EACH c IN USClasses WHERE classname(c) = "North Carolina"
   FOR EACH b IN BBShips WHERE class(b) = c
                          AND   homeport(b) = "Tahiti"
       PRINT shipname(b)
```

When a relation is nonfunctional, a slightly different syntax is used. Suppose ships were the inverse of class (ships is not a new relation, but rather a renaming of an existing relation which is treated differently by the syntax of DAPLEX). Ships is a nonfunctional relation from USClasses to BBShips. The following query would also find the names of North Carolina class battleships based in Tahiti:

```
FOR EACH c IN USClasses WHERE classname(c) = "North Carolina"
   FOR EACH b IN BBShips WHERE b ISIN ships(c)
                          AND   homeport(b) = "Tahiti"
       PRINT shipname(b)
```

Note that there is more than one syntax for specifying a join between BBShips and USClasses, viz., class(b) = c and b ISIN ships(c).

A "set constructor" can appear wherever an entity set can appear in the language. The following is another way of finding all Tahiti-based North Carolina-class battleships:

```
FOR EACH c IN USClasses WHERE classname(c) = "North Carolina"
   FOR EACH b IN (b´ IN BBShips WHERE b´ ISIN ships(c)
                          AND   homeport(b´) = "Tahiti")
       PRINT shipname(b)
```

The expression in parenthesis is a set constructor. In the previous queries, b iterates over all battleships, but only those with the desired class and homeport qualify to be printed. In the above, the set of Tahiti-based North Carolina-class ships is formed, and b iterates over these.

The language also supports "composed functional" notation. The following query finds the names of all North Carolina-class battleships:

```
FOR EACH c IN USClasses WHERE classname(c) = "North Carolina"
   FOR EACH name IN shipname(ships(c))
       PRINT name
```

A query with a set constructor or composed function can always be replaced by a query with nested FOR EACH statements only, except in a single case. Consider the following two queries to find the classes of Tahiti-based battleships:

```
FOR EACH b IN BBShips WHERE homeport(b) = "Tahiti"
    FOR EACH c IN USClasses WHERE c = class(b)
        PRINT classname(c)

FOR EACH c IN class(b IN BBShips WHERE homeport(b) = "Tahiti")
    PRINT classname(c)
```

There is a subtle difference in the output of these two queries. If there are two North Carolina-class battleships in Tahiti, then "North Carolina" will appear twice in the first, but only once in the second. The latter eliminates duplicates when forming the set of classes with battleships in Tahiti (i.e., F(set) is also a set).

These examples illustrate the problems of specifying views in DAPLEX. The varied syntax leads to some complications in substituting an object's definition for the object. Duplicate elimination causes more problems: more critically, the output of a query does not eliminate duplicates, yet it is usually desired to eliminate duplicates from views. The language lacks closure in the sense that a virtual object cannot be formed from the output of a query. It is not possible to directly specify a relation as the result of a query, nor is it possible to create a new entity set from the composition of existing entity sets (e.g., shipclass from ship joined with class). This ability is crucial for successful view processing. However, a virtual object could be defined as the result of a "load program" in the DAPLEX update language. We have not found it possible to adopt the query modification paradigm for views so defined. Finally, we need to support new virtual objects, such as generalization hierarchies (e.g., USShips isa Ship and URShips isa Ship), which are not currently supported within the language.

4. View Definition Language for DAPLEX

Our approach to view definition borrows heavily from the relational analog. First, we place the view definition into a simplified "flattened form", which eliminates some of the variability of the DAPLEX syntax. It is formed by performing the following: (1) qualifications are conjunctively collected and appended to the innermost iteration, (2) set constructors are moved to the qualification, so that each entity variable may only range over an entity set, and (3) composed functions are "unwound": $F(G(x)) = z \Rightarrow$ FOR EACH y IN Y WHERE $G(x) = y$ AND $F(y) = z$. Further, we adopt relational duplicate elimination semantics for views, so that duplicates are always eliminated on output and FOR EACH statements represent QUEL-like range statements rather than iterations over sets. Eventually, we intend to support duplicate elimination in a more flexible way [KATZ81].

As an example, the query

```
FOR EACH c IN class(b IN BBShips WHERE homeport(b) = "Tahiti")
    PRINT classname(c)
```

becomes

```
FOR EACH b in BBShips
    FOR EACH c in USClasses WHERE homeport(b) = "Tahiti"
                            AND   c = class(b)
            PRINT classname(c)
```

Note the similarity between flattened queries and QUEL queries.

4.1 Virtual Entity Set Definition

The schematic definition of a virtual entity set is:

```
FOR EACH e_1 IN E_1
    .
    .
    .
    FOR EACH e_n IN E_n WHERE Q(e_1,...,e_n)
        V <= <e_1,...,e_n>
```

A virtual entity set V is formed from the composition of base entity sets $E_1,...,E_n$. For example, the view of American battleships, based on the American ships schema of Section 1, could be specified as:

```
FOR EACH s IN USShips
    FOR EACH c IN USClasses WHERE shipclass(s) = classname(c)
                            AND   type(c) = "BB"
        BBShips <= <s,c>
```

In defining relations over a virtual entity set, it will be useful to reference a specific "component" entity set from which it has been derived. We define π_i for this purpose: for an entity v in V, $\pi_i(v)$ is e_i.

4.2 Virtual Relation Definition

Two types of virtual relations can be distinguished: relations from entity sets or value sets to value sets (called scalar-valued), and relations from entity sets to entity sets (called entity-valued). The latter type is used to specify joins between entity sets, and can only appear in Q. Relations are subsets of the Cartesian product of the sets over which they are defined. The sets play different roles: one is the domain (from), the other is the co-domain (to). The relation can be functional in either direction, but need not be.

A scalar-valued relation is specified as:

```
    FOR EACH e IN E
       F <= (e,f(e))
```

where f(e) is scalar-valued. For example, the function shipname from BBShips to shipnames is defined as:

```
    FOR EACH b IN BBShips
       shipname <= (b, shipname($\pi_1$(b))
```

π_1(b) evaluates to an entity variable ranging over USShips (i.e., the first component of the virtual entity set BBShips). Also, the function speed from BBShips to numbers is defined as:

```
    FOR EACH b IN BBShips
       speed <= (b, speed($\pi_2$(b)))
```

π_2 evaluates to an entity variable ranging over USClasses (i.e., the second component over the virtual entity set BBShips). Entity-valued relations are defined similarly. For example, the relation class from BBShips to USShips could be defined by:

```
    FOR EACH s IN BBShips
       FOR EACH c IN USClasses WHERE classname(c) = shipclass(s)
          class <= (s,c)
```

Because a virtual relation can be defined as the result of a query, the language is closed. This allows us to adopt the relational approach of query modification for view processing.

4.3   <u>Virtual</u> <u>Generalization</u> <u>Hierarchy</u> <u>Definition</u>

     The final view type is virtual generalization hierarchies and conditional
relations defined over them. A generalization object is formed from the (disjoint) union of specific objects. Relations over a generalization are conditionally defined over the constituent specific objects.

     As an example, consider the databases of U.S. and Russian ships:

     USShips(shipname, speed, captain)
     URShips(shipname, speed, displacement)

A virtual Ship object can be defined with shipnames and speeds. Only compatible relations over all specific objects can be defined for the generalized
object (i.e., upwards inheritance).

     The schematic definition of a generalized object G over specific objects
$S_1,...,S_n$ is:

     FOR EACH s IN S_1 U ... U S_n

        G <= s

Ships is defined as:

     FOR EACH s IN USShips U URShips
        Ships <= s

For the scalar-valued relations, the definition is:

     FOR EACH g IN G
        CASE OF g
           WHEN g ISIN S_1 => F <= (g, $f_1(g)$)
              .
              .
              .
           WHEN g ISIN S_n => F <= (g, $f_n(g)$)

where each f_i is scalar-valued. Thus the relations shipname and speeds are
defined as:

```
FOR EACH s IN Ships
   CASE OF s
      WHEN s ISIN USShips => shipname <= (s, shipname(s))
      WHEN s ISIN URShips => shipname <= (s, shipname(s))

FOR EACH s IN Ships
   CASE OF s
      WHEN s ISIN USShips => speed <= (s, speed(s))
      WHEN s ISIN URShips => speed <= (s, speed(s))
```

For an entity-valued relation F <u>from</u> G <u>to</u> H, the specification is:

```
FOR EACH g IN G
   FOR EACH h IN H WHERE
      (CASE OF g
         WHEN g ISIN S₁ => P₁(g,h)
            .
            .
            .
         WHEN g ISIN Sₙ => Pₙ(g,h))

         F <= (g,h)
```

Thus the relation class is defined as:

```
FOR EACH s IN Ships
   FOR EACH c IN Classes
      (CASE OF s,c
          WHEN s ISIN USShips AND c ISIN USClasses
             => c = USclass(s)
          WHEN s ISIN URShips AND c ISIN URClasses
             => c = URclass(s))
                class <= (s,c)
```

5. Query Modification Algorithm

View processing proceeds in two stages. First, virtual objects are replaced by their definitions (<u>substitution</u>). Second, the resulting query is simplified (<u>simplification</u>).

Throughout the section, it will be assumed that the user query has been expressed in the "flattened" form of the previous section. The FOR EACH part is called the RANGE, the predicate is called the QUALIFICATION, and the print statement is called the TARGET LIST.

5.1   Substitution

Generalization hierarchies are dealt with first by substituting the union of queries over specific objects for the query over the generalization, which is itself the union of specific objects. For each relation defined over a generalized object, there is a case for the ith specific object. We shall refer to this as the ith definition.

The processing steps are introduced with an example. To print the names of fast Ships, the query is:


```
FOR EACH s IN Ships WHERE speed(s) > 25
    PRINT shipname(s)
```


View processing should yield the following union of queries:


```
FOR EACH s IN USShips WHERE speed(s) > 25
    PRINT shipname(s)
```


union


```
FOR EACH s IN URShips WHERE speed(s) > 25
    PRINT shipname(s)
```


The processing steps for handling virtual generalization hierarchies are:
Step 1: For each generalization hierarchy G referred to in the query, substitute the specific objects $G_1,...,G_n$ for G. Create a query for each G_i and perform steps 2 and 3 for each.

Step 2: For each conditionally defined scalar relation over G, substitute the ith definition if the query refers to G_i. Replace the relation by the range component of its specification, substituting the actual domain entity variable for the dummy in the definition, wherever the relation appears in the QUALIFICATION or the TARGET LIST.

Step 3: For each conditionally defined entity relation over G, substitute the ith definition if the query refers to G_i. Replace the predicate in the QUALIFICATION with the predicate from the definition, substituting actual entity variables for the dummies in the definition.

Note that the method described above essentially places the query into dis-
junctive normal form. If a relation is not defined for a particular G_i, then
the query which references it is unsatisfiable, and can be eliminated from
further processing. This is tantamount to conjoining FALSE to the QUALIFICA-
TION.

Once generalizations and conditional relations have been eliminated, the
next step is to substitute for virtual relations and entity sets. Again, we
motivate the steps with an example. The query to find the North Carolina
class of battleships is written as:

```
FOR EACH c IN USClasses
    FOR EACH b IN BBShips
        WHERE classname(c) = "North Carolina"
        AND   c = class(b)
            PRINT shipname(b)
```

The query is processed as follows. Shipname(b) is substituted for first:

```
FOR EACH c IN USClasses
    FOR EACH b IN BBShips
        WHERE classname(c) = "North Carolina"
        AND   c = class(b)
            PRINT shipname($\pi_1$(b))
```

Then the clause "c = class(b)" is replaced:

```
FOR EACH c IN USClasses
    FOR EACH b IN BBShips
        WHERE classname(c) = "North Carolina"
        AND   classname(c) = shipclass("$_1$(b))

            PRINT shipname($\pi_1$(b))
```

Lastly, b is replaced by $\langle x_1, x_2 \rangle$ which iterate over USShips and USClasses:

```
FOR EACH c IN USClasses
    FOR EACH x₁ IN USShips

        FOR EACH x₂ IN USClasses

            WHERE classname(c) = "North Carolina"
            AND   classname(c) = shipclass(x₁)

            AND   classname(x₂) = shipclass(x₁)

            AND   type(x₂) = "BB"

            PRINT shipname(x₁)
```

Redundant clauses and variables have been introduced into the query. These will be candidates for later simplification.

The processing steps are:

Step 4: For each scalar-valued virtual relation in the QUALIFICATION or TARGET LIST, substitute the relation's range specification (second component) for the relation, replacing the actual domain entity variable for the dummy variable of the specification.

Step 5: For each entity-valued virtual relation in the QUALIFICATION, replace the clause involving the relation with the predicate of its definition, substituting the actual domain and range entity variables for the dummy variables of the specification.

Step 6: For each virtual entity set in the RANGE,
  (i) Replace the range (FOR EACH) over the virtual object by a (multivariable) range over base objects specified in the view definition. Assign unique names to entity variables derived from the definition.

  (ii) Syntactically replace each reference to the virtual entity variable by the object's component vector. Evaluate π_i operators while performing this replacement.

  (iii) Append the predicate of the virtual entity's definition to the query's QUALIFICATION, replacing dummy entity variables with those chosen in (i).

5.2 Correctness of Query Modification

Query modification can be thought of as a relation which maps queries into queries. Query modification is "correct" if the result of a query expressed over a view is the same as the result of a modified query expressed over the schema from which the view is derived. The relationship between schemas and queries is shown in Figure 2.

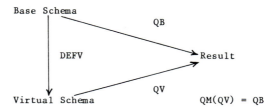

Figure 2. Query Modification

The correctness of query modification can be demonstrated because of the closure of the extended language. A virtual entity set or relation is defined as the result of a query. A query over virtual objects is mapped into a query over base objects by substituting the definition for the view. A virtual entity set is replaced by an iteration over base entity sets, and the predicate of the definition is appended to the query to restrict the iteration to the valid combinations that make up the view. Similarly, a clause referring to a virtual relation is replaced by the predicate which restricts the domain and range entity sets to those that participate in the relation. Thus, our query modification technique is correct by analogy with the relational approach.

5.3   Simplification

Queries which result from query modification are rarely in their simplest form. Many redundant clauses and iterations over entities have been introduced. Thus, it is useful to apply some techniques to remove the obvious redundancies, even though it is difficult to find the "simplest" query in general.

The method we use is a direct adaptation of the Tableaux method [AHO79a, AHO79b]. Rather than present the algorithm in detail, we illustrate its use with the sample query at the end of Section 3.

A Tableaux is nothing more than a matrix of rows and columns. There is one column for each entity set and scalar-valued relation used in the query. Additionally, there is a special column called TAG to indicate how rows have been derived. A row or collection of rows is used to encode the clauses of the query's predicate. Elements of the matrix fall into three classes:

distinguished variables (a_i) derived from print statements, nondistinguished variables (b_i) derived from entity variables and their relations, and constants (c_i) derived from restriction clauses.

The Tableaux for the example query is shown in Figure 3. A Tableaux is an unambiguous representation of the query, and it is always possible to map a DAPLEX query into a tableaux and to map a derived tableaux back into a DAPLEX query. Constraints on the database are used to identify variables that must be the same. We use functional dependency information to draw inferences about data in the database. For example, a ship has only a single shipclass (i.e., there is a functional dependency USShips --> shipclass), thus variables b3 and b5 must be the same. Further, rows 2 and 5 can be combined because they are identical (including the modified tag).

US Ships	ship name	ship class	US Classes	class name	type	TAG
			b1	"NC"		classname(c) = "NC"
b2		b3				shipclass(x1) = b3
			b1	b4		classname(c) = b4
		b3		b4		b3 = b4
b2		b5				shipclass(x1) = b5
			b6	b7		classname(x2) = b7
		b5		b7		b5 = b7
			b6		"BB"	type(x2) = "BB"
b2	a1					print shipname(x1)

Figure 3. Tableaux for Example Query

The functional dependencies over the sample database are readily apparent from the description in DAPLEX (see Section 1):

USShips --> shipname
shipname --> USShips
USClasses --> type
USClasses --> classname
classname --> USClasses
shipclass --> classname

The Tableaux is reduced as follows. First, the dependency USShips --> shipclass identifies b3 and b5. B5 is replaced by b3 in rows 5 and 7. Row 5 can be eliminated because it is now identical to row 2. Next, shipclass --> classname identifies b4 and b7. B7 becomes b4 in rows 6 and 7. Row 7 is identical with row 4 and can be removed. Next, classname --> USClasses identifies b1 and b6. B6 is renamed b1 in rows 6 and 8, and row 6 can now be dropped because it matches row 3. Finally, USClasses --> classname combines "NC" and b4. Constants have precedence in renaming, thus b4 is replaced by "NC" in rows 3 and 4. Now row 3 matches row 1, and can be removed. The final tableaux is in Figure 4. The simplified query is:

```
FOR EACH c IN USClasses
    FOR EACH x1 IN USShips
        WHERE classname(c) = "North Carolina"
        AND   shipclass(x1) = "North Carolina"
        AND   type(c) = "BB"
            PRINT shipname(x1)
```

Intuitively, this is the simplest query we could expect to derive.

US Ships	ship name	ship class	US Classes	class name	type	TAG
			b1	"NC"		classname(c) = "NC"
b2		b3				shipclass(x1) = b3
		b3		"NC"		b3 = "NC"
			b1		"BB"	type(c) = "BB"
b2	a1					print shipname(x1)

Figure 4. Final Tableaux for Example Query

6. Conclusions and Observations

In this paper, we have described a language for view definition and a method by which queries over virtual objects can be mapped into queries over base schema objects. Our method is founded upon the application of well-known relational technology for view support in the new realm of functional/entity-relationship data models. Several difficulties due to the new environment are handled by the query modification method we have proposed. Methods to support new types of virtual objects, such as generalization hierarchies, and to simplify modified queries were also described.

DAPLEX was initially chosen as the language of MULTIBASE because of the ease with which it can be mapped into the languages supported by existing database systems. However, issues related to its suitability for specifying database integration were not fully understood. Since the architecture is based on constructing the global schema as a view over the local schemas, view support is crucial to the success of MULTIBASE. The methods and algorithms described here have been successfully adapted and implemented in the system.

Our general observation is that well understood methods for the relational model can be adapted and extended for entity-based data models. The extension is nontrivial, but can be accomplished. Additionally, our work indicates that there is much to be said for the elegance and simplicity of relational style query languages. Attempts to extend these languages in almost any direction lead to difficulties and new avenues for research. More work is needed to gain a formal understanding of the languages proposed for entity-based data models.

7. <u>References</u>

[AHO 79a] Aho, A.V., C. Beeri and J.D. Ullman. "The Theory of Joins in Relational Databases". ACM Trans. on Database Sys., Vol. 4, No. 2, June 1979.

[AHO 79b] Aho, A.V., Y. Sagiv and J.D. Ullman. "Equivalence of Relational Expressions". SIAM Journal of Computing, Vol. 8, No. 2, 1979.

[BUNE79] Buneman, P. and R. Frankel. "FQL -- A Functional Query Language". Proc. ACM SIGMOD Conference, May 1979.

[CHEN76] Chen, P. P. "The Entity-Relationship Model -- Towards a Unified View of Data". ACM Trans. on Database Sys., Vol. 1, No. 1, March 1976.

[HELD75] Held, G. et. al. "INGRES -- A Relational Database Management System". Proc. AFIPS Natl. Comp. Conf., 1975.

[HOUS79] Housel, B., S.B. Yao and D. Waddle. "FDM -- Functional Data Model". Proc. Conf. on Very Large Databases, 1979.

[KATZ81] Katz, R. H. and N. Goodman. "On the Semantics of Duplicate Elimination and Outer Join in Functional Query Languages". In preparation.

[LUSK80]   Lusk, E. L. and Overbeek, R.A., A DML for entity-relationship models, in: Chen, P. P. (ed.), Entity-Relationship Approach to Systems Analysis and Design (North-Holland, Amsterdam, 1980).

[MCCU80]   McCue, D. and Poonen, G., Evaluation of E-R query language, in: Chen, P. P. (ed.), Entity-Relationship Approach to Systems Analysis and Design (North-Holland, Amsterdam, 1980).

[POON78]   Poonen, George, CLEAR: A conceptual language for entities and relationships, Proceedings of International Conference of Management of Data, Italy (August 1978); Technical Report, R&D Group, Digital Equipment Corporation.

[SHIP81]   Shipman, D. "The Functional Data Model and the Datalanguage DAPLEX". ACM Trans. on Database Sys., Vol. 6, No. 1, March 1981.

[SHOS78]   Shoshani, Arie, CABLE: A language based on the entity-relationship model, presented on the Conference of Database Management, Israel (August 1978)(oral presentation only); Working Paper, Computer Science and Applied Mathematics Department, Lawrence Berkeley Laboratory.

[SIBL77]   Sibley, E. and L. Kershberg. "Data Architecture and Data Model Consideration". Proc. AFIPS Natl. Comp. Conf., 1977.

[SMIT81]   Smith, J. et. al. "MULTIBASE -- Integrating Heterogeneous Distributed Database Systems". Proc. AFIPS Natl. Comp. Conf., 1981.

[STON75]   Stonebraker, M. "Implementation of Views and Integrity Constraints by Query Modification". Proc. ACM SIGMOD Conf., 1975.

Entity-Relationship Approach to
Information Modeling and Analysis, P.P. Chen (ed.)
Elsevier Science Publishers B.V. (North-Holland)
©ER Institute, 1983

A UNIFYING APPROACH FOR CONCEPTUAL SCHEMA
TO SUPPORT MULTIPLE DATA MODELS

Matthew Morgenstern

Department of Computer Science
Rutgers – The State University
New Brunswick, New Jersey 08903

ABSTRACT

This paper develops a uniform representation for the
conceptual schema which draws upon concepts from the Entity
Relationship Data Model and other common data models (n-ary
relational, network, hierarchical). We develop a directed
hypergraph as the basis for our representation, and show its
duality with a collection of mappings between sets of data
objects. Schemas in different data models are obtained by
different clustering of these underlying expressions, as
illustrated in the examples. Criteria are developed for
compatibility and equivalence between schemas, and an approach
for translating between logical schemas is described.

1. INTRODUCTION

The common data models share a set of fundamental concepts for
representing data, though the way in which each model expresses the schema
and the data differs. This paper considers these underlying concepts and
investigates a unifying representation for the conceptual schema. The
approach emphasizes Data Maps between sets of data objects, and the formation
of Clusters of Data Maps to represent semantically meaningful units of data.
We find that seemingly different data concepts can be uniformly represented
using this approach.

The common data models typically impart a distinct orientation to the
conceptual schema, and they often require that a choice be made among several
orthogonal representations for expressing the same data. If a need then
arises to integrate additional data concepts, it may be necessary to revise
previous choices and representations in a conceptual schema. For example,
what is considered a simple attribute in the conceptual schema at one point
in time may need to acquire an attribute of its own at a later time, perhaps
due to the addition of a new user's perspective. Still later, another user's
perspective may wish to expand the original attribute into an entity with its
own relationships. The need to change the conceptual schema in response to
revised user needs, and the extent of such change, is increased when there is
overcommittment to a particular perspective. It is felt that the current

approach reduces the impact of these and other changes due to incremental growth.

Several authors have noted the arbitrariness and ambiguity of classifying data by attributes, entities, and relationships. "Formal criteria do not exist for deciding what is an object, a property, or a relationship" [Lang]. An entity or "an object is anything about which assertions can be made" [Bil]. Yet "there is no absolute distinction between entities and values. To a car manufacturer, a colour is an attribute of one of its products: to the company that made the paint, a colour may well be an entity" [Hal].

Kent argues similarly that "there does not seem to be an effective way to characterize 'attributes' or to distinguish them from relationships. This need to map things into record-like terms seems to be the main force motivating a distinction between attributes and relationships" [Ke79]. Also, "apart from listing of examples, it is difficult to identify precise criteria for deciding whether something is an entity".

Perhaps, a database entity is best seen as a convenient formalism for grouping together relationships and attributes in a meaningful way. The notions of attributes, relationships, and entities provide us with a natural way of talking about the data. However, several different organizations of the data may be relevant. In fact, some of the apparent ambiguities in data base schema design may reflect the multiple orientations which are valid and needed by the different types of users. It may not be best to classify a data object as exclusively either an attribute, a relationship, or an entity. Some data objects may take on more than one role.

A number of interesting approaches for data modelling have appeared in the literature over the years. Some of these are listed in the references, and selected descriptions may be found in [Ull80], [McL78], and [Ke78]. Of particular relevance is Chen's work on the Entity Relationship Data Model [Chen76], and recent work by Shipman [Ship] on a functional data model and a concise language for expressing the attributes of entities and the relationships between them. The analyses by Kent [Ke77, Ke78, Ke79] explore the assumptions which often underlie data models, providing interesting perspectives and possible alternatives.

2.   THE FRAMEWORK FOR CONCEPTUAL SCHEMA

How then might we capture the multiple relationships, entities, attributes, and interdependencies of data objects which are to be supported by a conceptual schema? We see the fundamental structures to be (1) the data objects which are stored, (2) named mappings between data objects, and (3) organization of these data objects and mappings into semantically relevant units. Different organizations of the same data objects and mappings gives rise to different perspectives and models of the same data.

We define a <u>data</u> <u>object</u> to be a self-identifying data literal -- sometimes referred to as an attribute. (We also allow a data object to be a composite such as a month-day-year date.) The literal value is self-identifying in that it is associated with its data object type in the data base schema.

A named <u>Data</u> <u>Map</u> takes one or more data objects as an argument, and produces an association with another set of data objects. This resulting set may contain a single data instance for one or more different data object types -- in which case the Data Map is functional and yields a single vector as its value. Or it may produce a set of instances of this vector, so that we have a multi-valued Data Map. The arguments to the Data Map are called the Source, and the resulting data objects are called the Target.

For example, a Data Map named MARRIAGE may create an association from the NAME data objects for the husband and wife to data objects for the DATE and LOCATION. Thus given their names as arguments, this Data Map yields the associated date and location values describing the marriage. A multi-valued Data Map CHILDREN might take the NAMES of the husband and wife as arguments and yield a set of pairs (NAME, DATE), with one pair for each child giving that child's name and birthdate. In general, mappings capture single and multi-valued relationships and attributes, as well as the means by which data objects are qualified and referenced.

An important aspect of our data representation is the organization of these Data Maps -- and the data objects in them -- into semantically relevant collections of data called <u>Clusters</u>. Clusters may be named and may share data objects and Data Maps with other Clusters. Clusters may be used to represent entities, when an entity schema is desired. For example, a Cluster may include the Data Maps which describe the attributes and relationships of an entity. In this case, the Source of each of these Data Maps would include the data objects which uniquely identify an entity instance.

In general, we do not constrain Clusters to be disjoint, nor need they represent distinct real world objects. A cluster is a modular unit of data -- a chosen collection of mappings and data objects -- whether or not it describes an actual entity. A cluster node may be representative of some logical entity, or an n-ary relation, or a record or segment of a network or hierarchical schema.

The use of clusters of mappings, rather than the more structured concept of entities, allows more than one interpretation or perception of the same underlying data concepts. It thus facilitates integration of different data representations. It allows incremental growth of an application while minimizing the impact upon an existing conceptual schema.

At the user view level, a representation should provide visual and logical structure in accordance with the users' needs. Data should be grouped and aggregated into units which the user finds easy to think about. In contrast, however, the requirements for a conceptual schema framework should include flexibility and homogeneity -- it need not impose a structuring of the data for the user, as the user does not see it, nor could one structure serve all. It may be that a single data model formalism cannot serve both disparate purposes optimally.

The approach taken here is that it is desirable to use different representations for the conceptual schema and for the description of user views or subschema. This paper considers the conceptual schema representation and transformations which may be applied to it. A related facility for modular organization and presentation of data at the user interface is described in [Mor81a].

2.1 HYPERGRAPH REPRESENTATION

Entity-based data models, network models and binary relational models [Abr] often are represented in terms of directed line graphs. The directed edges which connect pairs of vertices play a primary role in such representations, but impose certain logical limitations on such models. We generalize these graphs, and show the equivalence between these new graphs and our Data Map expressions.

If an undirected edge is generalized to be a set (rather than a pair) of several vertices, we have the established concept of a hypergraph. A hypergraph H = (V,E) consists of a set V of vertices and a set E of edges, each edge being a subset of vertices [Ber]. Here we extend this classical hypergraph to obtain a directed hypergraph by designating each edge Ei to consist of two subsets of vertices, called the Source Si and the Target Ti, such that Si U Ti = Ei. Usually these subsets will be disjoint, though such is not required.

The meaning of a directed hypergraph edge is that there is an association from the data objects in the Source to the data objects in the Target. This is a generalization of the directed binary association represented by a directed edge in a line graph. It provides for a more natural expression of general non-binary relationships. Each directed hypergraph edge may be named. Multiple edges with different names may be defined over the same set of vertices. We may group certain edges which share some or all of their vertices, and we call this named collection a compound edge set.

There is a duality between this hypergraph representation and our Data Map expressions. In particular, if we let vertices represent data objects, then a named directed edge Ei of a hypergraph represents a named Data Map from data objects in the Source Si to the Target data objects in Ti. Similarly, a compound edge set represents a Cluster of Data Maps.

An incidence matrix of our directed hypergraph provides a representation which is easy to analyze and manipulate. Each column represents a vertex and is labelled with the data object type. Each row represents a directed edge or named mapping, and has a +1 or "S" for each source vertex and a negative number or "T" for each target vertex. The row is labelled with the name of the mapping, and functionality may be indicated by -1 or "T1" for each target vertex, and -n or "Tn" for non-functional mappings. A compound edge set corresponds to a set of rows from the incidence matrix.

Figure 1a shows a Hypergraph Incidence Matrix in which the first Data Map M1 is named SHIPMENT and represents a directed hypergraph edge from data objects PART# and SUPPLIER# to the Target data object QUANTITY. Map M2 represents an edge with name LOCATED which is directed from SUPPLIER# to SUPPLOCation. We may diagram a hypergraph by encircling each Source and Target set and directing a named arc from the Source to the Target subsets of each hypergraph edge. Figure 1b shows this for the above two maps. We shall return to this example later.

When several data maps are involved, hypergraphs might be difficult to draw in this manner. As an alternative, a representative line graph may be formed by defining a Cluster Node as a new graphical entity to represent a Cluster of Maps, or a Compound Edge Set of the hypergraph. Simple arcs are directed from each Source element (element in the Source of any data map in the cluster) to the cluster node. Outward arcs connect to each Target element. If the cluster of data maps is named in the incidence matrix of the hypergraph, so too will be the cluster node in this line graph.

Since this derived line graph represents collections of mappings, we refer to it as a Graph of Mappings or an M-Graph. It has some similarity to a graph of entities and relationships, but it is not the same either graphically or semantically, nor is it a user interface. It serves primarily as an intermediate step in the derivation of particular data model representations. A simple example of an M-Graph appears in Figure 2b and will be considered shortly.

The concept of an identifying set is defined next, and is similar to that of a key for functional maps. A discussion of the role of functional verses non-functional maps concludes this subsection.

The identifying set (id-set) of a Data Map is a subset of data objects from its Source, such that this id-set uniquely identifies an instance of the Map. The id-set of a multi-valued Map also uniquely identifies an instance of the Map, though the Target of that instance is a set of data objects. The id-set is minimal if it is not derivable from any of its subsets. A Data Map with a minimal id-set contains more information than other non-minimal Data Maps which may be derived from it. Unless otherwise stated, we assume that the Source of a Data Map will include just the minimal id-set.

For a Cluster of Data Maps the definitions are similar. The Source of a Cluster is the union of the Sources of its component Maps. And an id-set of a Cluster uniquely identifies an instance of each Map in the Cluster. When a Cluster is used to represent an Entity, the id-set uniquely identifies an instance of the Entity. If the Cluster represents an n-ary relation, the id-set(s) may serve as candidate keys if the mappings are functional.

Emphasis here has not been placed on functional mappings, though certainly we want to express functionality when it is present. At times we may be more interested in a set of objects, such as the set of cans of soda in a case, rather than in each can individually. Even when the members of a set could be uniquely identified, if the user needs to refer to the set as a whole -- such as the set of students in a class -- we wish to capture the fact that unique identification of the set is intended. To do otherwise might bias the user and the data base system unnecessarily.

Furthermore, functionality is sometimes relative to context. For example, part number 1234 is very specific and appears to functionally determine a part. But to the parts warehouse manager, this part number determines a type of part, such as a particular circuit board -- and the warehouse stores a set of these, some of which may have been produced at different plants, at different times, and with somewhat different costs. What does need to be represented is how some data objects are used in order to refer to other data objects, and which data maps may be clustered together to represent meaningful units of data.

2.2 TRANSFORMATIONS OF DATA MAPS

The Data Maps in a directed hypergraph are considered to be a **Base Set** if (a) the Source of each Data Map is a minimal identifying set, (b) no Data Map is derivable from another Data Map, and (c) the desired views are supported by (derivable from) this Base Set of Data Maps. Sometimes we refer to a hypergraph which satisfies (a) and (b) as a __minimal__ hypergraph -- it need not be unique.

The basic transformations which we use to obtain derivative Data Maps are: (1) omit one or more attributes (domains) from the Target of the Map; (2) a Source attribute may be repeated in the Target, or a Target attribute may be added to the Source; (3) an attribute may be deleted from the Source, creating a related data map which is multi-valued; (4) if a Data Map has more than one equivalent identifying set, either id-set may be used in place of the other. Transformations (2) and (3) together allow an attribute to be moved from the Source to the Target, yielding a multi-valued Map. These transformations allow the derivation of reduced maps from a Base Set. A more general form of these transformations (including composition of Maps) is available, but is not needed here.

To form a particular data model representation from a Base Set of Data Maps, we first may apply these transformations to obtain derivative maps. We then group selected Data Maps together into Clusters, and may express this intermediate result as an M-Graph. The syntactic rules associated with a data model formalism are applied to complete the organization of the data elements, thereby yielding data structured according to the desired model, as illustrated below.

It may be noted that our Data Maps are __not__ equivalent to the functional dependencies and multi-valued dependencies of relational database theory. Among other reasons, our Data Maps are named, so there can be more than one Data Map between the same sets of Source and Target domains. Thus some relational theory axioms would not have analogues for our Data Maps. For example, if a composition of our Data Maps happens to have the same Source and Target domains as another Data Map, it need not have the same meaning,

nor name, as this other Data Map. Nor do attributes need to be renamed based
upon which Data Map they participate in (as may be needed in a standard n-ary
relational model). When a composition of Data Maps should be equivalent to
another Data Map, this fact will be an explicit semantic constraint provided
by the database designer or user and recognized by the system.

2.3 EQUIVALENCE OF SCHEMAS

Different M-Graphs may be derived from the same directed hypergraph by
different clusterings of the Data Maps. These alternative M-Graphs give rise
to schemas in different data models, as is shown in the next section. Since
these schemas are derivable from the same underlying hypergraph, they
represent the same class of real world situations, but as seen from different
orientations.

Definition: Two schemas are compatible if they are both derivable from
a common directed hypergraph by appropriate clustering of the Data Maps.

One or both schemas may represent subsets or restrictions of the
underlying information; e.g., by omission of some Data Maps and/or data
objects. We say that two such schemas M1 and M2 are "compatible with respect
to Hypergraph H" if both M1 and M2 are derivable from H. When the derivation
process does not lose information we have equivalence, in that either is
derivable from the other.

Definition: Two schemas M1 and M2 are equivalent if they are compatible
with respect to some hypergraph H, and if H is derivable from M1 and from M2
individually.

Compatibility and equivalence apply to schemas from the same data model
as well as from different data models. A schema in one data model may be
translated to a different data model by means of its underlying directed
hypergraph. We translate the schema to the hypergraph representation and
recluster its Data Maps, possibly applying the above transformations to some
of these Data Maps. The new schema is then formed from these reclustered
Maps. We now proceed to discuss how a given directed hypergraph gives rise
to schemas in different data models.

3. TRANSLATIONS TO DIFFERENT DATA MODELS

We consider three data models: entity based, n-ary relational, and
network, and outline the translation process from a directed hypergraph to
each of them. A hierarchical model is a special case of a network model. We
focus on the essential structure of these models, and omit the details which
are not at the conceptual level. The key distinction between the models from
our point of view is the grouping of Data Maps into Clusters in the
underlying hypergraph.

In Figure 1a we show the hypergraph incidence matrix for the Parts and
Supplier classical example. Later we will present a more detailed example.
Each column represents a data object (attribute).   Each row represents a
mapping from Source objects (S) to Target objects which are denoted T1 for a
functional map or Tn for a multi-valued map. More than one Tn entry for a
given map means that the map yields a set of tuples, so that within each
tuple there is one instance of each target object. (We also allow "T?" to
mean that the multiplicity of a target object is not known.)

The "Shipment" Map M1 says that for each Part# and Supplier# there is a
single Quantity. Map M2 ("Located") associates a location with the Supplier.
M3 and M4 indicate that each part has several suppliers and each supplier is
responsible for several parts.   This hypergraph is not minimal. Rather a
hypergraph with just the Base Set of Data Maps M1 and M2 would be minimal,
since the source of M1 is a minimal id-set, and the other maps (except M2)
are derivable from it.

3.1 ENTITY MODEL

For an Entity-based model, we first cluster the Data Maps to correspond
to the semantic entities PART, SUPPLIER, and SHIPMENT. This intermediate
result may be shown as an M-Graph, as in Figure 2b, where each cluster is
represented by a square Cluster Node.   Then to obtain the Entity Schema, we
directly express the adjacency relationships between selected Cluster Nodes
which arise due to their having data objects in common. After "factoring"
these adjacency relationships, the Cluster Nodes may now be considered Entity
nodes.

We use the M-Graph as an intermediate expression of which clusters of
Data Maps are selected and their interrelationships. In Figure 2b, the
M-Graph connects each cluster node with each data object from the maps in the
cluster.   Arcs are directed from each Source element into the Cluster node
and out to Target elements. A single-headed arrow indicates functionality,
and a double-headed arrow indicates multiple data objects.

We capture the direction of the Data Maps so we can consider composition
of maps as a form of path following along the directed arcs. For an instance
of a Cluster there is just one instance of each Source element.   So a
functional arrowhead could also be directed outward to each Source element.
But this is not shown in an M-Graph as it can be deduced from the inward arc.
Note that cluster nodes are not connected to each other directly in the
M-Graph. Clusters are considered adjacent if they have data elements in
common.

We obtain the Entity Schema from this M-Graph by "factoring" the
adjacency relationships between Clusters which have common data objects. If
there is a path from cluster C1 through an attribute A to another cluster
node C2, it can be factored by explicitly representing the arc from C1 to C2.
It will be functional only when both original arcs were functional; else it
is multi-valued. It may inherit its name from the original Maps. Redundant
M-Graph arcs to data elements generally are removed so that each data element

is associated with an entity. By following this process we obtain the Entity Diagram in Figure 3.

3.2 RELATIONAL MODEL

To obtain a normalized relational data model, we start with a minimal hypergraph -- that is, the Source of each data map is a minimal identifying set and no map is directly derivable from another map. The Clusters which then are formed represent n-ary relations. To do this, functional maps having identical Sources may be combined into non-trivial clusters, with the Source elements as the key of the corresponding relation. A multi-valued map forms a relation of its own, with a key consisting of the Source and Target elements.

For the Parts-Supplier example, the minimal hypergraph is just maps M1 and M2 from Figure 1a. We consider each map as a separate cluster which represents a relation, and we underline the keys as in Figure 4a. In Figure 4b, we show the associated M-Graph representation. Since the hypergraphs for this Relational Schema and for the Entity Schema are derivable from each other (and thus from a common hypergraph), these schemas are equivalent.

3.3 NETWORK MODEL

We consider a network model consisting of "owner-coupled sets" which establish 1 to N (multi-valued) mappings between an owner record and its member records. This is characteristic of CODASYL DBTG schema.

Emphasis in the network model is on multi-valued maps, with a cluster node being formed for each chosen multi-map. It is possible to transform a map having more than one element in its identifying set into a new multi-map by moving an element from the id-set to the target: e.g., convert (ABC)--->(D) to (AB)--->>(CD). After Data Maps which are to be included in the model are chosen, we form the Clusters. A functional map should be included in a Cluster having the same id-set as this functional map, or if there is none, create a new cluster for the functional map. The resulting clusters of maps gives rise to the associated M-Graph. For our example, the clusters of maps and the M-Graph are shown in Figure 5a and 5b.

To form a Network Schema Diagram, there should be a record type which includes all Source attributes of a cluster. If such a record type does not already exist, create a new record type for these Source attributes. Also include in the record type all functional Target attributes associated with these Source attributes. Determine the partial ordering of clusters, with cluster C1 preceding C2 if the set of data objects in cluster C1 covers the id-set of cluster C2, and the latter id-set includes multi-valued Target attributes of C1. If C1 immediately preceeds C2, then the record type for C1 becomes the Owner for a DBTG set in which C2 is a Member record type.

A Member record type also is created for multi-valued Target attributes of a cluster that are not already in a Member record type. The name of the DBTG Set can default to the name of the cluster for the Member or the name of the multi-map from the cluster of the Owner. Attributes which appear in a predecessor record type can be omitted, in principle, from a successor as they are deducible from the DBTG set connections.

In Figure 5a the chosen maps from the hypergraph and the clusters are shown for our Parts-Supplier example. The resulting M-Graph is in Figure 5b, and 5c shows the final Network Schema. The Supplier# and Part# are optional in record type C1 (derived from cluster C1) as they are redundant. If we were deriving a hypergraph from a network schema, we would determine these "foreign keys" of record type C1 as the union of the keys in record type(s) superior to C1. This network schema represents all the primary maps from the hypergraph in Figure 1a. Thus this network schema is compatible with the Entity and Relational Schemas previously presented.

4.   INCREMENTAL GROWTH OF THE SCHEMA

As a database application expands in scope and size, existing user views may require revision and new user views may be added. The consequence usually is that the conceptual schema must be changed to support these new perspectives. This incremental growth or evolution can be troublesome for some systems, particularly so if frequent change becomes a way of life for a diversified application.

Seemingly different views may be expressed in a common representation using the directed hypergraph of Data Maps. Changes to user views which involve reorganization of the data and regrouping of the relationships are supported without changes to the directed hypergraph of Data Maps, and thus without changes to a conceptual schema expressed in this form. Addition of new data and relationships that previously were not in any view will require additional entries in the hypergraph, but with little impact upon existing entries for the schema. In this section we examine some types of changes and see their effect on the hypergraph representation of the conceptual schema.

4.1 ATTRIBUTE OF AN ATTRIBUTE

One user sees a simple attribute, while a new user sees a more refined object with an attribute of its own. We distinguish two cases for this need to introduce an attribute of an attribute. The first is a refinement of an attribute independent of its occurrence, such as associating a wavelength with the color red. This is just a new functional data map from color to wavelength, and has no effect on existing data maps.

The second case occurs when the new attribute depends on the occurrence of the first. For example if we consider tint to be an attribute of color, then the tint may be different for the red rose in the vase, the red car, and the red rose growing in the ground. To capture this, the data map to color may be logically expanded to now map to (color, tint) -- or, alternatively, a related Data Map may be added whose Target is Tint and whose Source are the data instances of the first Data Map.

If associating an attribute B to an attribute A suggests to one that A should be treated as an entity, this is fine. The data maps involving A need only be segregated and treated as a distinct cluster of the hypergraph to obtain this entity. Creation of this new entity does not change the data maps in the hypergraph.

4.2 ATTRIBUTE OF A RELATIONSHIP

An attribute is essentially a relationship between one data object and another, so this case is similar to the previous one. Thus to create an attribute of a relationship, we proceed similarly, and associate a new attribute value to an instance of a relationship by including this new attribute in the Target of the map associated with the relationship. For example, we may associate a date with a marriage relationship between two people by including the Date in the Target of the data map for that relationship. If we wish, instead, to associate an attribute with the name of the data map, independent of its occurrence, then we may do so with a new data map from the name of the relationship to the attribute.

Our use of the hypergraph of data maps as an underlying schema frees us from concern as to whether a relationship need now be treated as an entity because it has an attribute. That may be accomplished by clustering the data maps for the Entity if desired. Alternatively, the new attribute may be viewed simply as an additional component of the relationship. These choices have been relegated now to choices of presentation, as they should be, rather than treating these alternative interpretations as different conceptual schema.

4.3 RELATIONSHIPS BETWEEN RELATIONSHIPS

As an example, consider a situation where we have a relationship R1 between Person, Vehicle, and Date. And we have another relationship R2 between Task and its Location and Cost. We want to establish a new relationship for correspondences between instances of these two relationships.

In terms of our hypergraph model of the conceptual schema, there are separate data maps for relationships R1 and R2. To establish a relationship between these relationships, we form a new data map R3 whose Source is, in the general case, the union of the Source and Target for R1. The Target of R3 is the union of the Source and Target for R2. Functional Target attributes of R1 and R2 need not be included in R3.

For our example, the data map R3 would have Source attributes Person, Vehicle, and Date; and Target attributes Task, Location and Cost. If the Location and Cost are unique for a given Task Number, then the Target of R3 can be reduced to just this Task Number.

Whether each relationship is "entitized" into a separate entity or not is a matter of presentation. There is a single underlying conceptual representation from which we can directly present entities, or relationships, or the set of Tasks for which a Person used a specific Vehicle, or the set of pairs of (Vehicle, Task) uses by each Person. More than one organization of the data can be presented in a user view.

5. A NETWORK EXAMPLE

Here, a somewhat larger example is presented of how a DBTG style Network representation may be obtained from a conceptual schema expressed in terms of Data Maps. The process outlined in section 3.3 is applied here to a School database having data objects TITLE, NUMBER and CREDITS for each course. Also, each course may have several Required BOOKS and several Recommended BOOKS, and several numbered SECtions. For each student we have data objects for his or her unique SNUMber, SNAME, MAJOR, year (YR) of study, and the GRADE for each course taken. We allow for multiple students who happen to have the same SNAME.

The seven Data Maps shown in Figure 6a summarize the information from a directed hypergraph representation of the conceptual schema for this School database. A Data Map as represented here indicates the one or more minimal identifying sets of the Map (each in parenthesis) to the left of the arrow. A single-headed arrow means the named Map is functional; else it is multi-valued. The target attributes appear on the right. The i-th Data Map is named Mi by default, and may be given a semantic name also.

The first data map M1 describes the essential characteristics of a course; it states that the course's Title or Number each are an identifying set for each other and for Credits. Data map M1 also has an explicit semantic name, CLASS. Data map M2 is named STUDENT, and it states that a student's Number identifies one student's Name, Major and Year, while a student's Name may not always be unique according to Data Map M3. Data map M4 declares that the course Title and Student's Number uniquely determine the Grade that student received in that course and the Section which he attended. M5 says that each Section of each course has a set of students. M5 is related to the converse of Data Map M4. M6 and M7 relate the Course to its set of REQuired Books and its set of RECOMmended Books, respectively.

From these Data Maps, we can obtain the DBTG Sets and record types (Figure 7) by clustering these Maps and their derivatives. Each Cluster which contains a multi-valued Map becomes the basis for a DBTG Set whose Owner includes the Source attributes and whose Member record type includes the Target attributes.

The Data Map Clusters are shown in Figure 6b. Derivative maps are denoted a, b, c. There are six clusters, and five of them contain multi-maps and give rise to DBTG Sets. The Network Diagram of Figure 7 results from these Clusters and includes five record types and the five DBTG Sets.

The Owner record type for Cluster C1 includes the Source and functional Target attributes of map M1, and also serves as the Owner for the DBTG Sets resulting from Clusters C4 and C5. A separate Member record type is created for the multi-valued attribute BOOK of Clusters C4 and C5. The id-set of the Cluster C2 for Section contains the multi-valued Target attributes of Cluster C1, and thus the Source attributes of C2 may form a record type which is a Member with respect to the DBTG Set resulting from Cluster C1. Similarly, the id-set of the Cluster C3 includes the multi-valued Target attributes of C2, and so these attributes form a Member record type with respect to the DBTG Set resulting from Cluster C2. This record type also includes the functional Target attributes of the Grade Cluster C3, and so it serves as a Member with respect to the DBTG Set resulting from the Student Cluster C6.

The above seven Data Maps form a Base Set of Maps and contain sufficient information to support schema for this database expressed in the other data models -- these may be derived by the process described earler. More examples are provided in [Mor81b].

6. CONCLUSION

By generalizing an edge in a typical schema diagram, the notion of a directed hypergraph was developed. A directed hypergraph edge consists of a set (rather than a pair) of data objects, and represents a Data Map from one subset of data objects to another. The common data models provide different ways of portraying a collection of related hypergraph edges or Data Maps. Schema or subschema can be interpreted in terms of any of the common data models by appropriately clustering these Data Map expressions and adhering to the syntactic constraints of that data model formalism.

Compatibility and equivalence between schemas were defined in terms of this underlying hypergraph representation. An approach was discussed for translating between equivalent schemas, whether they are from the same or from different data models. The ability to integrate different data concepts easily into the Data Map representation can be important in reducing the impact of incremental growth and change on a conceptual schema.

REFERENCES

[Abr] J.R. Abrial, Data Semantics, in Data Base Management, eds. Klimbie and Koffeman, 1974, pp.1-60.

[Ber] Claude Berge, Graphs and Hypergraphs, North Holland, 1973.

[Bil] Horst Biller and E.Neuhold, Semantics of Data Bases, Infor Syst. vol.3, 1978, pp.11-30.

[Card80] Cardenas, A. and M.H. Pirahesh, The E-R model in heterogeneous database management systems network architecture, in: Chen, P. (ed.), Entity-Relationship Approach to Systems Analysis and Design (North-Holland, Amsterdam, 1980).

[Chen76] Peter P. Chen, The Entity-Relationship Model -- Toward a Unified View of Data, ACM Trans. on Database Systems, vol.1, no.1, pp.9-36, March 1976.

[Chen77] Chen, P.P., The entity-relationship approach to logical database design, Q.E.D. Monograph Series, No.6, Q.E.D. Information Sciences, Inc., Wellesley, Mass. (1977).

[Chu 80] Chu, W. and V. To, A hierarchical conceptual model for data translation in heterogeneous database environment, in: Chen, P. (ed.), Entity-Relationship Approach to Systems Analysis and Design (North-Holland, Amsterdam, 1980).

[Ha1] Patrick Hall, J.Owlett, and S.Todd, Relations and Entities, in Modelling in Data Base Mgt Systems, ed. G.M.Nijssen, 1976, pp.201-220.

[Ke77] William Kent, Entities and Relationships in Information, in Architecture and Models in Data Base Mgt Sys, ed. G.M. Nijssen, 1977, pp.67-91.

[Ke78] William Kent, Data and Reality, North Holland, 1978.

[Ke79] William Kent, Limitations of Record-Based Information Models, ACM Trans on Database Sys. vol.4, no.1, March 1979, pp.107-131.

[Lang] Borje Langefors, Comments on a Paper By Biller and Neuhold, Infor. Sys. vol.3, 1978, pp.31-34.

[McL78] D. McLeod, A Semantic Data Base Model and its Associated Structured User Interface, PhD Thesis, M.I.T. Lab for Comp Sci, 1978.

[Mor76] Matthew Morgenstern, Automated Design and Optimization of Management Information System Software, M.I.T. Laboratory for Computer Science (formally Project MAC), Ph.D. Thesis, 1976.

[Mor81a] Matthew Morgenstern, The User's View of a Database, Trends and Applications 1981: Advances in Software Technology, National Bureau of Standards, May 1981, pp.88-98.

[Mor81b] Matthew Morgenstern, A Unified Approach for Conceptual Schema to Support Multi-Model User Views, Dept of Computer Science, Rutgers Univ., New Brunswick, N.J., February 1981.

[Mor81c] Matthew Morgenstern, Strategies for Database Schema Acquisition and Design, ACM '81 Conference, Los Angeles, Calif., Nov. 1981.

[Pira78] Pirahesh, M.H., Database communication in heterogeneous environment, M.S. Thesis, Dept. of Computer Science, U.C.L.A., (1978)

[Ship] David W. Shipman, The Functional Data Model and the Data Language DAPLEX, ACM SIGMOD Conf, June 1979.

[Ull80] Jeffrey Ullman, Principles of Database Systems, Computer Science Press, 1980.

EDGE/MAP NAME		Part#	Supplier#	Quantity	SuppLoc
		-----	---------	--------	-------
SHIPMENT:	M1	S	S	T1	
LOCATED:	M2		S		T1
	M3	S	Tn	Tn	
SUPPLIES:	M4	Tn	S	Tn	
	M3´	S	Tn		
	M4´	Tn	S		

S = Source (domain) of map.
T1 = Target of functional map.
Tn = Target of non-functional map.
(above is not a minimal hypergraph)

A Hypergraph Incidence Matrix
for Parts and Supplier Example.

FIGURE 1a

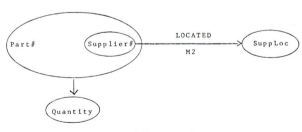

Diagram of Hypergraph
for Data Maps M1 & M2

FIGURE 1b

(a)   ENTITY Clusters:

CLUSTER   MAPS   DATA OBJECTS INVOLVED

      PART   M3'   Part#, Supplier#
      SUPPLIER   M2,M4'   Supplier#, SuppLoc, Part#
      SHIPMENT   M1   Part#, Supplier#, Quantity

(b)   Resulting M-Graph
      (edges are labelled with the names of the map(s) responsible
      for the edge; ID means ID-set of cluster node)

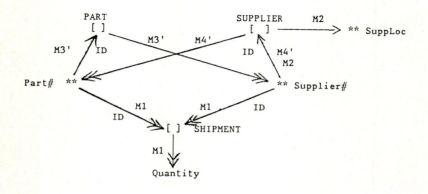

[ ] is a Cluster Node

Entity Clusters and Resulting M-Graph

FIGURE: 2a and b

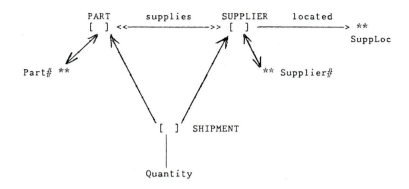

Entity Diagram Schema
(for M-Graph in Fig 2b)

FIGURE 3

RELATION	ATTRIBUTES
SUPPLY	(PART#, SUPPLIER#, QUANTITY)
SUPPLIER-LOC	(SUPPLIER#, SUPPLOC)

FIGURE 4a: Relational Schema

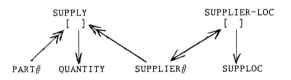

FIGURE 4b: M-Graph for Relational Schema

DERIVATION OF NETWORK SCHEMA

(a) Hypergraph Incidence Matrix

CLUSTER	MAP		PART#	SUPPLIER#	QUANTITY	SUPPLOC
C1	M1	:	S	S	T1	
C2	M2	:		S		T1
C2	M4	:	Tn	S	Tn	
C3	M3	:	S	Tn	Tn	

(b) M-GRAPH

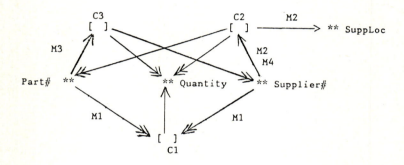

(c) Network Schema

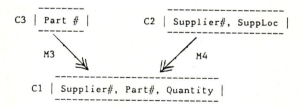

Supplier# and Part# are optional in C1

DERIVATION OF NETWORK SCHEMA

FIGURE 5

```
DATA MAPS:
    M1  CLASS   :   (TITLE),(NUMBER) ----> (TITLE, NUMBER, CREDITS)
    M2  STUDENT:        (SNUM)       ---->  (SNAME MAJOR YR)
    M3          :        (SNAME)      --->> (SNUM)
    M4  GRADES  :    (TITLE SNUM)    ---->  (GRADE SEC)
    M5  REGISTD:     (TITLE SEC)     --->>  (SNUM)
    M6  REQD    :       (TITLE)       --->> (BOOK)
    M7  RECOM   :       (TITLE)       --->> (BOOK)
```

FIGURE 6a: DATA MAPS for NETWORK SCHEMA

```
CLUSTERS
--------
C1: Course  { M1 : (TITLE),(NUMBER) --->  (TITLE, NUMBER, CREDITS)
            { M4a:      (TITLE)       --->> (SEC)

C2: Section { M5 :    (TITLE SEC)    --->> (SNUM)

C3: Grade   { M4b:   (TITLE SNUM)    --->  (GRADE)

C4: Reqd    { M6    REQD: (TITLE)    --->> (BOOK)

C5: Recom   { M7   RECOM: (TITLE)    --->> (BOOK)

C6: Student { M2 :       (SNUM)       --->  (SNAME MAJOR YR)
            { M4c:       (SNUM)       --->> (TITLE GRADE)
```

CLUSTERS OF DATA MAPS
FOR NETWORK SCHEMA

FIGURE 6b

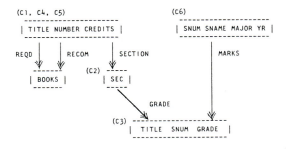

NETWORK DIAGRAM

FIGURE 7

Entity-Relationship Approach to
Information Modeling and Analysis, P.P. Chen (ed.)
Elsevier Science Publishers B.V. (North-Holland)
©ER Institute, 1983

CONCEPTUAL REPRESENTATION OF DATA AND LOGICAL IMS DESIGN

G. Caldiera   P. Quitadamo
ITALSIEL S.p.A.
Via Isonzo 21/B
00191 ROME
ITALY

Abstract : The topics of a conceptual representation of
data are presented using an E-R model enriched with
integrity constraints and hierarchies. Some rules are
also outlined to provide a logical representation
of the defined structures and a contral of the static
constraints through the features of IMS/DB.

I. INTRODUCTION

The growing complexity of the structure and management of data
bases has brought about a need for a representation of data
independent of the functions they support.

The data are seen and analyzed as a resource which is common to
various users and applicable to various functions.

This brings us to distinguish a level of representation referred
to as concepts and relationships between concepts, from a level of "lo
gical" a representation, where a decision is made as to which
connections to implement and how to implement them, taking into
consideration the efficiency of the system.

The conceptual model described in this paper uses an E-R
formalism derived from that of P.P.S. Chen (1) and enriched with
some characteristics which are essentially static integrity constraints.
This formalism is widely used in our company to provide a representation of data analysis. The E-R approach is a part of our general
integrated methodology of system analysis and design named DAFNE
(Data and Function Networking). ·

At the end of this paper we will show how to represent the defined structures and how to control the static constraints by using the features of IMS/DB.

II. FUNDAMENTALS OF CONCEPTUAL REPRESENTATION

When we refer not to individual objects existing in the real world, but to concepts, we are giving a conceptual representation of data. Reality is described, after a phase of preliminary analysis, by means of sentences in ordinary language (4) describing the context. We can consequently derive from this description a family of predicative forms with one or more variables:

$$P_1(x), P_2(x), \ldots, P_n(x)$$

$$P_1^2(x_1, x_2), P_2^2(x_1, x_2), \ldots, P_m^2(x_1, x_2)$$

$$\ldots\ldots\ldots\ldots\ldots\ldots\ldots\ldots\ldots\ldots\ldots$$

where the x's and the x_i's vary in the set Ω of the objects, or of the names of the objects, present in the context. If we fix the variables in a predicative form we obtain a statement which may be true in the analyzed context.

A concept defined by a predicative form with one variable $P_1(x)$ is called <u>entity</u>. Each entity E associated with P_1 is connected to the set of its occurrences, defined as the set $\Omega_{P_1} = \{x \in \Omega : P_1(x)$ is a true statement in the described context$\}$. Two entities, E_1 and E_2 , are considered <u>equal</u> if the predicative forms that define them are equivalent. Empty entities are obviously allowed, when the related set of occurrences is empty. Let us give an example: if, in the analyzed context, x varies over the names of the employees of a company and $P(x)$ is the predicative form "x is at the head of a finalized set of company activities", we can say that $P(x)$ defines the entity PROJECT HEAD whose occurrences are all the employees whose name, when substituted for x in $P(x)$, makes it a true statement. As can be seen, an entity must have a label (in our example it was PROJECT HEAD). This allows us to represent it in a diagram with a rectangle, with the label written inside.

On the other hand, the predicative froms with two or more

variables establish a connection between groups of elements of Ω. If, for example, x is an occurrence of the entity A and y is an occurrence of the entity B, we can say that (x,y) is an occurrence of the relationship $R_{P_1^2}$ between A and B if the statement $P_2^1 (x,y)$ is true.

A binary <u>relationship</u> is a concept defined by a predicative form with two variables referring to two entities. Relationships between more than two entities are defined analogously.

In the preceding example we can define two entities:

> WORKER : "X is an employee of the company assigned to production departments"

> MACHINE : "X is a mechanism finalized to an elementary productive function"

The predicative form $P^2 (x, y)$: "X works at Y" defines a relationship between the entities WORKER and MACHINE, which is assigned the label WORKS AT. The relationship WORKS AT is represented in the diagram with a diamond box attached to the entities entering the relationship, with the label written inside (Fig. 1).

Fig. 1

The conceptual schema of the data is a finite, connected, bipartite graph with nodes of one type, called entities, and nodes of an other type, called relationships: it may consist of a single entity, but a relationship cannot have unattached links (10).

In this way, we can point out the entities and the relationships we are interested in by representing the analyzed context in a diagram. If, for example, we want to represent the context of a library which lends books to card-holders, we shall adopt a graph like that of Fig. 2.

The predicative form that define these objects are:

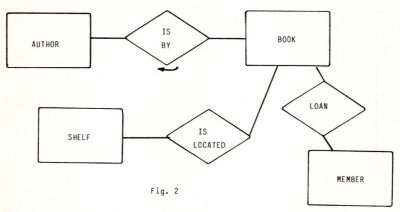

Fig. 2

BOOK   : "X is a publication, bound and in print"

MEMBER   : "X is a person holding a library card"

AUTHOR   : "X is a person who has written a book"

SHELF   : "X is a place to keep books"

IS LOCATED   : "X is located on Y"

IS BY   : "X was written by Y"

LOAN   : "X is on loan to Y"

Generalization hierarchies between entities are also allowed in our data model.

An entity A is hierarchically subordinated to an entity B if the predicative proposition defining A implies the one defining B.

This is represented in figure 3. It follows that the set of occurences O_A is still contained in O_B . A hierarchy is said to be complete if every occurrence of the "father" entity is required by one and only one "child" entity: this is represented by the black dot on the vertex of the triangle (Fig. 3).

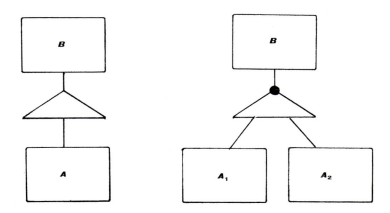

Fig. 3

This way of representing the relationship between the implying and implied predicative forms is also a way of defining the equality of entities: two entities A and B are equal if and only if A is hierarchically subordinated to B and, viceversa, B is subordinated to A. This fact implies automatically that the sets of occurrences σ_A and σ_B are equal.

Entities can also be defined starting with a many–variables predicative form. If A is an entity and P(x,y) is a predicative form where x varies in σ_A, for each $x \in \sigma_A$ the predicative form P(x,y) defines an entity: the set of these entities is a new entity B which is defined by the form "there exists an x, occurrence of A, such that P(x,y) is a true statement".

The occurrences of B exist, therefore, only if they are in relation to occurrences of A. The new entity thus defined is called a <u>weak entity</u> because it is defined on the basis of a relation with another entity. In an analogous way we can define weak entities dependent on a relationship between other entities. All the relationships used to define other entities are said existence relationships. For example, in the context of the library, which we mentioned previously, to define AUTHOR we have in fact used the relationship which ties it to BOOK: it is fairly obvious that the name of the author in the card–

catalog a library has no value if the library has none of his books.

Consequently, AUTHOR is a weak entity and the relationship IS BY is a relationship of existence. This is indicated by doubling the sides of the rectangle of the weak entity and by putting an E near the diamond box representing the relationship (Fig. 4).

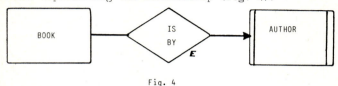

Fig. 4

These definitions determine the difference between the two types of entity nodes in the conceptual schema: strong entities and weak entities.

The first ones are, so to speak, the original ones; the other ones are derived concepts which may be attached to the original nodes. This difference is a integrity constraint in our model of data.

Let us look at other constraints we represent in the conceptual model.

Let $R_{P_i^n}$ be a relationship which connects the entities E_1, ..., E_n by means of the predicative form with n variables $P_i^n(x_1, ... x_n)$.

We say that the relationship R_{P^n} has multiplicity 1 with respect to the entity E_h ($1 \leqslant h \leqslant n$) if, however fixed an (n-1)-tuple of occurrences of the remaining entities, $\bar{x}_1 \in \mathcal{O}_{E_1}$, ..., $\bar{x}_n \in \mathcal{O}_{E_n}$, there is only one occurrence $\hat{x}_h$ of E_h such that the n-tuple $(\hat{x}_1, ..., \hat{x}_h, ..., \hat{x}_n)$ is an occurrence of the relationship. We see, for example, that the relationships LOAN of figure 2 has multiplicity 1 with regard to MEMBER, considering that the same book cannot be on loan to more than one person. However, we can say that the relationship has multiplicity N with regard to the entity E_h if there is a (n-1)-tuple of occurrences of the remaining entities such that there is more than one occurrence $\hat{x}_h$ of E_h for which the resulting n-tuple $(\bar{x}_1, ..., \hat{x}_h, ..., \bar{x}_n)$ is an occurrence of R_{P^n}. Let us establish in our example an occurrence of MEMBER who has borrowed more than one book: there will be at least two occurrences of BOOK in relation to this occurrence of MEMBER. Thus, the relationship LOAN has multiplicity 1 with regard to MEMBER and multiplicity N with regard to BOOK: consequently, it is a relationship 1-N and this is represented in figure 5.

Fig. 5

Analogously, relationships with three or more entities are represented with the respective multiplicities. For example, if the relazionship SUPPLY defined by the predicative form "the occurrence X of SUPPLIER sells the occurrence Y of PART to the occurrence Z of PROJECT" is a relationship 1-N-1, this is represented in figure 6.

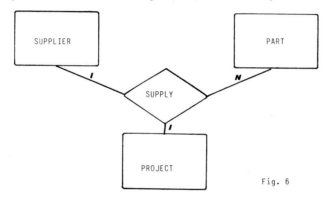

Fig. 6

In addition to multiplicity, the relationships have another important characteristic which we shall call "optionality".

We say that a relationship $R_{P_1^n}$ which connects the entities E_1, ..., E_n is optional with regard to the entity E_i if there is at least one occurrence $\bar{x}_i \in \mathcal{O}_{E_i}$ such that, for every $(n-1)$-tuple of the other entities $\bar{x}_1$, ..., $\bar{x}_n$, the resulting n-tuple $(\bar{x}_1$, ..., $\bar{x}_i$, ..., $\bar{x}_n)$ is not an occurrence of the relationship $R_{P_n^n}$. For example, in figure 6, if there were a project that did not buy parts from any suppliers, there would exist an occurrence of PROJECT that would satisfy the definition of optionality. The relationship SUPPLY is thus optional with regard to the entity PROJECT. In our diagrams we represent the non-optionality of a relationship with regard to an entity with a black dont at the root of the branch directed towards the entity.

In figure 6 the only entity for which the relatioship SUPPLY is not optional is SUPPLIER (all suppliers sell at least one part to at least one project), as represented in figure 7:

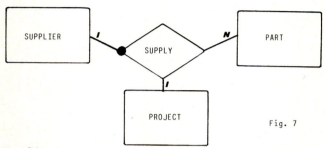

Fig. 7

Let σ be a set of occurrences of an entity E or of a relationship R. An <u>attribute</u> A of the entity E or of the relationship R is a function defined on a subset σ' of σ with values in a set **D** called the "domain" of the attribute.

$$A : \sigma' \subseteq \sigma \longrightarrow D$$

An attribute represents characteristics of the occurrence to which it is referred, characteristics that can generally be assigned to the entity or to the relationship. It has a label and is represented by means of a circle connected to the entity or to the relationship it is referred to. For example, the entity BOOK can have the attributes PUBLISHER, TITLE, YEAR OF PUBLICATION; the first two have as a domain a set of alphabetic strings with a pre-established maximum length, the last one has its domain a set of years.

The representation of the attributes is shown in figure 8:

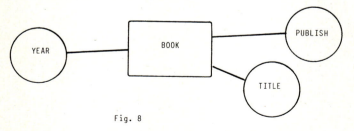

Fig. 8

We said that a relationship can also have attributes: for example LOAN has the attribute DATE which connects each pair of occurrences of BOOK and MEMBER to the date the book was lent (Fig. 9).

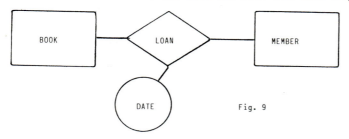

Fig. 9

Until now we have spoken about various occurrences of an entity or of a relationship without indicating how they can be distinguished. An attribute, or a family of attributes, such that it is a reversible function from the occurrences to the domain, allows for such a distinction and is called an identifier of the entity or of the relationship. In the example of figure 2 the MEMBER has as possible identifiers the attributes CARD–NUMBER or NAME; the SHELF has as a possible identifier the group of attributes ROOM NUMBER and SHELF NUMBER, and so on. If an entity is weak, two cases are possible: either it has an identifier or it does not, in the sense that it requires the identifier of the entity or of the relationship it depends on. In the latter case, the relationship that defines the entity is called an identification relationship.

The conceptual schema which represents the data of the analized context must be rather invariant from the different points of view of the people who draw it. We use for this purpose a normalized version of the conceptual schema, in which all implicit relationships are pointed out in a standard form.

A conceptual schema is said to be normalized (2) if:

i)   every attribute has a domain of atomic values;

ii)   the values of every attribute depend completely on the whole identifier and do not depend on any sub–set of the attributes the identifier is composed of;

iii)   there is no transitive dependency of an attribute on the identifier through another attribute.

This completes the presentation of the characteristics of our conceptual representation (7).

III. <u>LOGICAL PROJECT OF IMS DATA BASES: TECHNIQUES AND POSSIBILITIES</u>

In the definition of the Data Base Design phases there is often a confusion between "logical" and "physical" design: the logical design is considered as "high-level design" and the physical design as "low-level design". In this way it is left open which features of the target DBMS are to be considered at the "logical" rather than at the "physical" level (e.g., is an IMS secondary index a logical or a physical characteristic?).

In this paper, the implementation of the data structure represented at the conceptual level is seen as part of the logical design. In other words, the logical design is a mapping from the conceptual model (here the E-R model) to the DBMS model (here IMS/DB). The features of the target DBMS that are to be considered in this phase are only those that can be used for the implementation of the data structure, as well as all the features to which applications are sensitive. All other features must be taken into consideration at the physical design level.

For example, in an IMS data base the existence of a secondary index pointing to a target segment at a level other than the root level introduces the ability to see the parent as a child and the child as a parent. This of course changes the structure of the data; therefore applications must be aware of the existence of the secondary index. We are in the "logical design" phase.

On the other hand, the splitting of a data base into several "data set groups"(1,2,3,4...) is only a tuning consideration: it can be made during the data base "life", without any need to notify the user of the change. As much could be said concerning features such as organization (HISAM/HIDAM...), recording characteristics (e.g., size and structure of the Root Addressable Area in an HDAM data base, etc.). In such cases we are in the physical design phase.

In mapping an Entity-Relationship conceptual schema onto an

IMS–DB logical schema (3,5,6) it is best to begin by considering the strong entities and, therefore, by identifying the relationships of existence which are connected to them, that is the structures of the "Parent–Child" type existing in the conceptual schema; attention will subsequently be focused on the implementation of the relationships which do not imply existence and on the analysis of the semantic characteristics of the relationships and their implementation in the logical schema.

In the following paragraphs we shall analyze all the concectual structures seen in Section II and discuss their possible mappings into an IMS logical data model. We shall refer to the data model described in (9).

1. Entities and their attributes

    The strong entities appearing in the conceptual schema will be implemented as "root" segments of distinct physical data bases; the attributes of the entity will become search fields of the segment only if they are used for the definition of selection criteria by at least one transaction. Entities that are weak with respect to other entities are to be implemented as dependent segments, the relationship of "existence" becoming a "Parent–Child" connection between the segments.

    If the relationship is only of the existence type, direct access to the weak entity can be gained by building a secondary index on the identifier of the entity. Otherwise, the characteristic of identification ("ID"), in the case of such a relationship, can be implemented by using the "concatenated key" for the dependent segment.

2. Relationships which do not imply conditioning upon existence

    N–M Relationships :   an N–to–M–type relationship can be implemented by

                              – placing the two entities as roots of distinct physical data bases

                              – establishing a bidirectional logical relationship between the segments

- using the "Virtual Pairing" configuration,
taking into account which is the more
used   direction   of   the   relationship

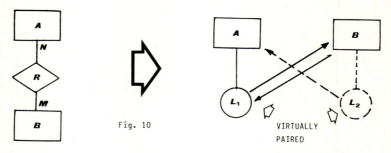

Fig. 10

VIRTUALLY
PAIRED

1-N Relationships :   a relationship 1 to N between A and B can
be seen as a particular case of N to M
relationships,   except   that   an   integrity
constraint will have to be placed on the
data base: we will have to prevent an
occurrence   of   B   from   having   a
correspondence with more than one segment
A in the inverse relationship. In an IMS
data base this constraint will have to be
enforced by imposing "POINTER=NOTWIN" on
the dependent segment which implements the
inverse relationship.

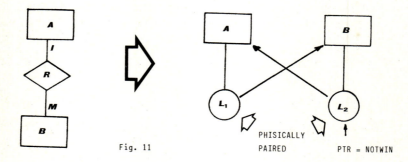

Fig. 11

PHISICALLY
PAIRED   PTR = NOTWIN

1-1 Relationships   :   there are two ways of implementing them:

          a) In case the percentage of entities that are involved in the relationship is large (> 60–70%) and access to one entity often implies access to the other, one can implement a single segment having as sequence field the identifier of the more used entity, and build a secondary index on the identifier of the other entity.

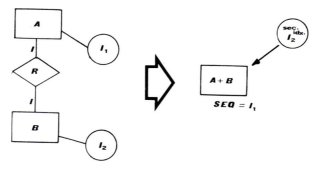

Fig. 12

          b) If the conditions in a) are not met the relationship will be implemented as a particular case of 1–N relationships, by imposing a double constraint on the uniqueness of the occurrences of the entities involved with the technique illustrated for 1–N relationships.

3. Relationships of Existence

The meaning og this type of relationship is that the deletion of a given entity must be propagated to all weak entities related to it through the existence relationship (s). This can be implemented in IMS/DB by using "Parent–Child" relationships and deletion rules as follows:

1-N Relationships   :   This type of relationship finds a natural implementation in IMS, which is based on hierarchical structures.

1-1 Relationships : They can be seen as a particular case of the preceding relationship type, by imposing "POINTER=NOTWIN" on the dependent segment to guarantee its uniqueness under a given parent.

N-M Relationships : To carry out automatically the deletion of an occurrence of an entity B when the last occurrence of an entity A, related to B, is deleted, one must:

- place the two entities as roots of distinct physical data bases

- establish a bidirectional logical relationship between the segment

- code "V" (Virtual) as the "Delete" rule of the segmente representing the weak entity

- code "V" as the "Delete" rule of the segments representing the relationship

- code "L" (Logical) as the "Insert" rule of the B segment

- prevent the insertion of B through the "Physical Path" with the specification of the "Processing Option" in the PCBs that have the B segment as a root

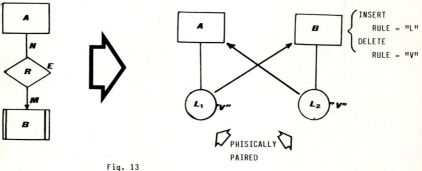

Fig. 13

4. Attributes of Relationships

The attributes of a relationship are treated as "fixed intersection data", that is, they are inserted in the segment implementing the logical relationship (i.e., the logical child).

In the case of N-M relationships, it best to make use of the feature of "Virtual Pairing" and to place the logical child under the segment defining the more used direction of the relationship (see Fig. 14).

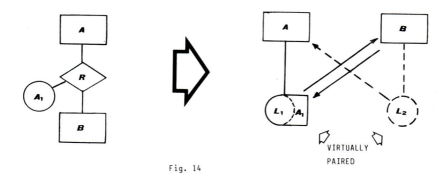

Fig. 14

5. Entities that are weak with respect to a relationship

In this case the entity will be treated as "Variable intersection data", that is, as a segment placed, under the segment that implements the logical relationship.

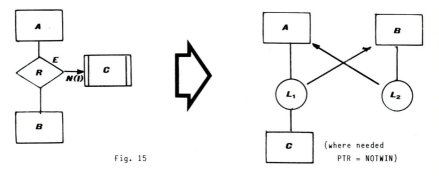

Fig. 15

6. Optionality of the relationship

As we have seen in section II it is bcth possibile and useful
to specify the non-optional character of a relationship even if the
relationship is not an existence relationship.

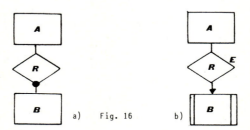

a)   Fig. 16   b)

While the representation of figure 16 b expresses a "Parent–Child"
relationship, i.e., it indicates that with the deletion of an
occurrence of A all the occurrences of B connected to A by R must
also be deleted, figure 16 a forces <u>not</u> to delete an occurrence of
the entity A if it is connected, by R, to occurrences of B.

This integrity constraint will be implemented by:

– making of the two entities two roots of physical data bases
  (note that both entities are "strong")

– establishing a bidirectional logical relationship between the
  entities

– indicating as the "Delete" rule of the A segment the option "P"
  (Physical), so that no occurrence of the A segment having
  "logical children" (occurrences of the relationship) can be
  cancelled

– indicating as the "Insert" rule of the A segment the "L" (Logical)
  option and by always performing the insertions of the A segment
  along with the insertion of the occurrence of the relationship
  that involves it (or, in other words, always through the "logical
  path")

– preventing the insertion of A through the "Physical Path", by
  checking the " processing option" of the PCBs having the A

segment as the root.

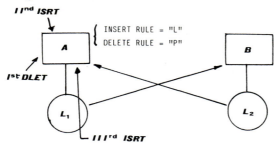

Fig. 17

I^{st} { dependents exist : refused

dependents do not exist : accepted

IInd : refused

IIIrd : accepted

7. Generalization Hierarchies

Let A_1 ... A_n be entities subordinated to A; let us look at the three possible implementations:

a) the hierarchy is implemented by means of a "Parent-Child" relationship, where entity A is the "parent" segment and entities A_i are distinct dependent segment where "POINTER= NOTWIN" is specified.

b) as in a), but representing each entity A_i as an occurrence of a sigle segment-type

c) the hierarchy is implemented with a sigle segment

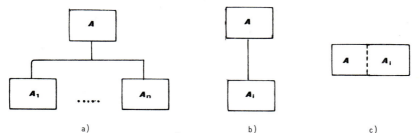

a)   b)   c)

Fig. 18

IV. CONCLUSIONS
     <u>   </u>

We have seen how, in mapping the conceptual model onto an IMS–DB
logical schema, it is possible to implement all the objects and the
characteristics of the proposed model; after this mapping a phase
of revision of the resulting logical schema will be necessary to
reduce the number of physical data bases and logical relationships,
thus achieving   an optimization of storage requirements and of
performance.

This phase can be carried out along the following lines:

- introduction of controlled redundancy in the data base

- elimination of the logical relationships representing directions of
  relationships not used by any transactions.

Once this process of revision is completed, one can undertake the
physical project, which consists in the definition of access parameters
and of storage characteristics which are never "seen" by application
programs.

BIBLIOGRAFY

(1) P.P.S. Chen, "The Entity – Relationship model: toward a unified view of data", ACM Transactions on Data Base Systems, vol. 1 n. 1 (1976), pp. 3-36.

(2) E.F. Codd: "Further normalization of the data base relational model". In "Data base Systems", Courant Computer Science Symposia 6, R. Rustin, Ed., Prentice Hall, Englewood Cliffs, N. J., 1971, p.p. 65-98.

(3) C.J. Date: An Introduction to Data base Systems, Addison – Wesley, 1977.

(4) H. Kansgassalo, "Logical and semantical properties of environmental situations for stating information requirements", Proceedings of the IFIP TC-8 "Working Conference on formal models and pratical tools for information systems design", Oxford, April 17-20, 1979.

(5) IBM, IMS/VS – System application and design guide.

(6) IBM, IMS/VS – Primer

(7) ITALSIEL, "Manuale di analisi dei dati", March 1981.

(8) Lusk, E.L. Overbeek, R.A. and Parrello, B. "A Practical Design Methodology For the Implementation of IMS Data bases, using the Entity – Relationship Model", Proceeding of ACM SIGMOD, May 1980.

(9) P. Scheuermann – G. Schiffner – H. Weber, "Abstraction capabilities and invariant properties modelling within the E-R approach", in "E-R approach to system analysis and design", P.P.S. Chen ed, North-Holland, 1980, pp. 121-140.

(10) J.F. Sowa: Conceptual graphs for a data base interface", IBM J. Res. Develop., Iuly 1976, pp. 336-357.

(11) Tsao, J.H. Enterprise schema – An approach to IMS logical database design, in Chen, P. (ed.), Entity – Relationship Approach to Systems Analysis and Design (North-Holland Amsterdam,1980).

Entity-Relationship Approach to
Information Modeling and Analysis, P.P. Chen (ed.)
Elsevier Science Publishers B.V. (North-Holland)
©ER Institute, 1983

Design Of Data Models For The ADABAS System
Using The Entity-Relationship Approach

Valdemar W. Setzer, René Lapyda

Instituto de Matemática e Estatística
Universidade de São Paulo
Brasil

The Entity-Relationship Model has been used as a design   tool
for database systems. In this paper we show how to convert the Entity-Relationship Diagram into the data model of the ADABAS system.
For this, a diagram for that system is introduced, a procedure for
the conversion is formally given, and choice criteria are stated,
advising the user about various minimization possibilities.

1. INTRODUCTION

As it was shown by many authors [4] the Entity-Relationship Model (ERM) [2]
may be used as a conceptual model for databases. By "conceptual model" we understand here a formal model which exists only in our mind, not necessarily im
plemented in a computer. It may be used as a model of the reality, and serves
as a step in the direction of a "concrete model", that is, one for which there
is an implementation. The main advantage of a conceptual model is its independ
ence on particular implementation constraints. In this paper, we show how to
convert the schema of the ERM into the data model for the ADABAS system [10],
as an example of the step conceptual model → concrete model. We presume   that
the reader is already familiar with the ERM. We give a brief introduction   to
the relevant ADABAS characteristics, and present a schema diagram for that sys
tem. A systematic procedure to convert the ERM diagram into the ADABAS diagram
is then introduced; optimization steps follow, where criteria are presented in
dicating possible factors to orient the choice of different solutions, minimiz
ing the number of files, access efficiency, etc. An abstract example is given
in the Appendix.

2. AN EXTENSION OF THE ERM DIAGRAM

We say that a relationship in the ERM between entity sets E_1 and E_2 is of a
m:c mapping, where c is a constant natural number, iff each element of E_2 is re
lated to any number of elements of E_1 and each element of E_1 is related[2] to at
$most$ c elements of E_2. An example of such a relationship is presented   in
Fig. 1. We may give [2] it the following interpretation: each instructor may be
teaching at most three courses, but a given course may be taught by any number
of instructors.

This research was partly done while the senior author was a Visiting Professor
a the Institut für Informatik, Univ. Stuttgart, under the CNPq-GMD program.

Fig. 1

In particular, we may have $c_1:c_2$ relationships, for $c_1,c_2 \in \mathbb{N}$, where analogous restrictions fall on both entities. With this extension, n:1 and 1:1 relationships have exactly the expected meaning and may be regarded as particularizations of the notation introduced here.

There exist interesting extensions to the ERM; for the sake of simplicity, in this paper we will use the original version [2] plus the attribute diagram of [3].

3. THE ADABAS DATA MODEL

We give here a brief introduction to the ADABAS data model, concerning mainly of its logical model, that is, as it is viewed by its users. This introduction will be made on a comparative basis, having the ERM notions as starting point. To make it easier to convert the ERM to the ADABAS model, we introduce new notions in the latter. ADABAS notions [10] are written between quotation marks, as for instance "field".

3.1. E-FILES

Corresponding to the entity sets of the ERM, we introduce ADABAS "files" which will be called *E-files*. The attributes of an entity set are converted into "fields" of the E-file. The value sets cannot be fully specified in ADABAS; they may be partially defined by the so called "standard length" and "standard format" specifications. For example, Fig. 2 introduces the characteristics of the entity set STUDENT, and Fig. 3 presents the (possible) corresponding ADABAS schema declaration in its basic data description language.

Each line of Fig. 3 declares a "file field"; the first specification is a level number as in COBOL or PL/I records; the second, the "field" name (2 letters); the third, the "standard length" of the "field"; the fourth, the "standard format" ('F'=fixed integer, 'A'=alphanumeric, etc.). 'DE' stands for "descriptor", declaring the "field" to be a key type with repeated values; only 'DE' "fields" may be qualified in "search-criteria" of efficient queries. ADABAS produces a partial inversion of this field, constructing an index file which points (conceptually) to the "file" records. Note the lack of total correspondence between ERM value sets (Fig. 2) and the "file" attributes of ADABAS. For instance, it is impossible to specify the value set {M,F} for attribute SEX; instead, one has to employ the specification '1,A'.

In some entity sets and in all relationship sets of the ERM composite keys occur with more than one attribute. The corresponding ADABAS construct is the "superdescriptor": one specifies a list of "descriptor fields" as a "superdescriptor", which may then be used in the "search criteria" as just one "descrip tor". In the sequel, we just consider "descriptors" in general.

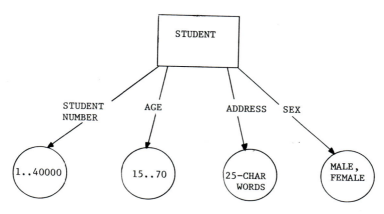

Fig. 2

STUDENTS

          01, SN, 5, F, DE   (student number)
          01, AG, 2, F   (age)
          01, AD, 25, A   (address)
          01, SX, 1, A   (sex)

Fig. 3

The diagramatic representation of an E-file is shown in Fig. 4.

3.2. RELATIONSHIPS

The ERM relationship sets will be implemented in ADABAS by two   different types of constructs: 1. The *implicit relationship* which uses solely the ADABAS relationship construct; 2. The *explicit relationship*, which uses   auxiliary "files" together with ADABAS relationships. In the sequel, we use the word *relationship* to denote an ERM relationship set and the expressions *implicit relationship*, *explicit relationship* and *ADABAS relationship* to denote the   corresponding ADABAS construct.

3.2.1. IMPLICIT RELATIONSHIPS

Implicit relationships are implementations of the ERM relationship sets   using the ADABAS construct "coupling". "Couplings" are relationships (in the   ERM sense) between "files" with the following characteristics:
a) "Couplings" correspond to binary relationships;

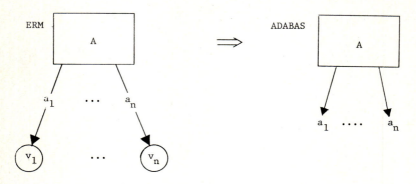

Fig. 4

b) "Couplings" have no names, that is, at most one "coupling" may exist between any two "files";
c) There exists no "self-coupling", that is, a "file" cannot be "coupled"   to itself;
d) "Couplings" have no attributes;
e) Any "file" may be "coupled" to a maximum of 80 (different) "files";
f) To build a "coupling" between files A and B, a special routine - the   "coupler" - is called dynamically, that is, between queries. One specifies to   the "coupler" 'DE' "fields" t_A and t_B of "files" A and B respectively. Elements   of A and B with equal values for t_A and t_B are then "coupled", that is, a relationship is created between them. ('DE' "fields" may also be specified dynamically.)

As a consequence of these characteristics "couplings" permit the (direct) implementation of 1:n relationship mappings without attributes. If a 'DE' "field" is furthermore declared to be of type 'MU' ("multiple field"), it may   assume up to 191 different values for a certain element (record) of the "file".   Thus, it may be used to implement m:191 mappings, without attributes. In particular, one may also implement $c_1:c_2$ relationships without attributes, where $1 \le c_1, c_2 \le 191$.

Figs. 5 and 6 show some occurrences of records in some "files", as examples of implicit relationships through 'DE' attributes. Fig. 7 shows an example with a 'DE', 'MU' attribute. To simplify the explanation, extended identifiers   are used, instead of the basic language 2-character names. Coupled elements are connected through arrows.

Note that in Fig. 5 the key of "file" DEPARTMENT was duplicated in   "file" EMPLOYEE, just for the sake of producing the "couplings". On the other hand, in Fig. 6 the "descriptors" are original attributes of both "files". In   Fig. 7, course codes were duplicated in "file" INSTRUCTOR as a 'DE', 'MU' "field", providing an m:191 relationship. It may be used as an implementation of Fig. 1, as long as TEACHING LOAD has no attributes.

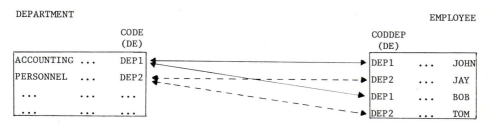

Fig. 5

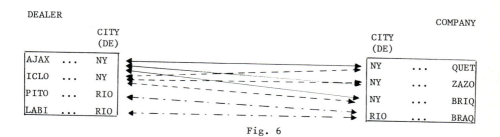

Fig. 6

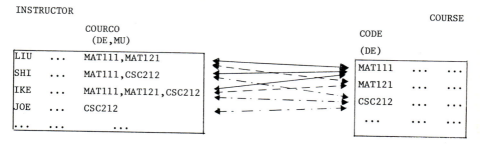

Fig. 7

Let us now introduce a graphical representation for the "couplings". Figs. 8 and 9 show this representation for the examples of Figs. 5 and 7, respectively. Notice that in the rounded-edge box we display the "descriptors" used in the "coupling". The 'MU' specification is detailed through a '*'.

Notice that in Fig. 8 we have drawn an arrow to represent in the ADABAS diagram an implementation of a 1:n relationship, as in the well-known "Data Structure Diagrams" [1]. Fig. 10 depicts various representations of implicit relationships.

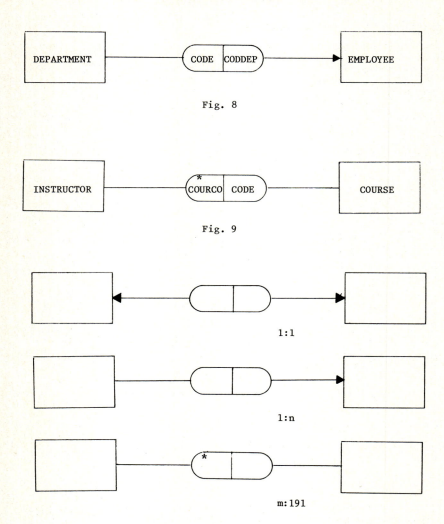

Fig. 8

Fig. 9

1:1

1:n

m:191

Fig. 10

3.2.2. EXPLICIT RELATIONSHIPS

Explicit relationships are implementations of ERM relationship sets through auxiliary ADABAS "files", which will be denoted *R-files*. To establish an explicit relationship between two "files" E_1 and E_2 (which will in general be E-files, with just one exception given in 4.2.2.2.) an R-file R and two "couplings" are introduced. One of the latter relates implicitly E_1 to R, and the other, E_2 to R. To implement these couplings, an attribute t_1 of E_1 and an attribute t_2 of E_2 are duplicated in R, originating attributes r_1 and r_2, respectively. A relationship between an element of E_1, with value v_1 of t_1, and an element of E_2, with value v_2 of t_2, is implemented by the introduction of an element of R with values v_1 for r_1 and v_2 for r_2. Fig. 11 shows an example of such relationships; E_1 corresponds to STUDENTS, E_2 to COURSES, R to TRANSCRIPT, t_1 to NUMBER, t_2 to CODE, r_1 to STNUM, r_2 to COCOD. An extra attribute of TRANSCRIPT, FINAL GRADE, shows the possibility of implementing relationship attri - butes through explicit relationships, which was not the case with implicit ones. Furthermore, notice that the couplings correspond to 1:n relationships, and that we have in fact an implementation of an ERM m:n relationship.

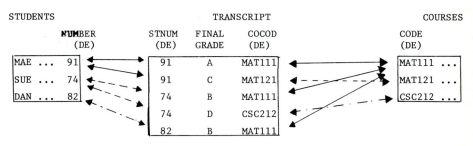

Fig. 11

Fig. 12 shows our diagramatic representation of this explicit relationship. R-files are represented by hexagons.

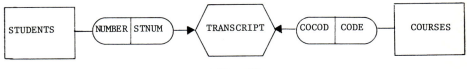

Fig. 12

Using explicit relationships, it is easy to implement ternary relationships connecting three entity sets. The corresponding E-files are each one "coupled" to a R-file. The same principle applies to n-ary relationships.

Notice that there should be no record in an R-file which is not related to every E-file participating in the explicit relationship. (This corresponds to "mandatory automatic" set-membership classes in the DBTG sense [7].)

3.3. QUERY LANGUAGES

We don't give here details of the various ADABAS query languages. It is just important to describe a fundamental characteristic of all these languages (basic language using host systems, ADASCRIPT direct query language and NATU-RAL, a powerful independent language). This characteristic has a strong impact on the simplicity of the query formulation and on the processing efficiency, and may be stated as follows: queries which refer to "couplings" permit the selection of elements of a certain "file" A subject only to qualifications on attributes of "files" $A_1, A_2, \ldots, A_n$ for $n \leq 5$, which are "coupled" *directly* to A.

For example, using ADASCRIPT one may formulate the following query for the files of Figs. 11 or 12:

> *find all records in file* TRANSCRIPT
> *with* FINAL_GRADE = 'C'
> *and coupled to file* STUDENTS
> *with* AGE=30 *and* SEX = 'M'
> *and coupled to file* COURSES
> *with* CREDITS=3

Notice that we have admitted the existence of attributes AGE and SEX in STUDENTS and CREDITS in COURSES.

It is impossible to *chain* references to "couplings", as for instance "give all records of file A coupled to records of file B which are coupled to file C". In Fig. 11, one of such queries would be the following: "find all students with final grade less than 'C' in courses with 3 credits".

4. ERM TO ADABAS CONVERSION

We present here a procedure to convert an ERM diagram to the ADABAS diagram introduced in the previous item. It has three steps: *initialization*, *generation* and *reduction* which are described using set notation. The second step consists of a systematic generation of ADABAS "files" and "couplings", where the ERM relationship sets are converted to explicit relationships. The third step consists of reducing the diagram, replacing some explicit relationships by implicit ones. Some guidelines for this step are given in form of efficiency criteria.

Two sets are constructed: F, with "files" and C, with "couplings". Set F will consist of E-, R- and X-files; the latter will be defined in item 4.2.2.2.

Suppose that the ERM-diagram to be converted consists of entity sets T_i, $i=1,2,\ldots,t$ and relationship sets L_i, $i=1,2,\ldots,l$.

4.1. INITIALIZATION

Execute $F:=\Phi$ and $C:=\Phi$, where Φ is the empty-set.

4.2. GENERATION

4.2.1. For each T_i, i=1,...,t
     - create an E-file E_i, with "fields" corresponding to the attributes of T_i; the key of T_i should be specified in E_i as 'DE';
     - execute $F:=F \cup \{E_i\}$

4.2.2. For each L_i, i=1,2,...,l

4.2.2.1. If L_i is not a self-relationship,

     -create an R-file R_i, establishing an explicit relationship among the E-files which represent the entity sets related through L_i. If L_i is a p-ary relationship this is done through "couplings" c_1^i, c_2^i,..., c_p^i; c_j^i couples E_j to L_i in a 1:n implicit relationship, as shown in Fig. 13. The key of E_j is duplicated in R_i.

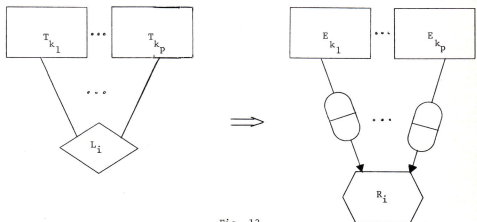

Fig. 13

     - execute $F:=F \cup \{R_i\}$; $C:=C \cup \{c_1^i, c_2^i,..., c_p^i\}$

4.2.2.2. If L_i is a binary self-relationship, relating an entity set T_j to itself
     - let E_j be the "file" corresponding to T_j. Create an auxiliary "file" X_i, whose type is denoted by *X-file*. It has just one attribute x_i which is a duplication of the key e_j of E_j (T_j). The values assumed by x_i will be those of e_j: Create a "coupling" c_o^i between E_j and X_i; c_o^i will be of type 1:1.
     - create a R-file R_i establishing an explicit relationship between E_j and X_i through "couplings" c_1^i and c_2^i which will be of type 1:n; the attributes of L_i are introduced in R_i;

- execute $F:=F\cup\{X_i,L_i\}$; $C:=C\cup\{c_o^i,c_1^i,c_2^i\}$.

Fig. 14 depicts this conversion. Observe the notation for X-files, as round-edge large boxes.

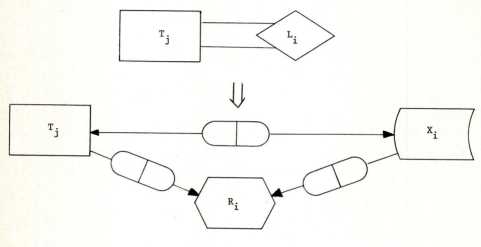

Fig. 14

Recalling that in the ERM the entity sets have *roles* in the relationships they take part [2], one may say that one of the roles T_j plays in L_i is implemented directly through a "coupling" to R_i; on the other hand, the other role is implemented indirectly through X_i. Notice that X_i introduces a redundancy in the database.

4.2.2.3. If L_i is a combination of self-relationships and non-self-relationships, the conversion is also a combination of the previous two techniques. Fig. 15 shows such a case. An example is a bank database where T_j is CLIENT, T_k is LOAN; the relationship expresses the fact that a client guarantees a loan of another client.

If one has an n-ary self-relationship, it is converted in one direct coupling to the correspondent R-file and n-1 indirect couplings through n-1 X-files.

4.3. REDUCTION

In this step, sets F and C are diminished, through the replacement of some explicit relationships by implicit ones. Recall that to each relationship set L_k there corresponds an R-file R_k, k=1,2,...,l.

4.3.1. For each pair of E-files E_i, $E_j \in F$, for which there exists *one and only one* explicit binary relationship through R_k and through couplings c_1^k and c_2^k

using attributes t_i of E_i and t_j of E_j

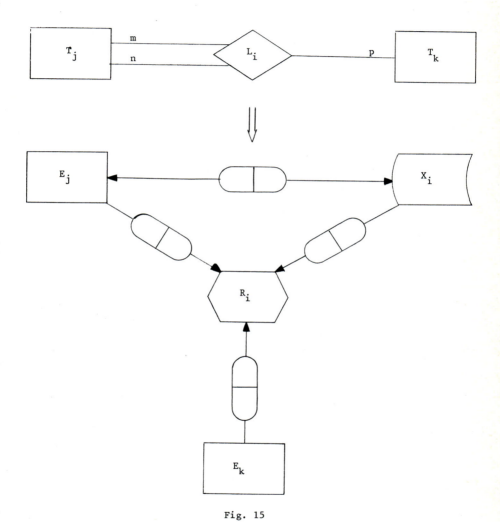

Fig. 15

4.3.1.1. If L_k is of type 1:1

      - choose one of the E-files, for instance E_i, according to one of the criteria described below, and duplicate in E_i the attribute t_j, originating t_i^j; introduce in E_i the attributes of R_k which were implementations of those of L_k;

      - execute procedure P (described in 4.3.1.5).

Choice criteria for E_i:

      - *Absence in the relationship set*: Let n_p be the estimated average number of E_p records which do not participate in the relationship, for $p=i,j$. Choose E_i if $n_i < n_j$.

Applying this criterion, the new attributes of E_i will have less empty values than the new attributes of E_j, had the duplication been done in the reverse direction. In particular, this criterion is not very important for the ADABAS system due to its compression facilities, which eliminate empty "fields".

      - *Query frequency*: For n queries to the database, one estimates an average of n_i (n_j) queries which locate records of E_i (E_j) using, among other attributes, qualifications over the key of E_j (E_i) and/or attributes of the relationship set. Choose E_i if $n_i > n_j$.

With this criterion, the number of queries which do not use the "coupling" will be maximized.

      - *Change of key values*: For n queries to the database, one estimates an average of n_i (n_j) changes in the keys of E_i (E_j). Choose E_i if $n_i > n_j$.

With this criterion, one minimizes the number of queries which alter both files simultaneously. Greater efficiency is obtained, and integrity problems are avoided.

      - *Presence stability in the relationship set*: For n queries to the database, one estimates an average of n_i (n_j) *exits* (cf. definition below) of records belonging to E_i (E_j) from the relationship between E_i and E_j. Choose E_i if $n_i < n_j$.

Given two "files" A_1 and A_2 related through some ADABAS relationship, we say that a record a_1 of A_1 *exits* this relationship iff, after some update operation, a_1 ceases to be related to some record of A_2.

With this criterion one minimizes the number of records which have to be changed due to *movements* of records in the relationship. There exists a *movement* of a record a_1 of "file" A related to b_1 of "file" B according to some relationship, when a_1 ceases to be related to b_1 and becomes related to b_2 of B, $b_1 \neq b_2$.

4.3.1.2. If L_k is of type 1:n according to Fig. 16,

      - duplicate in the E-file E_i the key t_j of E_j, originating t_i^j; introduce in E_i the attributes of R_k which are implementations of attributes of L_k;

- execute procedure P.

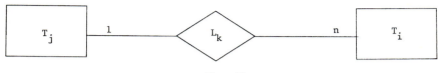

Fig. 16

Notice that there is a particular possibility of converting an explicit relationship into an implicit one: the case where L_k is of type 1:c without attributes, where $c \leq 191$ in the sense of item 2. In this case, we may choose to duplicate t_i in E_j, originating t_j^i. The latter has to be declared with the specification 'MU' (see 3.2.1). There exists an advantage in this organization: there will be a decrease of the processing time for queries which request just the values of t_i, that is, the key of T_i, using as a selection criterion values of attributes of E_j. In this case, the "coupling" is not used. On the other hand, a great disadvantage of this solution in comparison with the previous one, without 'MU', consists of the lack of automatic control over the 1:n characteristic of the relationship. With the 'MU' solution, this control has to be mantained by the user.

4.3.1.3. If L_k is of type m:c, where $1 \leq c \leq 191$, without attributes, according to Fig. 17,

- duplicate the key t_j of E_j in E_i, originating attribute t_j^i with specification 'MU';

- execute procedure P.

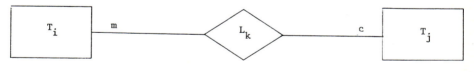

Fig. 17

4.3.1.4. If L_k is of type $c_1:c_2$ where $1 \leq c_1, c_2 \leq 191$, without attributes, accordding to Fig. 18,

- choose one of the E-files corresponding to T_i or T_j, for example E_i, according to one or more of the criteria described below; duplicate in E_i the key t_j of E_j, originating t_j^i with specification 'MU';

- execute procedure P.

Choice criteria for E_i:

- *Absence in the relationship set*: see 4.3.1.1.

- *Query frequency*: See 4.3.1.1; notice that in this case there are no attributes in the relationship set.

- *Change of key values*: For m queries to the database, it is estimated that an average of m_i (m_j) changes of key values in E_i (E_j) occur; furthermore, it is estimated that each record of E_i (E_j) is related to an average of n_i (n_j) records of E_j (E_i). Choose E_i if $m_i n_i > m_j n_j$.

- *Movement in the relationship set*: For n queries to the database, an average of n_i (n_j) movements (see 4.3.1.1) of records of E_i (E_j) occur in the relationship set L_k. Choose E_i if $n_i > n_j$.

This criterion has analogous effects of those of the presence stability criterion (see 4.3.1.1).

- *Record length*: it is estimated that each record of E_i (E_j) is related to an average of n_i (n_j) records of E_j (E_i); let s_i (s_j) be the length of the key t_i (t_j) of E_i (E_j). Choose E_i if $n_i s_j < n_j s_i$.

With this criterion, records of smaller length are obtained, relatively to the variable part due to the multiplicity degree of the 'MU' attribute.

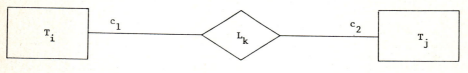

Fig. 18

4.3.1.5. *Procedure* P:

- create an implicit relationship between E_i and E_j, using t_j^i and t_j, originating 'coupling' c_o^k;
- execute $F:=F-\{R_k\}$; $C:=C \cup \{c_o^k\}-\{c_1^k, c_2^k\}$.

4.3.2. For each pair of E-files E_i, E_j for which there exist two or more explicit binary relationships $R_{k1}, R_{k2}, \ldots, R_{kr}$, $r \geq 2$, corresponding to relationships $L_{k1}, L_{k2}, \ldots, L_{kr}$ respectively,

4.3.2.1. If there exists one and only one relationship set L_{kp}, $p=1,2,\ldots,r$ satisfying restriction 4.3.1.g, $1 \leq g \leq 4$, execute the procedure L_{kp} described in item 4.3.1.g.

Notice that if L_{kp} has attributes, these will be implemented in an E-file. This fact may cause problems for other relationship sets, because these will have nothing to do with the L_{kp} attributes. Thus, one may eventually decide to ignore step 4.3.2.1 for some L_{kp} of these cases.

4.3.2.2. If there exist relationship sets $L_{kp_1}, L_{kp_2}, \ldots, L_{kp_q}$, $1 \leq p_h \leq r$, $q \geq 1$,

$1 \leq h \leq q$, each one satisfying one of the restrictions 4.3.1.1,...,4.3.1.4, select one L_{kp_h}, following one or more of the criteria described below; execute the procedure specified for the restriction satisfied by L_{kp_h}.

    – *Space*: Select the L_{kp_h} whose R-file is estimated to be the greatest in terms of required storage space.

    – *Efficiency*: Select that relationship L_{kp_h} for which it is estimated that its conversion from an explicit into an implicit relationship will produce the greatest increase in efficiency.

This general criterion depends not only on the types of queries, but also on the frequency of each type compared with that of other types.

    – *Absence of attributes*: Choose one of the relationship sets which has the smallest number of attributes.

With this criterion one diminishes the undesirable effects mentioned in 4.3.2.1.

5. CONCLUSIONS AND FURTHER RESEARCH

We believe that this work shows the possibilities presented by the ERM as a design tool for commercial database packages. The chosen system, ADABAS, is, in fact, very simple, quite uniformly defined and thus suitable to formalization, but other systems should also be suitable to the treatment described here. As an example, see the paper by Iossiphidis [8], with an application to System 2000 using a different approach. In particular, the concepts of implicit and explicit relationships should help in understanding how to implement relationship sets in a concrete system.

A research topic consists of mechanizing the conversion process. For this, the user should specify some parameters which would be used in the reduction process; some optimization techniques may eventually be used to obtain "minimal" sets of "files" and "couplings". Similar ideas were implemented by Iossiphidis.

A second research topic would consist of proving that the reduction process produces ADABAS files which, regarded as relations in the Relational Model [5], are in general in 3rd Normal Form [6]. Following Chen's considerations about the ERM and 3NF [2], one may say that the generation step produces these kind of relations. It is clear that implicit relationships obtained after the reduction process employing the 'MU' specification are not in 3NF; in fact, these relations are not even in 1NF. The correspondence of ADABAS with the Relational Model has been investigated by Renaud [9], without reference to a design methodology. Using the ERM one would eventually obtain a "top-down" design methodology of normalized relations implemented in the ADABAS system, as opposed to "bottom-up" synthesis methodologies.

6. REFERENCES

[1] Bachman, C.W. – "Data Structure Diagrams", *Database* (journal of the ACM SIGBDP) 1, 2, 1969, pp. 4-10.

[2] Chen, P.P.-S. "The Entity-Relationship Model - Toward a Unified View of

Data", *ACM Transactions on Data Base Systems* 1,1, Mar. 1976, pp. 9-36.

[3]   Chen, P.P.-S. "The Entity-Relationship Model - a basis for the   enterprise
      view of data", Proc. AFIPS 1977 NCC, Vol.46, AFIPS Press,   Montvale,
      pp. 77-84.

[4]   Chen, P.P.-S. (Ed.) - *Entity-Relationship Approach to Systems Analysis and
      Design*, North Holland, Amsterdam 1980.

[5]   Codd, E.F. "A Relational Model of Data for Large Shared Data Banks", *Comm.
      ACM* 13, June 1970, pp. 377-387.

[6]   Codd, E.F. "Further Normalization of the Data Base Relational Model",   in
      Rustin, R. (Ed.) *Data Base Systems*, Courant Computer Science Symposium 6,
      Prentice-Hall, Englewood Cliffs 1972.

[7]   Data Base Task Group of CODASYL Programming Language Committee   - *Report*,
      ACM, N. York, April 1971.

[8]   Iossiphidis, J. "A Translator to Convert the DDL of ERM to the DDL of Sys-
      tem 2000", in [4].

[9]   Renaud, D. "ADABAS and the Relational Model", 3rd International ADABAS Us-
      er's Conference, San Francisco May 1976, pp. 177-185.

[10] ADABAS Publications: ADABAS Introduction, Mar. 1979, ADASCRIPT+ Reference
      Manual, Mar. 1979, ADABAS Ref. Manual, Sept. 1976, NATURAL Ref. Manual,
      Jan. 1980, Software AG, Darmstadt.

7. APPENDIX

We present here a small abstract example, just to show the design process. No
tice the coupling characteristics shown in the ADABAS diagram after   generation
step. We have supposed that L_3 has no attributes and that the addition of attri
bute a_1 to E_2 is more convenient than its addition to E_1. ER Diagram:

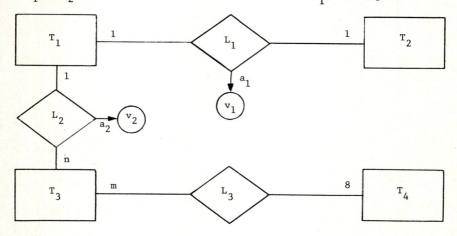

Generated ADABAS Diagram:

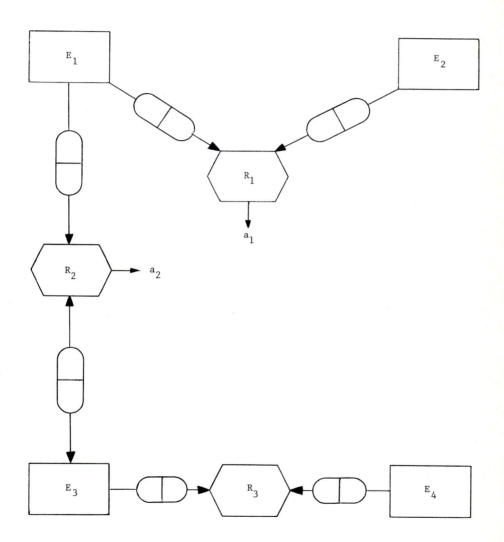

Reduced ADABAS Diagram:

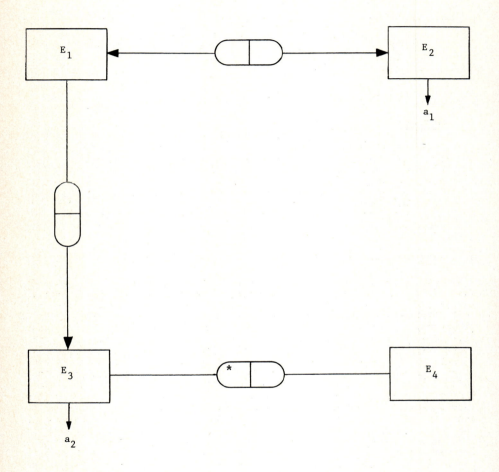

Entity-Relationship Approach to
Information Modeling and Analysis, P.P. Chen (ed.)
Elsevier Science Publishers B.V. (North-Holland)
©ER Institute, 1983

SCHEMA TRANSLATION USING THE ENTITY-RELATIONSHIP APPROACH

Surya R. Dumpala and Sudhir K. Arora
Department of Electrical and Computer Engineering
McMaster University
Hamilton, Ontario, Canada L8S 4L7

ABSTRACT

Entity-relationship (E-R) model was introduced in 1976 and since then has attracted considerable attention. Some work in the literature has been devoted to translating a schema in the E-R model to the three major data models - Network, Relational and Hierarchical. Translation in the other direction, namely, from the major data models to the E-R model is reported in this paper. Also alternate methods for doing the former type of translation are presented.

1. INTRODUCTION

Ever since entity-relationship (E-R) model was introduced by Chen [CHEN 76], it attracted considerable attention in systems modelling and database design [CHAN 80], [CHEN 77]. A lot of work has been reported in these areas in the literature. Also, the semantic simplicity and ease of derivability of other models from this model, make it a suitable candidate for conceptual level modelling of a data base. For example, it has been adopted as a data model for the conceptual level in GDBMS [DOGAC 80] and WCRC [ARORA 81]. Adoption of E-R model as the conceptual model calls for transformation of this model into external schemas in other data models. Some work has been reported in the literature addressing the problem. In [SAKAI 79], the conversion of E-R model to hierarchical model and the database design based on it, have been described. In [Wong 77], the logical design and schema conversion of E-R model to relational and DBTG data bases have been put forward. However, to the best of our knowledge, no work has been reported to convert schemas in the three major data models into E-R schemas. This is particularly of interest in an ANSI/SPARC data base architecture [ANSI 75], where user views have to be converted into views on the conceptual schema. This is necessary to enforce those integrity and security constraints, defined only at the conceptual level.

Some conversion schemes proposed in the literature are discussed briefly. In [SAKAI 79], functional dependancies, first order hierarchical dependencies and transitive dependencies among the entity sets have been employed to convert the E-R model to the hierarchical model. This approach is important because it is one of the first to use interrelational dependencies, embedded in the relationship relations. However, the approach has the following limitations. If dependencies are not available, the method relies on "the weight matrix", which is based on query statistics. In "global translation" a nonunique solution is possible and there are no criteria to choose one from the other. Also, the binary M:N relationships when converted into a tree on the basis of "the weight matrix" become arbitrarily 1:N. Further, it is not clear as to what happens to the attributes of the relationship sets.

In [WONG 79], a variant of entity relationship model is proposed as the data model. Mapping rules have been suggested to convert this modified E-R model into relational and DBTG models based on "single valued relationships", "associations" and "general relationships". However, the conversion schemes do not consider the weak entity sets. The author claims that the relational schema obtained by the mapping rules is always in 4NF. This appears to be a logical consequence of the E-R model which does not recognize multivalued dependencies.

This paper proposes algorithms for converting external schemas (subschemas) in three major data models - relational, network and heirarchical - into the entity relationship model. It also suggests alternate conversion methods for transforming the E-R model into the three major data models.

2. CONVERSION OF MAJOR DATA MODELS INTO E-R MODEL

2.1 Mapping relational Views into E-R Model

The views in the relational model consist of a set of relations, where each relation satisfies the following conditions. All the non-key attributes are fully functionally dependent on the key attributes and the non-key attributes are independent of each other; i.e., the relations are in 3NF. Before the mapping rules are presented formally, a set of definitions are presented to facilitate further discussion.

Definition: A relation whose key (primary) does not contain a key of another relation is called a primary relation (PR).

Definition: A relation, whose primary key is fully or partially formed by concatenation of primary keys or other relations, is called a secondary relation (SR). A secondary relation whose key is formed fully by concatenation of primary keys of other primary relations is said to be of type 1 (SR1). The secondary relations with primary key formed fully by concatenations of primary keys of primary and secondary relations are referred to as type 2 (SR2). The secondary relation which is neither type 1 nor type 2 is called type 3 (SR3). The key attributes in secondary relations which are part of a key of some primary relation, are referred to as KAP type while the rest are KAI type.

Definition: The non primary key attributes of a relation may be classified into three types. Those non primary key attributes of a relation which do not participate in any other relation are called NKA1 type. The non primary key attributes of a relation which form a part of some primary relation are termed as NKA2 type. The rest are called NKA3 type, i.e., the non primary key attributes that are part of some secondary relation and not involved in any primary relation. For this classification the designer must consider the semantics of the relations because, for example, an NKA2 type attribute may have different names in different relations.

Based on this formalism, the transformation rules, from relational views to E-R views are described below.

Transformation Rules

1) For each primary relation, define a corresponding entity set and identify it by the primary key. Define its NKA1 type attributes as the attributes of the entity sets and set up the domains as value sets.

2) For each secondary relation SR1 define a relationship set among the entity sets involved, identify it by the primary key, and identify the association as binary or k-ary depending upon the number of entity sets involved. Define the NKA1 type attributes as attributes of the relationship set.

3) For each secondary relation SR2 define a weak entity set and identify its primary key and the NKA1 type attributes as the attributes of the weak entity set. Here we may have a weak entity set supported by more than one k-ary relationship set among other entity sets.

4) For each secondary relation SR3 define an entity set for each of the KAI type attributes. Define a k-ary relationship set between all the entity sets that fall out of the key of this relation. The NKA1 attributes form the attributes of this k-ary relationship set.

5) For each NKA2 type attribute of a primary relation, define a relationship set between the entity sets involved.

6) For each binary relationship set obtained above, check whether there is a functional dependency (FD), $E_1 \rightarrow E_2$, $E_2 \rightarrow E_1$, or both. If there is, identify the type of relationship set as N:1, 1:N, or 1:1, respectively. If none of the above FD's exist, identify the type as M:N.

7) All NKA3 type attributes are associated with the corresponding entity set or relationship set after appropriate renaming.

An algorithm based on the transformation rules is presented here in an ALGOL-like language.

The Algorithm

Input: {S}, a set of primary and secondary relations,
 {F}, a set of functional dependencies.

<u>Output</u>: {E}, a set of entity sets where E_i ϵ{E} is of the form $E_i(ID, (A_i))$,
ID being the identifier of the entity set and (A), the set of
attributes of the entity set.

{R}, a set of relationship sets where R_i is of the form $R_i(ID, t,$
(A)), t being the type of the relationship set.

<u>Procedure</u>   TRANS_RE (S,F)

<u>begin</u>

    <u>For</u> each PR ϵ S <u>do</u>

    <u>begin</u>

     Define an E_i;

     E_i (ID) $\leftarrow$ key (PR);

     {E} $\leftarrow$ E_i;

     <u>For</u> each domain D_i ϵ PR <u>do</u>

     <u>begin</u>

      <u>IF</u> D_i ϵ NKA1$\cup$ NKA3 <u>then</u> $E_i(A_i)$ $\leftarrow$ D_i

        <u>else</u>

          <u>begin</u>

           <u>If</u> D_i ϵ NKA2 <u>then</u>

                   <u>begin</u>

                    Define a R_i

                    Identify t_i;

                    $R_i(ID)$ $\leftarrow$ (key, D_i);

                    $R_i(A_i)$ $\leftarrow$ ϕ;

                    <u>If</u> $R_i \notin$ {R} <u>then</u> {R_i} $\leftarrow$ R;

                    <u>else</u> (skip)

                 <u>end</u>

           <u>else</u> (skip)

         <u>end</u>

       <u>end</u>

      <u>end</u>

     <u>end</u>;

    <u>For</u> each SR2 ϵ S <u>do</u>

     <u>begin</u>

      Define a weak E_i;

E_i (ID) ← key (SR2);

{E} ← E_i

For each D_i ε SR2 do

  begin

    If D_i NKA1 ∪ NKA3 then $E_i(A_i)$ ← D_i

    else (skip)

  end

end;

For each SR3 ε S do

  begin

  Define KAI as E_i;

  E_i(ID) ← KAI;

  {E} ← E_i

  Define a relationship set R_i;

  R_i(ID) ← key (SR_2);

  Identify the type, t_i;

  If $R_i \not\subseteq$ {R} then {R} ← R_i

  else (skip)

  For each NKA1 ∪ NKA3 ← SR_2 do $R_i(A_i)$ ← D_i

  end;

For each R_i ε {R} do

  begin

  If R_i is binary then

            begin

             If $E_i \leftrightarrow E_j$ then R_i (t_i) ← 1:1

             else if $E_i \rightarrow E_j$ then $R_i(t_i)$ ← N:1

                else $R_i(t_i)$ ← M:N

          end

  else $R_i(t_i)$ ← M:N

  end

end (procedure)

As an example, consider the relational view shown in Fig. 1. The EMP relation describes a set of employees, giving the name, salary, manager, department number and the commission for each employee. The DEPT relation

gives the department number and the location. The SALES and NEW SALES
relations describe the items sold by the department in the past and the
present and their volume. The relation SUPPLY gives the information about the
companies that supply items to the departments and their volume. The relation
CLASS describes the type of each item. The keys of these relations are marked
in Fig. 1 by underlining. According to this information given in Fig. 1, the
above algorithm yields the E-R view shown in Fig. 2.

2.2 Mapping Network Views into E-R Model

A network view may consist of several record types and links as in the
general network model [TSICHRITZIS 77]. All the links are binary and are of
type 1:1, 1:N or N:M. Some record types may have recursive links defined on
themselves. A recursive link refers to a link defined on a single record
type. For example, a link "COMPONENT" is a recursive link defined on a record
type, "PART", implying that a part is made up of other parts. The
transformation rules for network views described above, are the following.

Transformation Rules

1)   For each record type, define a corresponding entity set and identify the
     data items (d) as the attributes of the entity set.

2)   For each link, define a relationship set and label the association type
     (t).

3)   For a recursive link, define a relationship set on the same entity set.

An algorithm for such a mapping is presented here.

The Algorithm

Input   {RT}, a set of record types,
         {L}, a set of links.
Output   {E}, a set of entity sets,
         {R}, a set of relationship sets.

Procedure TRANS_NE (RT,L)

Begin

For each $\gamma \in$ RT do

begin

Define an E_i;

For each $d_i \in \gamma$ do $E_i(A_i) \leftarrow d_i$;

E_i (ID) $\leftarrow$ key (γ);

{E} $\leftarrow E_i$

end;

For each $\ell \in L$ do
  begin
    Define a R_i;
    Identify the type, t_i;
    $R_i(ID) \leftarrow$ key (γ_i), key (γ_j);
    $\{\gamma_i$ and γ_j are the record types linked by $\ell\}$
    $\{R\} \leftarrow R_i$
  end;
end (procedure)

As an example, consider a network view of some hypothetical data base as shown in Fig. 3. It consists of record types, EMP, PROJ, DEPT, SUPPLY, PART, describing the projects and the associated information and record types SPOUSE and CHILD describing personal information about the employees. The links between the records are labelled in Fig. 3. The corresponding E-R schema obtained by applying the above algorithm is shown in Fig. 4. For simplicity, the attributes are not shown in the figure. Only entity sets and the relationship sets are identified.

2.3 Mapping Heirarchical Views into E-R Model

The hierarchical views are represented by a set of trees, where each tree has a set of record types as nodes. The links from a parent node to its child nodes are either 1:1 or 1:N type. The transformation rules for such a hierarchical forest into an E-R diagram are given below.

Transformation Rules

1) If two trees in the forest have common but renamed nodes, connect them at these nodes. Repeat this until the forest becomes connected but not necessarily acyclic graphs.

2) Replace all nodes in the graphs, by entity sets and edges by relationship sets. Identify the type of the relationship sets (either 1:N or 1:1).

An algorithm for the above mapping is given below. For the sake of simplicity, the details like attributes and relationship sets are omitted.

The Algorithm

Input   {F}, a forest of hierarchical trees with edges (e_i) as 1:1 or 1:N and nodes n_i.

Output   {E}, a set of entity sets,
       {R}, a set of relationship sets.

```
Procedure  TRANS_HE (F)
      begin
          G ← t;  (G is a graph; t is some tree in F)
          For each tree s ε (F-G) do
          begin
             For each node n ε s do
               begin
                  For each node m ε G do
                  begin
                     If n = m then NJOIN (G,s,n)
                     else (skip)
                  end
               end
             For each node n ε G do
               REPLACE (n,E);
             For each edge e ε G do
               REPLACE (e,R);
      end (procedure)
```

NJOIN (G,s,n)   – is a function which performs the joining of the graph G to
                     the tree s at the node n,

REPLACE (n/e,E/R) – is a function which replaces nodes by entity sets and
                    edges by relationship sets and outputs the entity sets and
                    relationship sets.

The above algorithm is illustrated by the example shown in Fig. 5. The hierarchical model in this figure consists of records STUDENT, COURSE, TEACHER, CLASS, ROOM. It is a view of some data base concerning a university. Each student in this view, may take several courses. Each course is taught by one teacher and held in one class room. But a teacher can offer more than one course and take several classes, where each class may have a number of students. Also, a class is taught by several teachers. These pieces of information are represented as hierarchies, as shown in Fig. 5. The corresponding graph and the E-R diagram are shown in Figs. 6a and 6b. For the sake of simplicity, the attributes are not shown in any of these diagrams. Note, the algorithm may sometimes give rise to a disconnected E-R diagram.

3. DERIVATION OF MAJOR DATA MODELS FROM THE E-R MODEL

The relational model is easily derivable from the E-R model. The entity and the relationship relations correspond to 3NF relations in the relational model. The semantic information of functional dependencies (FD's) is maintained as FD's among the entity and the relationship relations (ER's and RR's). The corresponding relational model is free of many semantic problems addressed by the normalization theory.

A relational model schema may be obtained from the E-R model schema by the following conversion algorithm.

Algorithm for E-R Model to Relational Model Conversion

Step 1: For each <u>entity set</u>, define a corresponding relation in the relational model.

Step 2: For each <u>k-ary</u> relationship set, generate a corresponding relation.

Step 3: For each <u>binary</u> relationship set <u>with</u> attributes, generate a relation in the relational model.

Step 4: For each <u>binary</u> relationship set <u>without</u> attributes, generate a relation only if it is of the type N:M. If it is of the type 1:N or 1:1, associate the key of the source entity set as an attribute with the relation corresponding to the target entity set. (We define the source and target entity sets as follows. Let E_1 and E_2 by the entity sets involved in a relationship set R, of type 1:N. Then E_1 is referred to as the source entity set and E_2, the target entity set. Note, for 1:1 type relationship set, E_1 and E_2 are both the source and the target entity sets.

Step 5: For each <u>weak entity</u> set, generate a relation in the relational model, whose key is formed by concatenation of its own "key" and the key of the supporting entity set.

An example illustrating the relational equivalent of the E-R model of Fig. 7 is shown in Fig. 8. The relations obtained may have null values.

The network model can be derived from E-R model by treating entity relations as recorded types and relationship relations as links. The data structure diagram [BACHMAN 69] representation of the network model can be obtained from E-R model by the following algorithm.

Algorithm: E-R Diagram to Data Structure Diagram Conversion

Step 1: Represent every entity set as a record type in the data structure diagram.

Step 2: For each 1:N binary relationship set draw unidirectional arrows in the diagram from the record type for the source entity to the target entity set. For 1:1 relationship set, draw a bidirectional arrow. The attributes of the 1:N relationship set go with the source while they go with both record types for 1:1.

Step 3:   For each N:M relationship set, create a new record type and draw pointed arrows from the record types of entity sets involved. The same holds good for k-ary relationship sets (k > 2). The attributes go with the new record type.

Step 4:   For each weak entity set, create a new record type and identify it by the "key" of the weak and the supporting entity sets.

As an illustration the output of the algorithm for the example in Fig. 7 is shown in Fig. 9.

The following algorithm converts an E-R model into an equivalent hierarchical model.

Algorithm to Convert E-R Model into Hierarchical Model

Step 1:   In cases of more than one relationship set between entity sets, rename and create new entity sets and relationship sets till there is only one relationship set between any two entity sets.

Step 2:   Convert all 1:N relationship sets into one-level trees with source entity sets as the roots. For 1:1 relationship sets merge the two entity sets and create a new node. The attributes of 1:N relationship sets go with the parent node.

Step 3:   For N:M relationship sets define a new node as the parent node and make the two entity sets as child nodes. The attributes of the relationship set go with the parent node.

Step 4:   Convert a k-ary relationship set into a one-level tree with a newly defined node as the root and the k nodes as leaves. The new node is a record consisting of the keys of the k nodes and attributes of the relationship set.

Step 5:   Combine all the trees obtained above at the common nodes. This may give rise to a forest of hierarchical trees.

The above algorithm yields the hierarchical model shown in Fig. 10 for the example shown in Fig. 7.

4.   CONCLUDING REMARKS

The entity-relationship model has attracted widespread attention. For example, it has been adopted as the conceptual model in GDBMS [DOGAC 80] and WCRC [ARORA 81]. Some work in the literature has been reported on converting schemas in the E-R model to the relational, the network and the hierarchical

model. Some of the limitations of this work are: weak entity sets are not
considered; attributes of relationship sets are not considered; sometimes a
non unique result is possible, etc. In this paper we have presented schema
translation methods which address these limitations. Further no work in the
literature has been reported on translation of schemas in the other direction,
i.e. from the relational, the network and the hierarchical model to the E-R
model. In this paper we have presented algorithms to address this problem.
One question that remains is the following. Given a schema in the E-R model,
we translate it to the relational, the network or the hierarchical models to
get a new schema. Now if we translate the new schema back to the E-R model it
is likely that we will not get the original schema we started with. Thus the
algorithms are in a sense not "reversible".

5. REFERENCES

[ANSI 75]
ANSI/X3/SPARC "Interim Report ANSI/X3/SPARC Study group on Data Base Management Systems", FDT 7 (2), Vol. 7, No. 2, 1975.

[ARORA 81]
Arora, S.K., Dumpala, S.R., Smith, K.C., "WCRC: An ANSI SPARC Machine Archi-
tecture for Data Base Management", To appear, Proc. International Symposium on
Computer Architecture, Minneapolis, May 12-14, 1981.

[BACHMAN 69]
Bachman, C.W., "Data Structure Diagrams", Data Base 1 (2), 1969, pp. 4-10.

[CHAN 80]
Chan, E.P.F. and Lochovsky, F.H., "A Graphical data base design aid using the
entity-relationship model", in: Chen, P. (ed.), Entity-Relationship Approach
to Systems Analysis and Design (North-Holland, Amsterdam, 1980).

[CHEN 76]
Chen, P.P.S., "The Entity Relationship Model - Towards a Unified View of
Data", ACM Trans. on Data Base Systems, March 1976, Vol. 1, No. 1, pp. 9-36.

[CHEN 77]
Chen, P.P.S, "The Entity Relationship Approach to Logical Database Design",
Q.E.D. Monograph Series, No. 6, Q.E.D. Information Sciences, Inc., Wellesley
(1977).

[DOGAC 80]
Dogac, A., Ozkarahan, E.A., "A Generalized DBMS Implementation on a Data Base
Machine", ACM SIGMOD, Santa Monica, California, May 1980, pp. 133-143.

[SAKAI 75]
Sakai, H., "A Unified Approach to the Logical Deisgn of a Hierarchical Data
Model", Proc. of the Int. Conf. on Entity-relationship Approach to Systems
Analysis and Design, Los Angeles, Dec. 10-12, 1979, pp. 61-74.

[TSICHRITZIS 77]
Tsichritzis, D.C., Lochovsky, F.H., "Data Base Management Systems", Academic
Press, 1977.

[WONG 79]
Wong, E., Katz, R.H., "Logical Design and Schema Conversion for Relational and
DBTG Data Bases", Proc. of the Int. Conf. on Entity-Relationship Approach to
Systems Analysis and Design, Los Angeles, Dec. 1979, pp. 311-322.

EMP (Name, sal, Mgr, Dept#, Comm)

DEPT (Dept#, Building, Floor)

SALES (Dept#, Item, Cvol)

SUPPLY (Company, Item, Dept#, Vol)

CLASS (Item, Type)

NEW SALES (Dept#, Item, Volume)

Figure 1: A Relational View of a Hypothetical Data Base

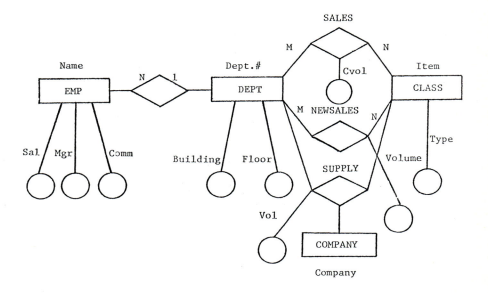

Fig. 2   The E-R View Corresponding to Fig. 1

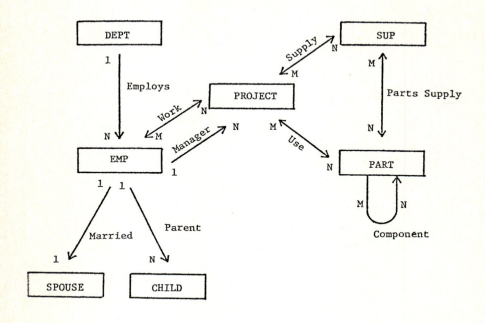

Fig. 3   A Network View of a Hypothetical Data Base

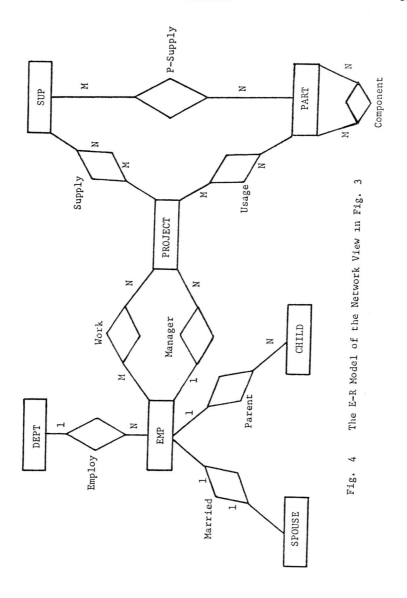

Fig. 4   The E-R Model of the Network View in Fig. 3

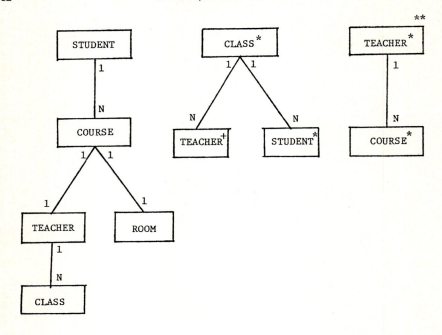

Fig.   5   A Hierarchical View of a University Data Base

(** Some teachers may offer courses, but there may not be any
   classes taking them. Such information is shown in this tree)

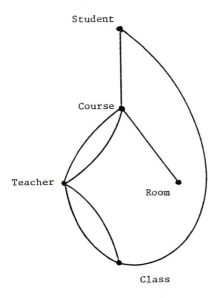

Fig. 6a   A Graph Corresponding to Fig. 5

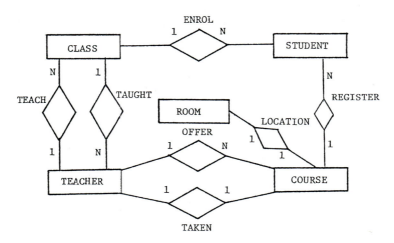

Fig. 6b   The E-R Model Corresponding to Fig. 5

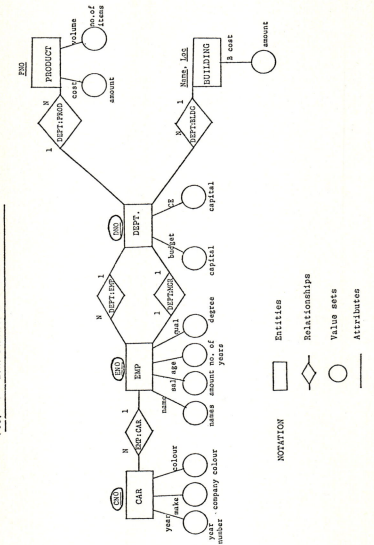

FIG, 7   E.R, DIAGRAM OF CORPORATE DATABASE

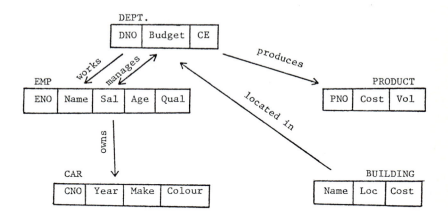

Fig. 9   Network Equivalent of the Corporate Data Base

Relations

DEPT.   (<u>DNO</u>, Budget, CE, MGR.ENO, BUILDING.NAME, BUILDING.LOC)

EMP.   (<u>ENO</u>, Name, Sal, Age, Qual, EMP.DNO, MGR.DNO)

PRODUCT   (<u>PNO</u>, cost, volume, DNO)

BUILDING   (<u>Name</u>,<u>LOC</u>, cost)

CAR   (<u>CNC</u>, year, make, colour, ENO)

Fig. 8:   Relational Equivalent of the Corporate Database

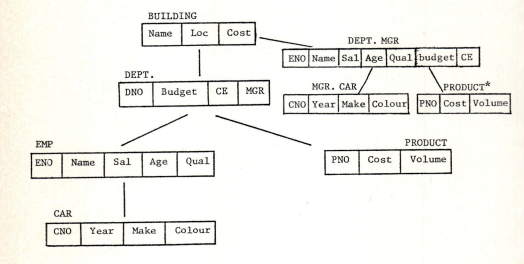

Fig. 10   Hierarchical Equivalent to the Corporate Data Base

Entity-Relationship Approach to
Information Modeling and Analysis, P.P. Chen (ed.)
Elsevier Science Publishers B.V. (North-Holland)
©ER Institute, 1983

ENTITY-RELATIONSHIP MODEL IN THE ANSI/SPARC FRAMEWORK*

Asuman Dogac[†]   and   Peter Pin-Shan Chen

Middle East Technical University   Graduate School of Management
        Ankara, Turkey   University of California, Los Angeles
                                             Los Angeles, California   90024
                                                        U.S.A.

ABSTRACT

The purpose of this paper is threefold: First, the semantic properties of the Entity-Relationship model are reviewed to
include the recent extensions to the model. Second, by considering these extensions the procedures transforming the Entity-
Relationship model into the conventional data models are refined. Finally, in light of these discussions, it is shown that
the Entity-Relationship model is a proper choice for the conceptual denominator of the ANSI/ X3/SPARC framework.

1. INTRODUCTION

The Entity-Relationship model has been tried in the ANSI/SPARC Framework both at the theoretical level [5, 6, 7, 20, 21, 23, 27] and at the
implementation level [8, 9, 10], and recently Ullman [25] showed how to
represent data in the three well-known data models starting with the
Entity-Relationship model. Elmasri et al. used the Entity-Category-Relationship (ECR) model, which is a generalization of the Entity-Relationship
model, in an experimental system called DDTS (Distributed Database Testbed
System) being developed in Honeywell [12]. Arora et al. adopted the
Entity-Relationship model for the conceptual level in WCRC, and ANSI/SPARC
machine architecture [1]. All of these works have contributed significantly to understanding the semantics of the data models and in comparing
their capabilities in modeling the real-world and also demonstrated that
the Entity-Relationship model is a very good choice as the conceptual
common denominator in the ANSI/SPARC framework.

However, we feel that some of the important semantic captured by the
Entity-Relationship model has been left out in the transformation procedures presented in the previous work. Recently, the Entity-Relationship
model is extended to include data base abstractions [21, 22], and also the
relationship types have been differentiated as partial, total or ordinary
[22] which have been found very useful in preserving existence dependency

*   This research was supported in part by NSF Grant No. MCS78-20005.

†   This research was performed when this author was a post doctoral
      scholar at UCLA from October 1980 to June 1981.

information and also in automating the update propagation in a data base [11]. Some of this information can be readily represented in the conventional data models whereas some require additional integrity constraints.

In this paper, after briefly going over some of the concepts in the Entity-Relationship model, we will refine the procedures transforming the Entity-Relationship model into the conventional data models. These procedures are actually used as a part of an experimental generalized data base management system, METUGDBMS [9, 10].

Still another important point is the following: the design experience with the experimental data base management system, METUGDBMS revealed the fact that the relations obtained through the Entity-Relationship model can adequately support conventional data models at the abstract level without requiring any extra set of data structures.

In section 2, we give an overview of the semantic properties of the Entity-Relationship model. Section 3 describes how to represent some of the semantic properties of the Entity-Relationship model in conventional data models. Finally, section 4 discusses other design advantages gained by using the Entity-Relationship model as the conceptual denominator of the ANSI/ SPARC framework.

2.   A FURTHER STUDY OF THE SEMANTIC PROPERTIES OF THE ENTITY-RELATIONSHIP MODEL

In the following some of the semantic properties of the Entity-Relationship model will be revised.

(a) In the Entity-Relationship model, there may be entity occurrences in the data base which do not participate in any relationship occurrences but, in order for a relationship occurrence to exist, the participating entity occurrences should be present in the data base.

The implications of this semantic integrity rule for storage operations are as follows:

(1) When an entity occurrence is deleted, the corresponding relationship occurrence should also be deleted.

(2) An insertion to a relationship is rejected unless the participating entity occurrences exist.

(3) In order to preserve data base integrity with the rules declared above, modifications to the key attributes of entities and relationships are accomplished as deletions followed by insertions.

(b) Existence dependency information is expressed through different entity and relationship types in the Entity-Relationship model.

In order to gain an insight into the possible forms of existence dependency, let us consider the following simple binary relationship:

(1) A total relationship between these two entities which is total on employee's side implies that each employee must work for at least one project. In other words, the information about an employee can exist in the data base only if he works for a project.

As a natural consequence of this fact, deletion of a project implies the deletion of the employees working only for that project. Diagrammatically a total relationship is represented by including a dot on the edge of the relationship connected with the total entity [22], as shown in figure 1.

(2) A weak relationship between the entities of the example above which is weak on employee's side is described as follows: Each employee is working for at least one project, and when a project is deleted all the employees working for that project should also be deleted.

The following example is helpful in differentiating the semantic implied by a total relationship and a weak relationship:

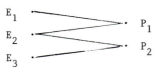

If the relationship between EMPLOYEE and PROJECT is total, then when P_1 is deleted, only E_1 will be deleted, whereas if the relationship is weak, then deletion of P_1 will imply the deletion of both E_1 and E_2.

A weak relationship is denoted with a diamond box with double-lines in the Entity-Relationship diagram as illustrated in figure 1.

(3) A weak entity: In (1) and (2), it is assumed that an employee has the freedom to resign. In other words, employees can be deleted from the data base. But there are real life cases [6] where the deletion of an entity is not allowed unless the relationship it is involved in is deleted. This semantic fact is expressed in the Entity-Relationship model through a weak entity. A weak entity is denoted by a rectangular box with double lines in the Entity-Relationship diagram, as illustrated in figure 1.

(4) An ordinary relationship between EMPLOYEE and PROJECT implies that employees have existence independent of the projects, in other words employees can be inserted and deleted freely. The same argument is also true for the projects.

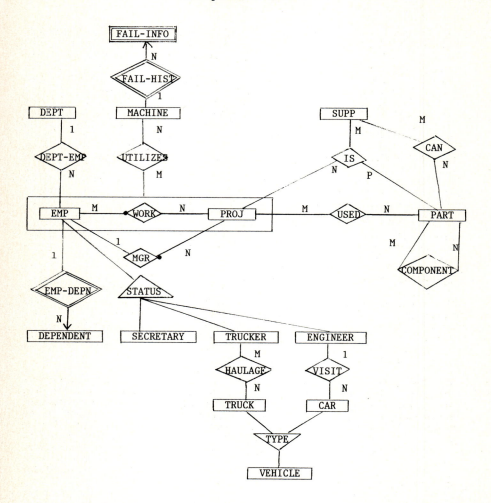

FIGURE 1. Entity-Relationship diagram of an example data base depicting the representation of the data base abstractions and different relationship types.

(c) Data base abstractions in the Entity-Relationship model: Aggregation refers to an abstraction in which a relationship between objects is regarded as a higher level object [24]. The relationship definition in the Entity-Relationship model is very similar to this definition. When the definition of relationships between the aggregations are also allowed, the semantic expressed by the model becomes clearer, although there is always a form of an Entity-Relationship diagram which will express the same semantics as that of aggregations by using relationships only.

It is not natural to expect entities to have uniform attributes, but a data model should be able to handle the differing attributes of the same type of an entity. In other words, a data model is expected to treat a set of similar objects as a generic object while at the same time preserving the information about the individual objects. A generic object may get involved in relationships where the differing attributes do not matter, whereas individual objects may also be involved in relationships where differences among them is important as shown in figure 1.

This kind of semantic is efficiently supported within the Entity-Relationship model. Pictorially, triangular boxes in the data structure diagram denote the existence of generalizations, as depicted in figure 1.

(d) Entity-Relationship model provides a natural starting point in organizing data. The information about entities and the relationships between them are inherent in the nature of the data, and furthermore, Entity-Relationship model does not place any restrictions in organizing this data. In other words, any number of relationships between any number of entities and also relationships, are allowed. Thus, the user of the model is not restricted with a template to fit his data in but he is provided with a general and flexible tool to organize his data.

The Entity-Relationship model just like data base abstractions provides a different point of view in organizing data than synthesis or decomposition approaches. Both the Entity-Relationship model and the data base abstractions make use of the information inherent in the data in forming the semantic clusters of the model. Decomposition and synthesis approaches on the other hand make use of the universal relation assumption and universal relation scheme assumption respectively and the theory about these assumptions has not yet settled down. And incorporating data base abstractions into the Entity-Relationship model made it even a more powerful tool for data base design process.

(e) Consistent data bases are only possible with propagating the update operations properly. Proper update propagation, on the other hand, requires the existence dependency information and information on how the rest of the data base is effected by the update. The Entity-Relationship model provides a useful tool for automating update propagation. Although the Entity-Relationship diagram is a non-directed graph, when the existence dependency information is considered, a directed graph is obtained. This graph is then used to guide update propagation [11].

3. TRANSFORMING THE ENTITY/RELATIONSHIP MODEL INTO THE RELATIONAL, NET-
WORK AND HIERARCHICAL DATA MODELS

The procedures and algorithms transforming the Entity-Relationship model in all or one of the conventional data models can be found in [5, 6, 7, 9, 10, 15, 16, 23, 25, 27]. In the following, we will cover a part of the transformation process which includes the properties of the Entity-Relationship model covered in section 2.

3.1 Representing the Entity-Relationship Model in the Relational Model

The basic constructs of the Entity-Relationship model, that is, the entities, relationships, aggregations and generalizations, can be directly represented in the relational model and the resulting relations have better update properties [7].

Now, let's try to see how some other properties of the Entity-Relationship model, which is discussed in section 2, map into the relational model:

(a) Consider the EMP, PROJ, entities and WORK relationship of figure 1. This information is represented by two sorts of relations in the relational model [25]. The relations EMP and PROJ are obtained from the corresponding entity sets EMP and PROJ, and each consists of all the attributes of corresponding entity sets. The relationship WORK is represented by a relation which is also called WORK and it consists of the attributes in the keys of the entity sets EMP and PROJ [22]. But there is also another semantic fact expressed by the E-R diagram that WORK relationship is total on employees side, which implies that, when a PROJ occurence is deleted from the data base, all the related occurences in the relations WORK and EMP should also be deleted. In order to express this semantic fact in the relational model, we need explicit integrity assertions.

The trigger definition introduced in System R paper [2] is a generalization of the concept of assertions and is an effective way of expressing this type of integrity constraints. Trigger definitions include information about when to enforce the constraint and also dictate the action to be taken. Therefore, we choose triggers to express and enforce these assertions. Then along with the relations

        EMP (END, NAME, SAL)
        WORK (END, PJNO)
        PROJ (PJNO, PDESCP, BUDGET)

created from corresponding entities and relationships, the following trigger definitions are also generated

```
DEFINE TRIGGER T1
     ON DELETION OF PROJ
          (DELETE EMP
           WHERE   ENO =
                 (SELECT END
                  FROM    WORK
                  WHERE   PJNO = 'X')
     AND END  ¬ =
                 (SELECT END
                  FROM    WORK
                  WHERE   PJNO  ¬ = 'X'))

DEFINE  TRIGGER  T2
     ON DELETION OF PROJ
          (DELETE WORK
           WHERE PJNO = 'X')
```

There are a few observations about this trigger definitions.

(1) 'X' is the project number of the project that has been deleted and should be supplied by the DBMS at the execution time.

(2) In order to clarify the meaning of first trigger definition assume the following data

```
E1    PJ1
E1    PJ2
E2    PJ2
```

and assume that PJ2 is deleted, that is, X is PJ2. As a result of the first part of qualification expression of the WHERE clause both E1 and E2 qualify for deletion. But we want E1 to remain in the data base. The second part of qualification expression selects those employees working for projects other than PJ2, and requires candidate employees for deletion to be different than this. Thus E1 remains in the data base, because he is working for PJ1.

(3) Another important point is the enforcement sequence of these assertion conditions. If trigger definition T2 is enforced before trigger definition T1, then T2 will not be able to find any tuples to delete in any case, that is, the entity occurrences.

(b) The semantic declared through the weak relationships in the Entity-Relationship model can be preserved in the relational model with the similar integrity constraints as described above.

Let us consider the weak relationship EMP-DEPN and the involved entities EMP and DEPENDENT of figure 1. The resulting trigger definitions would be:

```
DEFINE TRIGGER T1
     ON DELETION OF EMP
          (DELETE DEPENDENT
          WHERE  DEPNNO =
                      (SELECT DEPNNO
                       FROM    EMP_DEPN
                       WHERE   END = 'X'))

DEFINE TRIGGER T2
     ON DELETION OF EMP
          (DELETE EMP_DEPN
          WHERE   END = 'X')
```

(c) The semantic declared through weak entities can be preserved through
the use of a security constraint: Access to weak entities is defined as
READ ONLY, thus they cannot be deleted by the user. A weak entity is then
deleted by the DBA according to its type of relationship with other entities.

(d) Aggregations and generalizations as presented in the Entity-Relationship model can be transformed directly into relational model relations
and some of the relational invariants are already implied by the Entity-
Relationship model. Before going into the topic of how to enforce these
conditions in the relational model, let us briefly review the relational
invariants and the properties of the Entity-Relationship model which
expresses the same semantic. The first relational invariant states that
each parent aggregation should have the corresponding child aggregation.
As an example consider the VISIT aggregation in figure 1. If there is an
occurrence in this aggregation stating that a certain engineer is using a
certain car during his visit, the corresponding engineer and car occurrences should exist in the data base. The same semantic is available in the
Entity-Relationship model as discussed in section 2a.

Second relational invariant states that the tuple occurrences should be
unique within each aggregation which is also implied by the Entity-Relationship model.

Third and fourth relational invariants state that the parent and child
generalizations should be consistent. In other words, a child generalization should have the proper image in the parent generalization and a
parent generalization should have the corresponding child image.

And the last relationship invariant states that the groups formed by
generic objects should have mutually exclusive classes. The next step is
expressing and enforcing these rules in relational model.

Expressing semantic with a data model is important, but a DDL is also
expected to have the features to explicitly state how to enforce these
rules. It seems that none of the existing DDL languages for the relational model is powerful enough to express the wide variety integrity
constraints such as the ones above. As an example, the ASSERTION commands
of SEQUEL need to be improved in the following respects:

(1)   Inclusion of conditional commands.
(2)   Information on when to check if the constraint holds.
(3)   Inclusion of variables in the predicates.
(4)   Specifying a corrective action when the constraint fails to hold.

In this respect, TRIGGER definitions are better but still they fail to express conditional situations.

In the following, we will present a modified version of the TRIGGER definitions through examples to express and to enforce the above integrity constraints.

The first relational invariant can be enforced with the following two trigger definitions:

```
DEFINE    TRIGGER   T4   ON   INSERTION   OF   VISIT
          CHECK     (ENGNO    EXIST    IN   ENGINEER)
   IF     NOT   TRUE    THEN    REJECT    INSERTION
DEFINE    TRIGGER   T5   ON   DELETION   OF   ENGINEER
          CHECK     (ENGNO    EXIST    IN   VISIT)
   IF     TRUE   THEN   REJECT    DELETION
```

It should be pointed out at this point that insertions and deletions are to be made in a proper sequence:

1)   Before inserting a relationship (or an aggregation), the entities (or the child aggregations) are inserted first.

2)   While deleting an entity (or a child aggregation), the relationship (or the parent aggregation) is deleted first.

The second relational invariant can be expressed with the following trigger:

```
DEFINE    TRIGGER   T6   ON   INSERTION   OF   VEHICLE
          CHECK     (VEHICLENO    EXIST   IN   VEHICLE)
   IF   TRUE   THEN   REJECT    INSERTION
```

Generalizations are different than aggregations in the following sense: there is no proper sequence of insertions, parent generalization require the child image to be in the data base. Therefore if the integrity is to be checked after an insertion of any of these occurrences, it will not hold. One possible solution is considering the insertions into the parent and the child generalization as a single transaction and checking the integrity after this transaction is executed. The related trigger definitions would then be as follows:

```
DEFINE    TRIGGER   T7   ON   INSERTION   OF   EMP
          CHECK     (EMPNO    EXIST    IN   ENGINEER)
   IF   NOT   TRUE   THEN   REJECT    INSERTION;
DEFINE    TRIGGER   T8   ON   INSERTION   OF   ENGINEER
          CHECK     (EMPNO    EXIST    IN   EMP)
   IF   NOT   TRUE   THEN   REJECT    INSERTION
```

In order to express the last relational invariant, several integrity constraints are necessary one of which is the following:

DEFINE   TRIGGER   T9   ON   INSERTION   OF   ENGINEER
          CHECK   (EMPNO   EXIST   IN   SECRETARY
             OR   EMPNO   EXIST   IN   TRUCKER)
     IF   TRUE   REJECT   INSERTION;

This guarantees that an insertion into the entity ENGINEER would not violate the fifth relational invariant.

3.2 Representing the Entity-Relationship Model in the DBTG Network Model

Given an Entity-Relationship schema, the corresponding network schema is not unique. Representing the Entity-Relationship model entities and relationships with record types and set types in network model are given in [6, 9, 10, 23, 25]. In order to have a working DBTG schema some more information about the membership classes, location modes, set selection modes of the record and set types is necessary. A part of this information such as location modes or set selection modes, is dependent upon the requirements of a particular application and also storage organization. Still another part of the information, such as removal classes, denotes that existence dependency information is available through the Entity-Relationship model.

The properties of the Entity-Relationship model, discussed in section 2, map into the DBTG model as follows:

(a) The type of relationship in the Entity-Relationship model determines the type of removal class of the set types in the DBTG Network model.

The removal class of a set type generated from a weak relationship is FIXED. Let us briefly explain why this is so. If the removal class of a record type is FIXED in a set type, then the occurrences of this record type cannot be removed to another set occurrence. In other words, if an owner occurrence is deleted from the data base, all the associated member occurrences are also deleted. The semantic preserved by the weak relationship is exactly like this.

The removal class of a set type generated from an ordinary relationship is OPTIONAL.

When it comes to representing a total relationship in the Network data model, the MANDATORY removal class is not enough. Here a problem arises because of the fact that although M:N relationships are directly representable in the Entity-Relationship model, they can only be represented through the use of a link record type in the Network model. This point will become clearer by considering the example data base in figure 2.

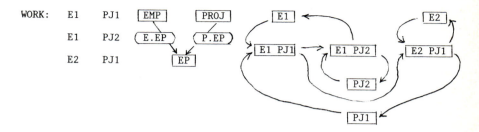

```
WORK:    E1    PJ1
         E1    PJ2
         E2    PJ1
```

FIGURE 2 An M:N Relationship and its representation in the Network model

Although the M:N relationship between the entities employee and project is directly representable in the Entity-Relationship model, it is necessary to introduce a link record type EP in the Network model. When the WORK relationship is declared to be total on the employees side; deletion of project PJ1 would require the deletion of employee E2. However when the membership of EP is MANDATORY in the set E-EP, deletion of PJ1 would only imply the deletion of link record type E2 PJ1. Actually since the removal classes are defined for member record types, it is impossible to delete the owner record types (and hence E2) in this way.

For 1:N relationships, however, total relationship has the same meaning as the MANDATORY removal class.

One more point to be noted here is that storage class (AUTOMATIC/ MANUAL) has meaning only when the record occurrence concerned is actually being created; it is irrelevant thereafter and for this reason cannot be used to preserve semantics.

(b) In representing the generalizations in the network model, there are several possibilities. Smith & Smith [24] suggested that generic object to be the owner and individual objects to be the members. But in such a case, each set instance would have exactly one member instance which seems to violate the one-to-many nature of the owner-member relationship in the Network model. Consider the generalization EMPLOYEE of figure 1, for example. For the employee occurrence "E25 John Doe 36" there would correspond a unique member occurrence either in ENGINEER or in TRUCKER or in SECRETARY. This is dictated by the fifth relational invariant which requires that the groups formed by generic objects have mutually exclusive classes.

Another possible representation is to merge the individual record types with the generic object [23], but this would complicate the representation of relationships between individual objects.

We suggest that individual objects be the owners and generic objects be the members. Thus, the members of the generic objects which have the same characteristics as individual objects will be clustered under the same owner.

Network data model has a powerful facility for providing integrity, that
is, CALL procedures. The integrity constraints specified by the Entity-
Relationship model can easily be specified with this facility. For example, for the data base of figure 1, the declaration of record VISIT could
include the clause CALL CHECK-VISIT BEFORE STORE. The procedure CHECK-
VISIT will then be automatically invoked whenever a new VISIT occurrence
is about to be stored. It can then perform any processing, for example,
it may check that the ENGNO and CARNO values match those in the relevant
ENGINEER and CAR occurrences. Actually this is the constraint for the
first relational invariant.

The rest of the integrity constraints including the relational invariants
can be expressed and enforced in the same manner.

3.3 Representing the Entity-Relationship Model in the Hierarchical Data
     Model

     A detailed discussion about designing a hierarchical schema from the
Entity-Relationship model is presented in [25]. In the following, we are
going to discuss how the other properties of the Entity-Relationship model
may be represented in the hierarchical data model.

     When it comes to representing different types of relationships (weak,
total or ordinary), only total relationships can be expressed in the
hierarchical data model, because actually a relationship between two
record types in the hierarchical data model is always a total relationship. This is obvious from the basic rule in a hierarchy that a child
record occurrence can have existence in the database only if the parent
record occurrence exists.

     A possible way of representing generalizations in hierarchical data
model is shown in figure 3.

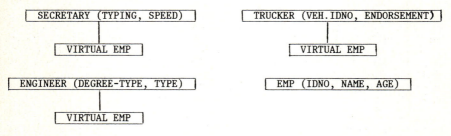

FIGURE 3.   Representing Generalizations in Hierarchical Data Model

     This schema has the following advantages:

a)   The employees having the same characteristics are clustered
      under the same parent.

b) Since employee record type exists as a root by itself, it can easily be processed without the need to process the three tree structures where it appears as a leaf node.

In a hierarchical data base management like IMS, there are two features of the system for handling integrity. The first guarantees the uniqueness of key values which correspond to the second relational invariant. The second feature is actually the integrity constraint, which is inherent in the model, that is, the child record type cannot exist without a parent. If we compare this with the semantic preserved in the E-R model, we see that it is not the same. For example, a generalization requires both child image and parent image to exist, whereas in a hierarchy, only existence of a parent record type suffices.

IMS has also been extended to include logical relationships which are the means of implementing the Entity-Relationship model in this system. For example, if an ordinary relationship exists between two entities, the implementation alternatives would be uni-directional logical relationship or bidirectional logical relationship. In addition to this, IMS's delete rules provide a mechanism for managing update propogation across relationships. However these properties are specific to IMS.

Generally the integrity provisions provided for the hierarchical data model are specifically tailored according to the inherent semantic in this model and are not sufficient to express any general integrity constraint. They therefore fail to capture some of the semantics expressed in the E-R model.

4. ENTITY-RELATIONSHIP MODEL AS A CONCEPTUAL DATA MODEL IN THE ANSI/SPARC FRAMEWORK

In section 3, we have indicated the previous work for representing data in conventional data models by using the Entity-Relationship model and also demonstrated how more semantic properties of the E-R model can be mapped into these models. From this discussion, it is clear that the Entity-Relationship model creates ease and efficiency in generating the three popular data models and thus it is a proper choice for the conceptual common denominator in the ANSI/SPARC framework.

Furthermore, experience with a generalized data base management system implementation which has a similar structure to that of ANSI/SPARC revealed the fact that the Entity-Relationship model provides further design and implementation advantages. Before discussing these advantages, we are going to survey the system very briefly.

4.1 A Generalized Data Base Management System: METUGDBMS

METUGDBMS [9, 10] is a software package coded in FORTRAN IV on an IBM
370/145 and has the framework shown in figure 4.

The universe of discourse, (that is, the information of interest) is
defined in the conceptual common denominator by using the concepts of the
Entity/Relationship model. The system accepts this definition and then
creates the data description in one of the three data models (network,
relational or hierarchical) according to user request. The user, by
observing the data description can code his queries in the associated data
manipulation language (SEQUEL for the relational model, LSL for the Network model, MRI System 2000 DML for the hierarchical model).

The system is designed on a data base machine RAP (Relational Associative Processor) [17, 18] and a software emulator [26] is used in the
implementation. RAP data base machine directly supports the relational
data model.

4.2 The Entity-Relationship Model at the Conceptual Common Denominator of METUGDBMS

In METUGDBMS, the relation definitions that exist in the data base
machine are not an ordinary set of relation definitions; they are generated automatically by the system from the Entity-Relationship definition
of the data and passed to the data base machine. These relation definitions suffice to support the three conventional data models at the abstract level along with the associated data manipulation languages without
requiring for any extra set of data structures. This is not a coinci-
dence. The Entity-Relationship model explicitly identifies the relationships between the entities which can be used as the owner-member relationship in the network model and the parent-child relationship in the hierarchical data model.

An ordinary set of relations does not have this property. As an
example, consider the well-known set of relations:

    EMP (NAME, SAL, MGR, DEPTNO)
    SALES (DEPTNO, ITEM, VOL)
    SUPPLY (COMPANY, DEPTNO, ITEM, VOL)

It seems very difficult to support a hierarchical or a network schema
with these relations because there are no identifiable owner-member or
parent-child relationships between them. Such a relationship is not taken
into consideration when these relations are formed in the first place.

If, however, we want to express the same information in the Entity-
Relationship model, we are forced to identify the entities and relationships between them explicitly. A possible E-R diagram for this case might
be as shown in figure 5.

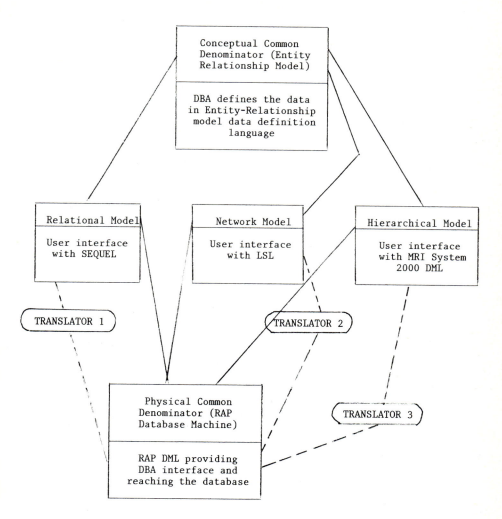

FIGURE 4.   METUGDBMS Architecture (Solid lines denote structural trans-
                 formations, broken lines depict language translations.)

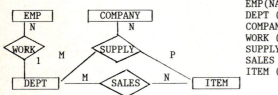

```
EMP(NAME, SAL, MGR)
DEPT (DEPTNO)
COMPANY (CNAME)
WORK (DEPTNO, NAME)
SUPPLY   (CNAME,DEPTNO,ITEMNO,VOL)
SALES (CNAME, ITEMNO, VOL)
ITEM (ITEMNO)
```

FIGURE 5.   The Entity-Relationship diagram for the example data base and
             the corresponding relations.

It has been shown in the METUGDBMS implementation that a set of
relations, like that of figure 5, is sufficient to support the hierarchical and the network data models at the abstract level and also to process
any query that has been coded in the associated DML like LSL or MRI system
20C0 DML [9, 10].   Thus, the design advantages provided by the Entity-
Relationship model are clear.

5.   CONCLUSION

ANSI/X3/SPARC proposal became widely accepted for the generalized
DBMS design since its publication and several data models have been suggested as the conceptual model.

In this paper, we have reviewed the semantic properties of the
Entity-Relationship model and showed that it is a proper choice for the
conceptual data model of ANSI/X3/SPARC framework for the following reasons:

1.   "It is intuitively clear that the Entity-Relationship model does an
     adequate albeit imperfect job of modeling the real world situations
     such as business enterprises or the records kept by the schools,
     hospitals, governments, and so on, where data base systems are likely
     to be used" [25].

2.   The Entity-Relationship can be easily transformed into the three
     popular data models, and also the relations obtained through the
     Entity-Relationship model have better update properties.

3.   If a relational DBMS is used as a physical common denominator, the
     relations obtained through the Entity-Relationship model would suf-
     fice to support hierarchical and network data models at the abstract
     level in the external schema.

REFERENCES

1. Arora, S.K., Dumpala, S.R., and Smith, K.C., WCRC: An ANSI SPARC
    machine Architecture for Data Base Management, to appear, Proc. Int'l
    Symposium on Computer Architecture, Minneapolis, May, 1981.

2. Astrahan, M.M. et al., System R: Relational Approach to Database
    Management, ACM TODS, Vol. 1, No. 2, June 1976, pp. 97-137.

3. Bernstein, A.P., Synthesizing Third Normal Form Relations from Func-
    tional Dependencies, ACM TODS, Vol. 1, No. 4, 1976, pp. 277-298.

4. Bernstein, A.P., What Does Boyce-Codd Normal Form Do?, Proc. of VLDB,
    1980, pp. 245-259.

5. Cardenas, A.F., Pirahesh, M.H., The E.R. Model a Heterogeneous Data
    Base Management System Network Architecture, in Chen, P. (ed.),
    Entity Relationship Approach to Systems Analysis and Design, North
    Holland, Amsterdam, 1980, pp. 577-583.

6. Chen, P.P., The Entity Relationship Model Toward A Unified View of
    Data, ACM TODS, Vol. 1, No. 1, 1976, pp. 9-36.

7. Chen, P.P., Chung, I., Nakamura, F., Entity-Relationship Normal
    Forms, IS Working Paper #5-81, UCLA.

8. Chiang, T.C., Bergeron, R.F., A Data Base Management System with an
    E-R Conceptual Model, in Chen, P. (ed.), Entity-Relationship Approach
    to Systems Analysis and Design, North Holland, Amsterdam, 1980,
    pp. 467-476.

9. Dogac, A., Ozkarahan, E.A., A Generalized DBMS Implementation on a
    Data Base Machine, Proc. Of ACM.SIGMOD, May 1980, pp. 133-143.

10. Dogac, A., Design and Implementation of a Generalized Data Base
    Management System - METUGDBMS, Ph.D. Thesis, Department of Computer
    Engineering, Middle East Technical University, Turkey, September
    1980.

11. Dogac, A., Chen P.P., Automating Update Propogation in a Data Base by
    using the Entity-Relationship Model, Information Systems Working
    Paper #9-81., UCLA.

12. Elmasri, R., Devor, Cog and Rahimi, S., Notes on DDTS: An Apparatus
    for Experimental Research in Distributed Database Management Systems,
    ACM SIGMOD RECORD, Vol. 11, No. 4, pp. 32-49.

13. Fagin, R., Multivalued Dependencies And a New Normal Form for Rela-
    tional Data Bases, ACM TODS, Vol. 2, No. 3, 1977, pp. 262-278.

14. Interim Report ANSI/X3/SPARC Study Group on Data Base Management
    Systems, FDT 7 No. 2, ACM, New York, 1975.

15. Iossiphidis, J., A Translator to Convert the DDL of ERM to the DDL of System 2000, in Chen, P. (ed.), Entity-Relationship Approach to Systems Analysis and Design, North Holland, Amsterdam, 1980, pp. 477-504.

16. Lusk, E.L., Overbeek, R.A., Parello, B., A Practical Design Methodology for the Implementation of IMS Data Bases, using the Entity-Relationship Model, Proc. of ACM-SIGMOD, May 1980 pp. 9-21.

17. Ozkarahan, E.A., An Associative Processor for Relational Data Bases--RAP, Ph.D. Thesis, Department of Computer Science, University of Toronto, January, 1976.

18. Ozkarahan, E.A., Schuster, S.A., Smith, K.C., RAP--An Associative Processor for Data Base Management, AFIPS Proc., Vol. 44, 1975, pp. 379-387.

19. Sakai, H., A Unified Approach to the Logical Design of Hierarchical Data Model, in Chen, P. (ed.), Entity-Relationship Approach to Systems Analysis and Design, North Holland, Amsterdam, 1980, pp. 61-74.

20. Sakai, H., Entity-Relationship Approach to the Conceptual Schema Design, Proc. of ACM-SIGMOD, May 1980, pp. 18.

21. Santos, C.S., Neuhold, E.J., Furtado, A.L., A Data Type Approach to the Entity-Relationship Model, in Chen, P. (ed.), Entity-Relationship Approach to Systems Analysis and Design, North Holland, Amsterdam, 1980, pp. 103-119.

22. Scheuermann, P., Schiffner, G., Weber, H., Abstraction Capabilities and Invariant Properties Modelling within the Entity-Relationship Approach, in Chen, P. (ed.), Entity-Relationship Approach to Systems Analysis and Design, North Holland, Amsterdam, 1980, pp. 121-140.

23. Schiffner, G., Scheuermann, P., Multiple Views and Abstractions with an Extended Entity-Relationship Model, Journal of Computer Languages, Vol. 4, pp. 139-154.

24. Smith, J.M., Smith, D., Data Base Abstractions: Aggregation and Generalization, ACM TODS, Vol. 2, No. 2, 1977, pp. 105-113.

25. Ullman, J.D., Principles of Data Base Systems, Computer Science Press, 1980.

26. Unlu, S., Design and Implementation of a Software Emulator for the Relational Associative Processor--RAP, M.SC. Thesis, Dept. of Computer Engineering, METU, August, 1979.

27. Wong, E., Katz, H.R., Logical Design and Schema Conversion for Relational and DBTG Databases, in Chen, P. (ed.), Entity-Relationship Approach to Systems Analysis and Design, North Holland, Amsterdam, 1980, pp. 311-321.

Entity-Relationship Approach to
Information Modeling and Analysis, P.P. Chen (ed.)
Elsevier Science Publishers B.V. (North-Holland)
©ER Institute, 1983

INCOD: A SYSTEM FOR CONCEPTUAL DESIGN OF DATA AND TRANSACTIONS IN THE ENTITY - RELATIONSHIP MODEL

P. ATZENI(1), C. BATINI, M. LENZERINI(2), F. VILLANELLI(1).

Istituto di Automatica - Facoltà di Ingegneria - Via Eudossiana, 18/00184 Roma ITALY-Tel. 06/484441.

Abstract
        The general structure of a computer aided system for INteractive COnceptual Design (INCOD) of Data Bases is described. INCOD is a tool for the incremental definition of the conceptual schema of a Data Base. Both the static aspects and the dynamic ones are taken into account. An enriched Entity-Relationship model is assumed for the representation of static aspects, and a specific language is used for the representation of dynamic aspects.

1. Introduction
        In the last years, the Entity-Relationship (E-R) Model [C1] has been widely studied and used in the area of the methodologies for information analysis and modelling and, particularly, for data base design (see, for instance, [C2]).
        A methodology for data base design may be seen as a set of tools, methods and techniques to:
1.   Collect user requirements.
2.   Design a data base application that consistently and efficiently implement user needs.
3.   Plan the development activity.
4.   Turn out a documentation that can be useful both during the design and during the prcduction phase (e.g. in occurrence of possible restructurings) of the application life cycle.
        Area 2 is seen [NO] as dealing with three separate subareas:
2.1 Information analysis and definition (conceptual design).
2.2 Implementation design.
2.3 Physical design.
        This paper is concerned with the conceptual design phase, whose goal is "to obtain an integrated, formal, implementation-independent specification of application-specific enterprise information" [K]. This formal specification (often called *Conceptual Schema*) is based on a specific model that is usually chosen among the so called semantic models (or second generation models).
        These models often provide formalisms to represent, besides the static

(1) P.Atzeni and F.Villanelli are supported by an ITALSIEL S.p.A. grant.
(2) M.Lenzerini is supported by an Olivetti S.p.A. grant.

requirements of the application, also the dynamic ones. Modelling transactions
(see [K]) in the conceptual design phase is useful for:
- Identifying deficiencies in the conceptual schema, i.e. finding additional
  schema constructs that are needed to execute the operations expressed in user
  requirements.
- Determining relative access frequencies along functional paths; this informa
  tion is useful for logical and physical design phase.
- Providing formal specification for detailed application development.

For such reasons, it is usually accepted that the conceptual schema be
the formalized representaiton of both the static and the dynamic requirements
of the application and that a methodology for conceptual data base design consider both.

The aim of this paper is to describe INCOD, a system, whose design and
implementation are in progress, for the aid to the conceptual data base design,
based on an extended E-R model. INCOD provides a set of tools that support the
designer during the phase of conceptualization of the static and dynamic requi
rements, automatically checking the consistency of the design process and simplifying the management of the corresponding documentation. An earlier version
of INCOD is described in [BL].

In Section 2 we give motivations for a system like INCOD, that allows
the incremental definition of a conceptual schema, according both to a top-down
and to a bottom-up strategy.

In Section 3 we describe the conceptual model: with regard to the static
aspects we define an enriched E-R model; with regard to the dynamic aspects we
use a specific, high level language to express transactions in the E-R model.

In Section 4 we describe INCOD's architecture and modules.

In Section 5 we show a detailed example of design session using INCOD.

2. General features of INCOD

As we said in the introduction, INCOD is a computer aided system to sup
port the designer of a data base in the formal description of user requirements
in terms of a conceptual model. Such description has to be obtained by means of
incremental enrichements needed by the complexity of the formalization process.

Different points of view exist in the literature concerning the process
by which the formal description be built. The different methods proposed can be
divided into two distinct classes: Top-Down Methods (TD methods) and Bottom-Up
Methods (BU methods).

It is our opinion that two different meanings can be attached to the
terms TD methods and BU methods in the conceptual design.

a) In *the first meaning* [BD] BU refer to those methods that proceed to the formal representation of the conceptual schema (CS) by means of two steps (see
   fig. 1):
1. View modelling;

2. View integration.

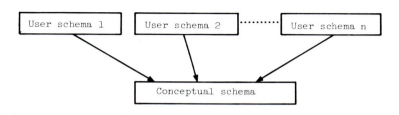

Fig. 1

        The first step results in a formal representation of each application or
user view (in the following *user schema* (US)) of interest to the enterprise.
During the second step the different user schemata are integrated into one conceptual schema of the data base.
        By TD methods we mean methods where the conceptual schema is initially
produced and only subsequently are the user schemata derived (see fig. 2).

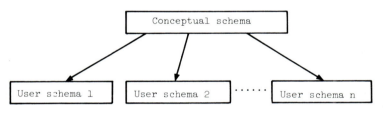

Fig. 2

In this first meaning the process that generated the CS is influenced by the *or
ganization of the enterprise into groups of users*.
b) The *second meaning* [DDS] refers to those methods in which the creation of CS
    and/or USs is influenced by the *organization of concepts according to their
    abstraction level*.
        The schemata are obtained by a *process of object enrichement* (where by
object we mean any concept primitive in the model chosen to represent the schema) which can be seen as disciplined by a set of *enrichement primitives*.
        The objects of interest to the enterprise may often be categorized accor
ding to various abstraction hierachies. It is commonly agreed in the literature
that such abstraction hierachies be explicitly incorporated into the definition
of the model used to represent the real world.
        In BU methods [BCPB] the initial objects chosen to enrich the schema are
atomic, non-decomposable objects. Subsequently, higher level objects are found

and explicitely added, as the abstraction hierachies are ascended (see fig. 3).

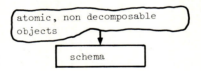

Fig. 3

In TD methods [BS] the process of schema generation is seen as being com‐
posed of a set of refinement steps for the representation of real world details
in the schema, so that to every refinement corresponds the substitution of an
object by an object structure refining it (see fig. 4).

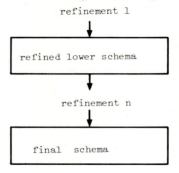

Fig. 4

The interaction between the two different meanings of TD-BU is visua‐
lized in Fig. 5. We'll associate to the first meaning x axis: BU methos run
along x axis to the right, TD methods to the left. Y axis will be associated
to the second meaning: BU methods run along it from the bottom to the top, TD
methods from the top to the bottom.

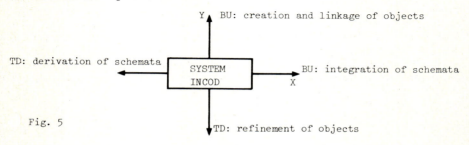

Fig. 5

INCOD provides the design of the environment "user schemata; conceptual schema" with a set of tools that match all the above described strategies:

- with regard to X asis, INCOD allows both the integration of user schemata into a global schema and derivation of user schemata from a global schema.
- with regard to Y axis, the system provides a set of commands that allow the design of a single schema with both a top-down (refinement of objects) and a bottom-up (creation and linkage of objects) strategy.

3. *The Conceptual Model*

For the reasons discussed in the introduction, the conceptual model adopted in INCOD allows the formalization of both the static and the dynamic aspects of the application of interest, at the same level of abstraction.

With regard to the static aspects, various extensions of the E-R model have been recently proposed (see, for instance, [SSW], [FNS]). Some of them, particularly meaningful in the conceptual design, are adopted in INCOD's data model.

With regard to the dynamic aspects, some proposals of E-R-oriented languages exist in the literature (see, for instance, [P], [S]). Their goal was the definition of transactions against an already designed E-R schema. On the contrary, the language we propose, that allows the formal description of both retrieval and manipulation operations, has been conceived to be used both in the design phase and during the life cycle of the data base.

In the following of this section the two formalisms, called respectively *data model* and *transaction model*, are described.

3.1 *The Data Model*

The data model used in INCOD is an extension of the E-R Model proposed by Chen [Cl]. A brief description of the model follows.

Three different *classes of objects* exist in the model: entities, relationships and attributes. Each object is represented and uniquely identified by an *object name* (entity name, relationship name, attribute name); moreover it may have associated both a set of synonyms and an explicative text in natural language.

Entities represent those classes of objects in the real world involved in the application. An elementary object within a class will be referred to as an *occurrence* (or *instance*) *of an entity*.

Relationships represent classes of logical associations between entities. An element of one of these classes will be referred to as an *occurrence of a relationship* (*). The model can describe the cardinality (type) of each relationship,

(*) We use the term "entity" ("relationship") as a synonym of the term "entity set" ("relationship set") of [Cl].

i.e. it can distinguish between 1:1, 1:n, m:n (binary) relationships. A 1:n relationship associates each occurrence of one of the entities with at most one occurrence of the other one. A 1:1 relationship satisfies the above property and its inverse. A binary relationship that is neither 1:1 nor 1:n is an m:n relationship. The extention of the concept of cardinality to relationships involving more than two entities is easy and therefore omitted.

Attributes represent properties of entities or relationships; an attribute is a mathematical function: the domain is the set of occurrences of an entity or a relationship and the codomain is a set of values. At present we do not distinguish in INCOD between attributes and value-sets [C1]. The set of attributes of an entity that uniquely identifies its occurrences is the *key* of the entity.

We now extend the original model defining two abstraction hierarchies. They could hold for entities as well as for relationships, but we define them for entities only.

The first type of hierarchy is the *subset relationship* (inversely *superset relationship*); an entity ε1 is a subset of another entity ε2 if every occurrence of ε1 is also an occurrence of ε2.

The second type of hierarchy is *generalization*; an entity ε is a generalization of the entities ε1,...,εn if each occurrence of ε is also an occurrence of one and only one of the entities ε1,...,εn. The partition over the occurrences of ε established by generalization may be seen as induced by a property of ε. This may be explicitly represented by an attribute of ε: in this case it will be referred to as *underlying attribute*.

Both in subset relationship and in generalization, attributes of the entity at the upper level of a hierarchy are also attributes of the entities at its lower level. Entities at the lower level will generally have additional attributes with respect to the entity at the upper level: in the model we explicitly represent only such attributes. The same holds for the relationships.

An E-R schema will be represented in the following by means of the diagrammatic representation of table 1.

OBJECT	REPRESENTATION
Entity	▭
Relationship	◇
Attribute	———○
Key attribute	———●
Generalization relationship with underlying attribute	⬡ (hexagon with ⇑ above)
Subset relationship	⇑

Table 1: The Diagrammatic Representation

3.2. *The Transaction Model*

The language we assume for the formalization of transactions is briefly described here. For a complete description of this version see [AV]. The syntax appears in Appendix 3. An improved version has been more recently developed and is discussed in [AC].

The language allows the specification of transactions directly referring to the data model described in section 3.1. It can be useful in two situations:

- in the conceptual design phase as a means of implementation-independent formalization of transactions;
- during the life of the data base, as a high-level DML.

The specification of both queries and manipulation operations is allowed by the language. Since manipulations are usually performed on data to be previously retrieved, the structure of the language is based on queries and allows the specification of updates on their results. So we describe the queries' structure first and the manipulations' then.

Queries

Each query is expressed in terms of a certain number of steps, each corresponding to one of the following two constucts:

1. *Relationship-crossing,* which has the syntax:

    FIND < entity name 1 > [<clauses>]
    [NOT] THROUGH < relationship name > [<clauses>]
    [NOT] HAVING $\left[\left\{ {EACH \atop HALL} \right\}\right]$ FOUND < entity name 2 > [<clauses>]

    where <> brackets and {} brackets have their usual meaning and [ ] brackets include optional phrases. Two different types of clause exist: the first one, DISPLAY (<attribute list>), specificies the attributes whose values must appear in the result, the second one, WITH (<predicate>), specifies a condition for the selection of the instance of the involved object.

2. *Hierarchy-crossing,* which has the syntax:

    FIND < entity name 1 > [<clauses>]
    [NOT] $\left\{ {ASCENDING \atop DESCENDING} \right\}$ <hierarchy-id>
    [NOT] HAVING FOUND <entity name 2> [<clauses>]

    where <hierarchy-id> is either the name of an underlying attribute or one of the keywords SUBSET, SUPERSET.
    For the semantics of the hierarchies (see section 3.1), the explicit specification of steps of this type can be omitted in many queries, but it is useful in the design phase, to compare transactions and data schemata.

The elementary constructs can be repeatedly combined according to the three following rules:

a. *Chaining.*

   Two subqueries can be combined using the output of the first one as the input for the second one:

   .
   .
   .

   THROUGH <relationship name 1> [<clauses>]
   HAVING FOUND <entity name> [<clauses>]
           THROUGH <relationship name 2> [<clauses>]

   .
   .
   .

b. *Branching.*

   Two or more subqueries can converge on the same entity or relationship:
   b1. *Branching on relationship.*

:
:

```
TRHOUGH <relationship name> [<clauses>]
BEGIN HAVING FOUND <entity name 1> [<clauses>]
```

:
:

$\left\{ \begin{matrix} AND \\ OR \end{matrix} \right\}$ HAVING FOUND <entity name 2> [<clauses>]

:
:

```
END
```

b2. *Branching on entity.*

```
FIND <entity name> [<clauses>]
BEGIN [NOT] THROUGH <relationship name 1> [<clauses>]
```

:
:

$\left\{ \begin{matrix} AND \\ OR \end{matrix} \right\}$ [NOT] THROUGH <relationship name 2> [<clauses>]

:
:

```
END
```

c. *Nesting.*

Among the terms of a selection predicate there may appear terms referring to the results of other subqueries:

...WITH (...<attribute name 1> ϑ <attribute name 2> OF THAT...)
where ϑ is one of the comparison operators $=, \neq, >, \geqslant, <, \leqslant$ and a subquery follows the keywords OF THAT.

Manipulations

As we said at the beginning of this section, manipulations are usually performed on data retrieved by means of queries. They have the following structures:

1. Deletion of one or more occurrences of an entity or relationship:
   DELETE FOUND .....

2. Modification of values of attributes in one or more occurrences of an entity or relationship:
   MODIFY (<attribute name>:=<value>,...) IN FOUND...

3. Insertion of an occurrence of an entity:
   INSERT <entity name> (<attribute name>:=<value>,...)

4. Creation of one or more instances of a relationship between occurrences of the related entities, already present in the data base:

```
CREATE <relationship name> (<attribute-name>:=<value>,...)
   BETWEEN FOUND <entity name 1> ...
                         :
                         :
                         :
AND    FOUND <entity name 2>...
                         :
                         :
                         :
END
```

The input values can be replaced by the keyword INPUT.

For reason to be explained later we call *executable* a transaction expressed in the language described in this section.

We show now two examples of transactions, which refer to the schema shown in Figure 6. For each of them we give the natural language text and the specification in the transaction language.

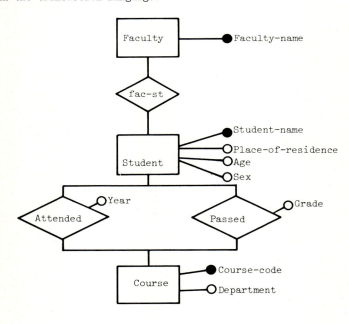

Fig. 6

Example 1

"Find the students that have been enrolled to a certain course for more than one year and have not yet passed the corresponding exam".

```
TRANSACTION bad-students
FIND student
BEGIN THROUGH attended WITH (year ≤ 1979)
       HAVING FOUND course WITH (course-code='CS')
AND    NOT THROUGH passed
       HAVING FOUND course WITH (course-code='CS')
END
```

Example 2
"Insert a student and enroll him in a certain faculty"

```
TRANSACTION enroll-student
INSERT student (student-name:='ROSSI'; place of residence:="ROMA";
                age:='19'; sex:='M')
CREATE fac-st
BETWEEN FOUND student WITH (student-name:='ROSSI")
AND     FOUND faculty WITH (faculty-name:='ENGINEERING')
END
```

Example 3
"Find all the courses attended by students that live in a given city and enrolled in a certain faculty".

```
TRANSACTION courses
FIND course
THROUGH attended
HAVING FOUND student WITH (place of residence = INPUT)
       THROUGH fac-st
       HAVING FOUND faculty WITH (faculty-name = INPUT)
```

   Further examples will be shown in section 5.

4. *Description of system's architecture and modules.*

   Figure 7 shows the architecture of INCOD. Every block represents a part
of the system responsible of a given function (*module*).
Continuous lines represent logical connections between modules, while dashed li
nes represent interactions between the designer and the system.
For each module a special purpose language is defined that allows such interaction.

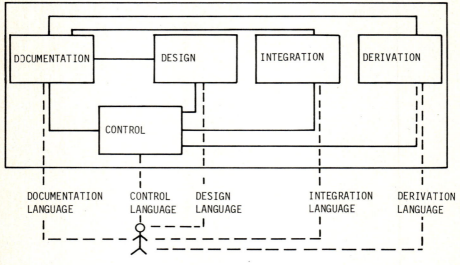

Fig. 7

A brief description of INCOD's modules follows.

1. The *Control module* supports the designer during initialization of the design, access and release of other modules.
2. The *design module* is used by the designer during the design of a schema.
3. The *integration module* is used by the designer during user schemata integration.
4. The *derivation module* is used by the designer during the process of extraction of user schemata from the conceptual schema.
5. The *documentation module* supports the designer in organizing documentation.

As we said in the introduction, the design of INCOD is in progress. At present we have defined the functional specification of the control, the design, the integration and the documentation modules and we are working at the specification of the derivation module: so we won't deal with this module in the following.

In this section we give more details about INCOD's modules and languages; the general syntactic structure and the semantics of the languages are shown in tables 2-5.
A more detailed description of the languages appears in [BLS], [ABLV].

4.1. *The control module.*

The commands of the control language allow creation and deletion of schema, access and release of the other modules of the system. Table 2 shows syntax and semantics of each command.

SYNTAX	SEMANTICS
*CREATE <schema>	Create a new schema (whose name is) <schema>
*DELETE <schema>	Delete the schema <schema>
*UPDATE <schema>	Enter the design module: a design session of the schema <schema> begins
*INTEGRATE <schema 1>, <schema 2> INTO <schema 3>	Enter the integration module: the schemata <schema 1> and <schema 2> are integrated into a new schema <schema 3>
*DOC	Enter the documentation module
*RETURN	Return to the control module

Table 2: The control language

4.2. *The design module.*

The purpose of this module is to help the designer to build a schema by means of successive enrichments. Such enrichments correspond to new knowledge obtained by the designer about the application: such new knowledge may concern both data and transactions.

The allowed enrichments are organized as a set of primitives, the commands of the *design language*.
Suppose that a given set of commands has been used to create a "partial" schema S+. When a new command (concerning either data or transaction) is applied on S+, the consistency of the corresponding *transformation* is checked with respect to the preexisting schema. On the whole, the types of inconsistencies that can be revealed during the conceptual design depend on:
1. The formalism to express data.
2. The formalism to express transactions.
3. The allowed transformations of the schema.

The above concepts will be clarified in the following two sections, in which we describe data and transactions specification commands respectively.

4.2.1. Data specification commands.

The operands of the data specification commands are the objects of a sche ma; such commands allow:

1. creating and deleting objects (entities, relationships, subsets and generali zations);
2. expanding objects, i.e. refining them into sets of objects that inherit their logical links;
3. giving a structure to entities and relationships (i.e. defining their attri butes and identifiers).

When a command is applied, the system checks the consistency of the cor responding transformation. We distinguish between *explicit and potential incon sistences.*

Explicit inconsistencies are those automatically detected by an inspection of the schema and the transformation; a general classification of explicit incon sistencies the system may check is the following:

1. Naming inconsistencies, arising when two objects of the same type have the sa me name.
2. Type inconsistencies, arising when two objects with different types have the same name.
3. Subset and generalization inconsistencies, when the structure of such rela tionships in the schema does not agree with their semantics (see in figure 8 an example of such inconsistency: E is a subset of two entities whose instan ces are mutually exclusive).

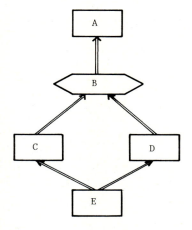

Fig. 8

Example 4

    Assume that the schema in fig. 9 has been previously created:

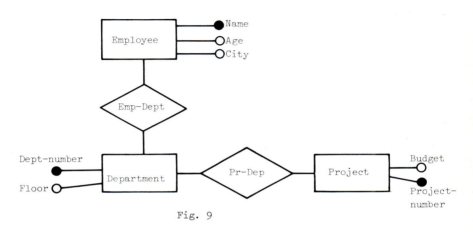

Fig. 9

    Suppose now the designer tries to create a new entity "City" with attributes City-name, State, Zip-Code. An inconsistency is now dectected by the system, because the object City has two different types in the schema.

    INCOD aids the designer to solve inconsistencies, providing several scenarios for each type of them. Such scenarios suggest *possible interpretations of the inconsistency.* To each interpretation a consequent solution corresponds. The designer can accept one of the scenarios or reject all of them. In the first case the corresponding solution is automatically performed; in the second case the command that generated the inconsistency is cancelled.

Example 5

    There are two interpretations corresponding to the inconsistency described in Example 4:

a. the new entity and the attribute are homonymous: the corresponding solution is to change one of the names;
b. the attribute represents a logical link between the entity Employee and the new entity: in this case the solution is to delete the attribute and represent the logical link by means of a relationship between the two entities.

With regard to *potential inconsistencies,* they correspond to situations in which *indications exist* of possible:

1. synonymies
2. hidden hierarchies
3. redundancies

Example 6

    Suppose the designer defines a relationship City-State between the entities City and State of the schema described in figure 10.

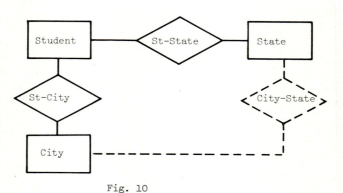

Fig. 10

A cycle is introduced in the schema: a warning message is printed in this case by the system so that the designer can detect the existence of a redundancy.

    A side effect of the application of a command concerns the update of the transactions already defined during the design and referring objects involved in the transformation.

    The designer can update such transactions with a suitable transaction specification command (see later). In case of default, system INCOD "suspends" the transactions, and the designer can defer their update.

4.2.2. *Transaction specification commands.*

    In order to make the designer's task easier during the formalization of the dynamic requirements and their comparison with the data schema, INCOD allows the definition of transactions at three different levels of refinement. So, the design of a transaction may be carried out by means of successive enrichments (see fig. 11)

Natural language transaction

↓

Conceptual transaction

↓

Navigational transaction

↓

Executable transaction

Fig. 11

With *Conceptual transaction* we mean a specification of the transaction in which only the involved objects are declared together with their types. With *Navigational transaction* we mean a specification of the transaction whose structu re is analogous to the executable one but in which only the involved objects and the access path ("navigation") are specified. (See Appendix 1,2 for the syntax of the conceptual and navigational transaction languages and Section 5 for examples of their use). We call executable the transactions at the lower level, because their expressive power is the same as an usual query and update language.

The transaction specification commands allow:

1. *creating new transactions* at any level of specification (conceptual, naviga- tional, executable) and matching them with the current data schema, i.e. che cking their consistency. If inconsistencies arise, then scenarios are shown suggesting possible solutions. The designer can choose either to suspend the transaction or to modify the schema. In the last case, the solution of an in consistency may require the modification of the data schema and/or of the transaction. If the data schema is modified, then (similary to what happens for data specification commands) transactions reffering to objects involved in the modification can be updated or suspended.

2. *matching suspended transaction* with the current data schema.

3. *refining* previously defined transactions, in order to obtain versions at a lower level in the hierarchy of fig. 11.

Example 5

Consider again the schema in figure 9.
The following transaction: "Find all the Names of Employees involved in a project with a given project-number", expressed in the language described in section 3:

        FIND Employee DISPLAY (Name)
        THROUGH Emp-proj
        HAVING FOUND Project WITH (Project-number=INPUT).

is now matched with the schema. An inconsistency arises because the transaction refers to a relationship that doesn't exist in the schema. The possible inter- pretations of the inconsistency are the following:

a. the logical link represented by the relationship Emp-Proj is missing in the schema: the solution is to create it.

b. the logical link referred to in the transaction is represented in the schema
   by the relationships Pr-Dept and Emp-Dept; the corresponding solution is to
   modify the transaction as follows:

```
FIND Employee DISPLAY (Name)
THROUGH Emp-Dep
HAVING FOUND Department
        THROUGH Pr-Dept
        HAVING FOUND Project WITH (Project-number=INPUT).
```

4.2.3. The Design Language.

In Table 3 the set of commands of the design language is described.

SINTAX	SEMANTICS
CREATE \<type\>: \<object\> where \<type\> can be: ENT, REL, ATT	An object with type \<type\> is created
EXPAND: \<obj\> INTO \<list of obj\>	The object \<obj\> is expanded in the objects in \<list of obj\> which inherit its logical links
STRUCT: \<obj\> BY \<list of att\>	The attributes of object (entity or relationship) \<obj\> are speci<u></u>fied
DELETE: \<obj\>	The object \<obj\> and its logical links are deleted
HELP	When an explicit inconsistency is detected the corresponding scenarios are shown
MATCH \<type of trans\> TRANS(ACTION): \<name\> [\<transaction declaration\>] where \<type of trans\> can be: CONCEPTUAL, NAVIGATIONAL or EXECUTABLE	When \<transaction declaration\> is present, a new transaction is crea ted and matched with the current data schema; when it is missing, a suspended transaction is matched.
REFINE \<name of trans\>	A new version of the transaction is interactively built.
DELETE \<name of trans\>	The transaction is deleted

Table 3. The Design Language

In Table 3 <transaction declaration> is a description of the transaction expressed in terms of the corresponding language.

4.3. *The integration module.*

The integration process, in INCOD, is guided by the system. It takes as input two schemata and builds the integrated schema by incremental aggregation of their objects; other schemata may be integrated one at a time by successive integration steps.

Any explicit or potential inconsistency arising during the integration is shown to the designer, who is forced to solve the explicit ones.

The system is able to:
- give information about the schemata (command * DOC);
- help the designer to solve inconsistencies by showing the corresponding scena rios (command HELP).

The integration process may be logically divided into four steps:
1. Aggregation of entities and their attributes;
2. Aggregation of relationships and their attributes;
3. Conclusive tests;
4. Update of transactions.

During the first step homonymies, synonymies and hidden hierarchies between entities are analysed: indications for synonymies exist when two entities have at least a common attribute; two entities having the same names and different attributes are shown as potential homonymous. Similar checks are performed in the second step with regard to relationships; further indications of possible synonymies between entities may arise in this phase: for instance, two entities not analysed during the first step and connected to the same entity by a relationship, are shown as potential synonymous.

In the third step, type inconsistencies are analysed and solved. In the fourth step, all the transactions defined in the schemata, in order to match them with the integrated schema, are modified according to the transformations performed to solve the inconsistencies.

During integration, all the commands of the design language can be used: further specific commands of the integration language are shown in Table 4.

SYNTAX	SEMANTICS
MERGE <obj$_1$>, <obj$_2$>: <obj$_3$>	<obj$_1$> and <obj$_2$> are merged into a unique object, whose name is <obj$_3$>
SPLIT <obj>: <obj$_1$>, <obj$_2$>	<obj> is split into the objects <obj$_1$> and <obj$_2$>

Table 4: The integration language

4.4. *The documentation module.*

The designer may obtain from the documentation module information concer
ning both the schemata managed by the system at a given moment and the objects
and transactions of the schemata. In the following we'll only refer to the second kind of information.

Syntax and semantics of the commands of the documentation language are
shown in Table 5.

Commands 1,1' are used to request general information about the schema,
commands 2,2' about an object or transaction.

Commands 3-5 concern with a given object; the semantics of command 5, in
particular, depends on the type of the specified object: neighbour of an attribute is considered the entity (or the relationship) it belongs to; neighbours of
an entity are its attributes and the entities connected to it by a relationship
or a subset relationship; neighbours of a relationship are its attributes and
the entities it connects.

SYNTAX	SEMANTICS
1. \<class of objects>: LIST where class of objects can be: ENTI-TIES, RELARIONSHIPS, ATTRIBUTES.	Display the list of \<class of objects>
1'.TRANSACTIONS: LIST	Display the list of transactions
2. \<object>: TEXT	Display the natural language text associated to \<object>
2'.\<transaction>: TEXT	Display the natural language text associated to \<transaction>
3. \<object>: UP	Display the object whose expansion produced \<object>
4. \<object>: DOWN	Display the expansion of \<object>
5. \<object>: NEIGH(BOURS)	Display the neighbours of \<object>
6. \<object list>: PATH	Display the logical paths connecting the objects of \<object list>
7. \<object>: HELP	Display all the information about \<object>
7'.\<transaction>: HELP	Display all the information about \<transaction>
8. \<schema>: HELP	Display all the information about \<schema>

Table 5: The documentation language

Comand 6 displays the logical paths connecting the given set of objects; facilities exist to select those paths having certain properties. Commands 7,7' are used to obtain all possible information about an object or a transaction. Command 8 displays a data schema, in the diagrammatic representation. The design of an E-R oriented graphic package is in progress. An E-R data definition language representation will be also provided.

5. *Example*

In this section we present an example of design session using INCOD.

Suppose that a schema, called student-schema, has been previously designed: the corresponding data schema is shown in fig. 6, transactions are those described in Example 1 and 3.

From interviews in the department, a new schema is now created by means of the following dialogue (here and in the following dialogues are enclosed within boxes, symbol '>' precedes the commands of the designer and symbols '***' precede the messages of the system):

```
>* CREATE    department-schema.
>* UPDATE    department-schema.
```

A design session of the schema begins:

```
> CREATE ENTITY: department-schema.
> EXPAND: department-schema INTO RELATIONSHIP dept-teacher
        BETWEEN department, teacher-schema.
```

An entity is created (schema 1 of fig. 12) and expanded into a relationship between two new entities (schema 2).

```
> EXPAND:  teacher-schema INTO RELATIONSHIP teacher-course
        BETWEEN teacher, course; LINK POINT: teacher.
```

The entity teacher-schema is expanded into a relationship; the new entity teacher is declared as link point: only this entity inherits the logical links of the refined entity teacher-schema (schema 3).

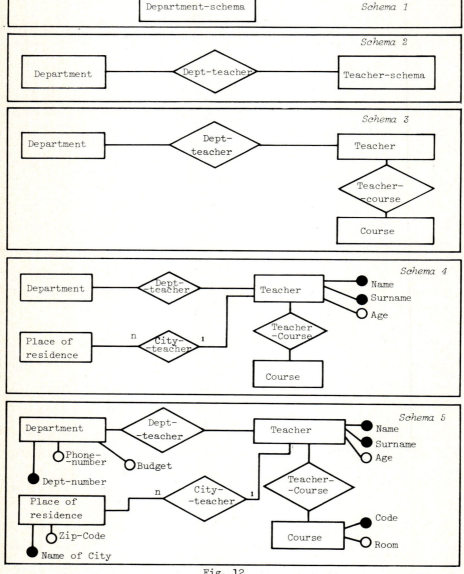

Fig. 12

```
> MATCH  NAVIGATIONAL  TRANSACTION  course-list

        FIND   course
        THROUGH   teacher-course
        HAVING FOUND   teacher  INVOLVING (name).
```

A transaction is declared at the navigational level, whose natural language
text is: "Display all the courses given by a teacher with a certain name".

```
*** INCONSISTENCY: THE ATTRIBUTES OF THE ENTITY teacher ARE NOT YET DEFINED.

> HELP.

    ***SCENARIOS:
    1. THE ATTRIBUTE name FOR THE ENTITY teacher MUST BE DEFINED.

    2. THE TRANSACTION MUST BE MODIFIED DELETING name IN THE CLAUSE
       "INVOLVING".

    3. THE TRANSACTION MUST BE SUSPENDED.

> 3.
```

An inconsistency is detected by the system. The designer asks for the correspon
ding scenarios and chooses the third one.

```
> CREATE ENTITY: place-of-residence.
> CREATE RELATIONSHIP: city-teacher BETWEEN teacher, place-of-residence;
                       TYPE: n,1.
> STRUCT: teacher WITH name, surname # age, department.

*** INCONSISTENCY: department HAS BEEN PREVIOUSLY DEFINED AS AN ENTITY.
```

```
> HELP.

    ***SCENARIOS:
    1. THE ATTRIBUTE department AND THE ENTITY department ARE HOMONYMOUS: A
       NEW NAME MUST BE DEFINED FOR THE ATTRIBUTE.

    2. THE ATTRIBUTE department REPRESENTS THE SAME LOGICAL LINK AS RELATION
       SHIP dept-teacher: THE ATTRIBUTE MUST BE DELETED.

    3. THE ATTRIBUTE department REPRESENTS A NEW LOGICAL LINK BETWEEN THE
       ENTITIES teacher AND department: A NEW RELATIONSHIP MUST BE CREATED
       AND THE ATTRIBUTE MUST BE DELETED.

> 2.
```

An entity and a relationship are now created; the type of the relationship is
declared: it relates n instances of the entity teacher with 1 instances of the
entity place-of-residence (schema 4). Then the attributes of the entity teacher
are defined by the command STRUCT: symbol '#' divides key attributes (on the
left) from the others (on the right).

   A new inconsistency is detected by the system: the designer accepts the
solution suggested by the second scenario and the attribute department is dele
ted by the system.

   Then the temporary schema is completed by means of the following commands
(schema 5).

```
> STRUCT : course  WITH  code # room.
> STRUCT : place-of-residence  WITH  name-of-city # zip-code.
> STRUCT : department  WITH  dept-number # phone-number, budget.
```

Suppose now that the following transaction must be checked over the schema:
"For every department with budget greater than a certain value print name, sur
name and age of teachers with more than 10 years of seniority and with age less
than a certain value, and the codes of the courses in which they have been involved.

```
> MATCH  CONCEPTUAL  TRANSACTION  old-teacher

        budget: ATT OF department: ENT;
        name, surname, age: ATT OF senior-teacher: ENT;
        code: ATT OF course: ENT.

*** INCONSISTENCIES:
1.   THE ENTITY senior-teacher HAS NOT BEEN DEFINED IN THE SCHEMA.

2.   name, surname, age ARE ATTRIBUTES OF THE ENTITY teacher.

> CREATE HIERARCHY: senior-teacher SUBSET OF teacher.
> MATCH CONCEPTUAL TRANSACTION old-teacher.
```

First the transaction is defined at the conceptual level: two inconsistencies
arise. Such inconsistencies are solved by creating a subset relationship between
the entities senior-teacher and teacher.

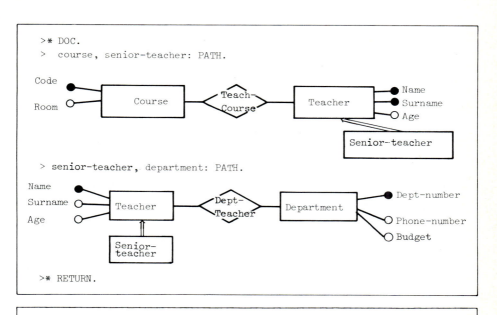

```
>* DOC.
>  course, senior-teacher: PATH.
```

```
>  senior-teacher, department: PATH.
```

```
>* RETURN.
```

```
> REFINE TRANSACTION  old-teacher.

*** THE TRANSACTION old-teacher IS DEFINED AT THE CONCEPTUAL LEVEL:

          budget: ATT of department: ENT;
          name, surname, age: ATT OF senior-teacher: ENT;
          code: ATT OF course: ENT.

   DO YOU WANT TO BUILD THE NAVIGATIONAL OR THE EXECUTABLE VERSION?

> NAVIGATIONAL:

       FIND course INVOLVING (code)
       THROUGH teacher-course
       HAVING FOUND senior-teacher INVOLVING (name, surname, age)
           THROUGH dept-teacher
           HAVING FOUND department INVOLVING (budget).
```

The design of the corresponding navigational version begins.
During the design, the documentation commands are used to obtain information
about the logical links existing among the objects referred to in the transaction.
Note that in the navigational version the designer has omitted the specification
of the hierarchy crossing.

```
> REFINE TRANSACTION old teacher.
*** THE TRANSACTION old-teacher IS DEFINED AT THE NAVIGATIONAL LEVEL:

    FIND course INVOLVING (code)
    THROUGH teacher-course
    HAVING FOUND senior-teacher INVOLVING (name, surname, age)
            THROUGH dept-teacher
            HAVING FOUND department INVOLVING (budget).
*** HOW DO YOU REFINE  INVOLVING (code) ?

> DISPLAY (code).
```

```
*** HOW DO YOU REFINE  INVOLVING (name, surname, age) ?

> DISPLAY (name, surname, age) WITH (age < INPUT).

*** HOW DO YOU REFINE INVOLVING (budget) ?

> WITH (budget ≥ INPUT).

 *** THE EXECUTABLE VERSION OF THE TRANSACTION old-teacher IS:

    FIND course DISPLAY (code)
    THROUGH teacher-course
    HAVING FOUND senior-teacher DISPLAY (name, surname, age) WITH (age < INPUT)
            THROUGH dept-teacher
            HAVING FOUND department WITH (budget ≥ INPUT).
```

The design of the executable version of the transaction old-teacher is completed.

```
>* DOC.
>   TRANSACTION: LIST.
  *** TRANSACTION TABLE:
```

TRANSACTION NAME	LEVEL	STATE
course-list	NAVIGATIONAL	SUSPENDED
old-teacher	EXECUTABLE	MATCHED

```
>* RETURN.
>   REFINE TRANSACTION course-list.
  *** THE TRANSACTION course-list IS DEFINED AT THE NAVIGATIONAL LEVEL:

        FIND course
        THROUGH teacher-course
        HAVING FOUND teacher INVOLVING (name).
```

```
  *** HOW DO YOU REFINE   INVOLVING (name) ?
> WITH (name = INPUT).

  *** THE EXECUTABLE VERSION OF THE TRANSACTION course-list  IS:

          FIND course
          THROUGH teacher-course
          HAVING FOUND teacher WITH (name = INPUT).

>* RETURN.
```

The designer requests documentation about the transactions defined during the design and then defines the executable version of the transaction course-list. Finally, the design module is released. The complete conceptual schema is shown in Fig. 13; transactions are described at the executable level.

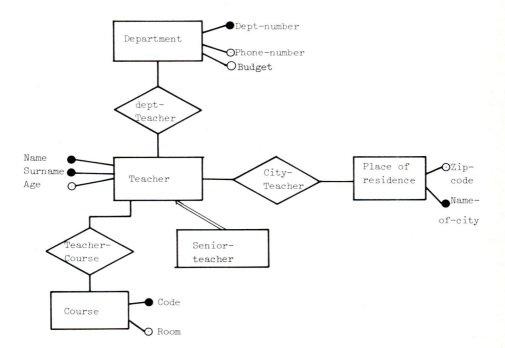

```
TRANSACTION  course-list:

        FIND  course
        THROUGH  teacher-course
        HAVING FOUND  teacher WITH (name = INPUT).

TRANSACTION  old-teacher

        FIND  course  DISPLAY (code)
        THROUGH  teacher-course
        HAVING FOUND senior-teacher DISPLAY(name, surname, age)WITH(age<INPUT).
            THROUGH  dept-teacher
            HAVING FOUND  department WITH (budget ⩾ INPUT).
```

Fig. 13

The two schemata, student-schema and department-schema, are now integrated to
obtain the global schema called university-schema.

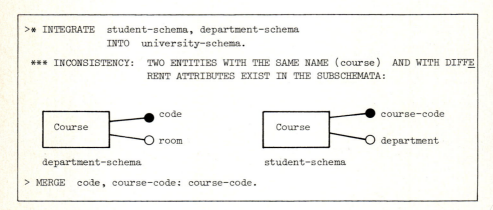

```
>* INTEGRATE   student-schema, department-schema
            INTO   university-schema.

 *** INCONSISTENCY:  TWO ENTITIES WITH THE SAME NAME (course)  AND WITH DIFFE
                    RENT ATTRIBUTES EXIST IN THE SUBSCHEMATA:
```

department-schema   student-schema

```
> MERGE   code, course-code: course-code.
```

The integration process is guided by the system. The first inconsistency detected concerns with the first step of the integration process (see section 4.3):
two entities with the same name and different attributes exist in the subschema
ta. The inconsistency is solved by declaring the key attributes (code and cour-
se-code) as synonymous (command MERGE): the system builds the integrated entity
by aggregation the remaining attributes.

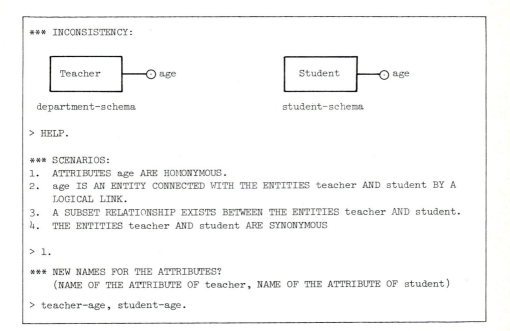

```
*** INCONSISTENCY:
```

department-schema   student-schema

```
> HELP.

*** SCENARIOS:
1.  ATTRIBUTES age ARE HOMONYMOUS.
2.  age IS AN ENTITY CONNECTED WITH THE ENTITIES teacher AND student BY A
    LOGICAL LINK.
3.  A SUBSET RELATIONSHIP EXISTS BETWEEN THE ENTITIES teacher AND student.
4.  THE ENTITIES teacher AND student ARE SYNONYMOUS

> 1.

*** NEW NAMES FOR THE ATTRIBUTES?
    (NAME OF THE ATTRIBUTE OF teacher, NAME OF THE ATTRIBUTE OF student)

> teacher-age, student-age.
```

The new incosistency refers to the entities student and teacher: the designer
asks 'or the scenarios and chooses the first one.

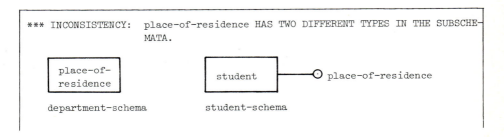

```
*** INCONSISTENCY:   place-of-residence HAS TWO DIFFERENT TYPES IN THE SUBSCHE-
                     MATA.
```

department-schema   student-schema

> HELP.

*** SCENARIOS:

1. THE ENTITY AND THE ATTRIBUTE ARE HOMONYMOUS.
2. THE ATTRIBUTE place-of-residence REPRESENTS A LOGICAL LINK BETWEEN THE
    ENTITIES student AND place-of-residence.

> 2.

*** NAME FOR THE NEW RELATIONSHIP?

> st-city.

*** INCONSISTENCY: department HAS TWO DIFFERENT TYPES IN THE SUBSCHEMATA.

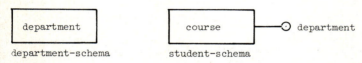

department-schema   student-schema

>* DOC.
>   department, course: PATH.

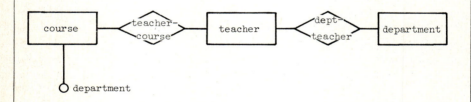

>* RETURN.

Type inconsistencies are now shown to the designer. In one case he asks for do
cumentation about the temporary integrated schema.

> DELETE: department.

*** IN WHICH SUBSCHEMATA?

> student-schema.

The designer recognizes that the attribute department of the entity course represents the same logical link as the path existing between the entities course
and department: so he deletes the attribute department.
Now the fourth step of the integration process begins: all the transactions defined in the two subschemata must be defined in terms of the integrated schema,
which is shown to the designer:

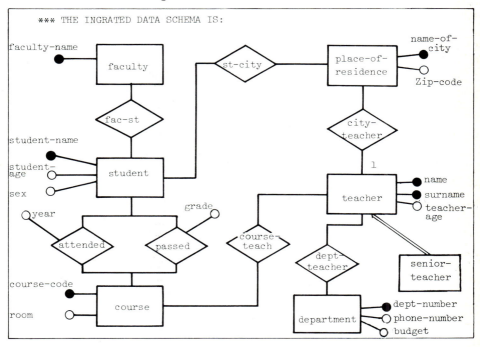

```
*** THE FOLLOWING TRANSACTION MUST BE UPDATED:

    EXECUTABLE TRANSACTION course

        FIND  course
        THROUGH  attended
        HAVING FOUND  student  WITH  (place-of-residence = INPUT)
                THROUGH  fac-st
                HAVING FOUND  faculty  WITH  (faculty-name = INPUT).


 *** INCONSISTENCY:  place-of-residence IS DEFINED IN THE INTEGRATED SCHEMA
                     AS AN ENTITY.

 > HELP.

 *** SCENARIO:

 1.  NEW VERSION OF TRANSACTION:

        FIND  course
        THROUGH  attended
        HAVING FOUND  student
                BEGIN
                    THROUGH  st-city
                    HAVING FOUND  place-of-residence WITH (name-of-city=INPUT)
                AND
                    THROUGH  fac-st
                    HAVING FOUND  faculty WITH (faculty-name = INPUT)
                END.

 > 1.
        END OF THE INTEGRATION.

 >* RETURN.
```

The designer accepts the solution suggested by the system: the transaction is
now consistent with the integrated schema. Finally the integration module is re
leased.

6. *Conclusions.*

In this paper the general characteristics of INCOD have been described.
At present, a prototypal implementation of the control, design, documentation and integration module is in progress.
With regard to the use of INCOD in a design environment, we are investigating which kind of tools could be used in the phase of Requirement Analysis in an integrated methodology that make use of INCOD in the phase of Conceptual Design.

References.

[ABLV] P. ATZENI, C.BATINI, M.LENZERINI, F.VILLANELLI – INCOD: A System for conceptual design of data and transactions in the Entity-Relationship Model: extended description. Technical Report-Ist. Automatica, Roma, Italy, In print.

[AC] P.ATZENI, P.CHEN – A Preliminary Definition of the Completeness of Query Languages for the Entity Relationship Model. This Volume.

[AV] P.ATZENI, F.VILLANELLI – A query and manipulation language for the E-R Model – Proc. of AICA Congress, Italy, 1981.

[BD] A.P.BUCHMANN, A.G.DALE – Evaluation criteria for logical data base design methodologies – CAD, Vol. 11, n. 3, 1979.

[BCBP] C.BALDISSERA, S.CERI, G.PELAGATTI, G.BRACCHI – Interactive specification and formal verification of user views in data base design – Proc. VLDB Conf., Rio de Janeiro, 1979.

[BL] C.BATINI, M.LENZERINI – INCOD: A System for interactive conceptual data base design. Proc. of IEEE Design Automation Conf., Nashville, 1981.

[BLS] C.BATINI, M.LENZERINI, G.SANTUCCI – Computer aided methodology for conceptual data base design: extended description – Technical Report DATAID-RT-80-CSCCA-1 Ist. di Automatica, Roma, Italy, 1980.

[BS] C.BATINI, G.SANTUCCI – Top-Down design in the Entity-Relationship model, in [C2].

[C1] P.CHEN – The Entity-Relationship model: toward a unified view of data – Trans. on Data Base Systems, Vol. 1, n. 1, 1976.

[C2] P.CHEN (ed.) – Entity-Relationship approach to Systems Analysis and Design – North Holland, 1980.

[CPB] S.CERI, G.PELAGATTI, G.BRACCHI – A structured methodology for defining static and dynamic aspects of data base applications.-Information Systems, 1981.

[DDS]   Data Dictionary System Working Party - Journal of Development DDSWP, London, 1979.

[K]   L.KERSCHEBERG et al. - Information modelling tools for data base design - Data base directions, Fort Lauredale, Florida, 1980.

[FNS]   A.L.FURTADO, E.J.NEUHOLD,C.S.DOS SANTOS - A data type approach to Entity -Relationship model - In [C2].

[NO]   1978 New Orleans Data Base Design Workshop Report - IBM Report RJ2554 (33154).

[P]   G.POONEN - CLEAR: a conceptual language for entities and relationships. - ICMOD, Milano, 1978.

[S]   A.SHOSHANI - CABLE: A language based on the Entity-Relationship model. - Rep. UCID-8005, Univ. of California, Berkeley, 1978.

[SS]   G.SHIFFNER, P.SHEUERMANN - Multiple views and abstraction with an extended Entity-Relationship model - Journal of Computer Languages, 1980.

[SSW]   P.SHEUERMANN, G.SHIFFNER, H.WEBER - Abstraction capabilities and invariant properties modelling within the Entity-Relationship approach. - In [C2].

APPENDIX 1

Syntax of the Conceptual Transaction Language

```
<conceptual-trans>::= <obj-declaration> [;<conceptual-trans>]
<obj-declaration>::= <name>:<type>
<type>::=?|ENT|<attribute>|<relationship>
<attribute>::= <attr-specification>OF<name>:<attr-operand>
<attr-specification>::= ATT|ATKEY|ATNK|KEY
<attr-operand>::=?|ENT|<relationship>
<relationship>::= REL AMONG <name>: ENT {<name>:ENT}^n_1
<name>::=<char> [<name>]
<char>::= A|B|C|...
```

APPENDIX 2

Syntax of the Navigational Transaction Language

```
<navigational-trans>:: [FUNCTION]<retrieve>
                       DELETE <retrieve>
                       MODIFY (<id-list>) IN <retrieve>
                       INSERT <id> (<id-list>) [SON OF <outent>]
                       CREATE <id> (<id-list>) BETWEEN
                         <outent> {AND<outent>}^n_1 END
```

`<retrieve>::=<outent>|<outrel>`

$$\text{<outrel>::=} \left\{ \begin{array}{l} \text{FIND} \\ \text{FOUND} \end{array} \right\} \text{<rel> [<having-expr>]}$$

$$\text{<outent>::=} \left\{ \begin{array}{l} \text{FIND} \\ \text{FOUND} \end{array} \right\} \text{<ent> [<through-expr>]}$$

`<having-expr>::=<having-term>|` BEGIN `<having-expr>` AND
`<having-expr>` END

`<having-term>::=` HAVING `<outent>`

`<through-expr>::= <through-term>|` BEGIN `<through-expr>` AND
`<through-expr>` END

`<through-term>::=` THROUGH HAVING `<rel>|`
$$\left\{ \begin{array}{l} \text{<through-clause>} \\ \text{<hierarchy-clause>} \end{array} \right\} \text{<having-expr>}$$

`<through-clause>::=` THROUGH `<rel>`

$$\text{<hierarchy-clause>::=} \begin{array}{l} \text{ASCENDING} \\ \text{DESCENDING} \end{array} \text{<hierarchy>}$$

`<ent>::=<id> [ INVOLVING (<ent-pred>)]`

`<rel>::=<id> [ INVOLVING (<rel-pred>)]`

`<hierarchy>::= <id>|` SUBSET| SUPERSET

`<ent-pred>::= <id-list>|`

$$[\text{<id-list>;]} \left\{ \text{<id> VERSUS [FUNCTION]<id>OF} \left\{ \begin{array}{l} \text{THAT} \\ \text{THOSE} \\ \text{<retrieve>} \end{array} \right\} \text{<ent-ret>;} \right\}_1^n$$

`<ent-ret>::=` FOUND `<through-expr>`

`<rel-pred>::= <id-list>|`

$$[\text{<id-list>]} \left\{ \text{<id> VERSUS [FUNCTION]<id> OF} \left\{ \begin{array}{l} \text{THAT} \\ \text{THOSE} \\ \text{<retrieve>} \end{array} \right\} \text{<rel-ret>;} \right\}_1^n$$

`<rel-ret>::=` FOUND `<having-expr>`

`<id-list>::= <id> [ <id-list>]`

`<id>::= <char> [ <id>]`

APPENDIX 3

Syntax of the Executable Transaction Language

`<executable-trans>::= [ <function>] <retrieve>|`
DELETE `<retrieve>|`
MODIFY (`<value-list>`) IN `<retrieve>|`
INSERT `<id>` (`<value-list>`) [SON OF `<outent>`] |
CREATE `<id>` [(`<value-list>`)] BETWEEN
`<outent>` {AND `<outent>`}$_1^n$ END

```
<retrieve>::= <outent>|<outrel>
<outrel>::=  {FIND  }  <rel> [<having-expr>]
             {FOUND }

<outent>::=  {FIND  }  <ent> [<through-expr>]
             {FOUND }
<having-expr>::= [NOT] <having-term>|
        [NOT] BEGIN <having-expr><bool-op><having-op> END
<having-term>::= HAVING  {{EACH}}  <outent>
                         {{ALL }}

<through-expr>::= [NOT] <through-term>|
        [NOT] BEGIN <through-term><bool-op><through-term> END
<through-term>::= THROUGH HAVING <rel>|
                  {<through-clause> }  <having-expr>
                  {<hierarchy-clause>}
<through-clause>::= THROUGH <rel>
<hierarchy-clause>::=  {ASCENDING }  <hierarchy>
                       {DESCENDING}
<ent>::= <id> [<manip-clause>][WITH (<ent-pred>)]
<rel>::= <id> [<manip-clause>][WITH (<rel-pred>)]
<hierarchy>::= <id>|SUBSET|SUPERSET
<ent-pred>::= <ent-term> [<bool-op><ent-term>]
<ent-term>::= (<ent-pred>)|NOT (<pred-ent>|<id><comp-op> {<id>   } |
                                                         {<const>}
              |<id><comp-op>  {         <id> OF{ {{THAT  }
                              {<function> ON{ {{THOSE{ <ent-ret>}
                                                  <retrieve>}

<ent-ret>::= WITH (<ent-pred>)|FOUND <through-expr>
<rel-pred>::= <rel-term> [<bool-op><rel-term>]
<rel-term>::= (<rel-pred>)|NOT (<rel-pred>|<id><comp-op> {<id>   } |
                                                        {<const>}
              {          <id> OF{ {{THAT  }
              {<function> ON{ {{THOSE{ <rel-ret>}
                                <retrieve>}

<rel-ret>::= WITH (<rel-pred>)|FOUND <having-expr>
<manip-clause>::= DISPLAY (<id-list>) [DELETE] | DELETE
<bool-op>::= AND|OR
<id-list>::= <id> [<id-list>]
<function>::= MAX|MIN|COUNT|AVG (<id>)|EXIST
<comp-op>::==|≠|<|≤|>|≥
<id>::= <char> [<id>]
<value-list>::= <id>:= <const> {;<id>: = <const>}
<const>::= INPUT|'<id>'
```

Entity-Relationship Approach to
Information Modeling and Analysis, P.P. Chen (ed.)
Elsevier Science Publishers B.V. (North-Holland)
©ER Institute, 1983

A Development of a Conceptual Schema Design Aid
in the Entity—Relationship Model

Hirotaka Sakai* Hidefumi Kondo** Zenshiro Kawasaki**

 * Hitachi Institute of Technology, Hitachi,Ltd., Tokyo, JAPAN
** Systems Development Laboratory, Hitachi,Ltd., Kawasaki, JAPAN

ABSTRACT

The development of CSDA, a tool for the conceptual schema
design of databases based on the Entity—Relationship approach, is
described. The data dictionary CSD, as the kernel of CSDA, stores
the comprehensive elements of the schema. Designers can
interactively handle these elements through the command language
CSDL. In this article, the capabilities of CSD and the language
interface are described. The usefulness of the
Entity—Relationship approach to the implementation of CSDA itself
is also discussed.

1. INTRODUCTION

The conceptual schema design using the ER (Entity—Relationship) model has
now culminated in one of the most attractive approaches in the logical design
of databases[1]. In order to establish a truly useful design methodology
based on the ER approach, we need a design aid for analysts and designers to
support the information analysis and structural design activities. We
developed the Conceptual Schema Design Aid (abbr. CSDA) for this purpose.

The capabilities required for CSDA are :

(a) to design stepwise and interactively the conceptual schema in the
framework of the ER model.

(b) to design views independently of each other, and integrate them step by
step into a single conceptual schema.

(c) to optionally use several user interface facilities such as the command
language, the graphics, and the table format interface.

(d) to easily update and maintain the meta data(i.e. the data for the
conceptual schema) in response to changes of requirements.

(e) to flexibly name the components of the schema, allowing the use of
synonyms (different names of the same thing) and homonyms (different

things with the same name).

(f) to describe the meanings of and the integrity constraints on the components of the schema.

In our database design approach, the fundamental means to describe the conceptual schema are the ER schema description and the ER diagram.

In addition to the notions proposed by Chen[2,3], we use the schema description by Sakai[4,5], and the notions on the extended ER model proposed by Santos-Neuhold-Furtado[7], Scheuermann-Schiffner-Weber[8], and Schiffner-Scheuermann[9].

CSDA was developed as a data dictionary system. The data dictionary is called the Conceptual Schema Dictionary (abbr. CSD).

In this article, we describe about CSD and the user interface called the Conceptual Schema Definition Language(abbr. CSDL).

Besides CSDL, the graphic and tabular interfaces are also a part of the CSDA which has yet to be implemented.

2.   THE ER MODEL AND THE ER DIAGRAM

We present very brief summary of the ER model. A more complete description can be found in other literature [2,3,4,5].

In the ER model, information is presented using the three conceptual elements : entities, relationships among entities, and values. The set of similar entities, similar relationships, and similar values in certain contexts are called an E set, an R set, and a V set respectively.

An E set is described in the form $E(A1/V1, A2/V2,...,An/Vn)$, where E is a name of the E set, Ai/Vi ($i = 1,2,...,n$) is an attribute/V set pair. The attribute Ai is a property of an E set, and is defined as a function from E into the V set Vi. When $X = \{A1,A2,...,Ak\}$ is a minimal set of attributes which gives one-to-one mapping from E into the Cartesian product $V1 \times V2 \times ... \times Vk$, we call X an identifier of E. The description of an E set is simply denoted $E(\underline{A1,A2,...,Ak},Ak+1,...,An)$ in which the identifier is underscored. If there exist more than one identifier, we arbitrarily select one and underscore it.

An R set is a set to relate several (not necessarily distinct) E sets E1, E2, ..., and Em. It is a set of tuples $(e1,e2,...,em)$ of mutually related entities ei of Ei($i = 1,2,...,m$). An R set is described in the form $R(E1/L1,E2/L2,...,Em/Lm :A1/V1,A2/V2,...An/Vn)$. R is a name of the R set. Ei/Li ($i = 1,2,...,m$) is an E set/role pair where Li is a name of the role that Ei plays in R. An R set may have attribute/V set pairs Aj/Vj ($j =$

1,2,...,n) too. In this case, the attribute Aj is a function from R into Vj. The simple version of the R set description is denoted R(E1,E2,...,Em : A1,A2,...,An).

The ER model is constructed as a set of E sets and R sets, and is illustrated in the ER diagram, in which an E set and an R set are represented by rectangular- and diamond-shaped boxes respectively. Participation of an E set in an R set is indicated by an arc connecting the two.

In the R set R(E1, E2, ..., Em : A1, A2, ..., An), the mapping ratio is defined as follows.

For an entity ei of Ei (i = 1,2,...,m), the mapping ratio of ei with respect to R is defined as the number of tuples (e1, e2, ..., ei, ..., em) of R with the i-th component ei fixed, and denoted m(ei, R). The mean, minimum, and maximum mapping ratios of Ei with respect to R are defined as the mean, minimum, and maximum values of m(ei, R) in Ei, and denoted m(Ei, R), $\underline{m}$(Ei, R), and $\overline{m}$(Ei, R) respectively.

E sets and R sets are often generalized or specialized[10]. The generalization is an abstraction which enables a class of individual E sets(or R sets) under a certain category to be thought of generally as a single E set (or R set). Conversely the specialization is a partitioning of a single E set (or R set) into several disjoint E sets (or R sets) under a certain category. In the ER diagram, categories are represented by ovals, and the generalization is indicated by an arrow from the oval to the E set (or R set) that is generalized.

We do not go into the procedure how the conceptual schema in the ER model should be constructed. However, we assume the design steps generally taken are: (1) Define the view for each application, (2) Integrate the views into a single conceptual schema, and (3) Refine the conceptual schema under appropriate notions.

3.   CONCEPTUAL SCHEMA DICTIONARY : CSD

The heart of the design tool CSDA is CSD, a repository to store various elements about the conceptual schema. All the information recognized in each of the design steps should be stored and maintained in the data dictionary. Not only the structured information of the schema elements such as E sets, R sets, categories, V sets, and attributes, but also the unformatted information such as the meanings and the integrity constraints regarding the elements are stored in the form of text descriptions.

CSD is structured in the framework of the ER model. TOTAL was chosen as the underlying database management system to implement CSD, because of the straightforwardness of the translation from the ER model to the TOTAL network model.

Considering that the conceptual schema is integrated from a family of views which in turn consist of E sets and R sets, the schema of CSD is represented as a hierarchy of 'schema', 'view', and 'E or R set'. This structure is illustrated in Fig.1. The description of the elements are given below.

[E sets]

(1) schema : S(SNAME,DESIGNER,VERSION,DATE,COMMENT)

(2) view : W(WNAME,DESIGNER,VERSION,DATE,COMMENT)

(3) E or R set : ER(WNAME,ERNAME,ER-INDICATOR)

The name of E sets and R sets are qualified with the view name. The E or R set 'ER' is specialized into the E set 'E' and the R set 'R' under the category 'ER-CAT'.

[R sets]

(4) schema and its constituent views : S-W(S,W : COMMENT)

(5) view and its constituent E sets and R sets : W-ER(W,ER : COMMENT)

[categories]

(6)   category   to   spcialize   'ER'   into   'E'   and   'R'   :
       ER-CAT(ER/GENERIC,E/SPECIFIC,R/SPECIFIC : ER-INDICATOR)

The more detailed version of the schema of CSD, i.e. the version after the specialization of 'ER', is illustrated in Fig.2. Their descriptions are as follows.

[E sets]

(7) E set : E(WNAME,ENAME,CARDINALITY,COMMENT)

(8) R set :R(WNAME,RNAME,CARDINALITY,COMMENT)

(9) category :C(WNAME,CNAME,COMMENT)

(10) V set :V(WNAME,VNAME,TYPE,RANGE,COMMENT)

(11) attribute :A(WNAME,ERNAME,ANAME,RANGE,COMMENT)

WNAME, ENAME, RNAME, CNAME, VNAME, ANAME, and ERNAME are attributes representing the names of views, E sets, R sets, categories, V sets, attributes, and E or R sets respectively. The names of E sets, R sets, categories,and V sets are qualified with the view name. Namely, these names should be unique in the same view, while it is allowed the same name can

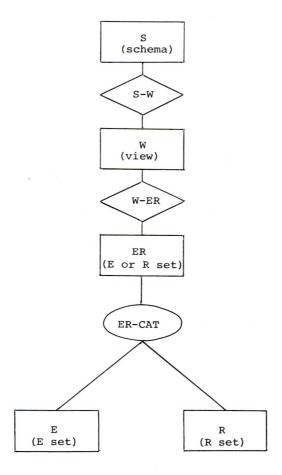

Fig. 1   The ER Diagram of CSD.

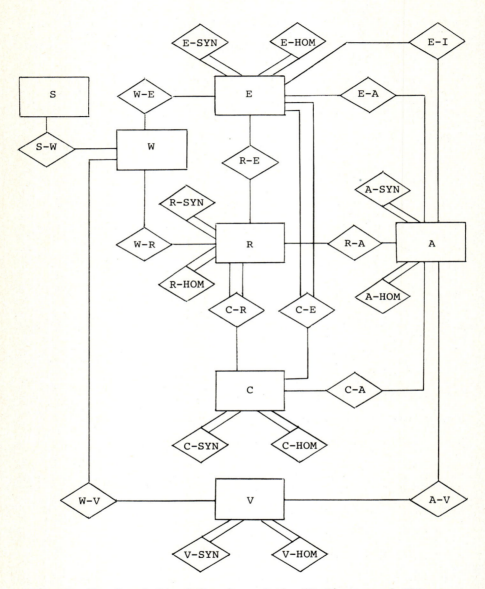

Fig. 2   The Specialized Version of the ER Diagram of CSD.

appear in different views with different meanings(homonym). The name of attributes are qualified with the view name and the E or R set name. The same attribute name can appear in different E sets or R sets with different meanings even in the same view.

On the other hand, synonyms can appear for each element from (7) to (11). For the elements from (7) to (10), different names representing the same thing can be used in different views, and for the element of (11), different names representing the same attribute can be used in the same view.

[R sets]

(12) E set and its attributes : E-A(E,A:COMMENT)

(13) E set and its identifier : E-I(E,A:COMMENT)

(14) R set and its attributes : R-A(R,A:COMMENT)

(15) R set and related E sets : R-E(R,E:ROLE, MAPPING-RATIO,COMMENT)

(16) attribute and its associated V set : A-V(A,V:RANGE,COMMENT)

(17) category and E sets : C-E(C,E/GENERIC,E/SPECIFIC:COMMENT)

(18) category and R sets : C-R(C,R/GENERIC,R/SPECIFIC:COMMENT)

'C-E' (or'C-R') represents the relationships among the category C, the generalized E set E/GENERIC (or R set R/GENERIC), and the specialized E set E/SPECIFIC (or R set R/SPECIFIC).

(19) category and its associated attributes of the generalized E or R set : C-A(C,A:COMMENT)

(20) view and its constituent E sets : W-E(W,E:COMMENT)

(21) view and its constituent R sets : W-R(W,R:COMMENT)

(22) view and its constituent V sets : W-V(W,V:COMMENT)

For each of the E sets 'E', 'R', 'C', 'V', and 'A', there exist R sets 'E-SYN', 'R-SYN', 'C-SYN', 'V-SYN', and 'A-SYN' respectively, maintaining the synonym chains. By the same token, the R sets 'E-HOM', 'R-HOM', 'C-HOM', 'V-HOM' and 'A-HOM' maintain the homonym chains. Only the descriptions of 'E-SYN' and 'E-HOM' are given here.

(23) E set synonym : E-SYN(E,E:COMMENT)

(24) E set homonym : E-HOM(E,E:SD-INDICATOR,COMMENT)

SD-INDICATOR is the attribute to indicate whether two E sets with the same name are same or different things.

4. CONCEPTUAL SCHEMA DEFINITION LANGUAGE : CSDL

CSDL is an interactive command language to stepwise construct the
conceptual schema. By the execution of CSDL commands in TSS mode, the
elements of CSD are created, retrieved, modified, or deleted. The objects of
the command operations are the elements of CSD such as 'E'(E set), 'R'(R set),
'C'(category), 'V'(V set), 'A'(attribute), 'S'(schema), 'W'(view),
'Y'(synonym), and 'H'(homonym), though the last two elements, 'Y' and 'H' are
not explicitly defined as E sets in CSD. On these objects, four types of
operations, 'C'(Create), 'G'(Get), 'M'(Modify), and 'D'(Delete) are executed.
The CSDL command codes are provided in combined forms of the objects and
operations. For example, the code 'GE' stands for 'Get E set'. The whole
codes are listed in Fig.3.

	Create	Get	Modify	Delete
S(schema)	CS	GS	MS	DS
W(view)	CW	GW	MW	DW
Y(synonym)	CY	GY	MY	DY
H(homonym)	CH	GH	MH	DH
E(E-set)	CE	GE	ME	DE
R(R-set)	CR	GR	MR	DR
C(category)	CC	GC	MC	DC
V(V-set)	CV	GV	MV	DV
A(attribute)	CA	–	MA	DA

Fig. 3   CSDL Command Code Table.

The basic form of CSDL commands is written as :

    OP   object-name
         SP   sequence-of-names or string
         ....
         SP   sequence-of-names or string

'OP' is a command code and 'object-name' is a name of a schema element.
The command code is often followed by one or more specifications. 'SP' is a

specifier   code   which   represents   the   type   of   the   specification   for
'sequence-of-names' or 'string'.

For example, the following is the syntax of 'CR'(Create R set) command.

```
CR   r-set
     E   e-set1[/role1][:map-ratio1]
         e-set2[/role2][:map-ratio2]
         ..........
         e-setn[/role n][:map-ratio n]
     [A  att1/v-set1[R(range1)]
         att2/v-set2[R(range2)]
         ..........
         attk/v-setk[R(rangek)]]
     [X  "any string"]
```

In this command, 'E' and 'A' specify the E sets to be related by 'r-set'
and the attributes of 'r-set' respectively. In the specification of E sets,
the roles and (mean) mapping ratios may optionally be specified. In the
specification of attributes, the restrictions on value ranges of the
associated V sets in the form (lower-bound, upper-bound) may optionally be
specified. 'X' is the specifier representing a text. Any text description
can be attached to each command in the form :

     X "any string"

We shall explain the usages of the commands taking the case to create the
schema. Let us consider the view 'airline-reservation' illustrated in Fig.4.
Names of the schema elements are written in small letters for visual
convenience.

We first present the expected outline of meta data which will be stored in
CSD by the execution of a sequence of creation commands. The meta data
consists of the following E sets and R sets.

[E sets]

```
E = {passenger, open-flight}
R = {reserve}
V = {person-name, address, phone-no, no-of-seats, flt-no, date}
A = {name, address, phone, no-of-seats, flt#, flt-date,
     no-of-seats-available}
```

[R sets]

```
E-A = {(passenger,name), (passenger,address), (passenger,phone),
       (open-flight,flt#), (open-flight,flt-date),
       (open-flight,no-of-seats-available)}
E-I = {(passenger,name), (passenger,address), (open-flight,flt#),
       (open-flight,flt-date)}
R-A = {(reserve,no-of-seats)}
```

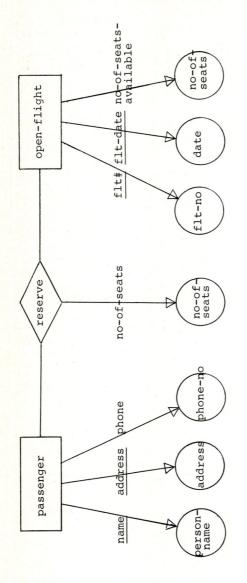

view : 'airline-reservation'

Fig. 4   An Example of the Conceptual Schema.

The meta data described above are created through the execution of the commands in Fig.5(a). In the 'CR'(Create R set) command (04), E sets to be related are specified together with their roles like 'passenger/requestor'. In 'CV'(Create V set) command (05), the types and value ranges of V sets are specified in the form :

    v-set   T("any string")   R("any string")

In 'CA'(Create Attribute) commands (06 to 08), attributes of E sets or R sets are specified together with the associated V sets like 'name/person-name'. In the case of E sets, the identifiers are also specified. The 'CV' and 'CA'commands (05 to 08), which supply the information about the detailed structures of E sets and R sets, could be executed later separately from the associated 'CE' and 'CR' commands (02 to 04). On the other hand, if the objects had been well analyzed, these information could be supplied within the 'CE' and 'CR' commands. For example, the commands 02 and 06 in Fig.5(a) can be combined into a single command as shown in Fig.5(b).

Next we consider the generalization/specialization of E sets as exemplified in Fig.6. This information is created through the commands in Fig.5(c) which define the view 'personnel'.

Synonyms and homonyms are also specified through 'CY'(Create Synonym) and 'CH'(Create Homonym) commands. For example, suppose that the E set name 'flying' in the view 'personnel' were used to refer to the same E set as 'open-flight' in the view 'airline-reservation'. Then 'flying' of 'personnel' should be specified to be a synonym of 'open-flight' of 'airline-reservation' by the command in Fig.5(d). The names specified in 'CY' command are linked each other making up a synonym chain in CSD. Similarly, 'CH' command is used to generate a homonym chain.

Several views are integrated into a schema through 'CS'(Create Schema) command. In our example, two views are integrated into a schema 'airline-database' through the command in Fig.5(e).

5.   TRANSACTION DESCRIPTIONS OF CSDL COMMANDS

For convenience of the implementation of the CSDL processor, the procedural steps that CSDL commands should take internally are described in the form of transaction descriptions.

Originally, the transaction description has been introduced in [6] as a general purpose method to formally describe the behavioral properties in conceptual schemas. By this means, the characteristics of transactions such as types, precedence, and propagations of operations on the database are made clear.

Since CSDL commands can be thought as transactions forwarded to CSD, the function of each command is represented in the transaction description. This

```
01   CW   airline-reservation   X "Create a new view."
02   CE   passenger
03   CE   open-flight
04   CR   reserve
     E    passenger/requestor   open-flight/reserved
05   CV   person-name    T("string of length under 20")
          address        T("string of length under 20")
          no-of-seats    T("integer") R("depends on plane type")
          flt-no         T("XX999")
          date           T("MMDDYY")
06   CA   E  passenger
          I  name   address
          A  name/person-name   address/address   phone/phone-no
07   CA   E  open-flight
          I  flt#   flt-date
          A  flt#/flt-no   flt-date/date
             no-of-seats-available/no-of-seats
08   CA   R  reserve
          A  no-of-seats/no-of-seats
```

Fig. 5(a)   A Sequence of Create Commands.


```
09   CE   passenger
          I  name   address
          A  name/person-name   address/address   phone/phone-no
          X  "Create E set together with its identifier(I) and
             attributes(A)."
```

Fig. 5(b) 'CE' Command including 'I' and 'A' Specification.

```
10   CW   personnel
11   CE   employee
12   CE   pilot
13   CE   stewardess
14   CE   operator
15   CC   job-class
          GE   employee
          SE   pilot   stewardess   operator
          X    "Create Category to specialize 'employee' into
               'pilot', 'stewardess', and 'operator'."
16   CE   flying
17   CR   assign
          E   employee/work   flying/worked-for
```

Fig. 5(c)   Commands for Generalization/Specialization.

```
18   CY   E   personnel.flying   airline-reservation.open-flight
```

Fig. 5(d)   Command for Synonym Definition.

```
19   CS   airline-database
          W   airline-reservation   personnel
```

Fig. 5(e)   Commands for View Integration.

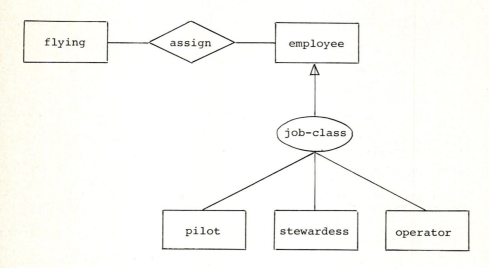

view : 'personnel'

Fig. 6   An Example of the Generalization/Specialization.

is a practically useful and easy-to-understand means to express the effect of
the command execution, particularly to express its update propagation. The
transaction description can be translated systematically into the TOTAL data
manipulation language. It is straightforward therefore to implement each CSDL
command as a sequence of TOTAL data manipulation commands.

In order to show a few sample transaction descriptions for the CSDL
commands, we shall first give a brief explanation of the transaction
description.

Query and update requests for a database are called transactions. A
transaction which refers to at most one R set is said a simple transaction.
Any transaction T is decomposed into a sequecnce of simple transactions S1,
S2, ..., Sn. We write this fact T = S1 S2 ... Sn.

A simple transaction is described in either the primary or the secondary form.

(1) the primary form

$S = op(U)$.

In this form, op and U are the type and the object of operations respectively. The form of op is any of the codes 'get', 'cr'(create), 'del'(delete), and 'mod'(modify). The primary form has the following functional meanngs depending on the op types.

(a) $S = get(E)$, or $S = cr(E)$.

Retrieve entities from, or add entities to the E set E. The entities which are retrieved from or added to E are called the object space of S, and denoted $\underline{S}$.

(b) $S = del(\underline{S}')$, or $S = mod(\underline{S}')$.

Delete or modify the object space $\underline{S}'$ of the simple transaction S'. $\underline{S}'$ could be an object space of the secondary form. In this case, $\underline{S}'$ is a subset of an E set or an R set.

Consider for example a general transaction Ta requesting update operations on the 'airline-reservation' database in Fig. 4, stating "Reduce the no-of-seats-available of 'JL001' on 'October 10' to zero." Then Ta is described in the form :

Ta = Sa1 Sa2,

where Sa1 = get(open-flight), and Sa2 = mod($\underline{Sa1}$).

(2) the secondary form

$S = \underline{S1}\ \underline{S2}\ ...\ \underline{Sk}(R) : op(U)$.

In this form, op and U represent the type and the object of operations respectively. The code for op is either 'get' or 'cr'. Si (i = 1,2,...,k) is the simple transaction which should have been executed before S, and $\underline{Si}$ is its object space. R is a name of the R set to be referred to. Si itself could be a secondary form. In such a case, the object space $\underline{Si}$ represent the set of elements which are retrieved from or added to U by the operation 'get' or 'cr'.

The meaning of the secondary form is as follows.

(a) $S = \underline{S1}\ \underline{S2}\ ...\ \underline{Sk}(R) : get(U)$.

Retrieve the entities from the E set U which are related to $\underline{S1}$, $\underline{S2}$, ..., and <u>Sk</u> by the R set R, or retrieve the relationships from the R set U which include <u>S1</u>, <u>S2</u>, ..., and <u>Sk</u> as participants in U.

(b) S = <u>S1 S2 ... Sk</u>(R) : cr(R).

Create the relationships of the R set R which relate <u>S1</u>, <u>S2</u>, ..., and <u>Sk</u> in terms of R, and add them to R.

Consider the reconfirmation transaction Tb forwarded to the 'airline-reservation' database in Fig. 4, stating "Reconfirm the reservation status of 'JL001' on 'December 10' for the passenger 'A'." This transaction requires to retrieve the relevant entities from the E sets 'passenger' and 'open-flight' respectively, and retrieve the relationship of the R set 'reserve' which relates them. Thus we have the following descriptions :

Tb = Sb1 Sb2 Sb3.

The three simple transactions are given by :

Sb1 = get(passenger),

Sb2 = get(open-flight),

Sb3 = <u>Sb1 Sb2</u>(reserve) : get(reserve).

For a simple transasction S, the notation S* represents that S is repeatedly executed. Further, the notation [S] means that S may or may not be executed depending on cicumstantial conditions.

Applying the transaction descriptions to each CSDL command, its procedural steps are formally expressed.

<u>Example 1</u> Consider the simple version of 'CR'(Create R set) command :

        CR   r-set
        E   e-set1/role1 e-set2/role2 ... e-setn/rolen

The effect of this command is described in the following sequence of simple transaction descriptions.

T('CR') = S1* S2 S3*.

S1 = get(E)

S2 = cr(R)

S3 = <u>S1 S2</u>(E-R) : cr(E-R)

It is assumed that the entities 'e-seti' (i = 1,2,...,n) already exist in the E set 'E' in CSD. S1 represent that the entity 'e-seti' should be retrieved from 'E' in CSD. S1 should be executed repeatedly for i =

1,2,...,n. S2 states that the entity 'r-set' should be added to the E set 'R'. In S3, the relationship which relates <u>S1</u> ('e-seti' of 'E') and <u>S2</u>('r-set' of 'R') in terms of the R set 'E-R' is created and added to 'E-R'. S3 should also be repeated n times.

Example 2 'CA'(Create Attribute) command
```
        CA  E    e-set
            [I   att1  att2  ...  attk]
            A    att1/v-set1
                 att2/v-set2
                 ..........
                 attn/v-setn
```

The transaction description for this command is given by :

T('CA') = S1 S2* [S3*] S4* S5* S6*.

S1 = get(E)

S2 = cr(A)

S3 = <u>S1</u> <u>S2</u>(E-I) : cr(E-I)

S4 = <u>S1</u> <u>S2</u>(E-A) : cr(E-A)

S5 = get(V)

S6 = <u>S2</u> <u>S5</u>(A-V) : cr(A-V)

Each of the simple descriptions are almost self-explanatory. It is assumed that the entity 'e-set' of 'E' and entities 'v-seti' of 'V' have been created before the execution of 'CA'. The description S3, which represents the creation of the relationship between 'e-set' and its identifier 'atti', may or may not be executed depending on the existence of the specifier 'I'.

The transaction descriptions claim the usefulness particularly for the 'Delete' commands which cause a fair amount of update propagation.

6.   CONCLUSION

The development of the Conceptual Schema Design Aid CSDA based on the ER approach, consisting of the data dictionary CSD and three types of interactive user interface facilities, was introduced.

CSD stores the comprehensive elements of the conceptual schema, such as E sets, R sets, categories, V sets, attributes, views, synonyms, homonyms, and relationships between them. CSD itself was described in terms of the ER model. This has proved the effectiveness of the ER approach to the database design of CSD.

   Among three types of interface facilities, the functions of the Conceptual
Schema Definition Language CSDL to create, get, modify, and delete the
elements of CSD were described.   The transaction descriptions on the CSDL
commands has also turned out to be a useful means to reduce the implemetation
cost.

   In order to make CSDA more practically useful, the systematic procedure for
the conceptual schema design and semi-automatic data translator from ER to
other data models, which work cooperatively with CSDA, are required.

7. REFERENCES

[1] P.P.Chen ed.   : Entity-Relationship Approach to Systems Analysis and
     Design(North-Holland, Amsterdam, 1980).

[2] P.P.Chen: The Entity-Relationship Model : Towards a Unified View of Data,
     Transactions on Database Systems Vol.1,No.1 pp.9-36(1976).

[3] P.P.Chen : The Entity-Relationship Model : A Basis for the Enterprise View
     of Data, AFIPS Conf. Proc. Vol.46, AFIPS Press, pp.77-84(1977).

[4] H.Sakai : On the Optimization of the Entity-Relationship Model, 3rd
     USA-JAPAN Computer Conf. Proc. pp.145-149(1978).

[5] H.Sakai : Entity-Relationship Approach to the Conceptual Schema Design,
     Proc. ACM-SIGMOD 1980, Santa Monica, California, pp.1-8(1980).

[6] H.Sakai : A Method for Defining Information Structures and Transactions in
     Conceptual Schema Design, Proc. 7th International Conf. on Very Large
     Data Bases(1981).

[7] C.S.dos Santos, E.J.Neuhold, A.L.Furtado : A Data Type Approach to the
     Entity-Relationship Model, in : Entity-Relationship Approach to Systems
     Analysis and Design, pp.103-119(North-Holland, Amsterdam, 1980).

[8] P.Scheuermann, G.Schiffner, H.Weber : Abstraction Capabilities and
     Invariant Properties Modelling within the Entity-Relationship Approach,
     in : Entity-Relationship Approach to Systems Analysis and Design,
     pp.121-140 (North-Holland, Amsterdam, 1980).

[9] G.Schiffner, P.Scheuermann : Multiple Views and Abstractions with an
     Extended-Entity-Relationship Model, Journal of Computer Languages, Vol.4,
     pp.139-154(1979).

[10] J.M.Smith, D.C.Smith : Database Abstractions : Aggregation and
     Generalization, Transactions on Database Systems Vol.2, No.2
     pp.105-133(1977).

Entity-Relationship Approach to
Information Modeling and Analysis, P.P. Chen (ed.)
Elsevier Science Publishers B.V. (North-Holland)
©ER Institute, 1983

An Interactive Query and Definition Facility for Semantic Dictionaries

Erich J. Neuhold
Institut für Informatik
University of Stuttgart
Stuttgart, Fed. Rep. of Germany

Yongxing Qi
On Research Visit from the
Computing Centre of the Ministry for
Metallurgical Industry
Peking, Peoples Republic of China

Data base laymen but also data base designers have to know about the semantic information contained in a data base system. To represent this information, semantic views and conceptual schemas have been developed using various semantic modelling techniques, as for example the Entity-Relationship Model (P. Chen), the Semantic Association Model (S. Su and D. Lo), the Object-Type Model (H. Biller and E. Neuhold) etc. In this paper we represent a form driven dialog facility, which allows a user to specify semantic models, i.e. semantic views and conceptual schemas in a simple and system controlled way. We choose the Semantic Association Model to illustrate the technique which is currently being realized on top of the distributed data base system POREL.

1. INTRODUCTION AND BASIC PRINCIPLES

What objects are stored in a data base? What properties do they have? What relationships exist between these objects? What rules must be observed when manipulating objects?

Questions like these must be answered whenever somebody wants to utilize the data base. Actually these questions are not concerned with the data structures and data values as they are kept in the data base, rather they are oriented towards the semantic data model, i.e. the conceptual description of the data base system, which expresses the meaning of these data and structures as seen by an enterprise. This knowledge is not only important to the data base user, but also to the designer, i.e. the data base administrator, who has to adjust the data base system to the ever changing requirements of a well-functioning enterprise.

We cannot expect the user or designer of a data base to know
or remember all the concepts and structures kept in the data
base system. Therefore, before he will be able to use the data
base or change the semantic data base model, he will have to
inform himself about the properties of the data kept in the
system. In this paper we propose a form-driven dialog technique
which can be utilized for querying, but also for changing and
extending the semantic data base description.

The data base designer will use the technique for querying
and changing both the semantic description of the total data
base - the conceptual schema - and the semantic views of the
data base as provided for the different user categories. A user
on the other hand will be restricted by the system to queries
about his semantic view only. In general, he will be excluded
from changing or extending his view of the data base, as such
changes could indirectly influence the conceptual schema and
therefore the design decisions made by the data base administrator for the whole enterprise.

The conceptual data model and the semantic views will be kept
in the data dictionary. Depending on the modelling principle
chosen, e.g. the Semantic Association Model by S. Su and D. Lo
[7], the Entity-Relationship Model by P. Chen [4] etc., for
describing the meaning of data and data structures kept in the
data base, the data dictionary will allow its user to

a) store information about all the basic and derived semantic
   concepts, entities and relationships composing the semantic
   model,
b) retrieve information about and descriptions of these components,
c) delete, modify and augment the semantic data model,
d) describe the "meta"-concepts, i.e. the principles used in
   representing the semantic data model.

Especially the last property is often forgotten or treated
inadequately when a data dictionary is proposed. We feel, however, that a user who starts with very little knowledge about
data bases, will have to be able to get the meaning of the concepts used in describing the semantic information through the
same means he later will employ to query the data model itself.
For us the data dictionary consists of two parts which we shall
call the model dictionary and the notation dictionary, where the
first describes the semantic model of the data base and the
second contains all the definitional concepts used in representing the model.

We could now have chosen P. Chen's model for our form-driven
data base schema description, as it is composed of a small number
of powerful concepts that lead to a very compact semantic repre-

sentation. However, the user requires for his understanding a
rather detailed description of the real world situation. Consequently, it will be beneficial to select a semantic modelling
technique, where many different concepts already are part of the
technique itself and do not have to be added when using it for
the model dictionary. The Semantic Association Model (SAM) by
S. Su and D.H. Lo [7,8] best satisfied these requirements, and
we have chosen it as our primary semantic representation technique.

SAM explicitly distinguishes a large number of semantic
associations between the different so-called concepts abstracted from the real world. The semantic association types are
based on differences in structural properties, semantic integrity constraints, and operational characteristics of the data
representing the enterprise, and they can be thought of forming
a semantic net as frequently used in information systems. Every
labelled node in the net describes a non-atomic concept (the
atomic concepts being the abstracted actual facts represented in
the data base, e.g. employee name "Ed Brown") and is defined by
the different semantic associations existing in the system. The
edges of the net identify the different relationships between
these concepts, and they will be labelled by the specific semantic roles the relations play in representing the semantic data
base model. We shall not further explain the details of the
Semantic Association Model, but refer the reader to its discussion in S. Su and D.H. Lo [7].

However, the data definition language (DDL) given in that
paper is not sufficient to represent all the information which
has to be included in the semantic dictionary, and we shall have
to extend the language accordingly. In addition, the context concepts of SAM can be seen to either apply to a context layer of a
non-atomic concept or to a definition layer. How can such a fact
be represented? Let us take a subnetwork example from the sample
data base of [4] (Figure 1). The meaning of a concept, e.g.
assignment, is described essentially by labelled arrows to other
concepts.

In contrast to SAM we think that the edges in the semantic net
should be directed to reflect the two aspects "context" and
"definition" more immediately. The concepts of the definition
layer are identified by arrows leading to them. They encompass
all those concepts in the net which contribute to the meaning of
a concept. In the sense of the Data Abstraction Model by Smith &
Smith [6] they describe how a concept is classified, generalized or aggregated by concepts of the definition layer. The
concepts of the context layer and especially the labelled arrows
coming from them describe the role the concept has to play in
the construction of even more complex non-atomic concepts.

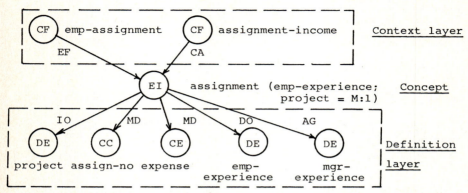

Figure 1: The Context- and Definition-Layers of a Concept

In explaining a concept, we therefore have to specify its name and type but also both the context and the definition layers in addition to any explanatory text required to make the concept meaningful to the user or to the data base designer.

In our discussions we shall use the example given in Figure 2 which represents a segment of the sample data base introduced by Su & Lo [7]. The Set-Relationship type (SR) 'model-dictionary' is defined by the two Subset links (SB) to the concept types Entity-Interaction (EI) and Set-Relationship (SR) of 'assignment', respectively 'all-employee'. The Set-Relationship type 'all-employee' in turn is defined by the two Subset links to the Defined Entity (DE) types 'emp-experience' and 'mgr-experience' together with the Set-Relationship (ST) to the Defined Entity type 'employee'. This ensures that descriptions of an employee in 'emp-experience', respectively 'mgr-experience' only can exist when corresponding occurrences exist in 'employee'. For a detailed description of SAM and a discussion of all the acronyms we again refer to [7,8] as we shall not need a deep understanding of the various SAM features for our further investigations.

We have added the three high level concepts data-dictionary, model-dictionary, and notation-dictionary to the semantic net in order to allow a user to start with these concepts when he wants to gather knowledge about his semantic model without even knowing a single concept name.

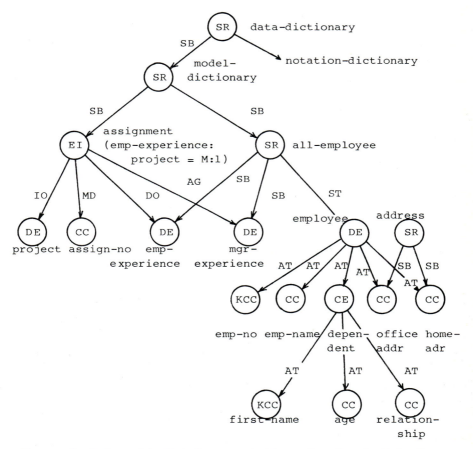

Figure 2: A Semantic Net Representation of a Sample Data Base

2. THE MODEL DICTIONARY

The complete information about the semantic data model of a data base is contained in the model dictionary. In case of SAM, each entry will describe an association type, which may be a concept class (CC), defined entity type (DE) e.t.c. We shall call an entry in the model dictionary an explanation of a concept. (Explanations of what association types may be used in the model dictionary will be contained in the notation dictionary.)

An explanation is composed of a number of sections and each section of one or more paragraphs. Of the different possible sections

                    concept-name
                    concept-type
                    synonym
                    definition
                    identification
                    context
                    comment

only the concept-name section is indispensable, all the others are optional. The comment section may appear more than once. It may actually follow each one of the paragraphs of an explanation. The complete syntax of an explanation is given in Appendix A. In our discussion we only introduce those parts necessary for the examples given at the end of this section.

Concept Name

This section contains only one paragraph which is governed by the syntactic rule

                    name <concept-identifier>

where <concept-identifier> is further explained in the notation dictionary, e.g. we may use any alphanumeric string up to some maximum length. Concept identifiers have to be unique in the model dictionary, i.e. they must uniquely identify the entries in the dictionary and therefore the nodes in the corresponding semantic net.

Concept Type

This section consists of a single paragraph which specifies the semantic type of the explained association where the allowed types are explained in the notation dictionary. In case of SAM these types are

                    concept-class (CC)
                    key-concept-class (KCC)
                    defined-entity (DE)
                    characterizing-entity (CE)
                    entity-interaction (EI)
                    set-relationship (SR)
                    composition (CP)
                    causation (CF)
                    action-means (AM)
                    action-purpose (AP)
                    logical-relation-of-implication (LRI).

In SAM the designer of the data base may introduce new additional concept types. In doing so, he would have to include corresponding notation explanations into the notation dictionary.

Synonym

A concept contained in a dictionary is allowed to have different names. The different names for a specific concept form a synonym class. The synonym section is used to represent the synonym class. One of the names of the class is selected as the concept name of a dictionary entry where the full description of the concept is found. The other names only appear as synonym concepts in the dictionary.

In the first case the synonym section specifies all the synonym names contained in the synonym class of the explained concept. For a synonym entry in the dictionary the synonym section identifies the dictionary entry where the concept associated with the synonym is explained.

Definition

In the definition section the composition of the described concept from more primitive components is explained. In addition the definition section contains assert rules and triggers associated with the described concept.

We distinguish between the definition of a concept-class and the definition of all the other association types.

The concept-class is defined by specifying its domain which is a set of atomic concepts either explicitly specified via enumeration or implicitly by data type and range specifications as found in data base schema definitions. The allowed data types and range specifications are explained in the notation part of the semantic dictionary.

The definition section of the other association types contains a number of paragraphs each describing one of the defining concepts together with its semantic role and an optional specification of its occurrence frequency

<semantic-role> : <concept-name> [<occurrence-spec>]

The possible semantic roles again are explained in the notation dictionary. In case of defined entities the only role possible is Attribute (AT).

In the definition section explicit semantic integrity constraints may be included. Of course, many such constraints are already contained implicitly in our semantic association model

through the specification of the various association types and
occurrence requirements. Further constraints, however, may be
required, and they can be included as additional paragraphs in
the definition section. We distinguish between two types of explicit semantic constraints <u>assert rules</u> and <u>triggers</u> (see also
Su and Lo [7,8].

For example assert rules and triggers which could be attached
to an employee explanation could have the form

> <u>assert</u> (1) <u>on</u> update <u>of</u> dependent:
> · · · test action to be performed
> (2) <u>on</u> update <u>of</u> office-addr:
> · · · test action to be performed
> <u>trigger</u>   <u>on</u> delete <u>of</u> emp-no
> · · · delete actions to be performed

Identification

This section contains one or more paragraphs specifying means
for uniquely identifying the different occurrences of an association type. The first paragraph has the form

> <u>primary</u> <identifying-concept-name>-list

and lists those components of the definition of a concept which
are to be used as <u>primary-keys</u> to identify the different
instances of the concept. The second, third, etc. paragraphs, if
present, have the format

> <u>secondary</u> <identifying-concept-name>-list

and they identify the secondary keys of the explained concept.

Context

The context section describes all those concepts where the
explained concept is used. To identify such a concept properly,
both the semantic role and the concept-name are given in a
paragraph. Of course, the context section could always be
constructed using the definition sections of the different dictionary entries alone. However, for ease of reference, the context section may be included explicitly in the concept
explanation. Each of its paragraphs has the form

> <semantic role> : <concept-name>

where the allowed semantic roles again are explained in the notation dictionary.

Comment

    Comments may follow both sections and paragraphs, and they
contain textual explanations about the purpose and meaning of the
different specified components of a concept explanation.

    A comment following a paragraph has the form

                /p* ... text not containing */ ... */

and a comment following a section has the form

                /s* ... text not containing */ ... */

and they are considered to further explain in terms even casual
users will understand the concepts and concept components contained in the semantic model of the enterprise.

A Sample Model Dictionary

    The model dictionary of the data base model given in Figure 2
will be given (partially) next, whereby the different dictionary
entries have been ordered lexicographically. In reality, many
more comments will have to be given, but for space reasons we
restrict ourselves to only a few.

```
name address
   type set-relationship
   definition SB : office address
              SB : home address
   /s* The home and office addresses may overlap if an employee
       works at home. */

name age
   type concept class
   definition DEC(3) (0<age<150)

name all-employee
   type set-relationship
   definition ST : employee
              SB : mgr-experience
              SB : emp-experience
   context    SB : model-dictionary

name angestellter
   synonym ↑ employee
```

```
name assignment
   type entity-interaction (emp-experience: project = m:1)
   definition AG : mgr-experience
              DO : emp-experience
              ID : project
              MD : assign-no   unique
   identification primary assign_no
   context    SB : model-dictionary

name emp
   synonym ↑ employee

name employee
   type defined-entity
   synonym emp, angestellter
   definition  AT : emp-no   unique
               AT : emp-name
               AT : dependent   multiple
               AT : office-addr
               AT : home-addr
   identification primary   emp-no
                  secondary emp-name   office-addr
   context    ST : all-employee
.
.
.
name relationship
   type concept-class
   definition father, mother, wife, son, daughter
   /s* The domain values e.g. father, mother, etc. can be
       extended whenever the need arises. */
```

3. THE NOTATION DICTIONARY

Whenever a layman or the data base designer wants to use the
semantic data model of a data base he has to understand the
modelling technique used in its representation. In our case we
have chosen SAM, and the principles to be understood include
elements like <concept-name>, <concept-definition>, action-
purpose, attribute, subset etc., that is, all elements used to
build the semantic model.

The notation dictionary - a part of the data dictionary - provides the basis for this information. The entries (their full
syntax is given in Appendix A) enable a layman or data base
designer to understand and use the definitional concepts. In
addition, by adding or modifying entries in the notation dictionary, it becomes possible to easily extend the semantic modelling technique. In SAM, for example, we may add new concept
types, data types or semantic roles to the notation dictionary

and therefore to our modelling tool. In addition, the notation dictionary allows the description of other semantic modelling techniques. We have used the same principles to describe the semantic data modelling tool given by Biller and Neuhold [2] and have tried them successfully with other techniques as described for example in Biller and Neuhold [1].

The notation dictionary has a structure very similar to the model dictionary itself, but entries now are identified by the key word <u>notation</u>.

A notational concept may be an atomic concept or it may itself be derived from more primitive notational concepts. The definition section of the dictionary entry distinguishes these situations. In the first case, an entry may have the form

> <u>notation</u> trigger
>   <u>type</u> meta-concept
> <u>definition</u> <u>basic</u>

In SAM other notational types are for example data-type or syntactic-concept. The last type identifies the notation name as a syntactic element, as for example a non-terminal used in the syntactic description of the data dictionary.

In the second case, the definition section lists all the notation names that are used in its definition, as for example

> <u>notation</u> concept-type
>   <u>type</u> meta-concept
> <u>definition</u> <u>is</u> <u>one</u> <u>of</u> CC, KCC, DE, CE, EI, SR, CP,
>   <u>CF</u>, <u>AM</u>, <u>LRI</u>

where CC, KCC, ... themselves identify entries in the notation dictionary where further explanations can be found.

We may also introduce synonyms for a notational concept e.g.

> <u>notation</u> action-means-association
>   <u>synonym</u> AM, action-means-concept

using a construct very similar to the one used in the model dictionary.

The comment section in case of the notation dictionary plays an even more important role than in case of the model dictionary. It is supposed to give a <u>precise</u> and <u>understandable</u> definition of the properties of a notational concept. Based on these explanations the user of the system has to be able to understand, query and eventually manipulate the conceptual data base model and/or his semantic data base view and through these manipulations gain knowledge about the data stored in the data base system.

4. THE INTERACTIVE DIALOG

The command language QDC (Query and Definition Commands) provides a query and definition facility for the conceptual model of
a data base system. It assumes that the semantic information
about the data base is stored in a data dictionary as discussed
in Sections 2 and 3 of this paper. The language is form-based and
dialog oriented and uses the screen format illustrated in Figure
3. It assumes a system where at least horizontal and vertical
lines can be drawn, but does not require a full graphic terminal.
So far the implementation of the system on top of the distributed
data base management system POREL [5] has not been completed, but
first results about its applicability show large improvements
in interacting with the data base system. Users feel much more
secure about understanding the contents of the data base, and
interactions with the data base therefore become less error-
prone and more reliable.

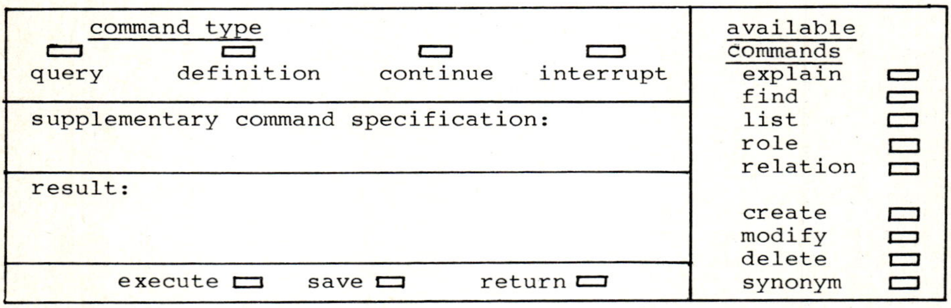

Figure 3: The QDC form

There exist four basic command types: query, definition, continue and interrupt.

The query command type includes commands such as explain a
concept, find the concept names of a category, list the concept
names for a morpheme, query the semantic roles of and the relationships between several concepts. We shall give a more
detailed discussion of these commands in Section 5 and shall
illustrate them with examples.

The definition commands allow us to create concepts, augment
and modify existing concept explanations, delete concepts or
parts of concepts or define existing concepts as synonyms. In
Section 6 we shall discuss these commands and give examples.

In additon to these commands two system control commands exist:

The <u>continue</u> command repeats the previous command or executes a new command in the context created by the previous execution. In this fashion it becomes possible to navigate through the semantic net. For example, if an explain command should produce the concepts to be found in the definition section of the explained concept, then a continue command will produce the explanations for these concepts. Similarly it is possible to follow the links in the semantic net by using a command to query the relationship between concepts and have it followed by a continue command, thus repeating the search for relationships and thereby spreading further and further throughout the net. However, we may also specify a new command together with the continue command. In this case, the result of the new command will be added to the result field of the already existing form allowing to display an ever increasing part of the semantic net and therefore of the semantic description of the data the enterprise uses.

The <u>interrupt</u> command allows us to interrupt the execution of a command and to set the dialog processor to the initial state.

A complete example for a semantic information session is given in Appendix B.

5. THE QUERY FACILITIES OF QDC

The query commands of QDC work both on the model dictionary and the notation dictionary.

5.1 The Explain Command

When using the explain command, the query and explain boxes of the QDC-form have to be tagged. The supplementary command specification part of the form will then show two lines identified by 'explanation:' and 'sections:' to indicate that they have to be filled with the concept- or notation-name to be explained and the segment and/or paragraph names of the components to be shown on the screen. The command will be executed as soon as the execute-box will be marked. In the result field the corresponding section descriptions or error messages will appear. The error messages may also contain suggestions on how the command could be executed successfully. That is, the system will attempt to propose a correction of the error which arose during the execution of the command.

If no section-name is specified, all sections of the explanation will be shown.

An example of a valid supplementary specification (for space reasons not shown inside of the complete form) is

```
explanation: employee
sections: concept-type, identification
```

which will produce the result field

```
type: defined-entity
identification primary emp-no
             secondary emp-name  office-addr
```

If comment sections would have been associated with the displayed sections and paragraphs, they would also have been displayed.

5.2 The Find Command

The find command is used to display the concept-name list found in the definition section of the concept identified by the explanation name specified in the QDC-form. With the aid of this command, we are able to search the data dictionary for components of concepts.

Examples (again not using complete QDC-forms)

1. query ✷   find ✷
   explanation: all-employee
   result: role : ST   type : DE   employee
             role : SB   type : DE   emp-experience
             role : SB   type : DE   mgr-experience

2. Using the result of the example above, we may now specify a continue command and identify one of the three concept names, e.g. employee, in the result field and we would get

   query ✷   continue ✷   find ✷
   explanation: employee
   result: role : AT   type : KCC   emp-no
           ... (for all components)

3. And again using emp-no

   query ✷ continue ✷ find ✷
   explanation: emp-no
   result: No further components: To see the details of
           emp-no use the explain command.

If we assume the concept 'data-dictionary' to be included as the highest concept in every semantic net, a most uninformed user can always start with this concept to gather knowledge about his semantic view or the complete conceptual model (if he is allowed to do so) by repeatedly using the find command.

5.3 The List Command

The list command allows a user to specify only a substring of some explanation name - a morpheme - to gather information about all explanation names which contain that substring. With the list command it is therefore possible to get explanations for concepts which one cannot identify completely, but also to gather information about concepts which have similar names in the semantic model.

Example (not using complete QDC-forms)

```
query ⌨ list ⌨
explanation:    emp..
result:   type : DE    emp-experience
          type : DE    employee
          type : KCC   emp-no
          type : CC    emp-name
```

Note: The concept name all-employee is not displayed, as the dots .. are used to indicate how the morpheme has to be completed for an explanation name to be shown.

5.4 The Role Command

The role command may be used whenever we want to inform ourselves about the different semantic roles a concept plays in the semantic net or reversely find concepts which play a specific role in the semantic model.

The general format of the supplementary command specification part for this command is given in Figure 4 where the QDC-form segment is shown as it will represent itself after the role command has been selected, i.e. tagged.

```
concept name (high):            all    ▭

role:                           some   ▭

concept name (low):
```

Figure 4: The Supplementary Command Specification for the Role Command

By specifying some of the lines in the supplementary command
specification part of the form and leaving others empty, the
desired information can be extracted from the semantic net. We
shall not discuss all the possibilities of this command as they
seem quite evident, but again restrict ourselves to a few
illustrations.

As a result this command produces parts of the semantic net,
which will be displayed in net-form in the result field of the
screen (if the screen allows such graphic forms).

Examples (not using complete QDC-forms)

1. query ⬧ role ⬧
   concept name (high): all-employee   all ⬧
   role: subset   some ☐
   concept name (low):
   result:

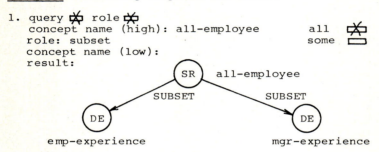

2. query ⬧ role ⬧
   concept name (high):   all ⬧
   role: some ☐
   concept name (low): mgr-experience
   result

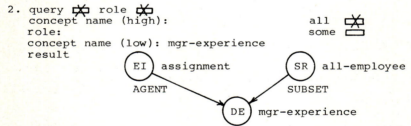

3. query ⬧ role ⬧
   concept name (high): emp-no   all ☐
   role: member   some ☐
   concept name (low): 1265
   result: yes

This query only determines whether 1265 is a possible, i.e.
well-formed, employee number. It does not determine whether
such an employee number actually exists in the data base.
A data base query command of the data base manipulation language, e.g. SQL [3], has to be used to query and manipulate
the actual data base. Our commands only refer to the conceptual
schema respectively the semantic views of a data base system.

4. query ✠ role ✠
   ```
   concept name (high): all-employee        ill  ▭
   role:                                    ome  ✠
   concept name (low): office-addr
   result: No direct relationship exists. Use the continue
           command to ask about indirect relationships starting
           with either the high or the low concept name. Another
           command which could be used is the relation command.
   ```

Especially Examples 1 and 2 can be used to find for a specific concept name its context and/or definition, that is concepts
which incorporate this concept name in some semantic role or are
part of it. The role command allows to traverse the semantic net
in an upward or downward fashion. Using the continue command and
selecting one or even more of the concepts displayed in the result field, navigation through the net will be simple and fast.

Notice that the user may always enquire about possible role
names, the meaning of a specific role name or any other notational term by referring to the notation part of the data dictionary. Using the <u>save</u> field in the QDC-form he is able to
temporarily save the form, then use other QDC-facilities for his
work and later return to the saved QDC-form by tagging the
<u>return</u> field of the QDC-form he then uses. So far we have not
introduced any form-naming facility which would allow a user to
directly return to a specific previous form, but if the usefulness of such a facility should be demonstrated, it could
easily be incorporated into QDC.

5.5 The Relation Command

The relation command can be used to query the semantic model
about the relationship of two arbitrary concepts. This relationship can be direct or indirect, and the command will display
those parts of the net which are involved in the relationship.

The supplementary command specification section of the relation command is shown in Figure 5. If the net that has to be
displayed, as the result of the command does not fit into the
result field of the form, only a part is shown and using function keys, the other parts can be displayed in a continuous
sequence until the full chain of relationships has been
displayed.

```
concept name 1:              direct    ▭

concept name 2:              indirect  ▭
```

Figure 5: The Supplementary Command Specification
          for the Relation Command

Note, however, that only the shortest path(s) will be displayed: more indirect relationships can be shown by using the
continue command.

Example (not using complete QDC-forms)

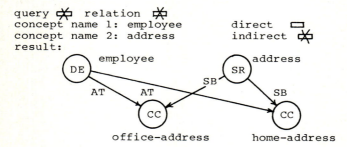

5. 6 The Processing of Synonyms

The dialog system processes any synonyms identically to the
semantic or notational concept they express. For the user of the
system no difference exists between the various names used for a
concept.

6. THE DEFINITION FACILITIES OF QDC

As in the case of the query facility of QDC all the definition
commands of QDC can be used on the model dictionary and the notation dictionary. They are form oriented, and the system will perform extensive tests to ensure the consistency of the specified
data model and notations (see section 6.5).

6.1 The Create Command

With this command, a new concept explanation or notation
explanation can be created. The form used for this command is
shown in Figure 6. The boxes identifying optional sections have
to be marked if a section is to be included. Comment sections may
be inserted after every section or paragraph. The system editor
will adjust the spacing such that even extensive descriptions can
easily be given. The check field can be used to start extensive
consistency checking by the system. Therefore it is possible to
enter with consecutive commands individually inconsistent explanations into the system. Only local checks will be made immediately, all others are delayed until the check-box is tagged.

```
┌──────────────────────────────────────────────┬─────────────────┐
│  command type                                  │  available       │
│  ┌─┐          ☒            ┌─┐         ┌─┐     │  commands         │
│  query     definition   continue   interrupt  │   explain  ┌─┐    │
│                                                │   find     ┌─┐    │
│        concept name:                           │   list     ┌─┐    │
│                                                │   role     ┌─┐    │
│  ┌─┐ concept type:                             │   relation ┌─┐    │
│                                                │                   │
│  ┌─┐ synonym:                                  │                   │
│                                                │   create   ☒      │
│  ┌─┐ definition:                               │   modify   ┌─┐    │
│                                                │   delete   ┌─┐    │
│  ┌─┐ identification:                           │   synonym  ┌─┐    │
│                                                │                   │
│  ┌─┐ context:                                  │                   │
│ ──────────────────────────────────────────────│                   │
│      execute ┌─┐  save ┌─┐ return ┌─┐ check ┌─┐│                   │
└──────────────────────────────────────────────┴─────────────────┘
```

Figure 6: The Create Command

6.2 The Modify Command

The form used for this command is similar to the one shown for
the create command in Figure 7. However, after the concept name
is specified the system will display the explanation as it already exists in the data dictionary. We can then extend the
description, change part of it, even delete paragraphs and (optional) sections. However, the command cannot be used to delete
a complete explanation. For this purpose the delete command
(Section 6.3) has to be used. The changes will become permanent,
when the execute-box will be tagged. The check-box will be used
identically to its use in the create command.

6.3 The Delete Command

The delete command causes the deletion of an explanation frome
the data dictionary and therefore the semantic model.

We feel that delete actions have to be guarded carefully and,
therefore, only a single explanation can be deleted with a single
command execution. A consistency check will be performed immediately. If no consistency violation arises from the execution
of the command, the deletion becomes permanent, otherwise the
system displays all the consistency violations and asks the user
to confirm his intention to delete the explanation. After he
confirms, the deletion becomes permanent but he now has to proceed and delete, create, modify other explanations until he re-
creates a new consistent semantic model.

The same technique could have been applied to the modify-
command, but we wanted to offer with the modify command a facility which allows a knowledgeable user to manipulate the schema
without continuous extensive testing and therefore with increase
performance. Using the check-box tagging principle he himself ca
specify all the checks he thinks are necessary when modifying th
data dictionary.

6.4 The Synonym Command

The synonym command can be used to identify two or more concepts already existing in the semantic net as synonyms of each
other. The concept name and the list of synonyms has to be given
The system will check whether the explanations given for the
identified concepts actually allow them to be synonyms of each
other. If differences exist, they will be displayed and will hav
to be changed first (via using the modify command) before the
execution of the synonym command can be completed successfully.
This checking even includes comment sections, in order to ensure
that semantic properties not formally expressed but only explained via comments do not get lost when synonyms are formed.

If the user wants to introduce a new synonym concept he cannot
use the synonym command, instead he has to use the create command
as described in Section 6.1.

6.5 The Consistency Checking Mechanism

The consistency checking mechanism heavily depends on the
semantic modelling technique chosen. In case of SAM which we have
used throughout this paper, many different checks can be performed. They are a direct result of the meaning of the various
notational concepts involved, but also include other properties.
For example, for every concept name appearing in a definition
section a corresponding explanation has to exist. In addition,
the context section of that concept has to contain the presently
explained concept name with the appropriate semantic role.

If the consistency checking mechanism detects any inconsistencies, they will be displayed and advice will be given how they
could probably be corrected. The checking mechanism currently
does not automatically correct inconsistencies, e.g. by including
a concept automatically in the context section. Making changes in
the semantic model of an enterprise requires great care and automation tends to hide to the designer the consequences of such
changes. We have therefore decided to make all the changes explicitly dependent on positive actions of the data base designer.

7. SUMMARY

In this paper we have presented a form-driven dialog facility
to create and manipulate semantic data base models. We have
illustrated its use on the basis of the Semantic Association
Model of S. Su and D. Lo, but feel confident that the same principles can be applied to other modelling techniques.

The facility will be implemented on top of the distributed
data base system POREL, which is currently in its completion stages at the University of Stuttgart.

Possible extensions of the proposed technique could allow the
specification of such information as a data base designer has to
provide to the data base management system in order to create an
efficient and reliable data base. These could include facilities
for defining the internal schema and the mapping between conceptual and internal schemas. We feel the data base designer should
have a single tool to cover all the various tasks he has to perform, and a form driven facility seems to offer considerable
advantage for handling the sometimes very complex information
the designer has to supply to the system.

References

[1] Biller, H., Neuhold, E.J.: Concepts for the Conceptual
    Schema.- Proc. of IFIP Working Conference "Modelling in
    Data Base Management Systems", Nijssen, G.M. (ed.),
    North Holland (1977)

[2] Biller, H., Neuhold, E.J.: Semantics of Data Bases: The Seman-
    tics of Data Models.- Information Systems, 3, 1 (1978)

[3] Chamberlin, D.D. (et al.): SEQUEL 2: A Unified Approach to
    Data Definition, Manipulation and Control.-
    IBM Journal R & D 20, 6 (1976)

[4] Chen, P.P.: The Entity-Relationship Model - Towards a Unified
    View of Data.- ACM TODS, 1, 1 (1976)

[5] Fauser, U., Neuhold, E.J.: System Architecture of the Dis-
    tributed Relational DBMS POREL.- Proc. of the IGDD Work-
    shop on Distributed Data Sharing Systems, Aix-en-Provence,
    INRIA (1979)

[6] Smith, J., Smith, D.: Database Abstractions: Aggregation and
    Generalization.- ACM TODS 5, 2 (1980)

[7] Su, S.Y.W., Lo, D.H.: A Semantic Association Model for Con-
    ceptual Data Base Design.- Proc. of the Conf. on "Entity-
    Relationship Approach to Systems Analysis and Design",
    Chen, P.P. (ed.), North Holland (1980)

[8] Su, S.Y.W., Lo, D.H.: A Multi-Level Semantic Model and its
    Semantic Integrity Control.- Tech.Rep. CIS-7778-12,
    Dept. of Comp. & Inf. Sciences, University of Florida,
    Gainsville (1978)

Appendix A: The Syntax of the Data Dictionary

```
<data-dictionary> ::= <model-dictionary><notation-dictionary>
<model-dictionary>     ::= <concept-explanation> - list
<concept-explanation> ::= <concept-name-section>
                          [<concept-type-section>]
                          [<concept-synonym-section>]
                          [<concept-identification-section>]
                          [<comment-section>]
                          [<concept-definition-section>]
                          [<concept-context-section>]
```

  Note: A comment-section may appear after any section or
        paragraph.

```
<concept-name-section>::= name <concept-name>
<concept-type-section>::= type <concept-type>
<concept-synonym-section> ::= synonym <concept-name> - list |
                              synonym ↑ <concept-name>
<concept-identification-section> ::=
    identification primary <identifying-concept-name-group>
            <secondary-identification> - list
<secondary-identification> ::=
    secondary <identifying-concept-name-group>
<identifying-concept-name-group> ::= <concept-name> - list
<comment-section>        ::= /p* <any-string without */> */ |
                             /s* <any-string without */> */
<concept-definition-section> ::= definition <description>
                                 [<constraints>]
<description>            ::= <concept-class-description> |
                            <derived-concept-description>
<concept-class-description> ::= <data-type>[<domain>]| <domain>
<data-type>             ::= DEC (<range>) | CHAR (<integer>)
<range>                 ::= <integer>,<integer> | <integer>
<domain>                ::= <string-domain> | <numeric-domain>
<string-domain>         ::= <alphanumeric-string> - list |
                            <numeric-string> - list
<numeric-domain>        ::= <numeric-range> - list
<numeric-range>         ::= <number><rel-op><concept-name> |
                <number><rel-op><concept-name><rel-op><number>
<rel-op>                ::= = | < | ≤ | = | > | ≥
```

```
<derived-concept-description> ::= <defining-concept-spec> - list
<defining-concept-spec> ::= <semantic-role > :
                    <concept-name>[<occurrence-specification>]
<occurrence-specification> ::= unique | multiple | multiple unique
<constraints>              ::= <assert-rules> [<triggers>] | <triggers>
<assert-rules>            ::= assert <assert> - list
<assert>                  ::= (<assert-order>)
                             [on <assert-condition>] : <assert-body>
            Note: <assert-body> not further specified.
<assert-condition>        ::= <operation> of <concept-name>
<assert-order>            ::= <integer>
<operation>               ::= insert | delete | query | update |
                             comparison | .....
<triggers>                ::= trigger <trigger> - list
<trigger>                 ::= (<trigger-order>)
                             [on <trigger-condition>]: <trigger-body>
            Note: <trigger-body> not further specified.
<trigger-condition>      ::= <assert-condition>
<trigger-order>          ::= <integer>
<concept-context-section> ::=
                    context <context-concept-spec> - list
<context-concept-spec> ::= <semantic-role> : <concept-name>

<notation-dictionary> ::= <notation-explanation> - list
<notation-explanation>::= <notation-name-section>
                          [<notation-type-section>]
                          [<notation-synonym-section>]
                          [<notation-definition-section>]
                          [<notation-comment-section>]
<notation-name-section> ::= notation <notation-name>
<notation-type-section> ::= type <notation-type>
<notation-type>  ::= syntactic-concept | data-type |
                     section-identifier | paragraph-identifier |
                     meta-concept |
    Note: May be extended depending on the semantic modelling
          principle chosen.
<notation-synonym-section> ::= synonym <notation-name> - list |
                               synonym ↑ <notation-name>
<notation-definition-section> ::= definition <defining-notation>
<defining-notation>    ::= basic |
                           is one of <notation-name> - list
<notation-comment-section> ::= /* <any string without */> */
```

Appendix B: A Dialog Session Example

In the following, we give an example of a dialog as it could
occur when using the conceptual schema of a data base. In the
forms shown shaded areas are always meant to have the same content as displayed by the preceding form.

```
    command type                          available
  ⊠        ▭           ▭          ▭        commands
query    definition  continue  interrupt   explain   ▭
                                            find      ⊠
explanation: model-dictionary               list      ▭
                                            role      ▭
                                            relation  ▭
result:
                                            create    ▭
                                            modify    ▭
                                            delete    ▭
                                            synonym   ▭
        execute ⊠   save ▭   return ▭
```

```
result:
   role: SB   type: EI   assignment
   role: SB   type: SR   all-employee ⊠
        execute ⊠   save ⊠   return ▭
```

```
result:
   role: SB   type: DE   emp-experience
   role: SB   type: DE   mgr-experience
   role: ST   type: DE   employee
        execute ▭   save ▭   return ⊠
```

```
result:
   role: SB   type: EI   assignment    ⊠
   role: SB   type: SR   all-employee
        execute ⊠   save ▭ return ▭
```

```
result:
   role: IO   type: DE   project
   role: MD   type: CC   assign-no
   role: DO   type: DE   emp-experience
   role: AG   type: DE   mgr-experience
        execute ▭   save ▭ return ▭
```

```
///////////////////////////////////////
| concept name 1: project          |  find  ▭  |
| concept name 2: employee         |           |
|----------------------------------| relation ✳ |
| result:                          |           |
|----------------------------------|           |
|     execute ✳   save ▭ return ▭  |           |
```

```
/////////////////////////////////////////////
|              ╭────╮                        |
|              │ SR │ model dictionary        |
|              ╰────╯                        |
|         SB  ╱        ╲  SB                  |
|       ╭────╮          ╭────╮                |
|       │ EI │ assignment (emp-experience: │ SR │ all-    |
|       ╰────╯   project = M:1)    ╰────╯  employee       |
|    ID   DO    AG      SB     SB    ST       |
|  ╭────╮   ╭────╮   ╭────╮        ╭────╮     |
|  │ DE │   │ DE │   │ DE │        │ DE │     |
|  ╰────╯   ╰────╯   ╰────╯        ╰────╯     |
|  project  emp-experience mgr-experience  employee |
|     execute ▭    save ▭ return ▭           |
```

```
///////////////////////////////////////
| explanation: employee            | explain  ✳ |
| sections: concept-name           | relation ▭  |
|           definition             |           |
|----------------------------------|           |
| result:                          |           |
|----------------------------------|           |
|     execute ✳   save ▭ return ▭  |           |
```

```
/////////////////////////////////////
| concept name: employee           |           |
| definition: AT: emp-no      unique |         |
|             AT: emp-name          |           |
|             AT: dependent   multiple |       |
|             AT: office-addr       |           |
|             AT: home-addr         |           |
|     execute ▭    save ▭ return ▭  |           |
```

```
/////////////////////////////////////
|        command type              |           |
|   ▭         ▭           ▭      ✳  |           |
| query   definition  continue interrupt |     |
```

Entity-Relationship Approach to
Information Modeling and Analysis, P.P. Chen (ed.)
Elsevier Science Publishers B.V. (North-Holland)
©ER Institute, 1983

AN EXTENDED ENTITY RELATIONSHIP MODEL
WITH MULTI LEVEL EXTERNAL VIEWS

Prabuddha De
College of Administrative Science
Ohio State University
Columbus, Ohio 43210

Arun Sen
College of Business Administration
University of South Carolina
Columbia, South Carolina 29208

Ehud Gudes
Wang Laboratories
Lowell, Massachusetts 01851

In this paper an extension to the Entity Relationship (ER) model
is proposed. The extension, which we call a Concept Relationship
(CR) model, uses a multi level interdependent architecture for the
design of external schemas. The objective is to capture information
requirements for various levels of the organizational hierarchy.The
CR model also provides more semantic information than the ER model,
and incorporates mechanisms for dependency resolution among related
items.

1. INTRODUCTION

The importance of abstraction in data base design can be derived from its
importance in systems design. A system is defined as a group of elements that
exhibit a set of interrelationships among themselves and interact together
toward one or more goals. Similarly, a data base consists of data types and
their interrelationships and has a common goal of satisfying the users' requirements. In the design of a system, we use models to abstract some of its
features. Similarly, in the design of a data base, we use abstractions so
that the data base can be intellectually manageable. A number of models can
be used, ranging from mathematical models, set-theoretic models, informational
models to semantic models.

The traditional data models (e.g., relational, network) allow a user to
deal with the representation of contrived items rather than the reality itself
[12,16]. This proposes an increased burden on the data base designer and increased difficulty in maintaining the consistency of the data base to mirror
real-world events. In order to bridge this gap and thus describe the semantic
structure of the real world, several conceptual schema models have been proposed in the past few years [13].

The Entity Relationship (ER) model, proposed by Chen [5], has many of the
desired features for modeling the conceptual schema. It is easy to formulate,
it is easy to understand, and it includes a concise diagramatic technique
which can be used by the designer to communicate the user requirements.

However, several criticisms can be raised against the ER model. First,
every organization has users at different levels of the organizational hierar-

chy [1]. Depending upon the levels, their need for data changes. The data
are more generalized and aggregated at a higher level than at a lower level.
Chen never really investigated this possibility, although he mentions the use
of relationship sets recursively to generate regular entity sets [5,6]. We
discuss the need of this extension in more detail in Section 2.

Second, at the discourse level, it may not be fair to expect the users to
articulate their requirements very precisely, noting each time the entity sets
and the relationship sets. At most, we can expect them to describe only the
regular entity sets and how they are interrelated. Moreover, these interrela-
tions may not be articulated as precisely as the ER model requires.

Third, can the designer determine all the entity sets that are dependent
on one? This is an important issue as sometimes the decision makers themselves may not be able to provide this information. This may cause some inconsistency in the logical data base. For example, if we have a PARTS entity
set and a SUPPLY entity set, we need to include also the SUPPLIER set to make
the logical data base meaningful.

In this paper we try to resolve these drawbacks by proposing a new model
which could be looked upon as an extension of the ER model[1]. We shall call
this new model the Concept Relationship (CR) model.

2.   ORGANIZATIONAL HIERARCHY AND ITS IMPACT ON DATA MODELING

Any organization can be thought of as an information generating process,
where the information is generated for the internal and external activities of
the organization. The internal activities include, among others, production,
marketing and finance, whereas the external activities are labor relations,
tax reporting, demand analysis and so on. Whatever the activities are, they
are the sole reason why the users in an organization need data. So, an effective design of a logical data base requires an analysis of these activities.

Following Anthony [1], the user activities in an organization can be
classified in three categories: strategic planning, managerial control and
operational control. Strategic planning is the process of deciding the objectives of the organization, the resources to be used to attain these objectives,
and the policies that govern the acquisition, use, and disposition of these
resources. Thus, strategic planning is the process of formulating long-range
plans and policies that determine the character of an organization. Management control is the process by which managers assure that resources are obtained and used efficiently in the accomplishment of the organizational objectives. And finally, operational control is the process of assuring that tasks
are carried out efficiently. This typology hints at the different information
needs for different organizational levels. The information needed by the
strategic planners is aggregate, and the scope and variety of this information
vary extensively. By contrast, for operational control we require detailed

------

[1]Another proposal for extending the ER model can be found in [15].

information of a well-defined and narrow scope. The information requirements
for management control fall in magnitude between those of strategic planning
and operational control. Table 1 shows examples of the types of activities and
data requirements at each of these levels.

The above classification makes it evident that the users at different levels will have different views. The views at the operational control level will
have data with maximum detail; they become less detailed as they move from operational control to strategic planning, making the decision-making views hierarchical. But after integraing these external views, the resulting conceptual
view will be flat (nonhierarchical), as shown in Figure 1. The boxes at the
external level represent the external views of the data base. The notation
" <--> " shows the external-conceptual mapping, while the notation " ·--· "
shows the mapping between individual external views.

Note that Figure 1 is a generalization of the widely accepted ANSI/X3/
SPARC data base architecture [2]. The external level of this new architecture
has (at most) three levels. Although the mappings between the views at the external level are shown explicitly in Figure 1, the users never see these mappings once the data base has been built.

3. THE CONCEPT RELATIONSHIP (CR) MODEL

Section 2 suggests that the organization imposes a hierarchy of external
views on the data base architecture. This hierarchy, alongwith the objections
raised earlier against the ER model, motivates us to propose an extended model
called the Concept Relationship (CR) model.

Like the ER model, this model abstracts knowledge about the data base
through discourses. In order to do that, it uses a semantic network made up of
concepts and relationships. The nodes of the network are the concepts, while
the directed edges are the relationships. The use of a semantic network is
needed to make the logical data base independent of any conventional data model
(relational, hierarchical or network [9]). However, once the semantic network
is constructed, it can be translated to any of these data models.

3.1 Concepts

We assume that the user abstracts data by their properties only. That
means, an abstract data item SUPPLIER is conceived by the user as a collection
of properties such as supplier identifier, supplier address, service supplied
and so on. This abstract data item is called a concept. So, a concept C_i (i =
1,2,3,...,N) is an abstraction regarding something that can be distinctively
identified by its properties or attributes. That is, $C_i = \{a_{i,j}\}$ where C_i is
the ith concept, $a_{i,j}$ is the jth attribute and is unique for C_i; $\{a_{i,j}\}$ is the
set of all attributes (j = 1,2,...,n). Figure 2 shows how to represent a concept in terms of its attributes. For simplicity, it is assumed that the names
of the attributes are not the same as the name of the concept C_i. But their
names include the concept name. For example, a concept EMPLOYEE should have
attributes with names as employee identifier, employee name and employee ad-

dress instead of just identifier, name and address. This is shown in Figure 3. This attribute naming convention avoids the confusion of having false relationships among concepts arising out of the same attribute names but with different meanings. However, one can expect two entirely different attribute names to mean the same.

Note the way the concept C_i is defined. One can identify this with the regular entity set in the ER model [5,6]. It is also identifiable with the object in Smith and Smith's model [20,21], or with the concept of Roussopoulos and Mylopoulos' model [14].

The properties of a concept are described below in the form of propositions.

Proposition 1. Two concepts are semantically identical if they mean the same and have semantically equivalent attributes. That is $C_1 = C_2$ if (a) they mean the same, and (b) $\forall k$ $\exists \ell$ such that $a_{1k} = a_{2\ell}$ and $\forall \ell$ $\exists k$ such that $a_{2\ell} = a_{1k}$.

The symbol = indicates "semantic equivalence." Two attributes are defined to be semantically equivalent if they are either identical or mean the same.

Proposition 2. Two concepts are semantically semi-identical if they have at least one pair of attributes such that one element of the pair is semantically equivalent to the other element of the pair. That is, $C_1 \simeq C_2$ if there exists at least a pair $a_{1,k}$ ($\epsilon\ C_1$) and $a_{2,\ell}$ ($\epsilon\ C_2$) such that $a_{1,k} = a_{2,\ell}$, where the sign $\simeq$ means "semantically semi-identical to."

Proposition 3. Two concepts are semantically different if they do not have any semantically equivalent attributes. That is $C_1 \neq C_2$ if $\forall k$ $\neg\exists \ell$ such that $a_{1,k} = a_{2,\ell}$ and $\forall \ell$ $\neg\exists k$ such that $a_{2,\ell} = a_{1,k}$. The symbol $\neq$ indicates "semantically not equivalent to."

Proposition 4. Two concepts are semantically related if they are either semantically identical or semi-identical.

The concepts are named according to a naming convention: (a) If two concepts are semantically identical, they may have identical names; (b) If two concepts are not semantically identical (that means they are either semantically semi-identical or semantically different), they should have different names. So, we cannot possibly have concepts with the same name and with different attributes.

Some examples will illustrate the earlier propositions and the naming convention. Let us take three concepts

SUPPLY = {supply supplier id., supply service id., supply amount of services},

SUPPLIER = {supplier id., supplier address, supplier service id.}, and
PROVIDER = {provider id., provider service id., provider address}.
Here, SUPPLY and SUPPLIER concepts differ semantically in one attribute and are
semantically semi-identical. Hence, they have different names. The concepts
SUPPLIER and PROVIDER mean the same and have semantically equivalent attributes.
So, these concepts are semantically identical and could be named the same.

The concept key of a concept is an attribute or a set of attributes that
uniquely determines an occurrence of that concept. In case several keys exist,
a semantically meaningful concept key would be chosen and called the "primary
concept key". An example of the primary concept key is shown in Figure 3.

3.2 Relationships

The data items in a data base are frequently related. These relationships
can be translated into interrelationships among concepts at the logical level.
There can be several types of these relationships, each with a definite purpose.

Our model recognizes the hierarchy of abstraction as described in Section
2. Note that this hierarchy is similar to Smith and Smith's abstraction hierarchy [20,21] with some differences. First, the CR hierarchy recognizes the
three levels of organizational activities, and so can have at most three levels.
Secondly, the hierarchy of abstraction in the CR model is at the external level
and not at the conceptual level as in Smith and Smith [20,21]. Each user has a
view of data and because of different levels of users' activities, it is only
proper to have hierarchical views at the external level.

As we will see later, we do not use relationships the way Chen has used in
his ER model [5]. Chen defines a new abstraction for them. In the CR model,
we do not differentiate between entities and relationships. For all practical
purposes, they are called concepts. The relationships, that we use, come out
of the inherent relationships among data items and of the structural relationships that are required to support the data requirements of the users.

These relationships can be represented in two ways. The first is by a
separate construct, such as the SET construct in the CODASYL model [9]. This
construct is a list of pointers from the occurrence of one concept to the other.
The second is by inheritance of attributes. This is not new and can be found
in the relational model [7,8]. The idea is to inherit some attributes of a concept A by a concept B, if A and B are related and the relationship is directed
from A to B. For this research, the second approach is chosen.

It should be clear by now that the CR model assumes that the concepts and
the relationships among them are given. Some of these relationships are user-
defined and some are organization dependent. In order to differentiate our relationships with those suggested by other researchers, ours will be called modeling functions.

A hierarchical view modeling process entails two major types of modeling
functions: horizontal and vertical. Horizontal modeling functions are those
that are used among concepts in one level. Vertical modeling functions are
used among concepts at different levels. We use four types of horizontal mod-

eling functions: logical horizontal integrity constraint (logical HIC), and three different causal horizontal integrity constraints (causal HIC's) which we call type I, type II and type III. The vertical functions are of four types also: logical vertical integrity constraint (vertical HIC), mathematical vertical integrity constraint (mathematical VIC), part-whole vertical masking function and classificatory vertical masking function.

3.2.1. Logical HIC: A logical HIC is used between semantically related concepts at the same level of the hierarchical view. It is denoted by

$$C_i \xleftrightarrow[\text{Logical HIC}]{\langle a_{i,1}; a_{i',1} \rangle} C_{i'}$$

where C_i and $C_{i'}$ are two semantically related concepts, and $a_{i,1}$ and $a_{i',1}$ are

the attributes of C_i and $C_{i'}$ respectively over which the concepts are semantically related.

There may be more than one attribute over which the concepts can be semantically related. Hence, the lgoical HIC also acts over a set of attributes. Some examples of the use of the logical HIC are given in Figures 4-6. Figures 4 and 5 show the logical HIC between semantically identical concepts. Figure 6 shows an instance where a logical HIC is used between semantically semi-identical concepts. It is important to note that not every semantically semi-identical concept is related by a logical HIC. That is, being semi-identical is only a necessary condition and not a sufficient one for a logical HIC to exist. Actually, only the user requirements and the designer's involvements determine the presence of the logical HIC.

3.2.2. Causal HIC's: In a typical data base, some concepts can be related by causal relationships. A causal relationship indicates a cause and effect connection among different concepts. It has been studied extensively in linguistics [4,10], cognitive psychology [11], artificial intelligence [3], and computer linguistics [19].

A concept taking part in a causal relationship can either be an object or an action [11]. Objects are things that occupy space. "Subcontractor", "order", and "elderly people" are examples of the object concept. Actions are things that occupy a position or an interval of time, and many involve some kind of a change. Examples of actions are "supply" and "serve". (Objects are usually nouns and actions are verbs.) An action can be further classified into a resultive action and a process [11]. The resultive action always produces a change in the state of a system. For example, a supplier "supplies" some items to a department. Here "supplies" is a resultive action and it changes the inventory of a department. A process does not produce a change in the system. Examples are: "breathe", "walk", "play", and "know".

We will assume that all causal relationships occur between concepts at the same level. They can be categorized into several groups depending on the degree of dependence of the "effect" concept on the "cause" concept [10,11].

3.2.2.1. Type-1 Causal HIC: One such group of causal relations consists of an

Agent relationship (also known as the Immediate Cause relationship) [11].

The agent relationship is used between two concepts C_i and C_j, in the direction of C_i to C_j, if C_i is an <u>immediate</u> object causing the resultive action C_j.

The term immediate means that there is no other concept besides C_i that can cause C_j. For example, the concept ORDER can cause a resultive action SUPPLY.

The relationship is denoted by $C_i \xrightarrow[\text{HIC-C1}]{\{a\}} C_j$. To represent the relationship, C_j must inherit some attributes of C_i, that is, the inheritance is in the direction of the arrow. So, if $C_i = \{a_{i,k}\}$ and $C_j = \{a_{j,\ell}\}$, $1 \leq k \leq m$, $1 \leq \ell \leq n$, and there is a type-1 HIC between them in the direction as shown, then

(i) The total number of attributes in C_j changes to n' from n, where $n' \geq n$.

(ii) $\overline{\{a_{i,k}\}} \cap \{a_{j,\ell}\} = \{a\}$, $1 \leq k \leq m$, $1 \leq \ell \leq n'$.

(iii) For every occurrence of C_i, there is at most one occurrence of C_j.

Here, $\{a\}$ is at least one key attribute (or attributes) of C_i. Note that C_j might already contain some of the attributes of $\{a\}$. In that case, no inheritance for these attributes will take place explicitly, but we will still consider these attributes of C_j as inherited attributes. As every occurrence of C_j is caused by an occurrence of C_i, there must be a relationship between the occurrences as described by the third condition.

Let us take our earlier example of ORDER and SUPPLY. The two concepts are shown in Figure 7. Because each supply has to have an order number, the "order number" should be inherited from the ORDER concept by the SUPPLY concept. But we see that the SUPPLY concept already has an attribute "supply order number" which is semantically equivalent to the "order number". So no explicit attribute inheritance takes place, but we consider the "supply order number" as an inherited attribute.

In the example of Figure 8, a resource acquisition for a service organization is abstracted by the RESOURCE concept. The acquisition is caused by a demand of services. The latter is abstracted by the SERVICE concept. Since a resource that is acquired depends upon the service type, the year the service is performed, the location of the service organization and the demand, these attributes of the SERVICE concept are the attributes to be inherited by the RESOURCE concept. Since, in general, the resource is acquired to help perform a service at a given time, the two attributes "service year" and "resource year" have a common domain and the "service year" need not be explicitly inherited. However, we will treat the "resource year" as an inherited attribute.

3.2.2.2. <u>Type-2 Causal HIC</u>: The second group of causal relations contains two similar types of relationships: Instrument (IN) and Patient (PT)[2] [11].

The IN relationship is defined between two concepts C_i and C_j, and works from C_i to C_j, if C_i is an immediate object <u>involved</u> in a resultive action C_j that is caused by some other concept C_k ($k \neq j$).

An example will be a SUPPLIER concept involved in a SUPPLY action which is actually caused by another concept ORDER.

The PT relationship is also between two concepts C_i and C_j, in the direction of C_i to C_j, if C_i is an immediate object <u>involved</u> in a process C_j.

For example, a SUPPLIER is involved in the SUPPLY process.

These two relationships can be denoted by $C_i \xrightarrow[\text{HIC-C2}]{\{a\}} C_j$. As before, to represent this relationship, C_j must inherit some attributes $\{a\}$ of C_i. Using the earlier notations, we find that the first two conditions of type-2 HIC are the same as (i) and (ii) of type-1, with the third condition as follows:

(iii) For every occurrence of C_i, there may be any number of occurrences of C_j (a 1:N mapping in the direction of the arrow, $N \geq 0$).

The existence of $\{a\}$ is needed as in the case of type 1 HIC. Also, as a single occurrence of C_i can initiate or can get involved with a number of occurrences of C_j, the third condition is important.

Let us take the earlier example of SUPPLIER and SUPPLY. This is shown in Figure 9. Here, we have used an example which does not need explicit attribute inheritance as "supplier identifier" and "supply supplier identifier" attributes are semantically equivalent. Cases can be shown, as in Figure 8, where actual inheritance is needed.

3.2.2.3. <u>Type-3 Causal HIC</u>: The last group of causal relations contains two more types of relationships: Affected Object (AO) and Related Object (RO)[3] [11].

The AO relationship is used between two concepts C_i and C_j, and is from C_i to C_j, if C_j is an immediate object <u>affected</u> by the resultive action C_i that is caused by some other concept C_k ($k \neq i$).

For example, a SUPPLY which is caused by an ORDER affects a DEPARTMENT, as it changes the inventory level.

The RO relationship works between two concepts C_i and C_j, in the direction

---

[2] The fact that two different semantic relationships (i.e. IN and PT) will lead to the same modeling function indicates that our model may not be rich enough semantically. We leave this question for future research.

[3] Again, we have the same problem as described in Footnote 2.

of C_i to C_j, if C_j is an immediate object <u>affected</u> by the process C_i.

The two concepts SUPPLY and DEPARTMENT can again be used to explain an RO relationship, if the SUPPLY is looked upon as a process affecting (the inventory level of) a DEPARTMENT.

The relationships are denoted by $C_i \xrightarrow[\text{HIC-C3}]{\{a\}} C_j$. As before, it is repre-

sented by the inheritance of some attributes {a} of C_i by C_j. The first two conditions of type-3 HIC are the same as those of type-1 or type-2. The third condition is as follows:

(iii) For every occurrence of C_i, there is one occurrence of C_j (an n:1 mapping in the direction of the arrow).

This last condition needs some explanation. As C_i is the affected concept, any change in C_i should introduce a one-to-one change in C_j. For example, one can have as many orders as possible, but the SUPPLY concept remains unaffected unless there is some real supply. As soon as a supply is available, it is earmarked for a specific department and the DEPARTMENT concept gets affected. This is shown in Figure 10 with proper inheritance of attributes.

3.2.3. Logical VIC: A logical VIC is used between semantically related concepts at different levels of the hierarchical view. We introduce a second subscript to the concept notation to denote the level. So $C_{i,j}$ now stands for the ith concept at the jth level. Using this notation, the logical VIC is denoted by

$$C_{i,j} \xleftarrow[\text{Logical VIC}]{\langle a_{i,j,1}; a_{i',j',1} \rangle} C_{i',j'}$$

where $C_{i,j}$ and $C_{i',j'}$ are two semantically related concepts at jth and j'th levels respectively, and $a_{i,j,1}$ and $a_{i',j',1}$ are the attributes of $C_{i,j}$ and $C_{i',j'}$ respectively, over which the concepts are semantically related. As in a Logical HIC, there can be more than one attribute over which the concepts can be semantically related. So, the Logical VIC also acts over a set of attributes. An example of the use of a logical VIC is shown in Figure 11. The figure shows that the logical VIC works on both semantically identical and semi-identical concepts. As in the case of a logical HIC, being semi-identical is only a necessary condition and not a sufficient one for a logical VIC to exist.

3.2.4. Mathematical VIC: Mathematical VIC's are used when the value of an attribute of one concept is dependent upon the values of the attributes of another concept (or concepts) at a different level (or at different levels). Using the earlier notations of representing a concept in a logical VIC, we see that the mathematical VIC between concepts can be represented as

$$C_{i,j} \xrightarrow[\text{Math VIC}]{\langle \{a'\}; a \rangle} C_{x,y}$$

where $C_{i,j}$ is a concept at level j, $C_{x,y}$ is another concept at level y, and a $(\epsilon C_{x,y})$ = f ({a'}), {a'} being the set of attributes from $C_{i,j}$ that are needed to calculate the value of the attribute a of $C_{x,y}$.

This definition of the mathematical VIC can be generalized to include several concepts in the left-hand side of the arrow. The generalization will be needed if a ($\varepsilon C_{x,y}$) is a function of attributes of several concepts in different levels. The function f is a mathematical operator, like addition, subtraction, or percentage.

An example at this point will be helpful. Figure 12 shows two concepts CLIENT and SERVICE. As the attribute "service total no. of persons" of the SERVICE concept indicates the total number of persons served and its value is calculated from the "client number" attribute of the CLIENT concept, the above two concepts are connected by a mathematical VIC and the direction is from CLIENT to SERVICE.

There is a restriction that one should observe for mathematical VIC's: there should not be a mathematical VIC between two concepts such that its domain (range) is the range (domain) of another mathematical VIC between the same two concepts. In terms of previously defined attributes, it means that if $a_{x,y,1} = f_1 (a_{i,j,1})$ then one should not accept another mathematical VIC such that $a_{i,j,1} = f_2 (a_{x,y,1})$. This is introduced for the sake of simplicity and consistency.

It is possible that between two concepts at different levels there exist both logical and mathematical VIC's. The situation is shown in Figure 12 where the concept SERVICE has an attribute which is semantically identical to an attribute of the concept CLIENT.

The last two modeling functions are the vertical masking functions (VMF's): part-whole and classificatory. These modeling functions mask out the details of the data as we go from operations level to strategic planning level. Similar ideas have been discussed by Smith and Smith [20,21] and Scheuermann et al. [17], and will not be repeated here.

4. USE OF THE CR MODEL FOR DIFFERENT MANAGEMENT LEVELS

In Section 2 we described Anthony's classification of management activities in an organization [1]. According to him, these activities can be classified in three levels: strategic planning, managerial control, and operational control. These levels have different data requirements. The requirements are typically more detailed at a lower level, and become less detailed as we move up.

The CR model can be used to capture the various data requirements of an organization. Every user (or every group of users) has an external view (See Figure 1) that describes the data requirements for that user. Using the CR model, a view can be defined as a collection of concepts and their interrelationships.[4]

[4] Actually, we can also have a view that contains just some concepts, and no interrelationships. However, for obvious reasons the reverse situation is not plausible.

We use HIC's, both logical and causal, to model these interrelationships within the view. Note that causal HIC's form distinct systems or frames. For example, an ORDER causes a SUPPLY, in which is involved a SUPPLIER and which affects a DEPARTMENT. Here, the ORDER is connected to the SUPPLY by a type-1 HIC, the SUPPLIER is connected to the SUPPLY by a type-2 HIC, and the SUPPLY is connected to the DEPARTMENT by a type-3 HIC. The advantage of this frame is that the user can be notified if he (or she) forgets to mention a concept in the frame while describing his (or her) data requirements.

Figure 1 shows that the views are hierarchical. This is in accordance with Anthony's hierarchy of activities. We define an activity as a collection of views. This definition assumes that for the logical data base design process, an activity is analyzed to extract its data requirements. As the activities are arranged in hierarchics, the concepts of these activities, too, have hierarchical connections. These hierarchical connections are modeled by logical VIC's, mathematical VIC's and VMF's.

So, we see that the CR model can be effectively used to abstract data requirements for the entire organizational hierarchy.

5. CONCLUSIONS

This paper is concerned with the development of a new type of abstraction which is more general than Chen's ER model. The proposed CR model uses a semantic network structure to abstract different user needs. A concept in the CR model can be identified with a regular entity in the ER model. However, the relationships among concepts are handled differently. Here, unlike the ER model, the relationships, or modeling functions, are treated as edges of a network with the concepts as the nodes. Eight different types of modeling functions are used to connect different types of concepts.

We raised three criticisms against the ER model. Let us now see how they are avoided in the CR model. First, using the VIC and VMF modeling functions, and three levels of external view structure, the model recognizes the importance of the organizational hierarchy. The VMF's are used to suppress details of data at higher levels.

Second, at the discourse level, we should not expect a user to articulate all requirements very precisely. The modeling functions in our model are semantically broader than associations of the ER model, and they should ease the process of articulation.

Third, the above modeling functions can be used to accurately represent the dependency structures of concepts. This has been demonstrated in [18].

The CR model has been successfully utilized to develop a data base for the Department of Aging in Pennsylvania. A description of that study can be found in [18].

REFERENCES

[1]   Anthony, R. N. Planning and Control Systems: A Framework for Analysis,
      Graduate School of Business Administration, Harvard University, Boston,
      1965.

[2]   ANSI/X3/SPARC, Study Group on Data Base Management Systems, Interim Report,
      FDT Bulletin of ACM SIGMOD 7, No. 21, 1975.

[3]   Bruce, B. "Case Systems for Natural Language," Artificial Intelligence,
      Vol. 6, No. 4, pp. 327-360, 1975.

[4]   Chafe, W. Meaning and the Structure of Language, Chicago: University of
      Chicago Press, 1970.

[5]   Chen, P. P. S. "The Entity-Relationship Model - Toward a Unified View of
      Data," ACM Transactions on Database Systems, Vol. 1, No. 1, pp. 9-36, 1976.

[6]   Chen, P. P. S. "Applications of the Entity-Relationship Model," Proceed-
      ings of New York University Symposium on Data Base Design, New York, pp.
      25-33, 1978.

[7]   Codd, E. F. "A Relational Model of Data for Large Shared Data Banks," Com-
      munication of the ACM, Vol. 13, No. 6, pp. 377-387, 1970.

[8]   Codd, E. F. "Further Normalization of the Data Base Relational Model," Da-
      ta Base Systems, Courant Computer Science Symposia Series, Vol. 6,
      Prentice-Hall, 1972.

[9]   Date, C. J. An Introduction to Database Systems, 3rd edition, Addison-
      Wesley, 1981.

[10] Fillmore, C. "The Case for Case," in Universals in Linguistic Theory, B.
      Bach and B. Harons (eds.), Holt, Rinehart and Winston, 1968.

[11] Fredericksen, C. H. "Representing Logical and Semantic Structure of Knowl-
      edge Acquired from Discourse," Cognitive Psychology, Vol. 7, pp. 371-398,
      1975.

[12] Hammer, M. and McLeod, D. "The Semantic Data Model: A Modeling Mechanism
      for Data Base Applications," Proceedings of ACM SIGMOD International Con-
      ference on the Management of Data, Austin, 1978, pp. 26-36.

[13] Kerschberg, L., A. Klug and D. Tsichritzis. "A Taxonomy of Data Models,"
      Technical Report CSRG-70, Computer Systems Research Group, University of
      Toronto, 1976.

[14] Roussopoulos, N. and J. Mylopoulos. "Using Semantic Networks for Data Base
      Management," Proceedings of V.L.D.B. Conference, Boston, 1975.

[15] Santos, C. S. dos, Neuhold, E. J. and Furtado, A. L. "A Data Type Approach to the Entity-Relationship Model" in Entity-Relationship Approach to Systems Analysis and Design, P. Chen (ed.), North-Holland, 1980.

[16] Schmid, H. A. and Swenson, J. R. "On the Semantics of the Relational Data Model, Proceedings of ACM SIGMOD International Conference on the Management of Data, San Jose, pp. 211-223, 1975.

[17] Scheuermann, P., G. Schiffner, and H. Weber. "Abstraction Capabilities and Invariant Properties Modeling within the Entity-Relationship Approach," Proceedings of International Conference on Entity-Relationship Approach to Systems Analysis and Design, Peter P. Chen (ed.), Los Angeles, pp. 121-140, 1979.

[18] Sen, A. On the Theory of Logical Data Base Design for a Decision Support System, Ph.D. Thesis, Pennsylvania State University, 1979.

[19] Simmons, R. F. "Some Semantic Structures for Representing English Meanings," in Language Comprehension and Acquisition of Knowledge, R. Freedle and J. B. Carroll (eds.), Freeman, 1973.

[20] Smith, J. M. and D. C. P. Smith. "Database Abstractions: Aggregation and Generalization," ACM Transactions on Database Systems, Vol. 2, No. 2, pp. 105-133, 1977.

[21] Smith, J. M. and D. C. P. Smith. "Database Abstractions: Aggregation," Communications of the ACM, Vol. 20, No. 6, pp. 405-413, 1977.

TABLE 1

DISTINCTIONS BETWEEN THE THREE LEVELS OF MANAGERIAL ACTIVITIES

	Strategic Planning	Managerial Control	Operational Control
Examples of the types of activities in an organization	(a) Decision on objectives of the organization	Formulating budgets	--
	(b) --	Measuring, appraising mgmt. performance	Measuring, appraising workers' efficiency
	(c) Planning the organization	Planning staff levels	Controlling credit extensions
	(d) --	Formulating decision rules for operational control	Controlling inventory
Characteristics of data			
(a) Source	External, Internal ———————————————————————————————————→		Largely internal
(b) Scope	Very wide ——→		Well defined, narrow
(c) Level of aggregation	Aggregate ——→		Detailed
(d) Time horizon	Future ———→		Historical
(e) Currency	Old ——→		Highly current
(f) Frequency of use	Infrequent ——→		Very frequent

Source: R. N. Anthony, "Planning and Control Systems: A Framework for Analysis,"

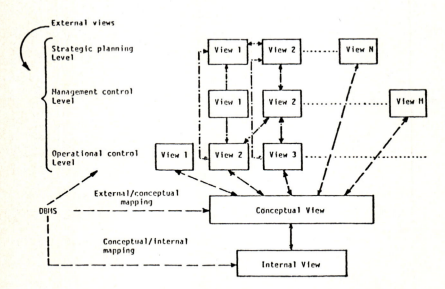

FIGURE 1.   DATA BASE ARCHITECTURE BASED ON MANAGEMENT ACTIVITIES

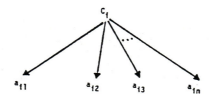

FIGURE 2. A REPRESENTATION OF A CONCEPT C_1

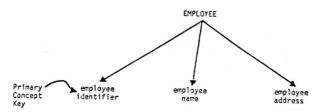

FIGURE 3. AN EXAMPLE OF THE CONCEPT "EMPLOYEE"

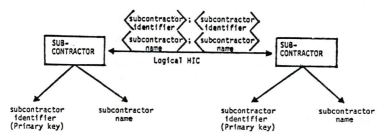

FIGURE 4. AN EXAMPLE OF A LOGICAL HIC BETWEEN TWO SEMANTICALLY IDENTICAL CONCEPTS (WITH THE SAME NAME)

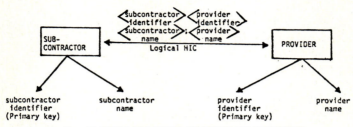

FIGURE 5. AN EXAMPLE OF A LOGICAL HIC BETWEEN TWO SEMANTICALLY IDENTICAL CONCEPTS (WITH DIFFERENT NAMES)

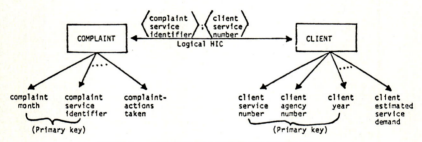

FIGURE 6. AN EXAMPLE OF A LOGICAL HIC BETWEEN TWO SEMANTICALLY SEMI-IDENTICAL CONCEPTS

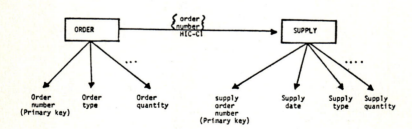

FIGURE 7. TWO CONCEPTS CONNECTED BY A HIC-C1 (WITHOUT EXPLICIT INHERITENCE)

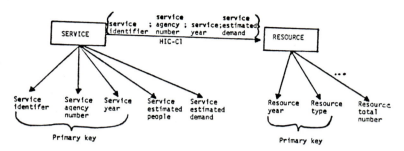

FIGURE 8. TWO CONCEPTS CONNECTED BY A HIC-C1
(WITH EXPLICIT INHERITENCE)

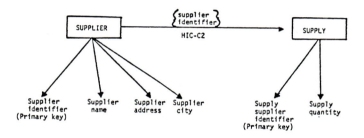

FIGURE 9. TWO CONCEPTS CONNECTED BY A HIC-C2

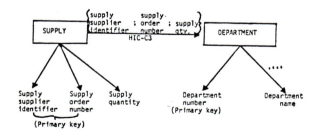

FIGURE 10. TWO CONCEPTS CONNECTED BY A HIC-C3

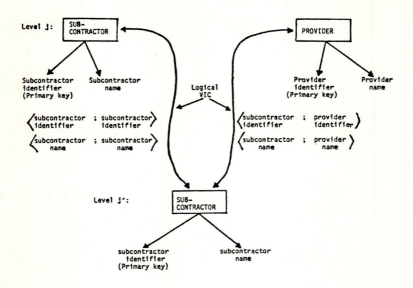

FIGURE 11. AN EXAMPLE OF THE USE OF THE LOGICAL VIC

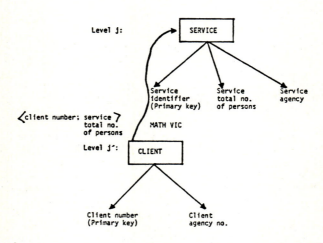

FIGURE 12. AN EXAMPLE OF THE USE OF THE MATHEMATICAL VIC

Entity-Relationship Approach to
Information Modeling and Analysis, P.P. Chen (ed.)
Elsevier Science Publishers B.V. (North-Holland)
©ER Institute, 1983

Term: An Approach to Include the Time Dimension in the Entity–Relationship Model

Manfred R. Klopprogge

Fakultät für Informatik, Universität Karlsruhe,
Postfach 6380, D-7500 Karlsruhe, Germany

The entity-relationship model (ERM) is augmented
by a time-dimension. The resulting data model TERM
allows the definition of application specific patterns of temporal change including concepts for the
treatment of incomplete or unprecise data (history
structures). Furthermore, TERM supplies two concepts
for data manipulation, namely, completion for continuing histories (instead of overwriting states), and
correction for altering erroneous data.

1. INTRODUCTION

Designing an information system means to model some portion
of the real world, a so-called mini world, in a suitable way,
such that the model can be implemented on a computer. Implementing the model implies finding a computer representation (data
definition) and providing mechanisms for maintenance and evaluation of that representation (data manipulation).

The tools for the modeling task are available in the form of
so-called data models. They provide the concepts and a corresponding formalism in which the real world image can be expressed.
Data models evolved from a description of *database interfaces*
such as the "network model" by DBTG [8] or the "relational model
of data" by E.F. Codd [6], to models for the description of the
sematics of a mini world. They are thus called *semantic data
models* or *second generation data models*. Examples are the "entity
-relationship model" by P. Chen [5], the "semantic data model"
by M. Hammer and D. McLeod [10], Legol 2.0 by Jones, Mason and
Stamper [11], [12], and many more.

Unfortunately, many data models are static in the sense that they presume the database to represent a single *current state* , so that they provide only *state transitions* that replace one database state by a updated current state. In many cases, however, one is not only interested in a representation of a present state, but also in the history of earlier states or a prognosis of future states.

The problem of changes in the mini world on the one hand and updating of databases on the other hand was first discussed by Schueler [15]. He argues that updating by overwriting destroys valuable information. Several authors have taken up his observations to the extent that they investigate how temporal change of data can be modeled. Consequently, they introduce the notion of *event* (B. Breutmann et al. [2], [3], Bubenko [4], Codd [7]. A. Flory und J. Kouloumdjian [9], and Hammer and McLeod [1Ø]. An event changes a state, and the new state is kept until the next event. Events may occur at integral valued time points (Breutmann) or real valued time points or intervals (Bubenko). Based on the notion of event, some authors allow the specification of consistency assertions, i.e. conditions under which events are valid. In the models of Bubenko and Flory patterns for valid sequences of events can be specified. For a large number of applications this is a good approach. However, there are other patterns of change, such as continuous change or fragmentary observation, where concepts based on events are not entirely meaningful.

It is the goal of this paper to introduce a model for data definition and data manipulation, that allows a general and rigorous treatment of time and, as a consequence, of incomplete data. Means must be available that allow to express very general patterns of change, and to define rules for the evaluation of fragmentary data. In Section 2 we give a number of examples for such patterns and evaluation methods. Patterns and Methods are not universal, but application specific, hence, they cannot be an inherent property of the model but must be definable by the information system designer. We provide him with a language that contains the necessary primitives. It uses the entity-relationship model for the "vertical" description of time aspects, and provides simple concepts for data manipulation accounting for both aspects. The model will be called the time-extended entity-relationship model (TERM).

In Section 3 we give a brief survey of the entity-relationship model. The extended model TERM is defined in Section 4. Its basic notions novel to data modelling, are discussed in Section

4. One of these is history, which is defined as a representation of the development of some fact over time. So-called history structures reflect patterns of temporal change. A discussion of idealized real observation of histories and their representation leads us to a distinction between observers and a referee. The observers are agents who may add sets of newly perceived states to the data base. The database system, or for that matter the observer, cannot verify the observations, however their plausibility can be checked since it is ruled by consistency assertions that may depend on times and values of new input states. It is suggested, that correction of "incorrect" data is confined to the referee; his perceptions are assumed to be a priori correct.

A discussion of the relationship between ("external") mini world history and ("internal") recording history concludes Section 4. In TERM the temporal orders of mini world times and of recording times are completely independent. This is in contrast to present day data base systems, where, aside from some "transmission delay", real world state and database state must always be assumed to refer to the same point in time (the "present").

In Section 5 we redefine some ERM notions, in such a way that the concepts of Section 4 can be integrated in a fairly straightforeward way. A syntax for data definition and data manipulation is given in Chapter 6 using a Pascal-like notation.

2. EXAMPLES FOR TIME-RELATED DATA MODELING PROBLEMS

In order to develop a feeling for the kind of concepts that allow to model temporal patterns we start out with a set of examples. Along with these, the need for dealing with incomplete and inaccurate data, with identification and with time-dependent consistency assertions, will become obvious.

Example 2.1 When a person moves his residence from one county to another, he must change the licence plate and registration-number of his car. This is an example for states that change only at discrete and identifiable events. The state following such an event is kept until the next event.

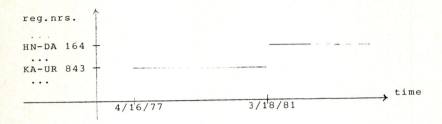

The example illustrates an interesting consequence of changing
states, namely, that the identification of an object may change
with a change of its state, i.e. it may vary over time.

Example 2.2 Consider a patient. Suppose that his blood temperature is taken twice a day. Then there is - within certain tolerance
levels - absolute confidence in the temperature values only for
certain points in time. The temperatures between these points
are usually approached by linear interpolation. Graphically this
looks as follows.

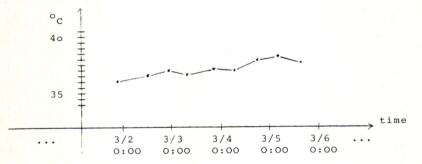

This is an example for continuous change, which is represented
by a finite set of measurements at real valued time points and an
induction formula to derive not explicitly measured states.

Example 2.3 Consider deposits and withdrawals from a banking
account. Usually one is interested in the money transfer only
within an accuracy of a day. Here we have a finite set of states,
namely desposits and withdrawals of a certain amount of money.
If one takes into account that transfers cannot take place on
weekends and holidays, then one may use a time scale of "banking

days" in place of the calendar days shown in the graph or one
may add assertions to the regular calendar restricting legal
banking days to weekdays.

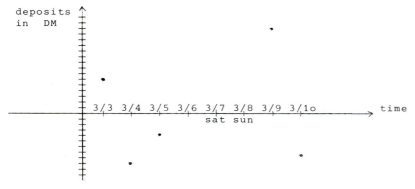

Example 2.4 Consider physical measurements, where times and
values are measured with some inaccurancy due to the properties
of the instruments. Let the accuracy of the clock be given by $\pm$
3 min., and the accuracy of the "valuemeter" by $\pm$ 5 %. The measuring results can be expressed by real valued coordinates.

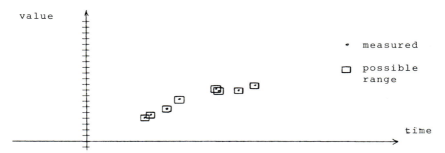

This example points to the difficulties in comparing states
or even events. Consider the two overlapping boxes. Do they
represent the same or different states? Data that is measured
with a potential uncertainty is frequently found in database
application problems.

3. THE ENTITY-RELATIONSHIP-MODEL (ERM)

The basic building block of the entity-relationship model (ERM) is the *entity*, which can be defined as something in the real world, that can exist and be described by certain *attributes* via certain *values*. Entities may be interrelated by a *relationship* in which each entity plays a certain *role*. Since a relationship can have attributes as well, relationships may again be interpreted as entities. Values are taken from the *value set* that is specific to the corresponding attribute. An entity is completely described by the values of all of its attributes, where some distinguished attribute or group of attributes, called *key attribute(s)*, has a value(s) *(key value(s)*) that determines the entity uniquely. In ERM the key value(s) of an entity must be time-invariant, so that the entity may be identified at different times with different states as the same entity. Similarly, a relationship is described by all attributes and roles (the value of a role is an entity represented by its key value) and is identified by key roles/attributes.

All entities (relationships) with identical attributes (attributes and roles) are said to be of the same *entity type* (*relationship type*). The set of all instantiations of an entity type (relation-ship type) is called an *entity set* (*a relationship set*).

4. FOUNDATIONS FOR AN EXTENSION OF ERM

4.1 Histories

In order to capture the aspect of time within the ERM, we introduce the notion of *history*. A history is called *atomic* if it can be formulated as a function from a time domain into some *range of values*. This function is supposed to represent the development of some fact over time (past, present, or future). Atomic histories are associated with the elementary concepts of the ERM, i.e., *attribute histories* and *role histories* are atomic. Furthermore, it should be possible to declare an entity or a relationship to exist even though the values of its components are still unknown. As a consequence, *existence histories* must separately be provided for both entities and relationships.

A history is called *composite* if it can be defined in terms of other (atomic or composite) histories. All composite histories are sets of histories: An *entity (relationship) history* consists of an existence history and the set of all its attribute (and role) histories. A *mini world history* is the set of all entity and relationship histories considered in the mini world.

The time domains of the atomic histories may be of different type, e.g., one may be a subset of another, or they may be completely disjoint. If the time structures of histories of components of one object type differ from each other then we must define a *transformation* to the time domain of the history of the object's existence description. The range of an attribute history is the set of values of some type. The range of all existence histories is the set of Boolean values. The range of a role history is, generally speaking, a set of entities or relationships, their precise representation raises some problems because the concept of key can not be maintained. A solution will be given in 5.3.

4.2 Idealized Perception and Representation

To give a more precise interpretation to the atomic history function we will investigate on how in general time, values and finally histories can be observed and represented.

Traditionally, physics has faced the problem of observation.
It has developed a theory of measurement, which we can exploit
for our problems of real world modeling (see e.g. [14]).

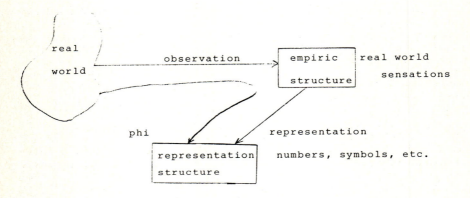

Fig.1 Observation and representation.

Some part of interest of the real world, the mini world, is
observed with sensors, such as eyes, ears or measuring instruments. The characteristics of such a sensor can be expressed by
an *empiric structure* , which consists of a set of possible real
world *sensations*, observable *relations* , and observable *operations*
among them. Two examples for empiric structures:

Example 4.1: A sensation of a balance for measuring weights is a
             position of the pointer. A perceptible relation is
             "heavier", an addition of weights leads to the
             observable operation "addition of pointer positions".

Example 4.2: An observer can recognize a set of persons. For
             each person there are many equivalent sensations,
             that enable the observer to identify a person uni-
             quely. The empiric structure here is just a set of
             sensations.

In order to communicate on sensations we need a representation.

In the case of an *idealized observation* , it is assumed, that
each real world fact leads to at most one sensation and each

sensation has at most one representation. Furthermore, observable relations and operations are mapped onto the representational level. In other words, phi of Fig. 3 must be homomorphic.

The image structure of such a phi is called a *representation structure*. A representation structure consists of a representation set and of relations and operators. In physics the real numbers are common representations, relations and operators on these can easily be defined. A representation structure for Example 4.1 is $(\mathbb{R}, <, +)$.

We will now extend the notion of observation. We say that *perception* is either an observation as defined above or any mental act of determining a mini world relevant fact. In other words, in the sequel we will use the term perception for anything that ultimately leads to a representation for the purpose of communication. Thus, we are confronted with more general structures than the real numbers. In Example 4.2 we can use as a representation structure a set of character strings for the persons' names with no operations or relations other than equality.

Note, that for each empiric structure there may exist a number of alternative representation structures. The balance of Example 4.1 may have a kilogram or a pound scale. The observer of Example 4.2 may use Latin or Greek characters.

Since empiric structures are specific to a sensor, it is clear, that there exists neither a universal empiric structure nor a universal representation structure.

4.3 Representation Structures for Time, for Values and for Attribute (Role, Existence) Histories

A representation structure for time is called a *time structure*, and a representation structure for values of attributes (including the existence "attribute") or roles is called a *value structure*.

A representation structure for histories of an attribute or a role is called a *history structure*. In our model we take as its representation set the powerset of the cross-product of the representation sets of a time structure and a value struture. Therefore, the representation of a history is a set of tuples

(time, value), which are called the states of the history. The
relations of the time structure induce corresponding relations
between states. Since an attribute history is a function, for
each time there exists at most one state.

The representation of histories poses one general problem. A
history may consist of an infinite number of states (as in Examples 2.1, 2.2, 2.4, but not in 2.3). What one needs in such a
case is the representation of a history by means of a finite set
of *characteristic states* and a function for the *derivation* of
not explicitly given states. For some history patterns it is
possible to identify characteristic states and to define a derivation function as part of the history structure. A set of states
is then a characteristic set with respect to some derivation
function if any perceptible state is either in the characteristic
set or in the set of derived states.

In Example 2.1 a value remains constant until there is some
"changing event" producing a new value. A characteristic set
here is the set of all states as observed immediately after the
changing event, i.e. {(4/16/77, KA-UR 843), (3/18/81,HN-DA 164)}.
A derivation function assigns to a given time point the value as
observed after the "most recent event".

In many cases it is not possible to specify a derivation
function. Instead, however, one may be able to specify algorithms
that approach the real world states by making more or less precise *assumption* . Examples are linear interpolation (as in Example
2.2), method of least squares, interval mathematics, and others.
Since those algorithms are specific to a history structure, they
must be defined as so-called *induction operators* .

Now let us turn to the operations and relations that are
meaningful for history structures. There is one *basic operation*
for attribute (role, existence) histories: the *addition* of the
representation of newly percepted states to old ones. Furthermore, there may be one derivation and several induction operators.

If the history consists of a finite set of states or if there
is a derivation function then there are two important relations,
namely, "equality" and "contradiction" of histories. Two histories of the same history structure are equal if all of their
states are equal. This is given if the set of characteristic
states of the one equals the corresponding states (characteristic
or derived) in the otherone and vice versa (by definition of
characteristic states, both histories are based on the same

derivation function). On the other hand, two histories contradict
if there exists a state in both histories with the same time but
different values.

The empiric structure of a sensor may be represented by two
or more different representation structures. As an example consider a time sensor and representations "Greenwich Mean Time" and
"Central Standard Time". In order to compare expressions of
different notation, they must be transformed (if such a transformation exists) into one common representation. A *transformation*
is a homomorphism from one representation structure into an
other.

4.4 Real Perception and Representation

It is an idealized assumption, that phi of Fig. 3 is homomorphic. In reality there are error sources, such as missing observations, postulation of perceptions that have no counterpart in
reality, transmission errors, criminal falsification, and the
like.

An information system designer who has well understood his
mini world may define criteria, for plausible representations of
real world facts. These criteria are commonly called *consistency
assertions*. Consistency assertions should be definable for the
histories of attributes, roles and existence description of
entities and relationships.

Plausible does not necessarily mean right. In general, it is
not decidable wether or not a representation corresponds to a
real world fact. But let us owe an idealistic approach and assume
that there may exist some *referee* whose observations are a priory
correct. Hence, he should be allowed to correct erroneous representations. In practise there will be some priviledged authority
in the organization who will act as if it were a referee.

4.5 Recording of Real World Facts in Databases

In our model to record perceptions of a mini world history means to file their representations in a database. We allow *observers* to *register* the mini world's history in two ways:

1) to *initiate* (i.e. to establish in the database representations of) new entities or relationships and to assign
initial histories to its attributes and/or roles,

2) to *complete* the knowledge about entities or relationships
by adding newly perceived (characteristic) states to previously recorded histories of attributes and/or roles (set
theoretic union). Note, that in order to derive those
states not explicitly recorded requires that the set of
registered states contains all characteristic states needed
for the derivation. The states added to the database may
refer to any points in time in the mini world ("past,
present, or future"), i.e. temporal order of real world
states and temporal order of their recording operations
are completely independent in TERM.

The registration operations of observers can be verified by testing the consistency assertions. Observation errors beyond the scope of consistency assertions must be detected in some other way. In this case, in order to *correct* , the *referee* is allowed

3) to *alter* erroneous histories by substituting erroneous
states by "correct" states or

4) to *erase* the stored representations of incorrectly inserted
entities or relationships.

Now we see, that besides the (external) mini world history there is an (internal) history of the recording operations. This history represents (like a log tape) the temporal sequence of initiate, complete, alter, or erase operations. A state of this *recording history* is an approach to the representation of the mini world history. Due to observational errors it is only an approach. The *latest state of a recording history* represents probably the best available approach to reality, since it inclu-des the latest perceptions of mini world facts. It tells us what we precently know of the mini world history, whereas previous states of the recording history tell us what we knew then. In

case there are only initiations and completions but no corrections, the set of database objects and the histories of each of
its components at a given recording time are included in the
respective sets of any later state of the recording history.

If we are not interested in earlier erroneous versions of
subsequently corrected data the corrections of the referee lead
to overwriting. In the language description of the following
sections it is assumed, that the database contains just such a
latest state of the recording history. Otherwise one had to add
constructs that allow to access previous recording states and
constructs to assign times to the execution of data manipulation
operations. Access to previous states of the recording history
should then be reserved to the referee.

5. TERM: A TIME-EXTENDED ENTITY-RELATIONSHIP MODEL

In Section 4 we introduced a number of further notions to
data modeling. In this section we will integrate them into ERM,
resulting in a number of important extensions. The value of an
attribute or a role is expanded to an atomic history. In history
structures we define how to cope with incomplete data. The introduction of consistency assertions and the distinction between
observers and a referee provides for a more systematic handling
of incorrect data. For identification of objects we will provide
more general means than keys, and, finally, we will include a
complete data manipulation language so that there is a self-contained formalism for data definition and data manipulation.

5.1 Entities and Relationships

With the remarks of Sections 3 and 4 in mind let us now redefine the ERM concepts entity and relationship. An *entity* (a
relationship) is something with an existence in its own right. A
relationship defines some interdependence between entities or
relationships. An entity (a relationship) is described by its
existence description, by *attributes* and *roles*. They may be
constant or *variable in time*. If they are time-invariant a *constant value* is associated, an *atomic history* otherwise. Attributes and roles are defined as in ERM, and existence, attribute

and role history as in Section 4.

The common structure of all entities (relationships) with identical attributes (and roles) is called an *entity type* (a *relationship type*). A definition of entity and relationship types together with all time, value, and history structures and transformations is called a *schema*.

5.2 Existence of Entities and Relationships

As mentioned earlier, the existence description of an entity or a relationship can be interpreted as a special attribute, the history of which has a Boolean value structure. A value false at time t means, that the entity does not exist in the mini world at time t and, consequently, none of its attributes or roles may have a defined value at t. There will be a built-in assertion for each component, guaranteeing that no characteristic state outside the object's existence is added to the component's history. Furthermore, derivation functions are implicitly restricted to those times where the existence attribute yields a value true.

5.3 Data Identification

The concept of key of the original ERM is not included in TERM, since a time-invariance of keys is a too strong restriction (cf. Example 2.1). We will provide more general means of identifying. We need an identification of entities and relationships for two reasons:

1) in order to avoid waste of storage space the value of a role should not be the duplicate of an object but rather a suitable *surrogate* to identify the respective *representation* of an object uniquely;

2) for the *retrieval* of objects there we allow identification by logical predicates. Such a predicate may identify an object uniquely or a possibly empty set of objects with identical relevant properties.

In both cases *pointers* to the stored representation of the

object serve the purpose. Consequently, roles have pointer values. Value structures for pointers need not explicitly be defined. There are no operations on pointers and the only relation
is equality. Equality of pointers is equivalent to equality of
the objects to which they refer. Note, that in TERM the pointer
value itself is invisible to the outside, visible are the objects
to which the pointers point. In Section 6.7 identifying expressions yielding a pointer value are discussed in more detail.

5.4 Data Manipulation

The data manipulation constructs are based on Pascal ([13]).
In addition to Pascal TERM includes concepts for database transactions, for non-deterministic set selection, and for predicate
logic qualification, not only of entities and relationships or
sets thereof, but also for the logic description of subsets or
elements of any set that can be constructed in TERM.

A *database transaction* is either a registration or a correction. A *registration* is a sequence of statements including <u>ini-
tiate</u> and/or <u>complete</u>-statements. For all attributes or roles
the history of which has been initialized or completed within
the transaction all assertions are tested. The transaction becomes effective only if all assertions are true. An *assertion* can
be defined for each attribute or role and is a Boolean expression
that can refer to the database as seen before the begin or at
the end of the transaction and/or to objects and partial histories that are added within the transaction. A *correction* transaction includes <u>erase</u> and <u>alter</u> statements, it is not controlled
by assertions.

TERM offers a *non-deterministic set selection operator* (<u>some</u>,
see 6.7) which can be employed for specifying any kind of non-
determinism.

6. THE TERM LANGUAGE

In the following we describe the TERM constructs. The language
here is restricted, with respect to what is described above, in
two ways: elements of representation sets must be describable by
Pascal-like types, and it is assumed, that only the latest state
of the recording history is accessible. In the subtitles we
refer to the syntax description in appendix A and to examples in
appendix B.

6.1 Definition of a Schema (A.1)

The schema consists of auxiliary declarations (for constants,
types, and functions, that are global to all other declarations)
and of definitions of structures, time structures, value structures, history structures, structure transformations, entity types,
and relationship types.

6.2 Definition of Time Structures and Values Structures (A.2,B.2, B.3)

TERM allows to define so-called structures. A structure is a
set with a number of relations between its elements and a number
of operators, that map elements of the set onto elements. The
structure set consists of elements of a given type. It can be
restricted by a where-clause containing a predicate (specified
as a Boolean expression) that must be true for all elements of
the structure set. The key-word element acts as a logical variable bound to the range of the type under consideration. A structure is an auxiliary construct, and in its definition it is not
said, which real world phenomenon can be representated by it.
The interrelation between real world and representation is defined by the usage of a structure as a time or a value structure.
Predefined structures are "Boolean", "integer", "real", "char",
and "pointer(↑)".

A time structure is defined as structure with a time interpretation. Its representation set is interpreted as set of time
elements (e.g. points or intervals). Accordingly, a value struc-

<u>ture</u> is a structure that represents values.

6.3 Definition of History Structures (A.2,B.6,B.7)

In the definition of a <u>history structure</u> we must specify the
set of histories, which is the powerset of the crossproduct of
the representation sets of a time structure and a value structure. The crossproduct, again, may be restricted by a <u>where</u>-clause
(see above), the words <u>history</u> and <u>state</u> are interpreted as
logical variables of the respective history or state type. Furthermore, we must define all history relations (other than equality and contradiction of histories) and history operations
(other than the base operation, see below). For each history
structure we assume as predefined types the following:

<u>type</u><history structure identifier>-state =
    <u>record</u> t:<time structure identifier>;
           v:<value structure identifier>
    <u>end</u>;
    <history structure identifier>-history =
    <u>set</u> <u>of</u> <history structure identifier>-state;

History relations are defined as Boolean functions of histories. As an example see B.4, where the relations "eqhist" and
"conthist", that are predefined in TERM are given in TERM syntax.

In 4.3 we distinguished three kinds of history operations,
namely, the base operation, a derivation and inductions.

To execute a base operation means to record new observations
or facts. For variable attributes an execution of the base operation results in the union of a set of new (characteristic) states
(representing new observations or facts) and the set of old
states (representing the previously percepted and registered
(characteristic) component history). For constant attributes the
base operation is an assignment and may be executed at most
once. Base operations are executed implicitly as part of a transaction statement. They are also implicitly defined.

A <u>history derivation</u> is a function that takes a set of characteristic states (the stored states of a history are assumed to
be characteristic) and a set of times and determines the state
for each time in the latter set. In many cases a history deriva-

tion will be a partial function. As mentioned in 5.2, its domain is the range of the object's existence. Examples for history derivations are found in B.5 and B.7. A history induction is a function that approximates not explicitly recordedd states (see B.6).

6.4 Definition of Transformations (A.1)

TERM allows to specify time structure transformations, value structure transformations, and history structure transformations. The functions accept input from one structure and produce output of another structure.

6.5 Definition of Entity Types and Relationship Types (A.3,B.7)

Entity type definitions and relationship type definitions only differ in that for the latter we require to specify roles. The existence description is treated, as if it were an attribute with the name existence. Attributes and roles may be constant or variable. A constant attribute requires an associated time-invariant value during the existence of the entity. We need not specify a history structure, since value plus existence history determine the attribute's history. For variable attributes a history structure must be specified.

Roles and attributes only differ in that the values of the histories of role are pointer values refering to entities or relationships.

For the atomic histories consistency assertions may be defined. The assert-clause names a predicate that has to be tested at the end of each registration transaction. Within the predicate the reserved word self refers to the object under consideration, whereas old refers to a component's history or to the set of all objects of some type before the begin of the transaction; new denotes the states of a history or elements of entity or relationship sets provisionally added within the transaction, and, finally, total is the union of old and new.

For all time-variable components (vc) we define as an implicit assertion (cf. 5.2):

> <u>assert</u> (<u>all</u> s <u>in</u> <u>new</u> self.vc)
> [<u>total</u> self.existence <u>at</u> s.t = true
> <u>and</u> s.v <> <u>nil</u>]

6.6 Construction of Sets (A.4)

The set concept in TERM is more general than in Pascal to the effect that within sets no ordering is assumed and more general operators are supplied. To denote this difference we will use ⟨ ⟩ instead of [ ] and disallow subrange expressions (in Pascal: <expression>..<expression>). Trivial sets are the empty set and sets with all elements explicitly ennumerated, furthermore the set of all initiated (and not erased) elements of one entity or relationship type, denoted by <u>set</u> <u>of</u> <u>all</u> <object type identi-fier>.

Set expressions are formed in the usual way (union, intersec-tion, set difference) or by predicates. For that reason we extend Pascal's Boolean expressions and introduce *first order predicate logic*. A more key-word oriented syntax is given to the common mathematical notation

$$(Q_n \ x_{n1}, \ldots, x_{nk_n} \ \in \ X_n) \ \ldots \ (Q_1 \ x_{11}, \ldots, x_{1k_1} \ \in \ X_1)$$

$$P(y_1, \ldots, y_m, x_{n1}, \ldots, x_{1k_1})$$

where Q_i stand for $\forall$ or $\exists$, x_{ij} are logical variables (see 6.8) of type x_i local to the predicate, and y_1 are (logical or other) variables global to the predicate. The predicate itself must be a TERM expression yielding a Boolean value. With the help of predicates subsets can be described as in the example:

{<u>those</u> y <u>in</u> Y <u>where</u> (<u>all</u> x <u>in</u> X)[y<x]}.

6.7 Identification of Set Elements (A.4)

The non-deterministic selector some returns one arbitrary
element from a non-empty set. It is not guaranteed, that two
calls of some on the same set will yield identical elements. A
special value nil is returned by a some call, if the set is
empty.

Deterministic identification of objects is similar to subset
description by predicates, the predicate, however, must yield
exactly one element, otherwise a value nil is returned. An example for an element identification is:

that x1 in X where (all x2 in X) [x1 < x2].

Expressions of the form that <logical variable declaration>
where <Boolean expression> can be used for unique selection of
an element of any given TERM set. It is especially useful for
the associative description of entities and relationships. Here
the evaluation of predicates results in a search procedure in
the database.

6.8 Variables

TERM extends the Pascal concept of variables in two ways.
Whereas Pascal distinguishes between *static* and *dynamic variables*
TERM also introduces *object variables* and *logical variables* .

Object variables are the representations for entities and
relationships, they are created by an initiate-statement and
normally have an infinite scope (except they are erased by the
referee). The scope of the object variable (its "accessability")
and the times where the object's existence equals "true" (its
real world existence) must not be confused. Like dynamic variables object variables can be referenced indirectly via pointers
bound to an entity or a relationship type. The initiate-statement
assigns an address value (cf. database key in the network model)
to a pointer variable. This value determines the object variable
uniquely during its accessability in the database. Other forms
of assignment to a pointer variable are like in the example:

```
var p,q,r:    person;
...
initiate(p);
q:= that pers in set of all person
     where pers.name = 'jones';
r:= some set of all pers;
```

Logical variables only occur within predicates, they must not stand on the left side of an assignment. For that reason we allow logical variables also to be of entity or relationship type (cf. pers in the above example).

6.9 History Expressions (A.4)

Reference to a history, a state or constant value of an attribute or role is made in a way similar to identification of record fields in Pascal, for example

```
var p:person; t:date; z:set of date;
    hp:project-history; hb:temp-history;
... p:= some set of all person;
if p.name = 'jones' and p.salary at t <=40000
then ...
                     %person has a constant attribute "name"
                     %and time variable attributes "salary, project
                     %involved", and "blood temperature"
...
z:= {those d in date where t1 < date < t2};
hp:= p.project-involved restricted to z;
hb:= p.blood-temperature restricted to z approached by lin-inter-
     pol;
                     %approximation by linear interpolation
```

For constant attributes or roles a history expression yields a value. If a history is restricted by an at clause, it yields the value at the time specified. Otherwise it is a set of states, either a complete history or the history restricted to the set of time elements, specified.

If for the time(s) specified in an at-clause (in a restricted to-clause) there is no explicit state in the registered (characteristic) history, then derivation of the stored history is invoked and the states will be implicitly derived, if possible

(nil otherwise). If approximation of missing and not derivable
states is desired an approached by-clause is required, where the
name of the induction function as defined in the respective
history structure must be specified.

6.10 Database Transactions (A.5)

A database transaction (register, correct) parenthesizes a
sequence of statements. erase and alter-statements may occur in
correct-transactions only; whereas initiate and complete-state-
ments may occur in correct or register-transactions. The data
manipulation operations within register are executed provisionally; at transaction end all assertions are tested, and, if they
all are true, the manipulations become permanent. There is a
predefined variable 'ta-status' which is set at the end of each
transaction allowing to test if the transaction was valid.

An initiate-statement creates a new object representation
together with an identifying pointer value. An initial history
may be defined for the new object. In any case a new object is
accessible via some-calls. A complete adds new observations to
existing objects. Initializing or completing an object's history
means executing a base operation for selected components.

An example:


```
var s1,s2: sal-state;
...
register begin
        s1.t.month:=jan;s1.t.year:=1981;s1.v=3100;
        s2.t.month:=oct;s2.t.year:=1981;s2.v=3250;
        complete (that p in set of all person
                where p.name = 'jones')
                begin salaray:={s1,s2}
                % executes a base operation for
                % salary of 'jones'; two new
                % characteristic states are added
                end
        % now assertions are tested and the value of
        % ta-status is determined
        end;
```

Remember that "update" or "delete" operators do not exist in TERM. There is, however, a concept for the correction of erroneous data. Correction is reserved to the referee. An <u>erase</u>-statement results in the deletion of the object, an <u>alter</u> results in the replacement of th object's history by a new history. The new history underlies no restriction, it may violate assertions.

<u>correct</u> <u>begin</u>
       <u>erase</u> (<u>that</u> p <u>in</u> <u>set</u> <u>of</u> <u>all</u> person
            <u>where</u> name='smith');
      <u>alter</u> (<u>that</u> p <u>in</u> <u>set</u> <u>of</u> <u>all</u> person
            <u>where</u> name='janes')
            <u>begin</u> name:'jones' <u>end</u>
     <u>end</u>;

6.11 Programs (A.5)

A TERM program is a schema definition (<u>define</u>), a generation or database program. Execution of a <u>generate</u> establishes a new database with empty object sets. Objects can be created, manipulated and evaluated by a <u>db-program</u> bound to the database by database and schema identifiers. Pascal is extended as described above. Everything defined in the associated schema is global to the program, global object variables are the entities and relationships of the database.

7. CONCLUSIONS

The goal of TERM is to give systems analysts and designers a tool that allows them to include the semantics of temporal aspects and the treatment of incomplete or incorrect data into the database schema, rather than dispersing it in application programs.

Starting from the idea, that databases should represent a history about a mini world rather than just a current state, we investigated on perception and representation of such histories. The understanding, that there is no universal pattern for temporal changes, lead us to the concept of problem dependent representation structures for time, values, and histories, that have to be defined for each application. This concept was then integrated into ERM, resulting in the datamodel TERM. TERM not only supplies all facilities for data definition, but also for data manipulation. The language is based on Pascal. There are two data manipulation concepts, namely, registration for adding of new facts and correction as a facility reserved for a priviledged agent, the referee. The language includes first order predicate logic for easy specification of sets and elements and non-determinism, thus supporting stepwise application program refinement.

ACKNOWLEDGEMENT

    The author is grateful to many helpful comments of Peter C. Lockemann and his colleagues.

APPENDIX A. A SYNTAX FOR TERM

A.1 Schema

schema

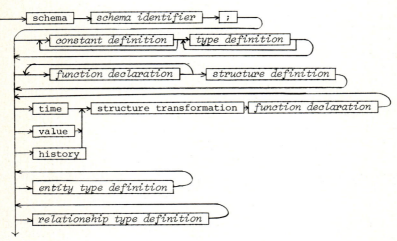

A.2 Structures

structure definition

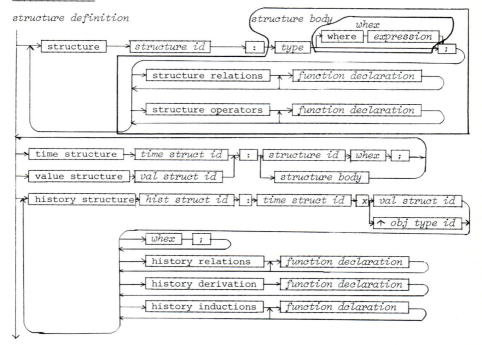

A.3 Entity Type and Relationship Type

entity type definition

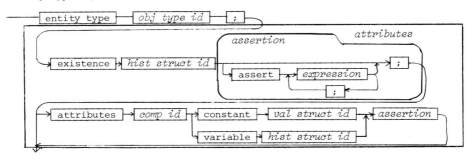

relationship type definition

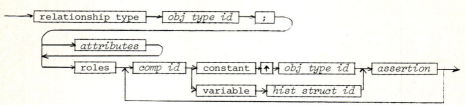

A.4 Expression

expression

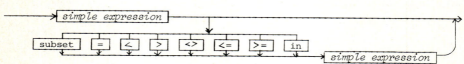

simple expression

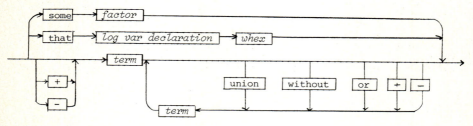

term

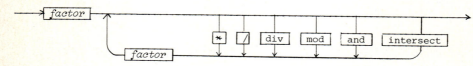

factor

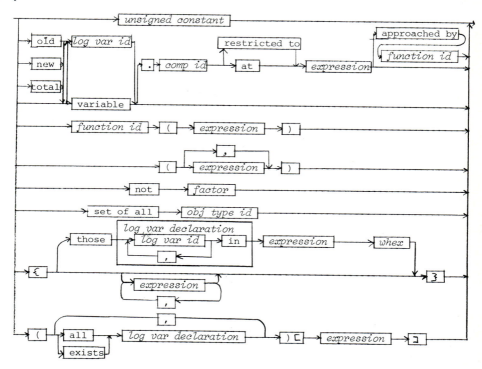

A.5 Program

program

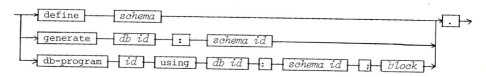

block

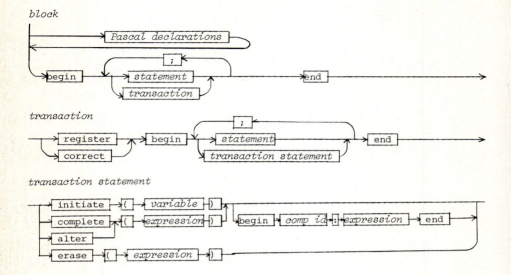

transaction

transaction statement

Syntactical variables not defined here are as in Pascal.

Appendix B. Examples

B.1 Structure: Real-Interval

This is an example for a structure. There we define a representation for unprecise data expressed as real-valued intervals. Definition of operators and relations are common in interval mathematics (cf. [1]).

```
structure   real-interval: record a,b: real end
                           where element.a <= element.b;
            % this restricts the representation set to true
            % intervals
structure   relations
function    less (rl,r2:real-interval):Boolean;   begin  less:=rl.b
            < r2.a end;
            % interval rl less than r2
function    equal (rl,r2: real-interval): Boolean;
```

```
              begin: equal:= rl.a=r2.a and rl.b=r2.b end;
              % equal intervals
function      leq (rl,r2:real-interval):Boolean;
              begin leq:= rl.ab <= r2.b end;
              % rl is less or equal r2
function      posseq (rl,r2: real-interval): Boolean;
              begin posseq:= not (less(rl,r2) or less (r2,rl)) end;
              % rl and r2 overlap
structure     operators
function      add (rl,r2: real-interval): real-interval;
              begin add.a:= rl.a+r2.a; add.b:= rl.b+r2.b end;
              % addition
function      sub (rl,r2: real-interval): real-interval;
              begin sub.a:= rl.a-r2.b; sub.b:= rl.b-r2.a end;
              % subtraction
function      merge (rl,r2:= real-interval): real-interval;
              begin if posseq (rl,r2)
                    then begin merge.a:= min ({rl.a,r2.a}).
                               merge.b:= max ({rl.b,r2.b}) end
                    else begin merge.a:= nil;
                               merge.b:= nil end
              end;
              % the function merges to intervals only if they
              % overlap, it is undefined (nil) otherwise
function      minim(s: set of real-interval);      % minimum
              begin minim:= that r in s            % r  is  logical  va-
                                            riable
                         where (exists rl in s, all r2 in s)
                               [leq(rl,r2) and r = rl];
                         % prealgorithmic expression, trivial
                         % implementation: nested loop over s
              end;
function      mixim(s: set of real-interval);      % maximum
              begin mixim:= that r in s
                         where (exists rl in s, all r2 in s)
% in interval mathematics a least four different distance
% functions are useful: maximal distance, minimal distance,
% average distance and normal distance
function max-dist (rl,r2: real-interval): real;
    begin max-dist:=max({rl.b,r2.b})-min({rl.a,r2.a}) end;
function min-dist (rl,r2:real-interval):real;
    begin min-dist:=max({0,rl.a-r2.b,r2.a-rl.b}) end;
function avg-dist(rl,r2: real-interval): real;
    begin    avg-dist:=abs(rl.a+(rl.a-rl.b)/2-r2.a-(r2.a-r2.b)/2)
    end;
function norm-dist (rl,r2: real-interval): real;
```

```
      begin norm-dist:=max.({abs(rl.a-r2.a),abs(rl.b-r2.b)})
end;
```

B.2 Time Structure: Date

This time structure describes calender dates.

```
time structure date:
        record m,d,y: integer end
                % month, day, year
        where not (element.m=2 and element.d = 29
                        and element.y mod 4 = o
                        and element.y <> 1900
                or element.m = 2 and element.d = 30
                or element.m in {2,4,6,9,11}
                        and element.d = 31
                or element.m > 12
                or element.d > 31);
        % disallows illegal dates
structure relations
function before (tl,t2:date): Boolean;       % temporal order
        begin before:= tl.y < t2.y
                        or tl.y = t2.y and tl.m < t2.m
                        or tl.y=t2.y and tl.m=t2.m and tl.d<t2.d
        end;
function contemp (tl,t2:date):Boolean;       % contemporary
        begin contemp:= tl.d = t2.d and tl.m = t2.m
        and tl.y = t2.y end;
function becon(tl,t2:date): Boolean;
        % before or contemporary
        begin becon:= before(tl,t2) or contemp(tl,t2) end;
structure operators
    function next-day(t:date):date;       %determines "tomorrow"
    begin next-day.y:= t.y; next-day.m:= t.m;
        if t.d < 28 then next-day.d:= t.d + 1
        else if t.d=28 and t.m = 2
                    then if t.y= 1900 or t.y mod 4<>0
                                    % leap-year?
                                    then begin next-day.d:= 1;
                                               next-day.m:= 3 end
                                    else next-day.d:= 29
            else if t.d = 29 and t,m =2
                        then begin next-day.d:=1; next-day.m:=3 end
```

```
            else if t.d<30  or t.d = 30 and t.m in {1,3,5,7,8,
                    10,12}
                    then next-day.d: = t.d + 1
            else if t.m <> 12 then begin next-day.d := 1;
                                         next-day.m := t.m+1
                                   end
        else begin next-day.d:= 1;
                   next-day.m:= 1;
                   next-day.y:= t.y + 1
              end
    end;
function prev-day(t.date): date;
        ... analoguous ...
function add(d:date, i:integer):date;       % adds a number  of
        days
        begin add:= d;
              while i>0 do
                    begin add:=next-day(add); i:= i-1 end;
              while i<0 do
                    begin add:= prev-day (add); i:= i+1 end.
        end;
function dist(d1,d2:date):integer;            % determines  the
                                                 number
        begin if  before  (d2,d1)       % of days between d1
              and d2
              then dist:= dist(d2,d1);
              while before (d1,d2) do
                    begin d1:= next-day (d1);
                          dist:= dist + 1 end
        end;
function maxd(t: set of date): date; % determines the maximum
        ...
function mind(t:=  set of date): date; % determines the mini-
        mum
        ...
function least-recent (t: set of date, z: date): date;
        % determines the left neighbor of z in t
        begin least-recent:= maxd({those x in t
                                   where becon (x,z)}) end;
function least-future (t: set of date, z: date):date;
        % right neighbor of z in t
        begin least-future:= mind ({those x in t
                                    where becon (z,x)}) end;
```

B.3 Value Structure: Registration-Numbers

This structure defines German licence plates (cf. Example 2.1)

```
value structure registration-numbers:
      record case car-registered: Boolean of
            true: (county: {KA,HN,F,MTK,BN,....}
                   middle: packed array [1,2] of char;
                   number: integer) end;
```

B.4 Predefined History Relations

Two relations are predefined for history structures, namely "eqhist" and "conthist".

```
function eqhist (g,h: <history structure identifier>): Boolean;
      % histories g and h are equal
      begin eqhist:= (all x in g, y in h)
                     [x.v = h at x.t and y.v = g at y.t]
      % the characteristic set of g must be derivable in h and
      % vice versa.
function conthist(g,h:<history structure identifier>): Boolean;
      % two histories are in contradiction.
      begin conthist := not eqhist(g,h) end;
```

B.5 History Structure: Staircase

This history structure models a pattern like in Example 2.1. Characteristic states are observed after each moving. History structures like this are typical for data models that are based on a notion of "event".

```
history structure staircase: date x registration-numbers;
```

% there are no particular relations besides the ones of B.4

```
history derivation
function derive(h:staircase-history, t: set of date):
                staircase-history;
```

```
     var s,l:staircase-state; z:date;
     begin derive:= {}; z:= some t; t:= t without {z};
          while z <> nil do
               s.t:= z;
               l:= least-recent (h,z)
               % least-recent is defined in date and im-
               % plicitly in staircase (left neighbor);
               if l=nil then s.v.car-registered:= false
                           else s.v:= l.v;
               extend:= extend union {s};
               z:= some t; t:= t without {z}
          end
     end;
```

B.6 History Structure: Measurement

This is a history structure for Example 2.4. There we have unprecise measurement of data and we cannot give a derivation formula.

```
const clockprec = 3; valprec = 5;    %precission of instruments
time structure mtim: real-interval
               where element.b = element.a + 2 * clockprec;
value structure val: real-interval
               where element.b =
                    element.a*(100+valprec)/(100-valprec);
history structure measurement: mtim x mval;
history relations
function uniq (h: measurement-history): Boolean;
          begin uniq:= (all s1,s2 in h)
                    [not posseq(s1.t, s2.t)
                     or posseq(s1.v, s2.v)] end;
          % possible equality of the times of any two states
          % requires possible equality of their states
function noncont(g,h: measurement-history): Boolean;
          begin noncont:= uniq(g union h) end;
          % two histories do not contradict if all of their states
          % with possibly equal times have possibly equal values
...
% many more relations could be defined, like "possible
% subhistory", "possible equality", etc.
...
history inductions
```

```
function lin-interpol (h: measurement-history, tm: set of  mtim):
                       measurement-history
        var s,l,r: measurement-state; z: mtim;
        begin lin-interpol:= { };
            z:= some tm; tm:= tm without {z};
            whilez <> nil do begin
                 s.t:= z;
                 l:= max({those x in h
                              where leq (x.t,z)});
                 % left neighbor
                 r:= min({those x in h
                              where leq (z,x.t)});
                 % right neighbor
                 if l = nil or r = nil
                 then begin
                      s.v.a:= nil; s.v.b:= nil end
                 else if equal (l,r)
                      then begin s.v.a:= l.v.a;
                            s.v.b:= l.v.b end
                      else begin
                            s.v.a:= (r.v.a-l.v.a) * (z.a-l.t.a)
                                    /(r.t.a - z.a) + l.v.a;
                            s.v.b:= s.v.a * (100 + valpec)
                                    /(100 - valprec) end;
                 lin-interpol:= lin-interpol union {s};
                 z:= some tm; tm:= tm without {z} end
                 end;
% other induction functions are also reasonable like
% "least-square", "spline", etc.
...
```


B.7 Entity and Relationship Type: Person, Company, Employment


```
history structure ex: date x Boolean
        where (exists b,e in history, all x in history)
             [x.v=false and (before(x,b) or becon (e,x))
             or x.v = true
             % b marks the begin, e the end of existence;
             % the existence history is completely defined
             or x.v = false and before (x,b) or x.v = true
             % the end of existence is still undefined
             or x.v = true and before (x,e) or x.v = false
             % the begin of existence is still undefined
```

```
            or history = { }
            % the existence history is undefined
            or x.v <> nil or least-recent (history, x) = nil
                        or least-future (history, x) = nil];
            % states with value nil are non-characteristic
history derivation
function derivex (h:ex, t: set of date): ex;
        var s,l,r: ex-state; z:date;
        begin derivex:= { }; z:= some t; t:= t without {z};
            while z <> nil do begin
                s.t:= z;
                l:= least-recent (h,z);
                r:= least-future (h,z);
                if l=nil and r.v=false % left margin
                    or l.v=false and r<>nil % past end
                    or l.v=false and r=nil % right  margin
                        and (exists x in h) [x.v = true]
                    then s.v:= false
                else if l.v=true and r<>nil % exists
                    then s.v:= true
                else s.v:= nil;             % who knows?
                derivex:= derivex union {s};
                z:= some t; t:= t without {z} end
        end;
    ...
entity type person;
existence ex;
attributes name constant string;       % alphabetical strings
        address variable location; % time:date; value:integer
entity type company;
existence ex;
attributes name constant string;
        address variable location;
        no-emp variable count; % time: date; value: integer
relationship type employment;
existence ex
        assert (all s in new self.existence)
            [not s.v = true
            or ( self.employer .existence at s.t and
                self.employee .existence at s.t)];
        % this guarantees that a person can be
        % employed only if person and company
        % exist
roles employer constant    company;
      employee constant    person;
```

REFERENCES

[1]   G. Alefeld, J. Herzberger, "Einführung in die Inter-
           vallrechnung", Bibliographisches Institut, Mannheim,
           1974.
[2]   B. Breutmann, E. Falkenberg, R. Mauer, "CSL: A Langua-
           ge for Defining Conceptual Schemas", Proc. IFIP WG
           2.6, Venice, 1979.
[3]   B. Breutmann, "The Temporal Dimension of Conceptual
           Schemas", Working Paper, IFIP WG 2.6, Munich, Mar
           1979.
[4]   J.A. Bubenko jr., "The Temporal Dimension in Informa-
           tion Processing", in "Architecture and Models in Data
           Base Management Systems", G.M. Nijssen, ed. North-
           Holland, 1977.
[5]   P.P.-S. Chen, "The Entity-Relationship Model – toward
           a Unified View of Data", ACM TODS, Vol1., No.1, Mar.
           1976.
[6]   E.F. Codd, "A relational model of data for large
           shared data banks," Comm.ACM 13,6, June 1970.
[7]   E.F. Codd, "Extending the Database Realtional Model
           to Capture More Meaning," ACM TODS, Vol.4, No.4, Dec.
           1979.
[8]   CODASYL Data Base Task Group, Apr. 1971 Report.
[9]   A. Flory, J. Kouloumdjian, "A Model for the Descrip-
           tion of the Information Systems Dynamics," Proc. ECI
           78, Springer Lecture Notes 65, Heidelberg, 1978.
[10]   M. Hammer, D.C. McLeod, "The Semantic Data Model: A
           Modelling Mechanism for Database Applications," Proc.
           SIGMOD Intn'l Conf. on Mod. of Data, June 1978.
[11]   S. Jones, P. Mason, R. Stamper, "LEGOL 2.0: A relatio-
           nal specification language for complex rules", Infor-
           mation Systems, Vol.4, No.4, Nov. 1979.
[12]   S. Jones, P. Mason, "Handling the Time-Dimension in a
           Data Base," Proc. Aberdeen Database Conference, July
           1980.
[13]   K. Jensen N. Wirth, "Pascal User Manual and Report",
           Springer, New York, 2nd. ed. 1975.
[14]   D.H. Krantz, R.D. Luce, P. Suppes, A. Tversky, "Foun-
           dations of Measurement", Vol.1, Academic Press, New
           York, 1971.
[15]   B.-M. Schueler, "Update Reconsidered", in Architecture
           and Models in DBMS, G.M. Nijssen ed., North-Holland,
           Amsterdam 77.

Entity-Relationship Approach to
Information Modeling and Analysis, P.P. Chen (ed.)
Elsevier Science Publishers B.V. (North-Holland)
©ER Institute, 1983

DATABASE VIEWS USING DATA ABSTRACTION

Burt Leavenworth
IBM Thomas J. Watson Research Center
Yorktown Heights, New York 10598

This paper is a further attempt to close the gap between programming languages and database management systems. It describes the use of a data abstraction language conjoined with a module interconnection language to define different views of an hierarchical data model (IMS), and transformations between that model and a relational model. This is done through the medium of an abstraction called a form. The internal representation of the form contains both the information for navigating the IMS database and for operating on form abstractions.

1. INTRODUCTION

Because of the great amount of interest in the relational model of data [5], and the continued popularity of the hierarchical model [19], in particular IMS [9], we are motivated to use data abstraction to represent both of these models and to describe transformations from one to the other. The approach is to start with an hierarchical database as a point of departure, and to develop user views which are also hierarchical, but are obtained by means of transformations which involve non-hierarchical structures as intermediate forms (which may or may not be pure relational). This approach suggests the coexistence of different models of data reflected by data abstractions with transformations between them to support different views.

A number of different approaches have been taken in an attempt to unify the disparate domains of programming languages and database management systems. The work by Date [6] is an example of a programming language designed specifically to deal with different data models (relational, hierarchical, and network). The SEQUEL2 [3] language embeds a query language into an existing host language, using a preprocessor to translate the database references into run time calls on the database system. On the other hand, a number of languages have been developed which exploit data abstractions and strong typing, but which are based on defining the relation as a primitive data type (see, for example [14]).

This paper describes the use of a module interconnection language to define a database schema, in conjunction with the use of data abstractions to define entity types and relationships. This can be characterized as using the notion of "programming in the large" [7] for the purpose of data definition, and that of "programming in the small" [7] for the purpose of data manipulation.

After introducing the ADAPT system [1] [11], we discuss a data abstraction called a <u>form</u> which allows different views of the hierarchical model and transformations between that model and the relational model. The interface between ADAPT and the hierarchical model is made explicit by considering IMS and DL/I (the data sublanguage of IMS). The internal representation of a form contains both the information for navigating the IMS database and for operating on form abstractions.

A previous paper [10] emphasized queries on a semantic net database, whereas this paper concentrates on data manipulation and user views on an hierarchical database.

2. THE ADAPT SYSTEM

We have developed an experimental programming system which supports data abstractions, and which has been heavily influenced by CLU [12]. The ADAPT System has two major components: (1) an External Structure [1], which is a module interconnection language, and (2) a programming language for specifying individual modules [11]. The ADAPT translator allows compilation of individual modules and consists of a type checker and code generator. The type checker has been running for over a year; the code generator is nearing completion. The current target language for this translator is PL/I.

There are three types of modules supported:

Procedure

ADAPT procedures are like conventional procedures except that parameters can be user defined types in addition to the primitive types provided by the language.

Capsule

Capsules allow the definition of abstract types in terms of the operations associated with those types. A capsule consists of the definition of the internal data representation for the abstract type, together with the definition of the operations (called encapsulated procedures) on this representation. Both of these components are hidden from the user.

Iterator

Iterators produce the elements of an aggregate data object, one element at a time, where the representation of the (abstract) data object is hidden.

There is also a means for defining Interface Modules which allow communication with modules written in standard PL/I. The purpose of the Interface Module is to allow an "escape" into PL/I code while preserving the type integrity of the overall program. This approach guarantees that an Interface Module cannot violate the data space of ADAPT programs.

For further details on the ADAPT System, see [11].

3. CONCEPTUAL SCHEMA SPECIFICATION

The idea of using a module interconnection language in conjunction with data abstractions to express the hierarchical structure of a database was developed independently by the author who recently found that this approach had been suggested by Weber [20]. In [10], we described how the conceptual schema for a semantic net data model could be specified by the module interconnection language used in our system, which we call the External Structure.

We will introduce the database example to be used in the remainder of the paper (which was taken from [17]) as a means to illustrate this specification. The database consists of departments (DEPT), and projects (PROJECTS) in a company. The schemas are shown below:

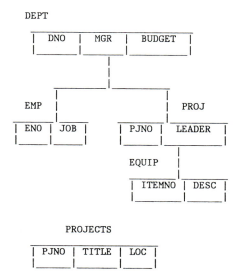

Each node representing an entity is shown below as a type definition in the External Structure with the names of the attributes as operations (value returning encapsulated procedures), and the return types as shown.

The notation * := DEPT means that the asterisk is used as a shorthand for the
DEPT type; it therefore acts like a macro substitution.

```
TYPE DEPT
 DEFINES
 ( * := DEPT
  DNO(*) -> STRING
  MGR(*) -> STRING
  BUDGET(*) -> INT
  EMP(*) -> FORM<<EMP>>
  PROJ(*) -> FORM<<PROJ>>
  CREATE(STRING,STRING,INT,FORM<<EMP>>,FORM<<PROJ>>) )

TYPE EMP
 DEFINES
 ( * := EMP
  ENO(*) -> STRING
  JOB(*) -> STRING

TYPE PROJ
 DEFINES
 ( * := PROJ
  PJNO(*) -> STRING
  LEADER(*) -> STRING
  EQUIP(*) -> FORM<<EQUIP>>
  CREATE(STRING,STRING,FORM<<EQUIP>>) -> * )

TYPE EQUIP
 DEFINES
 ( * := EQUIP
  ITEMNO(*) -> STRING
  DESC(*) -> STRING
  CREATE(STRING,STRING) )

TYPE PROJECTS
 DEFINES
 ( * := PROJECTS
  PJNO(*) -> STRING
  TITLE(*) -> STRING
  LOC(*) -> STRING )
```

Note that string bounds have not been shown for the sake of simplicity. Also,
note that the hierarchy is shown explicitly by value returning encapsulated
procedures whose return type is FORM<<entity-type-name>>. This will be
explained below. For the time being, think of this as representing a collection
of instances of the entity-type argument.

It may be useful at this point to indicate how the use of data abstractions in
ADAPT to model entities and their relationships can be related with the
Entity-Relationship model [4]. The elements of this model and corresponding
ADAPT features are shown below, together with a brief discussion.

E-R model	ADAPT model
Value	data object
Entity set	data abstraction or data type
Entity	instance of a data abstraction
Attribute	value returning encapsulated procedure (VREP) which maps an instance of a data abstraction to a data object

Relationship sets can be modelled using data abstractions and value returning encapsulated procedures (VREPs) as follows:

If the relationship R is 1:n between two entities (types) T1 and T2, then T1 can be modelled by a data abstraction named T1 having a VREP named T2 whose return type is FORM<<T2>>. If the relationship R is m:n between entities T1 and T2, then a relationship data abstraction named R can be defined having VREPs named T1 and T2 whose return types are T1 and T2.

Methods of translating the Entity-Relationship schema to the hierarchical model (IMS) are discussed in [13] [15] [18]. Another paper [16] shows the association between the E-R model and the theory of data types.

4. FORM ABSTRACTION

We will consider a data abstraction called a form which is based on the hierarchical data model. This abstraction was introduced by Housel and Shu [8]. A form will usually be shown in a two-dimensional format. Figure 1 depicts a form for the example database.

The name of a repeating group (or a child subtree) is enclosed in parentheses in the table. A section is defined as a form entry which represents a single hierarchical record. Thus, a section is one root instance with all its dependent instances (in IMS, this is called a database record). A form, then, consists of a sequence of sections of the form. In Figure 1, there are two sections, corresponding to the DNO values D1 and D4.

In [8], a set of nonprocedural form operations was defined where the operations require one or more forms as input arguments and produce an output form as a result. The most important of these operators for our purposes are:

SELECT - To select sections based on boolean qualification, project fields, and eliminate subtrees.

SLICE - To flatten a hierarchical branch to a flat table, possibly projecting only some of the items on that branch.

CONSOLIDATE - To build a hierarchy or flat table into a taller hierarchy by factoring out common parents.

GRAFT - To join two hierarchies at the root to form a bushier hierarchy

ELIMDUP - To eliminate duplicate sections

Examples of these operations in order to obtain different views of a database using the medium of data abstractions will be given shortly.

(DEPT)								
			(EMP)		(PROJ)			
							(EQUIP)	
DNO	MGR	BUDGET	ENO	JOB	PJNO	LEADER	ITEMNO	DESC
D1	DOE	40000	19	ENG	J6	RAE	221	COMPUTER
			41	SEC	J8	MEE	46	SCOPE
			52	TECH			317	LASER
			77	ENG	J11	FAR	271	COMPUTER
D4	SO	20000	60	CHEM	J9	LA	47	MICROSCOPE

Figure 1

An interesting special case of a form is a "flat table", i.e. a form that has no hierarchical structure. Figure 2 shows a non-hierarchical form representing the PROJECTS file. Henceforth, "flat table" will be used as a synonym for non-hierarchical form.

```
|        (PROJECTS)        |
|_____|
| PJNO | TITLE |  LOC  |
|_____|_____|_____|
|  J6  |   A   |  SF   |
|  J8  |   B   |  SJ   |
|  J9  |   C   |  LA   |
|  J11 |   D   |  SJ   |
|_____|_____|_____|
```

Figure 2

The External Structure (schema) for the PROJECTS file is shown below.

```
TYPE PROJECTS
 DEFINES
 ( * := PROJECTS
 PJNO(*) -> STRING
 TITLE(*) -> STRING
 LOC(*) -> STRING )
```

5. DATA RESTRUCTURING AND VIEWS

One of the requirements of applications programming is to develop a view of the database that differs from that originally developed during database design. The CONVERT operators [8] introduced above allow the applications programmer to generate new hierarchical structures from existing ones. As stated by Weber [20], "views may be considered as different schema abstractions. Different views may then incorporate different subsets of data base objects, may have objects in common, and may see the objects they share involved in different relationships".

Our strategy is to define a form data abstraction with its associated operators on forms. A form is viewed as being either hierarchical (H) or non-hierarchical (NH), and persistent (P) or non-persistent (NP). A persistent (permanent) object is one whose existence is independent of a single program execution, i.e. a data base object. A non-persistent (transient) object is one whose lifetime is not greater than the execution of a single program. We do not consider updating the original database in this paper.

Instead of defining nonprocedural operators in ADAPT corresponding to the CONVERT operators SELECT, SLICE and CONSOLIDATE, we define equivalent procedural algorithms (the reason for this is discussed later):

An algorithm (which is the equivalent of SELECT) operates on an hierarchical persistent form to produce an hierarchical non-persistent form. This can be shown schematically as:

    H/P --- SELECT ---> H/NP

This algorithm is the converse of the "deletion" algorithm [17] because a structure is being built up during the traversal of the source hierarchy, rather than eliminating subcomponents of a form (as in the CONVERT operation). A non-procedural form operator called SEL, however, will be defined which operates on flat tables.

An algorithm corresponding to SLICE has the following effect:

    H/P --- SLICE ---> NH/NP

The SELECT and SLICE algorithms navigate through the hierarchy in order to produce a form which is some subset or restructuring of the original database. Additional restructuring is performed using nonprocedural operations such as SEL, JOIN, which corresponds to GRAFT, and MAP which is used for projections. These operators are similar in effect to those of the relational algebra.

An algorithm corresponding to CONSOLIDATE has the effect:

    NH/NP --- CONSOLIDATE ---> H/NP

A form can thus be in one of four possible states:

H/P --- hierarchical database
H/NP --- temporary hierarchy
NH/P --- relational database
NH/NP --- temporary relation

We assume there is a nonprocedural operator (REL) to convert a temporary relation to a database relation.

    NH/NP --- REL ---> NH/P

The terms relational and relation are being used with the understanding that duplicate sections have been removed. This can always be done using the ELIMDUP operator.

Starting with a hierarchical database, then, differing views can be obtained in the following steps:

(1) Navigation is performed procedurally through the database, using the SLICE algorithm to produce a flat table (NH/NP).

(2) Nonprocedural operators, for example, SEL,JOIN,MAP, are applied to the flat tables to obtain different views.

(3) Finally, an hierarchical form can be produced by the CONSOLIDATE algorithm.

The application of these algorithms will be shown shortly. First, we will give the External Structure definition for the form abstraction and briefly describe the semantics of its operators.

```
TYPE FORM<<T:TYPE>>
 DEFINES
 ( * := FORM<<T>>
  /* The following are nonprocedural */
  /* operators on NH forms */
  ELIMDUP(*) -> *
  ONE<<T1:TYPE>>(*,PROC(T) -> T1) -> T1
  JOIN<<T1:TYPE,T2:TYPE>>
   (FORM<<T1>>,FORM<<T2>>,PROC(T1,T2)  -> BOOL)
     -> *
  SORT2<<T1:TYPE,T2:TYPE>>(*,PROC(T) -> T1,
    PROC(T) -> T2) -> *
  SEL(*,PROC(T) -> BOOL) -> *
  CREATE() -> *
  MAP<<T1:TYPE>>(*,PROC(T) -> T1) -> FORM<<T1>>
  GROUP ITER<<T1:TYPE>>(*,PROC(T) -> T1) => *
  EMPTY(*) -> BOOL
  ADD(*,T) -> *
  /* The following are procedural operators */
  /* on either NH or H forms  - the PCB type */
  /* is used specifically for H forms and */
  /* ignored for NH forms */
  EACH ITER(*,PCB) => T
  EACH_ROOT ITER(*,PCB) => T
  FILTER ITER(*,PROC(T) -> BOOL,PCB) => T )
```

FORM is an example of a generic type (has a type valued parameter) with the type parameter T. The form abstraction can be "instantiated" with any of the entity types already given by using the syntax FORM<<entity-type-name>>. We now give brief descriptions of the operators.

The ELIMDUP operator obtains a new form by removing duplicate sections from the form argument. The ONE operator obtains a value of type T1 in two steps: (1) it obtains a set of values using the second argument as a projection function, (2) it then selects one of these values (an error exception occurs if they are not all the same value). The JOIN operator obtains a new form by taking the natural join of the argument forms. The SORT2 operator obtains a new form by sorting the first argument with respect to the values selected by the second and third arguments. The SEL operator selects those sections of the first argument satisfying the predicate denoted by the second argument. The CREATE operator creates a non-persistent form. The MAP operator applies the second argument to each element of the first argument to obtain a new flat table. GROUP obtains a form in two steps: (1) obtains a set of values using the second argument as a projection function, (2) each iterator invocation yields a form such that all the above values are the same -- it is assumed that the first argument is sorted

with respect to these values. The EMPTY operator returns TRUE if its argument is
the empty form, and FALSE otherwise. ADD obtains a new form by adding a section
(second argument) to the given form (first argument).

The operators EACH, EACH_ROOT (applied only to the root segment of the
hierarchy), and FILTER are iterators, and are the basic mechanism for
interfacing with and navigating the database. The PCB (Program Control Block)
type represents a "pointer" to the buffer which is allocated by IMS in the
initialization phase and passed as a parameter to the application program. It
is needed for the DL/I calls discussed later.

We have already given an ADAPT schema (External Structure) for an application
consisting of departments and projects in a company. In this company, more than
one department can work on a project, and a department may be responsible for a
number of projects in different locations, although a project has only one
location. The application is to create a PROJDEPT file for projects located in
'SJ'. The schema for PROJDEPT is shown below:

```
TYPE PROJDEPT
 DEFINES
 ( * := PROJDEPT
 PJNO(*) -> STRING
 TITLE(*) -> STRING
 DEPT(*) -> FORM<<DEPT2>>
 CREATE(STRING,STRING,FORM<<DEPT2>>) -> * )

TYPE DEPT2
 DEFINES
 ( * := DEPT2
 DNO(*) -> STRING
 MGR(*) -> STRING
 BUDGET(*) -> INT
 LEADER(*) -> STRING
 EQUIP(*) -> FORM<<EQUIP2>>
 CREATE(STRING,STRING,INT,STRING,FORM<<EQUIP2>>) -> * )

TYPE EQUIP2
 DEFINES
 ( * := EQUIP2
 ITEMNO(*) -> STRING
 DESC(*) -> STRING
 CREATE(STRING,STRING) -> * )
```

This schema can also be represented by the hierarchy graph

```
                        PROJDEPT
                        ----------------
                        | PJNO | TITLE |
                        ----------------
                            |
                        DEPT |
                        --------------------------------
                        | DNO | MGR | BUDGET | LEADER |
                        --------------------------------
                            |
                        EQUIP |
                        ----------------
                        | ITEMNO | DESC |
                        ----------------
```

The first step is to produce a non-hierarchical form from the right hand branch (containing project information) of the DEPT hierarchy. This form has the structure:

```
TYPE T1
 DEFINES
 ( * := T1
 DNO(*) -> STRING
 MGR(*) -> STRING
 BUDGET(*) -> INT
 PJNO(*) -> STRING
 LEADER(*) -> STRING
 ITEMNO(*) -> STRING
 DESC(*) -> STRING
 CREATE(STRING,STRING,INT,STRING,STRING,STRING,STRING) -> * )
```

Starting with the declarations:

```
DCL DEPTS FORM<<DEPT>>;
DCL T1S FORM<<T1>>;
DCL T2S FORM<<T2>>;
DCL T3S FORM<<T3>>;
DCL INST_PROJECTS FORM<<PROJECTS>>;
DCL PROJDEPTS FORM<<PROJDEPT>>;
```

The SLICE algorithm can be performed by the following procedural program:

```
T1S=FORM<<T1>>¢CREATE();
FOR D IN FORM<<DEPT>>¢EACH_ROOT(DEPTS,PCB);
  FOR P IN FORM<<PROJ>>¢EACH(DEPT¢PROJ(D),PCB);
    FOR E IN FORM<<EQUIP>>¢EACH(PROJ¢EQUIP(P),PCB);
      T1S=FORM<<T1>>¢ADD(T1S,T1¢CREATE(DEPT¢DNO(D),
          DEPT¢MGR(D),DEPT¢BUDGET(D),PROJ¢PJNO(P),
          PROJ¢LEADER(P),EQUIP¢ITEMNO(E),EQUIP¢DESC(E)));
    END;
  END;
END;
```

The FOR statement works essentially as follows. The iterator (EACH_ROOT in this case) will select DEPTS and bind them one at a time to the variable D. Each time the iterator yields a DEPT, the body of the FOR statement is executed. This process is repeated until the iterator yields no further DEPTs.

One cannot tell in looking at the above program whether the forms one is manipulating are persistent or non_persistent; this information is contained in the internal representation of the form. These details will be discussed in the next section.

The expression FORM<<T1>>¢CREATE is a compound name with a prefix FORM<<T1>> and a suffix CREATE. The prefix represents a data abstraction (generic in this case) and the suffix represents the operation or encapsulated procedure associated with the abstraction. The use of these compound names makes the program somewhat difficult to read. This problem can be minimized by using generic declarations which have an effect similar to that of generic procedures in PL/I. The type prefix in compound names can be elided by using the types of the arguments in procedure invocations to select the full compound name. An example of a generic declaration is

        GENERIC DNO
         (WHEN (DEPT) DEPT¢NAME)

This means that when the operator DNO is applied to an argument of type DEPT, the compound name is inferred to be DEPT¢DNO. Similar declarations can be given for the operators MGR,BUDGET,PJNO,LEADER, ITEMNO and DESC which are encapsulated procedures of DEPT.

Two more examples using generic types will be given.

        GENERIC EACH<<T:TYPE>>
         (WHEN (FORM<<T>>) FORM<<T>>¢EACH)

        GENERIC ADD<<T:TYPE>>
         (WHEN (FORM<<T>>,T) FORM<<T>>¢ADD)

The generic declaration for EACH_ROOT is similar to that for EACH.

When these declarations are in force, the preceding program now reads as follows:

```
T1S = FORM<<T1>>¢CREATE();
FOR D IN EACH_ROOT(DEPTS,PCB);
 FOR P IN EACH(PROJ(D),PCB);
  FOR E IN EACH(EQUIP(P),PCB);
    T1S = ADD(T1S,CREATE(DNO(D),MGR(D),BUDGET(D),
       PJNO(P),LEADER(P),ITEMNO(E),DESC(E)));
   END;
  END;
END;
```

After performing the above algorithm, the target form looks like:

(T1)						
DNO	MGR	BUDGET	PJNO	LEADER	ITEMNO	DESC
D1	DOE	40000	J6	RAE	221	COMPUTER
D1	DOE	40000	J8	MEE	46	SCOPE
D1	DOE	40000	J8	MEE	317	LASER
D1	DOE	40000	J11	FAR	271	COMPUTER
D4	SO	20000	J9	LA	47	MICROSCOPE

Continuing the example application, the second step is to sort T1S:

T1S = SORT(T1S,T1¢PJNO,T1¢DNO);

This produces the same form as above except that the last and next to last rows are interchanged. Since the JOIN operation (see below) requires the matching of T1S and INST_PROJECTS on PJNO, it is only necessary to sort these forms on PJNO. However, since the final transformation requires its input to be sorted on PJNO and DNO, we perform this here in order to avoid another sort prior to the CONSOLIDATE algorithm (see below).

The application of SORT selects the compound name FORM<<T1>>¢SORT2 according to the generic declaration (assuming a maximum of two sort fields):

```
GENERIC SORT <<T:TYPE,T1:TYPE,T2:TYPE>
  (WHEN (FORM<<T>>,PROC(T) -> T1) FORM<<T>>¢SORT1,
  WHEN (FORM<<T>>,PROC(T) -> T1,PROC(T) -> T2) FORM<<T>>¢SORT2)
```

Note that the instantiation type T1 in the compound name is not the same T1 which appears in the generic declaration.

The next step is to join the result (using the natural join) with PROJECTS.

```
T2S = JOIN(INST_PROJECTS,T1S,(P:PROJECTS,T:T1 -> BOOL;
                       PJNO(P)=PJNO(T)));
```

The third argument of JOIN is a predicate having two parameters P and T of type PROJECTS and T1 respectively, which returns a Boolean value. The expression following the semicolon is called the body of the predicate.

The intermediate form T2 produced by this transformation is:

(T2)								
PJNO	TITLE	LOC	DNO	MGR	BUDGET	LEADER	ITEMNO	DESC
J6	A	SF	D1	DOE	40000	RAE	221	COMPUTER
J8	B	SJ	D1	DOE	40000	MEE	46	SCOPE
J8	B	SJ	D1	DOE	40000	MEE	317	LASER
J9	C	LA	D4	SO	20000	LA	47	MICROSCOPE
J11	D	SJ	D1	DOE	40000	FAR	271	COMPUTER

We can then select from T2S those projects located at 'SJ':

```
T2S = SEL(T2S,(T:T2 -> BOOL; LOC(T)='SJ'));
```

and project all fields except LOC (Type T3 has the same structure as T2 with the exception of the LOC field):

```
T3S = MAP(T2S,(X:T2 -> T3; T3¢CREATE(PJNO(X),TITLE(X),DNO(X),
              MGR(X),BUDGET(X),LEADER(X),ITEMNO(X),DESC(X))));
```

The final step is to build a hierarchical form (PROJDEPT) from the flat table T3.

We assume the declarations:

```
DCL PROJDEPTS FORM<<PROJDEPT>>;
DCL DEPT2S FORM<<DEPT2>>;
DCL EQUIP2S FORM<<EQUIP2>>;
DCL T3S FORM<<T3>>;
```

The CONSOLIDATE algorithm for this transformation is then:

```
PROJDEPTS = FORM<<PROJDEPT>>¢CREATE();
FOR T IN GROUP(T3S,T3¢PJNO);
  DEPT2S = FORM<<DEPT2>>¢CREATE();
  FOR D IN GROUP(T,T3¢DNO);
    EQUIP2S = MAP(D,(X:T3 -> EQUIP2;
                  CREATE(ITEMNO(X),DESC(X)));
    DEPT2S = ADD(DEPT2S,CREATE(ONE(D,T3¢DNO),ONE(D,T3¢MGR),
                          ONE(D,T3¢BUDGET),ONE(D,T3¢LEADER),
                          EQUIP2S));
  END;
  PROJDEPTS=ADD(PROJDEPTS,CREATE(ONE(T,T3¢PJNO),
                    ONE(T,T3¢TITLE),DEPT2S));
END;
```

The final result looks like:

(PROJDEPT)								
PJNO	TITLE	(DEPT)						
		DNO	MGR	BUDGET	LEADER	(EQUIP)		
						ITEMNO	DESC	
J8	B	D1	DOE	40000	MEE	46	SCOPE	
						317	LASER	
J11	D	D1	DOE	40000	FAR	271	COMPUTER	

This concludes the generation of the desired view.

To show the navigational procedure for the SELECT function, consider again the DEPT hierarchy, and assume we want to select DNO,MGR,PJNO,LEADER and ITEMNO from DEPT where DESC = 'COMPUTER'.

The target hierarchy would be defined as shown below.

```
TYPE T
 DEFINES
 ( * := T
 DNO(*) -> STRING
 MGR(*) -> STRING
 PROJ(*) -> FORM<<PROJ2>>
 CREATE(STRING,STRING,FORM<<PROJ2>>) -> * )

TYPE PROJ2
 DEFINES
 ( * := PROJ2
 PJNO(*) -> STRING
 LEADER(*) -> STRING
 EQUIP(*) -> FORM<<EQUIP3>>
 CREATE(STRING,STRING,FORM<<EQUIP3>>) -> * )

TYPE EQUIP3
 DEFINES
 ( * := EQUIP3
 ITEMNO(*) -> STRING
 CREATE(STRING) -> * )
```

Assuming the declarations:

```
DCL TS FORM<<T>>;
DCL PROJS FORM<<PROJ2>>;
DCL EQUIPS FORM<<EQUIP3>>;
```

the program could be written as follows:

```
TS = FORM<<T>>¢CREATE();
FOR D IN EACH_ROOT(DEPTS,PCB);
 PROJS = FORM<<PROJ2>>¢CREATE();
 FOR P IN EACH(PROJ(D),PCB);
  EQUIPS = FORM<<EQUIP3>>¢CREATE();
  FOR E IN FILTER(EQUIP(P),(EQ:EQUIP -> BOOL;
                  DESC(EQ) = 'COMPUTER'),PCB);
   EQUIPS = ADD(EQUIPS,CREATE(ITEMNO(E)));
  END;
  IF ¬EMPTY(EQUIPS) THEN
     PROJS = ADD(PROJS,CREATE(PJNO(P),LEADER(P),EQUIPS));
 END;
 IF ¬EMPTY(PROJS) THEN
    TS = ADD(TS,CREATE(DNO(D),MGR(D),PROJS));
END;
```

The resulting target form would then look like:

(T)				
DNO	MGR	(PROJ)		
		PJNO	LEADER	(EQUIP)
				ITEMNO
D1	DOE	J6	RAE	221
		J11	FAR	271

6. DATABASE INTERFACE

The interface between the ADAPT system and the database exists at two levels: at the level of the data model hierarchy ("programming in the large") and at the entity/data sublanguage level ("programming in the small"). Initially the database administrator defines an External Structure representing logical relationships in ADAPT based on the IMS database description (DBD). This ADAPT (logical) database is therefore a subset of the corresponding IMS physical database. This paper does not address the problem of defining an ADAPT hierarchy in terms of more than one physical database. However, logical databases in IMS provide essentially a static view of the enterprise data, whereas the approach presented here allows different views to be created dynamically.

The interface at the entity level is determined by the internal representation of forms and entities. The internal representation for a form is a discriminated union (ONEOF in ADAPT) which has two alternatives, one for a persistent form (IMS database), and the other for non-persistent data (temporary form). If persistent, the internal representation is a character string which denotes the segment name of the tree node. The representation for non-persistent data would be a matter of choice; if a linked list structure were desired, for example, the representation would most likely be a record with two fields: a value field and a link field.

The internal representation for an entity type is also a discriminated union which has two alternatives. If persistent, the representation is a record containing a character string which represents the I/O area for DL/I, and the segment names (character strings) for the children nodes. The representation for non-persistent data is a record containing values of the attributes (which may be scalar or non-scalar).

In order to understand the ADAPT/IMS interface, one must be aware that there are two hierarchies or trees: an ADAPT "virtual" tree and the IMS tree. The term "virtual" tree is used because the internal representation of an ADAPT entity contains the segment names of descendent nodes, allowing the continued navigation through the IMS tree; how this is done will explained shortly. The ADAPT node therefore implicitly represents the entire subtree of IMS because all descendent nodes are available recursively. The ADAPT tree is thus used to control sequencing and thereby navigation through the IMS database.

Sequencing through the IMS database is performed by two DL/I calls: GET UNIQUE and GET NEXT, using segment names as "unqualified segment search arguments " (SSAs) [9] for both calls. The GET UNIQUE call serves to set a position within the database for subsequent calls, and the GET NEXT call moves to the next segment in the database, following the standard hierarchical sequence (top to bottom, left to right). The use of an unqualified SSA restricts the search to only a particular segment type.

We show below the iterators EACH and EACH_ROOT, where the boxes enclose a pseudocode notation for DL/I calls and for the construction of the proper object to be returned by the iterator. The DL/I calls would be performed by Interface Modules.

```
EACH: ITERATOR(segment_name:STRING,mask:PCB) YIELDS(T);
      DO WHILE(status-code has blanks);
      _____
      | GN segment-name *V                       |
      | YIELD( f(I/O area,segment-name) );       |
      |_____|
      END;
END EACH;


EACH_ROOT: ITERATOR(segment-name:STRING,mask:PCB) YIELDS(T);
           _____
           | GU segment-name *V                       |
           | YIELD( f(I/O area,segment-name) );       |
           |_____|
```

```
        DO WHILE(status-code has blanks);
         _____
        | GN segment-name *V                       |
        | YIELD( f(I/O area,segment-name) );        |
        |_____|
        END;
END EACH_ROOT;
```

The notation f(I/O area,segment-name) means create an entity instance which is a function of the I/O area (updated by DL/I) and the segment-name. The internal representation of this instance will be a record, as outlined above, with values determined by the I/O area and with segment names of descendent nodes as determined as a function of the given segment-name argument. While not shown explicitly, the YIELD statement in the boxes can be considered to coerce the record type to an object of type T which is expected by the invoker of the iterator. The V command code (*V shown in the boxes) component of the DL/I call is used to prevent the position in the data base from being moved during a search of the hierarchical dependents of a segment. Otherwise, the search might continue in a subtree other than the one we are interested in (This is a detail of IMS).

The above process insures that the navigation of the ADAPT tree is always synchronized with the position in the IMS tree.

7. CONCLUSIONS

An attempt has been made to show the potential of data abstraction as a means for closing the gap between programming languages and database management systems. The form abstraction turned out to be a convenient vehicle for defining different user views and achieving a "dialogue" between different data models. Other abstractions could similarly be defined.

The interface between ADAPT and the database was achieved by using Interface Modules to communicate with the data sublanguage and/or architecture of the given database system. It should be emphasized that, although an Interface Module cannot violate the ADAPT data space, it is possible to return a type different from the one expected, thereby breaching the type integrity of ADAPT. Therefore this low level interface must be checked very carefully, since it is the weakest link in the type integrity chain.

The procedural algorithms called SELECT, SLICE and CONSOLIDATE were written as a replacement for the more general nonprocedural operators of CONVERT. This was done because type checking would not be as "strong" for these operators as they are for the operators defined to work on flat tables. It is assumed that extensions to the ADAPT language can be found which would allow the definitions of the hierarchical operators with the desired type checking properties; this is a subject for future research.

Although the algorithms in this paper are somewhat specialized for the particular example shown, it is our contention that they have a regular pattern which is easily learned and adapted to particular form patterns. General paradigms for these algorithms can be readily defined, but we have not bothered to do this here.

In summary, we would say that the advantages of using data abstractions in the database realm are the following:

The strong typing properties of ADAPT are imported into the database world and provide useful consistency checking.

We avoid the problem of glueing together a separate host language and query language.

Finally, the approach is not biased towards any particular data model or architecture.

We hope to have partially answered the question "What is the use of abstract data types in data bases?" [2].

ACKNOWLEDGMENTS

I am grateful to Bob Taylor for reading a draft of the paper and making valuable comments and suggestions, and also to Steve Perry who answered all my questions on IMS.

REFERENCES

[1] Archibald, Jerry L., The Yorktown External Structure User's Guide, Technical Memo No. 14, Software Technology Project, IBM Research Center, Yorktown Heights, N.Y. (Dec 1979).

[2] Brodie, M.L. and Schmidt, J.,"What is the use of Abstract Data Types in Data Bases?", Proceedings Fourth International Conference on Very Large Data Bases, West Berlin, Germany, 1978,139-141.

[3] Chamberlin, D.D. et al,"SEQUEL 2: A Unified Approach to Data Definition, Manipulation and Control", IBM Journal of Research and Development, Vol. 20, No. 6 (1976), 560-575.

[4] Chen, P.P.,"The Entity-Relationship Model: Toward a Unified View of Data", ACM Transactions on Database Systems 1,1 (March 1976),9-37.

[5] Codd, E.F.,"A Relational Model of Data for Large Shared Data Banks", CACM 13, 1970.

[6] Date, C.J.,"An Architecture for High-Level Language Database Extensions", Proceedings 1976 ACM SIGMOD International Conference on the Management of Data, 101-122.

[7] DeRemer, F. and Kron, H.,"Programming-in-the-Large versus Programming-in-the-Small", SIGPLAN Notices (June 1975), 114-121.

[8] Housel, Barron C. and Shu, Nan C.,"A High-level Data Manipulation Language for Hierarchical Data Structures", Proceedings of Conference on Data:Abstraction, Definition and Structure, Salt Lake City, Utah, March, 1976.

[9] IBM Corp. IMS/VS Application Programming Reference Manual, Form SH20-9026.

[10] Leavenworth, B.,An Integrated Database Programming Language, Report RC 8462, IBM Thomas J. Watson Research Center, September, 1980.

[11] Leavenworth, B., ADAPT Reference Manual, Technical Memo No. 19, Software Technology Project, IBM Research Center, Yorktown Heights, N.Y. (Aug. 1979).

[12] Liskov, B.H. et al,"Abstraction Mechanisms in CLU", CACM 20,8 (Aug. 1977), 564-576.

[13] Lusk, E.L., Overbeek, R.A. and Parrello, B.,"A Practical Design Methodology for the Implementation of IMS Databases, Using the Entity-Relationship Model, SIGMOD 1980, Santa Monica,9-21.

[14] Rowe, Lawrence A. and Shoens, Kurt A.,"Data Abstraction, Views and Updates in RIGEL",Proceedings ACM 1979 National Conference, 71-81.

[15] Sakai, H.,"A Unified Approach to the Logical Design of a Hierarchical Data Model", in: Chen, P. (ed.), Entity-Relationship Approach to Systems Analysis and Design (North-Holland, Amsterdam, 1980).

[16] Santos, C.S. dos, Neuhold, E.J. and Furtado, A.L.,"A Data Type Approach to the Entity-Relationship Model", in: Chen, P. (ed.), Entity-Relationship Approach to Systems Analysis and Design (North-Holland, Amsterdam, 1980).

[17] Shu, N.C. et al,"EXPRESS: A Data Extraction, Processing and Restructuring System, ACM TODS, Vol. 2,2 (June 1977),134-174.

[18] Tsao, J.H.,"Enterprise Schema--An Approach to IMS Logical Data Base Design", in: Chen, P. (ed.),Entity-Relationship Approach to Systems Analysis and Design (North-Holland, Amsterdam 1980).

[19] Tsichritizis, D.C. and Lochovsky, F.H.,"Hierarchical Data-Base Management",ACM Computing Surveys, Vol 8, No. 1 (March 1976),105-123.

[20] Weber, Herbert,"A Software Engineering View of Data Base Systems",Proceedings Fourth International Conference on Very Large Data Bases, West Berlin, 1978.

Entity-Relationship Approach to
Information Modeling and Analysis, P.P. Chen (ed.)
Elsevier Science Publishers B.V. (North-Holland)
©ER Institute, 1983

Design and Implementation of An E-R Data Base Management System (DBM-2)

T. C. Chiang
G. R. Rose

Bell Laboratories
Whippany, New Jersey 07981

ABSTRACT

DBM-2 is a data base management system designed for transaction systems that track activities in an enterprise. To support such applications in a production environment, DBM-2 is required to have high performance and flexibility. An Entity-Relationship (E-R) data model provides a basis for DBM-2 for meeting the requirements. This paper presents the design and implementation of DBM-2. Special attention is given to the implementation of "associations" between records, because the implementation is critical for supporting the E-R model.

1. INTRODUCTION

DBM-2 is a data base management system designed for transaction systems that track business activities in an enterprise. The first application is a transaction system for tracking repair activities of a telephone company. DBM-2 together with the application system has been in field trial since October 16, 1980, and will be deployed in most of the telephone companies in United States in 1982. Thus, DBM-2 is a real production system. DBM-2 is programmed in C [1], and runs under UNIX* [2] on a PDP 11/70 computer.

To support transaction systems and tracking applications in a production environment, DBM-2 is required to have high performance and flexibility. A transaction system is a system that has a defined set of tasks to be performed. A transaction performing a task normally is required to have a fast response time and may involve many data base retrievals and updates. A tracking system normally has a large data base and a heavy transaction load. These requirements put a premium on DBM-2 performance. Furthermore, the functional requirements of our application, probably typical of most, are ever changing. This implies that DBM-2 must provide data independence and enable easy change to the data base structure and definition. However, DBM-2 is not required to have a high level query language for arbitrary queries, since the tasks for a transaction system are well defined.

The data base that DBM-2 is managing in its telephone repair application is large in volume and complex in storage structures. It has about 300 million bytes of data in 30 files. There are 15 cross-record relationships, and up to 80 fields per record. The transaction load on the application system is rated at 4000 transactions per hour, where the transactions average 8 data base requests each. The availability of the application system is 22 hours per day. Many new fields as well as new perceptions of existing fields have been added to the data base. Files have been reorganized to improve performance. These changes have been made without requiring changes in the existing application programs. Some of the changes have been made without data base conversion.

An overview of DBM-2 has been presented in [3]. This paper focusses on how DBM-2 provides flexibility (mainly data independence and ease of change) without sacrificing performance. In particular, it includes discussions of the use of an Entity-Relationship (E-R) model, the internal data structures, the mapping between the internal and external structures,

---

* UNIX is a trademark of Bell Laboratories

and the program and process organizations. Special attention is given to the implementation of "associations" between records, because the implementation is critical for supporting the E-R model. Finally, some performance statistics are presented.

2. EXTERNAL VIEWS

DBM-2 supports multiple external views of the data base. An E-R model is used for the external views. The advantage of using an E-R model is that it provides: (1) rich enough constructs to capture the semantics of the application, (2) a simple user interface, (3) a high level of abstraction to hide internal data structures from user programs, (4) mechanisms for achieving performance, and (5) structures for ease of implementation.

From a user's (external) view, a data base is considered as a collection of files and a collection of "associations" among records. A record represents an entity in the real world, while an association represents a set of relationships among entities. A file is viewed as a two-dimensional table, where the columns are fields and the rows are records. A relationship is viewed as a named link between two records of perhaps two different files. The use of named links enables one to retrieve an associated record without a key search, and without needing to know the implementation of the link. Thus, an association provides a convenient way for a navigation of the data base. Furthermore, if the associated record is stored physically with a record that has already been retrieved into the main memory, additional disk accesses can be avoided. This is extremely important for performance. In addition to the use for navigation, associations are also used to express update dependencies. Update rules are defined as properties of an association. As described in [3], four "coupling factors" to represent four update rules have been identified so far. For example, a very tight coupling factor has the following definition:

Definition :

Given two files, E1 and E2, and an association A between them, A is said to have a very tight coupling factor if and only if:

1. insertion of a record e2 in E2 is permitted only if there is a record e1 in E1 that record e2 can be associated with,

2. deletion of a record e1 in E1 implies the deletion of all its associated e2's in E2,

3. no deletion of a record e2 in E2 is permitted independent of the associated e1 in E1.

The definitions for the other three types of coupling factors are relaxations of one or more items from the above definition. DBM-2 performs automatic updates of associated data items according to the declared update rules. This is not only convenient for programming, but also necessary for performance. Process and message switching overhead is saved. (Process organization around DBM-2 is discussed in Section 5.)

A Data Manipulation Language (DML) is provided for the application programmers to manipulate the data base via the E-R model. The DML is a set of commands for retrieval, insertion, modification, and deletion of data items in the data base. The set of DML commands is callable from a C program. There is a subset of DML commands referred to as "associated" DML that handles association operations. The following example illustrates a use of DML and associated DML.

Example

Suppose that a data base consists of two files: parts (P) and suppliers (S), and an association, part-supplier (PS), between P and S that associates a part with its suppliers. The schemata for P and S respectively are:

P(P#, P_name, P_color, P_size), and

S(S#, S_loc, S_name).

Let us assume that PS does not have any attributes for sake of simplicity. (PS could have QUANTITY as one of its attributes.) The graphical representation of the data base is shown in Figure 1.

PS

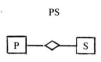

Figure 1. data base for the example

Let us suppose that one wants to retrieve the part name and the supplier name for a particular part that has part number (P#) value 100: one would issue the following commands for that purpose. (Note that a pseudo code is used.)

```
WORK_AREA *WA;
int r;
FILE p;

WA = {P_name, S_name}; /* define a user's view  - a projection*/
r = retrieve(P, WA, P# = = 100);
if (aretrieve(r, S, WA)<0)
        error();
else
        Print P_name, S_name;
```

Note that if PS is an association with very tight coupling, the aretrieve in the above example does not result in a disk access. More detailed illustration of DML usages can be founded in [3].

The data base administrators use the Data Definition Language (DDL) to define and change the information about the data base. The DDL has commands such as: (1) define file, (2) define field, and (3) define association. There are corresponding commands for changing files, fields, and associations.

3. INTERNAL VIEW AND DATA STRUCTURES

The internal view is a simple view of the otherwise quite complex internal data structures. It represents a view of the internal data structures as seen by the mapping function (see Section 4). The internal data structures include multi-level indexes, variable and fixed length records, variable and fixed length fields, records with variable numbers of fields, pointers among records, integration of two external records into one internal record, partition of one external record into several internal records, and up to 15 different field types (e.g. INTEGER and CHARACTER). The internal data structures are designed for high performance and conservation of disk space.

The internal view consists of a set of internal files (IFs), each of which consists of a set of internal records (IRs). The records have fixed formats, i.e., fixed record length, fixed field length, and fixed number of fields per record. There may be links between records. Links provide a formal mechanism for creating references from one IR to one or more distinct IRs. They may be viewed as replacing the pointers that traditionally appear in an internal view. Links are used to implement indexes, "associations", and "record partition". (Record partition is defined as the partition of an external record into two or more internal records.) Examples of such applications of links are illustrated in Section 4.

A link is a link-list data structure, which is the key to the simple representation of complex internal data structures in the internal view. A link consists of a header IR of a particular type and a set of member IRs of another type. The link header must be accessible by key, while the members may be accessed by key or via the link. For performance, a link may be stored on a common block of physical disk space. In this case, the link is referred to as a "closely-held" link. Normally, the members of a closely-held link can be accessed only via the link.

There are three software modules that construct the internal view: (1) Index Access Manager (IAM), (2) Data Format Manager (DFM), and (3) Record Access Manager (RAM). IAM and DFM deal with semantics of data structures, while RAM provides the access mechanism. More detailed description is given in Section 5.

4. MAPPING

DBM-2 hides the internal view from the users by providing a mapping function. The mapping between the internal and external views has two levels: (1) field level and (2) record level.

4.1 FIELD LEVEL MAPPING

At the field level the mapping function translates 15 different field types into null terminated character string format (as used in a C program) which is the canonical representation of an external field value. Semantically, an external field value can be of one of the many types, for example, ALPHANUMERIC, STANDARD_TIME, and LONG_TIME. The ALPHANUMERIC type is externally a string of letter and/or digits; STANDARD_TIME is a string with a specified format appropriate to time representation, and so on.

To support multiple external views of a field, one internal field type may be mapped into several different external field types. For example, an internal field that is a LONG (long integer, 32 bits for PDP 11/70) can be mapped into a STANDARD_TIME type (e.g. 01-01-81 0001A) or LONG_TIME type (e.g. 347145200, the number of seconds passed since the begining of 1/1/70).

A user can define his/her own field types by supplying the routine that interprets the new type. A relinking of DBM-2 and a change in DBCAT are neccessary then to establish the new type.

4.2 RECORD LEVEL MAPPING

At the record level, the mapping function handles record integration and record partition. In particular, it translates between "associations" and "links". There are three basic methods for the implementation of an association: (1) using links, (2) using embedded foreign keys, and (3) links of foreign keys. A link is a data structure that has been defined in Section 3. In a particular record, an embedded key is a key of another record embedded in the given record. A link of foreign keys is a link that consists of a header that is the given record and members that are keys of other records. Figure 2 shows examples for an embedded foreign key and a link of foreign keys, where r1 represents a record and ki, i=1,2,3, represents a key.

A variety of implementation methods can be derived from these three basic methods. For example, a one-to-many association between records of two different types can be implemented as an embedded key on one side of the association, and a link on the other side.

In case of record partition, a link connects two or more internal records of different types with one of the internal record being the header and the rest of the records being members of the link. The mapping function accesses the internal records through the link mechanism and

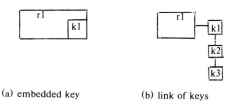

(a) embedded key   (b) link of keys

Figure 2. examples of foreign keys

"concatenate" all the internal records to make an external record.

5. SOFTWARE ARCHITECTURE

DBM-2 is implemented as a set of user processes under UNIX/TS+, a version of UNIX augmented for transaction applications with messages, shared memory, and a robust file system (CFS)*. DBM-2 processes communicate with other processes via messages and shared memory. The data sent between an application process and a DBM-2 process is in a well defined format [4] that is a list of <field name, field value> pairs. The list resides in a shared work-area between an application process and DBM-2. (The file system provides block I/O, concurrency control, and crash recovery.) Discussions on the UNIX/TS+ and the file system are beyond the scope of this paper.

The DBM-2 software has a modular design, which minimizes dependencies among the software modules. The DBM-2 software is functionally divided into several modules: (1) DML processor (DMLP), (2) Mapping Function (MAP), (3) Index Access Manager (IAM), (4) Data Format Manager (DFM), (5) Record Access Manager (RAM), (6) DDL processor (DDLP), and (7) Data Base editor (DBE). The interface between two modules is simple. This ensures flexible implementation strategy. Depending on memory size and excution time requirements, each module can be implemented as either a process or a subroutine. For example, in one version of DBM-2, RAM resided in the same address space as DMLP, MAP, and DFM. However, as the system evolved, the text space of the combined DBM-2 process was exhausted. Subsequently, RAM was moved to the CFS address space. Successive implementations of modules have had increased functionality. This is particularly true of RAM, for which the design of the most general version is discussed below.

In addition to these software modules, a table referred to as Data Base Catalog (DBCAT) stores information about the data base, e.g., file schemata and association definitions. The graphical representation of the software architecture for DBM-2 and the surounding processes is shown in Figure 3, where E1,...,En represent the external views in the application processes.

DBCAT is created by the Data Base Administrators (DBA) using DDL, and is updated by the DBA using DBE. The DDL processor has been implemented using YACC [5].

DMLP has two parts. The first part is a set of subroutines residing in the user program space. Within each of the subroutines, the parameters of a DML call are set up in the shared work-area and a message is sent to the second part of DMLP on the DBM-2 side. The second part of DMLP then interprets and executes the DML command by calling upon all the modules involved. The result is sent back to the first part of DMLP on the user side. The mapping function performs the translations that have been described previously.

---

* CFS is a transaction-oriented filing system developed for our high throughput applications with stringent data base consistency requirements.

Index Access Manager handles the semantics of access paths, e.g., the maintenance of indexes, by using the mechanism provided by RAM. For example, an index file that stored the indexes is just another internal file to RAM, but to IAM, it represents an access path to the data file. RAM provides access methods to both the index files and the data file, while IAM must maintain the consistency between all the index files and the corresponding data file.

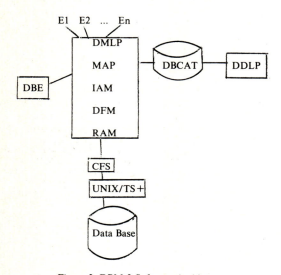

Figure 3. DBM-2 Software Architecture

The interface to IAM consists of a set of functions for retrieving and updating the indexes. For example, the function *getindex(file, select)* performs an optimal search and returns a set of indexes for *file*, according to the selection criteron, *select*.

Data Format Manager handles variable format records and data compression. Some flexibility can be achieved by using variable formatted records, because fields can be added, changed, and deleted without data conversion. Data compression coupled with variable formatted records conserves disk space, but consumes CPU time.

The Record Access Manager (RAM) provides data access and maintenance functions designed to support the internal view. These functions are above the level of the CFS.

RAM provides access to the IR's. Each IR is partitioned into a data area and an (optional) key area. Apart from this partitioning, no interpretation of content is performed by RAM.

The RAM architecture is a simple set of functions that provide for retrieving, adding, deleting and updating records via IF's and links. The basic record retrieval function *getrec(file, rcd, key)* illustrates this simplicity. All successful retrieval operations return a retrieval identifier *r* for use in subsequent linking and update operations. For example, the function *linkrec(link, r, r')* creates a link between the two IR's identified by *r* and *r'*. There are aproximately twelve functions in all.

The implementation approach for RAM IF operations is to provide a limited number of underlying physical file organizations and to map IF's onto physical files via control tables. This is accomplished by supplying a specific algorithm that corresponds to each general operation for each type of file. Initially two physical file organizations have been implemented.

The first is a binary-search organization that provides access to IR's via a full key and also, with pre-defined restrictions, to subsets of IR's that match the significant bytes of a given key. This file type, which is restricted to main memory applications, is designed to minimize retrieval time at the expense of insertion and deletion time.

The second is a hash organization intended primarily for disc files. It supports both fixed and variable length records and permits a mixture of record types to be recorded. The latter capability is the vehicle for providing closely-held records.

Links are implemented by reserving a fixed-length link area within each IR in which IR addresses are recorded. The standard format for IR addresses is *block* and *mark*, where *mark* is a unique identifier with respect to a particular block. Direct access is performed by reading the block and searching for the particular mark. This scheme permits IR's to be moved within a block for garbage collection.

There is also the concept of a *set* which is a subset of IR's in an IF with partial keys that match a given partial key. Once a set is defined, its IR's may be accessed sequentially.

6. PERFORMANCE

In general, a data base management system adds overhead to an application system in two areas: (1) main memory, and (2) processing time. The version of DBM-2 presently supporting the first application in the field requires about 95K bytes of main memory, of which about 30K bytes are in the data space. DBM-2 CPU time is discussed from two points of view: (1) absolute CPU time required to retrieve a single external record, (2) percentage of transaction CPU time that is spent in DBM-2.

The CPU time for DBM-2 to retrieve a set of fields of a record from a file is

$$t = 5 + 0.6f + I,$$

where t is the cpu time in ms, f is the number of fields specified by a user, and I the interprocess communication time. For example, retrieving 33 fields of a typical record of the application data base takes about 35 ms, of which 10 ms is in I. From a recent study [6] of system performance, the CPU time for a typical transaction is about 1273 ms, of which 363 ms are taken by DBM-2. (120 ms of this time are spent in inter-process communication.) So, DBM-2 requires about 28% of the total CPU time used by a typical transaction. The average fraction of CPU resources consumed by DBM-2 during a day of operation is about 22%.

7. CONCLUSION

In summary, DBM-2 provides the flexibility advantages of a data base management system to a production application. Fields can be added or changed without reprogramming, in most cases, without data conversion. Application programs are easier to write because of the encapsulation of internal structures. The cost of the added flexibility is increased CPU utilization: at most 20% to 30% for our application.

Acknowledgement

The development of the DBM-2 project has been done by the members of the Data Base Group in the Advanced Transaction Systems Department, under the direction of R.F. Bergeron. We would like to thank R.F. Bergeron for his support and advice. We would also like to thank the other members of the group for their contributions to the project. Special thanks go to A. Weinstein for his implementation of the Record Access Manager for the first application, and to D.H. Carter for his implementation of the robust file system.

REFERENCES

1. Kernighan, B.W., and Ritchie, D.M., *The C programming Language,* Prentice-Hall, Inc., Englewood Cliffs, New Jersey, 1978.

2. Ritchie, D.M., and Thompson, K., "The UNIX Time Sharing System," *Communication of ACM,* 17, No. 7, July 1974, pp. 365-375.

3. Chiang, T.C., and Bergeron, R.F., "A Data Base Management System with An E-R Conceptual Model", Proceedings of International Conference on Entity-Relationship Approach to System Design and Analysis, December, 1980.

4. M, Rochkind, "Packet Manipulation Language User's Manual". private communication.

5. Johnson, S.C., "YACC: Yet Another Compiler Compiler," Computing Science Technical Report No. 32, 1975, Bell Laboratories, Murray Hill, New Jersey.

6. J. Tsay, unpublished notes, November, 1980.

Entity-Relationship Approach to
Information Modeling and Analysis, P.P. Chen (ed.)
Elsevier Science Publishers B.V. (North-Holland)
©ER Institute, 1983

The Fact Database
An Entity-Based System using Inference

D.R.McGregor & J.R.Malone
Department of Computer Science
University of Strathclyde
Glasgow
Scotland

The Fact Database System is a general model for an information
handling system which we describe in terms of its data-structure
and an abstract machine which manipulates it. The combination of
data model and machine is capable of capturing much more semantic
detail than can systems based on present database models. The
internal representation of the information is completely hidden
from the external world and thus can be reorganised (to represent
the same information in a more general, compact or rapidly
accessible form) without this change being apparent at the
external user interface. The system's operations are
characterised by its use of inferential methods, which as a side
effect give it the ability to support 'naturalistic' user
languages. The practicality of the system has been demonstrated
by implementation.

1. INTRODUCTION

The Fact database is a model for a new type of information handling system
[McGREGOR80] [McGREGOR81] which we shall describe in terms of its main data-
structure (built from units of information called "Facts"), and a conceptual
machine which can manipulate the structure (the Fact machine).

The novel features of the Fact system arise because of the nature of its
internal knowledge structure which is fully assimilated by the machine. This
structure is a model of the real world described by the database. The
internal symbols and structures represent precise objects and concepts. The
precision and regularity of the internal data structure is much greater than
that of conventional relational or network systems. This, augmented by
information about set membership, enables the system to use inferential
methods in many aspects of its operations.

We shall show later how these features lead to a simple, flexible
interface, both to other computer systems and to 'user friendly' query
languages.

The "secret" internal representation of the information can be reorganised to represent the same information in a more general, compact or more rapidly accessible form. In manipulating the structure the machine forms simple hypotheses, which are fed back to the user for confirmation, rejection or investigation. Higher level constructs are also formed and similarly presented to the user for possible naming, and use in future.

While the machine can be implemented most efficiently using special-purpose hardware, we have demonstrated that it can also be realised with reasonable efficiency, on a conventional computer with ordinary moving-head disc backing-stores.

2. SYSTEM OVERVIEW

The major information handling processes (input, reorganisation and retrieval) are outlined diagramatically in figure 2.1.

New information is presented to the system as a series of records. Each field is a variable-length character string. The variable-length strings are first converted by a symbol table mechanism to fixed-length tokens. The second stage is the identification of the particular entities in the internal database model which are being referred to by the new data. When this identification has been completed satisfactorily it is possible to create an internal 'fact' which represents the new knowledge in a precise, language independent way.

Before finally adding the new 'fact' to the database, it is applied to the existing database as a query. At least a 'semantic rule' must be retrieved, otherwise the new fact is rejected (section 3.2).

In retrieving information also, the query is processed using the symbol table mechanism to convert each character string to its corresponding fixed-length identifier. The fixed-length identifiers are then used to retrieve matching associated data from the internal knowledge structure. Two types of information can be retrieved – either the required "answers", or a "rule" indicating that the query is feasible. A query which does not access at least one "rule" is not valid. In the case where data has been retrieved the information must now be translated into a valid external representation so that it can be returned to the user.

3. REPRESENTING KNOWLEDGE: THE FACT DATA MODEL

In our description of the model we use the terms Entity, Fact, Fact number, Subject, Relation and Object.

Following Senko [1975], any distinct 'thing' or concept is an Entity. It can be a concrete or abstract object. Each unique entity in the knowledge to be represented is given its own unique symbol in the system. An entity symbol

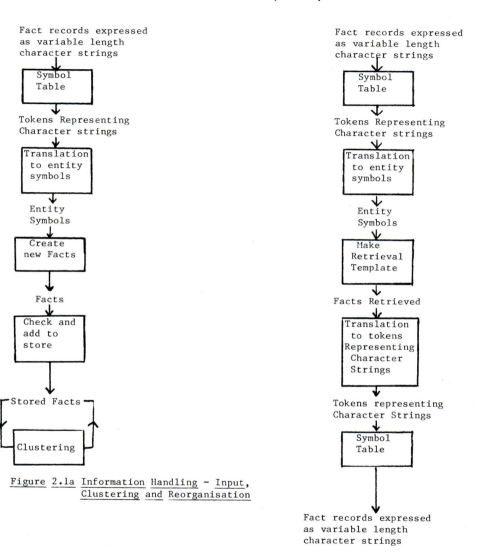

Figure 2.1a Information Handling – Input, Clustering and Reorganisation

Figure 2.1b Information Handling – Retrieval

can stand for a simple terminal object (e.g. a cup, spoon) or concept (e.g. a salary). In the following discussion we shall normally refer to `entity symbols´ as `entities´.

A quadruple structure plays the part of a molecule of information in our model — the smallest unit of free-standing information. We refer to the quadruple as a Fact. It is a named, directed association between two entities (referred to as Subject and Object), with the association in linking them (the Relation — also an entity) represented by a unique symbol — the Fact Number. This can be used to represent the Fact in more complex information structures. It is worth noting that the quadruple is irreducible — two different Facts can have the same entity symbols in Subject Relation and Object fields yet represent different Facts.

$$\text{Fact No., Subject, Relation, Object}$$
$$F1 \qquad X \qquad Y \qquad Z$$

Thus given only the above information the system would contain four entities X, Y, Z and F1. X, Y and Z would be simple or terminal entities, while F1 is a complex or non-terminal entity.

Suppose a system contained the following:

Factno	Subject	Relation	Object
F1	X	Y	Z
F2	Z	Y	Q
F3	F2	R	F1

In F3 we have a fact which uses the fact symbols F1 and F2 as entities. Data structures of any necessary complexity can be constructed in this way.

A number of workers have suggested entity (or object) based representations of knowledge [QUILLIAN69], a field reviewed by Winograd [1972]. We ourselves arrived at this representation through our work on relational database systems (e.g. McGregor, Thomson, Dawson [1976]). It is in the way the Fact machine accesses and automatically uses the data structure that our system differs from those of previous workers in this field.

3.1. CLASSES OF FACT : QUANTIFIERS

Facts are classed as either Deductive or Non-Deductive. Deductive Facts implicitly have the quantifier "forall" (∀) on each data field. Where an entity symbol appears in a Deductive Fact, the property indicated by the other fields is "inherited" by all members of the powerset of that entity symbol (as in all people being mortal). The effect is as though the data were stored explicitly with each member of the powerset. The use of Deductive Facts is illustrated in the description of the "Broom" concept (section 4.2).

Where the other quantifier "there exists" ($\dashv$) is given explicitly, the property is considered to be Non-Deductive, and is not inherited by set members. When a Fact is inserted as a Non-Deductive fact, a second fact is inserted automatically which indicates that the quantifier on each field of the Non-Deductive-Fact is $\dashv$ rather than $\forall$. Unless explicitly requested by the user, any Non-Deductive Facts will be automatically filtered out from his answers.

3.2. NON DEDUCTIVE FACTS AS SEMANTIC RULES

Non-Deductive Facts are used by the system as "Semantic Rules" to check the common-sense feasibility of new data being inserted. The simplest mode of action is that when any new fact is presented for insertion, the mechanism first treats the new information as a query (using the inferential fetch mechanism (Section 4.2)). At least one Non-Deductive Fact (the Semantic Rule) must be accessed.

Facts which do not match a semantic rule are not inserted by the system. A special operation is used to insert Non-Deductive Facts. In our present system insertions of the Non-Deductive Semantic Rules themselves are not checked. Suitable facts must be present which indicate the generic linkage between the new data being inserted, and the entities in the Semantic Rule.

4. THE FACT MACHINE

An overview of the functions of the Fact System are given in figure 4.1.

The machine can carry out two different types of operations, Tasks and Autonomous Activities. Tasks are carried out in response to external commands to the machine. They are the means by which data is retrieved, inserted or deleted. Autonomous Activities are carried out by the machine when it is not obeying Tasks. They are concerned with raising the level of the stored data structure, tidying it when an inconsistency can be resolved, suggesting possible hypotheses for resolution by the user community, reorganising the data to optimise performance and repair accidental damage.

In some ways Tasks could be likened to foreground processes of a computer system, while the Autonomous Activities are like background processes.

The major components of the machine are detailed in figure 4.2. We shall first describe some of the simplest "micro instructions" of the machine which are used in constructing the higher level interface.

4.1. PRIMITIVE MACHINE OPERATIONS

At this level, the machine operates only on fixed size entity symbols,

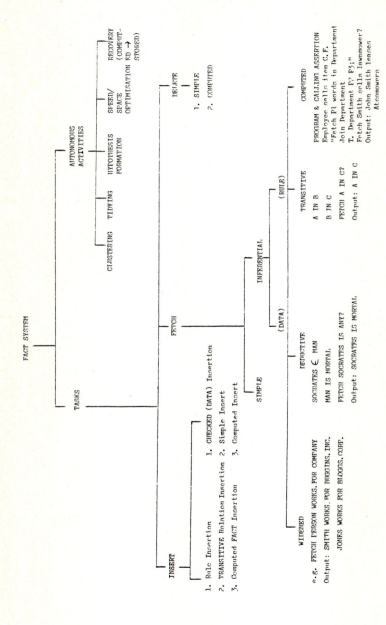

Figure 4.1 Functions of the Fact System

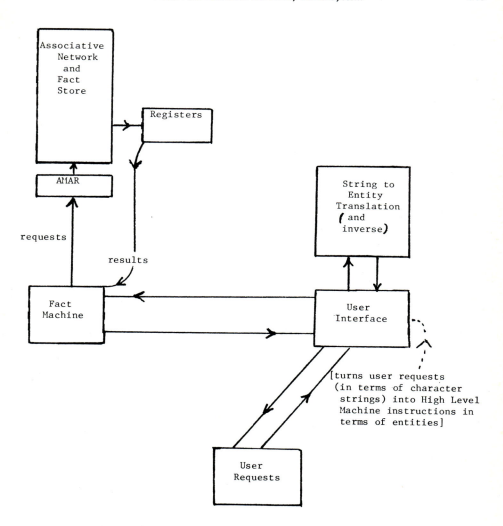

Figure 4.2 Major components of the Fact System

variable length strings being pre-processed by a scanner mechanism.

The heart of the machine is the associative store which has a quadruple structure corresponding to that of the Fact. Extraction of information to the output register is controlled by the Associative Memory Addressing Register (AMAR) and indirectly by the Input Register.

The Input and Output Registers are both multi-width (i.e. n Facts) and multi-depth (i.e. m Fact records deep). They hold the result of operations. Results may be output to the user via a post-processor mechanism, or operated on by various register manipulation commands.

Three instructions operate directly on the associative store to permit the manipulation of data.

The associative fetch retrieves data from the store. The AMAR is loaded with the required entity symbols, or 'don't care' fields. The machine responds by placing a copy of each Fact which matches the AMAR in the output register. The simple insert instruction places data into the store, all fields of the AMAR are loaded with the entity symbols to be inserted. A delete command removes data from the fact store. All fields of the AMAR are loaded with entity symbols, if the Fact exists it is removed from the store.

At this level of the machine we can provide instructions for all the relational operations [CODD70], and the machine can be shown to be "relationally complete".

4.2. INFERENTIAL FETCH : USE OF SET INFORMATION

In many situations it is very difficult for the external user or system making requests to be aware of the precise schema or terminology (e.g. filenames rolenames etc.) which are used inside the database. This is a problem which must be overcome if databases are ever to be flexibly linked up on a world wide basis.

Typical of the higher level instructions designed to overcome this problem is the Inferential Fetch instruction. This operation encapsulates the main ideas behind the Fact machine. It provides access to information via a "-self-adaptive standard interface" capable of matching correctly to "reasonable" requests for data.

A di-graph of generic information is given in figure 4.3. This kind of information is acted-on directly by the system in a number of ways :

    a) A query may use a denotation corresponding to a set of entities -

          "schoolteacher","employee","person","lecturer"

      - but the desired information in the database may be stored at a

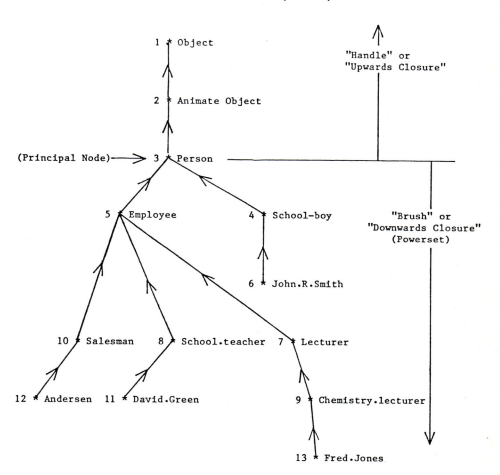

The Fact Database: An Entity-Based System 545

Figure 4.3 "Broom" of Generic information

different level. For instance it may be stored at the level of the
individual set members. We therefore need to "broaden" the terms
used in the enquiry to ensure that all relevant information in the
database is accessed irrespective of the level of generalisation at
which it is stored. A query about "person" should be concerned with
any subsets of person such as "employee", and <u>their</u> subsets
("lecturers") etc. To satisfy this requirement, the "broadening"
which we apply to the denotation used in the query is to attempt to
retrieve any member of the powerset of the term supplied (figure
4.3).

b) There is also the possibility that information is stored "higher up"
the generic hierarchy than the user requested term in the query.

If all people are mortal. It would be entirely reasonable for
the database to store the information in this form with the entity
representing the set of all people. On retrieval, we require that
queries requesting information about subsets (lecturers,
schoolteachers, chemistry lecturer etc.) or particular members of
those subsets − "Fred Jones is mortal?" −should elicit the stored
information. This requires simple deduction.

In order to do this, the query terms must therefore be
"broadened" upwards so that the stored information is accessed, at
whichever higher set it happens to be stored.

We call this the "upward closure" of the search term. It is a
relatively complex operation to visualise. Starting from the search
term (which we refer to as the Principal Node) it includes all sets
of which the Principal Node is a member, all sets containing any of
those sets as a member...and so on until no additional sets can be
accessed (figure 4.3). In our prototype system we have taken the
apparently arbitrary decision <u>not</u> to expand the set employees in the
above example. We believe that it is better to return information
to the user at as high a level as possible. The user has the
facilities to expand any set he wishes.

The entire "broadened" collection of search terms can be visualised as a
"Broom", consisting of the Principal Node, its powerset (or "Downward
Closure") −the "Brush", and its Upward Closure − the "Handle".

To ensure that all relevant information is accessed the Fact System thus
broadens each search term to the corresponding Broom, but selects information
only if it lies on the intersections of all required Brooms.

The importance of this procedure is that :

a) It provides a precise but flexible interface with the outside world.
The matching procedure seems to closely mirror the corresponding
human process, but is convenient for both computer systems and human

users.

b) It provides the system with the capability of restructuring its data, factoring common items and storing them higher up the generic structures, yet allowing users to access that information in a completely unchanged manner. We believe that this procedure is fundamental to any advanced database system.

The format of the input to the Inferential Fetch instruction is identical to that of the simple fetch. Instead of matching on a single entity or 'don't care' in each field, however, the simple single entity pattern is "broadened", so that it will match any entity in the "broom" of which the entity is the Principal Node.

Whereas the simple associative machine matches a single entity or 'don't care' pattern in each field the Fact machine "broadens" each entity, so that it will match any entity in the "broom" of which the entity is the Principal Node. A Fact is selected only if it joins entities each must one of which lie on the corresponding (Subject,Relation,Object) broom.

4.3. A SIMPLE EXAMPLE

When a character string is presented to the system as input, in general it represents more than one entity. Let us take a privileged look into the internal structure of out system. We find that it contains a number of entities including –

600	is the colour green
762	is a bowling green
886	is Mr. John Green

– in addition, the character string "green" is represented by entity number 245. (We can think of 245 as the symbol table's internal identifier for that character string).

We also have a number of Facts showing that the character string "green" is an acceptable input denotation for each of the above entities. For reasons which can be justified, we use the relation 'member of set' ($\in$) here. Thus we have –

1000:	600	$\in$	245
1001:	762	$\in$	245
1002:	886	$\in$	245

Use of the character string "green" in retrieving information would then be taken by the system to mean the entire set of entities {600, 762, 886, 245}. Thus each character string, in general, represents a set of entities inside the system. Each entity can have a multiple input representation, that is, it can be fetched in response to a number of different character strings presented as input.

If, however, we wish to present some additional information to be stored in the Fact system, to succeed we must be able to uniquely determine the actual entities involved.

```
Character input :      "Green          has_salary       $8000"
Identifiers :          245               120              130
Entity
Representation: 800:    886               211              765
of Fact   (Fact no)    (Subject)       (Relation)       (Object)
```

    Here   886 uniquely identifies this particular <u>real</u> Green
            765 uniquely identifies this particular sum of money
            211 determines this particular method of earning

The identification of the actual entities involved may well be a complex operation, involving additional information or interaction with the user. It is the chief problem for those storing information.

When trying to retrieve information from the system we have a different problem. As we have seen each character string presented stands for a set of entities. A Fact is at the intersection of 3 sets of entities, and a Fact is only fetched if it is at the intersection of the sets specified by the query. For example :   fetch "Green works_for company" Thus the given query specifies three sets. These sets are defined by the "brooms" stored in the associative network. Only the Facts actually in the common intersection of all three brooms are retrieved.

Entity symbols have secret internal codes. They must therefore be translated to meaningful character strings before being displayed to an external user. The output representation of a particular entity may well be stored explicitly within the database also as a Fact e.g.
                10004:   886   Rep_by 245

- indicating that entity 886 can be represented in English by 245 (the character string "green"). If an entity does not possess a character representation directly, the Fact system follows a number of possible routes until a representation is eventually located. The entity may be a Fact unit, the fact would be located and displayed, one field at a time. Another possibility is that the entity though unnamed, is a member of a set which has a name. The detailed mechanism of such a translation process is described elsewhere [McGREGOR82].

4.4. COMPUTED FACTS AND RELATIONS

A different, but equally powerful feature of the system permits any Fact to be tagged with a specific procedure which is obeyed whenever the Fact is accessed. This provides a convenient means of representing information by a program. This helps the Fact system to behave not merely as an assemblage of stored data but as a dynamic model in which functionally dependent variables are computed when required. The values of such variables are thus consistent with, and dependent on the most up-to-date stored information. The mechanism, which can be called recursively, is used to provide a wide range of facilities and play an important part in improving the accuracy and consistency of the data base.

On entry, the procedures have as parameters the operation code and data which caused the `trap' to occur. Typically, a set of results are returned. From the user's point of view the effect can be made indistinguishable from an operation accessing stored information.

In Computed Relations trapping action depends solely on the relation. For historical reasons, the prototype Fact machine handles two particular cases - Transitive and Reflexive Relations - as built-in primitive operations. Other Computed Relations are user-defined.

As a worked example consider the following case, where the stored data corresponds to the schema :

employee	works.in	department
department	stocks	items

If this example comes from a company which retails goods it may happen that users wish to present queries of the general form :

	salesman	sells	items
e.g.	John.Smith	sells	any
	person	sells	computers
	Brown	sells	bicycles

This type of question is valid as far as the questioner is concerned because it is normal English usage to say that a salesman sells something if he works in a department which stocks it for sale.

Without the ability to call a program to resolve this, users will receive invalid null responses - or the system will have to store duplicate data - both highly unsatisfactory outcomes.

The Fact system requires a 'Trigger' Fact, a program entity and a 'Link' Fact :-

Fa:	salesman	sells	items
P#:	"Fetch PSUBJ works_in department; join department to department stocks POBJ;"		
Fc:	Fa	Computed_Fact	P#

Computed_Fact is a special relation which causes the system to trap and enter the specified program. The system recognises this special relation whenever a Fact which has such a link is accessed by the inferential Fetch mechanism.

The terms PSUBJ, PREL and POBJ are macro substitution parameters which are replaced by the actual parameters of the request which caused the trap to occur.

As a procedure called in this way has access to the operation being performed, deletion and insertion operations can also be defined. Important database facilities can be implemented elegantly by this mechanism such as protected access to private information, and collection of access statistics.

5. AUTONOMOUS ACTIVITIES

Given the above retrieval mechanism, the flexibility of the data representation can be exploited by a set of background, or "autonomous activities" concerned with organising the secret internal data structure. They include:

1) Formation of additional new high level sets. These are shown to the user who can give them a name (external representation) which will be used in future, thus raising the level of the man-machine dialogue. These also save space by permitting factoring of the data.

2) Simplification of the database. When additional information becomes available indicating the equivalence of entities, the database may be simplified by removing the redundant information. In principle this can be performed as a task immediately. However it is preferable to equate the entities by a program, and perform the simplification as an autonomous activity.

3) Hypothesis formation. The process of clustering may enable the Fact machine to form a simple hypothesis that a number of different entity symbols represent the same real-world entity. The machine would do this when it finds that two entity symbols have a significant number of common properties and have an insignificant number of different properties, it would then converse with the user to determine if the hypothesis were correct. The system would be prevented from reconsidering rejected hypothesis by adding explicit 'denial of equivalence' Facts to the database.

4) Reversible conversion of stored data to computed data. Stored data can (sometimes) be replaced by an equivalent program. Conversely Computed Relations and Facts can be expanded to stored data in order to facilitate rapid operation.

5) Infrequently-used data could be moved to lower, less immediately accessible storage or could (with suitable control, and only if desired by the system manager) be eliminated altogether.

So far, we have investigated only the most basic one (a) with any thoroughness. The remainder are the subject of continued experimentation.

6. COMPLEXITY

The complexity of typical operations is dependent on the "interconnectedness" of the data. An important property which emerges by virtue of the associative nature of the Fact store is that the upper limit of the complexity of the inferential fetch operation is linearly dependent on the sum of the number of elements present in the brooms of each of the three fields. This complexity can be expressed in a variety of ways. These include:

a) The time taken by a single processor.

b) The time taken by multiple processors.

c) The volume of a complex data structure which keeps the brooms ready-formed for immediate look-up.

d) The interconnections of a diode containing network in which the flow of current (or fluid) shows up an entire broom in only a single operation taking just the propagation time of the signal.

7. IMPLEMENTATION METHODS

The two areas of particular difficulty in implementation are:

a) the expansions of each query term to its powerset and inverse powerset, given that we do not store them complete, in an explicit form.

b) the locating of information in the intersection of the expanded sets.

The performance of these expansion and intersection operations is absolutely critical to the performance of the system as a whole, and the future of this kind of system is completely dependent upon devising efficient mechanisms to implement them.

The most obvious method is to map the network of set hierarchies directly into backing-store, with sets located separately having all their members in one area. Our first attempt used this approach. It was much too slow because (even under ideal conditions using a hash index to locate each set) it required at least one backing-store access per entity in the powerset! It was particularly galling that a major proportion of these accesses were incurred checking that the bottom of the set hierarchy were actually at the bottom! — though ad hoc methods were soon introduced to limit this particular source of inefficiency. A breakthrough occurred when we realised that logically adjacent information should be stored in access-adjacent storage locations.

(The B-tree principle). This has transformed the prospects for efficient implementation.

Three implementation routes are now being investigated.

a) Direct implementation of a Generic Associative Memory by a special GAM chip implemented in VLSI.

b) Implementation by simulation of the hardware on a conventional system.

c) Implementation of the operations using an associative scanning-disc [BABB], [COPELAND], [HEATH], [LEA].

7.1. IMPLEMENTATION IN VLSI

It was observed at an early stage of the investigation that the generic hierarchy could be modelled by a wired network (figure 7.1). Applying a positive voltage to a particular node activates all others in the powerset, while a negative voltage can activate the corresponding inverse powerset. This is an exceedingly rapid operation, depending only on the speed of propagation of the signal, but the permanently-wired connections could only be produced automatically by a wiring machine! The permanently-connected circuit can, however, be transformed into an equivalent crossbar matrix of switches (figure 7.2). As in a telephone exchange the number of switches in a complete crossbar scheme is N^2 given N inputs and outputs. Only a small number of switches is actually required, so we have:

a) Replaced the large crossbar by a number of smaller crossbar memories acting as pieces of the larger matrix (figure 7.3).

b) Provided a mechanism to deal with the inevitable overflow of the sub-matrices, as the database grows.

c) Allocating internal entity symbols to network terminals so as to minimise the number of inter block overflows.

A 'switch matrix' with the geometry shown is not very suitable for production in LSI technology - a large number of lines are required to cross each other while at the same time not interfering with the logic of the switch circuits. It is therefore transformed into a topologically equivalent layout (figure 7.4) which leaves 'free' areas, where there is no other logic, in which the necessary interconnections can be formed. In both layouts each conductor comes physically adjacent to every other conductor at an active switch-point.

7.2. IMPLEMENTATION BY SIMULATION OF HARDWARE BY SOFTWARE

In investigating the usefulness of the proposed new hardware element, we

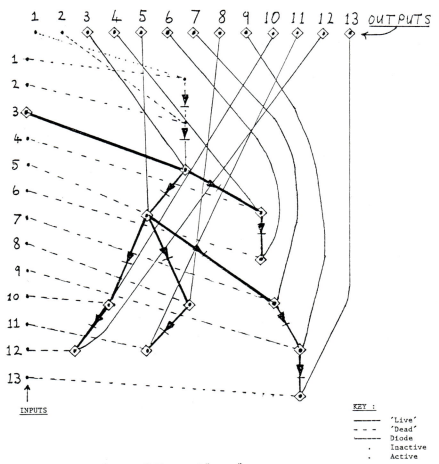

"Downward" Closure of "person"

A 'Wired' network

Figure 7.1

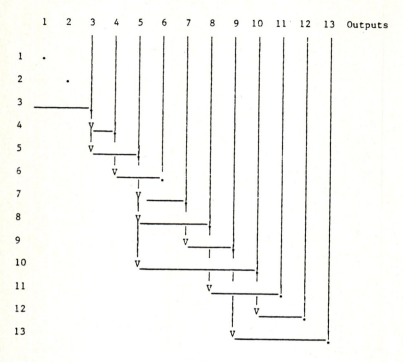

inputs

Data as Figure 7.1

KEY :

  V (diode) switched connection (open switches not shown)
    (wired) permanent connection
  •

Crossbar representation of network

Figure 7.2

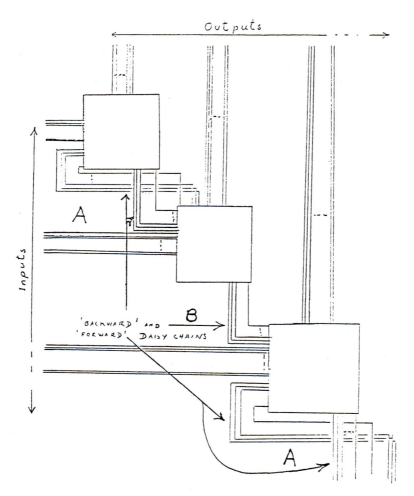

Note : Only a single set of (bi-directional) links is
actually required (B) to achieve the effect as
at (A). (i.e All links are bi-directional)

Figure 7.3

decided to implement a comprehensive simulation of a complete system in software. To our surprise this has produced the fastest systems we have implemented so far, partly because this produces an extremely compact representation of the data, but mainly because the allocation of entity information to blocks results in highly desirable clustering of logically associated information.

7.2.1. A DATA STRUCTURE FOR IMPLEMENTATION BY SOFTWARE

We shall now describe the data structure used by our software implementation. As is usual with database systems, data is presented to the system – and is returned from the system – in the form of variable-length character strings. These are converted by a scanner mechanism which uses a large backing-store file as a hash-table, and which returns a fixed-length identifier. In the case of a character string already present in the system, the identifier is of the form <net><line>. <net> is a datablock representing the hardware net switch matrix, <line> is the row of the matrix allocated to this symbol. The required initial datablock can thus be accessed directly and fetched into mainstore.

The structure of this datablock is given in (figure 7.5). It consists of an n x n square bit matrix, associated pointers, and 'buckets' containing data elements which can be chained to others making a cellular list. The bit matrix has one row for each entity which has been assigned to the net, the pointers refer to a descriptor of the additional information about the entity.

The structure is designed to store each piece of information as closely as possible to the other information with which it is associated. When a new entity comes into the system, the identifier allocated to it (which is also of the form <net><line>) is chosen to be one which :

   a) has sufficient space.

   b) contains associated data.

If no associated data is already present the new entity is allocated to a new or relatively empty block. When an new entity is associated with other information, but lack of space prevents it being allocated to the existing net, a connection or link must be made (using the pointers) from the existing net to a new net. A net is thus used as a small contiguous bucket to which entities can be assigned irrespective of their type. Although it may at first sight seem an untidy structure, it does in fact provide a good model for the clusters of associated items of information met in actual usage. It is particularly useful where we have to map the resultant data structure onto a backing store device.

7.2.2. IMPROVING INTERSECTION EFFICIENCY AND COMPACTNESS

As the database gets larger, the set information becomes a smaller

An alternative, but equivalent, topological arrangement,
more suitable for VLSI construction

Figure 7.4

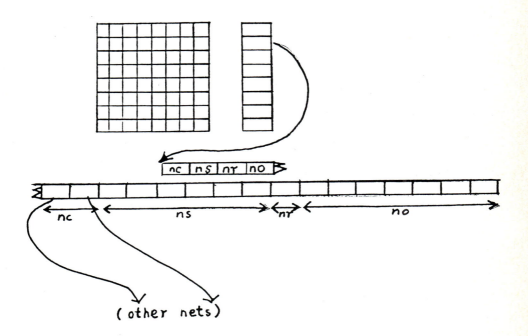

Structure of data block

Figure 7.5

proportion of the total. Actually extracting the basic assertions becomes the major part of the work. The 'Net' data structure described above can be further compacted if, instead of actual Fact record numbers the list contains the block numbers of blocks containing groups of logically associated records. These block number lists can be combined to give an approximate intersection, the small portion of the database thus selected is then scanned against the expanded sets of required entities in a reverse search, to yield the final accurate result.

7.3. IMPLEMENTATION USING HIGH-SPEED ASSOCIATIVE DISC DEVICES

We again require a two-phase retrieval operation, the first completing the generic closures, the second retrieving all the records within the intersections of these sets of search terms. First, we keep the set membership information physically distinct from the rest of the information. The device must have some means of recording two sets of 'hits' for each term in the query being conducted. [This could be implemented in CAM, microcoded hash-table in RAM, or even in bit-lists of sufficient size]. The records (set, setmember) are scanned, and checked on-the-fly against those already in the search lists. When a match is obtained, the other member of the pair is added to the set accumulating the appropriate closure.

If the data can be maintained in the form of partially-ordered, flattened trees (one for 'downwards', the other for 'upwards' closure) the closures can be accomplished in a single pass over both trees.

If this is too inconvenient, the ordering can be ignored, and the data scanned repeatedly until the closures are complete. Given the worst possible ordering of the data, such a system can accomplish the complete closure in n passes, where n is the the depth of the deepest tree in the generic tree accessed by the query. As has been noted by ourselves and others (e.g.Fahlman [1979]), these trees are invariably short and bushy. We find that in the Fact system depths rarely exceed three or four levels. Thus generic association seems relatively inexpensive and quite feasible at the current state of the art.

The second phase of retrieval is accomplished by scanning the remainder of the data against the expanded sets via an intermediate index as this enables the final scan to be limited to only a small section of the database.

An alternative would be to use the VLSI memory (section 3) to hold the generic information, using the associative disc to hold the major portion of the data.

8. IMPLEMENTATION – CURRENT STATUS

Working with a PDP11/34 minicomputer we have constructed prototype systems, with which we have been able to demonstrate the feasibility of the system concepts —the inferential fetch operation, use of Semantic Rules, computed Facts, transitive relations, internal reorganisation of the database, and simple hypothesis formation.

In recent months we have implemented a larger scale prototype on the ICL 2980 at ERCC, running under the EMAS operating system. This version is just becoming available and does not yet have the full range of facilities, but is already showing promise in its abilities to deal with large volumes of data. We are now concentrating on constructing a reliable full system, and benchmarking its performance against more conventional databases and information retrieval systems. We have just implemented the bucket selection, with reverse search for Fact records on our PDP11/34 implementation. This has greatly improved its performance, and its ability to deal with large databases. This system is now running with over 20000 Facts stored, and its ultimate size is now limited by our use of 16-bit words as distinct entity symbols. No such limitation exists on the ICL 2980 but a user's virtual store (which includes active files) is limited to a maximum of 24mbytes. Our aim is thus to get some experience in use of the system using the system implementations available now.

With regard to hardware developments, a 'breadboard' version of the memory circuit has been built, and we are co-operating with the MEMEX project [HEATH] investigating implementation by associative disc.

9. COMPARISON WITH OTHER SYSTEMS

We saw the model as a development of Senko's DIAMII [1975], and an extension of our own work on special-purpose hardware for database systems. Chen [1976], Smith and Smith [1977] have worked on Entity sets, and generic information. The work of Lea [1978] on associative hardware was also influential. After our initial developments we discovered the work by Sharman and Winterbottom [1979] and Chaing and Bergeron [1980], and were interested by the comparison between our basic associative Fact store and Feldman and Rovner's [1969] programming language LEAP. Recent works by Deliyani and Kowalski [1979] on logic and semantic networks is somewhat similar to our own in its use of deduction.

Semantic nets are a recognised method of representing knowledge in computer systems though they have only recently been applied to database systems [ROUSOPOLOUS75]. They have been found especially useful in the field of artificial intelligence where there is a wealth of literature describing various forms which they can take. A number of related systems have been developed by various workers – "networks" Woods [1975] "frames" Minsky [1975], "generalisation hierarchies" Winograd [1975]. There seems little doubt that nets are a powerful technique for the representation of information – though there is much debate on which representation is 'best' for a particular application.

In general, earlier implementations of semantic nets were unsuitable for use in large scale databases. Usually the data were held in mainstore, and explicit pointers were used to indicate links between nodes on the net. Later systems, in particular the implementation of Sharman and Winterbottom placed semantic nets on the backing store. Here however, the links between nodes were still explicit (address) pointers.

10. CONCLUSION

The most significant features of the Fact system are:-

a) The automatic implicit call of built-in or user-supplied program elements.

b) The fundamental simplicity of the information model, its secrecy and the consequent independence of application programs from the data structure.

c) The use of generic information and general pattern matching abilities, to provide a self-adaptive interface through which remote users or computer systems can immediately achieve effective communication.

d) The practical nature of the system which can be implemented to perform with reasonable efficiency, using a variety of different technologies.

We have presently refrained from pointing out the wider implications of this new model (for example to neurological systems).

11. ACKNOWLEDGEMENTS

We should like to thank our colleagues in the Department of Computer Science for their advice and helpful discussions. The work is supported in part by S.R.C Grant GR/A/3682.7.

12. REFERENCES

BABB,E., "Implementing a Relational Database by Means of Specialised Hardware", Trans. on Database Systems Vol. 4, No. 1, 1979, pp 1-29

CHEN,P.P.S., "The Entity-Relationship Model", Trans. on Database Systems Vol 1, No 1, 1976, pp 9-36

CHIANG,T.C.,BERGERON,R.F., "A database management system with an E-R conceptual model", in Entity-Relationship Approach to System Analysis and Design, ed P. Chen, North-Holland, Amsterdam, 1980

CODD,E.F., "A Relational Model of Data for Large Shared Data Banks", Comm. ACM Vol 13, 1970, pp 377-387

COPELAND,G.P.,LIPOVSKI,G.J.,SU,S.Y.W., "The Architecture of CASSM : A Cellular System for Non-numeric Processing", Proc. 1st. Annual Symp. on Computer Architecture, Dec. 1973, pp 121-128

DELIYANI,A.,KOWALSKI,R.A., "Logic and Semantic Networks", Comm. ACM vol 22, No 3, 1979, pp 184-192

FAHLMAN,S.E., A System for Representing and Using Real World Knowledge, MIT Press 1979

FELDMAN,J.A.,ROVNER,P.D., "An Algol Based Associative Language", Comm. ACM Vol 12, 1969, pp 439-449

LEA,R.M., "Associative Processing of Non Numerical Information", Proc. Summer Institute NATO ASI series c-32, 1978, pp 171-215

McGREGOR,D.R.,MALONE,J.R., "The Fact Database System", in Research and Development in Information Retrieval, eds C.J. Van rijsbergen, P.W. Williams, Butterworth 1980

McGREGOR,D.R.,MALONE,J.R., The Fact System : A System using Generic Associative Networks, to appear in Research and Development in Information Technology, Vol 1, no 1, Butterworth 1982

McGREGOR,D.R.,THOMSON,G.T.,DAWSON,W.D., High Performance Hardware for Database Systems, Proc. VLDB 1976, Preprints, pp 103-116

MINSKY,M., "A Framework for Representing Knowledge", in The Psychology of Computer Vision, ed P.H. Winston, McGraw-Hill, 1975

QUILLIAN,M.R., "The Teachable Language Comprehender : A Simulation Program and Theory of Language" Comm. ACM Vol 12, 1969, pp 459-476

ROUSOPOLOUS,N.,MYLOPOULOUS,J., "Using Semantic Networks for Database Management", Proc. VLDB 1975, pp 144-172

SENKO,M.E., "Specification of Stored Data Structures and Desired Results in DIAMII with FORAL", Proc. VLDB 1975, pp 557-571

SHARMAN,G.O.H.,WINTERBOTTOM,N., "NDB:Non-Programmer Database Facility", IBM Technical Report TR 12.179, England

SMITH,J.M.,SMITH,D.C.P., "Database Abstraction : Aggregation and Generalisation", Trans. on Database Systems Vol 2, No 2, 1977, pp 105-133

WALTZ,D.L., "An English Language Question Answering System for a Large Relational Database", Comm. ACM Vol 21, No 7, 1978, pp 526-539

WINOGRAD,T., in Understanding Natural Language, Edinburgh University Press, 1972

WINOGRAD,T., "Frame Representation and the Declarative/Procedural Controversy", in Representation and Understanding, eds D.G.Bobrow, A.Collins, Academic Press, 1975

WOODS,W., "Foundations for Semantic Networks", in Representation and Understanding, eds D.G.Bobrow and A.Collins, Academic Press, 1975

ZLOOF,M.M., "Query by Example: A Database Language", IBM System Journal Vol 16, no 4, 1977, pp 324-343

Entity-Relationship Approach to
Information Modeling and Analysis, P.P. Chen (ed.)
Elsevier Science Publishers B.V. (North-Holland)
©ER Institute, 1983

IMPLEMENTING A SELF-DEFINING ENTITY/RELATIONSHIP MODEL
TO HOLD CONCEPTUAL VIEW INFORMATION

Jerome M. Fox
J. Carlos Goti
Claude R. Miller
James M. Sagawa
IBM Santa Teresa Laboratory
San Jose, California

ABSTRACT

An approach to defining a conceptual view model of
entities and relationships using entities and relationships is discussed. The main concept consists of a
conceptual view using a set of entities and relationships to hold information about itself plus user defined
conceptual views simultaneously. The definition process
used to define such a model is documented followed by
an example of the models use. Finally some of the major
benefits of the model are high-lighted based on experience with a working version.

1.0 INTRODUCTION: THREE VIEWS OF INFORMATION

A helpful way to describe the information in an enterprise is to divide the
information into three classes or views: the conceptual view which describes
data as it exists in the enterprise, independent of how it is stored by the
Data Base Management System (DBMS) or used by applications; the storage view
which describes how the data elements defined in the conceptual view are
represented in the DBMS; and the logical view which describes the view of
data required by applications. This allows one to change how the data is
actually stored or to migrate to a new DBMS by redefining the storage view,
while the conceptual view and logical view remain unchanged.

In the conceptual view the enterprise may be described in terms of enterprise entities and relationships. Entities are defined as persons, places,
things, or events of interest to the enterprise. These entities are characterized by a set of attributes. For example: an employee is an entity;
and name, address, and current salary are attributes of an employee. A
collection of homogeneous entities is called an entity set. For example,
an employee is an entity and all employees are an entity set.

Relationships are directed binary connections between entities where the entities are members of the same or different entity sets. Relationships can also exist between relationships and entities and between relationships and relationships. Each relationship can have an inverse (opposite direction) relationship. Relationships do not hold data values in the same sense as entities, but they hold the information that two entity occurrences are "linked." Only entities hold actual data values.

In summary, the conceptual view is a description of enterprise data independent of how it is stored in the DBMS or used by applications.

2.0 SCOPE

This paper is based on a working system that has used the three view concept and the Entity/Relationship data model as its base. The components of each view in this system have been thought about and designed prior to implementation. This paper addresses data modelling in the conceptual view. It does not discuss other parts of the conceptual view or any part of the logical or storage views.

The conceptual view is a superset of what is sometimes termed the "enterprise schema" or "global schema." In the system upon which this paper is based, the conceptual view includes more than pure data modelling information. It also includes a policy model, which handles access security, data integrity, and data state triggering.

The logical view is a superset of what is sometimes termed the "external schema" or"application view." It includes a complete model of applications.

The storage view corresponds to what is sometimes termed the "internal schema."

3.1 ENTITY MODELS

An entity model is the generic description of the set of homogeneous entities which comprise an entity set. Entity Models are named and defined in the conceptual view. Every entity model must have one data field which contains a unique value for each entity in the set. This data field is called the entity identifier (e.g., employee name). Each entity model in the enterprise must have a unique name that is also the name of the entity set it models.

Entity models are used as a "map" of the entities in the entity set. The model is used to interpret and give meaning to the data in the entities. For example, employee entities may be understood or interpreted via the EMPLOYEE entity model. EMPLOYEE is the name of the entity model (and entity set); and name, address, and current salary are data fields in the entity model. The correspondence between the entity model, entity set, and entities is shown in Figure 1.

3.2 RELATIONSHIP MODELS

A relationship model is the generic description of a set of homogeneous relationships which form a relationship set. As stated before, relationships are:

1. Directed

    Each relationship model has a defined source and target. If relationship A is defined with entity X as its source, and entity Y as its target, then ALL occurrences of relationship A point "from" an occurrence of entity X and "to" an occurrence of entity Y.

2. Binary

    A given relationship model has one and only one source and target. In this context source and target mean any single entity or relationship model.

As with entity models, relationship models are defined and named in the conceptual view. Relationship models are used to interpret relationships in the same way that entity models are used to interpret entities. The main purpose of the relationship model is to state the source entity/relationship model and the target entity/relationship model. Once the source and target, models are defined, the individual relationships may be defined by stating the source entity/relationship identifier and the target entity/relationship identifier. For example, DEPARTMENTS and EMPLOYEES are both entity sets, and as application developers want to associate employees with their departments, a relationship model named WORKS is defined from the EMPLOYEE entity model to the DEPARTMENT entity model. This allows the definition of relationships that link specific employees with specific departments by stating an employee identifier and a department identifier. The correspondence between the relationship model, relationship set, and relationships is shown in Figure 2.

```
ENTITY NAME   = EMPLOYEE

ENTITY MODEL  : NAME───────────────>ADDRESS─────────────────────>SALARY─>
ENTITY-1      : Doe, John Q.        112233 State St.             10000
ENTITY-2      : Smith, Mary Z.      72 Main St.                  120000
ENTITY-3      : Jones, Tom X.       45678 59th Ave.              39000

ENTITY SET    : ENTITY-1, ENTITY-2, AND ENTITY-3
```

Figure 1: Example Entity Set

```
RELATIONSHIP NAME   = WORKS

RELATIONSHIP MODEL : SRC(EMPLOYEE)———>TRG(DEPARTMENT)——>
RELATIONSHIP-1a    : Doe, John Q.        63
RELATIONSHIP-2a    : Smith, Mary Z.      W9-22I
RELATIONSHIP-3a    : Jones, Tom X.       789V

RELATIONSHIP SET   : RELATIONSHIP-1a, RELATIONSHIP-2a, AND RELATIONSHIP-3a
```

Figure 2: Example Relationship Set

3.3 MODELLING INTERSECTION DATA

Intersection data is information that only has meaning to the intersection
of two other pieces of information. Intersection data is modelled by a
relationship from a relationship (which semantically represents the intersection) to an entity which contains the intersection data.

Continuing the example above, if an entity set named YEARS exists that holds
ranges of years, e.g. 72-73, 68-70, this information (the time or years an
employee worked in a department) may be added to the EMPLOYEE/DEPARTMENT
pairs as intersection data. The YEARS information is a candidate for
intersection data since it has no real meaning as part of an employee
entity or as part of a department entity. It only becomes meaningful when
thought of as an attribute of a employee/department pair.

Figure 3 illustrates this point using the above data. It assumes that
John Q. Doe worked in department 63 from 1968 through 1970 and that this
intersection data is modelled with the relationship TIME.

```
RELATIONSHIP NAME   = TIME

RELATIONSHIP MODEL : SRC(WORKS)————>TRG(YEARS)————>
RELATIONSHIP-1b    : Relationship-1a   68-70

RELATIONSHIP SET   : RELATIONSHIP-1b
```

Figure 3: Example Intersection Data

4.0 A SELF-DEFINING DATA MODEL

The result of modelling the enterprise conceptual view in terms of entities
and relationships yields a neat, clean picture of the enterprise data.
This solves one problem but creates another. How does one describe all the
entity and relationship modelling information in some accessible way? The

concept of using entities and relationships to model information may be
generalized to the point where a conceptual view can be defined (using
entities and relationships) that models entity and relationship definitions.
This leads to the need for an internal conceptual view, or a conceptual
view of conceptual views, which is the main topic of this paper.

Designing a conceptual view requires that a standard data base design be
done on the information involved. Any user thinking about his data at this
point must go through the process of deciding which information to model
with entities and which information to model with relationships. This same
process is needed when defining the internal conceptual view to hold conceptual view information. In this case the data consists of the definitions
of an entity and a relationship. This process is discussed in the remainder of the paper.

The first step is to define the conceptual view of an entity and of a
relationship. In general terms, the conceptual view of an entity consists
of general information about the entity set, e.g. key type, and the set of
field definitions that comprise each entity in the set.

The conceptual view of a relationship consists of general information about
the relationship set, e.g., relationship type (1-1, 1-many), source set,
target set, and the specific source and target of each relationship.

Entity models to hold entity and relationship model information must then be
defined. For purposes of illustration, these entity models (and other defined in later sections) will be given names. The entity model to hold
entity model information will be named ENTMOD, and the entity model to hold
relationship model information will be named RELMOD. ENTMOD holds information about all entity models in the conceptual view including its own.
RELMOD holds all the information required to define all relationships in the
conceptual view.

Once the models for entities and relationships are defined in terms of
entities and relationships, the model becomes SELF-DEFINING. This results
from treating the entity models for entities, relationships, departments,
employees, etc. in a standard consistent manner.

5.0   DESIGNING THE MODEL

5.1   LEVEL 1: A SIMPLE VERSION

The simplest version of the model would contain just two entities: one to
hold entity definitions and one to hold relationship definitions. However,
this format is not usable since it does not use any relationships. Relationships give the E/R model all its power and flexibility. A model with no
relationships will result in redundant data embedded or hard coded in the
entities.

The simplest usable model is shown in Figure 4.

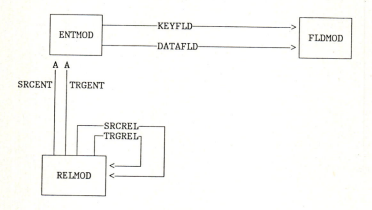

Figure 4: Simple CV Model

There are three entities: one for entities (ENTMOD), one for fields (FLDMOD), and one for relationships (RELMOD). As stated before, an entity definition is made up of some general information and a set of field definitions. The concept of a "field model" (FLDMOD) is introduced here to hold and consolidate the definitions of the fields that comprise the entities. The FLDMOD entity holds general information, e.g., maximum CV length, data type, display length, etc., about each field defined in the conceptual view. Figure 5 shows an example of a FLDMOD entity set.

```
ENTITY NAME   = FLDMOD

ENTITY MODEL : FIELDNAME————————>DATATYPE————————>MAXL->DISPL>
ENTITY-1     : Name              Character       18      18
ENTITY-2     : Address           Character       26      20
ENTITY-3     : Salary            Fixed bin       32      8
ENTITY-4     : Fieldname         Character       20      8
ENTITY-5     : Datatype          Character       16      12
ENTITY-6     : Maxl              Fixed bin       32      6
ENTITY-7     : Displ             Fixed bin       32      6

ENTITY SET   : ENTITY-1, ENTITY-2, -3, -4, -5, -6, AND ENTITY-7
```

Figure 5: Example Field Entity (FLDMOD) Set

The model in figure 4 allows the field definitions to be defined and held separately from the main entity definition allowing a field (with a matching definition) to be used in multiple entities without multiple definitions.

Each entity definition has one KEYFLD relationship between the entity name and the field which is the key for that entity and n DATAFLD relationships, with one relationship occurring between the entity name and each of the field definitions in the entity definition. Isolating the field definitions allows a field to be used in more than one entity without having the field name "hard coded" in the entity definition.

In the same manner relationship definitions are composed of general information about the relationship plus the source and target entity/relationship names. Since all entity names in the enterprise are in ENTMOD and all relationship names are in RELMOD, the source and targets may be connected to the relationship definition using relationships and not "hard coding" the entity/relationship names in the relationship definitions. These connections are made using the relationships SRCENT, SRCREL, TRGENT, and TRGREL. Each relationship model will have an occurrence of either SRCENT or SRCREL and TRGENT or TRGREL (two relationships in all).

5.2 LEVEL 2: ELIMINATING FIELD NAME UNIQUENESS

Field name uniqueness starts to become an obstacle as the model in Figure 4 is used over a period of time. All the attributes of a field are part of the field definition. Using a field name in entity-2 that has already been defined as part of entity-1 requires the use of the field as it has already been defined in entity-1. In order to use the field in entity-2, all the previously defined attributes of the field must be accepted. Since this is not always desired or reasonable, another field name is usually defined for entity-2 with its own set of attributes.

This scenerio generally will lead to new field names for each new entity; or in other words, it almost forces field name uniqueness across the conceptual view.

The model can be extended to ease this restriction, as shown in Figure 6. A new entity, ATTR, is added to hold field attributes. This entity is connected as intersection data from the relationship between entities and fields. ENTMOD holds the entity name, and FLDMOD holds the field name; so the relationship between them has a semantic meaning of "use of a field in an entity." Attributes of a field in an entity are "attached" to this relationship by the ATTRIBUTE relationship. Notice also that it was possible to combine the KEYFLD and DATAFLD relationships into one, since one of the attributes in ATTR could be "used as key/not used as key."

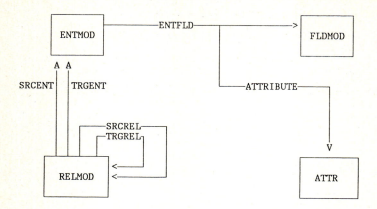

Figure 6: CV Model Without Field Name Uniqueness

5.3 LEVEL 3: ADDING RELATIONSHIP INVERSES

The next step in evolving towards a complete conceptual view model is the
question of relationship inverses. Since relationships have been defined
as "directed", the only way to reference a relationship in the reverse
direction is by defining an "inverse relationship."

An inverse relationship definition is held in the model just like any other
relationship definition. The main difference is that it has a very special
link with another relationship set. This special link is modelled with
another relationship in the model as shown in Figure 7.

The RELINV relationship is another relationship that has a relationship set
name as its source AND target. Since all relationship set names are held
in the relationship entity set name RELMOD, the RELINV relationship will
have RELMOD as its source and target as shown in Figure 7. This allows all
relationship definitions to remain in RELMOD.

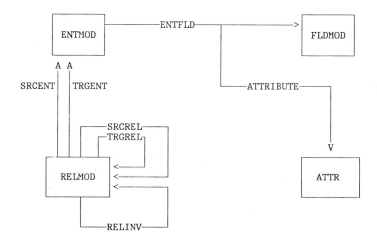

Figure 7: CV Model With Relationship Inverses

5.4 LEVEL 4: GENERALIZED TREATMENT OF ATTRIBUTES

Two small problems remain with the model in Figure 7. First, the RELINV
relationship is missing one important piece of information. Which relationship is the primary and which is the inverse? This is really "attribute"
information of the RELINV relationship. Secondly, ENTMOD and RELMOD still
hold general attribute information. It is also possible for FLDMOD to require some general (not dependent on inclusion in some entity set) attribute
information. The handling of attribute information can be generalized as
shown in Figure 8.

The first problem discussed above is solved by adding the RELINVA relationship. This allows for an intersection data attribute on the RELINV relationship. The attribute value could be "primary/inverse."

The second problem is solved with the addition of the ENTATTR, RELATTR, and
FLDATTR relationships directly from ENTMOD, RELMOD, and FLDMOD to ATTR.
This allows the general entity and relationship attributes to reside in
ATTR along with all the other attributes in the model.

Note that the model is further changed by combining the SRCENT and TRGENT
relationships (from RELMOD to ENTMOD) into one relationship named RELENT
with an intersection data relationship (RELENTA) added to hold, as an
attribute, the semantic information conveyed by the dual relationship.
The same is done for the new RELREL relationship.

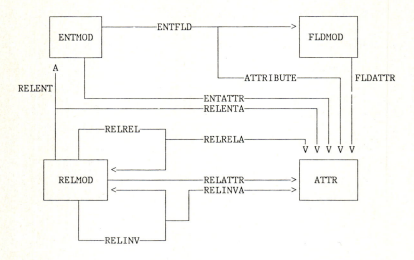

Figure 8: CV Model With Full Use Of ATTR

6.0 USING THE MODEL

Code can now be written that draws on the pool of information residing in
the conceptual view E/R model. The code can be "table driven" or actually
"entity/relationship" driven. The conceptual view model in Figure 8 (or
any previous figure for that matter) can be used as a map to guide the flow
of the logic manipulating the data. Knowledge of the conceptual view model
for conceptual views will be hard coded into the logic, but NO KNOWLEDGE OF
ANY OTHER DEFINED CONCEPTUAL VIEW IS REQUIRED. This is a very important
point because it allows a clean break between any existing code involved
with the conceptual view data and the enterprise conceptual view definition
itself. The enterprise conceptual view may change at any time without
affecting the code that manipulates this definition. Since the concept of
an enterprise conceptual view has been converted into entities and relationships, the code can access and manipulate any or all of the enterprise
conceptual view or the internal conceptual view definition while being
driven by the internal definition of a conceptual view that in turn is also
held in itself.

For example, if the EMPLOYEE entity set has already been defined, a new
employee entity could be manipulated by accessing the EMPLOYEE entity set
definition held in the conceptual view. In the same way a new entity set
may be manipulated by accessing the ENTMOD entity set definition.

6.1 EXAMPLE CONCEPTUAL VIEW MODEL CONTENTS

Some insight into the self-defining model can be gained by examining the
contents of the entity sets and relationship sets of Figure 4 after defining the three user entity sets and two relationship sets shown in Figure 9.

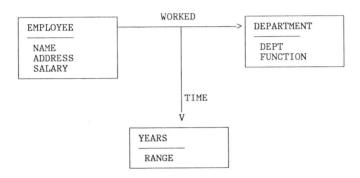

Figure 9: Example User CV Model

Notice that the internal definition of conceptual views and the enterprise
defined conceptual view data reside side by side in the entity and relationship sets. For clarity the entity set names under ENTMOD below are numbered and cross referenced with the field names under FLDMOD.

6.2 DICTIONARY "WHERE USED" INFORMATION

An interesting and useful by-product of the self-defining model is the
creation and maintenance of dictionary "where used" information, e.g.,
"What entities is field XYZ used in?", or "What relationship sets have
entity ABC as their source?"

This information is neatly held in the six conceptual view relationships.
Using the example above, the question, "What entities is field XYZ
used in?", can be answered by scanning the KEYFLD and DATAFLD relationship sets. The sources of all relationships with XYZ as the target is
the answer to the question. If only key fields were desired, only
the KEYFLD relationship set has to be scanned.

ENTITY CONTENTS

ENTMOD	FLDMOD	RELMOD
1-EMPLOYEE	NAME (1)	WORKED
2-DEPARTMENT	ADDRESS (1)	KEYFLD
3-ENTMOD	SALARY (1)	DATAFLD
4-FLDMOD	DEPT (2)	SRCENT
5-RELMOD	FUNCTION (2)	TRGENT
6-YEARS	ENTNAME (3)	SRCREL
	KEYTYPE (3)	TRGREL
	FLDNAME (4)	TIME
	FLDMAXLEN (4)	
	FLDTYPE (4)	
	RELNAME (5)	
	RELTYPE (5)	
	RELSRC (5)	
	RELTRG (5)	
	RANGE (6)	

RELATIONSHIP CONTENTS

KEYFLD		DATAFLD	
SRC (ENTMOD)	TRG (FLDMOD)	SRC (ENTMOD)	TRG (FLDMOD)
ENTMOD	ENTNAME	ENTMOD	KEYTYPE
FLDMOD	FLDNAME	FLDMOD	FLDMAXLEN
RELMOD	RELNAME		FLDTYPE
EMPLOYEE	NAME	RELMOD	RELTYPE
DEPARTMENT	DEPT		RELSRC
YEARS	RANGE		RELTRG
		EMPLOYEE	ADDRESS
			SALARY
		DEPARTMENT	FUNCTION

SRCENT		TRGENT	
SRC (RELMOD)	TRG (RELMOD)	SRC (RELMOD)	TRG (RELMOD)
SRCENT	RELMOD	SRCENT	ENTMOD
TRGENT	RELMOD	TRGENT	ENTMOD
SRCREL	RELMOD	SRCREL	RELMOD
TRGREL	RELMOD	TRGREL	RELMOD
KEYFLD	ENTMOD	KEYFLD	FLDMOD
DATAFLD	ENTMOD	DATAFLD	FLDMOD
WORKED	EMPLOYEE	WORKED	DEPARTMENT
		TIME	YEARS

SRCREL		TRGREL	
SRC (RELMOD)	TRG (RELMOD)	SRC (RELMOD)	TRG (RELMOD)
TIME	WORKED		

The second question, "What relationship sets have entity ABC as their source?" can be answered by scanning the SRCENT relationship set. The sources of all relationships with ABC as the target is the answer to this query.

7.0 SUMMARY

A part of an architecture for describing and holding data in a self-defining entity/relationship model was discussed. The information has been gathered and refined using an executing system incorporating these ideas.

The major breakthrough in this area of the system has been the use of a self-defining data model that holds its own (system) data in the same constructs as the user data. This allows the use of a common data access path to system and user data. Since information held in the entities and relationships may be "system data" when viewed in one way and "user data" when viewed in a different context, the ability to build and maintain such a system using itself becomes possible. The basic components of the executing system are now in place and current extensions are being made using the system itself.

In addition to the productivity advantage gained by the above approach, more control over the data is also achieved. If all additions, deletions, and changes to the enterprise conceptual view(s) are funneled through a facility that maintains the entities and relationships of the internal conceptual view of conceptual views, the answers to any number of important queries about the enterprise data will automatically be kept up to date. This is a major step in combining data definition and a base for queries used for change control.

8.0 ACKNOWLEDGEMENTS

The early architecture of this implementation was greatly influenced by Vernon L. Watts (IBM Santa Teresa Laboratory) and Dr. Christopher Wood (IBM Los Angeles Scientific Center).

9.0 BIBLIOGRAPHY

Chen, P.P. "The Entity-Relationship Model: Toward a Unified View of Data", ACM Tran. on Database Systems 1.1(March 1976) 9-37

Entity-Relationship Approach to
Information Modeling and Analysis, P.P. Chen (ed.)
Elsevier Science Publishers B.V. (North-Holland)
©ER Institute, 1983

Association:

A Database Abstraction for Semantic Modelling*

Michael L. Brodie

Department of Computer Science
University of Maryland
College Park, MD 20742

What is a good modelling concept? What is a good semantic
data model (SDM)? This paper addresses some of these important
open problems in the area of logical database design. SDM is
defined in terms of its constituent modelling concepts. Criteria
for evaluating and comparing modelling concepts and SDMs are
presented. The mathematical notion of set is considered as a fundamental modelling concept. It is demonstrated that although many
data models and SDMs are based on sets, their representation of
sets can be significantly improved. The contribution of this
paper is a new database abstraction called association. Association is a form of abstraction in which a collection of member
objects is considered as a higher level (more abstract) set
object. The concepts of association, member, and set are defined.
It is shown that they can be integrated into an SDM so that most
of the criteria for modelling concepts are satisfied.*

1. INTRODUCTION

Since the publication in 1974 of Abrial's landmark paper "Data Semantics"
[ABRI74], many modelling concepts have been proposed for the logical design of
database applications. Typically, database modelling concepts have been
presented in the context of semantic data models (SDMs). Due to a lack of

---

*This work was supported, in part, by the National Science Foundation under
grant number MCS 77-22509.

experience with both modelling concepts and their interrelationship in an SDM, there is a corresponding lack of evaluation criteria as well as open questions [BZ81] such as:

- What should be modelled?
- What is a good database modelling concept?
- What is a sufficient set of modelling concepts?
- What is a good SDM?
- How does one SDM resolve deficiencies in another SDM?

These increasingly important and practical questions arise not only in the database area but also in the areas of artificial intelligence and programming languages [BROD80a]. Although definitive answers to these questions cannot be expected, they should be addressed when modelling concepts or SDMs are introduced, evaluated, or compared.

In order to address the above questions, the concept of an SDM is defined in relation to its purposes and constituent modelling concepts. Particular emphasis is placed on the ability of an SDM to model both static and dynamic properties of database applications. A list of criteria is proposed for designing and evaluating modelling concepts on their own and within SDMs.

This paper introduces association, a new modelling concept. Association is a database abstraction based on the mathematical notion of set. Sets are fundamental modelling concepts that satisfy the defined criteria. Association supports a form of abstraction in which a collection of member objects is considered as a higher level set object. Although most data models and SDMs are based on set concepts, they do not directly support the properties of members, sets, and association in a way that satisfies the criteria.

Association and its related concepts, member and set, directly support the modelling of static and dynamic properties of sets of objects. These concepts are defined and are fully integrated into an SDM which satisfies such important SDM criteria as: abstraction, relativism, simplicity, and completeness (expressiveness).

2. SEMANTIC DATA MODELS

The design and development of database applications involves three distinct kinds of knowledge. These kinds of knowledge concern:

i. real or imagined situations to be modelled;
ii. representations of the situation, such as in schemas and programs;
iii. modelling concepts used to create and manipulate the representations.
   This third kind of knowledge concerns data models and SDMs.

A data model, as well as an SDM, is a collection of modelling concepts that provides a basis for:

i. modelling methodologies with which to identify static and dynamic objects and their properties;
ii. languages for precisely specifying properties of objects;
iii. languages for implementing specified objects directly on a computer.

Although the classical data models (hierarchic, network, and relational) are widely used as a basis for implementation, their modelling and specification roles can be enhanced significantly. To reduce the inherent complexity of data modelling and to increase precision, a new generation of data models, called semantic data models, was introduced. SDM concepts are intended to be more appropriate for modelling and for specifying real or imagined properties, whereas data model concepts are more appropriate for implementation.

A significant distinction between data models and SDMs is their relative ability to represent both structural and behavioural properties of objects. Structure refers to states and static properties (entities and their relationships). Behaviour refers to state transitions and dynamic properties (operations and their relationships). Data models provide concepts for modelling structure, but only primitive operations for modelling behaviour. Recent SDMs [BROD81c] [MBW80] provide concepts for modelling behaviour as well as structure.

An SDM is a collection of mathematically defined concepts with which to identify static and dynamic properties of real or imagined objects and to specify them using structural and behavioural means. Seven kinds of concepts constitute an SDM:

i. structural primitives: for specifying elementary structural properties, e.g., objects and object properties;
ii. structural relationships: for specifying relationships between and within objects, e.g., aggregation, generalization [SMIT77], functional relationships;
iii. structural abstractions: for specifying objects composed by structural relationships over structural primitives and abstractions;
iv. behavioural primitives: elementary accessing, derivation, and altering operations, e.g., insert, update, delete, find, and create.
v. behavioural relationships: control structures for specifying relationships among operations;
vi. behavioural abstractions: for specifying complex operations composed by behavioural relationships over behavioural primitives and abstractions, i.e., actions and transactions; and
vii. a predicate language for naming objects and for specifying queries as well as structural and behavioural constraints.

A constraint is a representation of a property of an application entity expressed in terms of the concepts of a particular data model or SDM. A constraint defines the values and operations acceptable in the representation. SDMs differ significantly in their expressible constraints and in the manner in which they are expressed. Constraints can be expressed inherently, explicitly, and implicitly.

   <u>Inherent constraints</u> are the basic (semantic) properties of the concepts that constitute the SDM.   These properties act as rules that cannot be violated by any representation based on the SDM. For example, the hierarchic data model permits only hierarchic relationships and the relational model does not permit duplicate tuples or ordering among tuples in a relation.

   An <u>explicit constraint</u> is a user-defined constraint sometimes called a semantic integrity constraint. SDM concepts can be used to define constraints that must be consistent with the inherent constraints. Examples of explicit constraints include: use of a relation and its attributes for a particular entity, use of primary and foreign keys.

   An <u>implicit constraint</u> is a logical consequence of (i.e., is derived from) other constraints. Implicit constraints are similar to side effects in programming languages. They are constraints that are neither inherent in the model nor expressed explicitly by the designer. Examples of implicit constraints include: triggered deletes of ancestors in hierarchies and fixed automatic owner-coupled sets, the transitive closure of a set of functional dependencies, and a logical consequence of a set of assertions.

   Although over 40 SDMs have been proposed [BROD80a], there are no widely accepted criteria for evaluating data modelling concepts on their own or collectively in SDMs. The remainder of this section proposes such criteria. The criteria provide a comparative basis for evaluating modelling concepts of SDMs, and guidance for designing new modelling concepts and SDMs.   The criteria are not objective; rather they are largely matters of taste and experience in using, comparing, and designing SDMs. The criteria are not mutually satisfiable; this shows the difficulty of SDM design. For a more detailed analysis than is presented here, the criteria should be considered with regard to the specific stages of the database life cycle [BROD81b].

SDM modelling concepts should support:

* abstraction [MCS81] – suppression of irrelevant detail; concentration on details essential to the properties at hand. For example: suppress implementation detail during specification; be able to concentrate on properties of objects and relationships for a particular view while ignoring all other properties.
* expressiveness – rich, inherent semantics to provide guidance; well-defined, explicit constraints to express all desired application properties to the necessary degree of precision. In some SDMs, expressive power has been achieved at the expense of simplicity and understandability.
* formality – definition of inherent and explicit constraints as a sound basis for semantic integrity analysis (perhaps automated) and for precise understanding.
* simplicity/elegance – small number of simple concepts to aid understanding,

design, and analysis.

- semantic relativism – ability to view the same information differently (e.g., as attributes, entities, relationships, functions, etc.) in different contexts as may be appropriate for different user views and for evolving applications.
- "natural" modelling concepts – modelling concepts common to the problem domain at hand and familiar to users and designers. Concepts that are close to the users' vocabulary and view of the application. This criteria could also be called understandability or application-orientation.
- structural and behavioural modelling concepts – provide means with which to specify static and dynamic properties.
- partitioning, modularity, and integration – support view design and view integration; the ability to decompose an application into distinct logical units that can be considered independently and as part of the whole application.
- high-level languages – support query, transaction, report, and definition languages that are non-procedural, free of unnecessary representation detail, and present users with application-oriented objects and operations.
- effective modelling methodologies.
- modelling directness – significant properties of the application should be representable directly, i.e., using a small number of modelling concepts. Directness contributes to elegance.
- modelling uniqueness – provide relatively few (e.g., one) ways of representing each property, i.e., the model is not too rich. Modelling concepts should not overlap in their ability to represent similar properties.
- provability – ability to verify a specification with respect to a corresponding implementation and validate the database with the schema; ability to derive all implicit constraints.
- independence of concepts – a clear separation of concepts so that properties may be specified independently and yet interact in a clearly defined way (e.g., consider aggregation and generalization independently).
- extensibility – ability to enhance or modify a database representation by adding, deleting, or modifying structures, behaviour, and constraints.
- picturability – lends itself to graphic representation for documentation.
- safe and efficient implementation – availability of safe and efficient implementation techniques for specified properties.

3. SETS ARE FUNDAMENTAL MODELLING CONCEPTS

Many structural and behavioural properties of real or imagined situations can be modelled naturally and directly with sets. There are three concepts for modelling structural properties of sets: member, set, and association. A member or set element is a primitive from which sets are defined. A set is a (possibly empty) collection of members that obey the set membership rule. Association is a form of abstraction in which a collection of members is considered as a higher level (more abstract) set. Association is used to represent the **member-of** relationship. A set is abstract since details of members are ignored when considering the set. Association can be repeated to specify an association hierarchy, i.e., sets, subsets, and sets of sets.

An SDM supporting the structural aspects of sets must provide member objects, set objects, and association. A <u>member object</u> is a structural primitive used in a schema to represent a member. A <u>set object</u> is a structural abstraction used in a schema to represent a set. Association is used to define the relationship between a set object and its constituent member object. Figure 1 depicts a set object S as an association (——>—>) of member objects of type M.

Figure 1: Object Scheme for Association

An SDM supporting sets must also provide concepts for modelling behavioural properties of sets. These include: behavioural primitives (elementary operations) and behavioural abstractions (actions and transactions) over members and sets, and behavioural relationships (control structures) with which to construct abstractions from primitives and other abstractions. Elementary member operations include create member, insert member into set, update member, and delete member from set. Elementary set operations include union, intersection, and difference. Complex operations can be expressed as behavioural abstractions in action and transaction procedures. The control structure inherent in association is repetition e.g.,

<u>For each</u> m <u>in</u> S <u>do</u> ... <u>end</u>.

However, sequence and choice can also be used.

Codd has shown [CODD71] that first order logic can be used as a predicate language over sets, to identify members and sets, and to specify queries and constraints.

To illustrate sets as modelling concepts, three examples are now given by means of object schemes. An object scheme is a directed graph in which nodes are strings denoting objects, and edges identify structural relationships between objects. Object schemes are discussed in more detail elsewhere [BROD81c]. In addition to association, the examples use aggregation and generalization relationships. Figure 2 illustrates the graphic notation of object schemes. The university committee example illustrates that sets and

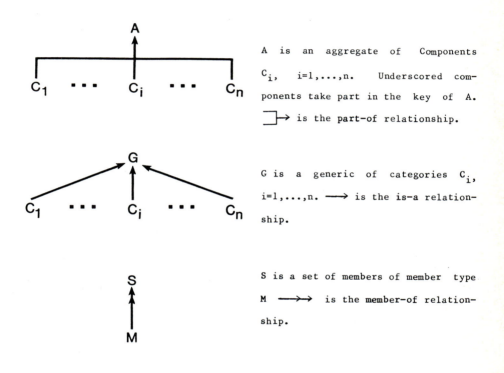

A is an aggregate of Components C_i, $i=1,\ldots,n$. Underscored components take part in the key of A.
⊐→ is the **part-of** relationship.

G is a generic of categories C_i, $i=1,\ldots,n$. ⟶ is the **is-a** relationship.

S is a set of members of member type M ⟶→ is the **member-of** relationship.

Figure 2: Object Scheme Notational Conventions

members have quite different structural properties. The university committee object scheme (Figure 3) contains the set object **people** which is composed by association from the member object **person**.

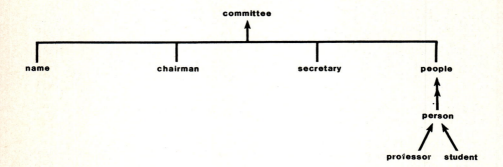

Figure 3: University Committee Object Scheme

Whereas person (Figure 4) has specific information pertaining to an individual
student or professor, people has information pertaining to a collection of
person. Clearly person.voting-record is a different kind of information than
people.voting-record.

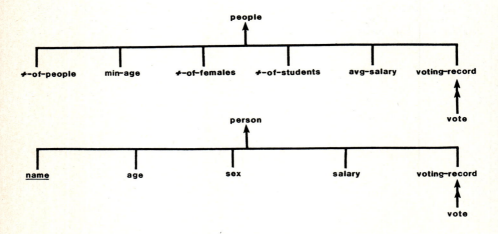

Figure 4: People and Person Object Schemes

Behavioural properties of sets and members also differ, i.e., have different effects on the database. Person has four actions defined: appoint, reappoint, dismiss, and update. People.appoint creates a person and assigns the person to a specified committee.people. Person.reappoint finds a person and assigns the person to a specified committee.people. Person.dismiss deletes a person from one committee.people and from the committee database if it was the only committee that the person was assigned to. Person.update permits person components to be updated. People has two actions: People.appoint creates an empty committee.people and repeatedly invokes person.appoint to populate it; people.dismiss repeatedly invokes person.dismiss to delete each person from committee.people.

Set objects are required in addition to member objects whenever specific set properties are of interest (and vice versa). Some set properties can be deduced directly from member properties, e.g., people.avg-salary from person.salary. However, some set properties are defined a priori hence they cannot be deduced from member properties, e.g., the definitional property that a given committee must consist of exactly 10 people including 5 students and 5 females. Further, the committee can redefine its composition policy.

The enterprise object scheme (Figure 5) illustrates the use of sets to represent layers of abstraction. Properties of sets are clearly distinguished from properties of members. This example violates Codd's notion of first normal form, since some components of aggregates are sets.

The soccer team example (Figure 6) illustrates the natural and frequent use of association in one object scheme. In each of the four sets, the set membership rule involves a contractual, legal relationship which can be specialized [MBW80] for each association and each member.

586 *M.L. Brodie*

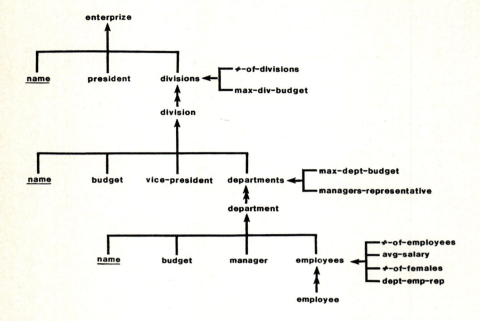

Figure 5: Enterprize Object Scheme

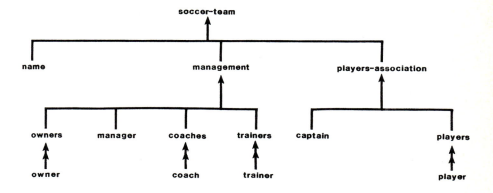

Figure 6: Soccer Team Object Scheme

The modelling concepts used to support sets satisfy the criteria given in Section 2.

- abstraction: Association permits details about members to be ignored when considering a set.
- expressiveness: The set membership rule can be defined as precisely as desired using first order logic.
- formality: Set theory and first order logic provide a formal basis for specifying properties inherently, explicitly, and implicitly.
- simplicity/elegance: Sets are modelled using three simple, integrated concepts: member, set, association.
- semantic relativism: Depending on the context, an object can be viewed as a member, as a set, as the result of an operation, and also as a component, category, generic, or aggregate (see Section 5).
- "natural" modelling concepts: Sets are broadly applicable in modelling many situations and are familiar to most users and designers. The major data models and SDMs support sets implicitly and indirectly.
- structural and behavioural modelling concepts associated with sets were described in Section 2.
- partitioning, modularity, and integration: The set membership rule can be used to partition members into sets which can further be partitioned into subsets. Each set can be treated independently in a modular fashion. Set theoretic operations can be used to combine subsets to form sets, and asso-

ciation can be used to form higher order sets, i.e., sets of sets.

- high-level languages: Set theory and predicate calculus (e.g., relational calculus) form a basis for high-level languages.
- modelling methodologies: Many database design methodologies are based on the notion of set, e.g., relations, entity sets, relationship sets, owner-coupled sets.
- modelling directness: If sets are "natural" then they support modelling directness.
- modelling uniqueness: Although sets are simple, natural, and direct modelling concepts, there may be many ways of modelling the same situation.
- provability: Consistency, verification, and validation can be based formally on set theory and first order logic.
- independence of concepts: Properties of sets and members are distinct, hence they may be considered independently. Though relativism, aggregate, generic, and set properties can be considered independently and can be fully integrated.
- extensibility: New subsets and supersets can be defined and set membership rules can be altered. Due to concept independence, constraints can be added or deleted.
- picturability: Object schemes depict static properties of sets, members, and association. Action schemes [BROD81c] depict behavioural properties of objects (i.e., actions and transactions).
- implementation: Sets as SDM concepts can be safely and efficiently implemented using both relational and CODASYL DMBSs.

4. SETS IN DATA MODELS AND SDMs

Most data models and SDMs support important aspects of sets. However, no model presents sets in a form that meets the criteria for modelling concepts. Although the classical data models can be used to implement sets, they do not support sets explicitly. Whereas most SDMs support sets implicitly, natural set properties are not directly supported.

4.1 SETS IN DATA MODELS

The relational model, which is based on set theory, supports many properties of sets. However, two aspects of the relational model reduce its effectiveness for modelling sets. The major deficiency is the lack of distinction between member and set properties. This is an example of semantic overloading; all structural properties are expressed in terms of one concept, the relation. A member corresponds to a tuple, and a set corresponds to a relation. Properties of members are represented as attributes of a relation. A particular member is presented by a single tuple. In the person---->->people

example (Figures 3 and 4), person (without voting-record) could be represented
in the relation:

person (<u>name</u>, age, sex, salary)

Although an instance of a person is a set of tuples (members), it is not possible to use person to represent set properties. A second relation people
(again without voting-record) would have to be used.

people(<u>group-name</u>, #-of-people, min-age,
       #-of-females, #-of-students, avg-salary)

One tuple of people represents a set, whereas an instance of people represents
a set of sets. The relational model provides no direct means of representing
association, e.g., person--->->people. Hardgrave's reformulation of the relational model in set theory [HARD80] clearly distinguishes member and set properties. On the behavioural side, there are no behavioural primitives, relationships, or abstractions. The powerful predicate language (i.e., relational
calculus) is set-oriented. Expressions over a single tuple (member) must be
specified over a relation (set) of one element. Expressions over sets of sets
cannot be specified in first order logic.

   A second deficiency of the relational model is the emphasis on first normal form and the lack of support of interrelational constraints. Considering
each aggregate object as a relation in the object schemes (Figures 3 through
6), all object schemes violate first normal form. In particular, since the
above relations person and people are in first normal form, the property
voting-record could not be represented. A disadvantage of first normal form
is that normalized relation schemes are a disjoint collection of relations
since interrelational dependencies are not directly expressible [DATE81].
Although joins and foreign keys can be used to connect relations, there is
little guidance or automatic support to ensure meaningful joins.

   Although the relational model does not directly support member and set
properties, it can be used to implement them indirectly. Two relations are
required; one to act as the set object representing set properties, and one to
act as the member object representing member properties. In addition, referential integrity [CODD79] must be supported to represent the association between
a set and its members. The behavioural primitives for tuples (members) and
relations (sets) are provided in many relational systems. A high-level programming language can be used in conjunction with the relational model to provide procedures for behavioural abstractions and control structures for
behavioural relationships. PASCAL/R [SCHM79] provides such facilities, e.g.,

<u>For</u> <u>each</u> r <u>in</u> rel <u>do</u> ... <u>end</u>.

Member and set properties are not inherent in the network (CODASYL) or
hierarchic data models. Sets can be represented using CODASYL's owner-coupled
sets and hierarchic parent-child relationships. These representations permit

set and member properties to be distinguished and association to be maintained. However, these structures are not sets. Members need not be distinct
and are ordered. On the behavioural side, there are no behavioural primitives
for sets, no behavioural relationships such as set-oriented control structures, and no behavioural abstractions. As with the relational data model, the
network and hierarchic models can be used to represent sets, but in a way that
does not meet the data modelling criteria of simplicity, naturalness, structure concepts, behaviour concepts, high-level language support, modelling
directness, and abstraction.

4.2 SETS IN SEMANTIC DATA MODELS

A host of SDMs has been proposed as extensions to data models in order to
resolve data modelling problems such as those discussed above. Six frequently
referenced SDMs are the semantic hierarchy model (SHM) [SMIT77] [SMIT80], the
entity-relationship model (ERM) [CHEN76], the semantic data model (SDM*)
[HMC78], the relational model/Tasmania (RM/T) [CODD79], TAXIS [MBW80], and
Beta [BROD80b]. These SDMs support sets indirectly, hence the data modelling
criteria are not met. In particular, no SDM supports the behavioural properties of sets and members. For each of the six models we will consider their
support of structural properties of members and sets.

4.2.1 SEMANTIC HIERARCHY MODEL

SHM provides concepts for modelling structural properties of individuals
or entities. There is one structural primitive for describing classes of individuals which we will call an object. An object, like a data type, defines a
class of individuals. An individual is an instance of an object. An object can
play the roles of a component or category, depending on its relationships with
other objects. SHM provides three structural relationships or forms of
abstraction: aggregation, generalization, and classification. Classification
is used to define objects from individuals. The structural abstractions are
aggregate objects which are composed by aggregation from component objects,
and generic objects that are composed by generalization from category objects.
Behavioural concepts are being developed for SHM [SMIT80].

SHM is an extension of the relational model and represents sets in the
same implicit way. The inherent constraints of SHM do not distinguish member
properties from set properties. The comments made for this lack of distinction
in the relational model apply directly to SHM. However, using the three forms
of abstraction, the explicit constraints of SHM can be used to represent some
structural properties of sets and members.

Although the three forms of abstraction involve sets, they do not directly support set and member properties given in Section 3. Classification abstracts a set of individuals to form an object, whereas association associates a set of individuals with a set instance or a set of objects with a set object. Aggregation groups a fixed number of distinct component objects but can be used to represent sets. Figure 7 illustrates two ways of representing a

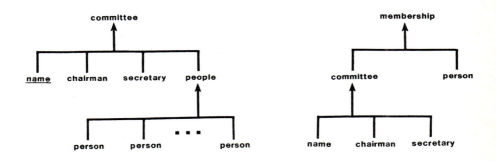

Figure 7: Two Object Schemes Associating People with Committee

set of people on a committee using SHM. The people aggregate is a fixed cardinality set. The membership aggregate could permit a variable number of person to committee relationships; in which case membership is treated as both a member and a set. In addition, membership is represented as a higher level abstraction than either committee or person when in fact a committee consists of people. Neither scheme represents such people properties as: #-of-people, avg-salary, #-of-females.

Generalization is a subset relationship among objects, e.g., person can be specialized into two categories student and professor. A generalization hierarchy represents the possible categories for one object. That object could describe members (e.g., student, professor, and person) or sets (e.g., students, professors, and people) as depicted in Figure 8. However, SHM provides no means for representing the association between members and sets.

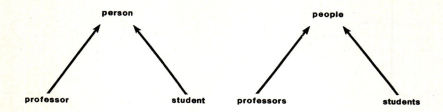

Figure 8: Person and People Object Schemes

4.2.2 ENTITY-RELATIONSHIP MODEL

ERM provides several concepts for modelling structural properties of entities. The main structural primitive is the attribute which is used to characterize properties of entities and relationships. The two structural abstractions are entity sets and relationship sets. ERM provides three forms of structural relationships. Implicitly, ERM provides classification between entity sets and entities and between relationship sets and relationships. Also implicitly, ERM supports attribute aggregation with which to aggregate attributes to compose entities or to add attributes to relationships. Explicitly, ERM provides entity aggregation with which to aggregate entities to form relationships. Behavioural concepts and further abstraction capabilities are being developed for ERM [SANT80] [SCHE80].

The inherent constraints of ERM do not directly support sets. Like SHM, ERM is a relational extension and does not distinguish member and set properties. Classification and aggregation do not directly support sets. However, unlike SHM, the association relationship between entity sets can be represented using a relationship set. For example, the membership of a set of people on a committee can be represented as shown in Figure 9.

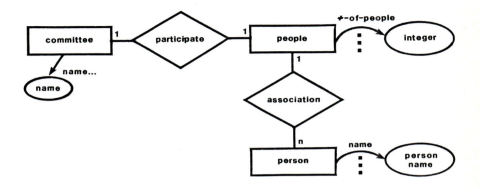

Figure 9: E-R Diagram for Committee Membership

Representations of sets using ERM distinguish entities and relationships, hence they do not exhibit relativism. Although it is a matter of opinion regarding the naturalness and simplicity of this distinction, the representation like those in SHM do not directly support sets or subsets.

4.2.3 THE SEMANTIC DATA MODEL

The main structural primitive of SDM* is the class. A class is a multiset of objects, events, or names. A class can be defined independently, in which case it is called a base class; or it can be defined using interclass connections over other classes. There are two structural relationships or interclass connections, each producing a different kind of structural abstraction. The subclass interconnection is similar to generalization and is used to define subclasses. A subclass is defined by restricting the attributes of a class or by explicitly including a class member in a subclass. Membership in a restricted subclass is derived much like CODASYL's automatic membership, whereas membership in a subset subclass is similar to CODASYL's manual membership. The second order class relationship is used to define (multi-) set classes. A set class is a set of classes and has classes as instances. A set class is either an abstraction or an aggregate. (This use of "aggregate" is unrelated to that in SHM.) Abstractions are generalizations with membership similar to restrict. Members of aggregates are given explicitly as with subset subclasses. For example, group could be defined as an aggregate of people. Members of group are particular sets of people: students, professors, secretaries, etc. An instance of students is implicitly a multi-set of student.

The inherent constraints of SDM* do not directly support sets. As with the earlier models, there is no distinction between set and member properties. For example, the class people is defined using properties of an individual person but has a set of people as an instance. The subclass connection, like generalization, does not support sets of objects, events, or names. However, SDM* does provide a more direct means of representing sets than the previous models, namely, aggregates. Aggregates do not represent simple sets of objects, events, and names. An aggregate is a second order class. An aggregate is a set of classes, and a class is a set of objects, events, or names. Classes like relations do not distinguish member and set properties. Set properties can be represented indirectly in several ways, for instance by using class, subclass, and set class. Although SDM* is more expressive than previous models, it is rather complex for modelling sets. SDM* does not provide concepts for modelling behaviour.

4.2.4 RELATIONAL MODEL/TASMANIA

RM/T, an extension of the relational model, provides means for expressing higher order relations. In RM/T, a relation functions both as the main structural primitive and structural abstraction. This is the case with SHM's object and SDM*'s class. RM/T adds to the relational model the three structural relationships: Cartesian aggregation, generalization (both as defined in SHM), and cover aggregation. Cover aggregation extends SDM*'s aggregate concept by permitting: (1) objects to be members in more than one cover and (2), cover aggregates with non-homogeneous members. RM/T does not extend the capabilities of SHM or SDM* to represent sets.

4.2.5 TAXIS

TAXIS provides one structural primitive, the class. A class is a collection of constants called tokens, which represent entities. There are two structural relationships: classification and is-a (generalization). Classification applied to tokens produces classes. Classification applied to classes produces meta-classes. A meta-class is a second order class as in SDM* (i.e., class of classes). An instance of a meta-class is a specific class such as **PROFESSOR**, **STUDENT** and **PERSON**. Such classes are instances of the meta-class **PERSON-CLASS**. Classes and metaclasses can be organized in generalization hierarchies using is-a (e.g., **PROFESSOR** is-a **PERSON** and **STUDENT** is-a **PERSON**.)

The inherent constraints of TAXIS do not support sets directly. Of the models considered, TAXIS makes the clearest distinction between set and member properties. Set properties can be associated with meta-classes and member properties can be associated with classes. For example, properties of **PERSON-CLASS** could include #-of-people, #-of-females, avg-salary etc., while properties of PERSON could include **name, age, sex,** and **salary**. Although properties of a class concern an individual token, a class instance is a set of tokens. Like SDM*'s second order classes, meta-classes do not represent sets. Also, classes of a meta-class are fixed and named. Introducing new classes (subsets) requires a redefinition of the meta-class. Hence, TAXIS presents no direct way of representing association.

4.2.6 BETA

Beta extends SHM with two structural relationships, map and set, which produce structural abstractions: map object and set object respectively. A map is any relationship between two objects that can be expressed in predicate calculus, such as **person married-to-person, person member-of committee**. A map between two objects produces a map object. Set corresponds to association. A set object is defined as a powerset of an underlying member object. For example, an instance of **people**, defined as a powerset of **person**, is a possibly empty set of **person** instances.

Although Beta directly supports association it does not provide means of associating set properties (e.g., #-of-people) with set objects. Secondly, since maps provide an alternate representation for sets (e.g., <member> member-of <set>), modelling uniqueness and simplicity is not satisfied. Finally, maps like relationships in ERM do not support relativism.

5. EXTENDED SEMANTIC HIERARCHY MODEL (SHM+)

SHM+ was designed to meet the SDM criteria given in Section 2. In particular, SHM+ provides concepts that support the modelling of structural and behavioural properties of databases. SHM+ extends SHM with concepts that directly support sets and behaviour modelling. This section summarizes SHM+ and describes its support of sets. The capabilities of SHM+ for modelling the behavioural semantics of databases are described elsewhere [BROD81c].

The main structural primitive in SHM+ is the class, similar to the class concept in SIMULA. A class includes a collection of objects (individuals or entities). Depending on its relationship with other classes, a class, seen as a primitive, can play the roles of a component class, a category class, and a member class. SHM+ provides four forms of abstraction or structural relationships: classification, aggregation, generalization, and association. <u>Classification</u> is a form of abstraction in which a collection of objects is considered as a higher level object class. An <u>object class</u> is a precise characterization of all properties shared by each object in the collection. An <u>object</u> is an instance of an object class if it has the properties defined in the class. Classification represents an **instance-of** relationship between an object class in a schema and an object in a database. For example, an object class **employee** with properties **employee-name**, **employee-number**, and salary may have as an instance the object with property values ´John Smith´, 402 and $20,000. Classification is used in structure modelling to identify, classify, and describe objects in terms of object classes. In the remainder of the paper, ´object´ is used to refer to object classes and the associated objects except when the two concepts must be distinguished.

Aggregation, generalization, and association are used to relate objects. Some properties of a object are determined by the role it plays in one or more of these relationships. <u>Aggregation</u> is a form of abstraction in which a relationship between <u>component objects</u> is considered as a higher level <u>aggregate object</u>. This is the **part-of** relationship. For example, an **employee** may be an aggregate of components **employee-number**, **employee-name**, and **salary**. <u>Generalization</u> is a form of abstraction in which a relationship between <u>category objects</u> is considered as a higher level <u>generic object</u>. This is the **is-a** relationship. For example, the generic **employee** may be a generalization of categories **secretary** and **manager**, i.e., **secretary is-a employee** and **manager is-a employee**. <u>Association</u> applied to objects produces a set class. For example, the set **people** is an association of **person** members. Aggregation, generalization, and association, applied to classes, produce the three structural abstractions, respectively: aggregate, generic, and set classes. Relativism is supported since a class can simultaneously play the roles of (have properties of) component, category, member, aggregate, generic, and set objects.

The behaviour modelling concepts of SHM+ are fully integrated with the structure modelling concepts. The behavioural primitives are: create, insert, update, and delete operations on classes. The primitive operations applied to a class must satisfy all roles that the class plays in agreement with the semantics of SHM+. The behavioural abstractions are actions and transactions which are similar to procedures. The behavioural relationships are control structures used to compose actions and transactions from behavioural primitives and abstractions. They are sequence, choice (e.g., <u>if then else</u> or <u>case</u> control structures), and repetition (e.g., <u>do while</u> or <u>for each</u> control structures). These are, respectively, the behavioural counterparts of aggregation, generalization, and association. This direct correspondence integrates structural with behavioural concepts and results in simplicity and elegance.

The inherent constraints of SHM+ directly and explicitly support sets. The semantic properties of the association of the member class M to form the set class S represented in the following object scheme are:

$$S$$

$$M$$

1. An instance of M is a single object from the M class.
2. An instance of S is a single object representing an element of the power-set of M Objects, i.e., a set of M objects.
3. M can be any SHM+ class.
4. S is an association of exactly one member class M.
5. Each M object must be a member of at least one S object.
6. M and S can simultaneously take part in aggregation, generalization, and association hierarchies. An association hierarchy results from the repeated application of association, e.g., M and S can be member classes in other associations, and M can be a set class in another association.
7. As with aggregation, properties are inherited upwards; properties of M are the basis of properties of S.
8. Aggregation must be used to represent set-oriented properties of S, otherwise an S object simply represents a set.
9. When considering an S object, set-oriented properties are considered, while properties of M are ignored.
10. The membership rule for S is either automatic or manual. Automatic membership is defined when S is defined using predicate calculus as a restriction of property values of M, or when member objects are explicitly enumerated. Manual membership is defined explicitly by inserting members into a set at run time.
11. An S object is uniquely identified by either component values, if it is also an aggregate, or by the membership rule (i.e., a value associated with the rule of the specific members of the set).
12. Association is used to form sets from members. Membership (applying or restricting the membership rule) is the inverse of association and is used to identify single members or subsets.
13. Behavioural primitives for M include insert into S and delete from S. Behavioural primitives for S include set union, intersection, and difference.
14. User-defined behavioural abstractions are defined over S for example:

```
        for each M in S do

            {operation composed primarily of M object actions}

        end for each
```

SHM+'s support of sets satisfies all of the SDM design criteria to some degree. The simplicity, elegance, and naturalness of sets was discussed in Section 3. Object schemes demonstrated picturability. SHM+ provides fully integrated concepts for modelling structural and behavioural properties. Set and member classes and association can be used to represent sets directly. A formal definition of SHM+ is being developed [BROD79] [RB81] using axiomatic and functional specification techniques as a basis for specifying database applications, and for proving implementations correct. Several applications designed using SHM+ and its associated design methodology ACM/PCM [BROD80b] have been implemented using PASCAL/R. The above 14 properties of sets address some of the criteria (for example, abstraction in 2, 7, and 9; partitioning and modelling methodologies in 12; relativism, extensibility, and concept independence in 3 and 6; and expressiveness in 10).

Since sets are natural, fundamental modelling concepts, association improves SHM+ as a whole. Association has a positive impact on almost all SDM criteria. Structural and behavioural properties of sets can be represented abstractly, elegantly, and directly.

SHM+ is based on three simple and natural forms of abstraction which have structural and behavioural counterparts: aggregation/sequence, generalization/choice, and association/repetition. The three concepts integrate structure and behaviour, provide an economy of concepts, and form a basis for a modelling methodology. The three concepts appear to be sufficient for modelling database applications. All primitive recursive functions can be constructed using sequence, choice, and repetition [DAVI58]. We believe that most useful database structures can be represented using aggregation, generalization, and association. These claims have been substantiated in using SHM+ to model six complex application systems for: university registration, hotel reservation, soccer team management, real estate management, criminal court scheduling, and IFIP conference management*. The criminal court scheduling system was implemented in 10,000 lines of PASCAL/R code.

---

*ACM/PCM and SHM+ have been used to specify a system for managing IFIP conferences as part of the IFIP's Comparative Review of Information Systems Design Methodologies.

6. CONCLUDING REMARKS

Sets are fundamental concepts for modelling structural and behavioural properties of database applications. This paper has presented criteria for evaluating the constituent modelling concepts of an SDM. It was demonstrated that the classical data models and six well-known SDMs do not meet the criteria established for sets. Association was introduced as a new database abstraction with which to compose sets from members. It was shown that association and the related concepts, set and member, directly support sets and can be integrated into an SDM. The resulting SDM, the extended semantic hierarchy model (SHM+), was described and was shown to meet the criteria established for sets.

SHM+ was developed in parallel with Active and Passive Component Modelling (ACM/PCM), a methodology for the design and development of database-intensive applications. ACM/PCM and SHM+ take advantage of concepts and methodologies from the areas of databases, programming languages, artificial intelligence, and software engineering. In particular, data, procedure, and control abstractions are used extensively to design active databases and expert systems.

SHM+ and ACM/PCM are a basis for research in four directions:

i. formal techniques for: specifying the semantics of both SDMs and database applications; analyzing specifications for consistency and completeness; and verifying implementations with respect to specifications [BROD79] [RB81].

ii. high-level languages for the design, specification, and implementation of database applications, as well as transaction and query languages having user friendly interfaces (e.g., screen-oriented).

iii. interactive tools to support logical and physical design methodologies of ACM/PCM.

iv. a database environment consisting of software tools that interact with a meta database to support each phase of the database system life cycle [BROD81b].

Acknowledgement

The author gratefully acknowledges the contributions of Dzenan Ridjanovic to the development of SHM+, ACM/PCM and to the implementation of the criminal court system. This paper was revised while the author was visiting the Computer Corporation of America.

7. REFERENCES

[ABRI74]
  Abrial, J.R. "Data Semantics". In Klimbie, J.W. and Koffman, K.L. (Eds.),
  Database Management, North-Holland, 1974, pp. 1-59.

[BROD79]
  Brodie, M.L. "Axiomatic Definitions of Data Model Semantics". Technical
  Report, Dept. of Computer Science, University of Maryland, December,
  1979.

[BROD80a]
  Brodie, M.L. (Ed.). Data Abstraction, Databases and Conceptual Modelling: An Annotated Bibliography, NBS Special Pub. 500-59, May 1980.

[BROD80b]
  Brodie, M.L. "The Application of Data Types to Database Semantic
  Integrity". Information Systems 5, 4 (1980).

[BROD81a]
  Brodie, M.L. "Data Abstraction for Designing Database-Intensive Applications". in [BZ81].

[BROD81b]
  Brodie, M.L. Database Design, course notes, Dept. of Computer Science,
  University of Maryland, Spring 1981.

[BROD81c]
  Brodie, M.L. "On Modelling Behavioural Semantics of Databases". Proc. 7th
  International Conf. on Very Large Databases, Cannes, France, September
  1981.

[BR81]
  Brodie, M.L. and D. Ridjanovic. "Extending a Relational Database Environment to Support Semantic Modelling". Dept. of Computer Science, University of Maryland, April 1981.

[BZ81]
  Brodie, M.L. and S.N. Zilles. (Eds). Proc. Workshop on Data Abstraction,
  Databases and Conceptual Modelling. SIGPLAN Notices 16, 1 (January
  1981).

[CHEN76]
  Chen, P.P.S. "The Entity-Relationship Model: Towards a Unified View of
  Data". ACM TODS 1, 1 (March 1976).

[CODD71]
Codd, E.F. "Relational Completeness of Data Base Sublanguages". In Rustin, R. (Ed.) Data Base Systems, Prentice-Hall, 1971.

[CODD79]
Codd, E.F. "Extending the Database Relational Model to Capture More Meaning". ACM TODS 4, 4 (December 1979).

[DATE81]
Date, C.J. "Referential Integrity". Proc. 7th International Conf. on Very Large Databases, Cannes, France, September 1981.

[DAVI58] Davis, M. Computability and Unsolvability. New York, McGraw-Hill, 1958.

[HMC78]
Hammer, M. and D. McLeod. "The Semantic Data Model". Proc. 1978 SIGMOD, Austin, May 1978.

[HARD80]
Hardgrave, W.T. "Positional Set Notation". Draft paper, National Bureau of Standards, February 1980.

[MCS81]
McLeod, D. and J.M. Smith. "Abstraction in Databases". in [BZ81].

[MBW80]
Mylopoulos, J., P.A. Bernstein and H.K.T. Wong. "A Language Facility for Designing Database-Intensive Applications". ACM TODS 5, 2 (June 1980).

[RB81]
Ridjanovic, D. and M.L. Brodie. "A Formal Definition of the Extended Semantic Hierarchy Model". Dept. of Computer Science, University of Maryland, in preparation.

[SANT80]
Santos, C.S. dos, E.J. Neuhold and A.L. Furtado. "A Data Type Approach to the Entity Relationship Model, in: Chen, P. (ed.), Entity-Relationship Approach to Systems Analysis and Design (North-Holland, Amsterdam, 1980).

[SCHE80]
Scheuermann, P., G. Schiffner and H. Weber. "Abstraction Capabilities and Invariant Properties Modeling within the Entity-Relationship Approach", Chen, P. (ed.), Entity-Relationship Approach to Systems Analysis and Design (North-Holland, Amsterdam, 1980).

[SCHM79]
Schmidt, J.W. "Some High Level Language Constructs for Data Type Relation". ACM TODS 2, 3 (September 1979).

[SMIT77]
    Smith, J.M. and D.C.P. Smith. "Database Abstraction: Aggregation and Gen-
    eralization". <u>ACM</u> <u>TODS</u> <u>2</u>, 2 (June 1977).

[SMIT80]
    Smith, J.M. and D.C.P. Smith. "A Database Approach to Software Specifica-
    tion". in W.E. Riddle and R.E. Fairley (eds.), <u>Software</u> <u>Development</u>
    <u>Tools</u>, Springer-Verlag, New York (1980).